Dedicated to

My Parents
Shri Sadanand Nachan and Smt Archana Nachan

My Sister
Miss Smita Nachan

My Wife
Mrs Sarika Nachan
and
Our Lovely New Born Baby Boy

About the Author

Nanddeep Nachan is a results-oriented Technology Architect with over 14 years of experience in Microsoft Technologies, especially in SharePoint, Office 365, MS Azure, and .NET. He is experienced in the design, implementation, configuration, and maintenance of several large-scale projects with career focuses included architectural design and implementation, website design and development, complete application development cycles, and intense focus on .NET technologies. He has experience in providing management expertise over a wide range of technical environments and industries, specialized in critical customer projects and complex technology deployments.

He has been working with SharePoint since the last 14 years and has exposure to SharePoint versions starting from SharePoint 2007 (MOSS).

He is a CSM (Certified Scrum Master), Microsoft Certified Professional with certifications in SharePoint, MS Azure, Office 365, and .NET. He is A 2-times C# Corner MVP and an Author. He is a regular speaker at various events. He is also an active contributor to technical communities like SharePoint Patterns and Practices (https://github.com/SharePoint/) and C# Corner (http://www.c-sharpcorner.com).

He is also a creative and technically sound photographer with experience in custom and specialized photography.

Mastering SharePoint Framework

*Master the SharePoint Framework
Development with Easy-to-Follow Examples*

by
Nanddeep Nachan

FIRST EDITION 2020

Copyright © BPB Publications, India

ISBN: 978-93-89328-875

All Rights Reserved. No part of this publication may be reproduced or distributed in any form or by any means or stored in a database or retrieval system, without the prior written permission of the publisher with the exception to the program listings which may be entered, stored and executed in a computer system, but they can not be reproduced by the means of publication.

LIMITS OF LIABILITY AND DISCLAIMER OF WARRANTY

The information contained in this book is true to correct and the best of author's & publisher's knowledge. The author has made every effort to ensure the accuracy of these publications, but cannot be held responsible for any loss or damage arising from any information in this book.

All trademarks referred to in the book are acknowledged as properties of their respective owners.

Distributors:

BPB PUBLICATIONS
20, Ansari Road, Darya Ganj
New Delhi-110002
Ph: 23254990/23254991

DECCAN AGENCIES
4-3-329, Bank Street,
Hyderabad-500195
Ph: 24756967/24756400

MICRO MEDIA
Shop No. 5, Mahendra Chambers,
150 DN Rd. Next to Capital Cinema,
V.T. (C.S.T.) Station, MUMBAI-400 001
Ph: 22078296/22078297

BPB BOOK CENTRE
376 Old Lajpat Rai Market,
Delhi-110006
Ph: 23861747

Published by Manish Jain for BPB Publications, 20 Ansari Road, Darya Ganj, New Delhi-110002 and Printed by him at Repro India Ltd, Mumbai

About the Reviewer

Priyaranjan is a Solution Architect based out of India who has been working with SharePoint since 2010. He is quite active in SharePoint, Office365 and Azure community activities and has been awarded as Microsoft MVP since 2018.

He is a tech enthusiast who believes in sharing knowledge and giving back to the community which will help in building better technical collaboration.

Acknowledgements

First and foremost, I would like to thank God for giving me the courage to write this book. I would like to thank everyone at BPB Publications for giving me this opportunity to publish my book.

I would also like to thank my loving and caring sister, Miss Smita Nachan, my wife, Mrs Sarika Nachan, and my parents for their endless support and helping me in numerous ways.

I would like to thank my mentors, Mr Hausen Henrik (Finland), Mr Priyranjan KS, all the other mentors, and my friend, Mr Ravi Kulkarni, for his useful discussions and suggestions, right from deciding topics, writing the concepts, framing exercises, etc.

Lastly, I would like to thank my critics. Without their criticism, I would never be able to write this book.

– Nanddeep Nachan

Preface

In the last few years, the SharePoint Framework has been very popular and has become the first choice of Modern SharePoint developers. SharePoint has become richer with its every release and eventually, a Modern SharePoint has evolved. The SharePoint Framework plays an important role in customizing Modern SharePoint. At the same time, it also supports classic SharePoint. The SPFx solutions are developed using open source toolchains, modern UI standards, and JavaScript libraries/frameworks like Angular JS, React JS, Knockout JS, etc.

The primary goal in the development of this book is to create a pedagogical sound and accessible book that emphasizes the core concepts of the SharePoint Framework. This book can be used to develop Modern SharePoint concepts easily. This book contains many examples to show the working of a particular code construct. This book is very helpful to learn the basic and advanced concepts of SharePoint programming.

This book targets SPFx features released until 1.9.1 version, which is the latest at the time of writing this book. The SharePoint Framework is ever growing and there will be more versions of it releasing in the future. After you finish reading this book, you will gain more insight that is useful over the SharePoint Framework and will enable you to set a foundation for future updates and learnings.

This book is divided into 56 chapters and it provides a detailed description of the core concepts of SharePoint Framework programming.

Chapter 1, Getting Started with SharePoint Framework introduces the concepts of the SharePoint Framework. SharePoint has become richer with its every release and eventually, a Modern SharePoint has evolved. It also explains the importance of using the SharePoint Framework.

Chapter 2, Develop Your First SPFx Web Part addresses the fundamental concepts of the SharePoint Framework. It describes the structure of the SharePoint Framework and the Yeoman generator to generate SPFx solutions.

Chapter 3, SPFx Web Part Property Pane introduces the concept of property panes in the SPFx web part. It also focuses on the core concepts of property pane metadata.

Chapter 4, Custom Controls for Web Part Property Pane addresses how to build custom controls for the SPFx web part property pane.

Chapter 5, PnP Controls for Web Part Property Pane discusses the uses of the option of using reusable PnP (Patterns and Practices) property pane controls. This chapter also focuses on the methods to use reusable PnP (Patterns and Practices) controls.

Chapter 6, CSS Considerations addresses the importance of CSS in the SPFx web part and common considerations. It also highlights how to override externally referenced CSS.

Chapter 7, Configure SPFx Web Part I condescribes the various ways to set the SPFx web part icon. It focuses on the concepts such as Office UI fabric icons, external icon image, base64 encoded image as an icon.

Chapter 8, Examine SPFx Web Parts on Modern SharePoint describes an option to test the SPFx web parts on an actual modern SharePoint page. This technique helps developers in many ways to carry out the page optimization, performance analytics and provides flexibility to test the web part along with the other content and web parts on the same page.

Chapter 9, Host SPFx Web Parts from MS Azure CDN addresses the concepts of hosting the SPFx web parts to the CDN location. It discusses the methods to host assets on MS Azure CDN.

Chapter 10, Host SPFx Web Parts from Office 365 Public CDN introduces the concept of Office 365 public CDN as an option to host the SPFx web part.

Chapter 11, Host SPFx Web Parts from SharePoint Document Library focuses on the importance and necessity of using CDN to host the SPFx web part. It describes the SharePoint document library as a hosting option.

Chapter 12, Integrating jQuery with SPFx Web Parts describes an option to coordinate jQuery with the SPFx web part and arrange required bundles and dependencies.

Chapter 13, CRUD Operations with No Framework focuses on No framework alternative to implementing the SPFx web part for CRUD (Create, Read, Update, and Delete) operations against the SharePoint list.

Chapter 14, CRUD Operations with React JS focuses on React JS alternative to implementing the SPFx web part for CRUD (Create, Read, Update, and Delete) operations against the SharePoint list.

Chapter 15, CRUD Operations with Angular JS focuses on Angular JS alternative to implementing the SPFx web part for CRUD (Create, Read, Update, and Delete) operations against the SharePoint list.

Chapter 16, CRUD Operations using Knockout JS focuses on Knockout JS alternative to implementing the SPFx web part for CRUD (Create, Read, Update, and Delete) operations against the SharePoint list.

Chapter 17, CRUD Operations with SP-PnP-JS focuses on SP-PnP-JS alternative to implementing the SPFx web part for CRUD (Create, Read, Update, and Delete) operations against the SharePoint list.

Chapter18, Transition to @pnp/sp from sp-pnp-js introduces the concept of transition to @pnp/sp from sp-pnp-js. It discusses why sp-pnp-js is deprecated and gives detailed information on how to transition.

Chapter19, SPFx Development with React JS focuses on the React library and explores why React works well with SPFx. It describes the concept of the virtual DOM and gives detailed information on React's primary building blocks such as React Element, React Props, React Component, React State, and JavaScript XML (.jsx).

Chapter 20, React Lifecycle Events in SPFx focuses on the React component life cycle, potential alternatives to fetch data in the React component with their advantages and disadvantages.

Chapter 21, Autobind Control Events in SPFx introduces the concept of the auto-binding event to control. It discusses the importance of binding actions to controls.

Chapter 22, Partial State Update for React-based SPFxWebParts focuses on the React State and its usage. It discusses the importance of the Spread operator to partially update the state.

Chapter 23, Using Office UI Fabric in SPFx introduces the concept of Office UI fabric components and focuses on using them in the SPFx web part for a consistent look and feel. It gives detailed information on how todevelop a robust and consistent design across SharePoint modern experiences.

Chapter 24, Provision SharePoint Assets in SPFx Solutions describes an option to provision SharePoint assets utilizing SPFx solutions. It discusses how to define the required structure to provision assets on the SharePoint site.

Chapter 25, Connect to MS Graph API with MSGraphClient addresses the concepts of MS Graph. It also highlights how to use it in the SPFx web part to retrieve helpful data like user information and so on with MSGraphClient.

Chapter 26, Connect to MS Graph API with AadHttpClient focuses on utilizing MS Graph API with AadHttpClient.

Chapter 27, SPFx Logging Mechanism addresses the importance of logging and gives detailed information on how to implement logging API.

Chapter 28, Debug SPFx Solutions describes the significance of troubleshooting/debugging and gives detailed information on how todebug the SPFx solutions with a browser, visual studio code debugger extension and troubleshoot the solution during development.

Chapter 29, Overview of SPFx Extensions introduces the concept of SPFx extensions and their types. It also highlights how SharePoint Framework extensions help to extend further the SharePoint modern UI.

Chapter 30, SPFx Extension - Application Customizer focuses onthe concept of application customizer SPFx extension and introduction of extension types.

Chapter 31, Extend Application Customizer with React Components focuses on implementing an application customizer utilizing the React component.

Chapter 32, SPFx Extension - Field Customizer introduces the concept of SPFx extensions field customizer and gives detailed information on how to modify the representation of the field in the SharePoint list.

Chapter 33, SPFx Extension - ListView Command Set introduces the concept of SPFx extensions ListView command set and gives detailed information on how toexpand the SharePoint list toolbar.

Chapter 34, Anonymously Call MS Azure Functions focuses on implementing an Azure function and anonymously call it inside the SPFx web part. It describes how perplexing or long-running processing can be executed from Azure functions.

Chapter 35, Securing Azure Function with Azure Active Directory describes the significance of protecting the Azure function with Azure active directory and gives detailed information on why the Azure functions deployed in a production environment should be secured.

Chapter 36, Consume Azure AD Secured Function with SPFx focuses on connecting to Azure active directory secured functions from SPFx solutions. It also highlights how AadHttpClient helps to connect securely to APIs without an OAuth implementation.

Chapter 37, Implementing Separation of Concerns (SoC) introduces the ideology of Separation of Concerns (SoC), actualizes it in an existing SPFx solution and gives detailed information on how SoC helps to isolate each section.

Chapter 38, Localization Support for SPFx addresses the concept of localization support for SPFx and localization alternatives with SPFx. It describes how localization fabricates a better substance for users around the world.

Chapter 39, Office 365 CLI introduces the concept of Office 365 CLI and gives detailed information on how it helps to manage Office 365 and SharePoint Framework solutions platform independently.

Chapter 40, SPFx Solutions Upgrade focuses on the upgrade procedure to a fresher adaptation of SPFx and gives detailed information on the importance of upgrade.

Chapter 41, SPFx Solution Upgrade with Office 365 CLI focuses on upgrading SPFx solutions with Office 365 CLI.

Chapter 42, Common Issues and Resolutions with Upgrading npm Packages outlines the necessity for npm bundle upgrade. It describes how to upgrade the npm bundles and basic issues, resolutions while refreshing to most recent npm bundles.

Chapter 43, Extend MS Teams with SPFx introduces the concept of the MS Teams tab advancement with SPFx and gives detailed information on how a similar web part arrangement can work with both SharePoint and Microsoft Teams depending upon the context under which it is running.

Chapter 44, Library Component Type introduces the ideology of a library component and gives detailed information on how to build our very own library component for code sharing and utilize it in the SPFx web part.

Chapter 45, Develop Custom App Pages with SPFx addresses the concept of developing custom app pages with SPFx. It describes how to utilize the custom page layouts built with SPFxall over the web part displaying hierarchical information in a tree view structure using React.

Chapter 46, Optimizing SPFx Solutions introduces the concept of optimizing SPFx solutions and gives detailed information on regularly observed practices and enhancement techniques to construct better SPFx solutions.

Chapter 47, Unit Test with Jest and Enzyme focuses on implementing a unit test with Jest and Enzyme. It describes how to automate the execution of the test cases using Azure DevOps.

Chapter 48, DevOps For SPFx addresses the concept ofDevOps For SPFx. It describes how to implement continuous integration and delivery pipelines for SharePoint Framework solutions with Azure DevOps.

Chapter 49, Query User Profile Details describes a practical scenario of retrieving the user profile details using Reactin the SPFx web part.

Chapter 50, Query SP Search Results describes the pragmatic situation of querying the list items utilizing Reactin the SPFx web part and gives detailed information on how to display search results utilizing SharePoint REST APIs.

Chapter 51, React-based Tree view describes practical scenarios of displaying hierarchical information in a tree view structure using React in the SPFx web part and gives detailed information on how toutilize third-party controls to address customer business requirements.

Chapter 52, React-based Carousel describes practical scenarios of displaying images in Carousel using Reactin the SPFx web part and gives detailed information on how to utilize third-party npm packages in SPFx solutions.

Chapter 53, React-based Organogram describes practical scenarios of displaying hierarchical information in an Org Chart format using React in the SPFx web part.

Chapter 54, Integrating Adaptive Cards with SPFx describes practical scenarios of integrating Adaptive Cards with SPFx, which exhibits the capacity of utilizing Adaptive Cards inside the SharePoint Framework.

Chapter 55, Integrating Google API with SPFx describes practical scenarios of integrating Google API with SPFx and gives detailed information on how Google Fit REST APIs can be expended in the SPFx web part to show the key wellness data (activity time spent, distance travelled, calories burned, step count) from the Google fit information source.

Chapter 56, SPFx Development with SharePoint On-Premises focuses on SPFx Development with SharePoint On-Premises and gives detailed information on SPFx readiness with SharePoint on-premises (SharePoint 2016 and 2019).

Downloading the code bundle and coloured images:

Please follow the link to download the
Code Bundle and the *Coloured Images* of the book:

https://rebrand.ly/384d6

Errata

We take immense pride in our work at BPB Publications and follow best practices to ensure the accuracy of our content to provide with an indulging reading experience to our subscribers. Our readers are our mirrors, and we use their inputs to reflect and improve upon human errors if any, occurred during the publishing processes involved. To let us maintain the quality and help us reach out to any readers who might be having difficulties due to any unforeseen errors, please write to us at :

errata@bpbonline.com

Your support, suggestions and feedbacks are highly appreciated by the BPB Publications' Family.

Table of Contents

1. **Getting Started with the SharePoint Framework 1**
   Structure 1
   Objectives 2
   SharePoint Evolution Across Versions 2
      SharePoint 2007: Full Trust Farm Solutions 2
      SharePoint 2010, SharePoint Online: Sandbox Solutions 3
      SharePoint 2013, SharePoint 2016, and SharePoint Online:
      App/Add-ins Model 4
   Birth of the SharePoint Framework 4
      How SPFx is different? 5
         Modern toolchain/Open source tooling 5
         Easy integration with SharePoint data 5
         Available in Cloud and On-Premises 5
         Client-side rendering 5
         Not dependent on JavaScript injection 5
         No iframe 5
   Key Features of the SharePoint Framework 5
   Script Editor WebPart vs App Part vs the SPFx WebPart 6
   Lightweight Components/Tools Used (SPFx Toolchain) 7
   ALM of the Client-side Web Part 9
   Setup the Developer Environment for SPFx 9
   Conclusion 11

2. **Develop Your First SPFx Web Part 13**
   Structure 13
   Objectives 13
   Features of SPFx Client-side Web Parts 14
      Develop Your First SPFx Solution 14
         Open Solution in Code Editor 17
         Run the WebPart on SharePoint local workbench 17
      Understand the Solution Structure 20
      Major Elements of the SPFx Solution 20

  Web Part Class (HelloWorldWebPart.ts) 21
  Property Type Interface (IHelloWorldWebPartProps) 21
 Conclusion 25

3. SPFx Web Part Property Pane 27
 Structure 27
 Objectives 27
 Property Pane Metadata 27
  SPFx Solution for the Property Pane 28
  Property Pane Code 29
 Supported Typed Object Properties 32
 Test the Property Pane 37
 Conclusion 38

4. Custom Control for the Web Part Property Pane 39
 Structure 39
 Objectives 39
 Build the List Dropdown Custom Control 40
 Define the Web Part Property 41
  Add the Dropdown Property Pane Control 45
   Define React Props for the dropdown 45
   Define the React State for the dropdown 46
   Define the DropDown React Component 46
  Add List Dropdown to the Property Pane Control 50
   Define internal properties for the dropdown property pane control 51
   Define the dropdown property pane control 51
 Use the Dropdown Property Pane Control in the Web Part 53
  Add the list information interface 53
   Reference the Dropdown Property Pane in the WebPart 54
 Test the Custom Property Pane 56
 Conclusion 56

5. PnP Control for the Web Part Property Pane 57
 Structure 57
 Objectives 57
 PnP Reusable Property Pane Controls 57

	Develop the SPFx Solution to use PnP Reusable Property Pane Controls 58
	Install PnP Property Controls 60
	Use List Picker Control in the Web Part Property Pane 60
	Conclusion 63
6.	**CSS Considerations** **65**
	Structure 65
	Objectives 65
	Manage CSS files in the SPFx solution 66
	Use of Sass 66
	Use CSS classes over id 66
	Use CSS Modules 67
	Override externally referenced CSS 69
	Conclusion 69
7.	**Configure the SPFx WebPart Icon** **71**
	Structure 71
	Objectives 71
	Out-of-the-box look and feel 72
	Office UI Fabric Icons 73
	Advantages of using an Office Fabric Icon 75
	Use an External Icon Image 75
	Advantages of using an external image as an icon 76
	Use the base64 Encoded Image 77
	Advantages of using the base64 encoded image 79
	General observation 80
	Conclusion 80
8.	**Examine SPFx WebParts on Modern SharePoint** **81**
	Structure 81
	Objectives 81
	Understand the SharePoint Workbench 81
	Local Workbench 82
	SharePoint Workbench 82
	Develop the SharePoint Framework Web Part 83

Configure SPFx web parts for Modern Pages 85
Conclusion 87

9. **Host SPFx WebParts from MS Azure CDN** 89
   Structure 89
   Objectives 90
   Configure the MS Azure Storage Account 90
   Configure the BLOB container 91
   Enable Azure CDN for Storage Account 93
   Configure the SPFx Solution to use Azure CDN 94
   Conclusion 98

10. **Host SPFx WebParts from the Office 365 Public CDN** 99
    Structure 99
    Objectives 100
    Configure the CDN for the Office 365 Tenant 100
    Setup the New Office 365 CDN 102
       Configure the SPFx Solution for the Office 365 CDN *103*
    Conclusion 106

11. **Host SPFx Web Parts From the SharePoint Document Library** 107
    Structure 107
    Objectives 107
    Deployment to CDN 108
    Configure the SharePoint Library as CDN 108
    Configure the SPFx Solution for the SharePoint Library CDN 108
    Conclusion 112

12. **Integrating jQuery with SPFx WebParts** 113
    Structure 113
    Objectives 113
    Integrate jQuery with the SPFx Web Part 113
    Configure the Required Packages and Dependencies 115
       Solution Changes for jQuery *116*
    Conclusion 121

13. CRUD Operations with No Framework 123
Structure 123
Objectives 123
Develop a SPFx Solution with No Framework for CRUD operations 123
Configure the Property for the List Name... 125
Conclusion 139

14. CRUD Operations with React JS 141
Structure 141
Objectives 141
Brief about React JS... 141
The SPFx Solution for CRUD operations with React JS 142
Configure the Property for the List Name... 144
Define a Model for List Item 148
Add Controls to the WebPart 149
Implement the Create Operation 153
Implement the Read Operation 154
Implement the Update Operation 156
Implement the Delete Operation 158
Create Operation 161
Read Operation 162
Update Operation 162
Delete Operation 163
Conclusion 163

15. CRUD Operations with AngularJS... 165
Structure 165
Objectives 165
Brief information about AngularJS.. 165
Create the SPFx Solution.. 166
Configure AngularJS.. 167
Configure the Property for List Name 169
Build an Angular application 172
Configure Data Service 172
Implement the Create Operation... 174

Implement the Read Operation 175
Implement the Update Operation 176
Implement the Delete Operation 177
Configure the Controller 178
Configure the Module 182
Add Controls to the WebPart 183
    Test the WebPart *185*
Create Operation 186
Read Operation 186
Update Operation 187
Delete Operation 187
    Troubleshooting *188*
Conclusion 188

16. CRUD Operations Using Knockout JS 189
Structure 189
Objectives 189
Brief information about KnockoutJS 189
Create the SPFx Solution 190
Configure Property for List Name 191
    Configure ViewModel *196*
Implement the Create Operation 197
Implement the Read Operation 198
Implement the Update Operation 199
Implement the Delete Operation 201
Add Controls to the Knockout template 203
Test the WebPart 205
Create Operation 205
Read Operation 206
Update Operation 206
Delete Operation 207
    Troubleshooting *207*
Conclusion 208

17. CRUD Operations with SP-PnP-JS 209

Structure 209
Objectives 209
Brief information about SP-PnP-JS 209
Create the SPFx Solution 210
Configure sp-pnp-js 212
Configure Property for List Name 212
Model for List Item 215
Add Controls to the WebPart 215
Import sp-pnp-js 218
Implement the Create Operation 218
Implement the Read Operation 218
Implement the Update Operation 219
Implement the Delete Operation 220
Test the WebPart 222
Create Operation 222
Read Operation 223
Update Operation 223
Delete Operation 224
Conclusion 224

18. Transition to @pnp/sp from sp-pnp-js 225

Structure 225
Objectives 225
Why sp-pnp-js is deprecated? 226
The SPFx WebPart with sp-pnp-js 226
Code the WebPart 227
Test the WebPart 228
Transition to @pnp/sp from sp-pnp-js 229
Test the web part after the @pnp/sp transition 231
Conclusion 231

19. SPFx Development with ReactJS 233

Structure 233
Objectives 233

Life with JavaScript before React JS 234
    Example of String Concatenation 234
    Templating Engines 234
    The era of Modern Toolchain 235
Overview of ReactJS 235
    Why React works well with SPFx? 235
React/Virtual DOM 236
Primary Building Blocks of React 237
    React Element 237
    React Props 237
    React Component - Stateful React Element 238
    React State 239
    JavaScript XML (.jsx) 239
Conclusion 240

20. React Lifecycle Events in SPFx 241
Structure 241
Objectives 241
React Component Life Cycle 241
Render Method of the React Component 242
    componentWillMount 243
    componentDidMount 244
Conclusion 245

21. Autobind Control Events in SPFx 247
Structure 247
Objectives 247
Develop the SPFx Web Part 247
    Development Scenario 249
        Define a State 249
        Add Controls to the Web Part 250
        Run the SPFx WebPart 252
Binding the event to the control 252
Binding all the events at once 253
Conclusion 254

22. Partial State Update for React-based SPFx WebParts 255
Structure 255
Objectives 255
React State 255
    Developthe SPFx Solution with React 256
    Definethe React State 257
    Code the WebPart 258
Spread operator 261
Test the WebPart 261
Conclusion 262

23. Using Office UI Fabric in SPFx 263
Structure 263
Objectives 263
The UI Challenges 264
Overview of Office UI Fabric 264
Office UI Fabric for the SharePoint Framework 264
    Create the SPFx Solution 264
Office UI Fabric Components 266
Use Office UI Fabric Components in the SPFx WebPart 267
Implement the Greet Message WebPart using Office UI Fabric 269
    Test the WebPart 271
Conclusion 272

24. Provision SharePoint Assets in SPFx Solutions 273
Structure 273
Objectives 273
SharePoint Assets 274
Create the SPFx Solution 275
Add SharePoint Assets to the SPFx Solution 277
    Custom Schema 279
Package the assets as part of the SPFx Solution 281
    Deploy and Testthe SPFx Web Part 282
Conclusion 284

25. Connect to the MS Graph API with MSGraphClient 285
Structure 285
Objectives 285
Brief information about Microsoft Graph 285
Develop the SPFx Solution to consume the MS Graph API with MSGraphClient 286
MSGraphClient to consume the Graph APIs..................................... 288
Retrieve User Information using MS Graph 291
Conclusion 293

26. Connect to the MS Graph API with AadHttpClient............................... 295
Structure 295
Objective 295
AadHttpClient vs MSGraphClient.. 295
Access MS Graph using AadHttpClient... 298
Get user details using MS Graph.. 300
Configureyour Office 365 Tenant as the First Release Tenant 301
API Management 302
Conclusion 303

27. SPFx Logging Mechanism.. 305
Structure 305
Objectives 305
Understand the Logging API 306
Developthe SPFx Solution for Implementing Logging 306
Exploring the Logging API... 308
Conclusion 309

28. Debug SPFx Solutions 311
Structure 311
Objectives 311
Develop the SharePoint Framework Web Part.................................. 312
Debugging with a Browser.. 314
Debug while developing.. 315
Debug with Visual Studio Code 316
Get the Debugger Extension 316

	Debugging on the Local Workbench	319
	Debugging on the Hosted Workbench	320
	Conclusion	321
29.	**Overview of SPFx Extensions**	**323**
	Structure	323
	Objectives	323
	SharePoint Framework Extensions	324
	Update the SPFxYeoman Generator	324
	Create the SharePoint Framework Extensions Project	325
	Conclusion	327
30.	**SPFx Extensions-Application Customizer**	**329**
	Structure	329
	Objectives	329
	Overview of an Application Customizer	329
	Page Placeholders:	*330*
	Application Customizer the SPFx Solution	330
	Solution Structure	*332*
	Implement the Application Customizer	333
	Conclusion	340
31.	**Extendan Application Customizer with React Components**	**341**
	Structure	341
	Objectives	341
	Generate the SPFx Solution for an Application Customizer	342
	Application Customizer Implementation	344
	Implement the React Component as the Footer	*346*
	Conclusion	350
32.	**SPFx Extensions-Field Customizer**	**351**
	Structure	351
	Objectives	351
	Overview of a Field Customizer	351
	Column Formatting VS SPFx Field Customizer	352
	Develop the SPFx Solution for a Field Customizer	352

        Solution Structure 354
        Implement the Field Customizer 355
        Debug Field Customizer 355
        Apply Field Customization 360
    Conclusion 362

33. SPFx Extensions-ListView Command Set 363
    Structure 363
    Objectives 363
    Overview of ListView Command Set 363
    Develop the ListView Command Set SPFx Solution 364
        Solution Structure 366
    Develop the ListView Command Set 367
    Debuggingthe List View Command Set 368
    Define the ListView Command Sets 371
    Implement the ListView Command Set Customization 373
    Conclusion 375

34. Anonymously Call MS Azure Functions 377
    Structure 377
    Objectives 377
    Introduction to Azure Functions 377
    Empower CORS for the Azure Function 380
    Call the Azure function from the SPFx Web Part 382
    Call Anonymous Azure Function from the Web Part 384
    Conclusion 387

35. Securing Azure Functions with Azure Active Directory 389
    Structure 389
    Objectives 389
    Azure Active Directory App Registration 389
        Set up the required permissions for App registration 391
        Assign consents for the App registration 392
        Implement the MS Azure Function 392
    CORS Enablement for Azure Function 396
    Develop the Azure Function with Visual Studio 398
    Conclusion 402

36. Consume Azure AD Secured Function with SPFx 403
Structure 403
Objectives 403
Consume the Azure function with the SPFx web part 403
Set permissions to the SPFx webpart 405
    Code the webpart 406
    Package the SPFx solution 408
Grant permissions to test the webpart 408
    Handle permission requests using Power Shell 409
Conclusion 410

37. Implementing Separation of Concerns (SoC) 411
Structure 411
Objectives 411
Separation of Concerns (SoC) 411
Developan SoC scenario 412
Mock data service implementation 415
Consume service inside the SPFx webpart 416
    Test the web part 417
Conclusion 418

38. Localization Support for SPFx 419
Structure 419
Objectives 419
Develop localization solutions for SPFx 419
Support for localization 421
    Test the web part property pane 425
Conclusion 425

39. Office 365 CLI 427
Structure 427
Objectives 427
Installation of the Office 365 CLI 428
Usage of the Office 365 CLI 428
Office 365 Tenant Management 428

Office 365 CLI Cmdlets 431
Office 365 CLI Upgrade 435
Conclusion 435

40. SPFx Solutions Upgrade 437
Structure 437
Objectives 437
The upgrade puzzle 437
Is the upgrade process simple? *438*
The basic strides to upgrade *438*
The upgrade plan 439
Conclusion 442

41. SPFx Solution Upgrade with the Office 365 CLI 443
Structure 443
Objective 443
Introduction to the Office 365 CLI 443
SPFx Solution Upgrade to the Latest Version 444
SPFx Solution Upgrade to a Specific Version 446
SPFx Solution Downgrade? *446*
Conclusion 447

42. Common Issues and Resolutions with Upgrading npn Packages 449
Structure 449
Objectives 449
Why to upgrade npm packages? 449
Upgrading npm packages *450*
Common Issues and Resolutions for npm Upgrade 450
Conclusion 452

43. Extend MS Teams with SPFx 453
Structure 453
Objectives 453
Develop the MS Teams Tab SPFx Solution 453
Support for MS Teams in SPFx 456
Handle MS Teams Context in the Web Part 457
Package and Deploy the web part to SharePoint 459

Make the web part accessible in MS Teams 461
Conclusion 464

44. Library Component Types 465
Structure 465
Objectives 465
Introduction to a Library Component 465
Create the Library Component 466
Develop the Library Component 468
Utilize the library component in the SPFx webpart 470
    Verify the webpart 472
Deploy a library to the tenant app catalog 472
Consume the Library from the Tenant App Catalog 473
Conclusion 473

45. Develop Custom App Pages with SPFx 475
Structure 475
Objective 475
Develop custom app pages with SPFx 475
Configure the web part for a single part page 477
Deploy the Package 478
    Deploy the package to the app catalog 478
Verify the Custom App Page Creation 479
Conclusion 481

46. Optimizing SPFx Solutions 483
Structure 483
Objective 483
SPFx implementation common issues 483
    Tip# 1: Splitting web parts to load individually 484
    Tip# 2: Dynamic loading of third-party libraries 485
    Tip# 3: Externally Reference External Libraries 486
    Tip# 4: Dissecting the SPFx Bundle 487
Conclusion 488

47. Unit Test with Jest and Enzyme 489
Structure 489
Objectives 489
Need of unit tests 490
Implement Unit Tests 490
    NPM Dependencies 493
    Setup Jest for SPFx: 493
    Include tests in the SPFxwebpart 494
    Execute Test Cases 496
Automate Unit Testing with Azure DevOps.. 496
    Azure DevOps Build Pipeline Configuration................................. 497
Conclusion 501

48. DevOps for SPFx... 503
Structure 503
Objectives 503
Continuous Integration (CI) 504
Create a Build Definition 504
Setup Deployment Trigger 518
Conclusion 519

49. Query User Profile Details 521
Structure 521
Objectives 521
User Profile Service Outline 521
Query User Profile Details from SPFx... 522
    Define Model representing User Profile Information 524
    Code the WebPart.. 526
Conclusion 528

50. Querying SP Search Results... 529
Structure 529
Objectives 529
SPFx Web Part to Query Search Results 529
    Define a Model for Search Result... 531
Implement Service to Query Search Results 535
Conclusion 537

51. React-based Tree View 539
Structure 539
Objectives 539
Develop a SPFx Solution for a React-based Tree View 539
Tree View Control 541
Conclusion 544

52. React-based Carousel 545
Structure 545
Objectives 545
Develop the SPFx Solution for Carousel 545
NPM Carousel Package 547
Conclusion 552

53. Implement a React-based Organogram 553
Structure 553
Objectives 553
Develop the SPFx Solution for an Organogram 553
Development Scenario 555
NPM Packages 556
Code the webpart 557
Conclusion 559

54. Integrating Adaptive Cards with SPFx 561
Structure 561
Objectives 561
Introduction to Adaptive Cards 561
Develop the SPFx web part for Adaptive Cards integration 562
NPM Packages 563
SharePoint Information Architecture 563
Conclusion 569

55. Integrating the Google API with SPFx 571
Structure 571
Objectives 571
Google Fit REST API 571

xxxii

    Overview of the Google Fit REST API 572

    Beginning with Google Fitness REST APIs 572

        Get Started with REST API 572

  Google Developer Playground 577

    List all data sources 580

        Get the Number of Steps 581

        Get the start date and end date 582

  Develop the SPFx web part to display Google Fit information 582

    NPM Packages Used 583

    Define State 584

    Implement the Service 585

    Code the web part 588

    Include Authorized JavaScript Origins 590

    Verify the web part 591

  Conclusion 591

56. SPFx Development with SharePoint On-Premises 593

  Structure 593

  Objectives 593

  Decide the SPFx Version 593

    Prepare SharePoint On-Premises for SPFx 594

    Develop the SPFx Web Part 594

        SPFx Support for SharePoint 2019 596

        Verify the SPFx webpart on the local SharePoint workbench 597

        Set up App Catalog 598

        Enable Scripting Capabilities (SharePoint 2019 only) 600

        Prepare the Package 600

        Upload the Package to the App Catalog 600

        Add the SPFx Solution to the SharePoint Site 601

        Place SPFx web part on the modern page 603

  Conclusion 605

Appendix 607

Glossary 613

Index 619

Recommendations, Resources & The Final Words 622

Chapter 1
Getting Started with the SharePoint Framework

SharePoint is evolving over the years. The SharePoint classic experience was introduced in late 2002. Since then, Microsoft continued adding new features on top of it. However, around the year 2017, Microsoft rolled out a new 'Modern' SharePoint based on new modern up-to-date web technologies. Modern SharePoint appeals to users with a fresh look and new modern experience, which is designed using modern web technologies. It works responsively on mobile devices and provides overall usability features.

Structure

- SharePoint Evolution Across Versions
- Birth of the SharePoint Framework
- Key Features of the SharePoint Framework
- Script editor web part vs App part vs SPFx web part
- Lightweight Components/Tools Used
- ALM of the Client-side Web Part
- Setup the Developer Environment for SPFx

Objectives

- Get introduced to Modern SharePoint customizations using the SharePoint Framework
- Overview of the **SharePoint Framework (SPFx)**
- Understand the SPFx Toolchain

SharePoint Evolution Across Versions

Before we deep dive into Modern SharePoint, let us look back in history to see how SharePoint has evolved over time. SharePoint 2007/MOSS supported the full trust server-side development. Over the years, the focus of development gradually shifted from server side to client side. Server and client-side development have their own advantages and limitations.

The following diagram shows how SharePoint has evolved across the versions:

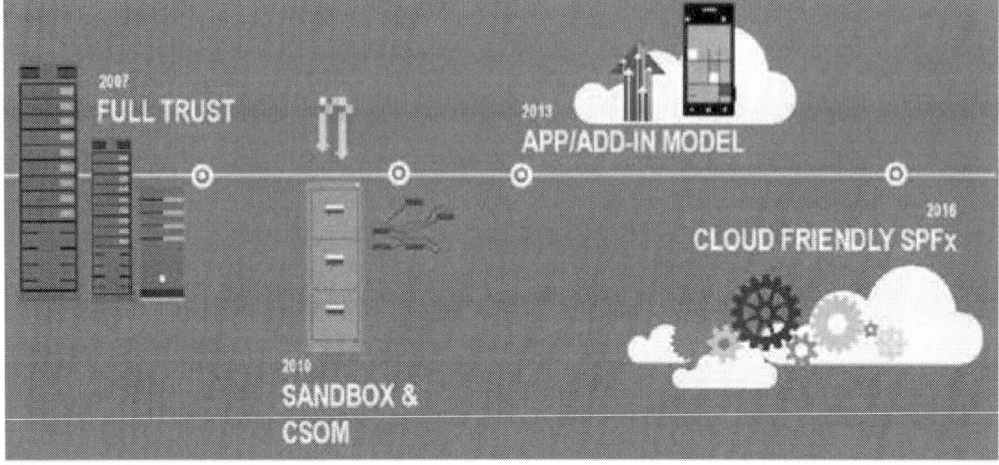

Figure: 1.1: SharePoint evolution across versions

SharePoint 2007: Full Trust Farm Solutions

In the days of MOSS, custom solutions were developed using 'Full Trust' or 'Farm Solutions', which supported the packaging and deployment of SharePoint customizations. The development approach was known as the SharePoint solution package, which bundled native .NET code and files with a .wsp extension. It containeda set of custom web parts, web templates, timer jobs, event receivers, etc. written in server-side languages like C#.

The server-side code had full permissions on the SharePoint farm. The SharePoint solution packages were formed using features, which could be turned on and off on SharePoint sites. One or more features were packaged together and deployed to SharePoint at various defined scopes like a farm, web application, site collection or a single site.

Full trust farm solutions enabled developers to customize or extend SharePoint as per business demands. As the code runs directly within the SharePoint server, the poorly designed code can affect the performance negatively, which might affect each and every application running as part of that SharePoint farm.Full trust farm solutions had imposed security concerns and risks as they had full permissions on the SharePoint farm.

SharePoint farm solutions are still supported for all SharePoint on-premises versions from 2007, 2010, 2013, 2016 and 2019. However, from the future compatibility perspective, it is not advisable to build SharePoint farm solutions.

> **Θ Note**
> A point to note that SharePoint solution packages (`.wsp`) are not supported in SharePoint online.

SharePoint 2010, SharePoint Online: Sandbox Solutions

Sandbox solutions are considered a subset of the farm solutions code development model. Sandbox solutions are more targeted to the specific site collection in SharePoint. It enables an individual site collection administrator to install and maintain custom solutions without the involvement of a farm administrator. Sandbox solutions had access toa limited subset of APIs, name spaces within the server-side object model and Microsoft .NET Framework 3.5 assemblies.

Later, Microsoft introduced the new SharePoint app model and eventually deprecated the use of custom managed code within the sandboxed solution. The app model was commonly used instead of a Sandbox solution managed code scenario. To start with the deprecation cycle, only the declarative markup in the form of XML and JavaScript was allowed in the Sandbox solution, which was famously known as no-code Sandboxed solutions (NCSS).Over time, all types of sandbox solutions were deprecated.

SharePoint 2013, SharePoint 2016, and SharePoint Online: App/Add-ins Model

The app model offers more flexibility and decouples SharePoint from the app runtime. It gives the ability to run the code in the external environment of your choice (e.g. IIS web site or MS Azure Web Apps). It is mainly supported by two types of deployment models, namely, SharePoint-hosted and Provider-hosted.

The SharePoint-hosted deployment type represents a way to deploy client-side, lightweight apps to SharePoint which contains no server-side components. They use SharePoint's data structure, including the separate subsite (called as **AppWeb**) and the actual SharePoint site (called as **HostWeb**). The user interface had to be built using CSS, HTML, and JavaScript. All assets were hosted within AppWeb to avoid cross-site scripting attack, thus providing more security.

Provider-hosted add-inshas server-side components contained within an ASP.NET application and you need to provide a separate environment to host them. This solution provided an approach to run the custom code outside SharePoint.

The add-ins infrastructure is clunky and relies heavily on JavaScript and asynchronous REST API calls/client-side object model calls to interact with the associated SharePoint context. The Add-in runs in a separate iframe. Even as of today,the add-ins model is supported; however, it did not progress much in the past few years.

Birth of the SharePoint Framework

The SharePoint custom development gradually shifted from server side to client side with the introduction of the client-side object model from Microsoft, which allowed you to connect to the SharePoint site remotely. **Managed Client-Side Object Model (CSOM)**, **JavaScript object model (JSOM)**, and REST APIs were being used effectively by SharePoint developers to carry out the customizations.

However, excessive use of JavaScript across the SharePoint sites (inside Script Editor or Content Editor web parts, custom actions) became unmanageable. Modern SharePoint does not support direct injection of JavaScript on the SharePoint site. The customizations are only allowed using SPFx web parts. An introduction to theSharePoint Framework brought in governance around this issue.

> ϴ **MSDN definition**
>
> The SharePoint Framework is a page and web part model that provides full support for the client-side SharePoint development, easy integration with SharePoint data, and support for open source tooling.

How SPFx is different?

The SharePoint framework is different from the classic JSOM development in many areas. Here are a few key points on how SPFx is different.

Modern toolchain/Open source tooling

SPFx supports open source tooling and modern toolchain, including Node.js, npm, Yeoman, Gulp, TypeScript, and so on.

Easy integration with SharePoint data

We can implement REST API wrapper classes for easy integration with SPFx.

Available in Cloud and On-Premises

SPFx is generally available in SharePoint Online. It also supports On-Premises from SP2016 onwards. Please note that in order to start using SPFx in the SharePoint Server 2016, you will need to install 'SharePoint 2016 Feature Pack 2' on the server. On the other hand, for the SharePoint Server 2019, SPFx is supported out of the box, without any installation of any pre-requisites.

Client-side rendering

SPFx does not rely on server side or compiled code written in C#. It is a development-platform agnostic framework. This means that it can be implemented on any operating system, including Windows, MacOS, etc. It natively supports multiple **integrated development environments (IDE)** like Visual Studio Code, Atom, and WebStorm.

Not dependent on JavaScript injection

Modern SharePoint does not allow injecting JavaScript directly on a page or using the custom action. At the same time, it leaves behind Script editor and Content editor web parts. Which in turn brings governance and more control.

No iframe

SPFx is like an add-in model that does not use an iframe to render. It has direct integration with the page model.

Key Features of the SharePoint Framework

- Unlike Add-in/App parts running inside iframes, the SPFx web part runs within the context of the currently logged in user and connection with the browser.

- All controls are rendered in the normal DOM enabling faster rendering on the browser.
- Controls are responsive.
- It does not support the elevation of privileges like in SharePoint in the full-trust code to overcome the permission model.
- It has full access to the lifecycle of the SharePoint Framework webpart, i.e. component (In it, render, load, serialize and deserialize, configuration changes, and so on).
- It is framework agnostic. Any framework like React, Angular, Knockout, and so oncan be used with SPFx.
- It supports open source development tools (npm, TypeScript, Yeoman, webpack, and Gulp).
- It can be used with both classic pages and modern pages.
- Safe and secure, tenant level access is required to deploy changes to the SPFx webpart.
- We can control the visibilityof the web part by deciding who can view in the App Catalog.
- Data models are unchanged. Earlier knowledge of CSOM can be transferred to the SPFx development.
- It is responsive in nature.

Script Editor WebPart vs App Part vs the SPFx WebPart

Custom development is an integral part of the SharePoint portal. With the increase in the use of the client-side development, JSOM has become the choice of developers. We have been using Script editors to inject scripts on pages or App parts to render themin an iframe.

- **Script Editor WebPart:**
    - Commonly used practice on classic SharePoint sites for customizing DOM.
    - Users with sufficient permissions can edit the script.
    - Sites with the 'NoScript' flag set do not support running scripts.
- **App Parts:**
    - Developed with the App/Add-ins model.
    - Runs inside an iframe. Due to this, it does not have access to the SharePoint page DOM.

- o   Development and deployment are comparatively complicated.
- **SPFx WebParts:**
  - o   Supports modern open source toolchain and JavaScript frameworks.
  - o   Works with both classic and modern SharePoint pages.
  - o   Provides modern experience, responsiveness out of the box.
  - o   Brings in governance to JavaScript injection.

Lightweight Components/Tools Used (SPFx Toolchain)

The toolchain for the SharePoint framework is based on open source tools and ideology. In this section, we will walk you through the necessary tools we should have in our toolchain to implement SharePoint framework solutions and compare them with equivalent tools used in the past in the server-side object model development.

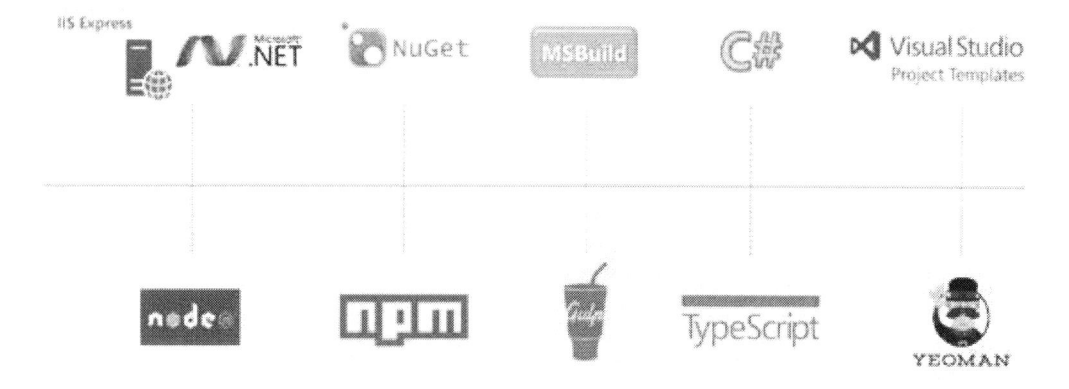

Figure 1.2: SharePoint Framework Toolchain (Server-side toolchain comparison)

- **Node.js:**
  - o   Open source JavaScript runtime
  - o   Responsible to build and run the applications
  - o   SPFx supports LTS (Long Term Support) version, preferably 8.x
- **NPM Packages:**
  - o   Stands for Node Package Manager
  - o   Package manager for JavaScript libraries
  - o   Maintains an online repository (npm registry) to find and deploy new packages

- o Installs packages and its dependencies
- o Packages can be installed globally (`-g switch`) or locally
- o Installed packages are available inside the `node_modules` folder

- **Gulp:**
  - o Automates SPFx development and deployment tasks
  - o Bundles and minifies JavaScript and CSS files
  - o Runs tools to call the bundling and minification tasks before each build
  - o Compiles LESS or SASS files to CSS
  - o Compiles TypeScript files to JavaScript
  - o Compiles, bundles and copies files to the deployment folder for packaging

- **Yeoman:**
  - o Relies on NPM and Gulp
  - o Scaffolding tool for Modern web apps
  - o SPFx solution generator
  - o 'yo' is the command line utility to build the project structure
  - o The Yeoman generator for creating the SharePoint framework project is available from Microsoft

- **TypeScript:**
  - o Strongly typed language
  - o Adds compile-time syntax and type checking for JavaScript
  - o Gets compiled to JavaScript code

- **Visual Studio Code:**
  - o Free, open source IDE for SPFx solutions
  - o Fast and lightweight
  - o Can work on any operating system, including Windows, Mac OS, and Linux
  - o Offers functionalities like IntelliSense, debugging, source control, and file management
  - o Supports third-party extensions
  - o Automatically updates itself

- **SharePoint Workbench:**
  - o The HTML page served by Node.js on a local file system
  - o It provides a sample canvas to add web parts

- o The local SharePoint Workbench is available as workbench.html on localhost
- o On the SharePoint site, it is available as `workbench.aspx` served from the hive folder
- o Responsive in nature

ALM of the Client-side Web Part

The **Application Lifecycle Management (ALM)** involves multiple tasks. The following diagram depicts the flow of the client-side web part from the installation of the needed npm packages for a solution, development of code to implement the functionality, test the solution on the workbench, and packaging and deployment of the solution to the SharePoint site.

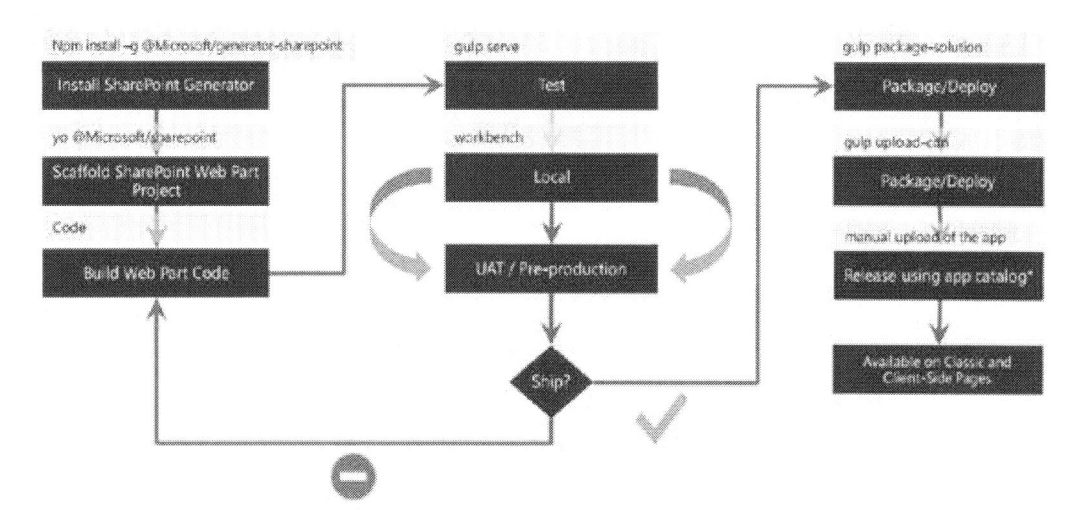

Figure 1.3: SharePoint Framework Client-side Web Part ALM

The SharePoint Framework also supports **continuous integration (CI)** and **continuous deployment (CD)**. We will deep dive into it in the upcoming chapters.

Setup the Developer Environment for SPFx

Perform the following set of commands to get your developer environment ready for SPFx.

1. **Install NodeJS:**
   - o Install the latest LTS version from **https://nodejs.org**.

- o If you already have NodeJS installed, check the version by running the following command:

```
node -v
```

2. **Install Yeoman and gulp:**
   - o Run the following command (to install globally):

```
npm install -g yo gulp
```

3. **Install Yeoman SharePoint Generator:**
   - o Run the following command:

```
npm install -g @microsoft/generator-sharepoint
```

   - o If you already have the Yeoman SharePoint Generator installed, check the version by running the following command:

```
npm ls @microsoft/generator-sharepoint -g --depth=0
```

> **Θ Note**
>
> You may create a batch file to install all the needed packages with specific versions for your development purpose and distribute it across the team so that everyone in the team has the same platform to start with the development.

4. **Install Code Editor:**

   Install any of the following code editors:
   1. Visual Studio Code **(https://code.visualstudio.com)**
   2. Atom **(https://atom.io)**
   3. Webstorm **(https://www.jetbrains.com/webstorm)**

5. **Update NPM packages:**

   Yo, Gulp, and the Yeoman SharePoint Generator get installed as NPM packages. Use the following commands to check and update them.

   To update NPM, use the following command:

```
npmi -g npm
```

To check the outdated packages, use the following command:

```
npm outdated -global
```

This command will report packages that need updates. Use the following command to update the reported packages:

```
npm update -g <package-name>
```

This book targets SPFx features released until 1.8.1 version, which is the latest at the time of writing this book. The SharePoint Framework is ever growing and there will be more versions of it releasing in the future.

Conclusion

In this chapter, we explored how SharePoint had become richer with its every release and eventually, a Modern SharePoint has evolved. The SharePoint Framework plays an important role in customizing Modern SharePoint. At the same time, it also supports classic SharePoint. It uses the modern open source toolchain.

We now have a basic understanding of the SharePoint framework and have configured our developer environment for SPFx. With this, we will start with the development of the SharePoint Framework in ourupcoming chapters.

CHAPTER 2
Develop Your First SPFx Web Part

Modern SharePoint development is evolving around the SharePoint Framework (SPFx). The SPFx client-side web parts are developed using the open source toolchain, modern UI standards, and JavaScript libraries/frameworks like Angular JS, React JS, Knockout JS, etc. The SPFx web part runs inside the context of the SharePoint page and is responsive in nature.

In this chapter, we will build a simple SPFx-based client-side web part. First, we need to follow the instructions discussed In the previous chapter to set up our development environment for SPFx.

Structure

- Features of SPFx Client-Side Web Parts
- Develop Your First SPFx Solution
- Understand the Solution Structure
- Major Elements of SPFx Solutions

Objectives

- Kick start the advancement of the SharePoint Framework
- Get acquainted with the SPFx arrangement structure

- Importance of each file and folder in SPFx solutions

Features of SPFx Client-side Web Parts

SPFx offers various features from the development and end user point of view:
- **Lightweight:** It uses JavaScript libraries (supports Angular JS, React JS, and KnockOut JS natively), SCSS, and HTML.
- **Responsive:** It renders on any device and supports various resolutions.
- **Environments:** It is supported on both SharePoint Online and On-Premises (SharePoint 2016 onwards).

Develop Your First SPFx Solution

SPFx supports the modern open source toolchain. The Yeoman generator for SPFx helps to scaffold the initial project structure. SPFx is framework agnostic. To start building the client-side web part, we can choose any of the JavaScript library or framework (No JavaScript Framework, React, and Knockout). Once developed, the SPFx web part can be tested on the SharePoint Workbench.

Open the command prompt. Perform the following steps to create the SPFx solution:

1. Create a directory for the SPFx solution.

   ```
   md firstspfx-webpart
   ```

2. Navigate to the above-created directory.

   ```
   cd firstspfx-webpart
   ```

3. Run the Yeoman SharePoint generator to create the SPFx solution.

   ```
   yo @microsoft/sharepoint
   ```

4. The Yeoman generator will run through the wizard by asking questions about the SPFx solution to be generated.

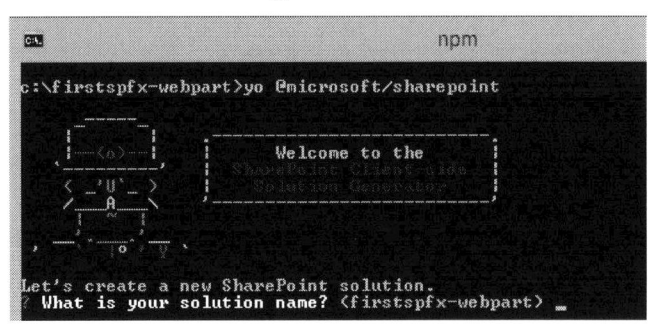

Figure 2.1: SPFx Yeoman generator

The SPFx Yeoman generator will display the following wizard of questions:

- **Solution Name:** Specify the name of the SPFx solution. Hit the *Enter* key to go ahead with the default name (firstspfx-webpart in this case) or type in any other name for your solution.
    - **Selected choice:** Hit *Enter* (default name)
- **The target for the component:** Specify the target environment to develop and deploy the SPFx solution. Choose from any of the SharePoint Online or SharePoint On-Premises environments.
    - **Selected choice:** SharePoint Online only (latest)
- **Place of files:** Choose the folder location for the SPFx project (either the same folder or a subfolder).
    - **Selected choice:** Same folder
- **Deployment option:** Specify Y to allow deployment of the app instantly to all the sites, N otherwise.
    - **Selected choice:** N (install on each site explicitly)
- **Type of client-side component to create:** Choose to create a client-side web part or an extension.
    - **Selected choice:** WebPart
- **Web part name:** Specify the name of the web part name. Hit the *Enter* key to go ahead with the default name or type in any other name.
    - **Selected choice:** Hit *Enter* (default name)
- **Web part description:** Specify the web part description. Hit the *Enter* key to go ahead with the default description or type in any other value.
    - **Selected choice:** Hit *Enter* (default description)
- **A framework to use:** Select a JavaScript framework to develop the component. The available choices are No JavaScript Framework, React, and Knockout.
    - **Selected choice:** No JavaScript Framework

5. The Yeoman generator will start the scaffolding process to create the solution. It will download the needed npm packages, and install the required dependencies. The solution creation will take a significant amount of time.

Figure 2.2: Yeoman scaffolding for the SPFx project

6. Once the scaffolding process is finished, Yeoman will show the following message:

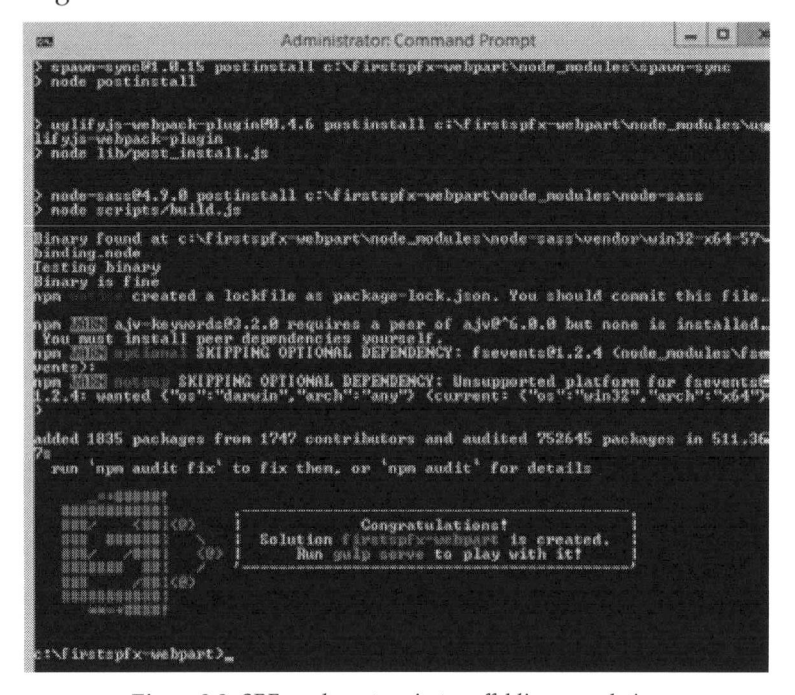

Figure 2.3: SPFx web part project scaffolding completion

Open Solution in Code Editor

Any of the following code editorial managers can be utilized to open the SPFx solution:
- Visual Studio Code **(https://code.visualstudio.com)**
- Particle **(https://atom.io)**
- Webstorm **(https://www.jetbrains.com/webstorm)**

Type the following command to open the SPFx solution in your choice of code editor:

```
code .
```

Run the WebPart on SharePoint local workbench

Since the client-side toolchain uses the HTTPS endpoint, we will need to install the developer certificate (part of the SPFx toolchain) as a one-time activity on the development environment.

1. To install a developer certificate, run the following command from the command prompt:

```
gulp trust-dev-cert
```

The following diagram shows the installation of the developer certificate:

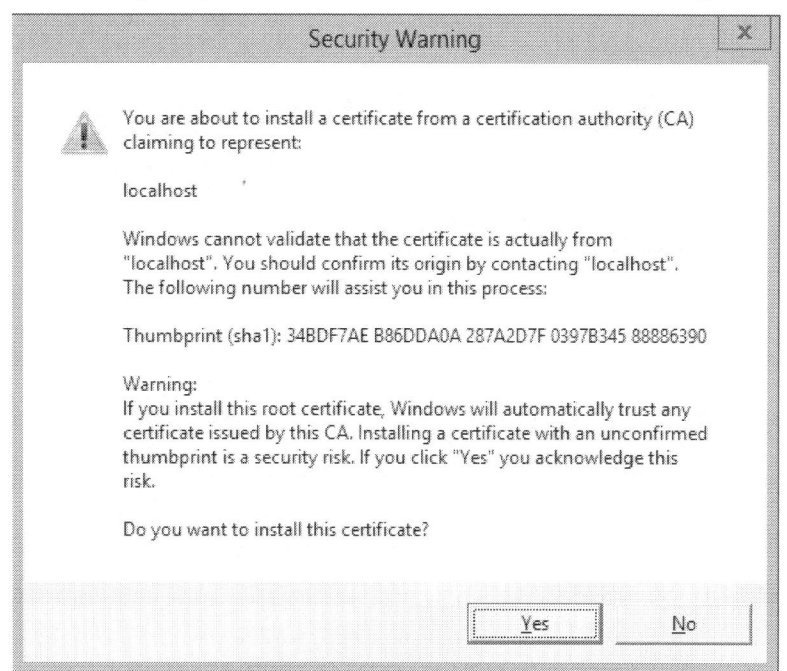

Figure 2.4: Developer certificate installation

2. Click on Yes to accept the security warning.
3. Run the following command to preview the web part in the browser:

```
gulp serve
```

The preceding command instructs Gulp to start the Node.js server and open the browser with a local SharePoint Workbench **(https://localhost:4321)**.

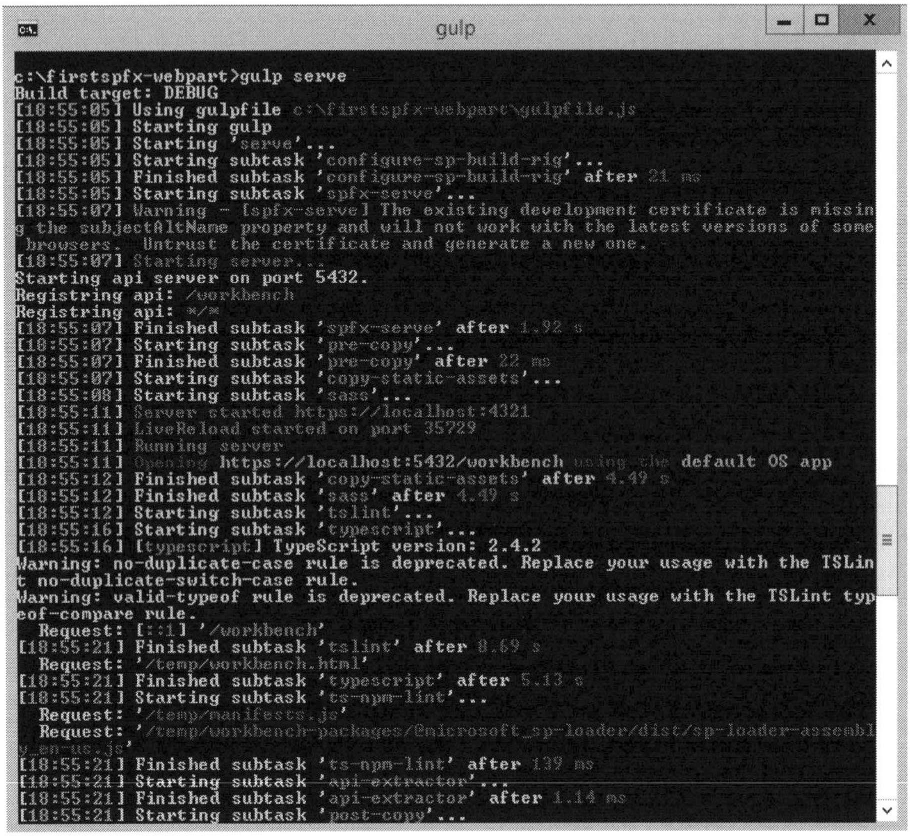

Figure 2.5: Gulp serve in action

This gulp serve command runs a series of the following gulp tasks:
- Minifies and bundles JavaScript and CSS files
- Compiles SASS (Syntactically Awesome Style Sheets) to CSS
- Compiles TypeScript to JavaScript

4. On successful compilation and running the gulp tasks, it will open the SharePoint local workbench. The SharePoint Local Workbench is an HTML page which helps to preview and test client-side web parts without deploying to SharePoint. It gets served locally on the following URL: **https://localhost:4321/temp/workbench.html**

Figure 2.6: SharePoint local workbench

5. Click on the Add (+) icon and select the web part to add it on the page.

Figure 2.7: Add the web part to SharePoint local workbench

Congratulations! The first client-side web part is ready to use.

6. Click on the Edit icon to modify the web part property (e.g. description) from the properties pane. The change in the description field will be reflected on the client-side web part as you type in.

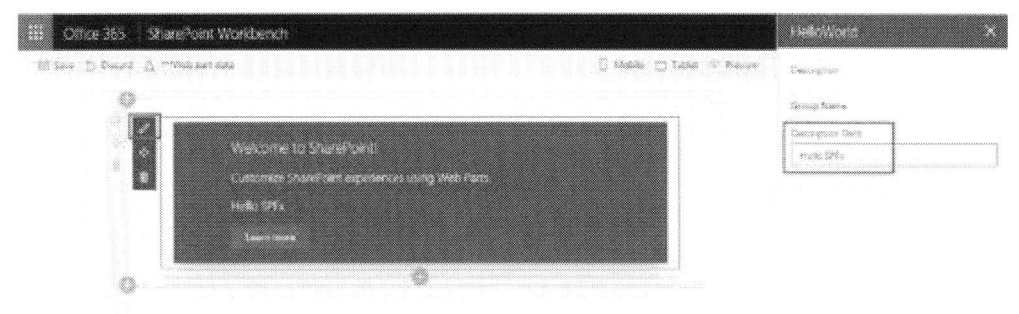

Figure 2.8: Edit properties of the SPFx web part

Understand the Solution Structure

Let us explore the solution structure of the SPFx client-side web part and understand the major elements.

Type the following command to open the SPFx solution in a code editor:

```
code .
```

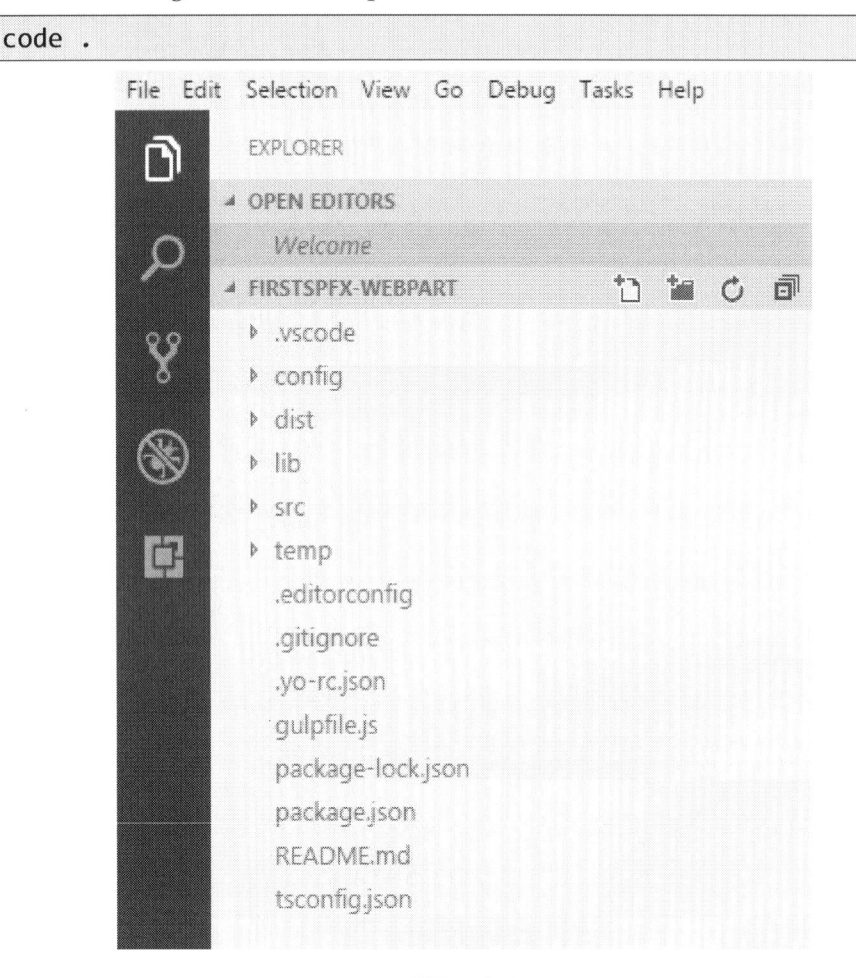

Figure 2.9: SPFx solution structure

The SPFx solution structure comprises different files and folders. The essential language utilized is TypeScript (which is a superset of JavaScript). The code for the most part uses classes, modules, and interfaces written in TypeScript.

Major Elements of the SPFx Solution

Here are the major folders of the solution:

Folder	Contents
config	Configuration files
dist	Distributable files (e.g. TypeScript files compiled into bundled JavaScript files)
lib	Intermediate files that are being used by SharePoint in the project build process
node_modules	Contains npm package dependencies in a complex hierarchy of files and folders
src	Contains source files
temp	Contains temporary files
typings	TypeScript typing information

The following files have great significance in the SPFx solution.

Web Part Class (HelloWorldWebPart.ts)

This class represents an entry point and is located on the src\webparts\helloWorld folder. Each client-side web part class should extend from Base ClientSideWebPart, which is responsible for primary working of the web part.

Property Type Interface (IHelloWorldWebPartProps)

This interface helps to define business-specific custom properties for the web part. We can include any of the following properties:
- Button
- Checkbox
- Choice group
- Dropdown
- Horizontal rule
- Label
- Link
- Slider
- Textbox
- Multi-line Textbox
- Toggle
- Custom

The properties can be used in the web part as follows:

TypeScript

```
<p class="${ styles.description }">${escape(this.properties.
description)}</p>
```

WebPart Manifest:

`HelloWorldWebPart.manifest.json` holds the metadata of the web part such as display name, `description`, `icon`, `version`, and `id`.

JSON

```
{
"$schema":"https://developer.microsoft.com/json-schemas/spfx/client-
side-web-part-manifest.schema.json",
"id": "a925e124-f0f8-4a26-a797-d384046cf5a7",
"alias": "HelloWorldWebPart",
"componentType": "WebPart",

// The "*" signifies that the version should be taken from the package.json
"version": "*",
"manifestVersion": 2,

// If true, the component can only be installed on sites where Custom
Script is allowed.
// Components that allow authors to embed arbitrary script code should
set this to true.
// https://support.office.com/en-us/article/Turn-scripting-capabilities-
on-or-off-1f2c515f-5d7e-448a-9fd7-835da935584f
"requiresCustomScript": false,

"preconfiguredEntries": [{
"groupId": "5c03119e-3074-46fd-976b-c60198311f70", // Other
"group": { "default": "Other" },
"title": { "default": "HelloWorld" },
"description": { "default": "HelloWorld description" },
"officeFabricIconFontName": "Page",
```

```json
"properties": {
"description": "HelloWorld"
    }
  }]
}
```

Config.json:

This file consists of information regarding components used in the SPFx solution, entry point of the SPFx solution, external JavaScript library references (for e.g. jQuery) and its dependencies, and localization resources.

JSON

```json
{
"$schema":"https://developer.microsoft.com/json-schemas/spfx-build/config.2.0.schema.json",
"version": "2.0",
"bundles": {
"hello-world-web-part": {
"components": [
    {
"entrypoint": "./lib/webparts/helloWorld/HelloWorldWebPart.js",
"manifest": "./src/webparts/helloWorld/HelloWorldWebPart.manifest.json"
    }
   ]
  }
 },
"externals": {},
"localizedResources": {
"HelloWorldWebPartStrings": "lib/webparts/helloWorld/loc/{locale}.js"
  }
}
```

deploy-azure-storage.json:

This file contains the Azure storage account details, which can be utilized during deployment of the SPFx web part to Azure CDN.

This record is utilized while sending the client-side web part to Azure CDN. This record contains Azure stockpiling record subtleties.

JSON

```json
{
"$schema":"https://developer.microsoft.com/json-schemas/spfx-build/deploy-azure-storage.schema.json",
"workingDir": "./temp/deploy/",
"account": "<!-- STORAGE ACCOUNT NAME -->",
"container": "spfxcontainer",
"accessKey": "<!—ACCESS KEY -->"
}
```

package-solution.json:

This file contains the solution path configurations.

JSON

```json
{
"$schema":"https://developer.microsoft.com/json-schemas/spfx-build/package-solution.schema.json",
"solution": {
"name": "spfx-helloworld-client-side-solution",
"id": "41c6825d-8ef2-45e1-b544-5f0d64a480e6",
"version": "1.0.0.0",
"includeClientSideAssets": false,
"skipFeatureDeployment": true
   },
"paths": {
"zippedPackage": "solution/spfx-helloworld.sppkg"
   }
}
```

gulpfile.js:

This file defines gulp tasks to be run.

package.json:

This file defines JavaScript library dependencies and their versions used by npm.

tsconfig.json:

This file defines settings for TypeScript compilation.

.editorconfig:

The Visual studio configuration file define show the editor works in this folder.

.gitignore:

This file instructs Git to ignore certain files.

.npmignore:

This file instructs npm to ignore certain files.

README.md:

This is a documentation file for Git repositories.

tsconfig.json:

This file configures TypeScript compilation options.

Conclusion

In this chapter, we started by developing our first SPFx solution. Yeoman generators help to generate the SPFx client-side web part solution. The solution has a predefined structure. Each folder and file has its own significance. It is important to understand the role of each file for better development. We used Visual Studio Code to view the generated project and run the project using Gulp to test in the local SharePoint Workbench. Finally, we took an in-depth look into the source files and project structure of the generated SPFx project.

CHAPTER 3
SPFx Web Part Property Pane

SharePoint web parts have properties that characterize the conduct of that web part. The conduct and presence of the web part can be changed by setting the properties. In the SharePoint Framework, properties are by and large alluded as property sheets.

Structure
- Property Pane Metadata
- Supported Typed Object Properties
- Test the Property Pane

Objectives
- Deep dive into understanding supported property fields
- Configure the property panes

Property Pane Metadata
The Property pane has the following metadata:
- **Pages:** This allows you to isolate complex interactions and divide them across one or multiple pages. Pages have sub-metadata defined as Header and Groups.

- **Header:** This characterizes the title of the property pane.
- **Groups:** This gathers different property fields together. The following is a list of out-of-the-box available property fields:

#	Property field	SPFx Typed Object
1	Label	`PropertyPaneLabel`
2	Textbox	`PropertyPaneTextField`
3	Multiple lines of text	`PropertyPaneTextField`
4	Link	`PropertyPaneLink`
5	Dropdown	`PropertyPaneDropdown`
6	Checkbox	`PropertyPaneCheckbox`
7	Choice	`PropertyPaneChoiceGroup`
8	Toggle	`PropertyPaneToggle`
9	Slider	`PropertyPaneSlider`
10	Button	`PropertyPaneButton`
11	Horizontal Rule	`PropertyPaneHorizontalRule`
12	Custom	Our own implementation using a combination of the above

SPFx Solution for the Property Pane

1. Create a directory for the SPFx solution:

   ```
   md spfx-oobpropertypanes
   ```

2. Navigate to the directory:

   ```
   cd spfx-oobpropertypanes
   ```

3. Run the Yeoman SharePoint Generator to create the solution:

   ```
   yo @microsoft/sharepoint
   ```

4. Provide the following values in the Yeoman generator wizard:
   - **Solution Name:** Specify the name of the SPFx solution. Hit the *Enter* key to go ahead with the default name (`spfx-oobpropertypanes` in this case) or type in any other name for your solution.
     o **Selected choice:** Hit *Enter* (default name)
   - **The target for the component:** Specify the target environment to develop and deploy the SPFx solution. Choose from any of SharePoint Online or SharePoint On-Premises environments.

- o **Selected choice:** SharePoint Online only (latest)
- **Place of files:** Choose the folder location for the SPFx project (either the same folder or a subfolder).
  - o **Selected choice:** Same folder
- **Deployment option:** Specify Y to allow deployment of the app instantly to all the sites, N otherwise.
  - o **Selected choice:** N (install on each site explicitly)
- **Type of client-side component to create:** Choose to create a client-side web part or an extension.
  - o **Selected choice:** WebPart
- **Web part name:** Specify the web part name. Hit the *Enter* key to go ahead with the default name or type in any other name.
  - o **Selected choice:** SPFX Property Pane
- **Web part description:** Specify the web part description. Hit the *Enter* key to proceed with the default description or type in any other value.
  - o **Selected choice:** Hit *Enter* (default description)
- **A framework to use:** Select a JavaScript system to build the part. Accessible decisions are (No JavaScript Framework, React, and Knockout).
  - o **Selected choice:** No JavaScript Framework

5. Once the Yeoman generator finishes scaffolding the SPFx solution, type `code .At the` command prompt to open the solution in your favorite code editor.

Property Pane Code

Open `SpfxPropertyPaneWebPart.ts` file located at `"\src\webparts\spfxPropertyPane"`.

The `getPropertyPaneConfiguration()` method contains the configuration to build the property pane.

TypeScript

```
protected getPropertyPaneConfiguration(): IPropertyPaneConfiguration {
return {
    pages: [
      {
        header: {
```

```
          description: strings.PropertyPaneDescription
        },
        groups: [
          {
            groupName: strings.BasicGroupName,
            groupFields: [
              PropertyPaneTextField('description', {
                label: strings.DescriptionFieldLabel
              })
            ]
          }
        ]
      }
    ]
  };
}
```

The `defaultSpfxPropertyPaneWebPartclass` accepts an interface of the `ISpfxPropertyPaneWebPartPropsproperty` type, which by default exposes the description as the string property. The property can be utilized in the render() method as follows:

TypeScript

```
${escape(this.properties.description)}
```

The `SpfxPropertyPaneWebPart` class looks as follows:

TypeScript

```
exportinterfaceISpfxPropertyPaneWebPartProps {

name: string;

}

exportdefaultclassSpfxPropertyPaneWebPartextendsBaseClientSide
WebPart<ISpfx PropertyPaneWebPartProps> {
```

```
publicrender(): void {
this.domElement.innerHTML = `
<div class="${styles.spfxPropertyPane}">
<div class="${styles.container}">
<div class="${styles.row}">
<div class="${styles.column}">
<span class="${styles.title}">Welcome to SharePoint!</span>
<p class="${styles.subTitle}">Customize SharePoint experiences using Web Parts.</p>
<p class="${styles.description}">Description: ${escape(this.properties.description)}</p>
<a href="https://aka.ms/spfx" class="${styles.button}">
<span class="${styles.label}">Learn more</span>
</a>
</div>
</div>
</div>
</div>`;
 }
   .
   .
   .
}
```

The import section has the property types defined as follows:

TypeScript

```
import {
BaseClientSideWebPart,
IPropertyPaneConfiguration,
PropertyPaneTextField
} from '@microsoft/sp-webpart-base';
```

Supported Typed Object Properties

Many properties can be defined for the SPFx web part with the default supported typed objects (e.g. textbox, checkbox, label, link, etc.):

1. In the `spfxPropertyPaneWebPart.ts` file located at "\src\webparts\spfxPropertyPane", import the corresponding typed objects:

   TypeScript
   ```
   import {
   BaseClientSideWebPart,
   IPropertyPaneConfiguration,
   PropertyPaneTextField,    // Textbox
   PropertyPaneCheckbox,     // Checkbox
   PropertyPaneLabel,        // Label
   PropertyPaneLink,         // Link
   PropertyPaneSlider,       // Slider
   PropertyPaneToggle,       // Toggle
   PropertyPaneDropdown// Dropdown
   } from'@microsoft/sp-webpart-base';
   ```

2. Modify the `ISpfxPropertyPaneWebPartProps` interface by adding new properties with the following code andby mapping fields to typed objects:

   TypeScript
   ```
   exportinterfaceISpfxPropertyPaneWebPartProps {
   name: string;
   description: string;
   Slider:string;
   Toggle:string;
   dropdowm:string;
   checkbox:string;
   URL:string;
   textbox:string;
   }
   ```

3. Add new property pane fields and map them to their respective typed objects in the getPropertyPaneConfiguration() method:

   TypeScript
   ```
   protectedtextBoxValidationMethod(value: string): string {
   ```

```
if (value.length<10) {
return"Name should be at least 10 characters!";
  }
else {
return"";
  }
}

protectedgetPropertyPaneConfiguration(): IPropertyPaneConfiguration
      {
return {
pages: [
      { //Page 1
header: {
description:"Page 1 - Name and Description"
         },
groups: [
          {
groupName:"Group one",
groupFields: [
PropertyPaneTextField('name', {
label:"Name",
multiline:false,
resizable:false,
onGetErrorMessage:this.textBoxValidationMethod,
errorMessage:"This is the error message",
deferredValidationTime:5000,
placeholder:"Please enter name","description":"Name property field"
             }),
PropertyPaneTextField('description', {
label:"Description",
multiline:true,
resizable:true,
placeholder:"Please enter description","description":"Description property field"
             })
```

```
            ]
          }
        ]
      }
    ]
  };
}
```

4. `pages[]` holds the page collection. It is like an array. Each page can have the Groups attribute that can hold the properties We can define multiple pages for the property pane as follows:

TypeScript
```
{ //Page 2
          header: {
             description:"Page 2 - Slider and Dropdown"
          },
          groups: [
            {
              groupName:"Group one",
              groupFields: [
                PropertyPaneSlider('Slider', {
                   label:'Slider',min:1,max:10
                }),
                PropertyPaneToggle('Toggle', {
                label:'Slider'
                })
              ]
            },
            {
  groupName:"Group Two",
              groupFields: [
                 PropertyPaneDropdown('dropdowm', {
                   label:'Drop Down',
                   options: [
                     { key:'Item1', text:'Item 1' },
                     { key:'Item2', text:'Item 2' },
```

```
                    { key:'Item3', text:'Item 3' }
                  ]
                }),
                PropertyPaneCheckbox('checkbox',
                    { text:'Yes/No'})
            ]
          }
        ]
      },
```

5. Setup one more page for the remaining fields. We can group related fields together on a page for their logical grouping. We can have multiple pages set in a property pane:

   TypeScript
   ```
   { //Page 3
     header: {
       description:"Page 3 - URL and Label"
     },
     groups: [
       {
           groupName:"Group One",
           groupFields: [
   PropertyPaneLink('URL',
                   { text:"Microsoft", href:'http://www.microsoft.
          com',target:'_blank'}),
               PropertyPaneLabel('label',
               { text:'Please enter designation',required:true}),
               PropertyPaneTextField('textbox',{})
         ]
       }
     ]
   }
   ```

6. Modify the render method to show the selected field values:

   TypeScript
   ```
   exportdefaultclassSpfxPropertyPaneWebPartextendsBaseCli
       entSideWebPart<ISpfxPropertyPaneWebPartProps> {
   ```

```
publicrender(): void {
this.domElement.innerHTML = `
<div class="${styles.spfxPropertyPane}">
<div class="${styles.container}">
<div class="${styles.row}">
<div class="${styles.column}">
<span class="${styles.title}">Welcome to SharePoint!</span>
<p class="${styles.subTitle}">Customize SharePoint experiences
      using Web Parts.</p>
<p class="${styles.description}">Name: ${escape(this.properties.
      name)}</p>
<p class="${styles.description}">Description: ${escape(this.
      properties.description)}</p>

<p class="${styles.description}">Slider: ${escape(this.
      properties.Slider)}</p>
<p class="${styles.description}">Toggle: ${escape(this.
      properties.Toggle)}</p>
<p class="${styles.description}">dropdowm: ${escape(this.
      properties.dropdowm)}</p>
<p class="${styles.description}">checkbox: ${escape(this.
      properties.checkbox)}</p>

<p class="${styles.description}">URL: ${escape(this.properties.
      URL)}</p>
<p class="${styles.description}">textbox: ${escape(this.
      properties.textbox)}</p>
<a href="https://aka.ms/spfx" class="${styles.button}">
<span class="${styles.label}">Learn more</span>
</a>
</div>
</div>
</div>
</div>`;
  }
  .
  .
  .
}
```

Test the Property Pane

Let us use the local SharePoint workbench to test the SPFx web part.

1. Open the command prompt.
2. Type `gulp serve`.
3. On the local SharePoint workbench, locate and add our web part named SPFxPropertyPane.

Figure 3.1: Add SPFx web part to SharePoint neighborhood workbench

4. Edit the web part to change property fields:

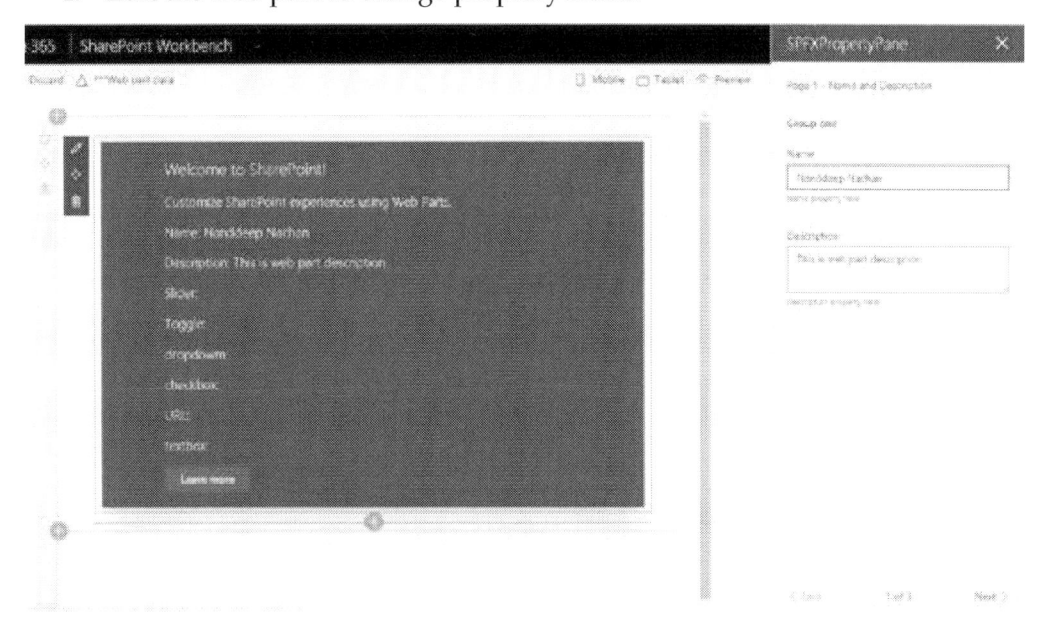

3.2: Alter SPFx web part to test property pane

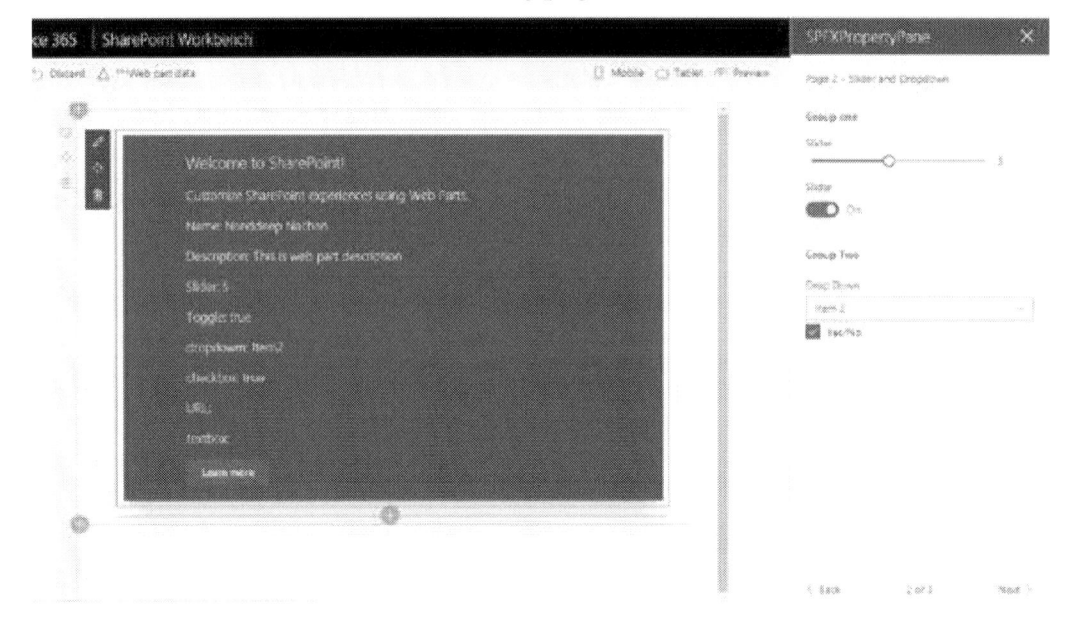

5. Click on **Next** to see the following page of fields:

Figure 3.3: SPFx property pane paging

Conclusion

In this chapter, we investigated the out of the case available property fields and arranged the property sheets. Property fields allowend clients to arrange the web part with a few properties. It allows a simple arrangement of the SPFx client-side web part. We can utilize predefined typed objects to define properties for the web part. Properties can be assembled by pages. A property sheet has three key metadata: a page, a discretionary header, and group. The SharePoint Framework contains a lot of standard controls for the property sheet.

CHAPTER 4
Custom Control for the Web Part Property Pane

The SharePoint Framework web parts support various predefined typed objects (e.g. textbox, checkbox, link, slider, etc.) to define properties for our SPFx web part. These predefined typed objects are sufficient in most cases; however, to meet certain business scenarios, we have to create our own custom controls. One classic example of this is list selection for the web part. We can have a simple textbox in the web part property pane to allow the user to enter the SharePoint list name. However, listing all available SharePoint lists in a dropdown will give a more seamless experience to the end users.

Structure
- Build Dropdown Custom Control for SharePoint List
- Define the Web Part Property
- Use Dropdown Property Pane Control in the Web Part
- Test the Custom Property Pane

Objectives
- Build custom controls for the property pane
- Develop the list dropdown selection property pane

Build the List Dropdown Custom Control

Open the command prompt. Perform the following steps to create the SPFx solution:

1. Create a directory for the SPFx solution:

   ```
   md spfx-customcontrol-propertypane
   ```

2. Navigate to the above-created directory:

   ```
   cd spfx-customcontrol-propertypane
   ```

3. Run the Yeoman SharePoint Generator to create the solution:

   ```
   yo @microsoft/sharepoint
   ```

4. The Yeoman generator will display the wizard by asking you questions about the solution to be created:

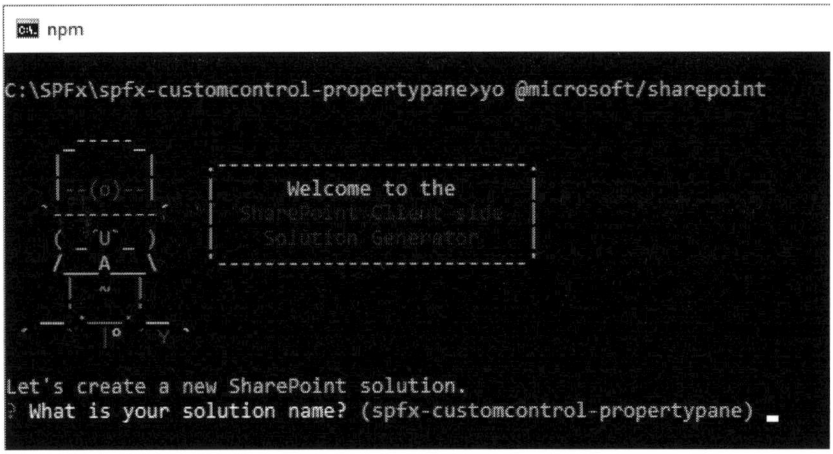

Figure 4.1: SPFx solution generation

The SPFx Yeoman generator will display the following wizard of questions:

- **Solution Name:** Specify the name of the SPFx solution. Hit the *Enter* key to go ahead with the default name (`spfx-customcontrol-propertypane` in this case) or type in any other name for your solution.
    - **Selected choice:** Hit *Enter*
- **The target for the component:** Select the target environment where we are planning to deploy the client web part i.e. SharePoint Online or SharePoint On-Premises (SharePoint 2016 onwards).
    - **Selected choice:** SharePoint Online only (latest)
- **Place of files:** Choose the folder location for the SPFx project (either the same folder or a subfolder).
    - **Selected choice:** Use the current folder

- **Deployment option:** Selecting Y will allow the app to be deployed instantly to all sites and will be accessible everywhere.
    - o **Selected choice:** Y
- **Permissions to access web APIs:** Check whether the components in the solution require permissions to access web APIs that are unique and not shared with other components in the tenant.
    - o **Selected choice:** N (solution contains unique permissions)
- **Type of client-side component to create:** Choose to create a client-side web part or an extension.
    - o **Selected choice:** WebPart
- **Web Part Name:** Specify the name of the web part name. Hit the *Enter* key to go ahead with the default name or type in any other name.
    - o **Selected choice:** CustomPropertyPaneDemo
- **Web part description:** Specify the name of the web part description. Hit *Enter* key to go ahead with the default description or type in any other value.
    - o **Selected choice:** Hit *Enter*
- **A framework to use:** Select any JavaScript framework to develop the component. Available choices are (No JavaScript Framework, React, and Knockout).
    - o **Selected choice:** React

5. After the scaffolding is finished, run the following command to lock down the version of project dependencies:
```
npm shrinkwrap
```

6. At the command prompt, type the following command to open the solution in the code editor of your choice:
```
code .
```

Define the Web Part Property

As a business scenario, we will build a custom control to render the available lists from the current SharePoint site in a dropdown as the web part property. Let us start by defining the web part property to store the user selected list from the web part property:

1. Open `CustomPropertyPaneDemoWebPart.manifest.json` under the "\src\webparts\customPropertyPaneDemo" folder.
2. Rename the default description property to `listName`:

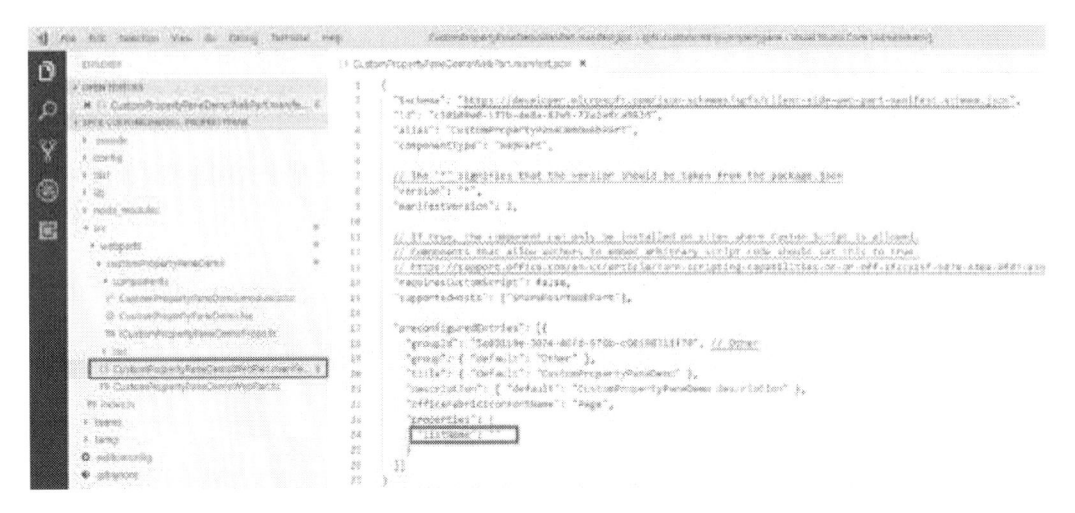

Figure 4.2: Define the list Name property

3. Open `ICustomPropertyPaneDemoProps.ts` under the "src\webparts\ customPropertyPaneDemo\components\" folder and update it to use the `listName` property:

   TypeScript

   ```typescript
   exportinterface ICustomPropertyPaneDemoProps {
     listName: string;
   }
   ```

4. In "\src\webparts\customPropertyPaneDemo\CustomPropertyPaneDemoWebPart.ts", update the `render()` method to use the `listName` property.

   TypeScript

   ```typescript
   public render(): void {

   const element: React.ReactElement<ICustomPropertyPaneDemoProps> = React.createElement(

       CustomPropertyPaneDemo,

       {

         listName: this.properties.listName

       }

     );

     ReactDom.render(element, this.domElement);

   }
   ```

5. Update the getPropertyPaneConfiguration() method to expose the list name as the web part property:

   TypeScript

   ```
   protected getPropertyPaneConfiguration(): IPropertyPaneConfiguration
   {
   return {
         pages: [
           {
             header: {
               description: strings.PropertyPaneDescription
             },
             groups: [
               {
                 groupName: strings.BasicGroupName,
                 groupFields: [
                   PropertyPaneTextField('listName', {
                     label: strings.ListFieldLabel
                   })
                 ]
               }
             ]
           }
         ]
      };
   }
   ```

6. Update the interface at "src\webparts\customPropertyPaneDemo\loc\mystrings.d.ts":

   TypeScript

   ```
   declareinterface ICustomPropertyPaneDemoWebPartStrings {
      PropertyPaneDescription: string;
   ```

```
    BasicGroupName: string;
    ListFieldLabel: string;
}
```

7. In the "src\webparts\customPropertyPaneDemo\loc\en-us.js", update the definition as follows:

TypeScript

```
define([], function() {
return {
"PropertyPaneDescription": "Description",
"BasicGroupName": "Group Name",
"ListFieldLabel": "List"
  }
});
```

8. In the "src\webparts\customPropertyPaneDemo\components\CustomPropertyPaneDemo.tsx", update the render() method to use the listName property field:

TypeScript

```
public render(): React.ReactElement<ICustomPropertyPaneDemoProps> {
return (
<divclassName={ styles.customPropertyPaneDemo }>
<divclassName={ styles.container }>
<divclassName={ styles.row }>
<divclassName={ styles.column }>
<spanclassName={ styles.title }>Welcome to SharePoint!</span>
<pclassName={ styles.subTitle }>Customize SharePoint experiences using Web Parts.</p>
<pclassName={ styles.description }>{escape(this.props.listName)}</p>
<ahref="https://aka.ms/spfx"className={ styles.button }>
<spanclassName={ styles.label }>Learn more</span>
```

```
        </a>
      </div>
    </div>
  </div>
</div>
);
}
```

9. At the command prompt, type `gulp serve` to see the new web part property in action:

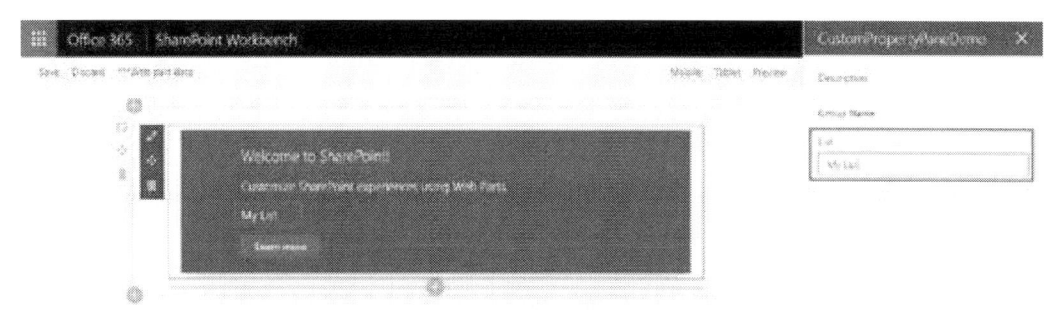

Figure 4.3: Test SPFx WebPart for property pane change

Add the Dropdown Property Pane Control

Let us implement a dropdown for showing lists from the SharePoint site.

Define React Props for the dropdown

Under "src\webparts\customPropertyPaneDemo\components", add the IList DropdownProps.ts file:

TypeScript

```
import { IDropdownOption } from 'office-ui-fabric-react/lib/components/Dropdown';

export interface IListDropdownProps {
  label: string;
  loadOptions: () => Promise<IDropdownOption[]>;
  onChanged: (option: IDropdownOption, index?: number) => void;
  selectedKey: string | number;
```

```
    disabled: boolean;
    stateKey: string;
}
```

The preceding class defines properties for the React component being used on the web part property pane:

- `label:` This is a label for the dropdown control.
- `loadOptions:` This is a delegate function to load available options.
- `onChanged:` This is a delegate function called upon user selection.
- `selectKey:` This is a user selected value.
- `disabled:` This defines whether the dropdown is disabled or not.
- `stateKey:` This re-renders the React component.

Define the React State for the dropdown

Under "src\webparts\customPropertyPaneDemo\components", add theIList DropdownState.tsfile:

TypeScript

```
import { IDropdownOption } from'office-ui-fabric-react/lib/components/Dropdown';

exportinterface IListDropdownState {
    loading: boolean;
    options: IDropdownOption[];
    error: string;
}
```

The preceding interface defines the state for the React component.

- **loading:** This defines if the component is loading its options.
- **options:** This holds all available dropdown options.
- **error:** This defines any error that has occurred.

Define the DropDown React Component

Under "src\webparts\customPropertyPaneDemo\components", add the List Dropdown.tsx file:

TypeScript

```
import *as React from 'react';

import { Dropdown, IDropdownOption } from 'office-ui-fabric-react/lib/components/Dropdown';

import { Spinner } from 'office-ui-fabric-react/lib/components/Spinner';

import { IListDropdownProps } from './IListDropdownProps';

import { IListDropdownState } from './IListDropdownState';


export default class ListDropdown extends React.Component<IListDropdownProps, IListDropdownState> {

private selectedKey: React.ReactText;

constructor(props: IListDropdownProps, state: IListDropdownState) {
super(props);
this.selectedKey = props.selectedKey;

this.state = {
    loading: false,
    options: undefined,
    error: undefined
  };
}

public componentDidMount(): void {
this.loadOptions();
  }

public componentDidUpdate(prevProps: IListDropdownProps, prevState: IListDropdownState): void {
if (this.props.disabled !== prevProps.disabled ||
this.props.stateKey !== prevProps.stateKey) {
```

```
        this.loadOptions();
    }
}

private loadOptions(): void {
    this.setState({
        loading: true,
        error: undefined,
        options: undefined
    });

    this.props.loadOptions()
        .then((options: IDropdownOption[]): void => {
            this.setState({
                loading: false,
                error: undefined,
                options: options
            });
        }, (error: any): void => {
            this.setState((prevState: IListDropdownState, props: IListDropdownProps): IListDropdownState => {
                prevState.loading = false;
                prevState.error = error;
                return prevState;
            });
        });
}

public render(): JSX.Element {
    const loading: JSX.Element = this.state.loading ? <div><Spinner label={'Loading options...'}/></div> : <div/>;
```

```
const error: JSX.Element = this.state.error !== undefined ?
<divclassName={'ms-TextField-errorMessage ms-u-slideDownIn20'}>Error
while loading items: {this.state.error}</div> : <div/>;

return (

<div>

<Dropdownlabel={this.props.label}

disabled={this.props.disabled || this.state.loading || this.state.error
!== undefined}

onChanged={this.onChanged.bind(this)}

selectedKey={this.selectedKey}

options={this.state.options}/>

{loading}

{error}

</div>

    );
  }


private onChanged(option: IDropdownOption, index?: number): void {

this.selectedKey = option.key;

// reset previously selected options

const options: IDropdownOption[] = this.state.options;

    options.forEach((o: IDropdownOption): void => {

if (o.key !== option.key) {

      o.selected = false;

    }

   });

this.setState((prevState: IListDropdownState, props: IListDropdownProps):
IListDropdownState => {

     prevState.options = options;

return prevState;

    });
```

```
if (this.props.onChanged) {
this.props.onChanged(option, index);
    }
  }
}
```

The `ListDropdown` class represents the React component to render the dropdown property pane control.

We are using the Office UI fabric React dropdown to render the options. All available options are loaded in the component by calling the `loadOptions()` method. The component state is updated to show the loaded options.

Add List Dropdown to the Property Pane Control

To define public properties for the dropdown property pane control, add the IPropertyPaneDropdownProps.ts file under the "src\webparts\customPropertyPaneDemo\components" folder:

TypeScript

```
import { IDropdownOption } from 'office-ui-fabric-react/lib/components/Dropdown';

exportinterface IPropertyPaneDropdownProps {
  label: string;
  loadOptions: () => Promise<IDropdownOption[]>;
  onPropertyChange: (propertyPath: string, newValue: any) => void;
  selectedKey: string | number;
  disabled?: boolean;
}
```

In the preceding interface:
- **label:** This is a label for the dropdown control.
- **loadOptions:** This is adelegate function to load available options.
- **onPropertyChange:** This is adelegate function called upon user selection.

- **selectKey:** This is a user selected value.
- **disabled:** This defines whether the dropdown is disabled or not.

Define internal properties for the dropdown property pane control

Create the new IPropertyPaneDropdownInternalProps.ts file under the "src\webparts\customPropertyPaneDemo\components\" folder:

TypeScript

```typescript
import { IPropertyPaneCustomFieldProps } from '@microsoft/sp-webpart-base';
import { IPropertyPaneDropdownProps } from './IPropertyPaneDropdownProps';


export interface IPropertyPaneDropdownInternalProps extends IPropertyPaneDropdownProps, IPropertyPaneCustomFieldProps {

}
```

This interface combines properties from the IPropertyPaneDropdownProps interface and the standard SharePoint Framework IPropertyPaneCustomFieldProps interface for the custom control to run correctly.

Define the dropdown property pane control

Create the new "PropertyPaneDropdown.ts" file under the "src\webparts\customPropertyPaneDemo\components\" folder:

TypeScript

```typescript
import * as React from 'react';
import * as ReactDom from 'react-dom';
import {
  IPropertyPaneField,
  PropertyPaneFieldType
} from '@microsoft/sp-webpart-base';
import { IDropdownOption } from 'office-ui-fabric-react/lib/components/Dropdown';
import { IPropertyPaneDropdownProps } from './IPropertyPaneDropdownProps';
import { IPropertyPaneDropdownInternalProps } from './IPropertyPaneDropdownInternalProps';
```

```
import ListDropdown from'./ListDropdown';

import { IListDropdownProps } from'./IListDropdownProps';


exportclass PropertyPaneDropdown implements IPropertyPaneField<IProperty
PaneDropdownProps> {

public type: PropertyPaneFieldType = PropertyPaneFieldType.Custom;

public targetProperty: string;

public properties: IPropertyPaneDropdownInternalProps;

private elem: HTMLElement;


constructor(targetProperty:string,properties:IPropertyPaneDropdownProps)
{

this.targetProperty = targetProperty;

this.properties = {

    key: properties.label,

    label: properties.label,

    loadOptions: properties.loadOptions,

    onPropertyChange: properties.onPropertyChange,

    selectedKey: properties.selectedKey,

    disabled: properties.disabled,

    onRender: this.onRender.bind(this)

  };
}

public render(): void {

if (!this.elem) {

return;

  }


this.onRender(this.elem);

}
```

```
private onRender(elem: HTMLElement): void {
if (!this.elem) {
this.elem = elem;
    }

const element: React.ReactElement<IListDropdownProps> = React.createElement
(ListDropdown, {
      label: this.properties.label,
      loadOptions: this.properties.loadOptions,
      onChanged: this.onChanged.bind(this),
      selectedKey: this.properties.selectedKey,
      disabled: this.properties.disabled,
// required to allow the component to be re-rendered by calling this.
render() externally
      stateKey: new Date().toString()
    });
    ReactDom.render(element, elem);
  }

private onChanged(option: IDropdownOption, index?: number): void {
this.properties.onPropertyChange(this.targetProperty, option.key);
  }
}
```

The preceding class implements the standard SharePoint Framework `IProperty PaneField` interface.

Use the Dropdown Property Pane Control in the Web Part

Add the list information interface

Let us define an interface that represents a SharePoint list.

Create a new `IListInfo.ts` file under the "src\webparts\customPropertyPane Demo" folder:

TypeScript

```
exportinterface IListInfo {
    Id: string;
    Title: string;
}
```

Reference the Dropdown Property Pane in the WebPart

In the webpart file `src\webparts\customPropertyPaneDemo\CustomPropertyPaneDemoWebPart.ts`, we need to make the following edits:

Import the `PropertyPaneDropdown` class:

TypeScript

```
import { PropertyPaneDropdown } from './components/PropertyPaneDropdown';
```

Add a reference to the interface and helper functions to work with the web part properties:

TypeScript

```
import { IDropdownOption } from 'office-ui-fabric-react/lib/components/Dropdown';
import { update, get } from '@microsoft/sp-lodash-subset';
```

Add the method `loadLists` to load available lists. For the sake of simplicity, we are using mock data here:

TypeScript

```
private loadLists(): Promise<IDropdownOption[]> {
returnnew Promise<IDropdownOption[]>((resolve: (options: IDropdownOption[]) => void, reject: (error: any) => void) => {
    setTimeout(() => {
      resolve([{
        key: 'sharedDocuments',
        text: 'Shared Documents'
      },
      {
        key: 'myDocuments',
        text: 'My Documents'
```

```
      }]);
    }, 2000);
  });
}
```

Add the method `onListChange` to handle the property dropdown value change:

TypeScript
```
private onListChange(propertyPath: string, newValue: any): void {
const oldValue: any = get(this.properties, propertyPath);
// store new value in web part properties
  update(this.properties, propertyPath, (): any => { return newValue; });
// refresh web part
this.render();
}
```

Update the get `PropertyPaneConfiguration()` method to use the dropdown property pane control to render the `listName` web part property:

TypeScript
```
protected getPropertyPaneConfiguration(): IPropertyPaneConfiguration {
return {
    pages: [
      {
        header: {
          description: strings.PropertyPaneDescription
        },
        groups: [
          {
            groupName: strings.BasicGroupName,
            groupFields: [
new PropertyPaneDropdown('listName', {
              label: strings.ListFieldLabel,
```

```
                loadOptions: this.loadLists.bind(this),
                onPropertyChange: this.onListChange.bind(this),
                selectedKey: this.properties.listName
              })
          ]
        }
      ]
    }
  ]
  };
}
```

Test the Custom Property Pane

At the command prompt, type `gulp serve`. Add the webpart and verify the property pane:

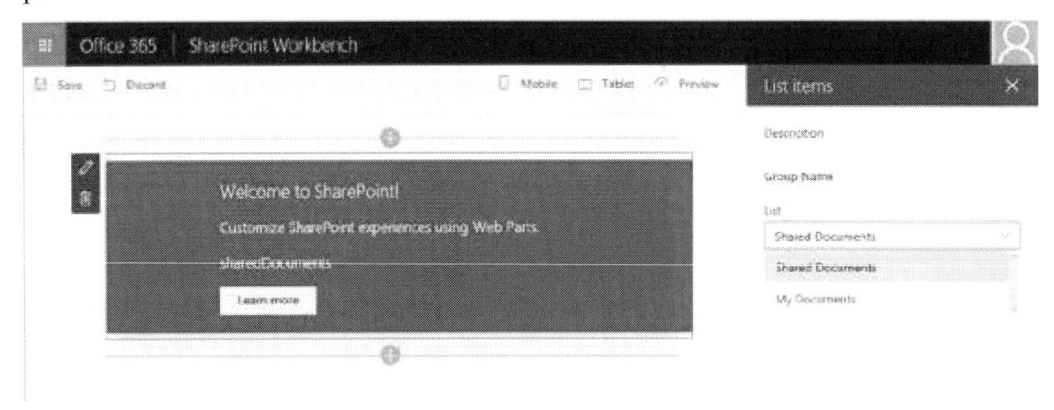

Figure 4.4: List dropdown custom control

Conclusion

In this chapter, we explored how to build a custom control for the SPFx web part property pane. The process to develop custom controls is a bit tedious to make it work. In the next chapter, we will explore how **Patterns and Practices (PnP)** have simplified the process by offering various property pane controls.

CHAPTER 5
PnP Control for the Web Part Property Pane

The SharePoint Framework supports various property pane controls, which can be used to meet the business requirements. If we need to go beyond this, then we have to develop our own custom property pane controls, as we saw in the previous chapter. However, developing custom controls requires custom code, additional efforts, maintenance overhead, and frequent upgrades. Patterns and Practices (PnP) have made available a set of reusable property pane controls, which can be easily imported to our SPFx solution.

Structure
- PnP Reusable Property Pane Controls
- Use List Picker Control in the Web Part Property Pane

Objectives
- Explore various property pane controls offered by PnP
- Install and start using them in our solution

PnP Reusable Property Pane Controls

PnP (Office 365 Patterns and Practices) have released a set of reusable property pane controls that can be used in SPFx solutions. Here are a few of the commonly used

controls offered by PnP:
- Color Picker
- Date and Time Selector
- List Selector
- People/Group Selector
- Spin Button
- Managed Metadata Term Selector
- Multi-value Selection
- Number Values
- Information Panel

In this chapter, we will use the list selector property pane control in our SPFx web part.

Develop the SPFx Solution to use PnP Reusable Property Pane Controls

Open the command prompt. Perform the following steps to create the SPFx solution:

1. Create a directory for the SPFx solution:
   ```
   md pnp-list-selector-propertypane
   ```

2. Navigate to the above-created directory:
   ```
   cd pnp-list-selector-propertypane
   ```

3. Run the Yeoman SharePoint Generator to create the SPFx solution:
   ```
   yo @microsoft/sharepoint
   ```

4. The Yeoman generator will run through the wizard by asking questions about the SPFx solution to be generated:

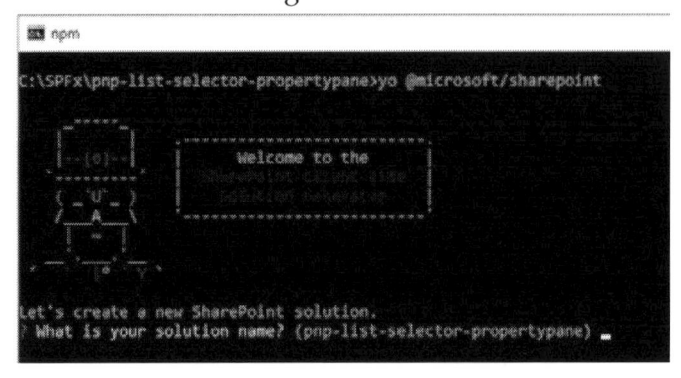

Figure 5.1: SPFx Yeoman generator

The SPFx Yeoman generator will display the following wizard of questions:
- **Solution Name:** Specify the name of the SPFx solution. Hit the *Enter* key to go ahead with the default name (pnp-list-selector-propertypane in this case) or type in any other name for your solution.
    - **Selected choice:** Hit *Enter*
- **The target for the component:** Specify the target environment to develop and deploy the SPFx solution. Choose from any of SharePoint Online or SharePoint On-Premises environments.
    - **Selected choice:** SharePoint Online only (latest)
- **Place of files:** Choose the folder location for the SPFx project (either the same folder or a subfolder).
    - **Selected choice:** Use the current folder
- **Deployment option:** Specify Y to allow the deployment of the app instantly to all the sites, N otherwise.
    - **Selected choice:** N (install on each site explicitly)
- **Permissions to access web APIs:** Check whether the components in the solution require permissions to access web APIs.
    - **Selected choice:** N (solution contains unique permissions)
- **Type of client-side component to create:** Choose to create a client-side web part or an extension.
    - **Selected choice:** WebPart, since single part app pages are web parts.
- **Web Part Name:** Specify the name of the web part name. Hit the *Enter* key to go ahead with the default name or type in any other name.
    - **Selected choice:** ListSelector
- **Web part description:** Specify the name of the web part description. Hit the *Enter* key to go ahead with the default description or type in any other value.
    - **Selected choice:** Hit *Enter*
- **A framework to use:** Select any JavaScript framework to develop the component. Available choices are (No JavaScript Framework, React, and Knockout)
    - **Selected choice:** No JavaScript Framework

5. The Yeoman generator will start the scaffolding process to create the solution. It will download the needed npm packages and install the required dependencies. The solution creation will take a significant amount of time.

Install PnP Property Controls

1. Run the following command to install PnP property pane controls:

   ```
   npm install @pnp/spfx-property-controls --save --save-exact
   ```

2. Run the following command to lock down the version of project dependencies:

   ```
   npm shrinkwrap
   ```

3. At the command prompt, type the following command to open the solution in the code editor of your choice:

   ```
   code .
   ```

Use List Picker Control in the Web Part Property Pane

In order to use the list picker property pane in the SPFx webpart, follow the given guidelines:

1. Open the web part file "src\webparts\listSelector\ListSelector WebPart.ts"
2. Import the following modules:

   TypeScript
   ```
   import { PropertyFieldListPicker, PropertyFieldListPickerOrderBy } from '@pnp/spfx-property-controls/lib/PropertyFieldListPicker';
   ```

3. Create a new property for the web part by updating the existing `IListSelectorWebPartProps` interface:

   TypeScript
   ```
   exportinterface IListSelectorWebPartProps {
     description: string;
     lists: string | string[]; // Stores the list ID(s)
   }
   ```

4. Add the custom property control to `groupFields` of the web part property pane configuration:

   TypeScript
   ```
   protected getPropertyPaneConfiguration(): IPropertyPaneConfiguration
       {
   return {
       pages: [
   ```

```
{
    header: {
        description: strings.PropertyPaneDescription
    },
    groups: [
      {
        groupName: strings.BasicGroupName,
        groupFields: [
          PropertyPaneTextField('description', {
            label: strings.DescriptionFieldLabel
          }),
          PropertyFieldListPicker('lists', {
            label: 'Select a list',
            selectedList: this.properties.lists,
            includeHidden: false,
            orderBy: PropertyFieldListPickerOrderBy.Title,
            disabled: false,
            onPropertyChange: this.onPropertyPaneFieldChanged.bind(this),
            properties: this.properties,
            context: this.context,
            onGetErrorMessage: null,
            deferredValidationTime: 0,
            key: 'listPickerFieldId'
          })
        ]
      }
    ]
  };
}
```

Test the Web Part:
1. At the command prompt, typethe following command to run the solution without opening the browser.

   ```
   gulp serve --nobrowser
   ```

2. Open the SharePoint site.
3. Navigate to `/_layouts/15/workbench.aspx`.
4. Add the web part to the page.
5. Edit the property pane:

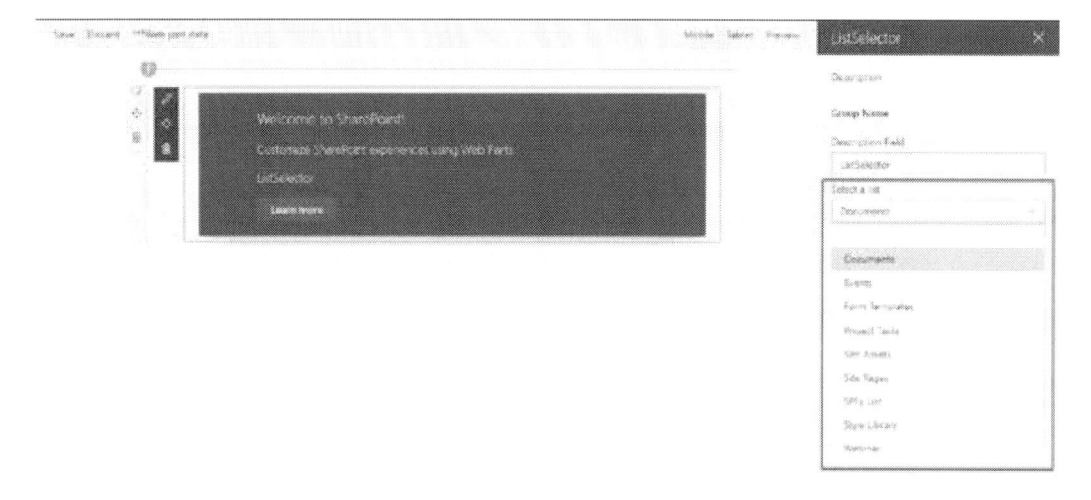

Figure 5.2: PnP reusable list selector control as the property pane control

The list dropdown shows the available lists from the SharePoint site. This makes it easy for users to select the list.

We can use any of the following PnP controls as property pane controls in the SPFx web part:
- Color picker
- Date and time selector
- List selector
- People/group selector
- Spin button
- Managed metadata term selector
- Multi-value selection

- Number values
- Information panel

Conclusion

In this chapter, we analyzed the option of using reusable **Patterns and Practices (PnP)** property pane controls. These controls are available as npm packages, which can be added to our SPFx project. It helps to reduce the code lines and brings in more stability.

Chapter 6
CSS Considerations

The look and feel defines the appearance of the web part on a page. The web part should have a matching look as that of the entire page to give a consistent user browsing experience. Since the classic SharePoint days, CSS has been playing an important role to define the overall look and feel of the web part.

In Modern SharePoint, we have more powerful support from Office UI Fabric, which helps to design consistent experience in Office 365. It provides various responsive controls to be used in the SPFx web part. Each control in Office UI Fabric has its own CSS classes defined. In some scenarios, we might have to overwrite the CSS classes from Office UI fabric to achieve the desired look.

Structure
- Manage CSS files in the SPFx solution
- Use of Sass
- Override external referenced CSS

Objectives
- Common CSS considerations for SPFx
- Override the behavior of classes from other components

Manage CSS files in the SPFx solution

The SPFx solution is composed of multiple components. Each component may have its visual appearance. The component uses CSS styles to define its appearance.

The recommended React-based SPFx solution structure that uses multiple components is as follows:

```
companyWebPart\components
        \employee
                \employee.tsx
                \employee.module.scss
        \department
                \department.tsx
                \department.module.scss
```

Figure 6.1: Sample SPFx solution structure

Use of Sass

SPFx supports Sass as well as CSS. **Syntactically Awesome Style Sheets (SASS)** is a superset of CSS and gets compiled to CSS. Sass allows using variables, rules, imports, and many more.

More information about Sass can be found at **https://sass-lang.com/**.

Use CSS classes over id

Each DOM element on a page is identified by its unique id or a CSS class attached to it. In the same way, each element in the SPFx web part has a corresponding id and class.

Referencing elements by its id inside the markup might not work well, as there might be multiple instances of the web part on a page or multiple web parts may have a common id given by the developer.

The following code uses the id to refer to an element and is not recommended to use:

TypeScript

```
export default class SPFxWebPart extends  BaseClientSideWebPart <IGetting StartedWebPartProps> {
  public render(): void {
```

```
    this.domElement.innerHTML = `
<div id="greetMessage">
        Welcome to SharePoint Framework
</div>`;
  }
}
```

It is recommended to refer to the elements by the CSS class as shown in the following code:

TypeScript

```
export default class GettingStartedWebPart extends BaseClientSideWebPart
<IGettingStartedWebPartProps> {
  public render(): void {
    this.domElement.innerHTML = `
<div class="${styles.greetMessage}">
        Welcome to SharePoint Framework
</div>`;
  }
}
```

Use CSS Modules

The SharePoint Framework web part is just one of the components on the SharePoint page along with other web parts or controls on the page. CSS styles of one of the SPFx web part may conflict with CSS styles of another SPFx web part or other controls on the page.

SPFx resolves this conflict issue by CSS modules. The SPFx toolchain processes all files with .module.scss extension and appends a unique hash value to each of the files.

For example, if you are referencing the following CSS style in the solution:

employee.module.scss

```
.employee {
    margin: 1em 0;
```

```scss
.text {
    font-weight: bold;
    font-size: 1em;
    }
}
```

The department CSS can be defined as follows.

department.module.scss

```scss
.department {
    padding: 0.5em 1em;

    .text {
        font-weight: italic;
        font-size: 0.5em;
    }
}
```

The .module.scss files get converted to CSS files inside the lib folder after the build process:

employee.module.css

```css
.employee_f6071de4 {
    margin: 1em 0;
}

.employee_f6071de4 .text_f6071de4 {
        font-weight: bold;
        font-size: 1em;
}
```

department.module.css

```css
.department_2f9c53f0 {
    padding: 0.5em 1em;
}
```

```
.department_2f9c53f0 .text_2f9c53f0 {
        font-weight: italic;
        font-size: 0.5em;
}
```

The hash value generated for each class makes the CSS class name unique; although the same CSS class name is referred to in multiple web parts.

Override externally referenced CSS

The SPFx web part refers to Office 365 UI Fabric or third-party UI components. Each of these components has its own predefined CSS, which we might have to override. The `global` keyword inside the `.module.scss` file can be used to achieve this as follows:

scss

```scss
// Full page width for workbench canvas
:global(#workbenchPageContent) {
    max-width: initial;
}


// Override third party SuperTreeView CSS
:global(.super-treeview>div>.super-treeview-node>.super-treeview-node-content>input[type=checkbox])
{
  -webkit-appearance: radio; /* Chrome, Safari, Opera */
  -moz-appearance: radio;    /* Firefox */
}
```

Conclusion

In this chapter, we understood the importance of CSS in the SPFx web part and its common considerations. SPFx supports both CSS and Sass. In SPFx, it is preferable to refer to elements by its CSS class. The global keyword can be used to override the external CSS styles.

CHAPTER 7
Configure the SPFx WebPart Icon

By the saying *A picture speaks a thousand words*, we should be able to represent our work in a pictorial view thatcan help the audiences to recognize the purpose behind the work. In the SharePoint terminology, if we are developing a component, the icon of the component should be self-explanatory.

The SharePoint Framework client web parts, when added to the page, display an icon and a title. The icon helps end users to build some perspective about the web part.

Structure
- Out-of-the-box look and feel of the SPFx web part
- Office UI Fabric Icons
- Use an External Icon Image as an Icon
- Use a base64 Encoded Image as an Icon

Objectives
- Configure icons for the SharePoint framework client web parts
- Various available mediums to define the web particon

Out-of-the-box look and feel

Let us start by exploring the default look and feel of the SPFx web part. In the previous chapters, we learned how to create the SPFx web part. We will either start by creating a new SPFx web part or use any existing web part solution created in the previous solutions.

Perform the following steps to test the look and feel of the SPFx web part:

1. Open the command prompt.
2. Navigate to the folder containing the SPFx solution.
3. At the command prompt, type the following command to download and install npm packages specified in the `package.json` file:

```
npm install
```

4. Once the npm packages are installed, type `gulp serve` at the command prompt.
5. Open the SharePoint site.
6. Navigate to `/_layouts/15/workbench.aspx`.
7. Add the webpart to the page:

Figure 7.1: SPFx default web part icon

The SPFx web part appears on the list with the default icon. A predefined entry inside the web part manifest defines the icon for the web part.

Figure 7.2: SPFx web part manifest

Let us explore the various ways to set a new icon for our web part.

Office UI Fabric Icons

Office UI Fabric provides various icons to be used in the SharePoint framework web parts. Here is a list of icons provided by Office UI Fabric **(https://developer.microsoft.com/en-us/fabric#/styles/icons)**.

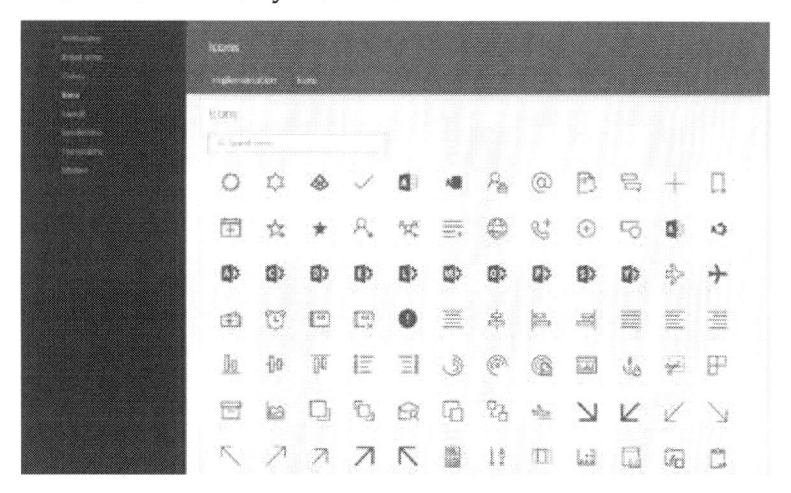

Figure 7.3: Office UI Fabric Icons

To use a specific icon, move the mouse over the icon to get the name of the icon and set it to the `officeFabricIconFontName` property in the web part manifest file, which defines the icon to use.

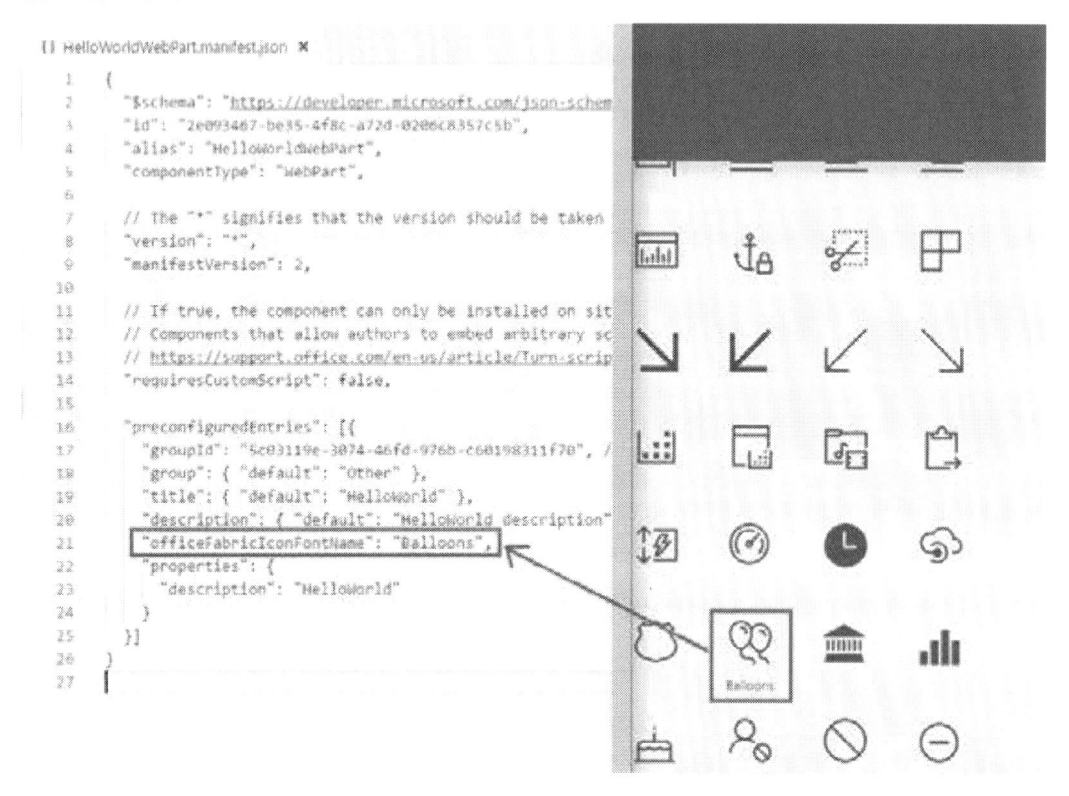

Figure 7.4: Referencethe Office UI Fabric icon in the SPFx web part

While adding the web part to the page, the following icon will be displayed:

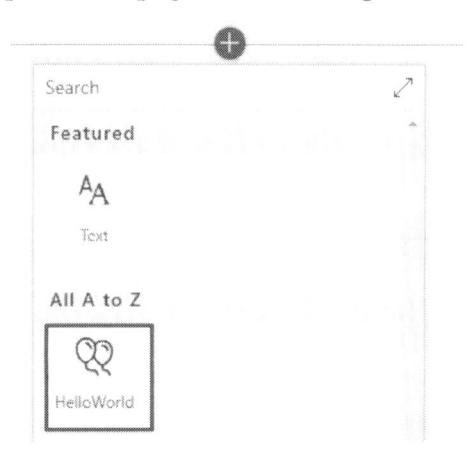

Figure 7.5: Office UI Fabric icon for SPFx

Advantages of using an Office Fabric Icon

Using an Office Fabric Icon offers below advantages:
- The icon need not be deployed along with web part assets.
- The icon automatically adjusts the screen resolution.

Use an External Icon Image

If we do not find any matching image from the Office UI fabric offerings, we can use our custom image as an icon. Any external icon can be specified in the iconImageUrl property as an absolute URL.

JSON

```json
{
"$schema":     "https://developer.microsoft.com/json-schemas/spfx/client-side-web-part-manifest.schema.json",

"id": "2e093467-be35-4f8c-a72d-0206c8357c5b",

"alias": "HelloWorldWebPart",

"componentType": "WebPart",


// The "*" signifies that the version should be taken from the package.json
"version": "*",

"manifestVersion": 2,


// If true, the component can only be installed on sites where Custom Script is allowed.

// Components that allow authors to embed arbitrary script code should set this to true.

// https://support.office.com/en-us/article/Turn-scripting-capabilities-on-or-off-1f2c515f-5d7e-448a-9fd7-835da935584f

"requiresCustomScript": false,


"preconfiguredEntries": [{

"groupId": "5c03119e-3074-46fd-976b-c60198311f70", // Other

"group": { "default": "Other" },
```

```
"title": { "default": "HelloWorld" },
"description": { "default": "HelloWorld description" },
"iconImageUrl": "https://contoso.sharepoint.com/PublishingImages/baloon.png",
"properties": {
"description": "HelloWorld"
    }
  }]
}
```

In this example, an image is uploaded to the SharePoint image library (e.g. **https://contoso.sharepoint.com/PublishingImages/baloon.png**) and this absolute path is specified in the `iconImageUrl` property of the web part manifest. Please note to take away the `officeFabricIconFontName` property from the web part manifest.

While adding the web part to the page, the following icon will be displayed:

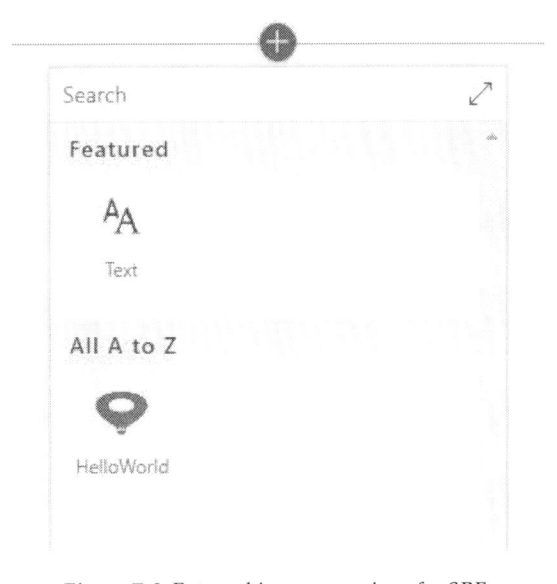

Figure 7.6: External image as an icon for SPFx

Advantages of using an external image as an icon

Using an external image as an icon offers below advantages:
- It gives the flexibility to choose our own image as an icon.

- The image has to be deployed as a web part asset.
- Our own custom image might lose quality on higher DPIs.

Use the base64 Encoded Image

We can also have our custom image base64 encoded and use the base64 string instead of an absolute URL to the image. We can use any of the online services to base64 encode our image. Here is an example of such an encoding service **https://www.base64-image.de/**.

Perform the following steps to encode the image:

1. In the browser, type https://**www.base64-image.de/**.
2. Upload the image:

Figure 7.7: Base64 encoding

3. Click on **show code** to get the base64 encoded string:

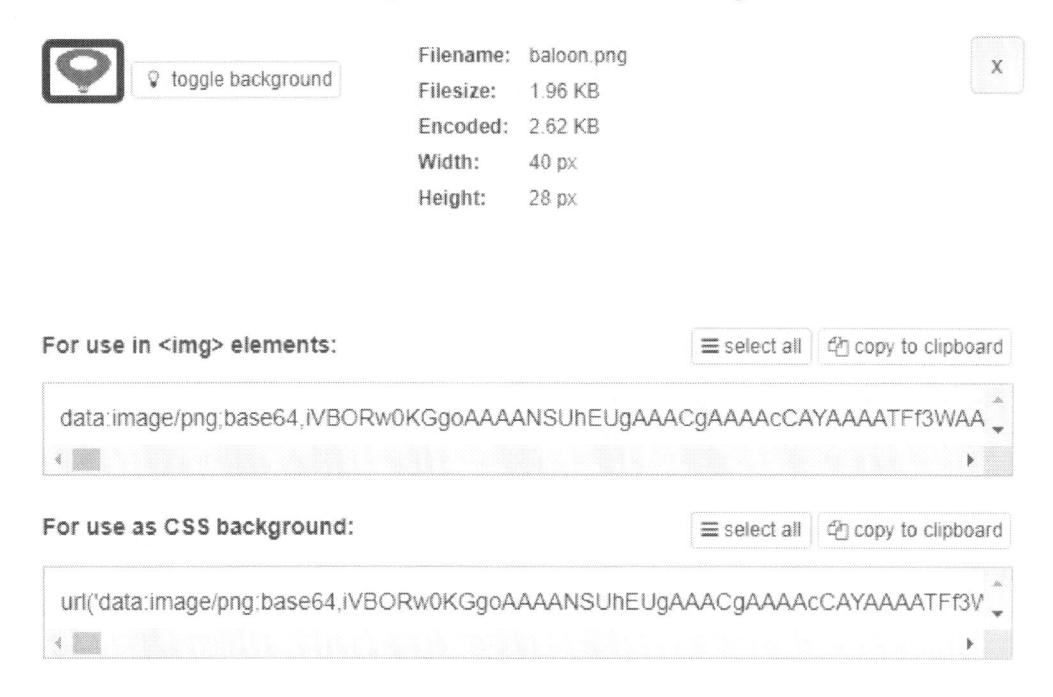

Figure 7.8: Base64 Encoded String

4. Click on **copy to clipboard** to get the base64 encoded string.
5. Set it to the `iconImageUrl` property in the web part manifest.

    JSON

    ```
    {
    "$schema": "https://developer.microsoft.com/json-schemas/spfx/client-side-web-part-manifest.schema.json",

    "id": "2e093467-be35-4f8c-a72d-0206c8357c5b",

    "alias": "HelloWorldWebPart",

    "componentType": "WebPart",


    // The "*" signifies that the version should be taken from the package.json

    "version": "*",

    "manifestVersion": 2,
    ```

```
// If true, the component can only be installed on sites where
Custom Script is allowed.

// Components that allow authors to embed arbitrary script code
should set this to true.

// https://support.office.com/en-us/article/Turn-scripting-
capabilities-on-or-off-1f2c515f-5d7e-448a-9fd7-835da935584f


"requiresCustomScript": false,


"preconfiguredEntries": [{

"groupId": "5c03119e-3074-46fd-976b-c60198311f70", // Other

"group": { "default": "Other" },

"title": { "default": "HelloWorld" },

"description": { "default": "HelloWorld description" },

"iconImageUrl": "data:image/png;base64,iVBORw0KGgoAAAANSUhEUgAAACg
AAAAcCAYAAAATFf3WAAAAAXNSR0IArs4c6QAAAARnQU1BAACxjwv8YQUAAAAJ
cEhZcwAADsQAAA7EAZUrDhsAAAAZdEVYdFNvZnR3YXJlAEFkb2JlIEltYWdlUmVh
ZHlxyWU8AAAHGE1EQVRYR6VXW4hVVRj+skJRqV

.
.
.

gPSVuRZ16qLQH/A+98fw3agBmCgAAAABJRU5ErkJggg==",

"properties": {

"description": "HelloWorld"

    }

  }]

}
```

Advantages of using the base64 encoded image

Using the base64 encoded image as an icon offers below advantages:
- Base 64 encoding works on almost all formats (e.g.,.bitmap, .jpg, .png, etc.)

- The image need not be deployed along with the web part assets.

General observation

If you specify both the `officeFabricIconFontName` and the `iconImageUrl` properties in the web part manifest, the icon specified in `officeFabricIconFontName` will be used.

Conclusion

In this chapter, we explored various ways to set the SPFx web part icon. Each web part should have an icon, which will speak about itself. It is recommended that you use Office UI fabric available icons in your web parts. An external icon image or base64 encoded image offers more flexibility to have your customized icon.

CHAPTER 8
Examine SPFx WebParts on Modern SharePoint

The SharePoint Framework web parts are supported on both modern and classic SharePoint sites. The workbench helps to test the SPFx web parts in isolation. However, in real scenarios, the SPFx web part should be tested on the page itself where it is supposed to be a part of. It helps us to provide a better view on how the web part fits into the page.

Structure
- Understand the SharePoint workbench
- Configure SPFx web parts for modern pages
- Test SPFx web parts on modern pages

Objectives
- Explore the SharePoint workbench
- Test the SharePoint framework web parts on a modern page instead of testing them on the workbench

Understand the SharePoint Workbench

The SharePoint workbench is developer design surface which helps the developer to preview and test the web part in isolation without deploying it to the actual SharePoint site. SharePoint offers two types of workbenches.

Local Workbench

Local workbench is an HTML-based page which mimics the SharePoint UI. It starts after running the gulp serve command and usually opens with the following URL: **https://localhost:4321/temp/workbench.html**

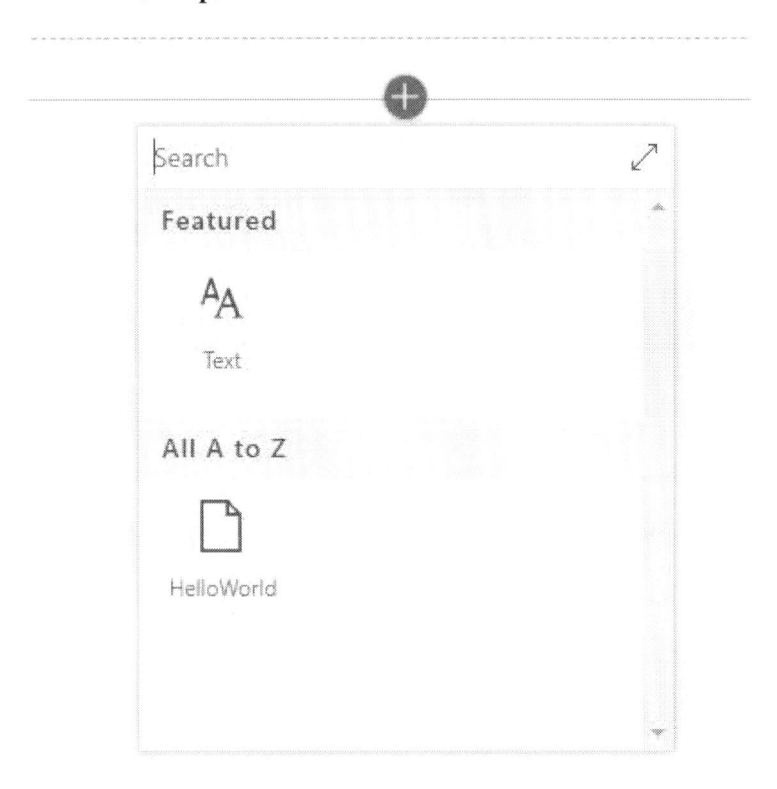

Figure 8.1: SharePoint local workbench

SharePoint Workbench

SharePoint workbench provides a SharePoint context to test the SPFx web part. It can be accessed from `/_layouts/15/workbench.aspx`. The gulp command can be run without opening a browser by using the `gulp serve --nobrowser` command.

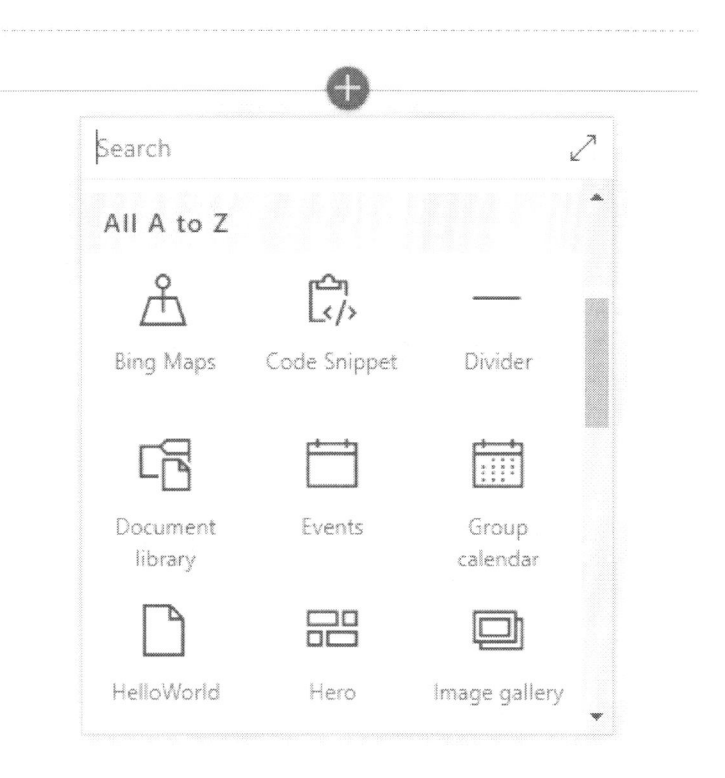

Figure 8.2: SharePoint workbench

Develop the SharePoint Framework Web Part

Open the command prompt. Perform the following steps to create the SPFx solution:

1. Create a directory for the SPFx solution:

   ```
   md spfx-hello-world
   ```

2. Navigate to the above-created directory:

   ```
   cd spfx-hello-world
   ```

3. Run the Yeoman SharePoint Generator to create the SPFx solution:

   ```
   yo @microsoft/sharepoint
   ```

4. The Yeoman generator will run through the wizard by asking questions about the SPFx solution to be generated.

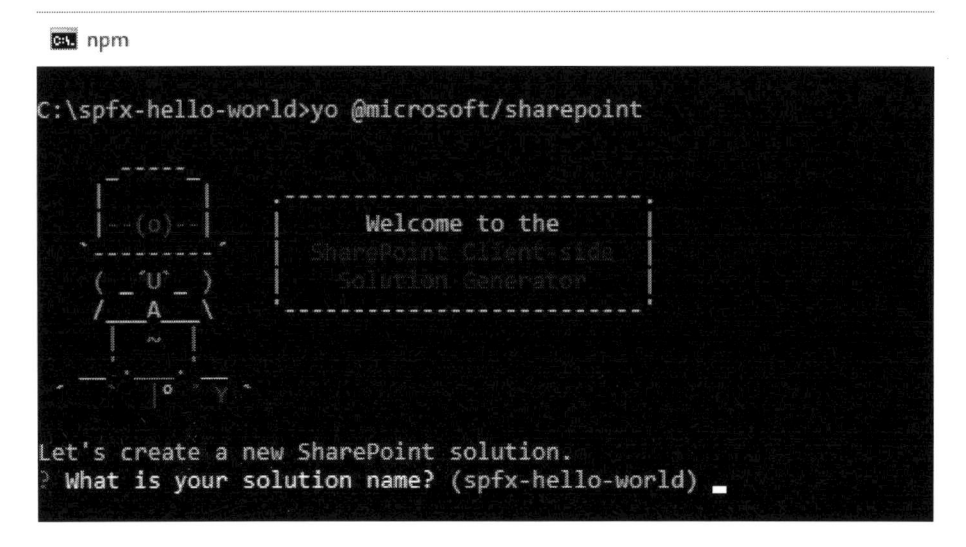

Figure 8.3: SPFx Yeoman generator

The SPFx Yeoman generator will display the following wizard of questions:

- **Solution Name:** Specify the name of the SPFx solution. Hit the *Enter* key to go ahead with the default name (spfx-hello-world in this case) or type in any other name for your solution.
    - **Selected choice:** Hit *Enter* (default name)
- **The target for the component:** Specify the target environment to develop and deploy the SPFx solution. Choose from any of SharePoint Online or SharePoint On-Premises environments.
    - **Selected choice:** SharePoint Online only (latest)
- **Place of files:** Choose the folder location for the SPFx project (either the same folder or a subfolder).
    - **Selected choice:** Same folder
- **Deployment option:** Specify Y to allow the deployment of the app instantly to all the sites, N otherwise.
    - **Selected choice:** N (install on each site explicitly)
- **Type of client-side component to create:** Choose to create a client-side web part or an extension.
    - **Selected choice:** WebPart

- **Web part name:** Specify the name of the web part name. Hit the *Enter* key to go ahead with the default name or type in any other name.
    - o **Selected choice:** HelloWorld
- **Web part description:** Specify the name of the web part description. Hit the *Enter* key to go ahead with the default description or type in any other value.
    - o **Selected choice:** Test SPFx on Modern Pages
- **A framework to use:** Select a JavaScript framework to develop the component. Available choices are (No JavaScript Framework, React, and Knockout)
    - o **Selected choice:** No JavaScript

5. The Yeoman generator will start the scaffolding process to create the solution. It will download the needed npm packages and install the required dependencies. The solution creation will take a significant amount of time.
6. Once the scaffolding process is completed, lock down the version of project dependencies by running the following command:

```
npm shrinkwrap
```

7. At the command prompt, type the following command to open the solution in the code editor of your choice:

```
code .
```

Configure SPFx web parts for Modern Pages

Follow below steps to configure SPFx web parts for Modern Pages:

1. At the command prompt, run the following command:

```
gulp serve
```

2. Or run the following command, without opening the browser instance:

```
gulp serve --nobrowser
```

3. In the browser, navigate to your SharePoint page. Append the following text to the URL in the browser:

```
?loadSPFX=true&debugManifestsFile=https://localhost:4321/temp/manifests.js
```

86 ■ *Mastering SharePoint Framework*

4. Click on **Load debug scripts** when prompted:

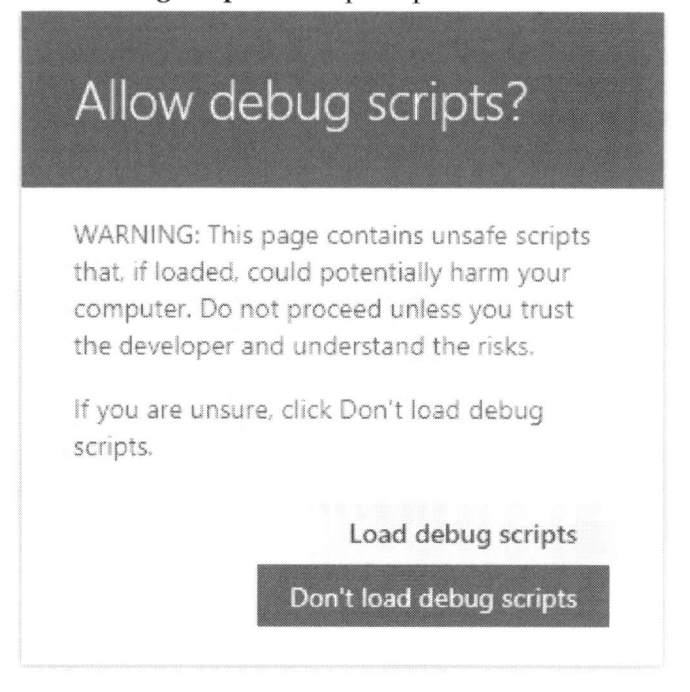

Figure 8.4: Allow debug scripts on the SharePoint page

5. Edit the page, and click on the Add icon to add the web part:

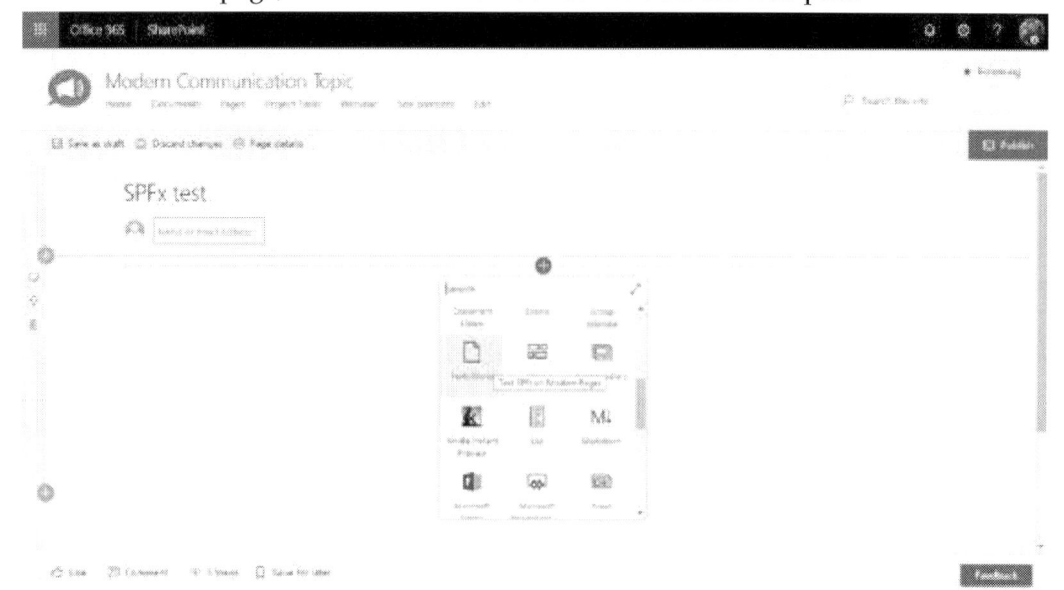

Figure 8.5: Add SPFx web part to the SharePoint page

6. Our SPFx web part is available in the list of web parts to be added.

The web part can be added to the page and can be tested along with other content on the page.

Conclusion

In this chapter, we explored an option to test the SPFx web part on an actual modern SharePoint page. This technique helps developers in many ways to carry out the page optimization, performance analytics and provides flexibility to test the web part along with other content and web parts on the same page.

CHAPTER 9
Host SPFx WebParts from MS Azure CDN

In the previous chapters, we have developed SPFx webparts and tested them locally on the SharePoint work bench. The local SharePoint work bench provides a platform to test the SPFx web part without the dependency on being deployed to SharePoint. In the real world, we have to provide a hosting environment to SPFx web parts from where it can be served to SharePoint.

Here are a few commonly used CDN (Content Delivery Network) options:
- MS Azure CDN
- Office 365 Public CDN
- SharePoint library inside Office 365 tenant

Structure
- Configure the MS Azure Storage Account
- Configure the BLOB Container
- Enable Azure CDN for Storage Account
- Configure the SPFx Solution to use Azure CDN

Objectives

- Configure the MS Azure Storage Account
- Deploy the SPFx web part to MS Azure CDN

Configure the MS Azure Storage Account

Perform the following steps to configure the MS Azure storage account:

1. Login to MS Azure **(https://portal.azure.com)**.
2. Click on **Create a resource**.
3. Click on **Storage account - blob, file, table, queue**:

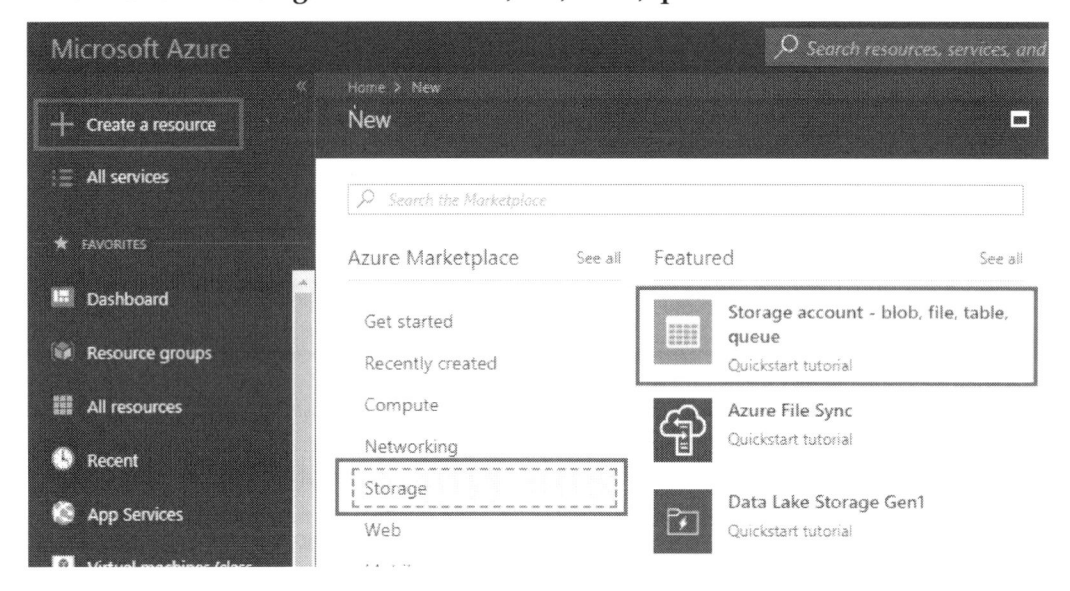

Figure 9.1: Create a storage account

4. Fill in the details:

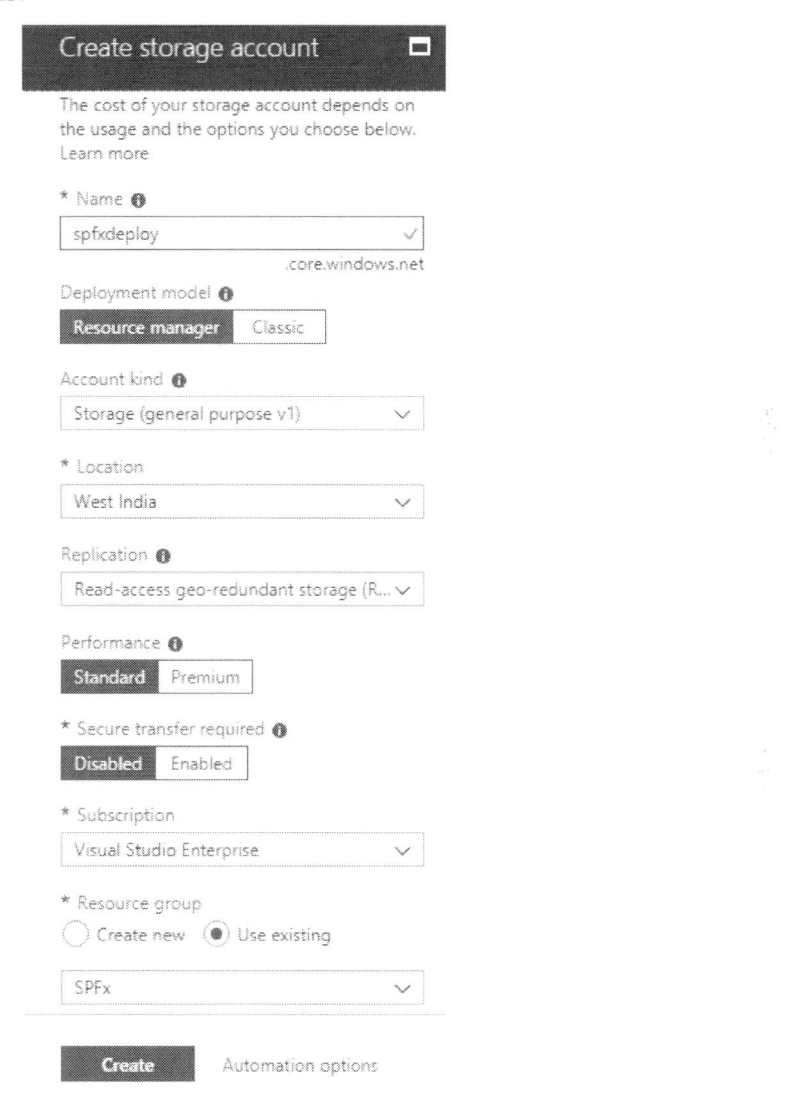

Figure 9.2: Create a storage account

5. Click on **Create**.
6. The storage account endpoint URI is formed as
   http://<StorageAccountName>.blob.core.windows.net.

Configure the BLOB container

Follow the given steps to configure the BLOB container:

1. From the Dashboard, select the storage account.
2. Click on **Blobs**:

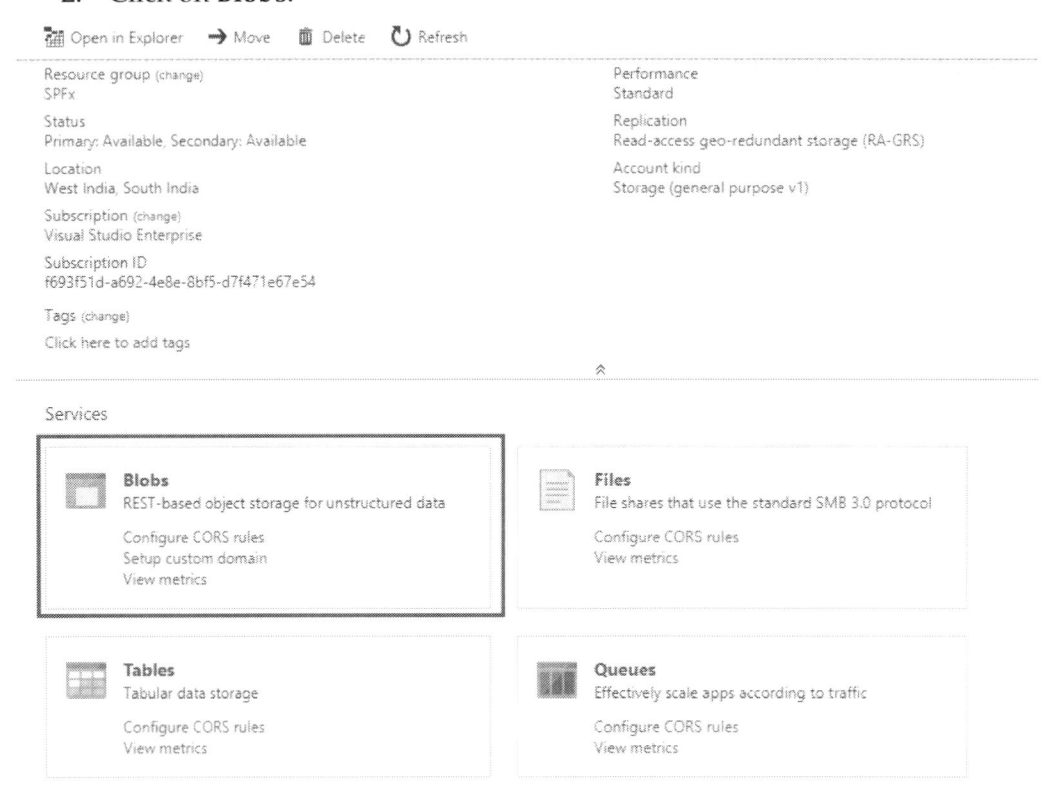

Figure 9.3: Create BLOB storage

3. Click on + **Container**:

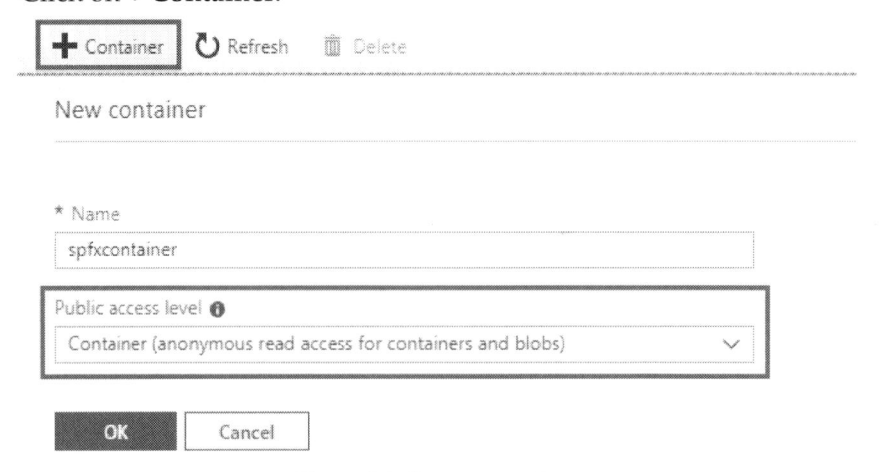

Figure 9.4: Create a container

4. Click on **Access keys**. Copy any one of **key1** or **key2** access keys:

Figure 9.5: Access keys

Enable Azure CDN for Storage Account

Follow the given steps to enable CDN for the storage account:
1. From the Dashboard, select the storage account.
2. Under **BLOB SERVICE**, select **Azure CDN**:

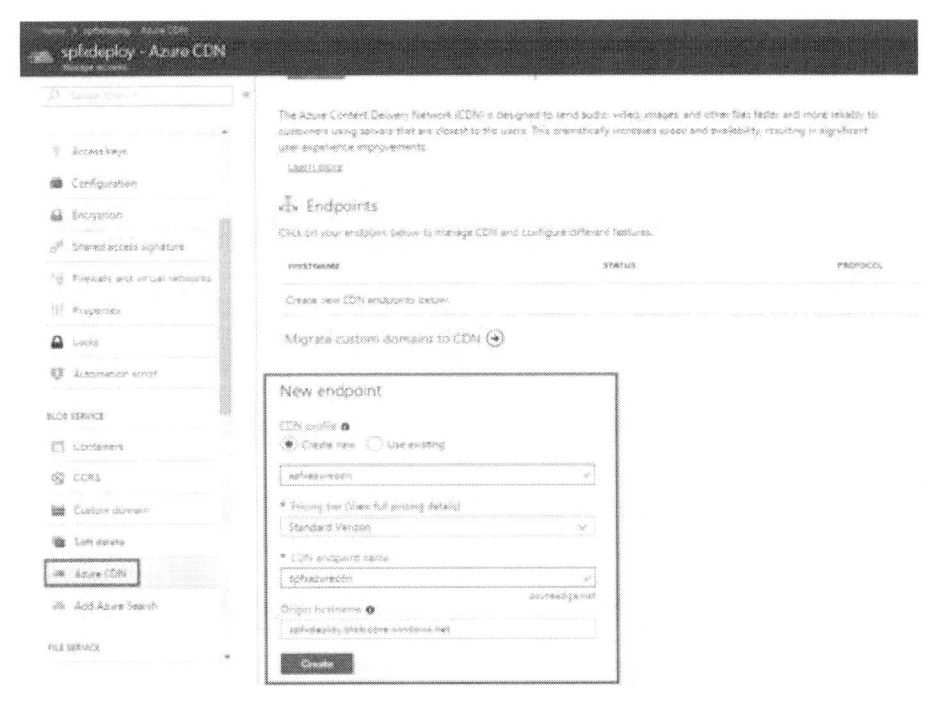

Figure 9.6: Enable Azure CDN

3. Click on **Create**.
4. The endpoint will be listed under the endpoint list:

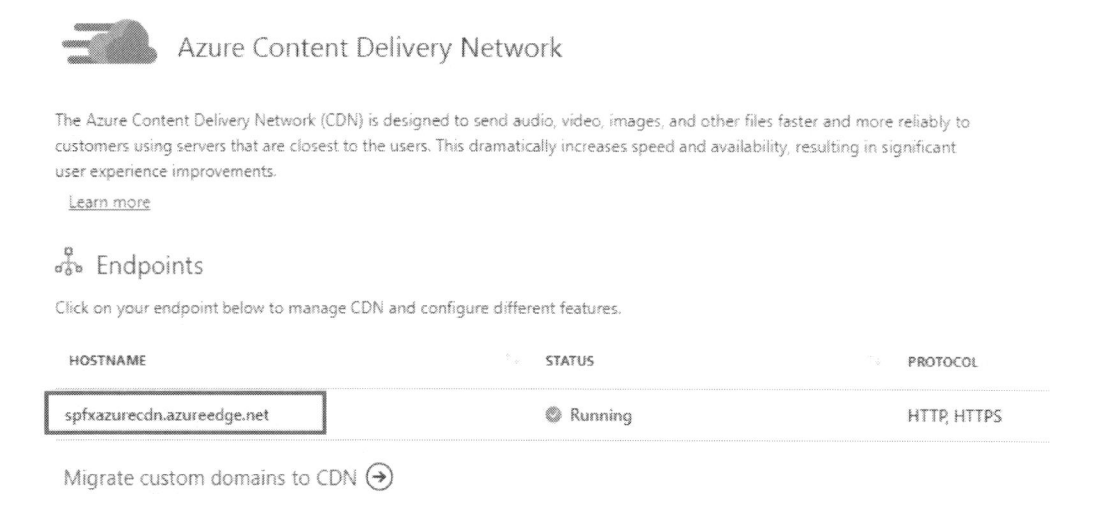

Figure 9.7: Endpoints

5. The BLOB container can be referred to as the following URL:

   `http://<EndpointName>.azureedge.net/<myPublicContainer>/<BlobName>`

Configure the SPFx Solution to use Azure CDN

- **Update the SPFx package details:**

  Follow below steps to update the package details to not include the client-side assets as part of the final package:

  1. Open a command prompt.
  2. Navigate to the SPFx solution folder.
  3. Type `code .` to open the solution in the code editor of your choice.
  4. Under the `config` folder, open the `package-solution.json` file. This file contains the solution packaging information.
  5. Set the `includeClientSideAssets` value as `false`. The client-side assets will not be packaged inside the final package (`.sppkg` file) and will be hosted on the external CDN:

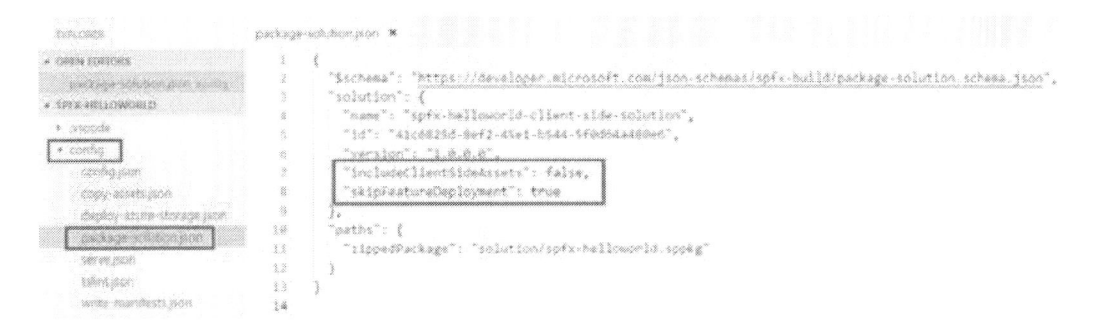

Figure 9.8: Configure the SPFx solution for Azure CDN

- **Update the Azure storage account details to Solution:**

  Follow below steps to specify the Azure storage account details:

  1. Under the `config` folder, open `deploy-azure-storage.json` and update the Azure storage account details.
  2. Update values as follows:
     - `account`: storage account name
     - `container`: BLOB container
     - `accessKey`: storage account access key (primary or secondary)

Figure 9.9: Update the Azure storage account details in the SPFx solution

- **Update the CDN Path:**

  Follow below steps to specify the CDN path used for client-side assets:

  1. Under the `config` folder, open `write-manifests.json`.

2. Specify the BLOB container endpoint as the CDN base path:

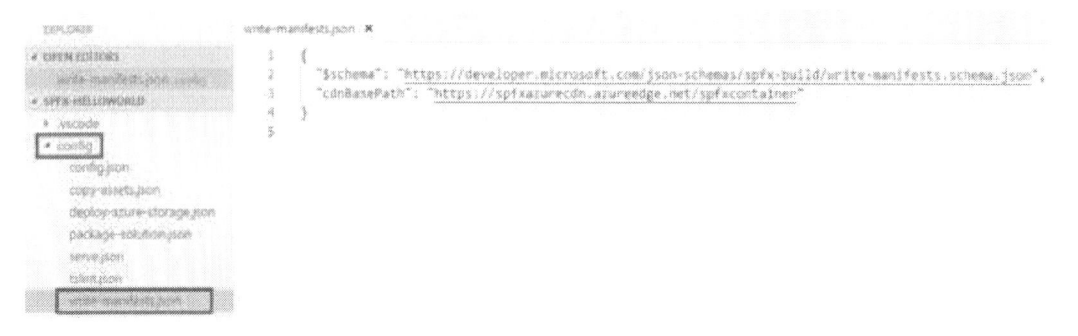

Figure 9.10: Update CDN path

- **Prepare the package:**

  Follow below steps to prepare the package to deploy. At the command prompt, type the following command:

  ```
  gulp bundle --ship
  ```

  This will minify the required assets to be uploaded to CDN. The ship switch represents distribution. The minified assets are located in the **temp\deploy** folder.

- **Deploy assets to Azure Storage:**

  Follow below steps to deploy the assets to Azure storage. At the command prompt, type the following command:

  ```
  gulp deploy-azure-storage
  ```

  This will deploy the assets (JavaScript, CSS files) to Azure CDN.

- **Deploy the Package to SharePoint:**

  The next step is to deploy the app package (.sppkg) to the SharePoint App catalog.

  At the command prompt, type the following command:

  ```
  gulp package-solution --ship
  ```

  This will create the solution package (.sppkg) in the sharepoint\solution folder.

- **Upload the package to the app catalog:**

  Follow below steps to upload the package to app catalog:

  1. Open the SharePoint app catalog site.

2. Upload the solution package (`.sppkg`) from the `sharepoint\solution` folder to app catalog.
 3. Check whether the URL is pointing to Azure CDN.

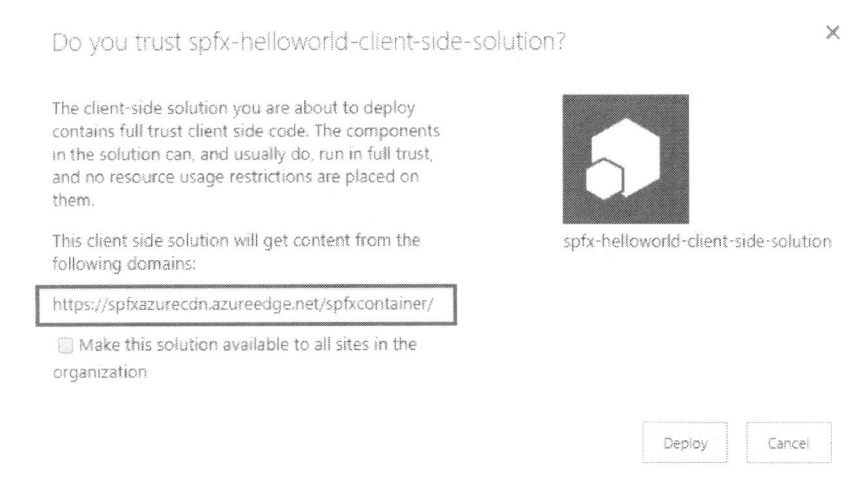

Figure 9.11: Upload the package to the app catalog

 4. Click on **Deploy**.

- **Test the web part:**

  Follow below steps to test the web part on the SharePoint page:

  1. Open any SharePoint site in your tenant.
  2. Add the App to your site from the **Add an App** menu.
  3. Edit any page and add the webpart.

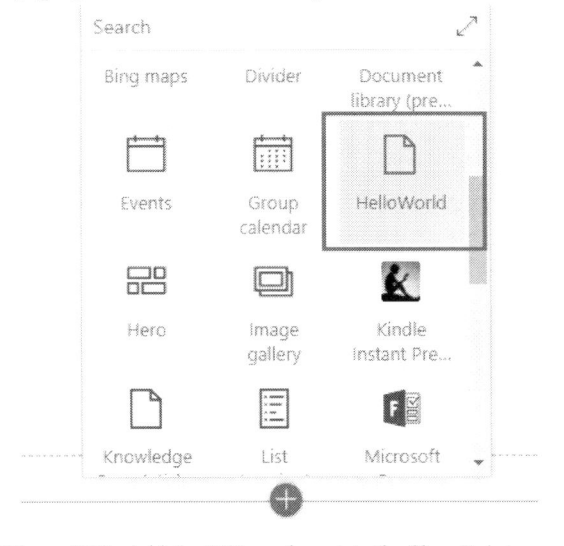

Figure 9.12: Add the SPFx web part to the SharePoint page

4. Click on *F12* to open the developer toolbar. Confirm that it is served from Azure CDN:

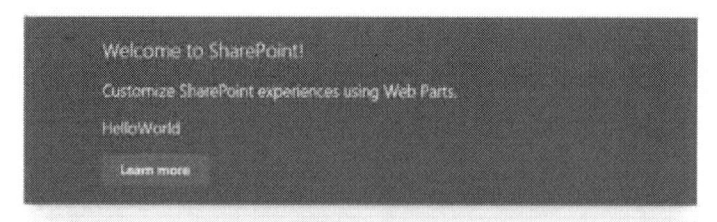

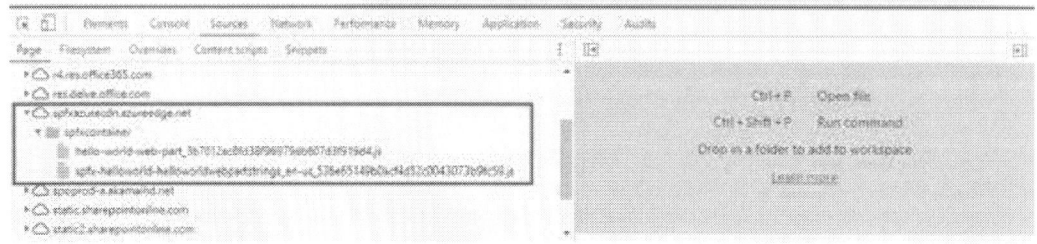

Figure 9.13: Verify the Azure CDN path

Conclusion

In this chapter, we explored the background of hosting SPFx web parts to the CDN location. Azure CDN is one of the options used to host the SPFx webpart. The SharePoint framework natively supports to deploy assets to Azure CDN. In case of any changes made to the CDN path in the future, the same can be updated in the SPFx solution and redeployed. Please note that the MS Azure CDN comes with a cost of the Storage Account.

In the next chapter, we will explore the Office 365 public CDN as an option to deploy SPFx web parts.

CHAPTER 10
Host SPFx WebParts from the Office 365 Public CDN

SPFx web parts can be tested locally on the SharePoint workbench. However, during the final deployment scenario, we have to provide a hosting environment from where it can be referenced in SharePoint.

Here are a few commonly used the **Content Delivery Network (CDN)** options:
- MS Azure CDN (previous chapter)
- Office 365 Public CDN (this chapter)
- SharePoint Library in your tenant (next chapter)

The Office 365 CDN is yet another promising option to host the SPFx web part. Compared to MS Azure, this option is more viable;the reason being it does not require any additional platform or configuration. A SharePoint document library can be used effectively to serve as the Office 365 Public CDN.

Structure
- Configure the CDN for the Office 365 Tenant
- Setup the New Office 365 CDN
- Configure a SPFx Solution for the Office 365 CDN

Objectives

- Configure the Office 365 Public CDN.
- Deploy SPFx webparts to the Office 365 CDN.

Configure the CDN for the Office 365 Tenant

A document library inside the SharePoint site can be used to serve as a CDN. The supporting JS files can be placed inside this document library to be available publicly. The SPFx web part can be configured to access the Office 365 Public CDN

Perform the following steps to configure the Office 365 CDN:

1. Download and install the latest version of the SharePoint Online Management Shell from **https://www.microsoft.com/en-us/download/details.aspx?id=35588**
2. Open the SharePoint Online Management Shell.
3. Use the following command to connect to the SharePoint Online tenant:

   ```
   Connect-SPOService -Url https://[tenant]-admin.sharepoint.com
   ```

   Replace the placeholder [tenant] with your O365 tenant name.

4. Run the following the set of commands:
   - **Get the CDN status:**

     ```
     Get-SPOTenantCdnEnabled -CdnType Public
     ```

     This command will return the status of the CDN. True if the CDN is enabled, False otherwise:

     ![Administrator: SharePoint Online Management Shell showing PS C:\> Get-SPOTenantCdnEnabled -CdnType Public, Value: False]

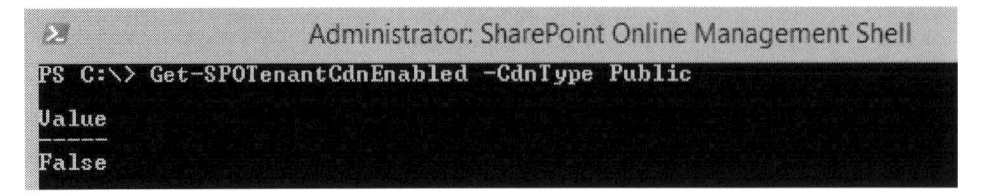

     Figure 10.1: Review the existing Office 365 public CDN settings

   - **Get location of the existing CDN origins:**

     ```
     Get-SPOTenantCdnOrigins -CdnType Public
     ```

This command will return the location of the existing CDN origins in the O365 tenant. Since the CDN is not yet set up, it might return a blank value on the first run:

Figure 10.2: Get location of existing CDN origins

- **Get policy settings for the CDN:**

    Get-SPOTenantCdnPolicies -CdnType Public

This command will return the CDN policy settings:

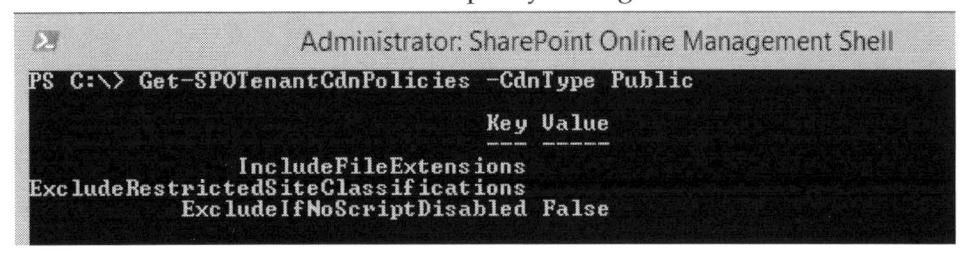

Figure 10.3: Get policy settings for the CDN

- **Enablethe CDN:**

    1. Run the following command to enable the CDN:

        Set-SPOTenantCdnEnabled -CdnType Public

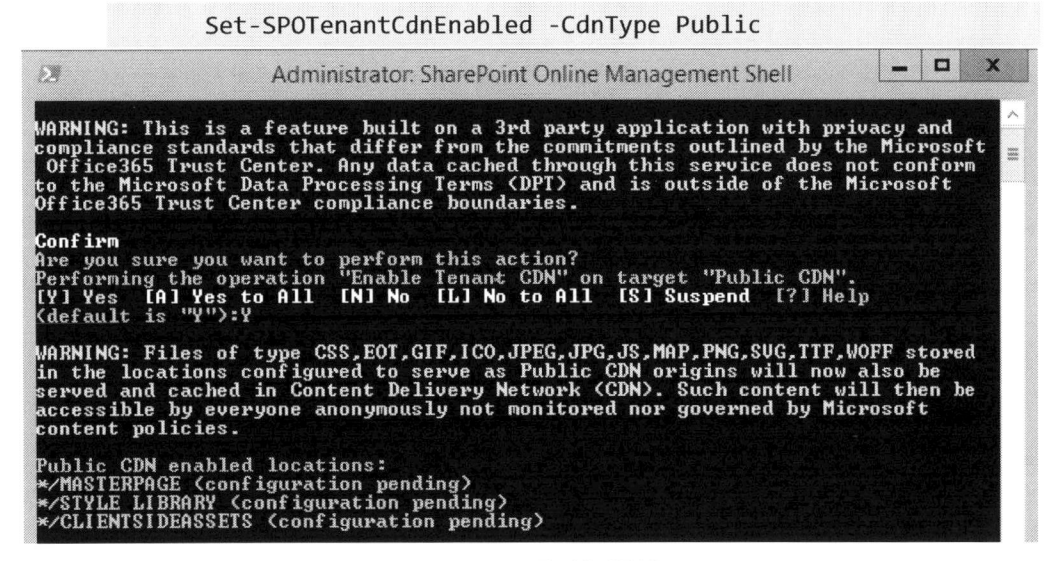

Figure 10.4: Enable CDN

The */CLIENTSIDEASSETS origin is by default available as a valid origin. By default, the allowed file extensions are: CSS, EOT, GIF, ICO, JPEG, JPG, JS, MAP, PNG, SVG, TTF, and WOFF.

The CDN configuration might take up to 15 to 20 minutes.

2. Use the following command to check the status of the CDN endpoints:

```
Get-SPOTenantCdnOrigins -CdnType Public
```

```
PS C:\> Get-SPOTenantCdnOrigins -CdnType Public
*/MASTERPAGE (configuration pending)
*/STYLE LIBRARY (configuration pending)
*/CLIENTSIDEASSETS (configuration pending)
PS C:\>
```

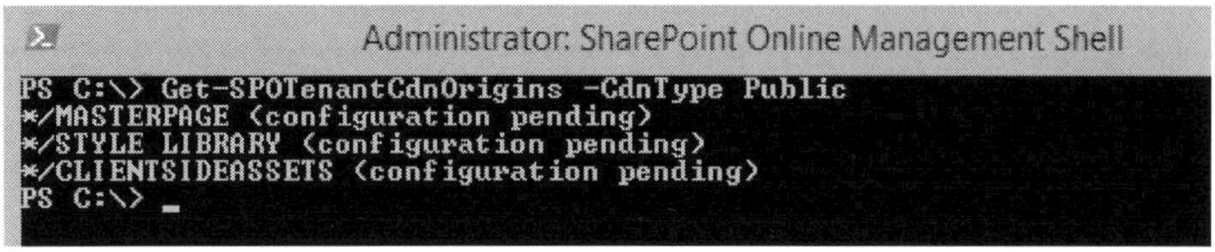

Figure 10.5: Get CDN origins

The origin will be displayed without (configuration pending) the status when ready.

Once the CDN origin is ready, the output will be as shown in the following screenshot:

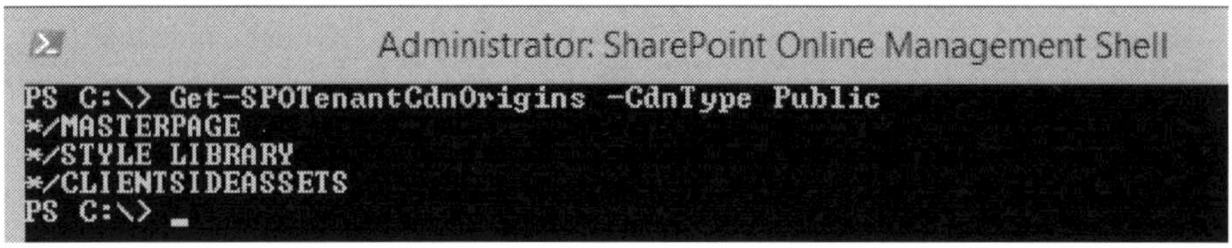

```
PS C:\> Get-SPOTenantCdnOrigins -CdnType Public
*/MASTERPAGE
*/STYLE LIBRARY
*/CLIENTSIDEASSETS
PS C:\>
```

Figure 10.6: Get the CDN origins

Setup the New Office 365 CDN

Perform the following steps to setup a new CDN location.

1. Open the SharePoint site. (e.g. **https://[tenant].sharepoint.com/sites/[site-collection-name]**)
2. Create a document library (e.g. CDN).
3. Run the following command in the SharePoint Online Management Shell:

```
Add-SPOTenantCdnOrigin -CdnType Public -OriginUrl sites/[site-collection-name]/ [document-library]
```

The OriginUrl is a relative URL. The new CDN origin configuration might take 15 to 20 minutes.

4. Run Get-SPOTenantCdnOrigins to check the status:

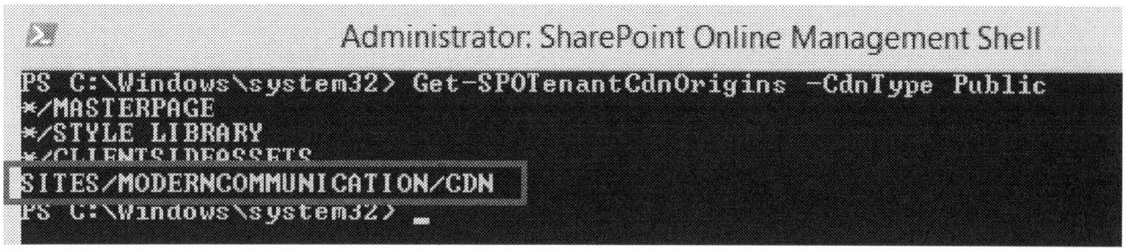

Figure 10.7: Get CDN origins

5. Create a folder inside the document library with the SPFx web part name (e.g. O365CDNDeploy).

6. To get the path of the CDN, type the following URL in the browser:
   ```
   https://[tenant].sharepoint.com/_vti_bin/publiccdn.ashx/url?itemurl=https:// [tenant].sharepoint.com/sites/[site-collection-name]/[document-library]/[folder]
   ```

Configure the SPFx Solution for the Office 365 CDN

Configuring the SPFx solution for Office 365 CDN requires below major steps.

- **Update package details:**

  Follow below steps to update the package details to not include the client-side assets as part of the final package:

1. Open the command prompt.
2. Navigate to the SPFx solution folder.
3. Type `code .` to open the solution in the code editor of your choice.
4. Under the config folder, open the `package-solution.json` file. This file contains the solution packaging information.
5. Set `includeClientSideAsserts value as false`. The client-side assets will not be packaged inside the final package (`.sppkg` file) and will be hosted on the external Office 365 public CDN:

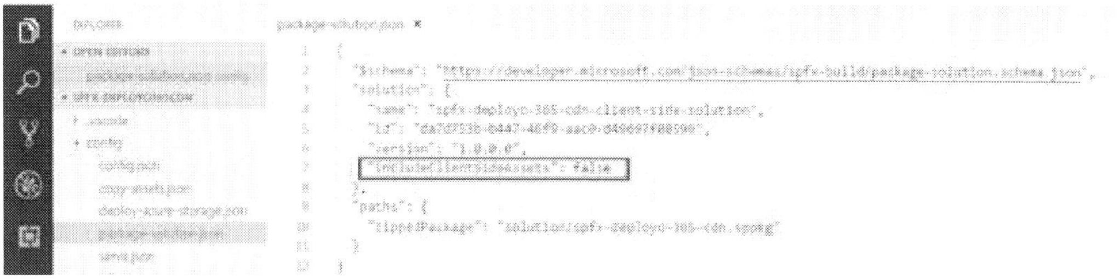

Figure 10.8: Update the SPFx package details

104 ■ *Mastering SharePoint Framework*

- **Update the CDN Path:**

Follow below steps to specify the CDN path used for client-side assets:

1. Under the `config` folder, open `write-manifests.json`.
2. Specify the Office 365 CDN endpoint as the CDN base path.

   https://publiccdn.sharepointonline.com/[tenant]/sites/[site-collection-name]/[document-library]/[folder]

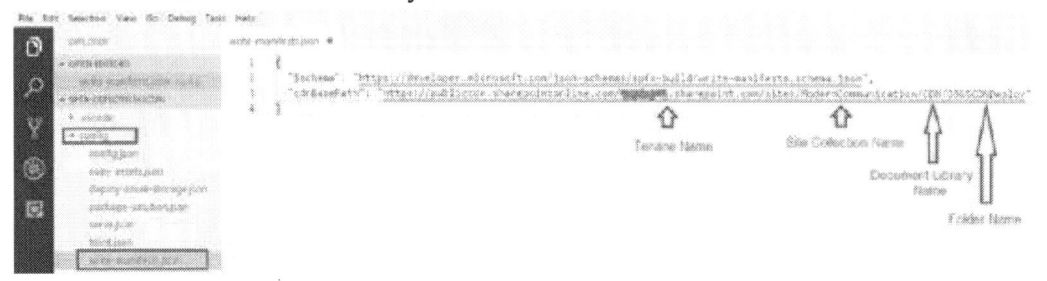

Figure 10.9: Update the CDN path in the SPFx solution

- **Prepare the package:**

  At the command prompt, type the following command:

  ```
  gulp bundle --ship
  ```

  This will minify the required assets to be uploaded to the CDN. The ship switch represents distribution. The minified assets are located on the `temp\deploy` folder.

  Upload the files from the `temp\deploy` folder to the Office 365 CDN (the SharePoint document library setup as CDN):

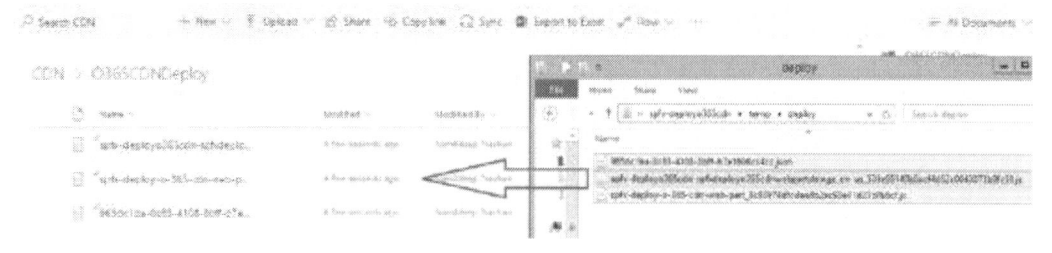

Figure 10.10: Upload files to the CDN

At the command prompt, type the folowing command:

```
gulp package-solution --ship
```

This will create the solution package (`.sppkg`) in the `sharepoint\solution` folder.

- **Upload package to the app catalog:**

    Follow below steps to upload the solution package to SharePoint app catalog:

    1. Open the SharePoint app catalog site.
    2. Upload the solution package (.sppkg) from the "\sharepoint\solution" folder to the app catalog.
    3. Validate whether the URL is pointing to the Office 365 CDN.

Figure 10.11: Upload the SPFx package to the app catalog

  4. Click on Deploy.

- **Test the web part:**

    Follow below steps to test the web part on the modern SharePoint page:

    1. Open any SharePoint site in your tenant.
    2. Add the App to your site from the **Add** an **App** menu.
    3. Edit any page and add the webpart.

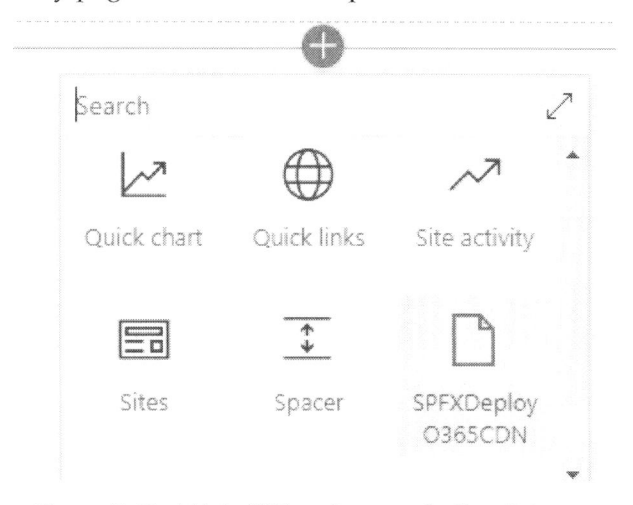

Figure 10.12: Add the SPFx web part to the SharePoint page

4. Click on F12 to open the developer toolbar. Confirm that it is served from the Office 365 Public CDN.

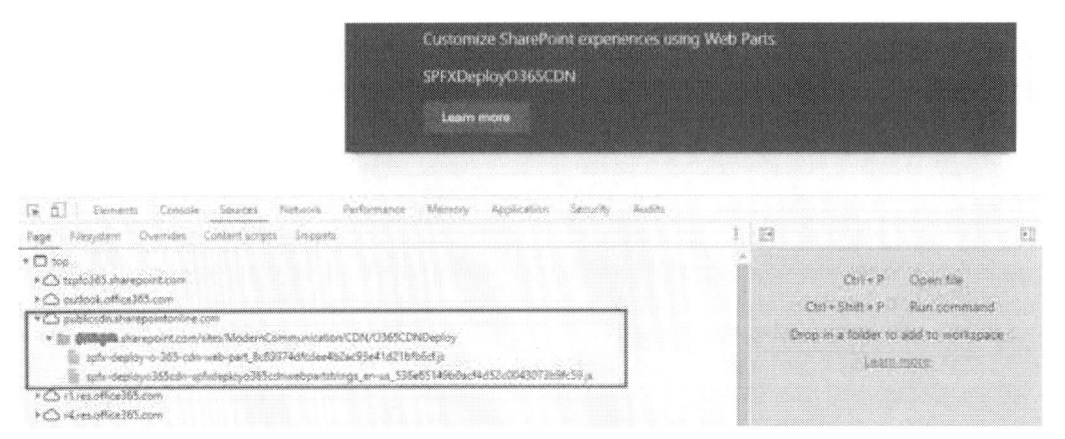

Figure 10.13: Verify the O365 public CDN location

Conclusion

In this chapter, we explored the Office 365 public CDN as an option to host the SPFx web part. It is a more convenient option than MS Azure, as it does not require any additional platform and a document library inside a SharePoint site can be served as a CDN. In case of any changes to the CDN path in the future, the same can be updated in SPFx solution and redeployed.

CHAPTER 11
Host SPFx Web Parts From the SharePoint Document Library

In the previous chapters, we explored options to host SPFx web parts on MS Azure CDN and Office 365 Public CDN. Each one has its own pros and cons. With this background, we will explore one simple option to host the SPFx web parts in the SharePoint document library.

Here are a few commonly used CDN (Content Delivery Network) options:

1. MS Azure CDN (previous chapter)
2. Office 365 Public CDN (previous chapter)
3. SharePoint library inside Office 365 tenant (this chapter)

Structure
- Configure the SharePoint Library as CDN
- Configure the SPFx Solution for the SharePoint Library CDN

Objectives
- Configure the SharePoint library as CDN
- Deploy SPFx webparts tothe SharePoint library

Deployment to CDN

The SPFx web part is packaged into a solution package (.sppkg file) and various scripts, CSS, and other asset files. The sppkg is deployed to the SharePoint app catalog and it includes the manifest with the URL pointing to the location of the script and asset files. It is necessary to deploy the corresponding script and asset files at the URL mentioned in the manifest for the smooth functioning of the SPFx web part.

The URL always refers to a location called CDN. The SharePoint Framework can be configured to use any public CDN, including MS Azure BLOB storage, Office 365 public CDN, or a SharePoint document library. Each of these has its own pros and cons in terms of scalability, performance, and cost. CDN serves as a central repository for the organizations having users across different geo-locations.

The `includeClientSideAssetsproperty` in the `package-solution.json` file if set to true includes the assets inside the `.sppkg` file. After the deployment, SharePoint unpacks the assets to the defined location.

Configure the SharePoint Library as CDN

Follow below steps to Configure the SharePoint Library as CDN:

1. Open the SharePoint site.
2. Navigate to **Settings** (gear icon) >**Add an App**>**Document Library**.
3. Give it a name `-SPFxDeploy`.
4. Click on **Settings** (gear icon) >**Library settings**.
5. Under **Permissions and Management**, click on **Permissions for this document library**.
6. Give read permission to all users (use built-in domain group `everyone`).

Configure the SPFx Solution for the SharePoint Library CDN

- **Update package details:**

    Follow below steps to update the package details to not include the client-side assets as part of the final package:

    1. Open a command prompt.
    2. Navigate to the SPFx solution folder.
    3. Type `code .` to open the solution in the code editor of your choice.

4. Open the `package-solution.json` file from the config folder, which contains the solution packaging information.

5. Set the `includeClientSideAssets` value as `false` to host the client-side assets inside the SharePoint document library instead of being packaged to the `.sppkg` file.

The following configuration inside `package-solution.json` represents the solution packaging information:

Figure 11.1: Update the SPFx solution for packaging

- **Update the CDN Path:**

  Follow the given steps to specify the SharePoint document library URL as the CDN base path:

  1. Under the `config` folder, open `write-manifests.json`.
  2. Specify the SharePoint document library URL as the CDN base path.

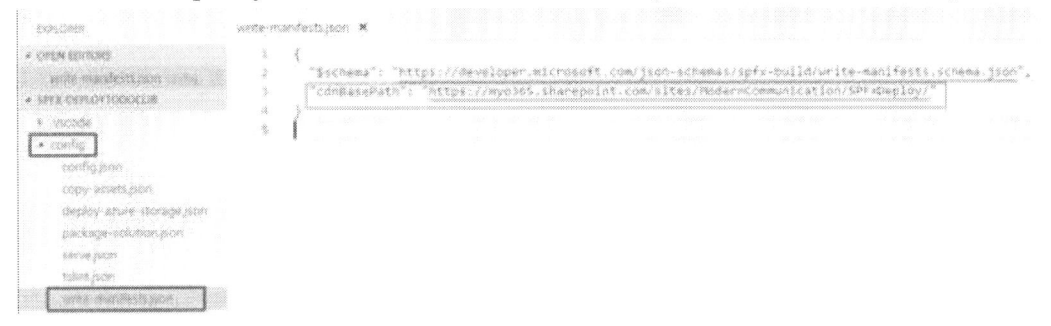

Figure 11.2: Update CDN path as SharePoint library

- **Prepare the package:**

  In the command prompt, type the following command:

  ```
  gulp bundle --ship
  ```

This command will help to minify the required assets to be uploaded to CDN. The `ship` switch denotes distribution. The minified assets are available in the `temp\deploy` folder.

Upload the files from the `temp\deploy` folder to the SharePoint document library:

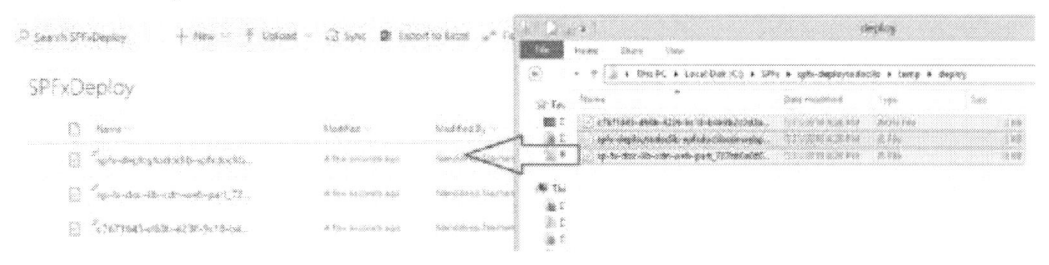

Figure 11.3: Upload files to CDN

- **Deploy Package to SharePoint:**

    In the command prompt, type the following command:

    ```
    gulp package-solution --ship
    ```

This will create the solution package (.sppkg) in the \sharepoint\solution folder.

- **Upload package to the app catalog:**
    1. Open the SharePoint app catalog site.
    2. Upload the solution package (`.sppkg`) from the \sharepoint\solution folder to the app catalog.
    3. Check whether the URL is pointing to the SharePoint library:

Figure 11.4: Deploy the package to the app catalog

4. Click on Deploy.
- **Test the web part:**
 1. Open any SharePoint site in your tenant.
 2. Add the App to your site from the **Add an App** menu.
 3. Edit any page and add the webpart:

Figure 11.5: Add the SPFx web part to the SharePoint page

 4. Open the developer toolbar (*F12* from keyboard) to confirm that it is being served from the SharePoint library:

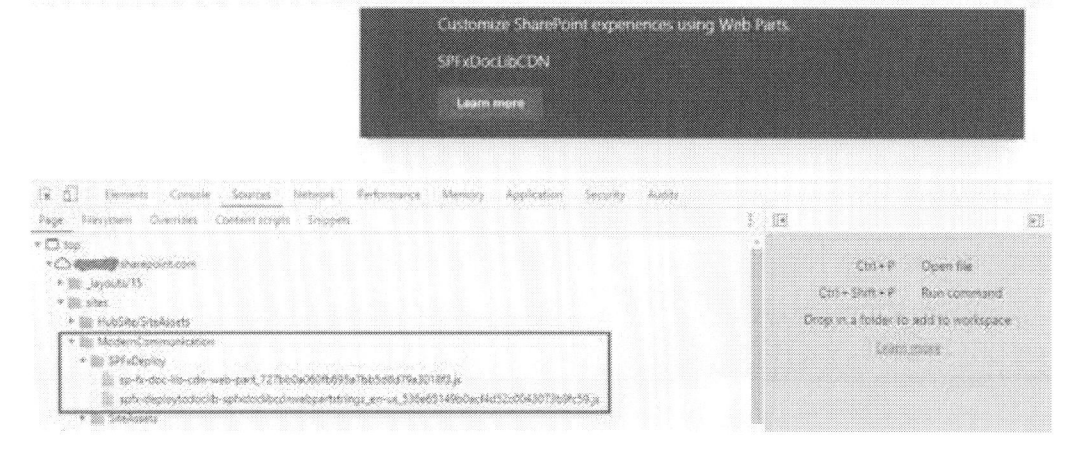

Figure 11.6: Verify the CDN location

Conclusion

In this chapter, we explored the importance and necessity of using CDN to host the SPFx web part. The SharePoint document library is a simpler option to use and configure. However, each CDN hosting option has its own pros and cons. Based on your business scenario and supported infrastructure, you need to choose the one that suits your needs better.

CHAPTER 12
Integrating jQuery with SPFx WebParts

The SharePoint Framework client-side web parts are created using a JavaScript framework. jQuery isone of the largely used JavaScript framework and is supported to create SPFx web parts. This alternative likewise broadens the chance to transform the classic jQuery-based JSOM to the modern SPFx web part.

Structure
- Integrate jQuery with the SPFx Web Part
- Configure the Required Packages and Dependencies

Objectives
- Integrate an external library (e.g. jQuery) with SPFx web parts
- Build the SPFx web part for jQuery Accordion

Integrate jQuery with the SPFx Web Part

Open the command prompt. Follow the given steps to create the SPFx solution:
1. Create a directory for the SPFx solution:

```
md spfx-jqueryintegration
```

2. Navigate to the above created directory:

   ```
   cd spfx-jqueryintegration
   ```

3. Run the Yeoman SharePoint Generator to create the solution:

   ```
   yo @microsoft/sharepoint
   ```

4. The Yeoman generator will display the wizard by asking you questions about the solution to be generated:

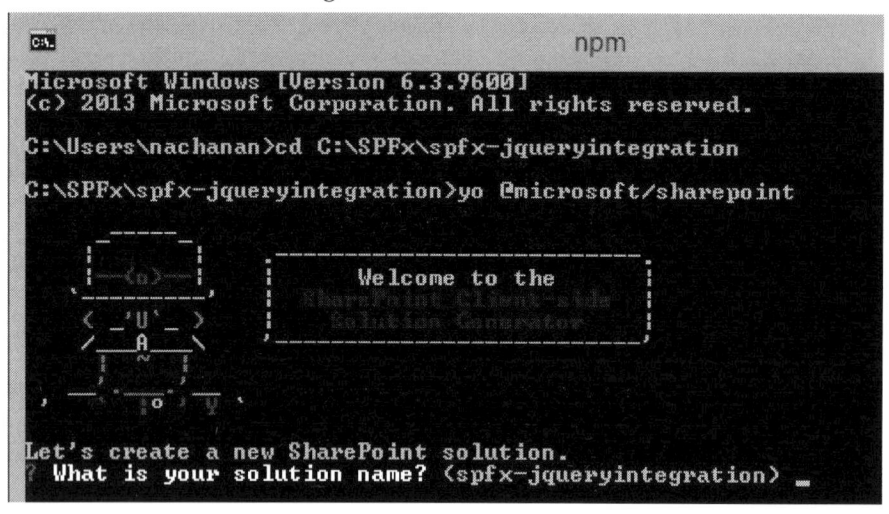

Figure 12.1: SPFx Yeoman generator

The SPFx Yeoman generator will display the following wizard of questions:

- **Solution Name:** Specify the name of the SPFx solution. Hit the *Enter* key to go ahead with the default name (`spfx-jquery integration` in this case) or type in any other name for your solution.
    - **Selected choice:** Hit *Enter*

- **The target for the component:** Specify the target environment to develop and deploy the SPFx solution. Choose from any of SharePoint Online or SharePoint On-Premises environments.
    - **Selected choice:** SharePoint Online only (latest)

- **Place of files:** Choose the folder location for the SPFx project (either the same folder or a subfolder).
    - **Selected choice:** Same folder

- **Deployment option:** Specify Y to allow the deployment of the app instantly to all the sites, N otherwise.
    - **Selected choice:** N (install on each site explicitly)
- **Type of client-side component to create:** Choose to create a client-side web part or an extension.
    - **Selected choice:** WebPart
- **Web part name:** Specify the name of the web part name. Hit the *Enter* key to go ahead with the default name or type in any other name.
    - **Selected choice:** SPFxJqueryIntegration
- **Web part description:** Specify the name of the web part description. Hit the *Enter* key to go ahead with the default description or type in any other value.
    - **Selected choice:** Hit *Enter* (default description)
- **A framework to use:** Select a JavaScript framework to develop the component. Available choices are (No JavaScript Framework, React, and Knockout).
    - **Selected choice:** No JavaScript Framework. We will integrate jQuery to this solution.

Configure the Required Packages and Dependencies

- **Include Packages:**

    At the command prompt, type the following command to include the jQuery package in our solution:

    ```
    npm install jquery jqueryui combokeys --save
    ```

    The `--save` option empowers NPM to incorporate the packages to the dependencies section of the package.json file.

- **Include Typings:**

    Typings will help for auto-complete while composing the code in the code editor. Type the following command:

    ```
    tsd install jquery jqueryui combokeys --save
    ```

- **Lockdown the package dependencies:**

    Execute the following command to lock down the package dependencies:

    ```
    npm shrink wrap
    ```

Solution Changes for jQuery

Follow below steps to add external references for jQuery:

1. At the command prompt, type the following command to open the SPFx solution in the code editor of your choice:

   ```
   code .
   ```

2. Expand the `node_module` folder to see the npm packages being added for jQuery:

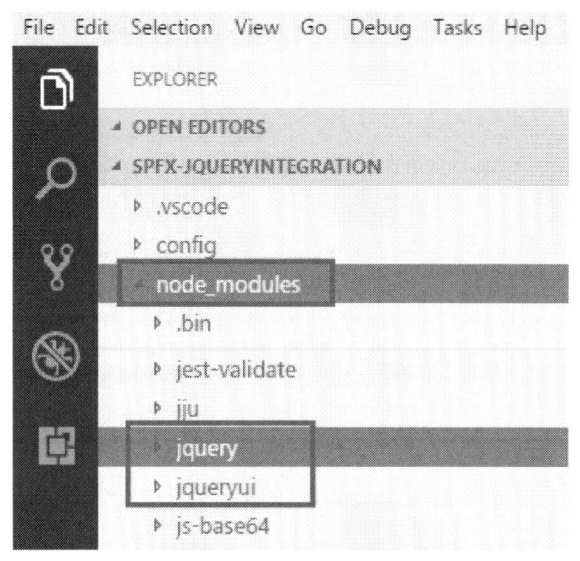

Figure 12.2: jQuery npm package

3. Open `config.js` on under the `config` folder.
4. Under the **externals** node, add jQuery references.

Figure 12.3: Add external references for jQuery

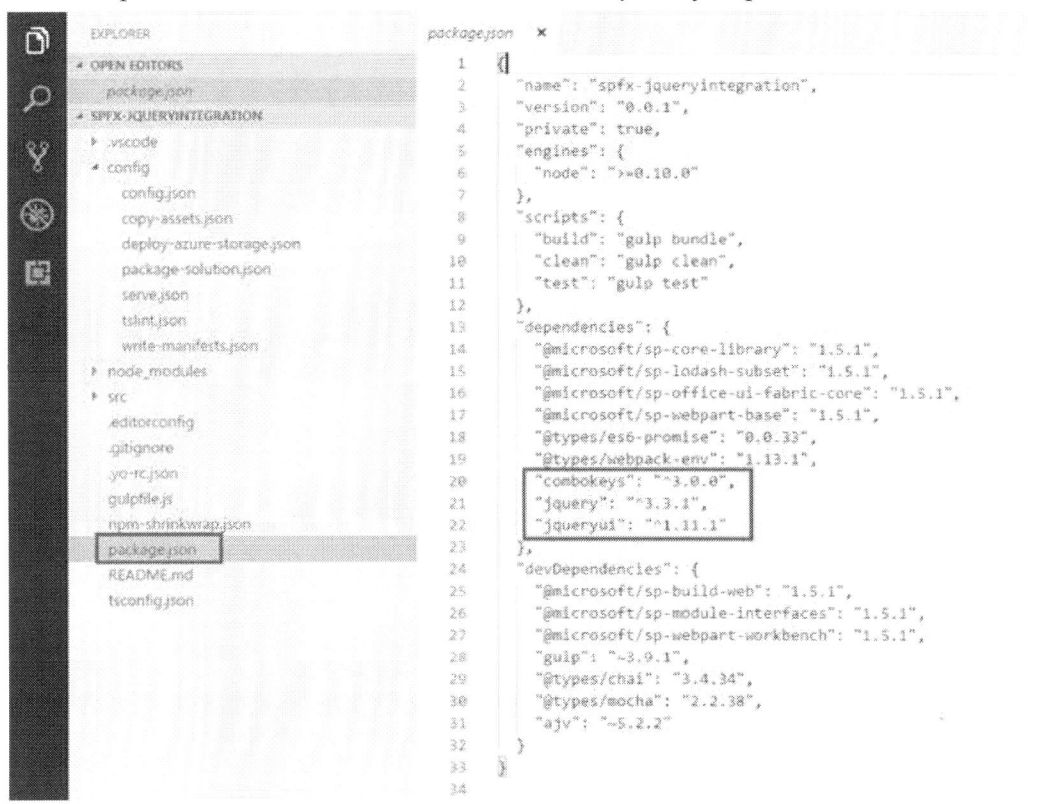

5. Open `package.json` and check whether jQuery dependencies are listed:

Figure 12.4: Verify jQuery dependencies

6. Open the webpart file `SpFxJQueryIntegrationWebPart.ts` and import jQuery:

Figure 12.5: Import jQuery to the SPFx web part

7. Define a constructor and load the external jQuery UI CSS from it:

```
export default class SpFxJQueryIntegrationWebPart extends BaseClientSideWebPart<ISpFxJQueryIntegrationWebPartProps> {
  public constructor() {
    super();
    SPComponentLoader.loadCss("//code.jquery.com/ui/1.12.0/themes/smoothness/jquery-ui.css");
  }
```

Figure 12.6: Load the external jQuery UI CSS

8. Right click on the `spFxJQueryIntegration` folder, and then click on **New File**:

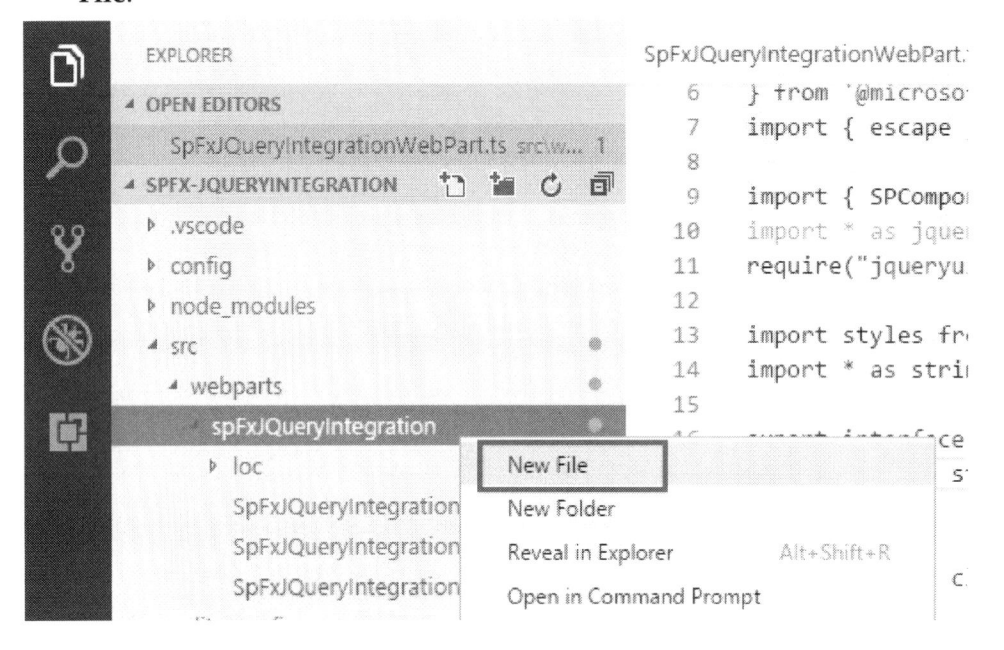

Figure 12.7: Add a new file

Integrating jQuery with SPFx WebParts ■ 119

9. Name the file as `AccordianTemplate.ts` with the following content:

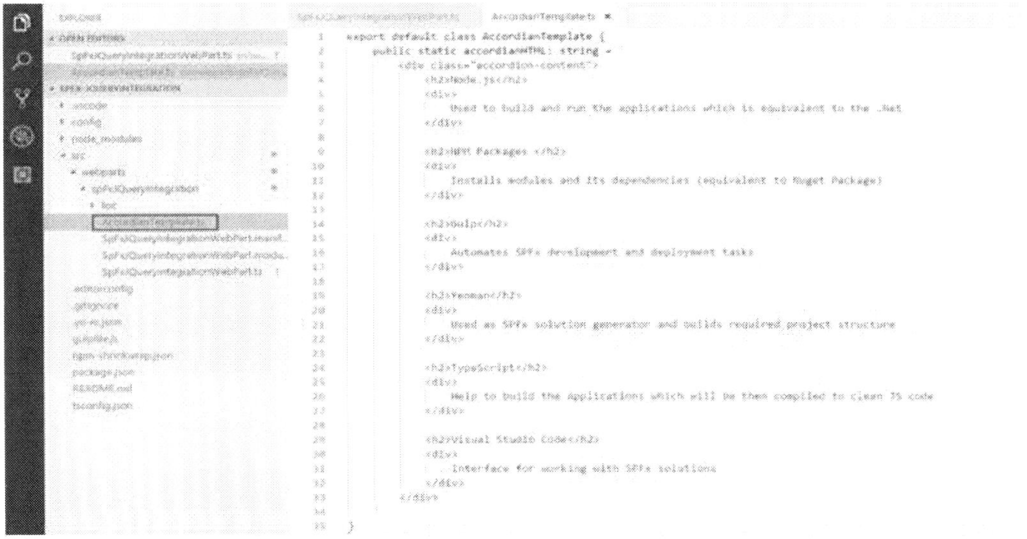

Figure 12.8: Add a new file Accordion Template.ts

10. Use the accordion template in the main webpart class:

Figure 12.9: Use the Accordion template in the SPFx web part

120 ■ *Mastering SharePoint Framework*

Test the web part:

1. At the command prompt, type `gulp serve`.
2. Open any SharePoint site in your tenant or use the SharePoint local workbench.
3. Add the App to your site from the `Add an App` menu.
4. Edit any page and add the webpart:

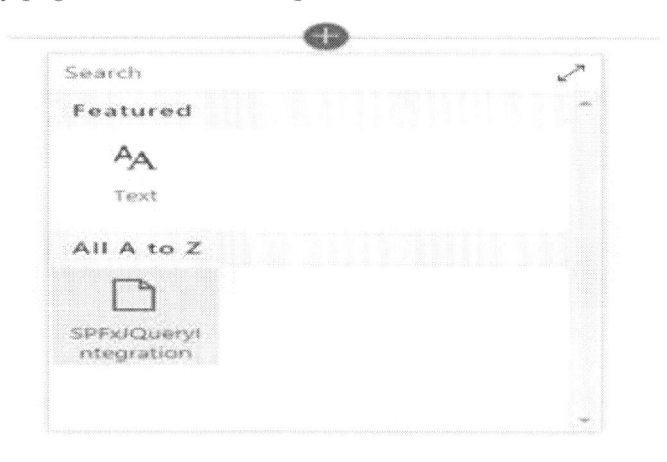

Figure 12.10: Add the SPFx web part to the SharePoint page

5. Check whether the webpart is working:

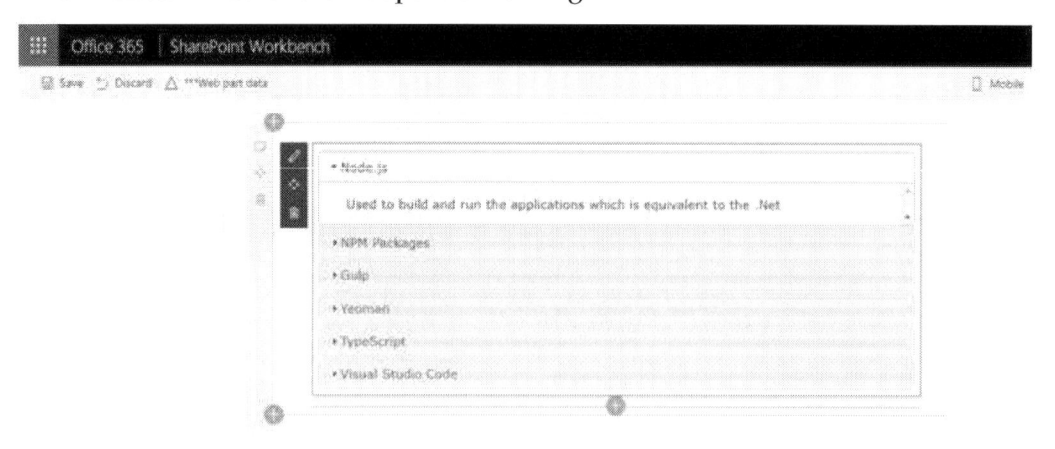

Figure 12.11: SPFxjQuery Accordion web part

Conclusion

In this chapter, we explored coordinating jQuery with the SPFx web part and arranged required bundles and dependencies. jQuery is one of the prominent JavaScript frameworks among SharePoint developers. JavaScript frameworks like jQuery can be effectively coordinated with SPFx client web parts. They additionally bolster typings which aides for IntelliSense while building the code in editors.

Chapter 13
CRUD Operations with No Framework

A common SharePoint portal business scenario mostly consists of involvement with the SharePoint site to retrieve and update the information. In this chapter, we will perform CRUD (Create, Read, Update, and Delete) operations against SharePoint utilizing the 'No Framework' course of action.

Structure
- CRUD tasks against SharePoint utilizing the 'No Framework' alternative
- Configure the Web Part Property for the List Name

Objectives
- Implement the SPFx web part utilizing the 'No Framework' alternative
- REST APIs support for CRUD operations

Develop a SPFx Solution with No Framework for CRUD operations

Open a command prompt. Follow the given steps to make the SPFx solution:

1. Make a folder for the SPFx solution:

```
md spfx-crud-nofw
```

2. Change the path to the above folder:

   ```
   cd spfx-crud-nofw
   ```

3. Execute the Yeoman Generator for SharePoint:

   ```
   yo @microsoft/sharepoint
   ```

4. The Yeoman generator will run through a wizard to ask questions about the SPFx solution creation:

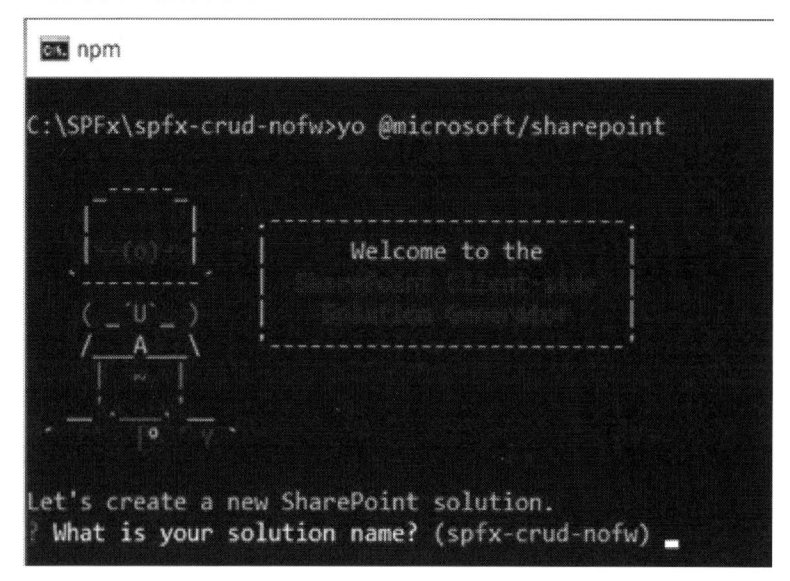

Figure 13.1: SPFx Yeoman generator

The SPFx Yeoman generator will display the following wizard of questions:

- **Solution Name:** Determine the SPFx solution name. Hit the *Enter* key to proceed with the default selection (spfx-crud-nofw in this case) or type another name.
    - **Chosen decision:** Hit *Enter*.
- **Target environment:** Specify the target environment to deploy the SPFx solution. Select any option from SharePoint Online or SharePoint On-Premises environments.
    - **Chosen decision:** SharePoint Online only (latest).
- **Place of files:** Choose the folder location for the SPFx project (either the same folder or a subfolder).
    - **Chosen decision:** Use the current folder.

- **Deployment option:** Specify Y to deploy the app instantly to all the sites, N otherwise.
    - **Chosen decision:** N (install on each site explicitly)
- **Consents to access web APIs:** Check whether the components in the solution need explicit permission to access web APIs that are unique and not shared with other components in the tenant.
    - **Chosen decision:** N (solution contains unique permissions)
- **Choice of client-side component:** Decide to develop a web part or an extension.
    - **Chosen decision:** WebPart
- **Web part name:** Provide the web part name. Hit the *Enter* key to proceed with the default choice or type another name.
    - **Chosen decision:** NoFwCRUD
- **Web part description:** Provide the web part description. Hit the *Enter* key to proceed with the default choice or type another value.
    - **Chosen decision:** CRUD operations with no framework
- **Choice of framework:** Choose a JavaScript framework to develop the component from choices of the No JavaScript Framework, React, and Knockout.
    - **Chosen decision:** No JavaScript Framework

5. After the scaffolding is finished, lock down the version of project dependencies by executing the following command:

```
npm shrinkwrap
```

6. At the command prompt, type the following command to open the solution in the code editor of your choice:

```
code .
```

Configure the Property for the List Name

The SPFx web part by default has the description property. Let us change the property name to list name. We will use this property to configure the list name to perform CRUD operations.

Follow below steps to change the property name to list name:

1. In the '\src\webparts\noFwCrud\loc\' folder, open the `mystrings.d.ts` file.

126 ■ *Mastering SharePoint Framework*

2. The `DescriptionFieldLabel` property should be changed to `ListNameFieldLabel`:

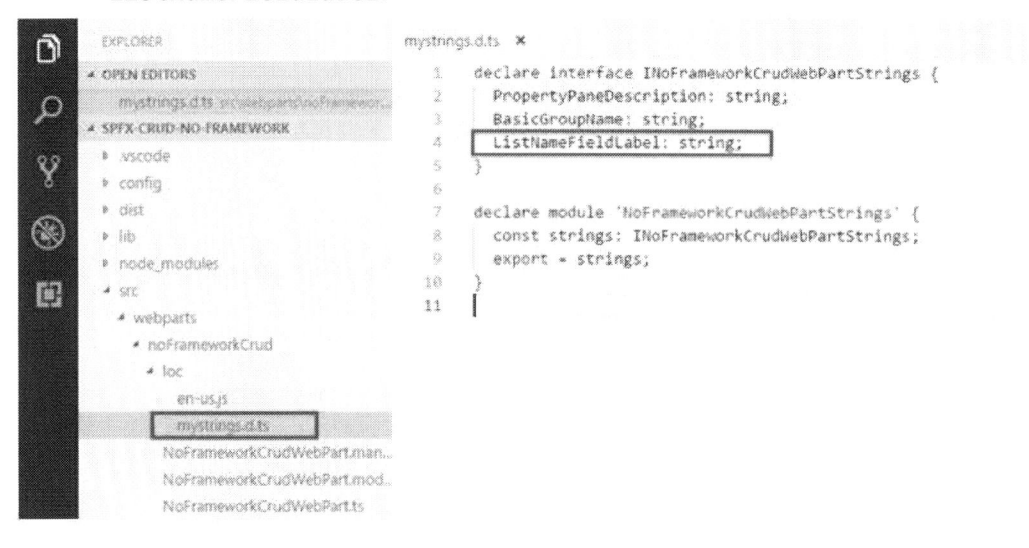

Figure 13.2: Description label renamed to list name

3. In the '\src\webparts\noFwCrud\loc\en-us.js' file, specify the default value to the `listName` property:

Figure 13.3: Property for List name

CRUD Operations with No Framework   127

4. Open the "\src\webparts\noFwCrud\NoFwCrudWebPart.ts" file.
5. The description property should be changed to listName.

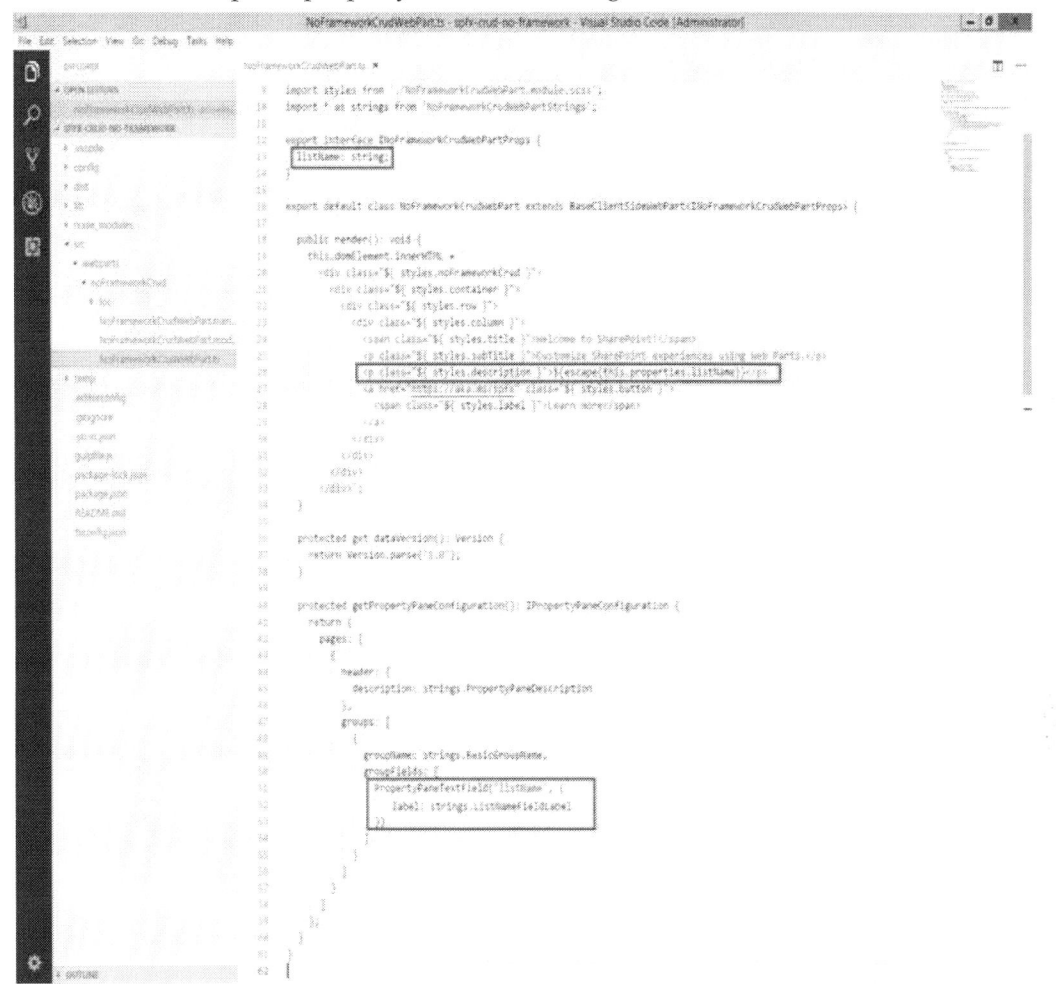

Figure 13.4: Configure the web part to use the list Name property

6. Execute the gulp serve command on the command prompt.
7. On the Local SharePoint workbench page, add our SPFx web part.

8. Verify the **List Name** web part property by editing it:

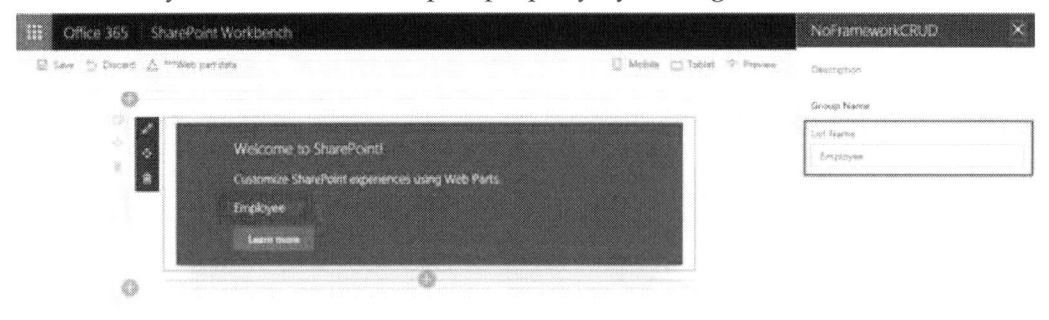

Figure 13.5: '*List Name*' *property*

Model to represent the List Item:

Add the `ISPListItem.ts` file to the solution to represent the list item. The `Title` and `Id` properties denote the fields of the Employee list schema and are used during REST API calls to perform the CRUD operations:

```
export interface ISPListItem {
    Title?: string;
    Id: number;
}
```

Figure 13.6: List item

Add Controls to the WebPart:

1. Open '\src\webparts\noFwCrud\NoFwCrudWebPart.ts' file.
2. In the Render method, include buttons with an event handler for CRUD operations:

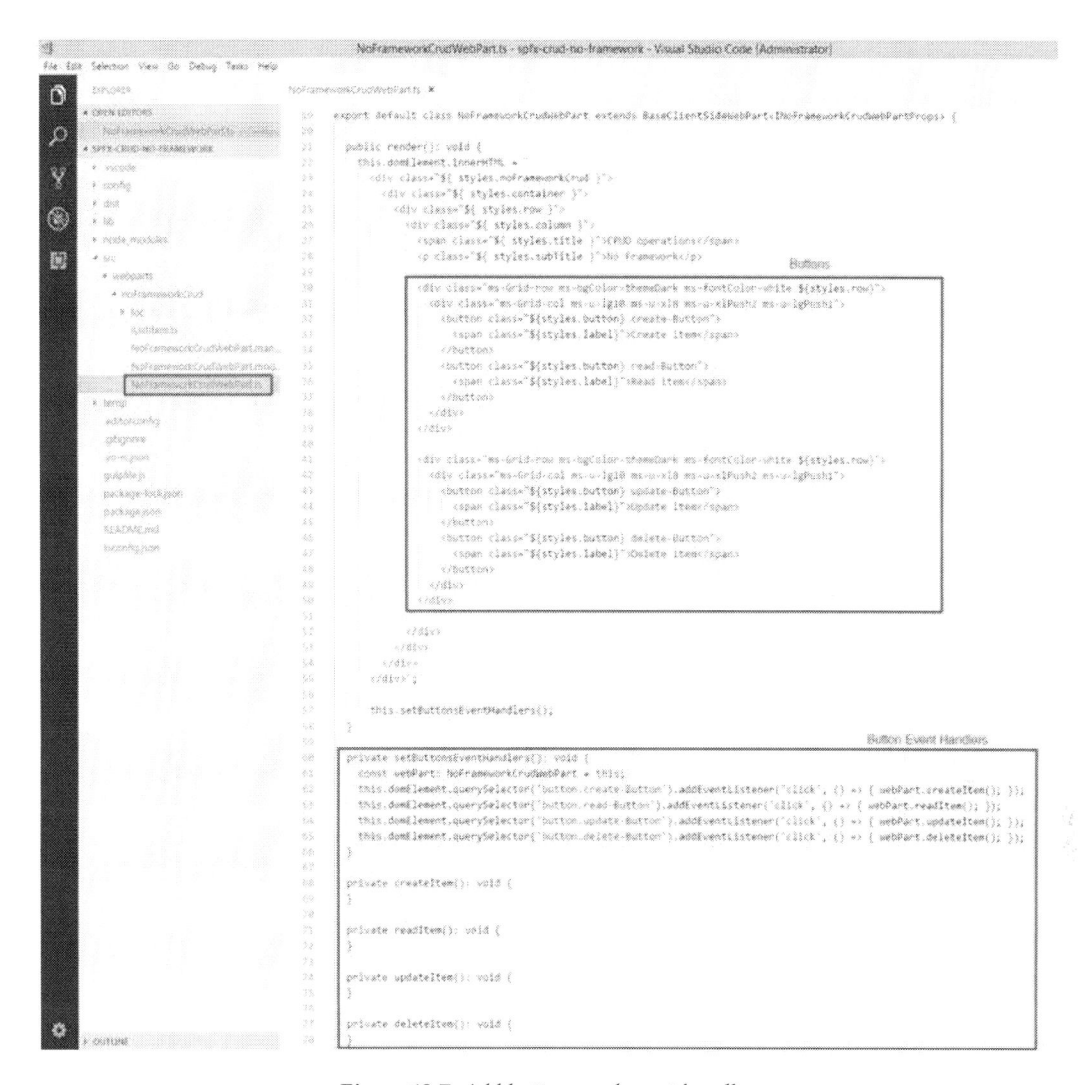

Figure 13.7: Add buttons and event handlers

3. Execute `gulp serve` on the command prompt. The webpart should appear with buttons placed on it:

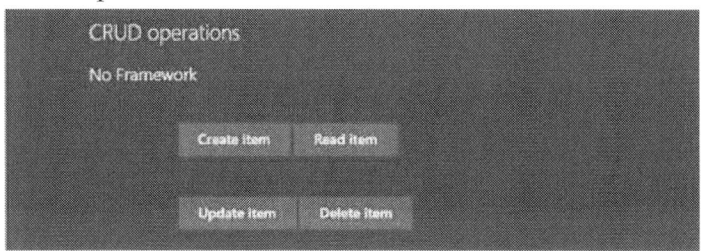

Figure 13.8: Test buttons on the SPFx web part

4. Develop a generic method to get the ID of the most recent item and execute Read, Update, and Delete operations on it:

TypeScript

```
private getRecentItemId(): Promise<number> {

returnnew Promise<number>((resolve: (itemId: number) => void, reject: (error: any) => void): void => {

this.context.spHttpClient.get(`${this.context.pageContext.web.absoluteUrl}/_api/web/lists/getbytitle('${this.properties.listName}')/items?$orderby=Id desc&$top=1&$select=id`,
      SPHttpClient.configurations.v1,
      {
        headers: {
'Accept': 'application/json;odata=nometadata',
'odata-version': ''
        }
      })
      .then((response: SPHttpClientResponse): Promise<{ value: { Id: number }[] }>=> {
return response.json();
      }, (error: any): void => {
        reject(error);
      })
      .then((response: { value: { Id: number }[] }): void => {
if (response.value.length === 0) {
          resolve(-1);
        }
    else {
          resolve(response.value[0].Id);
        }
      });
   });
}
```

The `SPHttpClient` class is used to perform REST calls against SharePoint.

Create Operation Implementation:

To add a new item to the list, make use of REST API:

TypeScript

```
private createItem(): void {
const body: string = JSON.stringify({
'Title': `Item ${new Date()}`
  });


this.context.spHttpClient.post(`${this.context.pageContext.web.absoluteUrl}/_api/web/lists/getbytitle('${this.properties.listName}')/items`,
  SPHttpClient.configurations.v1,
  {
    headers: {
'Accept': 'application/json;odata=nometadata',
'Content-type': 'application/json;odata=nometadata',
'odata-version': ''
    },
    body: body
  })
  .then((response: SPHttpClientResponse): Promise<ISPListItem>=> {
return response.json();
  })
  .then((item: ISPListItem): void => {
this.updateStatus(`Item '${item.Title}' (ID: ${item.Id}) successfully created`);
  }, (error: any): void => {
this.updateStatus('Error while creating the item: ' + error);
  });
}
```

Read Operation Implementation:

To read a recent item from the list, make use of REST API.

TypeScript

```
private readItem(): void {
this.getRecentItemId()
    .then((itemId: number): Promise<SPHttpClientResponse>=> {
if (itemId === -1) {
thrownew Error('No items found in the list');
    }

this.updateStatus(`Loading item with ID: ${itemId}...`);

returnthis.context.spHttpClient.get(`${this.context.pageContext.web.absoluteUrl}/_api/web/lists/getbytitle('${this.properties.listName}')/items(${itemId})?$select=Title,Id`,
        SPHttpClient.configurations.v1,
        {
          headers: {
'Accept': 'application/json;odata=nometadata',
'odata-version': ''
          }
        });
    })
    .then((response: SPHttpClientResponse): Promise<ISPListItem>=> {
return response.json();
    })
    .then((item: ISPListItem): void => {
this.updateStatus(`Item ID: ${item.Id}, Title: ${item.Title}`);
    }, (error: any): void => {
this.updateStatus('Failed to load recent item.Error: ' + error);
    });
}
```

Update Operation Implementation:

To update the recent item from the list, make use of REST API:

TypeScript

```
private updateItem(): void {
letrecentItemId: number = undefined;
this.updateStatus('Loading the recent item...');

this.getRecentItemId()
    .then((itemId: number): Promise<SPHttpClientResponse>=> {
if (itemId === -1) {
thrownew Error('No items present in the list');
    }

recentItemId = itemId;
this.updateStatus(`Loading item with ID: ${itemId}...`);

returnthis.context.spHttpClient.get(`${this.context.pageContext.web.absoluteUrl}/_api/web/lists/getbytitle('${this.properties.listName}')/items(${recentItemId})?$select=Title,Id`,
        SPHttpClient.configurations.v1,
        {
           headers: {
'Accept': 'application/json;odata=nometadata',
'odata-version': ''
        }
     });
   })
    .then((response: SPHttpClientResponse): Promise<ISPListItem>=> {
return response.json();
   })
    .then((item: ISPListItem): void => {
this.updateStatus(`Item ID1: ${item.Id}, Title: ${item.Title}`);
```

```
const body: string = JSON.stringify({
'Title': `Updated Item ${new Date()}`
      });

this.context.spHttpClient.post(`${this.context.pageContext.web.
absoluteUrl}/_api/web/lists/getbytitle('${this.properties.listName}')/
items(${item.Id})`,
         SPHttpClient.configurations.v1,
         {
           headers: {
'Accept': 'application/json;odata=nometadata',
'Content-type': 'application/json;odata=nometadata',
'odata-version': '',
'IF-MATCH': '*',
'X-HTTP-Method': 'MERGE'
         },
           body: body
      })
         .then((response: SPHttpClientResponse): void => {
this.updateStatus(`Successfully updated item with ID: ${recentItemId} `);
         }, (error: any): void => {
this.updateStatus(`Updating item failed. Error: ${error}`);
         });
      });
}
```

Delete Operation Implementation:

To delete the recent item from the list, make use of REST API:

TypeScript

```
private deleteItem(): void {
if (!window.confirm('Do you want to delete the recent item?')) {
return;
```

CRUD Operations with No Framework ▪ 135

```
     }

this.updateStatus('Loading therecent items...');
letrecentItemId: number = undefined;
let etag: string = undefined;
this.getRecentItemId()
    .then((itemId: number): Promise<SPHttpClientResponse>=> {
if (itemId === -1) {
thrownew Error('No items exists in the list');
      }

recentItemId = itemId;
this.updateStatus(`Loading item with ID: ${recentItemId}...`);
returnthis.context.spHttpClient.get(`${this.context.pageContext.web.absoluteUrl}/_api/web/lists/getbytitle('${this.properties.listName}')/items(${recentItemId})?$select=Id`,
        SPHttpClient.configurations.v1,
        {
          headers: {
'Accept': 'application/json;odata=nometadata',
'odata-version': ''
          }
        });
    })
    .then((response: SPHttpClientResponse): Promise<ISPListItem>=> {
etag = response.headers.get('ETag');
return response.json();
    })
    .then((item: ISPListItem): Promise<SPHttpClientResponse>=> {
this.updateStatus(`Deleting item by ID: ${recentItemId}...`);
returnthis.context.spHttpClient.post(`${this.context.pageContext.web.absoluteUrl}/_api/web/lists/getbytitle('${this.properties.listName}')/items(${item.Id})`,
      SPHttpClient.configurations.v1,
```

```
        {
            headers: {
'Accept': 'application/json;odata=nometadata',
'Content-type': 'application/json;odata=verbose',
'odata-version': '',
'IF-MATCH': etag,
'X-HTTP-Method': 'DELETE'
            }
        });
    })
    .then((response: SPHttpClientResponse): void => {
this.updateStatus(`Item with ID: ${recentItemId} successfully deleted`);
    }, (error: any): void => {
this.updateStatus(`Deleting item failed. Error: ${error}`);
    });
}
```

Test CRUD operations:

Follow below steps to test the CRUD operations:

1. With the gulp running on the command prompt, add the webpart to the SharePoint work bench.
2. Set the list name using the web part property:

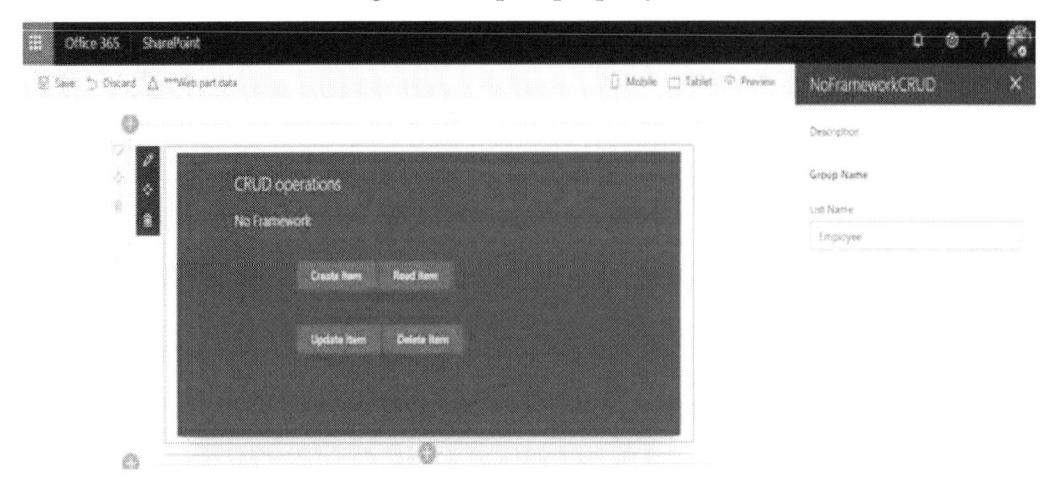

Figure 13.9: Add the SPFx web part to the SharePoint page

3. Test the CRUD functionality by clicking on each button.
   - **Create an item:**

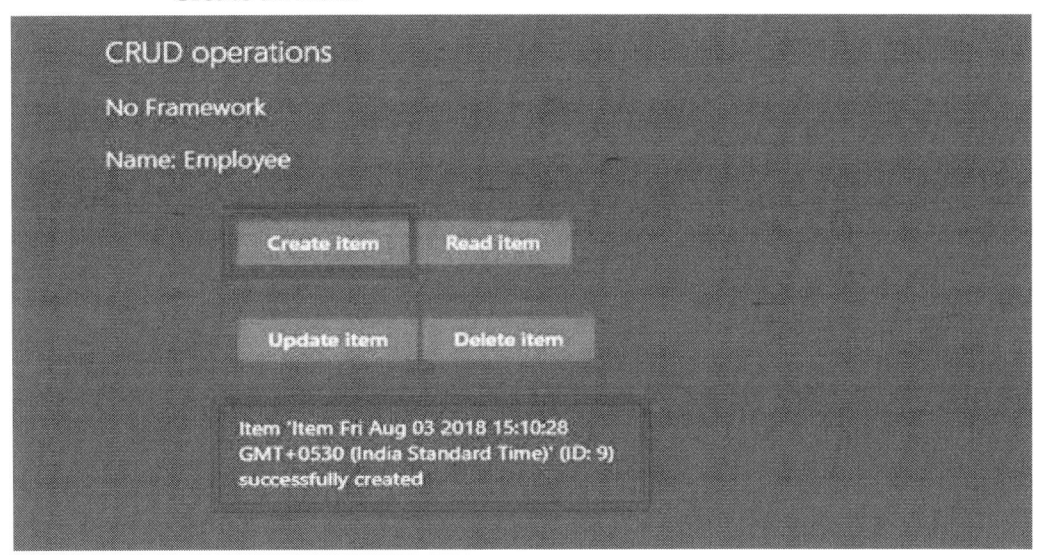

Figure 13.10: Create an item

   - **Read the recent item:**

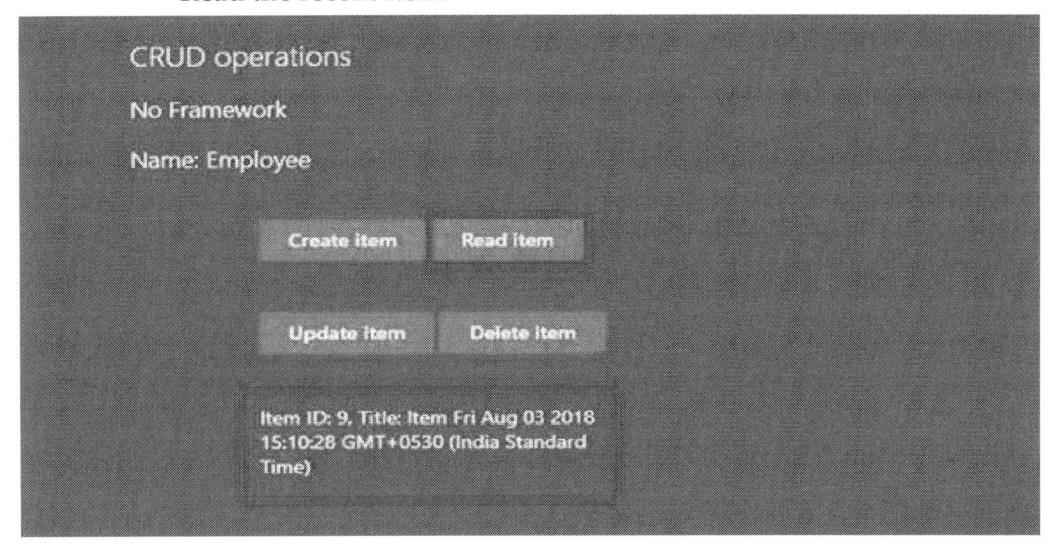

Figure 13.11: Read the recent item

138   ■   *Mastering SharePoint Framework*

- **Update the recent item:**

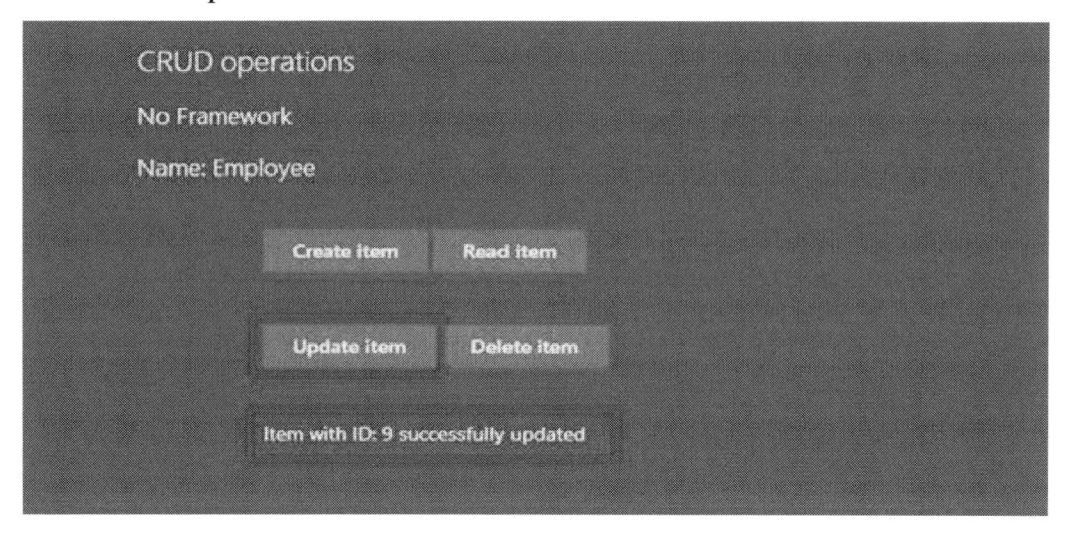

Figure 13.12: Update the recent item

- **Delete the recent item:**

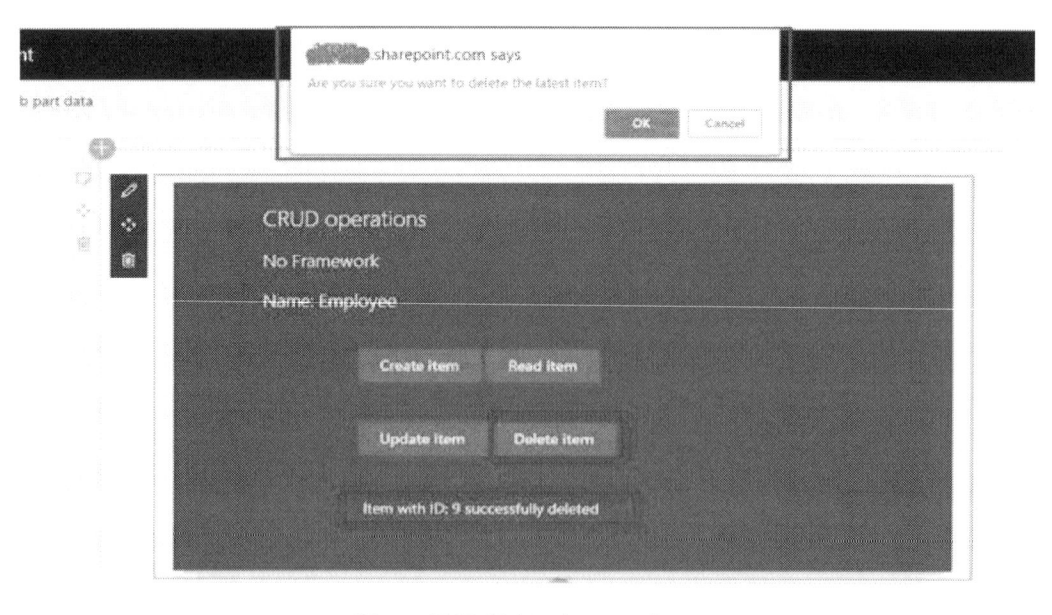

Figure 13.13: Delete the recent item

Conclusion

In this chapter, we explored the No framework alternative to implement the SPFx web part for **CRUD (Create, Read, Update, and Delete)** operations against the SharePoint list. The operations are carried out using REST APIs. 'No framework' demands to write more plumbing code than with any other supported JavaScript libraries. As an outcome, it generates relatively lengthier code.

CHAPTER 14
CRUD Operations with React JS

In this chapter, we will perform **Create, Read, Update,** and **Delete** (**CRUD**) operations against SharePoint using React JS. The SharePoint Framework natively supports React JS.

Structure

- React JS overview
- CRUD operations with React JS
- Configure the Web Part Property for List Name
- Add Controls to the Web Part
- Implement CRUD operations on the SharePoint List

Objectives

- SPFx web part development using React JS
- **Create, Read, Update,** and **Delete** (**CRUD**) operationson the SharePoint list

Brief about React JS

React JS is a JavaScript library developed and maintained by Facebook. It denotes **View (V)** in **Model View Controller** (**MVC**). React JS reacts to changes in the application state. The SharePoint Framework itself is developed using React JS. You can read more about React JS at **https://reactjs.org/**.

> **Ө Note**
>
> *Chapter 19* is dedicated toSPFx Development with React JS, which deep dives into the React library and focuses on why React works well with SPFx.

The SPFx Solution for CRUD operations with React JS

Open the command prompt. Follow the given steps to create the SPFx solution:

1. Create a directory for the SPFx solution:

   ```
   md spfx-crud-reactjs
   ```

2. Navigate to the above created directory:

   ```
   cd spfx-crud-reactjs
   ```

3. Run the Yeoman SharePoint Generator to create the SPFx solution:

   ```
   yo @microsoft/sharepoint
   ```

4. The Yeoman generator will run through the wizard by asking questions about the SPFx solution to be generated:

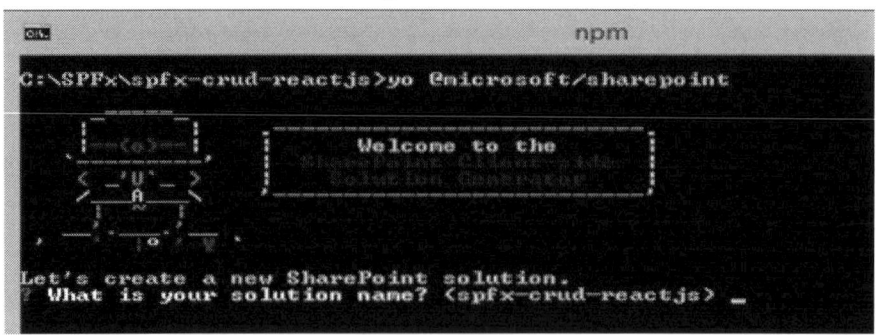

Figure 14.1: SPFx Yeoman generator

- **Solution Name:** Specify the name of the SPFx solution. Hit the *Enter* key to go ahead with the default name (`spfx-crud-reactjs` in this case) or type in any other name for your solution.
    - o **Selected choice:** Hit *Enter*

- **The target for the component:** Specify the target environment to develop and deploy the SPFx solution. Choose from any of SharePoint Online or SharePoint On-Premises environments.
    - o **Selected choice:** SharePoint Online only (latest)
- **Place of files:** Choose the folder location for the SPFx project (either the same folder or a subfolder).
    - o **Selected choice:** Same folder
- **Deployment option:** Specify Y to allow the deployment of the app instantly to all the sites, N otherwise.
    - o **Selected choice:** N (install on each site explicitly)
- **Type of client-side component to create:** Choose to create a client-side web part or an extension.
    - o **Selected choice:** WebPart
- **Web part name:** Specify the name of the web part. Hit the *Enter* key to go ahead with the default name or type in any other name.
    - o **Selected choice:** React CRUD
- **Web part description:** Specify the description of the web part. Hit the *Enter* key to go ahead with the default description or type in any other value.
    - o **Selected choice:** CRUD operations with React JS
- **A framework to use:** Select a JavaScript framework to develop the component. The available choices are No JavaScript Framework, React, and Knockout.
    - o **Selected choice:** React

5. The Yeoman generator will start the scaffolding process to create the solution. It will download the needed npm packages and install the required dependencies. The solution creation will take a significant amount of time.
6. Once the scaffolding process is completed, lock down the version of the project dependencies by running the following command:

```
npm shrinkwrap
```

7. At the command prompt, type the following command to open the solution in the code editor of your choice:

```
code .
```

Configure the Property for the List Name

The SPFx web part by default has a description property. Let us change the property name to list name. We will use this property to configure the list name to perform CRUD operations:

1. Under the `\src\webparts\reactCrud\loc\` folder, open the `mystrings.d.ts` file.
2. Rename `DescriptionFieldLabel` to `ListNameFieldLabel`:

Figure 14.2: Rename description label to list name

CRUD Operations with React JS ■ 145

3. In the en-us.js file under the \src\webparts\reactCrud \loc\folder, set the display name for the listName property:

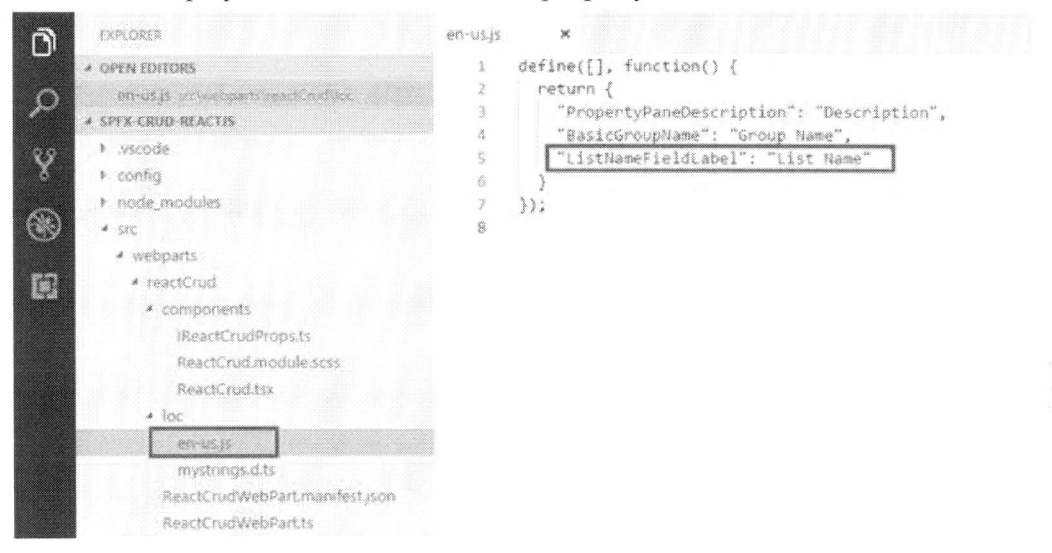

Figure 14.3: Set display name for list name property

4. In the IReactCrudProps.ts interface under the '\src\webparts\reactCrud\components\' folder, set the member name to listName:

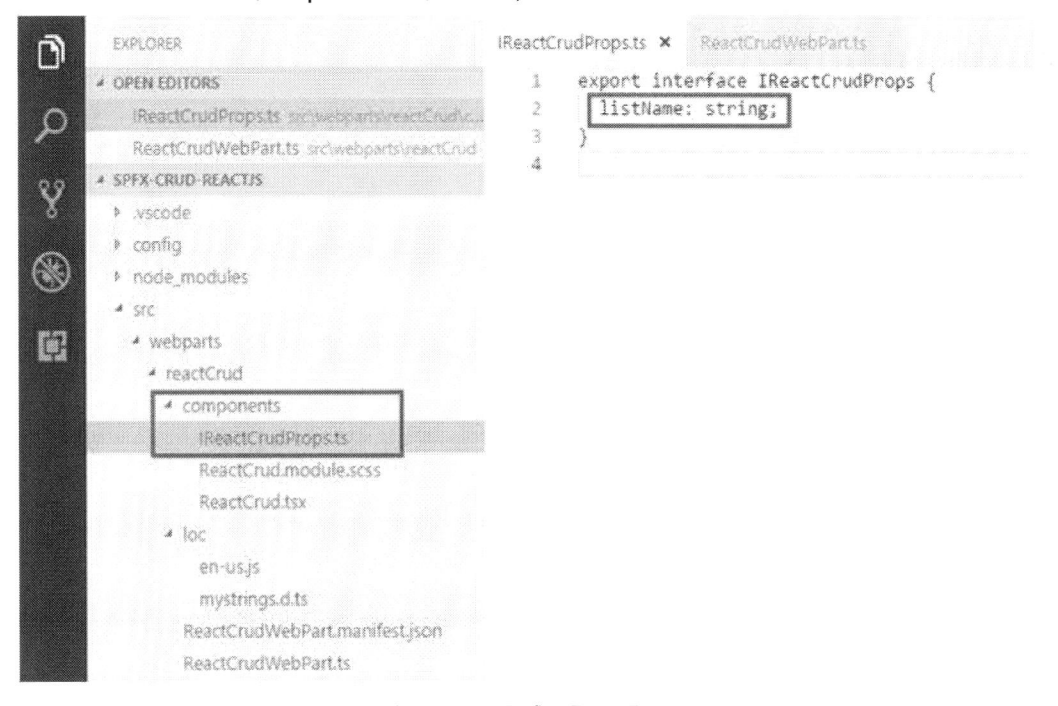

Figure 14.4: Define React Props

5. Open the main webpart file (`ReactCrudWebPart.ts`) under the `\src\webparts\reactCrud` folder.

6. Rename the description property pane field to `listName`:

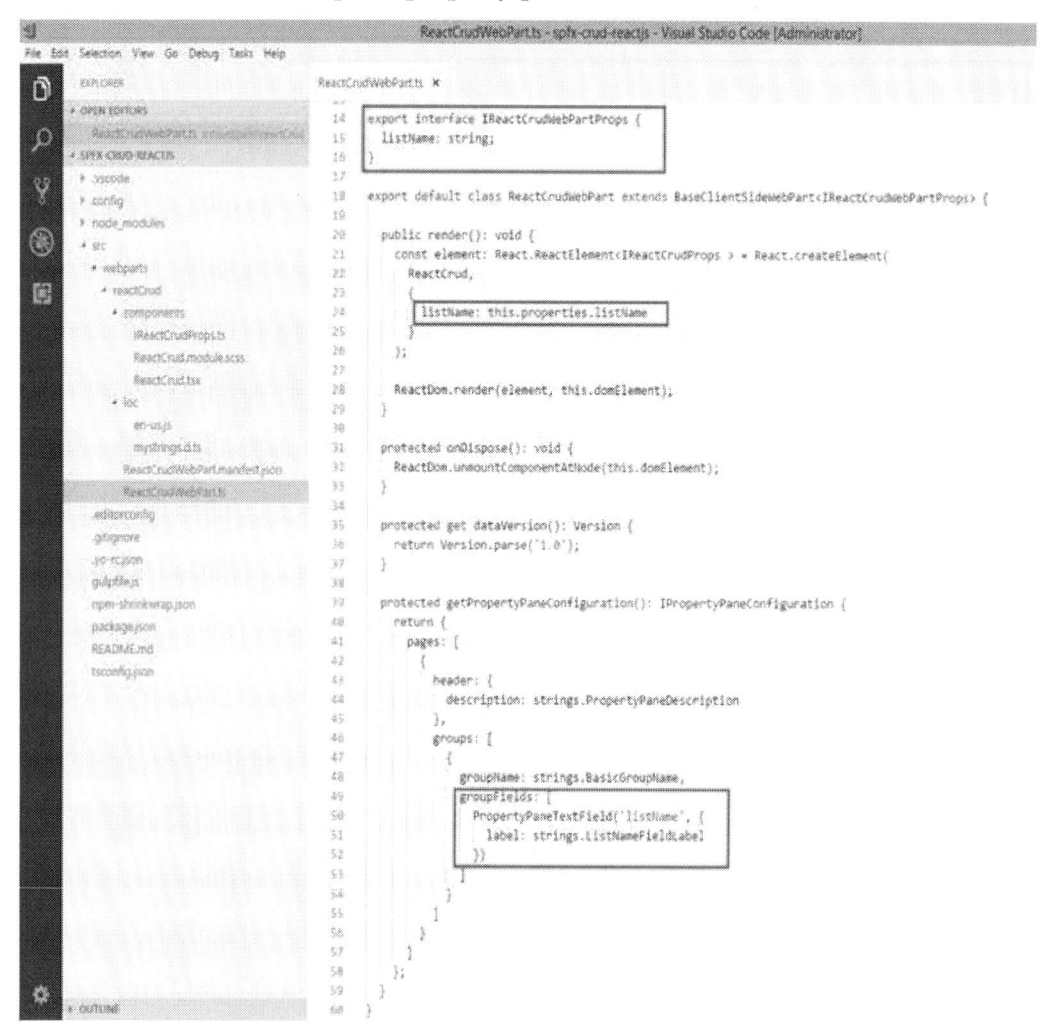

Figure 14.5: Use the list name property in the SPFx web part

7. The UI in React gets served from the `ReactCrud.tsx` component under '`\src\webparts\reactCrud\components\ReactCrud.tsx`'. Make the changes for the `listName` property in the component:

Figure 14.6: Use the list name property in the web part

8. At the command prompt, type gulp serve.
9. In the SharePoint local workbench page, add the web part.
10. Edit the web part to ensure the listName property pane field is getting reflected:

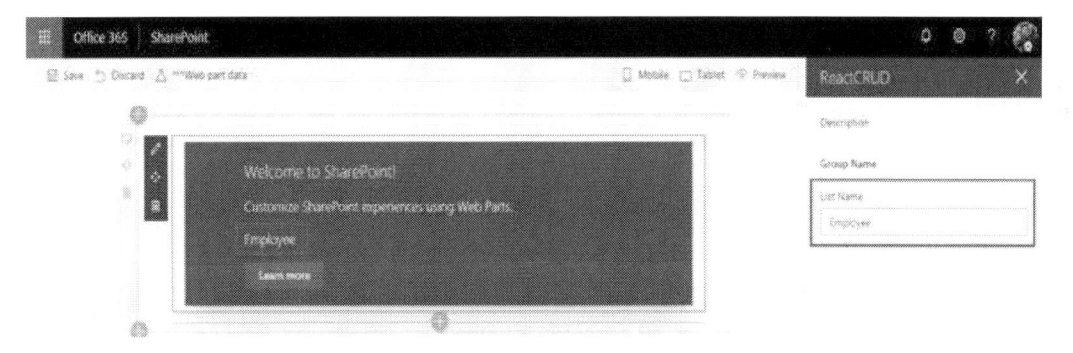

Figure 14.7: Test the SPFx web part for the list name property

148 ■ *Mastering SharePoint Framework*

Define a Model for List Item

Follow below steps to define a model to represent the SharePoint list item.

1. Add a class (`IListItem.ts`) representing the list item:

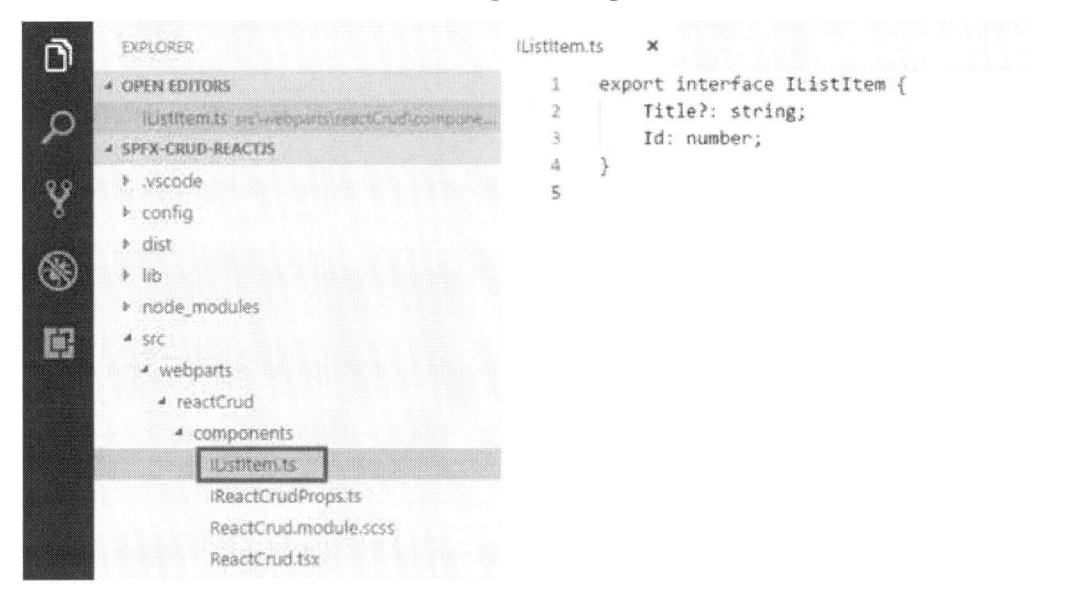

Figure 14.8: Model for list item

2. React JS acts on the state change. Let us add a state to our solution:

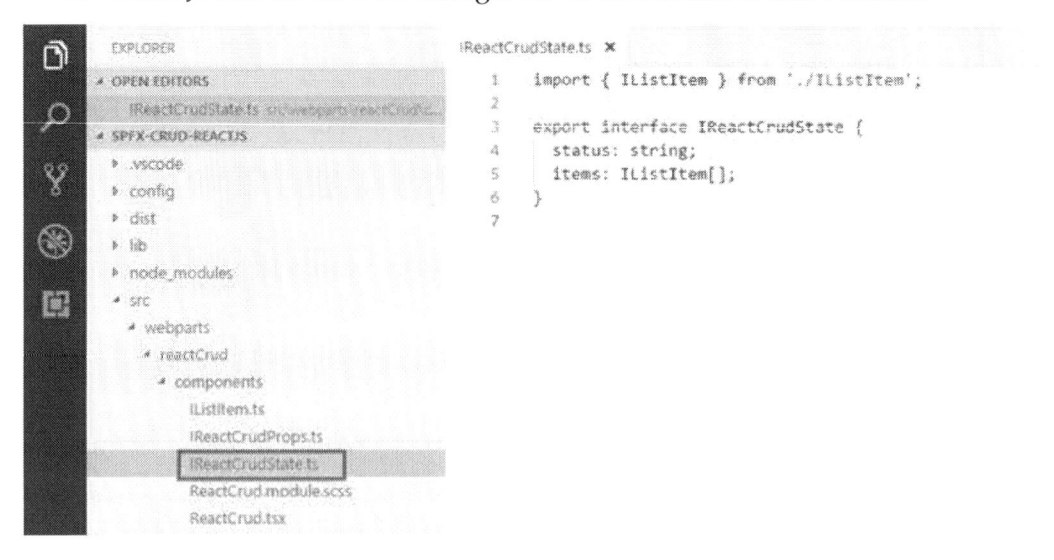

Figure 14.9: Define the React state

3. Configure `ReactCrud.tsx` for this state:

Figure 14.10: Configure the React component to use state

Add Controls to the WebPart

Follow below steps to add controls to perform CRUD operation:

1. Open `ReactCrud.tsx` under the `'\src\webparts\reactCrud\components\'` folder.

2. Modify the Render method to include buttons for CRUD operations and add event handlers to each of the buttons:

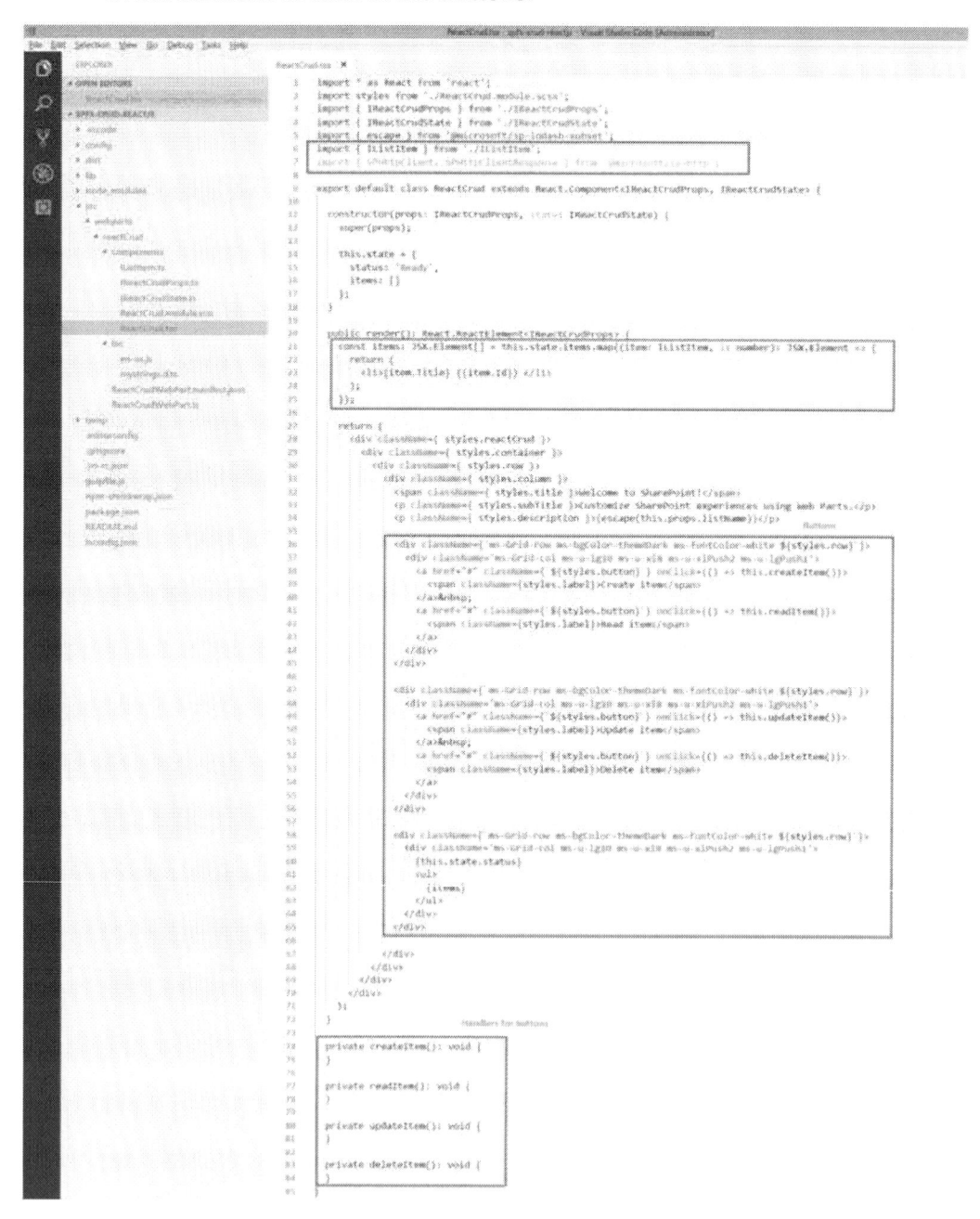

Figure 14.11: Add buttons and event handlers

3. At the command prompt, type `gulp serve` to see the buttons on the webpart:

Figure 14.12: Test buttons on the SPFx web part

4. The read, update and delete operations will be performed on the latest item. Update the `IReactCrudProps.ts` interface in '`\src\webparts\reactCrud\components\`' to include the site URL and `spHttpClient`:

Figure 14.13: Update the interface to include the site URL and spHttpClient

5. Update '\src\webparts\reactCrud\ReactCrudWebPart.ts' to initialize the site URL and spHttpClient:

Figure 14.14: Initialize the site url and spHttpClient

6. Let us implement a generic method which will return the id of the latest item from the given list:

    TypeScript

    private getLatestItemId(): Promise<number> {

    returnnew Promise<number>((resolve: (itemId: number) => void, reject: (error: any) => void): void => {

    this.props.spHttpClient.get(`${this.props.siteUrl}/_api/web/lists/getbytitle('${this.props.listName}')/items?$orderby=Id desc&$top=1&$select=id`,

    SPHttpClient.configurations.v1,

    {

      headers: {

    'Accept': 'application/json;odata=nometadata',

    'odata-version': ''

      }

    })

        .then((response: SPHttpClientResponse): Promise<{ value: { Id: number }[] }>=> {

    return response.json();

    }, (error: any): void => {

       reject(error);

```
        })
            .then((response: { value: { Id: number }[] }): void => {
    if (response.value.length === 0) {
            resolve(-1);
        }
    else {
            resolve(response.value[0].Id);
        }
        });
    });
}
```

Implement the Create Operation

We will use the REST API to add the item to the list:

TypeScript

```
private createItem(): void {
this.setState({
    status: 'Creating item...',
    items: []
  });

const body: string = JSON.stringify({
'Title': `Item ${new Date()}`
  });

this.props.spHttpClient.post(`${this.props.siteUrl}/_api/web/lists/
getbytitle('${this.props.listName}')/items`,
  SPHttpClient.configurations.v1,
  {
    headers: {
'Accept': 'application/json;odata=nometadata',
```

```
      'Content-type': 'application/json;odata=nometadata',
      'odata-version': ''
    },
    body: body
  })
    .then((response: SPHttpClientResponse): Promise<IListItem>=> {
      return response.json();
    })
    .then((item: IListItem): void => {
      this.setState({
        status: `Item '${item.Title}' (ID: ${item.Id}) successfully created`,
        items: []
      });
    }, (error: any): void => {
      this.setState({
        status: 'Error while creating the item: ' + error,
        items: []
      });
    });
}
```

Implement the Read Operation

We will use the REST API to read the latest item:

TypeScript

```
private readItem(): void {
  this.setState({
    status: 'Loading latest items...',
    items: []
  });
```

CRUD Operations with React JS   ▊   155

```
this.getLatestItemId()
    .then((itemId: number): Promise<SPHttpClientResponse>=> {
if (itemId === -1) {
thrownew Error('No items found in the list');
    }

this.setState({
      status: `Loading information about item ID: ${itemId}...`,
      items: []
    });
returnthis.props.spHttpClient.get(`${this.props.siteUrl}/_api/web/lists/getbytitle('${this.props.listName}')/items(${itemId})?$select=Title,Id`,
      SPHttpClient.configurations.v1,
      {
        headers: {
'Accept': 'application/json;odata=nometadata',
'odata-version': ''
        }
      });
  })
    .then((response: SPHttpClientResponse): Promise<IListItem>=> {
return response.json();
  })
    .then((item: IListItem): void => {
this.setState({
      status: `Item ID: ${item.Id}, Title: ${item.Title}`,
      items: []
    });
  }, (error: any): void => {
this.setState({
```

```
            status: 'Loading latest item failed with error: ' + error,
            items: []
        });
    });
}
```

Implement the Update Operation

We will use the REST API to update the latest item:

TypeScript

```
private updateItem(): void {
this.setState({
    status: 'Loading latest items...',
    items: []
  });


let latestItemId: number = undefined;


this.getLatestItemId()
    .then((itemId: number): Promise<SPHttpClientResponse>=> {
if (itemId === -1) {
thrownew Error('No items found in the list');
      }

      latestItemId = itemId;
this.setState({
        status: `Loading information about item ID: ${latestItemId}...`,
        items: []
      });


returnthis.props.spHttpClient.get(`${this.props.siteUrl}/_
```

CRUD Operations with React JS   157

```
api/web/lists/getbytitle('${this.props.listName}')/
items(${latestItemId})?$select=Title,Id`,
        SPHttpClient.configurations.v1,
        {
          headers: {
'Accept': 'application/json;odata=nometadata',
'odata-version': ''
          }
        });
    })
    .then((response: SPHttpClientResponse): Promise<IListItem>=> {
return response.json();
    })
    .then((item: IListItem): void => {
this.setState({
        status: 'Loading latest items...',
        items: []
      });

const body: string = JSON.stringify({
'Title': `Updated Item ${new Date()}`
    });

this.props.spHttpClient.post(`${this.props.siteUrl}/_api/web/lists/
getbytitle('${this.props.listName}')/items(${item.Id})`,
        SPHttpClient.configurations.v1,
        {
          headers: {
'Accept': 'application/json;odata=nometadata',
'Content-type': 'application/json;odata=nometadata',
'odata-version': '',
```

```
    'IF-MATCH': '*',
    'X-HTTP-Method': 'MERGE'
      },
      body: body
    })
      .then((response: SPHttpClientResponse): void => {
this.setState({
        status: `Item with ID: ${latestItemId} successfully updated`,
        items: []
      });
    }, (error: any): void => {
this.setState({
        status: `Error updating item: ${error}`,
        items: []
      });
    });
  });
}
```

Implement the Delete Operation

We will use the REST API to delete the latest item:

TypeScript

```
private deleteItem(): void {
if (!window.confirm('Are you sure you want to delete the latest item?')) {
return;
  }

this.setState({
    status: 'Loading latest items...',
```

```
      items: []
    });


let latestItemId: number = undefined;
let etag: string = undefined;
this.getLatestItemId()
    .then((itemId: number): Promise<SPHttpClientResponse>=> {
if (itemId === -1) {
thrownew Error('No items found in the list');
      }

      latestItemId = itemId;
this.setState({
        status: `Loading information about item ID: ${latestItemId}...`,
        items: []
      });

returnthis.props.spHttpClient.get(`${this.props.siteUrl}/_api/web/lists/getbytitle('${this.props.listName}')/items(${latestItemId})?$select=Id`,
        SPHttpClient.configurations.v1,
        {
          headers: {
'Accept': 'application/json;odata=nometadata',
'odata-version': ''
          }
        });
    })
    .then((response: SPHttpClientResponse): Promise<IListItem>=> {
etag = response.headers.get('ETag');
return response.json();
```

```
    })
        .then((item: IListItem): Promise<SPHttpClientResponse>=> {
this.setState({
        status: `Deleting item with ID: ${latestItemId}...`,
        items: []
    });

returnthis.props.spHttpClient.post(`${this.props.siteUrl}/_api/web/
lists/getbytitle('${this.props.listName}')/items(${item.Id})`,
        SPHttpClient.configurations.v1,
        {
           headers: {
'Accept': 'application/json;odata=nometadata',
'Content-type': 'application/json;odata=verbose',
'odata-version': '',
'IF-MATCH': etag,
'X-HTTP-Method': 'DELETE'
            }
        });
    })
        .then((response: SPHttpClientResponse): void => {
this.setState({
        status: `Item with ID: ${latestItemId} successfully deleted`,
        items: []
    });
    }, (error: any): void => {
this.setState({
status: `Error deleting item: ${error}`,
items: []
    });
```

    });
}

Test the WebPart:

Follow below steps to test the web part on the SharePoint page:

1. At the command prompt, type `gulp serve`.
2. Open the SharePoint site.
3. Navigate to `/_layouts/15/workbench.aspx`.
4. Add the webpart to the page.
5. Edit the webpart, in the properties pane, and type the list name.
6. Click on the buttons (**Create Item, Read Item, Update Item,** and **Delete Item**) one by one to test the webpart.
7. Check whether the operations are taking place in the SharePoint list.

Create Operation

Click on the Create item button to create an item inside the configured SharePoint list:

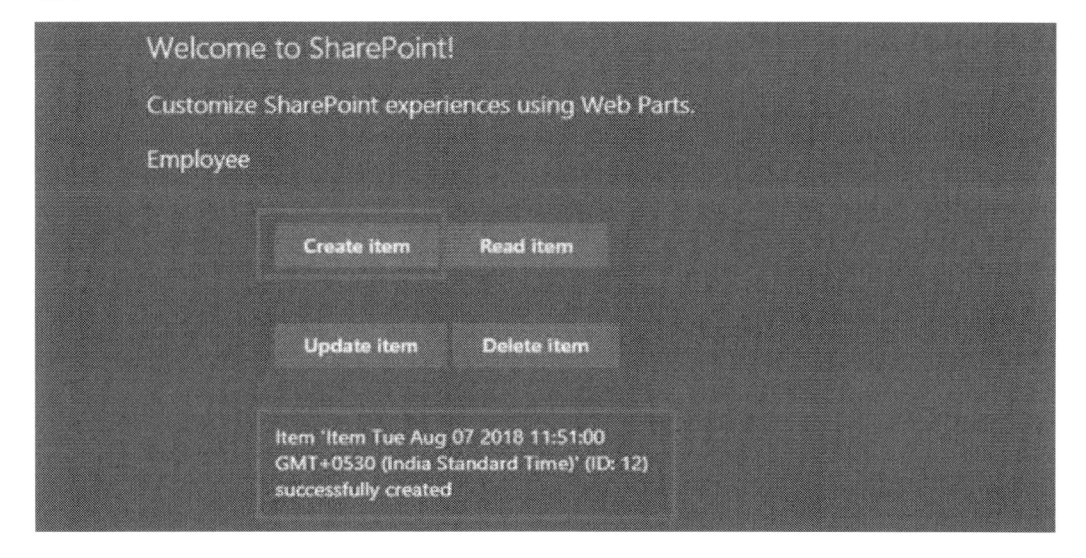

Figure 14.15: Create operation

Read Operation

Click on the **Read item** button to read the latest item from the configured SharePoint list:

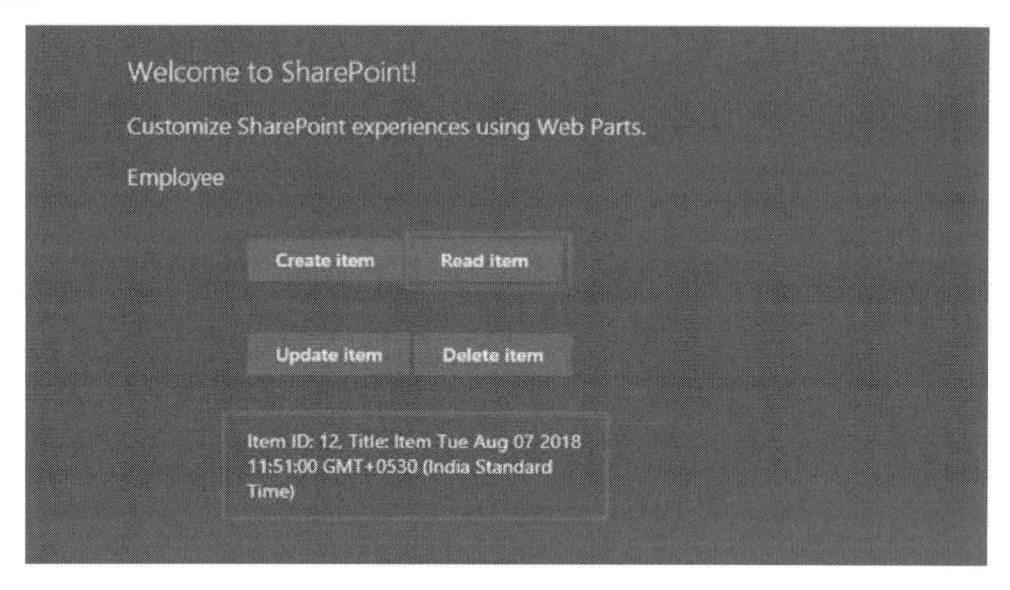

Figure 14.16: Read operation

Update Operation

Click on the **Update item** button to update the latest item from the configured SharePoint list:

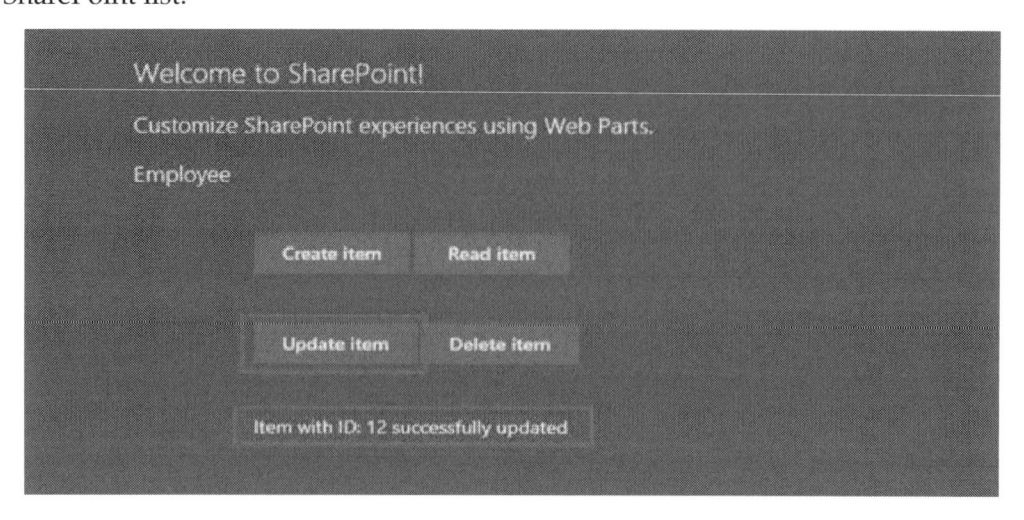

Figure 14.17: Update operation

Delete Operation

Click on the **Delete item** button to delete the latest item from the configured SharePoint list:

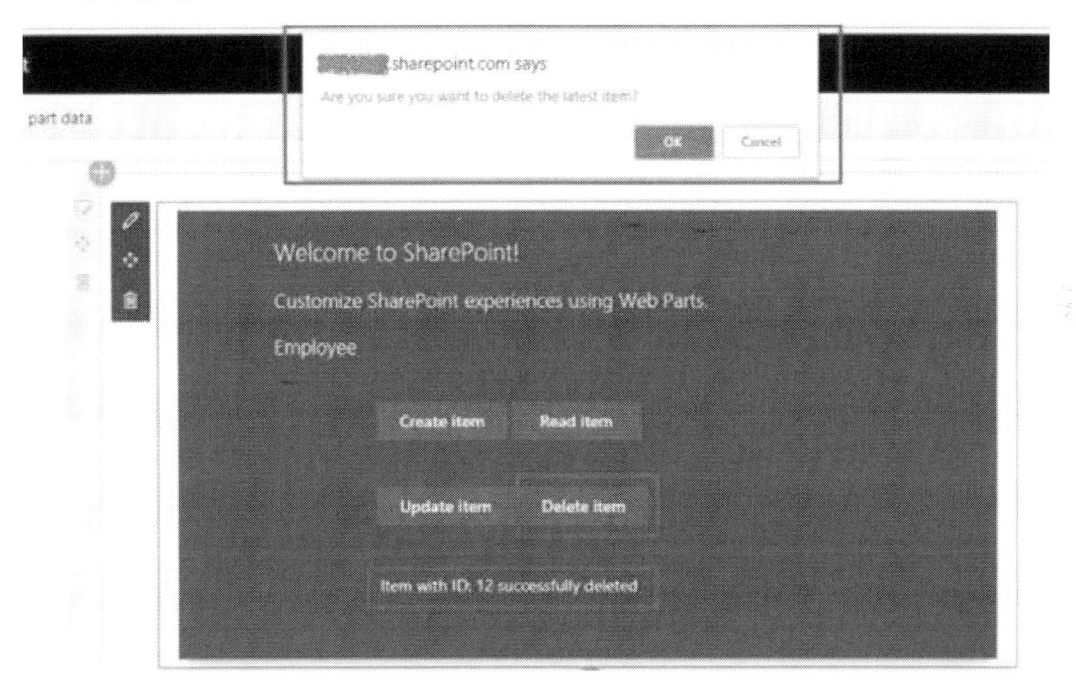

Figure 14.18: Delete operation

Conclusion

In this chapter, we developed the SPFx web part with React JS and interacted with the SharePoint list for **Create, Read, Update,** and **Delete (CRUD)** operations. React JS is natively supported by the SharePoint framework. SPFx generates all the React components for you to get started with the development. React JS supports the breaking of the application into small React components, which simplifies development and maintenance. React JS focuses more on the UI development.In contrast to Angular which is more famous for creating SPA (Single Page Applications). In the next chapter, we will perform CRUD operations using Angular JS.

Chapter 15
CRUD Operations with AngularJS

In this chapter, we will explore how to interact with the SharePoint list for **Create, Read, Update,** and **Delete (CRUD)** operations using AngularJS. React JS is not natively supported by the SharePoint Framework.

Structure
- Brief information about AngularJS
- Develop the SPFx Solution for CRUD operations with AngularJS
- Configure the Web Part Property for the List Name
- Add Controls to the Web Part
- Implement CRUD operations on the SharePoint List

Objectives
- Develop the SPFx web part with AngularJS
- Create, **Read, Update,** and **Delete (CRUD)** operations on the SharePoint list

Brief information about AngularJS

AngularJS is a JavaScript framework which extends HTML with new attributes. It is popular for creating a SPA (Single Page Application). You can read more about AngularJS at **https://angularjs.org/**.

Create the SPFx Solution

Open the command prompt. Follow the given steps to create the SPFx solution:

1. Create a directory for the SPFx solution:

   ```
   md spfx-crud-angularjs
   ```

2. Navigate to the above created directory:

   ```
   cd spfx-crud-angularjs
   ```

3. Run the Yeoman SharePoint Generator to create the SPFx solution:

   ```
   yo @microsoft/sharepoint
   ```

4. The Yeoman generator will run through the wizard by asking questions about the SPFx solution to be generated:

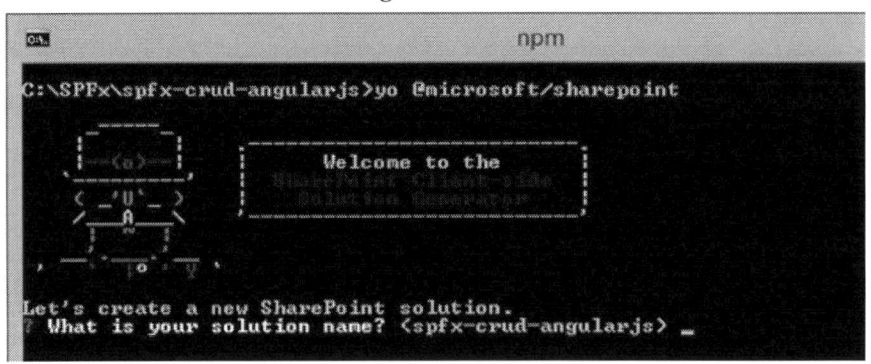

Figure 15.1: SPFx Yeoman generator

- **Solution Name:** Specify the name of the SPFx solution. Hit the *Enter* key to go ahead with the default name (`spfx-crud-angularjs` in this case) or type in any other name for your solution.
    - o **Selected choice:** Hit *Enter*
- **The target for the component:** Specify the target environment to develop and deploy the SPFx solution. Choose from any one of the SharePoint Online or SharePoint On-Premises environments.
    - o **Selected choice:** SharePoint Online only (latest)
- **Place of files:** Choose the folder location for the SPFx project (either the same folder or a subfolder).
    - o **Selected choice:** Same folder

- **Deployment option:** Specify Y to allow the deployment of the app instantly to all the sites, N otherwise.
    - **Selected choice:** N (install on each site explicitly)
- **Type of client-side component to create:** Choose to create a client-side web part or an extension.
    - **Selected choice:** WebPart
- **Web part name:** Specify the name of the web part. Hit the *Enter* key to go ahead with the default name or type in any other name.
    - **Selected choice:** AngularCRUD
- **Web part description:** Specify the description of the web part. Hit the *Enter* key to go ahead with the default description or type in any other value.
    - **Selected choice:** CRUD operations with AngularJS
- **A framework to use:** Select a JavaScript framework to develop the component. The available choices are No JavaScript Framework, React, and Knockout.
    - **Selected choice:** React

5. The Yeoman generator will start the scaffolding process to create the solution. It will download the needed npm packages and install the required dependencies. The solution creation will take a significant amount of time.

6. Once the scaffolding process is complete, lock down the version of project dependencies by running the following command:

    ```
    npm shrinkwrap
    ```

7. At the command prompt, type the following command to open the solution in the code editor of your choice:

    ```
    code .
    ```

Configure AngularJS

AngularJS is not natively supported by the SharePoint framework. At the command prompt, type the following command to add the NPM package reference:

```
npm install angular ng-office-ui-fabric --save
```

The `--save` option includes the packages to the dependencies section of the `package.json` file.

Install Angular typings for TypeScript. Typings enables Intellisense while writing the code in the code editor:

```
tsd install @types/angular --save
```

Expand the node_module folder to see the npm packages being added to Angular:

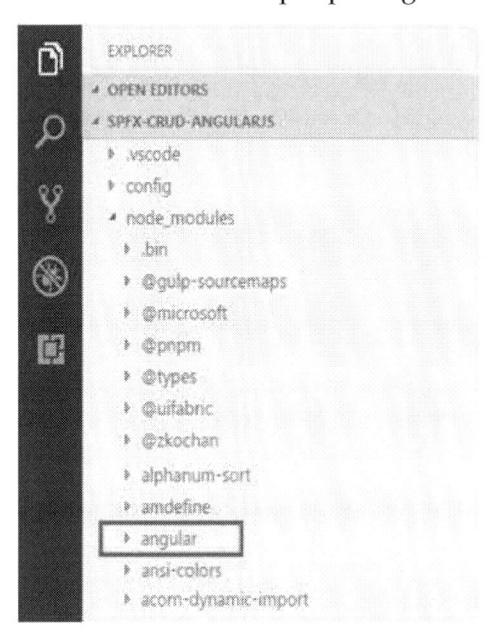

Figure 15.2: Angular npm package

Open the `config.json` under `config` folder. Under the externals node, add the Angular reference:

Figure 15.3: Add the external Angular reference

CRUD Operations with AngularJS   169

You may also add the path from the external CDN. Open `package.json` and check whether the Angular dependency is listed:

Figure 15.4: Verify the Angular dependency

Configure the Property for List Name

The SPFx solution by default has the description property that has been created. Let us change the property to list name. We will use this property to configure the list name on which the CRUD operation needsto be performed.

Follow below steps to Configure the Property for List Name:

1. Open mystrings.d.ts under the '\src\webparts\angularCrud\loc\' folder.
2. Rename `DescriptionFieldLabel` to `ListNameFieldLabel`:

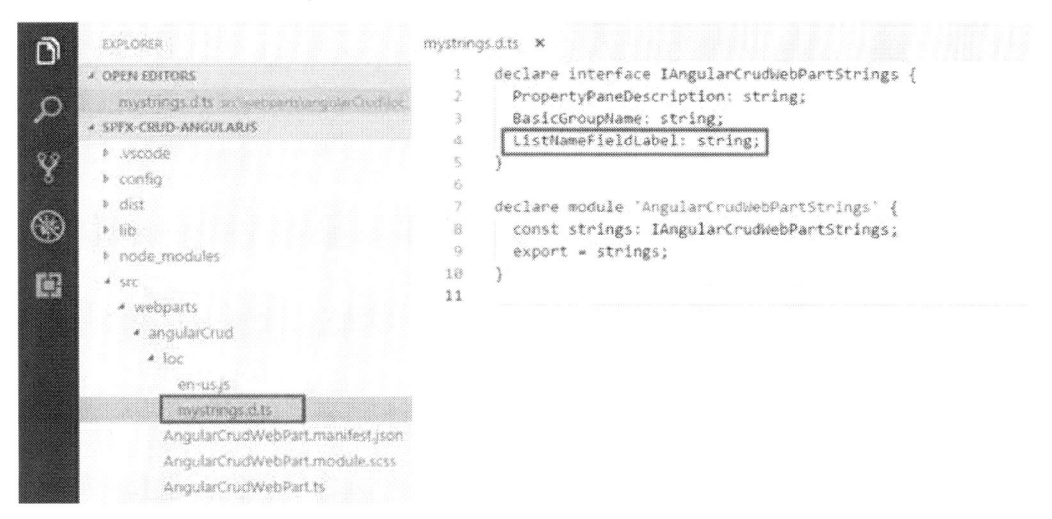

Figure 15.5: Rename description label to list name

3. In the en-us.js file under \src\webparts\angularCrud\loc\ folder, set the display name for the listName property:

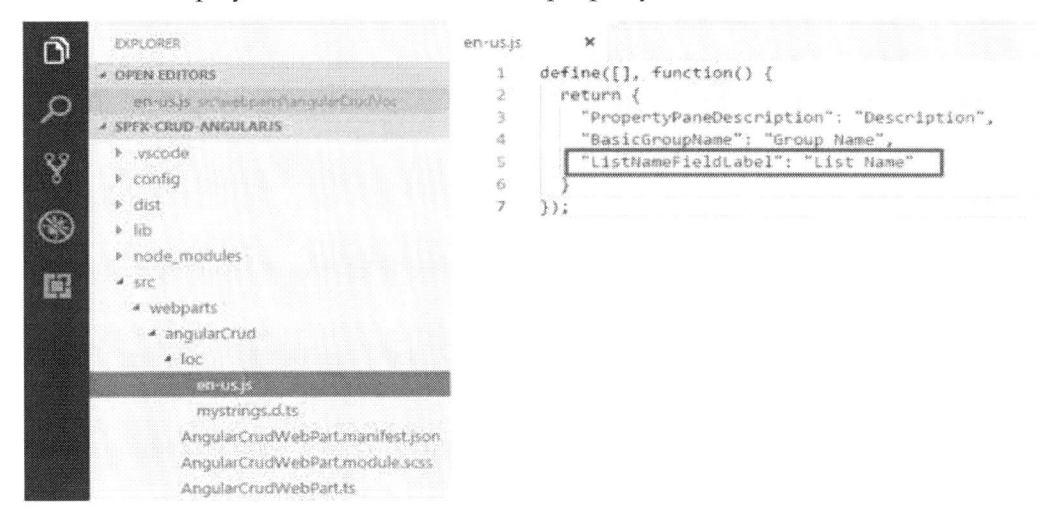

Figure 15.6: Set the display name for list name property

4. Open the main webpart file (AngularCrudWebPart.ts) under the \src\webparts\angularCrud folder.
5. Rename the description property pane field to listName:

TypeScript

exportinterface IAngularCrudWebPartProps {

  listName: string;

}

exportdefaultclass AngularCrudWebPart extends BaseClientSideWebPart<IAngularCrudWebPartProps> {

public render(): void {

this.domElement.innerHTML = `

<div class="${ styles.angularCrud }">

<div class="${ styles.container }">

<div class="${ styles.row }">

<div class="${ styles.column }">

<span class="${ styles.title }">Welcome to SharePoint!</span>

<p class="${ styles.subTitle }">Customize SharePoint experiences using Web Parts.</p>

```
            <p class="${ styles.description }">${escape(this.properties.
listName)}</p>
            <a href="https://aka.ms/spfx" class="${ styles.button }">
              <span class="${ styles.label }">Learn more</span>
            </a>
          </div>
        </div>
      </div>
    </div>`;
  }

  protectedget dataVersion(): Version {
    return Version.parse('1.0');
  }

  protected getPropertyPaneConfiguration(): IPropertyPaneConfiguration
{
    return {
      pages: [
        {
          header: {
            description: strings.PropertyPaneDescription
          },
          groups: [
            {
              groupName: strings.BasicGroupName,
              groupFields: [
                PropertyPaneTextField('listName', {
                  label: strings.ListNameFieldLabel
                })
              ]
```

```
            }
          ]
        }
      ]
    };
  }
}
```

6. At the command prompt, type `gulp serve`.
7. In the SharePoint local workbench page, add the web part.
8. Edit the web part to ensure the `listName` property pane field is getting reflected:

Figure 15.7: Test the SPFx web part for the list name property

Build an Angular application

Add a folder named app as the starting point for creating an Angular app.

Configure Data Service

Add the `DataService.ts` file under the app folder and define the data services we are going to perform:

TypeScript

```
exportinterface IListItem {
    Id: number;
    Title?: string;
```

}

exportinterface IDataService {

   createItem(title: string, webUrl: string, listName: string): angular.IPromise<IListItem>;

    readItem(itemId: number, webUrl: string, listName: string): angular.IPromise<IListItem>;

       getLatestItemId(webUrl: string, listName: string): angular.IPromise<number>;

  updateItem(item: IListItem, webUrl: string, listName: string): angular.IPromise<{}>;

  deleteItem(item: IListItem, webUrl: string, listName: string): angular.IPromise<{}>;

}

exportdefaultclass DataService implements IDataService {

publicstatic $inject: string[] = ['$q', '$http'];

constructor(private $q: angular.IQService, private $http: angular.IHttpService) {

}

public createItem(title: string, webUrl: string, listName: string): angular.IPromise<IListItem> {

const deferred: angular.IDeferred<IListItem> = this.$q.defer();

return deferred.promise;

}

public readItem(itemId: number, webUrl: string, listName: string): angular.IPromise<IListItem> {

const deferred: angular.IDeferred<IListItem> = this.$q.defer();

return deferred.promise;

}

public getLatestItemId(webUrl: string, listName: string): angular.IPromise<number> {

const deferred: angular.IDeferred<number> = this.$q.defer();

```
    return deferred.promise;

  }

public updateItem(item: IListItem, webUrl: string, listName: string):
angular.IPromise<{}> {

const deferred: angular.IDeferred<IListItem> = this.$q.defer();

return deferred.promise;

  }

public deleteItem(item: IListItem, webUrl: string, listName: string):
angular.IPromise<{}> {

const deferred: angular.IDeferred<IListItem> = this.$q.defer();

return deferred.promise;

  }
 }
```

Implement the Create Operation

We will use the REST API to add the item to the list:

TypeScript

```
public createItem(title: string, webUr l: string, listName: string):
angular.IPromise<IListItem> {

const deferred: angular.IDeferred<IListItem> = this.$q.defer();

const body: string = JSON.stringify({

'Title': `Item ${new Date()}`

      });


this.getRequestDigest(webUrl)

            .then((requestDigest: string): angular.IPromise<angular.
IHttpPromiseCallbackArg<IListItem>>=> {

returnthis.$http({

              url: `${webUrl}/_api/web/lists/getbytitle('${listName}')/
items`,
```

```
                method: 'POST',
                headers: {
"Accept": "application/json;odata=nometadata",
"Content-type": "application/json;odata=verbose",
"X-RequestDigest": requestDigest
                }
            });
        })
            .then((response: angular.IHttpPromiseCallbackArg<IListItem>): void => {
                deferred.resolve(response.data);
            }, (error: any): void => {
                deferred.reject(error);
            });
return deferred.promise;
}
```

Implement the Read Operation

We will use the REST API to read the latest item:

TypeScript

```
public readItem(itemId: number, webUrl: string, listName: string): angular.IPromise<IListItem> {
const deferred: angular.IDeferred<IListItem> = this.$q.defer();

this.$http({
        url: `${webUrl}/_api/web/lists/getbytitle('${listName}')/items(${itemId})`,
        method: 'GET',
        headers: {
'Accept': 'application/json;odata=nometadata'
        }
```

```typescript
        })
            .then((response: angular.IHttpPromiseCallbackArg<IListItem>): void => {
    const item: IListItem = response.data;
                item.ETag = response.headers('ETag');
                deferred.resolve(item);
            }, (error: any): void => {
    deferred.reject(error);
        });


    return deferred.promise;
}
```

Implement the Update Operation

We will use the REST API to update the latest item:

TypeScript

```typescript
public updateItem(item: IListItem, webUrl: string, listName: string): angular.IPromise<{}> {

const deferred: angular.IDeferred<IListItem> = this.$q.defer();


const body: string = JSON.stringify({
'Title': `Item ${new Date()}`
    });


this.$http({
                url: `${webUrl}/_api/web/lists/getbytitle('${listName}')/items(${item.Id})`,
        method: 'POST',
        headers: {
'Accept': 'application/json;odata=nometadata',
'Content-type': 'application/json;odata=nometadata',
```

```
'odata-version': '',
'IF-MATCH': '*',
'X-HTTP-Method': 'MERGE'
      },
      data: body
    })
  .then((result: {}): void => {
    deferred.resolve();
  }, (error: any): void => {
    deferred.reject(error);
  });


return deferred.promise;
}
```

Implement the Delete Operation

We will use the REST API to delete the latest item:

TypeScript

```
public deleteItem(item: IListItem, webUrl: string, listName: string): angular.IPromise<{}> {

const deferred: angular.IDeferred<IListItem> = this.$q.defer();

this.$http({
          url: `${webUrl}/_api/web/lists/getbytitle('${listName}')/items(${item.Id})`,
      method: 'POST',
      headers: {
'Accept': 'application/json;odata=nometadata',
'Content-type': 'application/json;odata=verbose',
'odata-version': '',
```

```
        'IF-MATCH': item.ETag,
        'X-HTTP-Method': 'DELETE'
            }
      })
        .then((result: {}): void => {
          deferred.resolve();
        }, (error: any): void => {
          deferred.reject(error);
        });
return deferred.promise;
}
```

Configure the Controller

Add the HomeController.tsfile under the app folder:

TypeScript

```
import { IDataService, IListItem } from'./DataService';

interface IConfigurationChangedArgs {
  webUrl: string;
  listName: string;
}

exportdefaultclass HomeController {
publicstatic $inject: string[] = ['DataService', '$window', '$rootScope', '$scope'];

public status: string = undefined;
public items: IListItem[] = [];

private webUrl: string = undefined;
private listName: string = undefined;
```

```typescript
constructor(private dataService: IDataService, private $window: angular.
IWindowService, private $rootScope: angular.IRootScopeService, private
$scope: angular.IScope) {

const vm: HomeController = this;

this.init(undefined, undefined, undefined);

    $rootScope.$on('configurationChanged',
        (event: angular.IAngularEvent, args: IConfigurationChangedArgs):
void => {
        vm.init(args.webUrl, args.listName, vm.$scope);
      });
  }

private init(webUrl: string, listName: string, $scope: angular.IScope):
void {
if (webUrl !== undefined&& webUrl.length >0&&
      listName !== undefined&& listName.length >0) {
this.webUrl = webUrl;
this.listName = listName;
    }

if ($scope) {
      $scope.$digest();
    }
  }

public createItem(): void {
const itemTitle: string = `Item ${new Date()}`;
this.status = 'Creating item...';
this.items.length = 0;
this.dataService.createItem(itemTitle, this.webUrl, this.listName)
      .then((item: IListItem): void => {
this.status = `Item '${item.Title}' (ID: ${item.Id}) successfully created`;
```

```typescript
        }, (error: any): void => {
            this.status = 'Error while creating the item: ' + error;
        });
    }

    public readItem(): void {
        this.status = 'Loading latest items...';
        this.items.length = 0;
        this.dataService.getLatestItemId(this.webUrl, this.listName)
            .then((itemId: number): angular.IPromise<IListItem>=> {
                if (itemId === -1) {
                    thrownew Error('No items found in the list');
                }

                this.status = `Loading information about item ID: ${itemId}...`;
                returnthis.dataService.readItem(itemId, this.webUrl, this.listName);
            })
            .then((item: IListItem): void => {
                this.status = `Item ID: ${item.Id}, Title: ${item.Title}`;
            }, (error: any): void => {
                this.status = 'Loading latest item failed with error: ' + error;
            });
    }

    public updateItem(): void {
        this.status = 'Loading latest items...';
        this.items.length = 0;
        let latestItemId: number = undefined;
        this.dataService.getLatestItemId(this.webUrl, this.listName)
            .then((itemId: number): angular.IPromise<IListItem>=> {
                if (itemId === -1) {
```

CRUD Operations with AngularJS   181

```
thrownew Error('No items found in the list');
      }

      latestItemId = itemId;
this.status = `Loading information about item ID: ${latestItemId}...`;


returnthis.dataService.readItem(latestItemId, this.webUrl, this.listName);
      })
      .then((latestItem: IListItem): angular.IPromise<{}>=> {
this.status = `Updating item with ID: ${latestItemId}...`;
      latestItem.Title = `Item ${new Date()}`;
returnthis.dataService.updateItem(latestItem, this.webUrl, this.listName);
      })
      .then((result: {}): void => {
this.status = `Item with ID: ${latestItemId} successfully updated`;
      }, (error: any): void => {
this.status = `Error updating item: ${error}`;
      });
  }

public deleteItem(): void {
if (!this.$window.confirm('Are you sure you want to delete this todo item?')) {
return;
    }

this.status = 'Loading latest items...';
this.items.length = 0;
let latestItemId: number = undefined;
this.dataService.getLatestItemId(this.webUrl, this.listName)
      .then((itemId: number): angular.IPromise<IListItem>=> {
if (itemId === -1) {
```

```
        thrownew Error('No items found in the list');
       }

            latestItemId = itemId;
this.status = `Loading information about item ID: ${latestItemId}...`;

returnthis.dataService.readItem(latestItemId,    this.webUrl,    this.listName);
      })
        .then((latestItem: IListItem): angular.IPromise<{}>=> {
this.status = `Deleting item with ID: ${latestItemId}...`;
returnthis.dataService.deleteItem(latestItem, this.webUrl, this.listName);
      })
        .then((result: {}): void => {
this.status = `Item with ID: ${latestItemId} successfully deleted`;
      }, (error: any): void => {
this.status = `Error deleting item: ${error}`;
      });
  }
}
```

Configure the Module

Add the app-module.ts file under the app folder:

TypeScript

```
import*as angular from'angular';
import HomeController from'./HomeController';
import DataService from'./DataService';

import'ng-office-ui-fabric';

const crudapp: ng.IModule = angular.module('crudapp', [
'officeuifabric.core',
```

```
'officeuifabric.components'
]);

crudapp
  .controller('HomeController', HomeController)
  .service('DataService', DataService);
```

Add Controls to the WebPart

Follow below steps to add controls to the web part:

1. Open `AngularCrudWebPart.ts` under the `\src\webparts\angularCrud\` folder.

2. Import the Angular module:

   TypeScript

   ```
   import*as angular from'angular';

   import'./app/app-module';
   ```

3. Modify the Render method to include buttons for CRUD operations and add event handlers to each of the buttons:

   TypeScript

   ```
   exportdefaultclass AngularCrudWebPart extends BaseClientSideWebPart<IAngularCrudWebPartProps> {

   private $injector: angular.auto.IInjectorService;

   public render(): void {

   if (this.renderedOnce === false) {

   this.domElement.innerHTML = `

   <div class="${styles.angularCrud}" data-ng-controller="HomeController as vm">

   <div class="${styles.container}">

   <div class="ms-Grid-row ms-bgColor-themeDark ms-fontColor-white ${styles.row}">

   <div class="ms-Grid-col ms-u-lg10 ms-u-xl8 ms-u-xlPush2 ms-u-lgPush1">
   ```

```html
        <span class="ms-font-xl ms-fontColor-white">
            Sample SharePoint CRUD operations in Angular
</span>
</div>
</div>
<div class="ms-Grid-row ms-bgColor-themeDark ms-fontColor-white ${styles.row}">
<div class="ms-Grid-col ms-u-lg10 ms-u-xl8 ms-u-xlPush2 ms-u-lgPush1">
<uif-button ng-click="vm.createItem()" ng-disabled="vm.listNotConfigured">Create item</uif-button>
<uif-button ng-click="vm.readItem()" ng-disabled="vm.listNotConfigured">Read item</uif-button>
</div>
</div>
<div class="ms-Grid-row ms-bgColor-themeDark ms-fontColor-white ${styles.row}">
<div class="ms-Grid-col ms-u-lg10 ms-u-xl8 ms-u-xlPush2 ms-u-lgPush1">
<uif-button ng-click="vm.readItems()" ng-disabled="vm.listNotConfigured">Read all items</uif-button>
</div>
</div>
<div class="ms-Grid-row ms-bgColor-themeDark ms-fontColor-white ${styles.row}">
<div class="ms-Grid-col ms-u-lg10 ms-u-xl8 ms-u-xlPush2 ms-u-lgPush1">
<uif-button ng-click="vm.updateItem()" ng-disabled="vm.listNotConfigured">Update item</uif-button>
<uif-button ng-click="vm.deleteItem()" ng-disabled="vm.listNotConfigured">Delete item</uif-button>
</div>
</div>
<div class="ms-Grid-row ms-bgColor-themeDark ms-fontColor-white ${styles.row}">
<div class="ms-Grid-col ms-u-lg10 ms-u-xl8 ms-u-xlPush2 ms-u-lgPush1">
```

```
<div>{{vm.status}}</div>
<ul>
<li ng-repeat="item in vm.items">{{item.Title}} ({{item.Id}})</li>
<ul>
</div>
</div>
</div>
</div>`;

this.$injector = angular.bootstrap(this.domElement, ['crudapp']);
    }

this.$injector.get('$rootScope').$broadcast('configurationChanged', {
        webUrl: this.context.pageContext.web.absoluteUrl,
        listName: this.properties.listName
    });
  }
}
```

Test the WebPart

Follow below steps to test the web part on the SharePoint page:

1. At the command prompt, type `gulp serve`.
2. Open the SharePoint site.
3. Navigate to `/_layouts/15/workbench.aspx`.
4. Add the webpart to the page.
5. Edit the webpart, in the properties pane, and type the list name.
6. Click on the buttons (**Create item**, **Read item**, **Update item**, and **Delete item**) one by one to test the webpart.
7. Check whether the operations are taking place in the SharePoint list.

Create Operation

Click on the **Create item** button to create an item inside the configured SharePoint list:

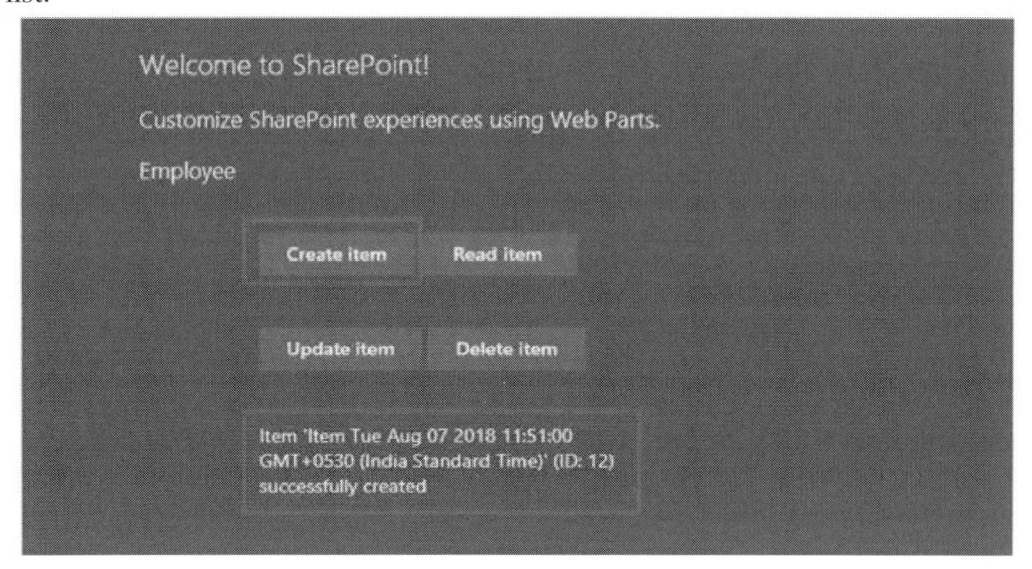

Figure 15.8: Create operation

Read Operation

Click on the **Read item** button to read the latest item from the configured SharePoint list:

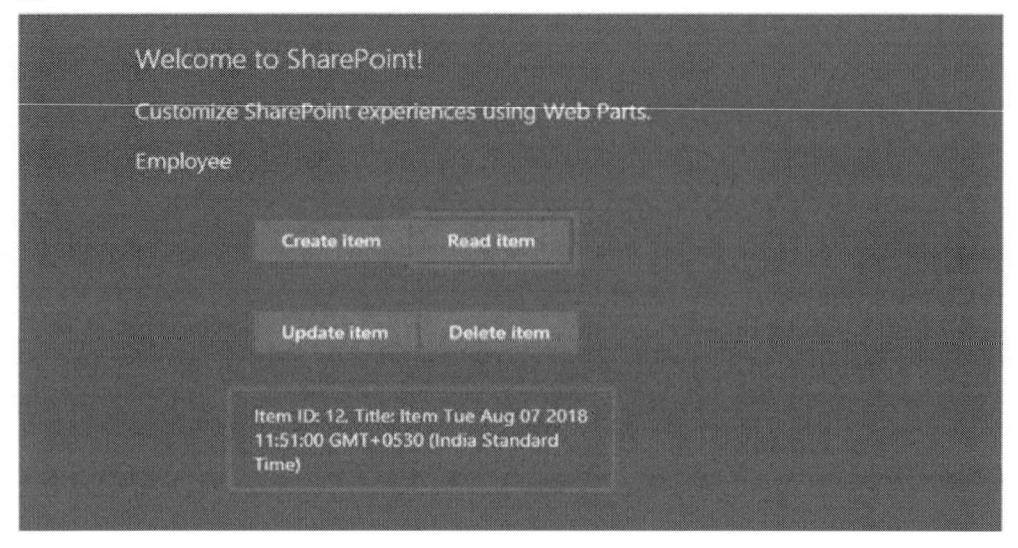

Figure 15.9: Read operation

Update Operation

Click on the **Update item** button to update the latest item from the configured SharePoint list:

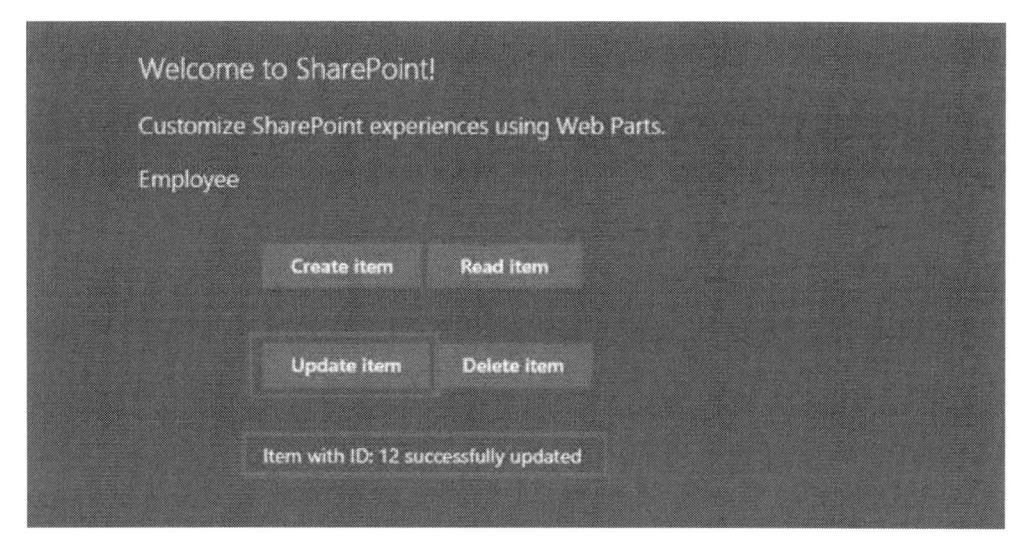

Figure 15.10: Update operation

Delete Operation

Click on the **Delete item** button to delete the latest item from the configured SharePoint list:

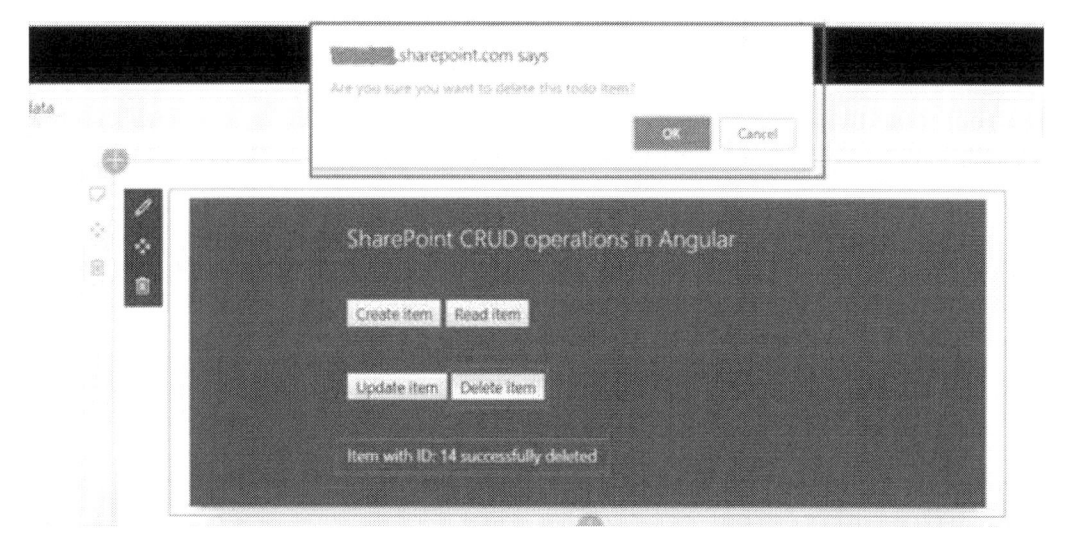

Figure 15.11: Delete operation

Troubleshooting

In some cases, the SharePoint workbench **(https://[tenant].sharepoint.com/_layouts/15/workbench.aspx)** shows the following error although 'gulp serve' is running:

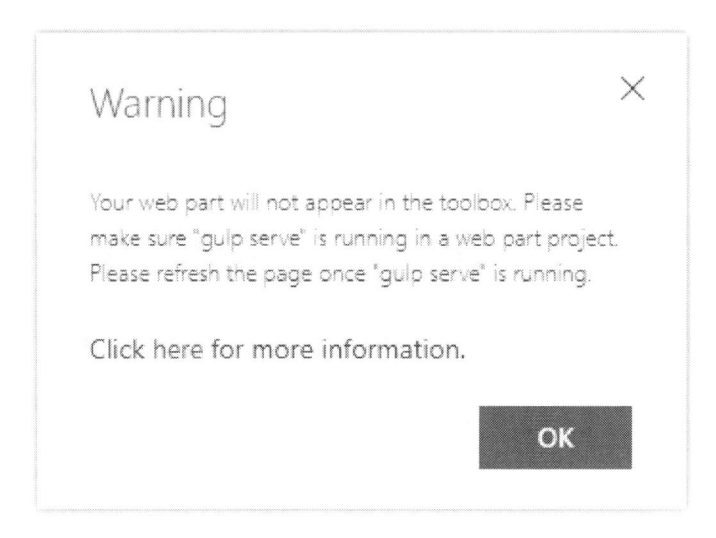

Figure 15.12: Troubleshooting

Open the following URL in the next tab of the browser and accept the warning message:

https://localhost:4321/temp/manifests.js

Conclusion

In this chapter, we developed the SPFx web part with AngularJS and interacted with the SharePoint list for **Create, Read, Update,** and **Delete (CRUD)** operations. AngularJS is more famous for creating a **Single Page Applications (SPA)**. It is not supported natively with the SharePoint framework.

In the next chapter, we will perform CRUD operations using Knockout JS.

CHAPTER 16
CRUD Operations Using Knockout JS

In this chapter, we will interact with the SharePoint list for **Create, Read, Update,** and **Delete (CRUD)** operations using **KnockoutJS (**aka **KO)**. KnockoutJS is natively supported by the SharePoint Framework.

Structure
- Brief information about KnockoutJS
- Develop the SPFx Solution for CRUD operations with KnockoutJS
- Configure the Web Part Property for the List Name
- Add Controls to the Web Part
- Implement CRUD operations on the SharePoint List

Objectives
- Develop the SPFx web part with KnockoutJS
- **Create, Read, Update,** and **Delete (CRUD)** operations on the SharePoint list

Brief information about KnockoutJS

KnockoutJS was developed and maintained as an open source project by Steve Sanderson, a Microsoft employee. KnockoutJS follows the JavaScript implementation of the Model-View-ViewModel pattern with templates. You can read more about KnockoutJS at **http://knockoutjs.com/**.

Create the SPFx Solution

Open the command prompt. Follow the given steps to create the SPFx solution:

1. Create a directory for the SPFx solution:

    ```
    md spfx-crud-knockoutjs
    ```

2. Navigate to the above created directory:

    ```
    cd spfx-crud-knockoutjs
    ```

3. Run the Yeoman SharePoint Generator to create the SPFx solution:

    ```
    yo @microsoft/sharepoint
    ```

4. The Yeoman generator will run through the wizard by asking questions about the SPFx solution to be generated:

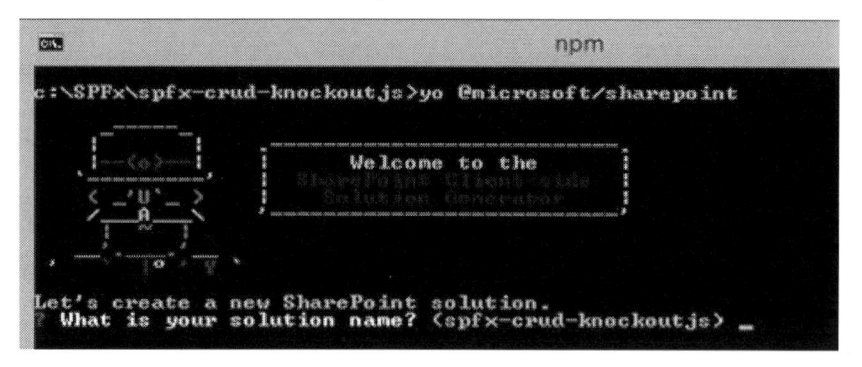

Figure 16.1: SPFx Yeoman generator

- **Solution Name:** Specify the name of the SPFx solution. Hit the *Enter* key to go ahead with the default name (`spfx-crud-knockoutjs` in this case) or type in any other name for your solution.
    - **Selected choice:** Hit *Enter*
- **The target for the component:** Specify the target environment to develop and deploy the SPFx solution. Choose from any one of the SharePoint Online or SharePoint On-Premises environments.
    - **Selected choice:** SharePoint Online only (latest)
- **Place of files:** Choose the folder location for the SPFx project (either the same folder or a subfolder).
    - **Selected choice:** Same folder

- **Deployment option:** Specify Y to allow the deployment of the app instantly to all the sites, N otherwise.
    - **Selected choice:** N (install on each site explicitly)
- **Type of client-side component to create:** Choose to create a client-side web part or an extension.
    - **Selected choice:** WebPart
- **Web part name:** Specify the name of the web part. Hit the *Enter* key to go ahead with the default name or type in any other name.
    - **Selected choice:** KnockoutCRUD
- **Web part description:** Specify the description of the web part. Hit the *Enter* key to go ahead with the default description or type in any other value.
    - **Selected choice:** CRUD operations with KnockoutJS
- **A framework to use:** Select a JavaScript framework to develop the component. The available choices are No JavaScript Framework, React, and Knockout.
    - **Selected choice:** Knockout

5. The Yeoman generator will start the scaffolding process to create the solution. It will download the needed npm packages and install the required dependencies. The solution creation will take a significant amount of time.

6. Once the scaffolding process is complete, lock down the version of the project dependencies by running the following command:

```
npm shrinkwrap
```

7. At the command prompt, type the following command to open the solution in the code editor of your choice:

```
code .
```

Configure Property for List Name

The SPFx web part by default has the description property. Let us change the property name to list name. We will use this property to configure the list name to perform CRUD operations.

Follow below steps to Configure the Property for List Name:

1. Under the '\src\webparts\knockoutCrud\loc\' folder, open the mystrings.d.ts file.

192 ■ *Mastering SharePoint Framework*

2. Rename `DescriptionFieldLabel` to `ListNameFieldLabel`:

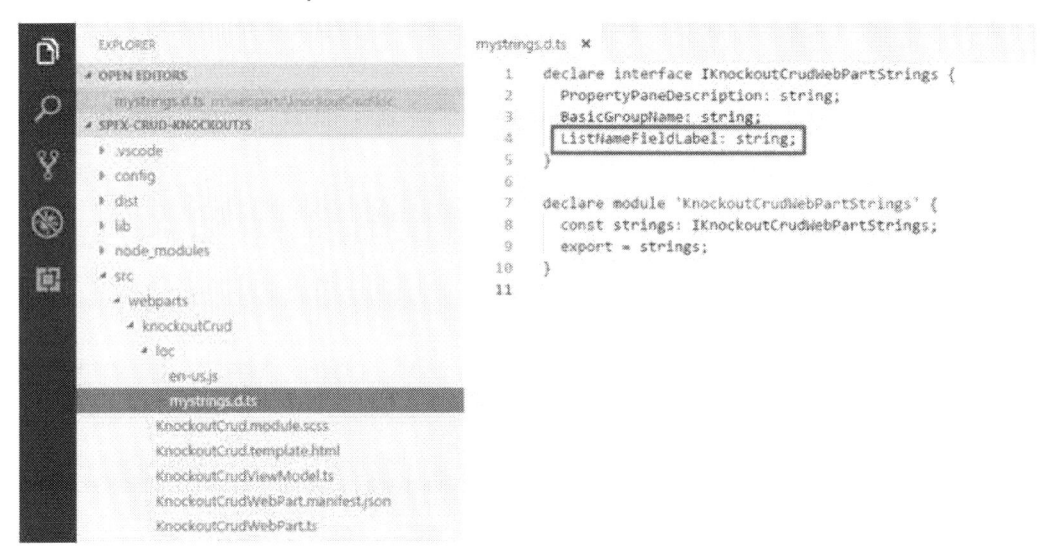

Figure 16.2: Description label renamed to list name.

3. In the en-us.js file under the \src\webparts\knockoutCrud\loc\ folder, set the display name for the listName property.

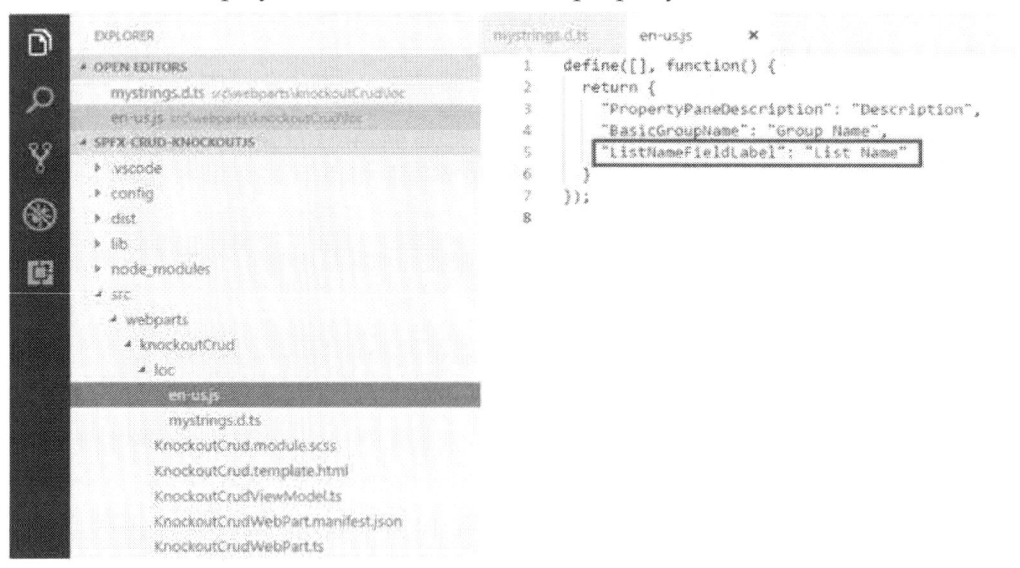

Figure 16.3: Set the display name for the list name property

4. Under the '\src\webparts\knockoutCrud' folder, open the main webpart file (`KnockoutCrudWebPart.ts`).

5. Rename the description property pane field to `listName`:

Figure 16.4: Rename description property to list name

6. Inside KnockoutCrudViewModel.ts, update the ViewModel to reflect the listName property:

TypeScript

```typescript
import * as ko from 'knockout';

import styles from './KnockoutCrud.module.scss';

import { IKnockoutCrudWebPartProps } from './KnockoutCrudWebPart';

export interface IKnockoutCrudBindingContext extends IKnockoutCrudWebPartProps {
    shouter: KnockoutSubscribable<{}>;
}


export default class KnockoutCrudViewModel {
public listName: KnockoutObservable<string> = ko.observable('');

public knockoutCrudClass: string = styles.knockoutCrud;
public containerClass: string = styles.container;
public rowClass: string = styles.row;
public columnClass: string = styles.column;
public titleClass: string = styles.title;
public subTitleClass: string = styles.subTitle;
public descriptionClass: string = styles.description;
public buttonClass: string = styles.button;
public labelClass: string = styles.label;


constructor(bindings: IKnockoutCrudBindingContext) {
this.listName(bindings.listName);


// When web part description is updated, change this view model's description.
    bindings.shouter.subscribe((value: string) => {
```

```
    this.listName(value);

        }, this, 'listName');

    }

}
```

7. In the template (KnockoutCrud.template.html), reflect the `listName` property:

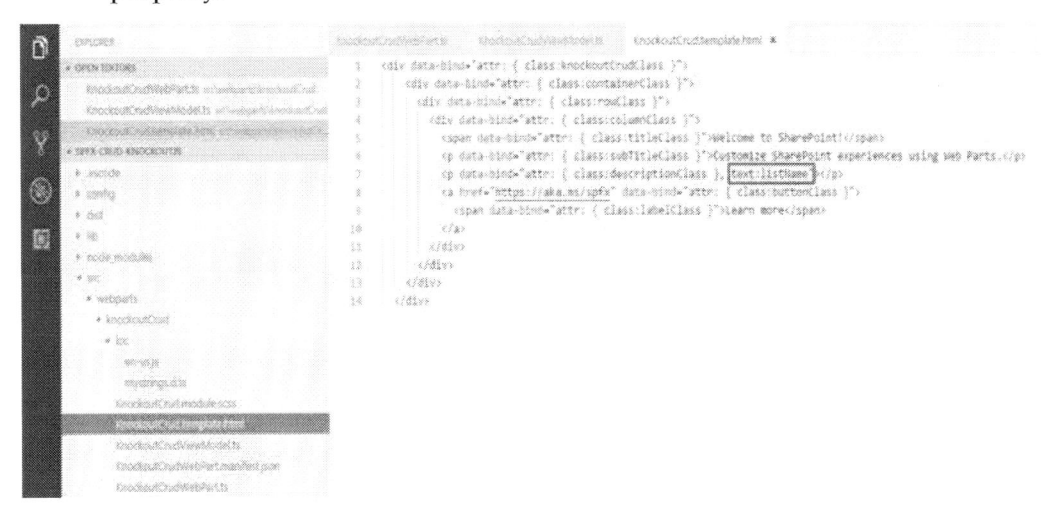

Figure 16.5: Reflect list name in the Knockout template

8. At the command prompt, type `gulp serve`.
9. In the SharePoint local workbench page, add the web part.
10. Edit the web part to ensure the `listName` property pane field is getting reflected:

Figure 16.6: Test SPFx web part for the list name property

Configure ViewModel

Follow below steps to Configure the ViewModel:

1. Open KnockoutCrudViewModel.ts, add import statements:

   TypeScript

   Import { IwebPartContext } from'@microsoft/sp-webpart-base';

   import { SPHttpClient, SPHttpClientResponse } from'@microsoft/sp-http';

2. Add context to interface IKnockoutCrudBindingContext:

   TypeScript

   exportinterface IKnockoutCrudBindingContext extends IKnockoutCrudWebPartProps {
     shouter: KnockoutSubscribable<{}>;
     context: IWebPartContext;
   }

3. Add an interface torepresent the SharePoint list item.

   TypeScript

   exportinterface IListItem {
     Id: number;
     Title: string;
   }

   The ViewModel looks as shown in the following screenshot:

```
KnockoutCrudViewModel.ts  ×
1   import * as ko from 'knockout';
2   import styles from './KnockoutCrud.module.scss';
3   import { IKnockoutCrudWebPartProps } from './KnockoutCrudWebPart';
4   import { IWebPartContext } from '@microsoft/sp-webpart-base';
5   import { SPHttpClient, SPHttpClientResponse } from '@microsoft/sp-http';
6
7   export interface IKnockoutCrudBindingContext extends IKnockoutCrudWebPartProps {
8     shouter: KnockoutSubscribable<{}>;
9     context: IWebPartContext;
10  }
11
12  export interface IListItem {
13    Id: number;
14    Title: string;
15  }
```

Figure 16.7: Knockout ViewModel

CRUD Operations Using KnockoutJS — 197

4. Add the following properties to bind to UI:

   TypeScript

   ```
   public message: KnockoutObservable<string> = ko.observable('');
   ```

5. Implement a generic method to get the latest item ID:

   TypeScript

   ```
   private getLatestItemId(): Promise<number> {
   returnthis._context.spHttpClient.get(this._context.pageContext["web"]["absoluteUrl"]
         + `/_api/web/lists/GetByTitle('${this.listName}')/items?$orderby=Id desc&$top=1&$select=id`, SPHttpClient.configurations.v1)
         .then((response: SPHttpClientResponse): Promise<any>=> {
   return response.json();
         })
         .then((data: any): number => {
   this.message("Load succeeded");
   return data;
         },
         (error: any) => {
   this.message("Load failed");
         }) as Promise<number>;
      }
   ```

Implement the Create Operation

We will use the REST API to add the item to the list:

TypeScript

```
private createItem(): void {
const body: string = JSON.stringify({
'Title': `Item ${new Date()}`
   });
this._context.spHttpClient.post(`${this._context.pageContext["web"]
```

```
["absoluteUrl"]}/_api/web/lists/getbytitle('${this._listName}')/items`,
  SPHttpClient.configurations.v1,
  {
    headers: {
'Accept': 'application/json;odata=nometadata',
'Content-type': 'application/json;odata=nometadata',
'odata-version': ''
    },
    body: body
  })
  .then((response: SPHttpClientResponse): Promise<IListItem>=> {
return response.json();
  })
  .then((item: IListItem): void => {
this.message(`Item '${item.Title}' (ID: ${item.Id}) successfully created`);
  }, (error: any): void => {
this.message('Error while creating the item: ' + error);
  });
}
```

Implement the Read Operation

We will use the REST API to read the latest item:

TypeScript

```
private readItem(): void {
this.getLatestItemId()
    .then((itemId: number): Promise<SPHttpClientResponse>=> {
if (itemId === -1) {
thrownew Error('No items found in the list');
      }
```

CRUD Operations Using KnockoutJS ▰ 199

```
this.message(`Loading information about item ID: ${itemId}...`);
returnthis._context.spHttpClient.get(`${this._context.pageContext["web"]
["absoluteUrl"]}/_api/web/lists/getbytitle('${this._listName}')/
items(${itemId})?$select=Title,Id`,
        SPHttpClient.configurations.v1,
        {
           headers: {
'Accept': 'application/json;odata=nometadata',
'odata-version': ''
           }
        });
    })
    .then((response: SPHttpClientResponse): Promise<IListItem>=> {
return response.json();
    })
    .then((item: IListItem): void => {
this.message(`Item ID: ${item.Id}, Title: ${item.Title}`);
    }, (error: any): void => {
this.message('Loading latest item failed with error: ' + error);
    });
}
```

Implement the Update Operation

We will use the REST API to update the latest item:

TypeScript

```
private updateItem(): void {
let latestItemId: number = undefined;
this.message('Loading latest item...');


this.getLatestItemId()
```

```typescript
    .then((itemId: number): Promise<SPHttpClientResponse>=> {
        if (itemId === -1) {
            thrownew Error('No items found in the list');
        }

        latestItemId = itemId;
        this.message(`Loading information about item ID: ${itemId}...`);

        returnthis._context.spHttpClient.get(`${this._context.pageContext["web"]["absoluteUrl"]}/_api/web/lists/getbytitle('${this._listName}')/items(${latestItemId})?$select=Title,Id`,
            SPHttpClient.configurations.v1,
            {
                headers: {
                    'Accept': 'application/json;odata=nometadata',
                    'odata-version': ''
                }
            });
    })
    .then((response: SPHttpClientResponse): Promise<IListItem>=> {
        return response.json();
    })
    .then((item: IListItem): void => {
        this.message(`Item ID1: ${item.Id}, Title: ${item.Title}`);

        const body: string = JSON.stringify({
            'Title': `Updated Item ${new Date()}`
        });

        this._context.spHttpClient.post(`${this._context.pageContext["web"]["absoluteUrl"]}/_api/web/lists/getbytitle('${this._listName}')/items(${item.Id})`,
            SPHttpClient.configurations.v1,
            {
```

```
            headers: {
'Accept': 'application/json;odata=nometadata',
'Content-type': 'application/json;odata=nometadata',
'odata-version': '',
'IF-MATCH': '*',
'X-HTTP-Method': 'MERGE'
        },
          body: body
      })
        .then((response: SPHttpClientResponse): void => {
this.message(`Item with ID: ${latestItemId} successfully updated`);
        }, (error: any): void => {
this.message(`Error updating item: ${error}`);
        });
    });
}
```

Implement the Delete Operation

We will use the REST API to delete the latest item:

TypeScript

```
private deleteItem(): void {
if (!window.confirm('Are you sure you want to delete the latest item?')) {
return;
    }

this.message('Loading latest items...');
let latestItemId: number = undefined;
let etag: string = undefined;
this.getLatestItemId()
    .then((itemId: number): Promise<SPHttpClientResponse>=> {
```

```
if (itemId === -1) {
thrownew Error('No items found in the list');
      }

      latestItemId = itemId;
this.message(`Loading information about item ID: ${latestItemId}...`);
returnthis._context.spHttpClient.get(`${this._context.pageContext["web"]["absoluteUrl"]}/_api/web/lists/getbytitle('${this._listName}')/items(${latestItemId})?$select=Id`,
        SPHttpClient.configurations.v1,
        {
          headers: {
'Accept': 'application/json;odata=nometadata',
'odata-version': ''
          }
        });
    })
    .then((response: SPHttpClientResponse): Promise<IListItem>=> {
etag = response.headers.get('ETag');
return response.json();
    })
    .then((item: IListItem): Promise<SPHttpClientResponse>=> {
this.message(`Deleting item with ID: ${latestItemId}...`);
returnthis._context.spHttpClient.post(`${this._context.pageContext["web"]["absoluteUrl"]}/_api/web/lists/getbytitle('${this._listName}')/items(${item.Id})`,
        SPHttpClient.configurations.v1,
        {
          headers: {
'Accept': 'application/json;odata=nometadata',
'Content-type': 'application/json;odata=verbose',
'odata-version': '',
```

```
            'IF-MATCH': etag,
        'X-HTTP-Method': 'DELETE'
            }
        });
    })
    .then((response: SPHttpClientResponse): void => {
this.message(`Item with ID: ${latestItemId} successfully deleted`);
    }, (error: any): void => {
this.message(`Error deleting item: ${error}`);
    });
}
```

In the `KnockoutCrudWebPart.ts` file, update the bindings in the `OnInit` method:

TypeScript

```
const bindings: IKnockoutCrudBindingContext = {
    listName: this.properties.listName,
    context: this.context,
    shouter: this._shouter
};
```

Add Controls to the Knockout template

Follow below steps to add controls to the Knockout template:

1. Open the `KnockoutCrud.template.html` under the `\src\webparts\knockoutCrud\` folder.
2. Update the HTML template to include buttons for CRUD operations and add event handlers to each of the buttons:

   TypeScript

   ```
   <div data-bind="attr: { class:knockoutCrudClass }">
       <div data-bind="attr: { class:containerClass }">
           <div data-bind="attr: { class:rowClass }">
               <div data-bind="attr: { class:columnClass }">
   ```

```html
        <span data-bind="attr: { class:titleClass }">Welcome to 
SharePoint!</span>
        <p data-bind="attr: { class:subTitleClass }">Customize 
SharePoint experiences using Web Parts.</p>
        <p data-bind="attr: { class:descriptionClass }, 
text:listName"></p>

        <div data-bind="attr: {class:rowClass}">
          <button data-bind="attr: {class: buttonClass}, click: 
createItem">
            <label class="attr: {class: labelClass}">Create item</
label>
          </button>
          <button data-bind="attr: {class: buttonClass}, click: 
readItem">
            <label class="attr: {class: labelClass}">Read item</
label>
          </button>
        </div>

        <div data-bind="attr: {class:rowClass}">
          <button data-bind="attr: {class: buttonClass}, click: 
updateItem">
            <label class="attr: {class: labelClass}">Update item</
label>
          </button>
          <button data-bind="attr: {class: buttonClass}, click: 
deleteItem">
            <label class="attr: {class: labelClass}">Delete item</
label>
          </button>
        </div>

        <div data-bind="attr: {class:rowClass}">
          <p class="ms-font-l" data-bind="{ css: 'ms-fontColor-
```

```
white', text: message }"></p>
        </div>
      </div>
    </div>
  </div>
</div>
```

Test the WebPart

Follow below steps to test the web part on the SharePoint page:

1. At the command prompt, type `gulp serve`.
2. Open the SharePoint site.
3. Navigate to `/_layouts/15/workbench.aspx`.
4. Add the webpart to the page.
5. Edit the webpart, in the properties pane, and type the list name.
6. Click on the buttons (**Create item, Read item, Update item,** and **Delete item**) one by one to test the webpart.
7. Check whether the operations are taking place in the SharePoint list.

Create Operation

Click on the **Create item** button to create an item inside the configured SharePoint list:

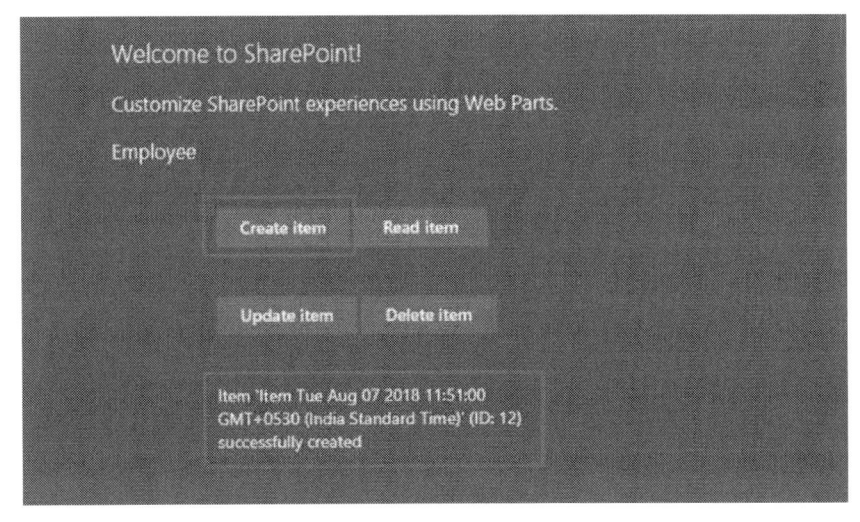

Figure 16.8: Create operation

Read Operation

Click on the **Read item** button to read the latest item from the configured SharePoint list:

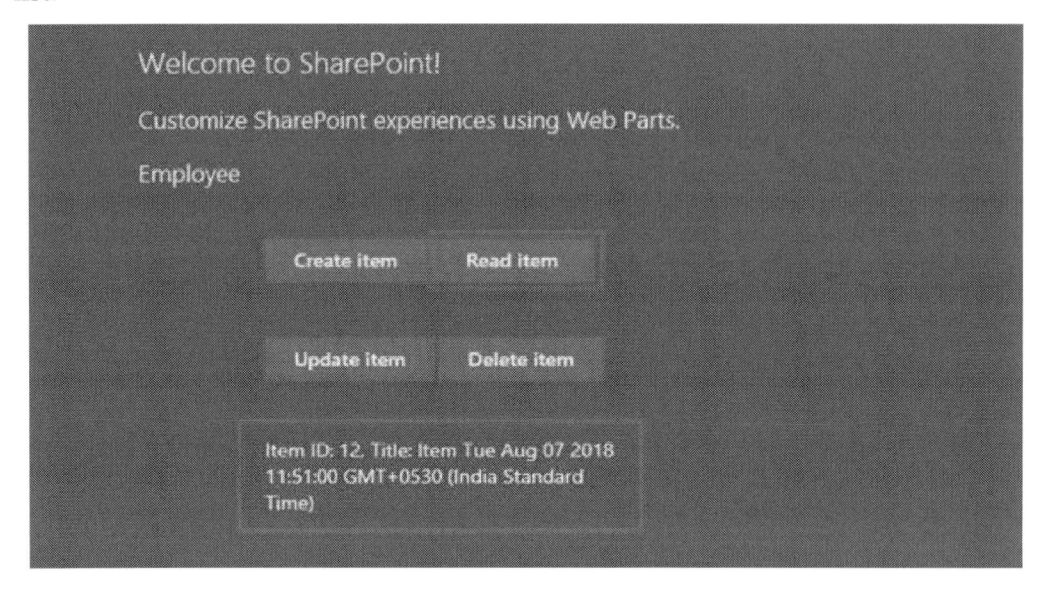

Figure 16.9: Read operation

Update Operation

Click on the **Update item** button to update the latest item from the configured SharePoint list:

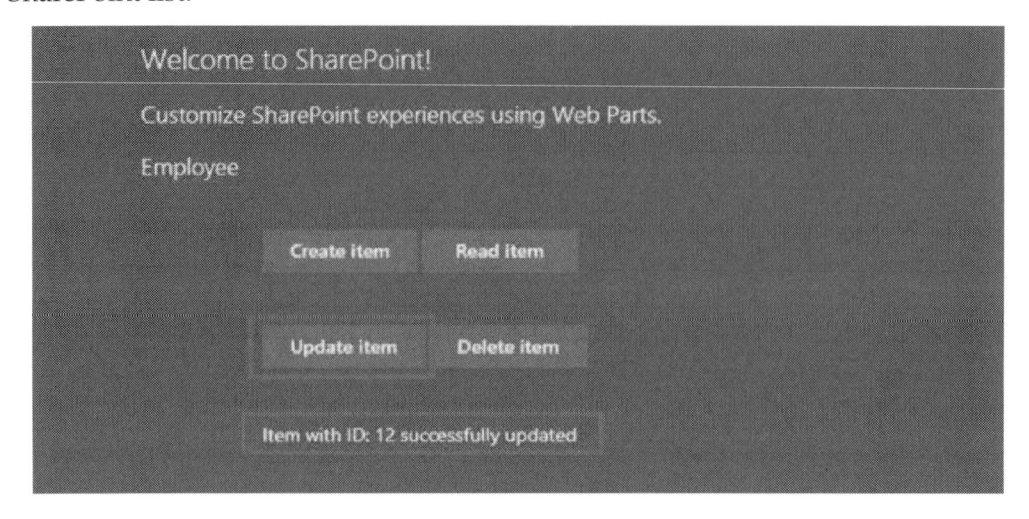

Figure 16.10: Update operation

Delete Operation

Click on the **Delete item** button to delete the latest item from the configured SharePoint list:

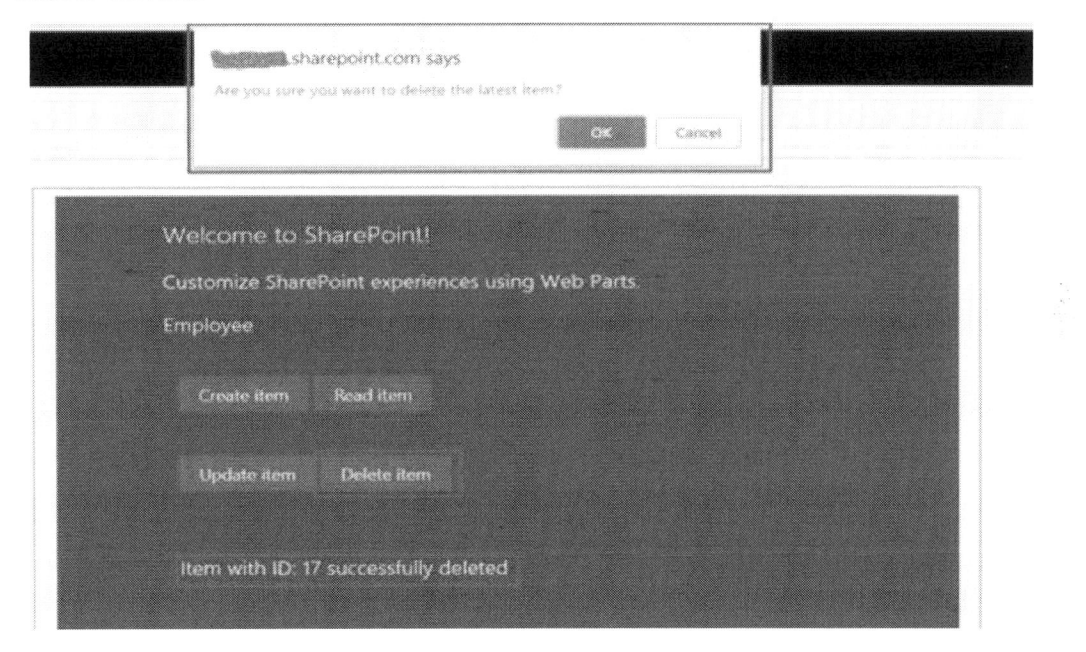

Figure 16.11: Delete operation

Troubleshooting

In some cases, the SharePoint workbench **(https://[tenant].sharepoint.com/_layouts/15/workbench.aspx)** shows the following error although 'gulp serve' is running:

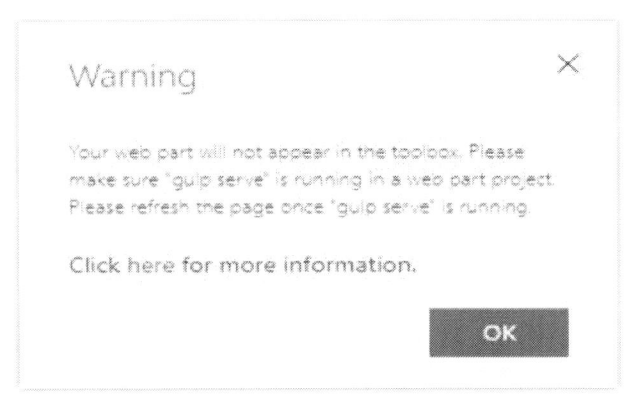

Figure 16.12: Troubleshooting

Open the following URL in the next tab of the browser and accept the warning message:

https://localhost:4321/temp/manifests.js.

Conclusion

In this chapter, we developed the SPFx web part with KnockoutJS and interacted with the SharePoint list for **Create, Read, Update,** and **Delete (CRUD)** operations. KnockoutJS is natively supported by the SharePoint Framework.

CHAPTER 17
CRUD Operations with SP-PnP-JS

In this chapter, we will interact with the SharePoint list for **Create, Read, Update,** and **Delete (CRUD)** operations using the external JavaScript library called sp-pnp-js.

Structure

- Brief information about SP-PnP-JS
- Develop the SPFx Solution for CRUD Operations with SP-PnP-JS
- Configure the Web Part Property for the List Name
- Add Controls to the Web Part
- Implement CRUD Operations on the SharePoint List

Objectives

- Learn about sp-pnp-js
- **Create, Read, Update,** and **Delete (CRUD)** operations on the SharePoint list

Brief information about SP-PnP-JS

SP-PnP-JS is patterns and practices that the core JavaScript library offers. They are simplified common operations with SharePoint to help developers concentrate on business logic without worrying much about the underlying technical implementation. It contains fluent APIs to work with SharePoint REST APIs. You can read more about it at - **https://www.npmjs.com/package/sp-pnp-js**.

> ⊖ **Note**
>
> SP-PnP-JS is deprecated and @pnp/sp is introduced by SharePoint **Patterns and Practices (PnP)** to simplify common operations with SharePoint and SPFx. However, in this chapter, I want to demonstrate the SP-PnP-JS capabilities. In the next chapter, we will explore the transition from `sp-pnp-js` to `@pnp/sp`.

Create the SPFx Solution

Open the command prompt. Follow the given steps to create the SPFx solution:

1. Create a directory for the SPFx solution:

   ```
   md spfx-crud-sppnpjs
   ```

2. Navigate to the above created directory:

   ```
   cd spfx-crud-sppnpjs
   ```

3. Run the Yeoman SharePoint Generator to create the SPFx solution:

   ```
   yo @microsoft/sharepoint
   ```

4. The Yeoman generator will run through the wizard by asking questions about the SPFx solution to be generated:

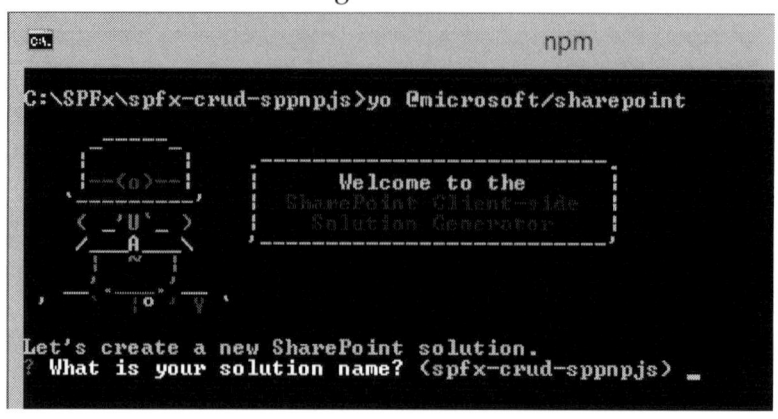

Figure 17.1: SPFx Yeoman generator

- **Solution Name:** Specify the name of the SPFx solution. Hit the *Enter* key to go ahead with the default name (`spfx-crud-sppnpjs` in this case) or type in any other name for your solution.
    - **Selected choice:** Hit *Enter*
- **The target for the component:** Specify the target environment to develop and deploy the SPFx solution. Choose from any one of SharePoint Online or SharePoint On-Premises environments.
    - **Selected choice:** SharePoint Online only (latest)
- **Place of files:** Choose the folder location for the SPFx project (either the same folder or a subfolder).
    - **Selected choice:** Same folder
- **Deployment option:** Specify Y to allow the deployment of the app instantly to all the sites, N otherwise.
    - **Selected choice:** N (install on each site explicitly)
- **Type of client-side component to create:** Choose to create a client-side web part or an extension.
    - **Selected choice:** WebPart
- **Web part name:** Specify the name of the web part. Hit the *Enter* key to go ahead with the default name or type in any other name.
    - **Selected choice:** SPPnPJSCRUD
- **Web part description:** Specify the description of the web part. Hit the *Enter* key to go ahead with the default description or type in any other value.
    - **Selected choice:** CRUD operations with SP PnP JS
- **A framework to use:** Select a JavaScript framework to develop the component. The available choices are No JavaScript Framework, React, and Knockout.
    - **Selected choice:** No JavaScript Framework

5. The Yeoman generator will start the scaffolding process to create the solution. It will download the needed npm packages and install the required dependencies. The solution creation will take a significant amount of time.

6. Once the scaffolding process is complete, lock down the version of project dependencies by running the following command:

```
npm shrinkwrap
```

7. At the command prompt, type the following command to open the solution in the code editor of your choice:

```
code .
```

Configure sp-pnp-js

At the command prompt, run the following command to install sp-pnp-js:

```
npm install sp-pnp-js --save
```

Configure Property for List Name

The SPFx solution by default has the description property that is created. Let us change the property to list name. We will use this property to configure the list name on which the CRUD operations need to be performed.

Follow below steps to Configure the Property for List Name:

1. Open `mystrings.d.ts` under the '\src\webparts\spPnPjscrud\loc\' folder.
2. Rename `DescriptionFieldLabel` to `ListNameFieldLabel`:

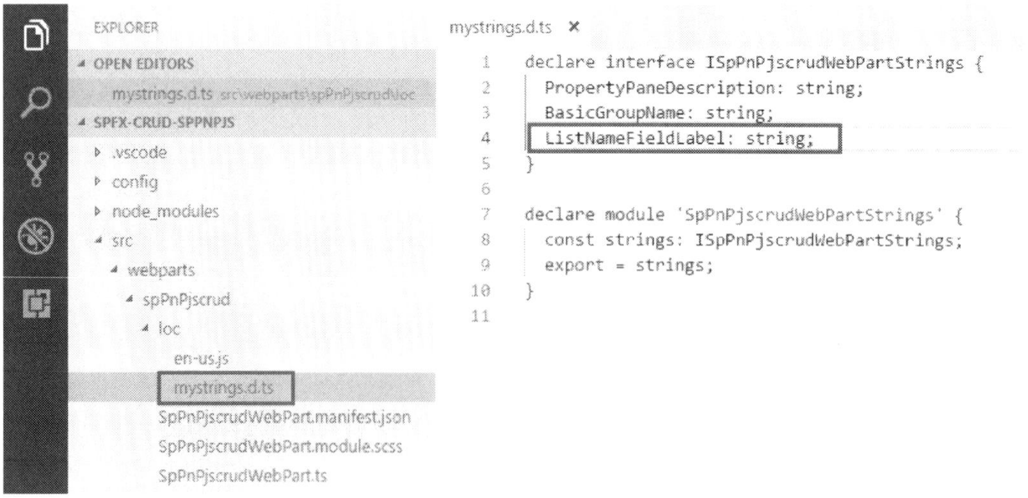

Figure 17.2: Rename description label to list name.

3. In the en-us.js file under \src\webparts\spPnPjscrud\loc\ folder, set the display name for the listName property:

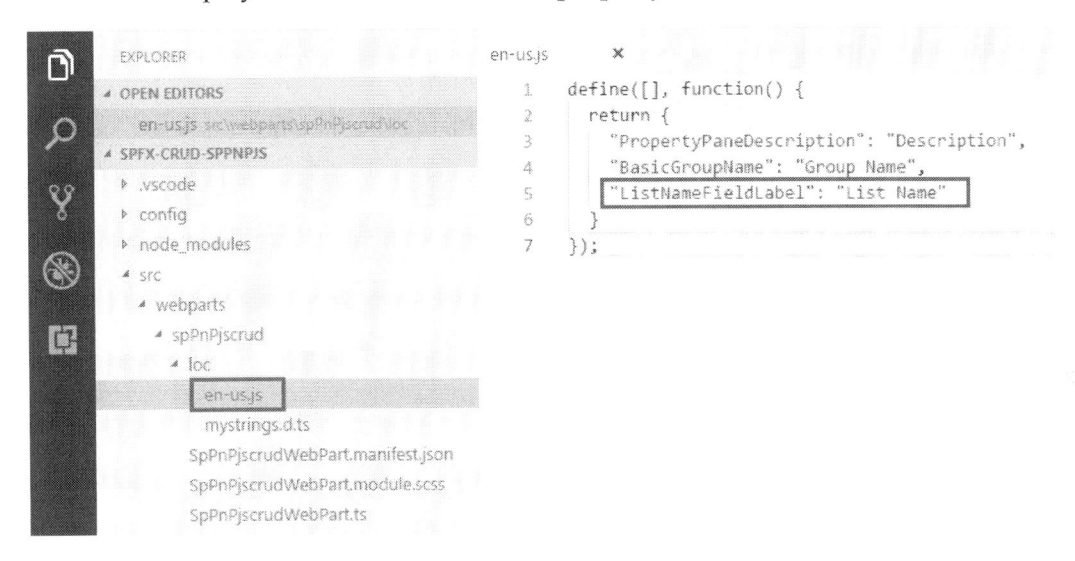

Figure 17.3: Set the display name for the list name property

4. Open the main webpart file (SpPnPjscrudWebPart.ts) under the \src\webparts\spPnPjscrud folder.

5. Rename the description property pane field to `listName`:

Figure 17.4: Use the list name property in the SPFx web part

6. At the command prompt, type `gulp serve`.
7. In the SharePoint local workbench page, add the web part.
8. Edit the web part to ensure the `listName` property pane field is getting reflected:

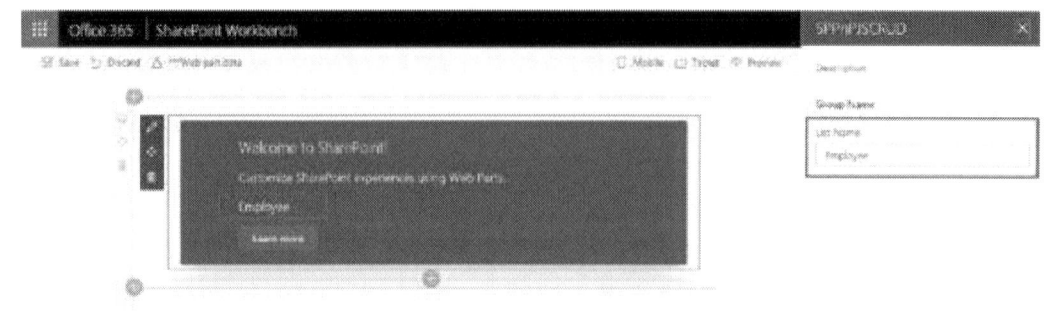

Figure 17.5: Test the SPFx web part for the list name property

Model for List Item

Add a class (`IListItem.ts`) representing the list item:

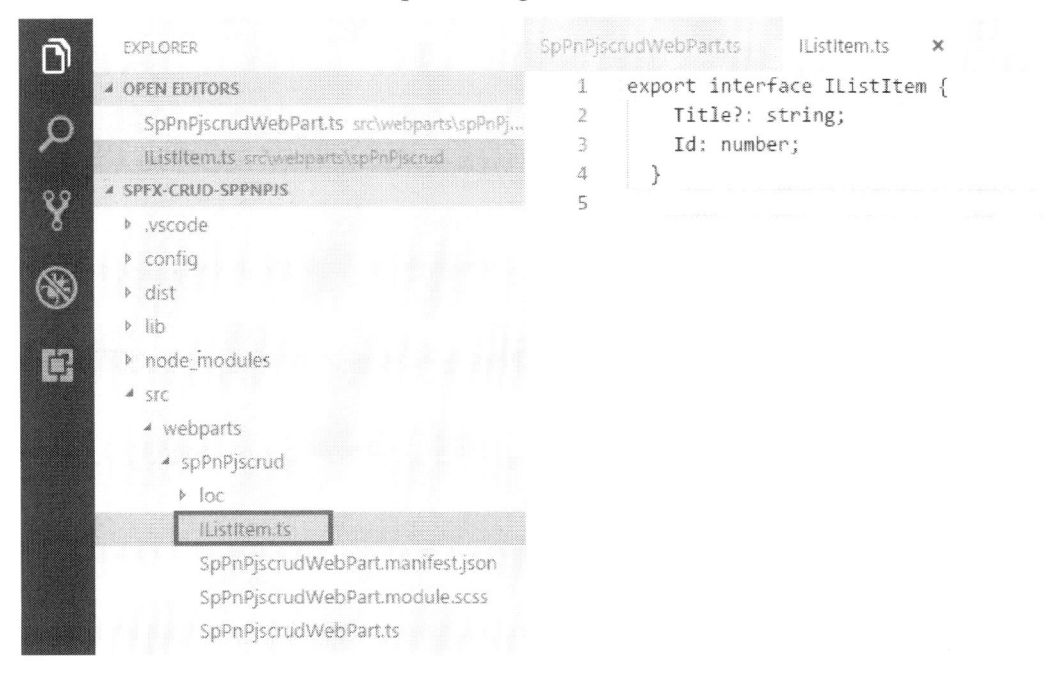

Figure 17.6: Model for list item

Add Controls to the WebPart

Follow below steps to add controls to the web part:

1. Open the main webpart file (`SpPnPjscrudWebPart.ts`) under the `\src\webparts\spPnPjscrud` folder.

216 ■ *Mastering SharePoint Framework*

2. Modify the Render method to include buttons for CRUD operations and add event handlers to each of the buttons:

Figure 17.7: Add buttons and event handlers

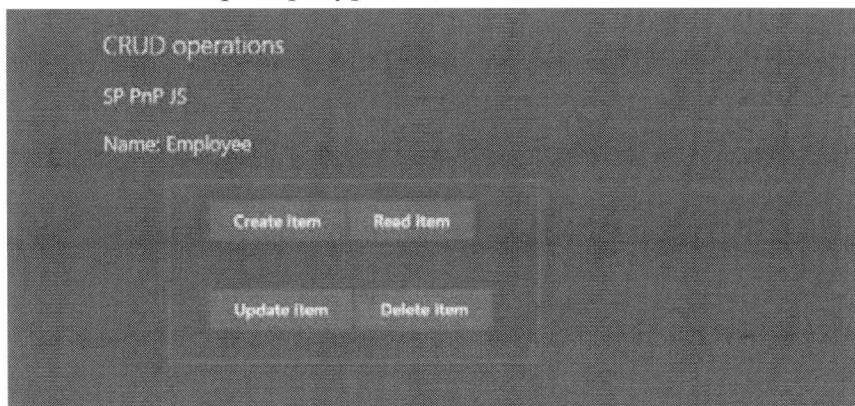

3. At the command prompt, type gulp serve to see the buttons on the webpart:

Figure 17.8: Test buttons on the SPFx web part

4. We will use the sp-pnp-js APIs to perform CRUD operations. Let us implement a generic method which will return the id of the latest item from the given list using sp-pnp-js APIs:

TypeScript

privategetLatestItemId(): Promise<number> {

returnnewPromise<number>((resolve: (itemId: number) =>void, reject: (error: any) =>void): void=> {

sp.web.lists.getByTitle(this.properties.listName)

    .items.orderBy('Id', false).top(1).select('Id').get()

    .then((items: { Id: number }[]): void=> {

if (items.length === 0) {

resolve(-1);

    }

else {

resolve(items[0].Id);

    }

    }, (error: any): void=> {

reject(error);

    });

  });

}

Import sp-pnp-js

Add the following import statements to the main web part at `src\webparts\spPnPjscrud\SpPnPjscrudWebPart.ts`:

TypeScript

```typescript
import { IListItem } from './IListItem';
importpnp, { sp, Item, ItemAddResult, ItemUpdateResult } from"sp-pnp-js";
```

Implement the Create Operation

We will use the `sp-pnp-js` API of `items.add` to add the item to the list:

TypeScript

```typescript
privatecreateItem(): void {
this.updateStatus('Creating item...');


sp.web.lists.getByTitle(this.properties.listName).items.add({
'Title':`Item ${newDate()}`
  }).then((result: ItemAddResult): void=> {
constitem: IListItem = result.dataasIListItem;
this.updateStatus(`Item '${item.Title}' (ID: ${item.Id}) successfully created`);
  }, (error: any): void=> {
this.updateStatus('Error while creating the item: ' + error);
  });
}
```

Implement the Read Operation

We will use `sp-pnp-js` API - `getById` to read the item:

TypeScript

```typescript
privatereadItem(): void {
this.updateStatus('Reading latest items...');

this.getLatestItemId()
```

```
            .then((itemId: number): Promise<IListItem>=> {
if (itemId === -1) {
thrownewError('No items found in the list');
    }

this.updateStatus(`Loading information about item ID: ${itemId}...`);
returnsp.web.lists.getByTitle(this.properties.listName)
        .items.getById(itemId).select('Title', 'Id').get();
    })
    .then((item: IListItem): void=> {
this.updateStatus(`Item ID: ${item.Id}, Title: ${item.Title}`);
    }, (error: any): void=> {
this.updateStatus('Loading latest item failed with error: ' + error);
    });
}
```

Implement the Update Operation

We will use sp-pnp-js API to update the item:

TypeScript

```
privateupdateItem(): void {
this.updateStatus('Loading latest items...');
letlatestItemId: number = undefined;
letetag: string = undefined;

this.getLatestItemId()
    .then((itemId: number): Promise<Item>=> {
if (itemId === -1) {
thrownewError('No items found in the list');
    }

latestItemId = itemId;
this.updateStatus(`Loading information about item ID: ${itemId}...`);
```

```typescript
returnsp.web.lists.getByTitle(this.properties.listName)
        .items.getById(itemId).get(undefined, {
headers: {
'Accept':'application/json;odata=minimalmetadata'
            }
        });
    })
    .then((item: Item): Promise<IListItem>=> {
etag = item["odata.etag"];
returnPromise.resolve((itemas any) asIListItem);
    })
    .then((item: IListItem): Promise<ItemUpdateResult>=> {
returnsp.web.lists.getByTitle(this.properties.listName)
        .items.getById(item.Id).update({
'Title':`Updated Item ${newDate()}`
        }, etag);
    })
    .then((result: ItemUpdateResult): void=> {
this.updateStatus(`Item with ID: ${latestItemId} successfully updated`);
    }, (error: any): void=> {
this.updateStatus('Loading latest item failed with error: ' + error);
    });
}
```

Implement the Delete Operation

We will use `sp-pnp-js` API to delete the item.

TypeScript

```typescript
privatedeleteItem(): void {
if (!window.confirm('Are you sure you want to delete the latest item?')) {
return;
    }
```

CRUD Operations with SP-PnP-JS ▪ 221

```
this.updateStatus('Loading latest items...');
letlatestItemId: number = undefined;
letetag: string = undefined;
this.getLatestItemId()
    .then((itemId: number): Promise<Item>=> {
if (itemId === -1) {
thrownewError('No items found in the list');
    }
latestItemId = itemId;
this.updateStatus(`Loading information about item ID: ${latestItemId}...`);
returnsp.web.lists.getByTitle(this.properties.listName)
        .items.getById(latestItemId).select('Id').get(undefined, {
headers: {
'Accept':'application/json;odata=minimalmetadata'
        }
      });
  })
    .then((item: Item): Promise<IListItem>=> {
etag = item["odata.etag"];
returnPromise.resolve((itemas any) asIListItem);
  })
    .then((item: IListItem): Promise<void>=> {
this.updateStatus(`Deleting item with ID: ${latestItemId}...`);
returnsp.web.lists.getByTitle(this.properties.listName)
        .items.getById(item.Id).delete(etag);
  })
    .then((): void=> {
this.updateStatus(`Item with ID: ${latestItemId} successfully deleted`);
  }, (error: any): void=> {
this.updateStatus(`Error deleting item: ${error}`);
```

        });
}

Test the WebPart

Follow below steps to test the web part on the SharePoint page:

1. At the command prompt, type `gulp serve`.
2. Open the SharePoint site.
3. Navigate to `/_layouts/15/workbench.aspx`.
4. Add the webpart to the page.
5. Edit the webpart, in the properties pane, and type the list name.
6. Click on the buttons (**Create item, Read item, Update item,** and **Delete item**) one by one to test the webpart.
7. Check whether the operations are taking place in the SharePoint list.

Create Operation

Click on the **Create item** button to create an item inside the configured SharePoint list:

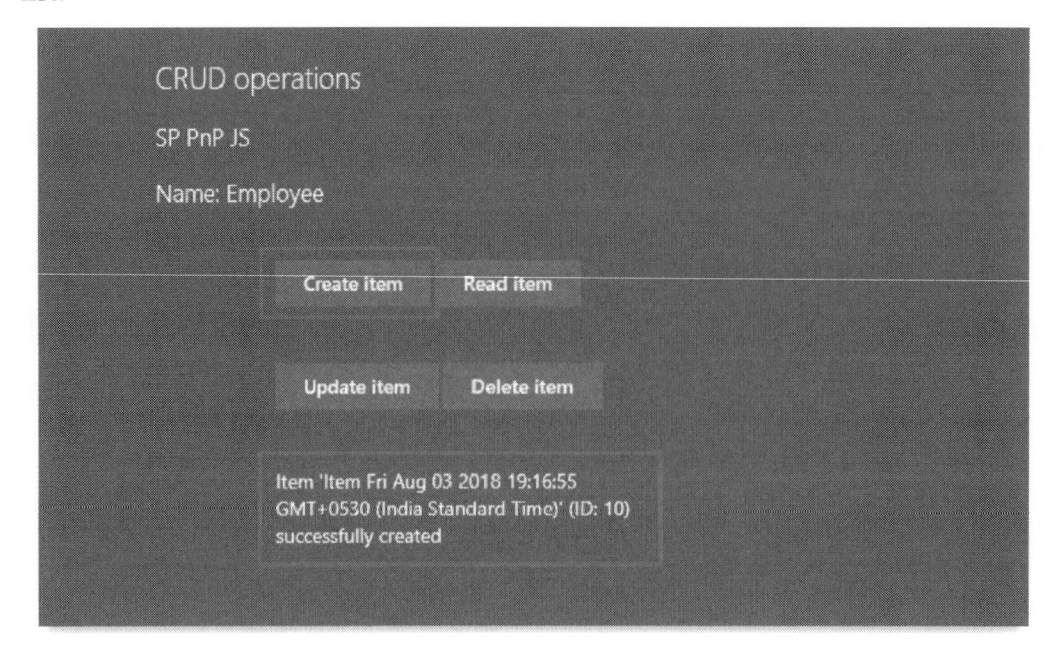

Figure 17.9: Create operation

Read Operation

Click on the **Read item** button to read the latest item from the configured SharePoint list:

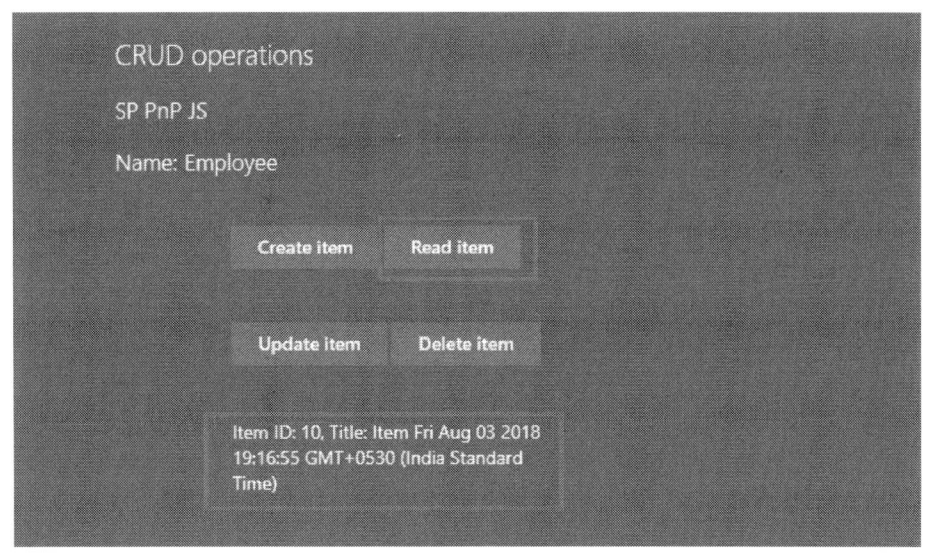

Figure 17.10: Read operation

Update Operation

Click on the **Update item** button to update the latest item from the configured SharePoint list:

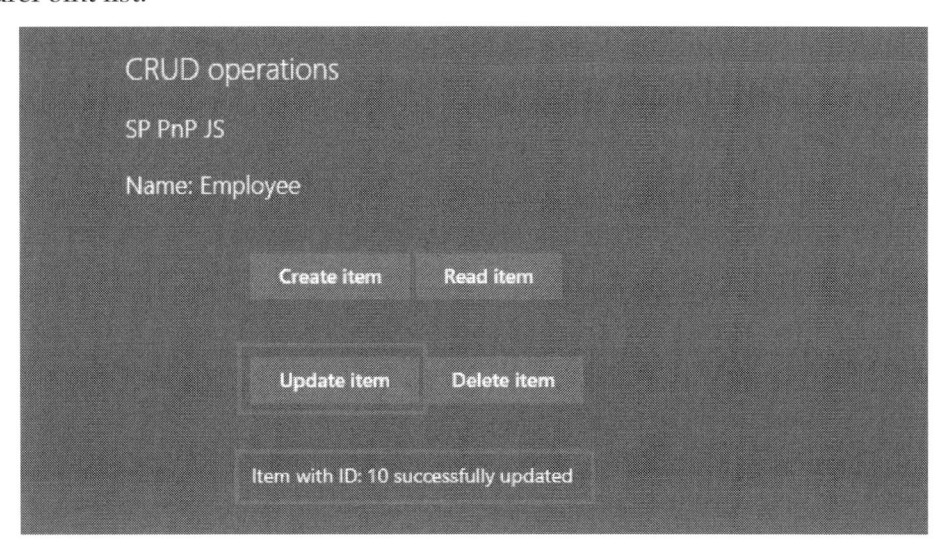

Figure 17.11: Update operation

Delete Operation

Click on the **Delete item** button to delete the latest item from the configured SharePoint list:

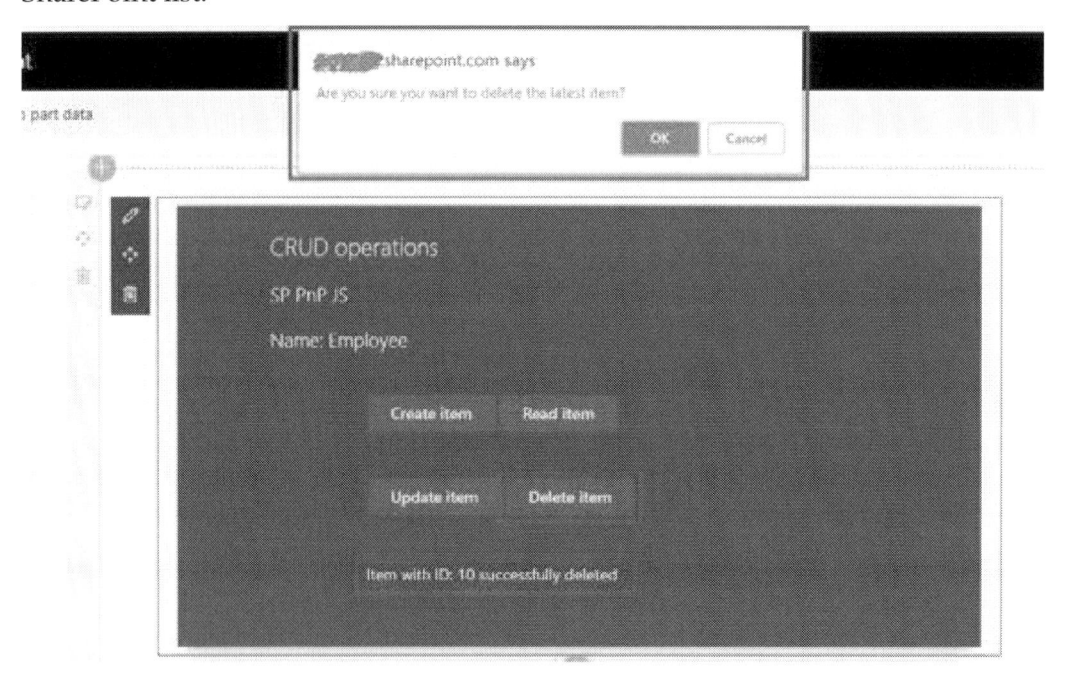

Figure 17.12: Delete operation

Conclusion

In this chapter, we interacted with the SharePoint list for **Create, Read, Update,** and **Delete (CRUD)** operations using sp-pnp-js. sp-pnp-js APIs help to perform common operations (like CRUD) with SharePoint easily. It makes the code lesser to maintain. A developer can concentrate on business logic rather than worrying about identifying and using various REST APIs to use in the code.

CHAPTER 18
Transition to @pnp/sp from sp-pnp-js

SharePoint **Patterns and Practices (PnP)** had introducedthe sp-pnp-jsto simplify basic activities with SharePoint and SPFx. The sp-pnp-js had given different wrapper APIs to perform activities with SharePoint in a viable manner and less code. The sp-pnp-js had removed the complicated work to frame REST demands, process the JSON reactions and let developers concentrate on the rationale of the real business.

Structure
- Why sp-pnp-js is Deprecated?
- Develop the SPFx Web Part with `sp-pnp-js`
- Transition to `@pnp/sp` from `sp-pnp-js`

Objectives
- Reasons behind deprecation of `sp-pnp-js`
- What is there in `@pnp/sp`
- Transition of our code from `sp-pnp-js` to `@pnp/sp`

Why sp-pnp-js is deprecated?

The `sp-pnp-js` library was an enormous bundle of a single JS taking care of different obligations (for example, perform SharePoint activities, logging, perform tasks with MS graph, taxonomy, and so on). Subsequently, it was a bulky package.

The single `sp-pnp-js` bundle is broken into various bundles that give developers more control and acquire just expected pieces to their solutions. This additionally gives the adaptability to update the required bundle independently.

The SPFx WebPart with sp-pnp-js

Open the command prompt. Follow the given steps to create the SPFx solution, if you have not had a prior project with `sp-pnp-js`:

1. Create a directory for the SPFx solution:

   ```
   md spfx-sp-pnp
   ```

2. Navigate to the above created directory:

   ```
   cd spfx- sp-pnp
   ```

3. Run the Yeoman SharePoint Generator to create the SPFx solution:

   ```
   yo @microsoft/sharepoint
   ```

4. The Yeoman generator will present you with the wizard by asking questions about the solution to be generated:

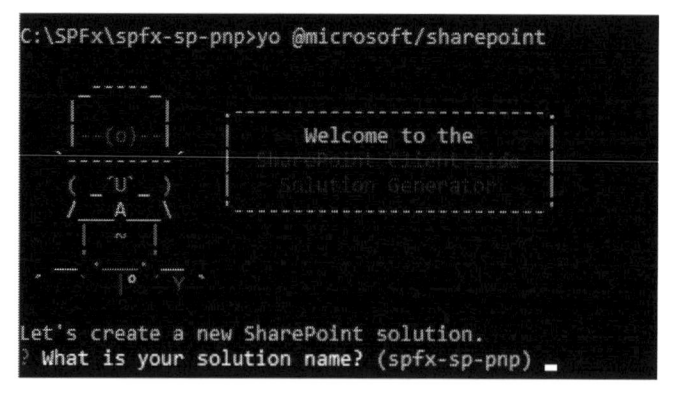

Figure 18.1: SPFx Yeoman generator

The SPFx Yeoman generator will display the following wizard of questions:

- **Solution Name:** Specify the name of the SPFx solution. Hit the *Enter* key to go ahead with the default name (`spfx-sp-pnp` in this case) or type in any other name for your solution.
    - o **Selected choice:** Hit *Enter*

- **The target for the component:** Specify the target environment to develop and deploy the SPFx solution. Choose from any one of SharePoint Online or SharePoint On-Premises environments.
    - **Selected choice:** SharePoint Online only (latest)
- **Place of files:** Choose the folder location for the SPFx project (either the same folder or a subfolder).
    - **Selected choice:** Use the current folder
- **Deployment option:** Specify Y to allow the deployment of the app instantly to all the sites, N otherwise.
    - **Selected choice:** Y
- **Permissions to access web APIs:** Check if the components in the solution require permissions to access web APIs that are unique and not shared with other components in the tenant.
    - **Selected choice:** N (solution contains unique permissions)
- **Type of client-side component to create:** Choose to create a client-side web part or an extension.
    - **Selected choice:** WebPart
- **Web Part Name:** Specify the name of the web part. Hit the *Enter* key to go ahead with the default name or type in any other name.
    - **Selected choice:** HelloPnP
- **Web part description:** Specify the description of the web part. Hit the *Enter* key to go ahead with the default description or type in any other value.
    - **Selected choice:** Hit *Enter*
- **A framework to use:** Select any JavaScript framework to develop the component. The available choices are No JavaScript Framework, React, and Knockout.
    - **Selected choice:** No JavaScript Framework

5. Open the command prompt, and type the following command to add the `sp-pnp-js` npm package to the project:

```
npm install sp-pnp-js --save
```

Code the WebPart

Follow below steps to use the sp-pnp-js:

1. At the command prompt, type the following command to open the solution in the code editor of your choice:

```
code .
```

2. Open the webpart file from `\src\webparts\helloPnP\HelloPnPWebPart.ts`.
3. Add the `sp-pnp-js` imports:

   TypeScript

   ```
   import pnp, { Web } from 'sp-pnp-js';
   ```

4. Write the `onInit()` method to configure the `spfx` context:

   TypeScript

   ```
   public onInit(): Promise<void> {
   // setup to use spfx context
   returnsuper.onInit().then(_ => {
       pnp.setup({
         spfxContext: this.context
       });
     });
   }
   ```

5. Implement the `render()` method:

   TypeScript

   ```
   public render(): void {
       pnp.sp.web.lists.select("Title").getAs<{ Title: string }[]>().then(lists => {
       this.domElement.innerHTML += `<hr/><h2>Lists in web</h2><ul>${lists.map(l => `<li>${l.Title}</li>`).join("")}</ul>`;
       });
   }
   ```

Test the WebPart

Follow below steps to test the web part on the SharePoint page:

1. At the command prompt, type `gulp serve`.
2. Open the SharePoint site.
3. Navigate to `/_layouts/15/workbench.aspx`.
4. Locate and add the webpart to the page:

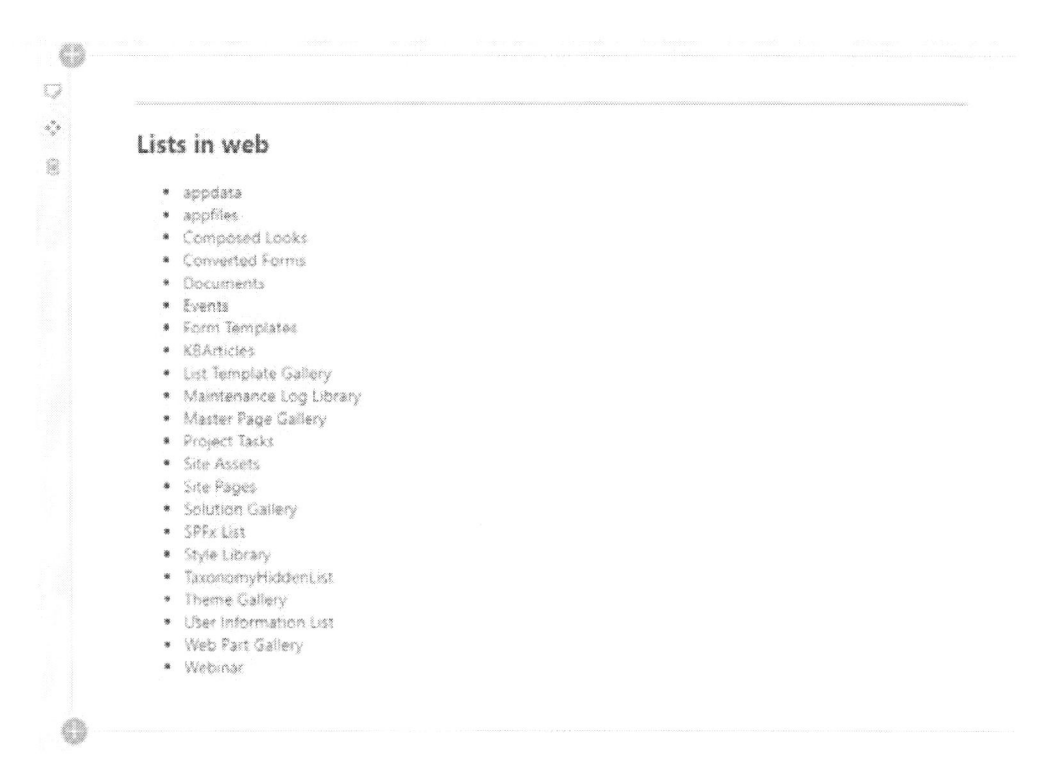

```
Lists in web

    • appdata
    • appfiles
    • Composed Looks
    • Converted Forms
    • Documents
    • Events
    • Form Templates
    • KBArticles
    • List Template Gallery
    • Maintenance Log Library
    • Master Page Gallery
    • Project Tasks
    • Site Assets
    • Site Pages
    • Solution Gallery
    • SPFx List
    • Style Library
    • TaxonomyHiddenList
    • Theme Gallery
    • User Information List
    • Web Part Gallery
    • Webinar
```

Figure 18.2: SPFx web part listing all lists in SharePoint site

Transition to @pnp/sp from sp-pnp-js

Follow below steps to transition the code from sp-pnp-js to @pnp/sp:

1. At the command prompt, type the following command to add the `sp-pnp-js` npm package to the project:

    ```
    npm i @pnp/logging @pnp/common @pnp/odata @pnp/sp --save
    ```

The new @pnp/sp package will appear under node_modules:

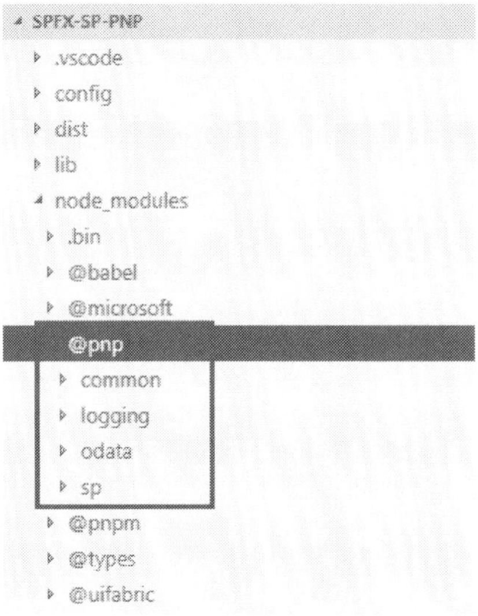

Figure 18.3: @pnp/sp package under node_modules

2. We will now update our imports to @pnp/sp:

   TypeScript

   ```
   // sp-pnp-js imports
   // import pnp, { Web } from 'sp-pnp-js';

   // @pnp/sp imports
   import { sp, Web } from'@pnp/sp';
   ```

3. Update the code to make use of the new @pnp/sp imports. The 'pnp' references are replaced with "sp".

4. Update the onInit() method:

   TypeScript

   ```
   public onInit(): Promise<void> {
   returnsuper.onInit().then(_ => {
       sp.setup({
         spfxContext: this.context
       });
     });
   }
   ```

5. Update the render() method:

   TypeScript

   ```
   public render(): void {
       sp.web.lists.select("Title").get<{ Title: string }[]>().then(lists => {
       this.domElement.innerHTML += `<hr/><h2>Lists in web</h2><ul>${lists.map(l =>`<li>${l.Title}</li>`).join("")}</ul>`;
       });
   }
   ```

Test the web part after the @pnp/sp transition

At the command prompt, type `gulp serve` to test the webpart after the `@pnp/sp` transition. On the UI front, it looks equivalent to it as in the past (with `sp-pnp-js` implementation). We have a redesigned the SPFx solution behind the scene to a newer package.

Conclusion

`sp-pnp-js` was acquainted with improved common operations with SharePoint and SPFx. It was one major cumber some package with all functionalities together. SharePoint **Patterns and Practices (PnP)** have broken it into numerous packages that give developers more control and get just expected pieces to their solutions. As the old sp-pnp-js bundle is deprecated, to line up with future updates, it is prudent to begin utilizing the new `@pnp/sp` bundle and begin changing old solutions for the new @pnp/sp bundle.

CHAPTER 19
SPFx Development with ReactJS

React JS is natively supported by the SharePoint Framework. In fact, SPFx itself is developed using React JS. React JS supports virtual or React DOM (document object model) which makes it very reactive and responsive.

Structure

- Life with JavaScript before ReactJS
- Overview of ReactJS
- React/Virtual DOM
- Primary Building Blocks of React

Objectives

- Understand React JS
- Find out why React works well with SPFx
- Virtual DOM
- Primary building blocks of React

Life with JavaScript before React JS

Most developers (including me) find JavaScript to be really cool. JavaScript is a great language for front end developers. However, as developers what we really wanted to do was to be able to manipulate things in the browser. That is where JavaScript came in. It is not a perfect language, but it worked. The reason why we are using JavaScript is that we want JavaScriptto build some business logic on top of a web page that will occur after the delivery of content to the browser. Very often we are taking that business logic and then manipulating the **document object model (DOM)** so that the page re-renders or aspects of the page change to reflect the changes in the business logic.

Example of String Concatenation

Below is an example of string concatenation:

JavaScript

```
$.each(data.News, function (i, item) {
  if (data.News[i].State != null) {
      trHTML += '<tr class="trNews">
            <td class="tdNews">' + data.News[i].State + '</td>
            <td class="tdNews">' + data.News[i].Header + '</td>
            <td class="tdNews">' + data.News[i].NewsDesc + '</td>
      </tr>';
  }
});


$('#divIncidents').append(trHTML);
```

In the past, we built this kind of code, which grabbed elements using something like jQuery or even old school vanilla JavaScript and then, we would do our business logic. We build up this weird HTML by tedious string concatenation to make something to work.

Templating Engines

A lot of developers built their own templating engine to create some sort of JavaScript methods or functions that would allow them to easily work with HTML. There are some good libraries available to create this HTML kind of templates (like Knockout, Handlebars). These HTML templates could then be easily bound to our JavaScript objects, and we could more quickly create the little custom interfaces in the DOM manipulation.

Yet when we were developing them, we got to work more with the standard HTML and did not have to use those ugly little weird string concatenations.

The era of Modern Toolchain

Then, Node.js came along and we sawJavaScript views to create application frameworks which were just completely insane. Then, Angular was introduced, which was more of a framework that confined all the MVC models such as the model, view, and the controller. Later, ReactJS came to concentrate only on view.

Overview of ReactJS

React is an open-source JavaScript library. Open source means that we can see all the code that makes it work, and we can help contribute to making it better. Microsoft has decided to use an open-source framework to help in the delivery of the new SharePoint framework. React helps us build user interfaces on top of our webpages. React was created and it's still maintained by Facebook.

The primary basis of React is creating the declarative views that are extremely fast. If you think about the MVC or MVVM models, where we have **Model View Control (MVC)** - React is only the view. It is not trying to provide anything else and because of that React is a library and it's not a framework. React only provides the view. It means, it is up to us to come up with a model and controller components. One of React's strict pillars is that it has one-way dataflow. Now,the dataflow idea was put into an architectural style that has been called flux. Flux is not the hard and fast only way to do things. It is more of an architectural style for this one-way data flow.

Why React works well with SPFx?

The possible reason why Microsoft decided to go with the React library instead of the Angular framework because they did not necessarily need all that Angular had to offer. Microsoft wanted to build itsown controller and modeling methodologies in order to work with the SharePoint data. They wanted a great library that would help them create a web interface for the web parts. Also, they wanted something reactive, quick and that is where React comes in because React is considered a very fast and leanlibrary. Since React is only providing the view, it is a little easier to debug. Based on my personal experience, ReactJS is a little simpler to learn because it is only providing the view.

React/Virtual DOM

The reason why React is so fast because it uses virtual DOM. Using virtual DOM, React is able to update the partial view which might have changed. **Virtual DOM** is an abstraction of the **Actual DOM**:

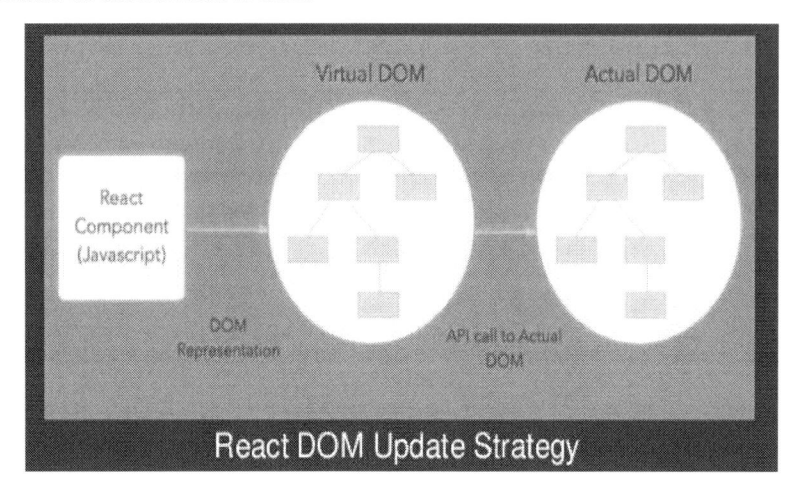

Figure 19.1 React DOM

React/Virtual DOM makes React extremely fast because only the component that you update within a view will actually get updated in the browser.

On every update to the component:
- React builds a new virtual DOM subtree.
- Analyzes the difference with actual DOM.
- Computes minimal DOM mutation.
- Executes batch updates.

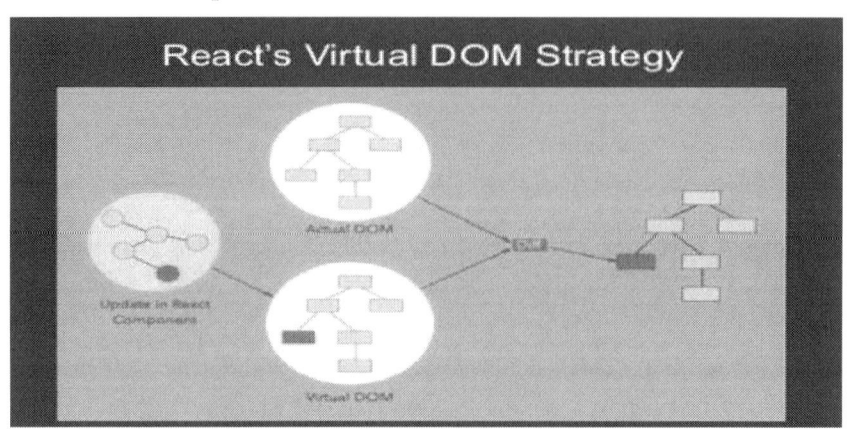

Figure 19.2 React's Virtual DOM Strategy

Primary Building Blocks of React
React Element

The React element is stateless which means that it does not store any state. It is just an object that will describe what it is that we want to display in the browser for that specific element. When we create a React element, we need to provide some sort of a type for that element which then gets tied into a rendering function that says how you are eventually going to get rendered. You want it to be able to send parameters and properties to your elements and you do not want it to be static.

Below is an example of React Element:

TypeScript

```
constelement: React.ReactElement<IReactSharePointCrudProps> = React.createElement(

ReactSharePointCrud,

{

basicHttpClient:this.context.httpClient,

description:this.properties.description

}

);
```

React Props

A props variable allows you to pass the properties and then the React element can use those properties to render the HTML.

Below are key considerations for React Props:
- Props are of key importance in component composition.
- It is the mechanism used for passing data from parent to child components.
- Props can't be changed inside the component.
- Props can be referred as component "configuration".

Below is an example of React Props:

TypeScript

```
exportinterfaceIAdaptiveCardsImageGalleryProps {
    serviceScope: ServiceScope;
    imageGalleryName: string;
```

```
          imagesToDisplay: number;
}

exportdefaultclassAdaptiveCardsImageGalleryextends
React.Component<IAdaptiveCardsImageGalleryProps,
IAdaptiveCardsImageGalleryState> {
          ...
}
```

React Component - Stateful React Element

React Component is very similar to the React element except that it stores the state. We use a method called `setState` that allows you to update the state of the components when the state is outdated. React is smart enough to go in the virtual DOM for us and re-render just what was changed.

To the React element, we can send some properties and some state. We can pre-define what the state should be when we start.

Below is an example of React Component:

TypeScript

```
exportdefaultclassReactSharePointCrudextendsReact.
Component<IReactSharePointCrudProps, IReactSharePointCrudState> {

constructor (props: IReactSharePointCrudProps, state:
IReactSharePointCrudState) {

super(props);

this.state = {

status:this.listNotConfigured(this.props) ? "Please configure list in web part properties" : "Ready";

items: [],

mystring:""
}
     }
   .
   .
   .
}
```

React State

Below are key considerations for React State:
- Mutable data that represents the component's internal state.
- When the state is updated, the component itself and its children are re-rendered.
- The state is initialized in the component constructor.
- Events can change the component state.

Below is an example of React State:

TypeScript

```
exportinterfaceIAdaptiveCardsImageGalleryState {
    galleryItems: any[];
    isLoading: boolean;
    showErrorMessage: boolean;
}

exportdefaultclassAdaptiveCardsImageGalleryextends
React.Component<IAdaptiveCardsImageGalleryProps,
IAdaptiveCardsImageGalleryState> {
    ...
}
```

JavaScript XML (.jsx)

JSX is a syntactic language for rendering templates. Use JSX to write React Views.

Below are key considerations for JSX:
- Adapted by TypeScript as well (.tsx) to allow similar coding.
- Not required by React, but makes life easier.
- JSX gets converted to JavaScript.

Below is an example of JSX:

JSX

```
<MyButtoncolor='Red'shadowSize='{5}'>
    Click Me!
</MyButton>
```

The precedingJSX gets compiled into the following code:

TypeScript

```
React.ReactElement(
MyButton,
{ color:'Red', shodowSize:'5' },
'Click Me!'
);
```

Conclusion

In this chapter, we deep dived into the React library and explored why React works well with SPFx. React is fast because it uses virtual DOM, which is an abstraction of the true DOM. React's primary building blocks are React Elements, React Props, React Components - Stateful React Elements, React States, and JavaScript XML (.jsx).

CHAPTER 20
React Lifecycle Events in SPFx

React JS is regularly used to create solutions in the **SharePoint Framework (SPFx)**. It is a typical practice to get the information from the SharePoint site, Office 365, MS Graph API, or from an outside administration like an external service and show it in the SharePoint framework web part. In any case, there is a confusion about which React method is the best place to fetch the data.

Structure
- React Component Lifecycle
- Render Method of the React Component
- component DidMount Method of the React Component

Objectives
- Explore all possible options to fetch data in the React component
- Pros and cons of each option

React Component Life Cycle

The React component experiences different stages throughout its life cycle. It gives different methods that advise us when a specific phase of the process happens.

These methods are called as **component's lifecycle methods** and they are conjured in a predictable order.

From the SharePoint framework point of view, we can focus on the following events:

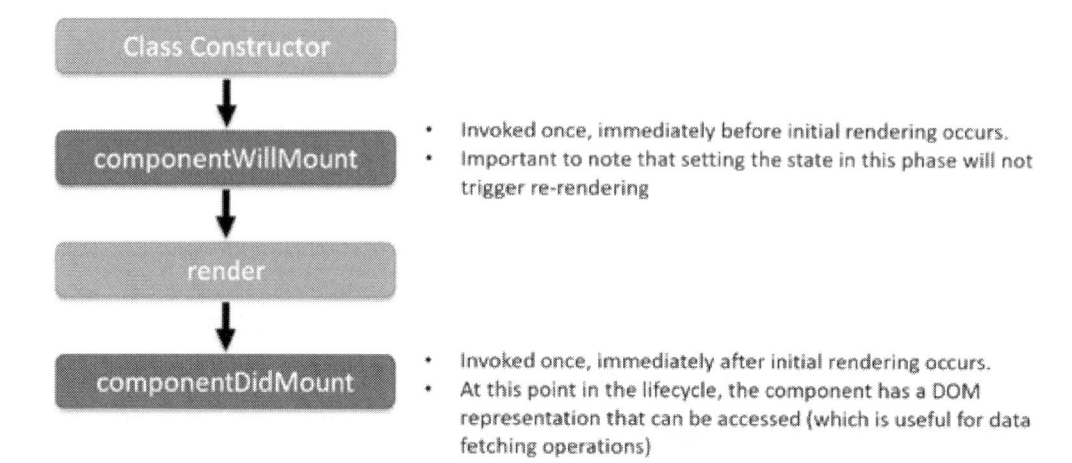

Figure 20.1: React component life cycle

The React component experiences the following different stages throughout its life cycle:

- **componentWillMount:** This method is executed before rendering on both the server and the client side.
- **componentDidMount:** This method is executed after the first render only on the client side.
- **componentWillReceiveProps:** This method is invoked as soon as the props are updated.
- **shouldComponentUpdate:** This method returns a `true` or `false` value to determine if the component will be updated or not.
- **componentWillUpdate:** This method is called just before rendering.
- **componentDidUpdate:** This method is called soon after rendering.
- **componentWillUnmount:** This method is called after the component is unmounted from the DOM.

Render Method of the React Component

Each React component has a Render method. The undeniable idea is to have a fetch mechanism inside the Render method. However, it is not a good place to fetch the data. The reason being that it causes the state to change. Also, it is not advisable to perform any asynchronous calling in the Render method.

componentWillMount

This method is called directly before the React component's first render event. Just by perusing this statement, it is enticing to have the data fetching logic implemented inside `componentWillMount`. But, wait! This place probably won't be perfect for fetching the information as asynchronous calls to get the information probably won't return before the Render method executes. This implies that there are high possibilities that the component will render empty data at least once.

We can neither delay the Render method until `componentWillMount` completes, nor can we return a promise from `componentWillMount`. To deal with this circumstance smoothly, we can set up the component's initial state.

Consider an example of fetching data from the service as follows:

TypeScript

```typescript
class Employee extends Component {
  componentWillMount() {
    dataService.get('/mydata').then(result => {
      this.setState({items: result.data});
    });
  }

  render() {
    return (
<ul>
      {this.state.items.map(item =>
<li key={item.id}>{item.name}</li>
      )}
</ul>
    );
  }
}
```

In this example, componentWillMount calls the dataService asynchronously which will result in empty data for the first occurrence.

To deal with this circumstance, we can set the initial state in the constructor:

TypeScript
```
constructor(props) {
    super(props);

    this.state = {
      items: []
    };
}
```

We can check for empty data inside the Render method:

TypeScript
```
render() {
  return (
<ul>
      {this.state && this.state.items && this.state.items.map(item =>
<li key={item.id}>{item.name}</li>
      )}
</ul>
  );
}
```

componentWillMount is now deprecated so it is not advisable to use this method.

componentDidMount

The React component gets rendered once before calling componentDidMount. It is ideal to utilize this method to fetch the data for the following reasons:
1. Data won't be loaded until after the initial render. This will make it mandatory to set up the initial state to avoid errors like undefined states.

2. In case the application needs server rendering, `componentWillMount` will be called twice (once on the server and once on the client). Having data fetching logic in `componentDidMount` will guarantee that we get the information just once on the client.

componentDidMount will dependably be approached by the client after the first render when it gets the information. Refrain from any kind of state change inside the componentDidMount method on the grounds that it will cause re-rendering of the component. As this will call `componentDidMount`, which will again call the Render method, and so on. This will cause an infinite loop.

componentDidMount can be utilized to set up long-running processes that can fetch data from SharePoint or any external service on a periodic basis.

TypeScript

```
componentDidMount() {
  this.interval = setInterval(this.fetchMyDaya, 3600000);
}
```

Conclusion

In this chapter, we explored the React component life cycle, potential alternatives to fetch data in the React component with their advantages and disadvantages. While creating the SharePoint Framework web part with React, it is recommended to utilize the `componentDidMount` method. We must refrain from utilizing the `componentWillMount` method as it is deprecated. The Render method is certifiably not a decent place for getting the information as it causes the state change.

CHAPTER 21
Autobind Control Events in SPFx

The SharePoint Framework (SPFx) web parts are key to implement custom solutions in modern SharePoint. A web part can contain different controls in it. A few controls help to get the inputs from end users (like textboxes, dropdowns, choices, and so on.). Likewise, a few controls produce events to process the user inputs (for example, the handle click event). The event characterizes what happens when a specific action is taken on the control. As a developer, we have to characterize the bit of code that should run when an action is triggered on the control.

Structure
- Binding events to controls
- Binding all events at once

Objectives
- Bind actions to controls in SPFx solutions developed using React
- Autobind the events to the control

Develop the SPFx Web Part
Open the command prompt. Follow the given steps to create the SPFx solution:

1. Create a directory for the SPFx solution:

   ```
   md spfx-react-autobind
   ```

2. Navigate to the above-created directory:

   ```
   cd spfx-react-autobind
   ```

3. Run the Yeoman SharePoint Generator to create the SPFx solution:

   ```
   yo @microsoft/sharepoint
   ```

4. The Yeoman generator will run through the wizard by asking questions about the SPFx solution to be generated:

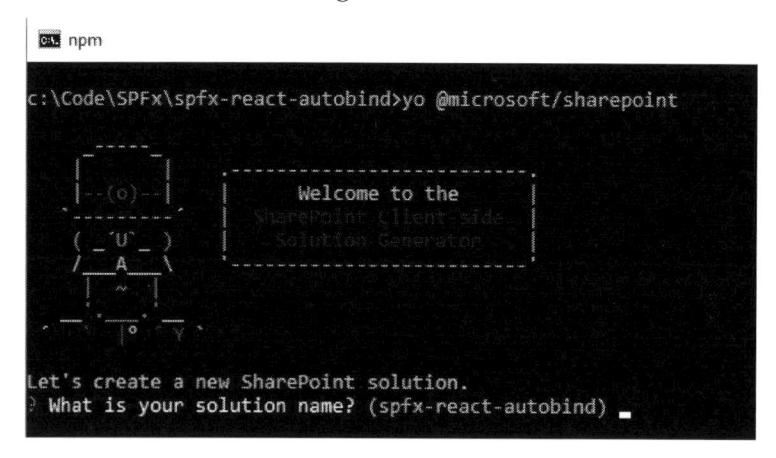

Figure 21.1: SPFx Yeoman generator

The SPFx Yeoman generator will display the following wizard of questions:

- **Solution Name:** Specify the name of the SPFx solution. Hit the *Enter* key to go ahead with the default name (spfx-react-autobind in this case) or type in any other name for your solution.
    - **Selected choice:** Hit *Enter*.
- **The target for the component:** Specify the target environment to develop and deploy the SPFx solution. Choose from any one of SharePoint Online or SharePoint On-Premises environments.
    - **Selected choice:** SharePoint Online only (latest).
- **Place of files:** Choose the folder location for the SPFx project (either the same folder or a subfolder).
    - **Selected choice:** Use the current folder.
- **Deployment option:** Specify Y to allow the deployment of the app instantly to all the sites, N otherwise.

- o **Selected choice:** N (install on each site explicitly)
- **Permissions to access Web APIs:** Check whether the components in the solution require permissions to access web APIs.
  - o **Selected choice:** N (No explicit permissions are required)
- **Type of client-side component to create:** Choose to create a client-side web part or an extension.
  - o **Selected choice:** WebPart
- **Web part name:** Specify the name of the web part. Hit the *Enter* key to go ahead with the default name or type in any other name.
  - o **Selected choice:** ReactAutoBind
- **Web part description:** Specify the description of the web part. Hit the *Enter* key to go ahead with the default description or type in any other value.
  - o **Selected choice:** Auto bind events in React
- **A framework to use:** Select any JavaScript framework to develop the component. The available choices are No JavaScript Framework, React, and Knockout.
  - o **Selected choice:** React
5. The Yeoman generator will perform scaffolding process to generate the solution. The scaffolding process will take a significant amount of time.
6. Once the scaffolding process is complete, lock down the version of project dependencies by running the following command:

```
npm shrinkwrap
```

7. At the command prompt, type the following command to open the solution in the code editor of your choice:

```
code .
```

Development Scenario

We will add a textbox and button to our web part. At the click of a button, we will display a greeting message with the text entered in a textbox.

Define a State

Let us define a state to store the user entered text. Add the `IReactAutoBindState.ts` file under the '\src\webparts\reactAutoBind\components\' folder:

TypeScript

```
exportinterfaceIReactAutoBindState {
```

```
userText: string;
}
```

Add Controls to the Web Part

Follow below steps to add controls to the web part:

1. Open ReactAutoBind.tsx under '\src\webparts\reactAutoBind\components\' folder.
2. Add the following imports:

   TypeScript

   ```
   // Import text field component
   import { TextField } from 'office-ui-fabric-react/lib/TextField';

   // Import button component
   import { IButtonProps, DefaultButton } from 'office-ui-fabric-react/lib/Button';
   ```

3. Define the textbox and button controls:

   TypeScript

   ```
   publicrender(): React.ReactElement<IReactAutoBindProps> {
   return (
   <divclassName={styles.reactAutoBind}>
   <divclassName={styles.container}>
   <divclassName={styles.row}>
   <divclassName={styles.column}>
   <spanclassName={styles.title}>Welcome to SharePoint!</span>
   <pclassName={styles.subTitle}>Autobind events demo</p>

   <TextField
   required={true}
   name="txtSearchText"
   placeholder="Search..."
   value={this.state.userText}
   onChanged={e=>this.setState({ userText:e })}
   />
   ```

```
         <DefaultButton
         data-automation-id="search"
         target="_blank"
         title="Greet"
         onClick={this.greetButtonClicked}
         >
                 Greet
         </DefaultButton>

         <div>{this.state.userText}</div>

         </div>
         </div>
         </div>
         </div>
            );
         }
```

4. Define the button click event:

   TypeScript

   ```
   privategreetButtonClicked(): void {
   alert("Hello " + this.state.userText);
   }
   ```

5. Define the constructor to set the initial state:

   TypeScript

   ```
   Constructor(props: IReactAutoBindProps, state: IReactAutoBindState) {
   super(props);

       this.state = {
   ```

```
userText:""
    }
}
```

Run the SPFx WebPart

Follow below steps to run the SPFxweb part:

1. At the command prompt, type `gulp serve`.
2. Open the SharePoint site.
3. Navigate to `/_layouts/15/workbench.aspx`.
4. Add the web part to the page.
5. Type in some text In the textbox.
6. Click on the **Greet** button:

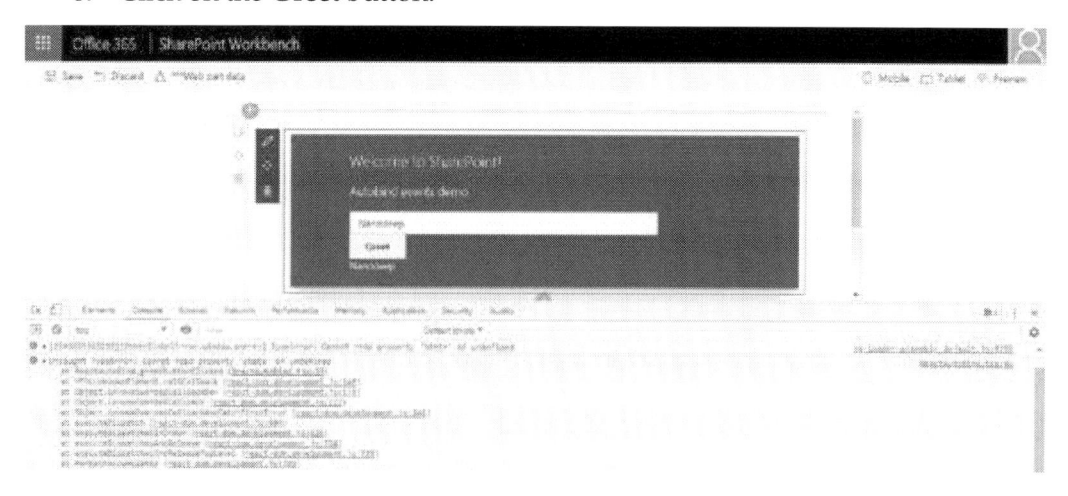

Figure 21.2: Test event binding of the control

We will see the alert message greeting in the text entered in the textbox. But nothing happens. If we observe the developer toolbar console, we have an error **"Cannot read property 'state' of undefined at ReactAutoBind.greetButtonClicked"**. This implies that the click event has not yet bound to our button control.

Binding the event to the control

In the constructor, add the following code:

TypeScript

```
constructor(props: IReactAutoBindProps, state: IReactAutoBindState) {
super(props);
```

```
this.state = {
userText:""
  }

this.greetButtonClicked = this.greetButtonClicked.bind(this);
}
```

Refresh the **SharePoint Workbench**. Add some text in the text box and click on the **Greet** button. As the event is bound to the button, we will see an alert:

Figure 21.3: Test event binding of the control

Binding all the events at once

There are chances that we may forget to include the bindings in the constructor for our controls. As the number of controls grows on the web part, there will be a significant amount of code only for the event binding. To deal with this in an elegant manner, we can utilize `autobind`.

Follow below steps to bind all the events at once:

1. Add the following import:

    Script

    ```
    import { autobind } from'office-ui-fabric-react';
    ```

2. Remove any bindings from the constructor.
3. Decorate the event with @autobind:

    Script

    ```
    @autobind
    ```

```
privategreetButtonClicked(): void {
alert("Hello " + this.state.userText);
}
```

Conclusion

In this chapter, we learned about auto binding the events to the control. It is important to bind actions to controls. An action can be bound to the control in the constructor separately. Autobind ties the action to the control by decorating the method.

CHAPTER 22
Partial State Update for React-based SPFx WebParts

React JS is natively supported by the SharePoint Framework. It means React JS is available as an out-of-the-box option to create a SPFx solution. One of the reasons why React might work best with SPFx is that instead of re-rendering the whole **Document Object Model (DOM)**, it updates the virtual DOM based on delta changes. The React component is one of the basic structures of React which has the state. When the state is modified, React JS automatically renders the changes. We can have immense data in the React state.

Structure
- Overview of the React State
- Introduction to the Spread Operator

Objectives
- Understand the React state
- Understand the Spread operator
- Partially update the React state in the SPFx webpart

React State
The state is alterable information (mutable data) representing the internal state of the component. When the state is refreshed, the component and its children are re-

rendered. It is perfect to initialize a state in the constructor. Any events occurring on the SPFx web part may change the state of the component. The state of the React component can be changed by calling the `setState` method.

Develop the SPFx Solution with React

Open the command prompt. Follow the given steps to make the SPFx solution:

1. Make a folder for the SPFx solution:

    ```
    md react-state-update-partial
    ```

2. Change the path to the above folder:

    ```
    cd react-state-update-partial
    ```

3. Execute the Yeoman Generator for SharePoint:

    ```
    yo @microsoft/sharepoint
    ```

4. The Yeoman generator will run through the following wizard to ask questions about the SPFx solution to be created:

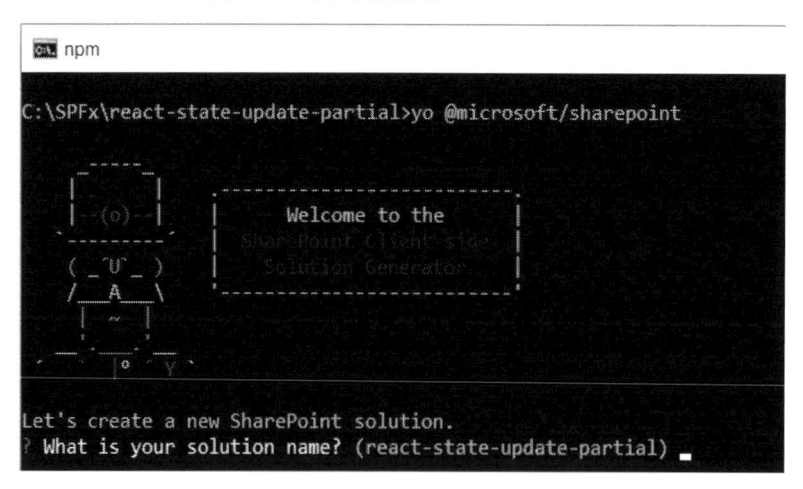

Figure 22.1: SPFx Yeoman generator

The SPFx Yeoman generator will display the following wizard of questions:

- **Solution Name:** Determine the SPFx solution name. Hit *Enter* key to proceed with the default selection (`react-state-update-partial`) or type another name.
    - o **Chosen decision:** Hit *Enter*.
- **Target environment:** Specify the target environment to deploy the SPFx solution. Select any option from SharePoint Online or SharePoint On-Premises environment.

- o **Chosen decision:** SharePoint Online only (latest)
- **Place of files:** Choose the folder location for the SPFx project (either the same folder or a subfolder).
  - o **Chosen decision:** Use the current folder
- **Deployment option:** Specify Y to deploy the app instantly to all the sites, N otherwise.
  - o **Chosen decision:** N (install on each site explicitly)
- **Consents to access web APIs:** Decide whether the components in the solution need an explicit permission to access web APIs that are unique and not shared with other components in the tenant.
  - o **Chosen decision:** N (solution contains unique permissions)
- **Choice of client-side component:** Decide to develop a web part or an extension.
  - o **Chosen decision:** WebPart
- **Web part name:** Provide the web part name. Hit the *Enter* key to proceed with the default choice or type another name.
  - o **Chosen decision:** `ReactStateUpdatePartial`
- **Web part description:** Provide the web part description. Hit the *Enter* key to proceed with the default choice or type another value.
  - o **Chosen decision:** Update React State Partially
- **Choice of framework:** Choose the JavaScript framework to develop the component from the available choices of No JavaScript Framework, React, and Knockout.
  - o **Chosen decision:** React

5. After the scaffolding is finished, lock down the version of project dependencies by executing the following command:
   ```
   npm shrinkwrap
   ```

6. At the command prompt, execute the following command to open the SPFx solution in the preferred code editor:
   ```
   code .
   ```

Definethe React State

Follow below steps to define the React State:

1. Under the '\src\webparts\reactStateUpdatePartial\components\' folder, create a new `IReactStateUpdatePartialState.ts` file:

TypeScript

```
exportinterfaceIReactStateUpdatePartialState {
presentDate: Date;
arbitraryNumber: number;
arbitraryText: string;
}
```

2. Update the React component "\src\webparts\reactStateUpdate Partial\components\ReactStateUpdatePartial.tsx" to use the above created state:

   TypeScript

```
import { IReactStateUpdatePartialState } from'./IReactStateUpdatePartialState';

exportdefaultclassReactStateUpdatePartialextendsReact.Component<IReactStateUpdatePartialProps, IReactStateUpdatePartialState> {

publicconstructor(props: IReactStateUpdatePartialProps, state: IReactStateUpdatePartialState) {
super(props);
this.state = {
presentDate:newDate(),
arbitraryNumber:0,
arbitraryText:""
};
}
}
```

Code the WebPart

Follow below steps to develop the web part:
1. Under '\src\webparts\reactStateUpdatePartial\components\' folder, open the `ReactStateUpdatePartial.tsx`webpart file.
2. Add the needed controls to the `render()` method:

TypeScript

```
public render(): React.ReactElement<IReactStateUpdatePartialProps> {
return (
<div className={styles.reactStateUpdatePartial}>
<div className={styles.container}>
<div className={styles.row}>
<div className={styles.column}>
<span className={styles.title}>Welcome to SharePoint!</span>
<p className={styles.subTitle}>Customize SharePoint experiences using Web Parts.</p>
<p className={styles.description}>{escape(this.props.description)}</p>
<div>
<a href="#" className={`${styles.button}`} onClick={() => this.clickShowDate()}>
<span className={styles.label}>Show Date</span>
</a>
 
Present Date: {this.state.presentDate.toDateString()}
</div>
<p></p>
<div>
<a href="#" className={`${styles.button}`} onClick={() => this.clickShowArbitraryNumber()}>
<span className={styles.label}>Generate Arbitrary Number</span>
</a>
 
Arbitrary Number: {this.state.arbitraryNumber}
</div>
<p></p>
```

```
<div>
<ahref="#"className={`${styles.button}`}onClick={() =>this.clickShowArbitraryString()}>
<spanclassName={styles.label}>Generate Arbitrary String</span>
</a>
 
Arbitrary Text: {this.state.arbitraryText}
</div>

</div>
</div>
</div>
</div>
  );
}
```

3. Implement the button click methods to set the state partially:

   TypeScript
   ```
   privateclickShowDate(): void {
   this.setState(() => {
   return {
        ...this.state,
   presentDate:newDate()
     };
    });
   }


   privateclickShowArbitraryNumber(): void {
   this.setState(() => {
   return {
   ```

```
        ...this.state,
arbitraryNumber:Math.floor(Math.random() * 10) + 1
    };
  });
}


  privateclickShowArbitraryString(): void {
  this.setState(() => {
  return {
        ...this.state,
arbitraryText:Math.random().toString(36).substring(2, 15) + Math.random().toString(36).substring(2, 15)
    };
  });
}
```

Spread operator

The spread operator (...) helps to copy the state of the object being passed to the component's state. The spread operator adds another element to the existing array by preserving the actual array.

Test the WebPart

Follow below steps to test the web part on the SharePoint page:

1. At the command prompt, type `gulp serve`.
2. On the SharePoint site, browse to `/_layouts/15/workbench.aspx`.
3. Add the webpart to the page.

4. Click on each button and verify the state:

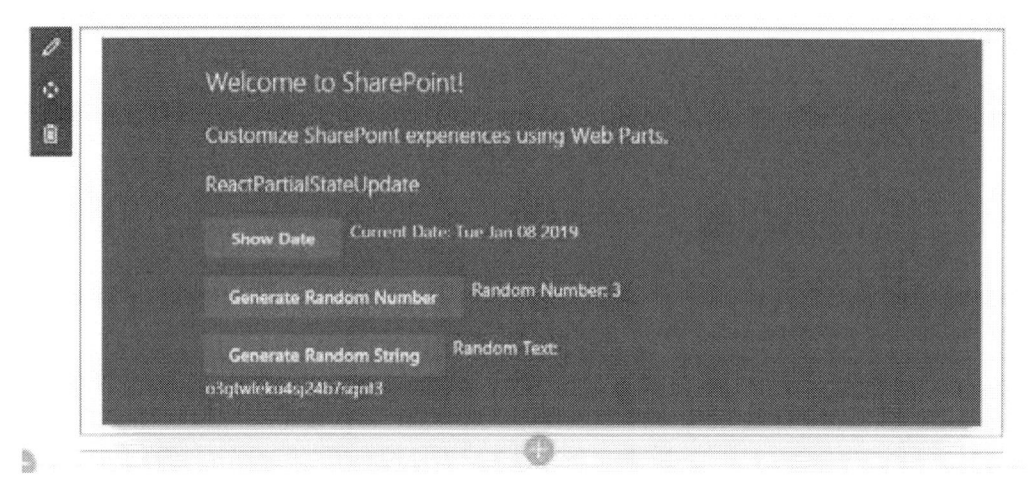

Figure 22.2: Verify partial state update

Conclusion

In this chapter, we learned about the React State and its usage. The spread operator partially updates the state. The spread operator permits replicating enumerable properties from one object to another. We can use the equivalent in the SPFx solution to partially update the React state.

CHAPTER 23
Using Office UI Fabric in SPFx

The **SharePoint Framework (SPFx)** solutions developed in React JS can take advantage of using Office UI Fabric as a front-end framework to develop user experiences. The components utilized in the SharePoint Framework web part ought to have a consistent look and feel to have better user engagement and keep up the consistency the whole way across Office 365. The Office UI Fabric control offers controls to give consistency to the SPFx web parts with Office 365.

Structure

- The UI Challenges
- Overview of Office UI Fabric
- Office UI Fabric for the SharePoint Framework
- Office UI Fabric Components

Objectives

- Explore Office UI Fabric for the SharePoint Framework
- Explore Office UI Fabric Components
- Use Office UI Fabric Components in the SPFx WebPart

The UI Challenges

In the SharePoint venture until this point, we have been creating custom web parts. Building the visual interface for each one of the custom web parts had included noteworthy endeavors from SharePoint developers as well UX designers and UI developers to make the web part resemble an indispensable piece of the SharePoint portal. Huge efforts were put behind to structure the CSS classes and place the required controls (like marks, textboxes, buttons, and so on.) on the web part. This likewise had its own challenge to rewrite while rebranding the SharePoint portals.

Office UI Fabric handles these difficulties gracefully for SharePoint developers and designers keeping in mind the goal that they can assemble the client-side web parts, which can resemble Office 365 and offer responsiveness.

Overview of Office UI Fabric

Office UI Fabric is an official front-end framework for developing user experiences in Office 365. It offers a collection of robust and responsive components. You can peruse about Office UI Fabric at **https://developer.microsoft.com/en-us/fabric**.

Office UI Fabric for the SharePoint Framework

The SharePoint Framework Fabric Core npm package (`@microsoft/sp-office-ui-fabric-core`) is a subset of Fabric core styles that can be effectively coordinated with the SharePoint Framework. The Yeoman generator for the SharePoint Framework (from version 1.3.4 onwards) supports Office UI Fabric by default.

To install the Fabric Core package in your existing project, run the following command:

```
npm install @microsoft/sp-office-ui-fabric-core –save
```

To use Fabric Core styles, use the following declaration:

```
@import '~@microsoft/sp-office-ui-fabric-core/dist/sass/SPFabricCore.scss';
```

However, it is recommended to use the Office UI Fabric React package with the SharePoint Framework.

Create the SPFx Solution

Open the command prompt. Follow the given steps to create the SPFx solution:

1. Create a directory for the SPFx solution:

   ```
   md spfx-officeuifabric
   ```

2. Navigate to the above created directory:

   ```
   cd spfx-officeuifabric
   ```

3. Run the Yeoman SharePoint Generator to create the SPFxsolution:

   ```
   yo @microsoft/sharepoint
   ```

4. The Yeoman generator will display the wizard by asking questions about the solution to be generated:

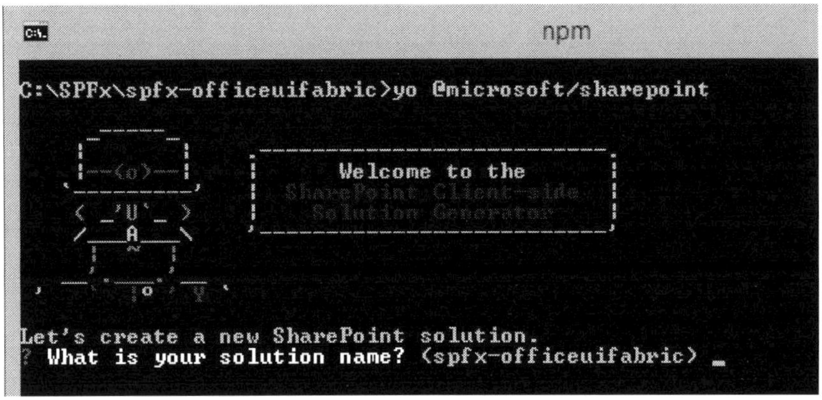

Figure 23.1: SPFx Yeoman generator

The SPFx Yeoman generator will display the following wizard of questions:

- **Solution Name:** Specify the name of the SPFx solution. Hit the *Enter* key to go ahead with the default name (`spfx-officeuifabric` in this case) or type in any other name for your solution.
    - **Selected choice:** Hit *Enter*
- **The target for the component:** Specify the target environment to develop and deploy the SPFx solution. Choose any from SharePoint Online or SharePoint On-Premises environment.
    - **Selected choice:** SharePoint Online only (latest)
- **Place of files:** Choose the folder location for the SPFx project (either the same folder or a subfolder).
    - **Selected choice:** Same folder
- **Deployment option:** Specify Y to allow the deployment of the app instantly to all the sites, N otherwise.
    - **Selected choice:** N (install on each site explicitly)

- **Permissions to access web APIs:** Decide whether the components in the solution require permissions to access web APIs that are unique and not shared with other components in the tenant.
    - **Selected choice:** N (solution contains unique permissions)
- **Type of client-side component to create:** Choose to create a client-side web part or an extension.
    - **Selected choice:** WebPart
- **Web part name:** Specify the name of the web part. Hit the *Enter* key to go ahead with the default name or type in any other name.
    - **Selected choice:** OfficeUIFabricExamples
- **Web part description:** Specify the description of the web part. Hit the *Enter* key to go ahead with the default description or type in any other value.
    - **Selected choice:** Office UI Fabric Integration with SPFx
- **A framework to use:** Select any JavaScript framework to develop the component. Available choices are No JavaScript Framework, React, and Knockout.
    - **Selected choice:** React

5. After the scaffolding is complete, run the following command to lock down the version of project dependencies:

```
npm shrinkwrap
```

6. At the command prompt, type the following command to open the solution in the code editor of your choice:

```
code .
```

Office UI Fabric Components

Office UI Fabric majorly has the following categorized components:

Basic Inputs:

- Button
- Checkbox
- Choice Group
- Combo Box
- Contextual Menu
- Dropdown
- Label
- Link
- Rating
- Slider
- Spin Button
- Text Field
- Toggle

Navigation:
- Breadcrumb
- Command Bar
- Nav
- Overflow Set
- Pivot
- Search Box

Content:
- Activity Item
- Calendar
- Details List
- Facepile
- Grouped List
- Icon
- Image
- List
- Persona

Pickers:
- Color Picker
- Date Picker
- People Picker
- Swatch Color Picker

Progress and Validation:
- Message Bar
- Progress Indicator
- Shimmer
- Spinner

Surfaces:
- Callout
- Dialog
- Document Card
- Hover Card
- Layer
- Modal
- Overlay
- Panel
- Scrollable Pane
- Teaching Bubble
- Tooltip
- Coachmark

Utilities:
- Focus Trap Zone
- Focus Zone
- Marquee Selection
- Resize Group
- Selection
- Themes

Use Office UI Fabric Components in the SPFx WebPart

Follow below steps to use the Office UI Fabric components in the SPFx web part:

1. Navigate to the Office UI Fabric Components site at **https://developer.microsoft.com/en-us/fabric#/components**.
2. Select and expand the Category of your component.
3. Click on the component node.
4. Here is an example of selecting a button component:

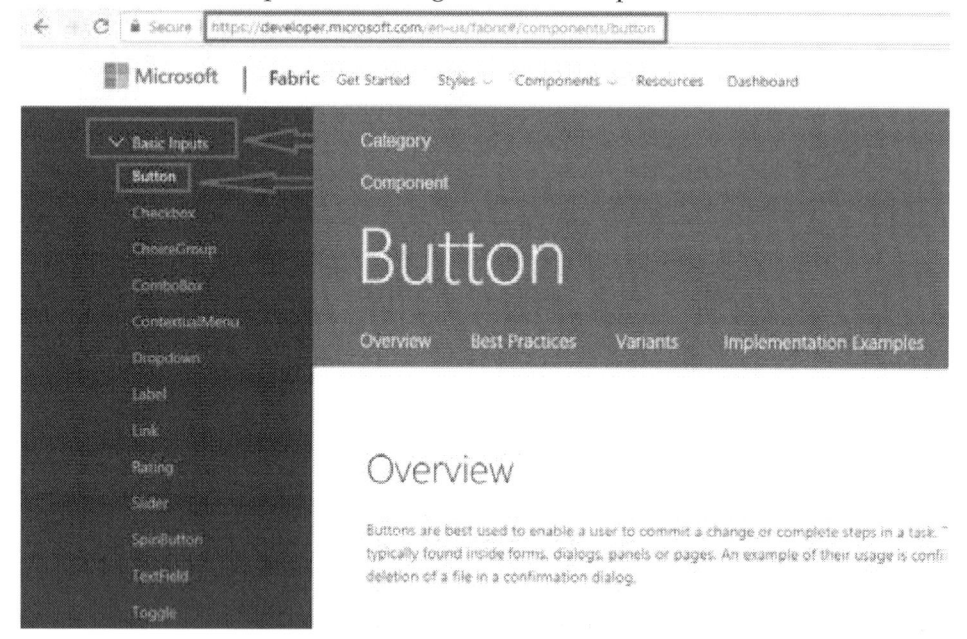

Figure 23.2: Office 365 UI Fabric Button component

5. Alternatively, search your component from the search box.
6. Click on the **Variants** tab to see the variations for use of the component:

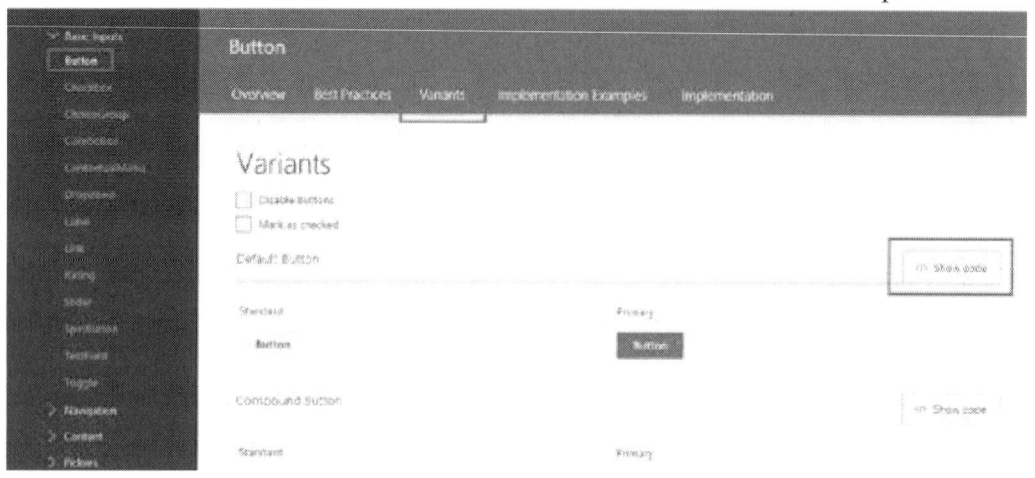

Figure 23.3: Office 365 UI Fabric component variations

7. Click on **Show code** to get the code for the component:

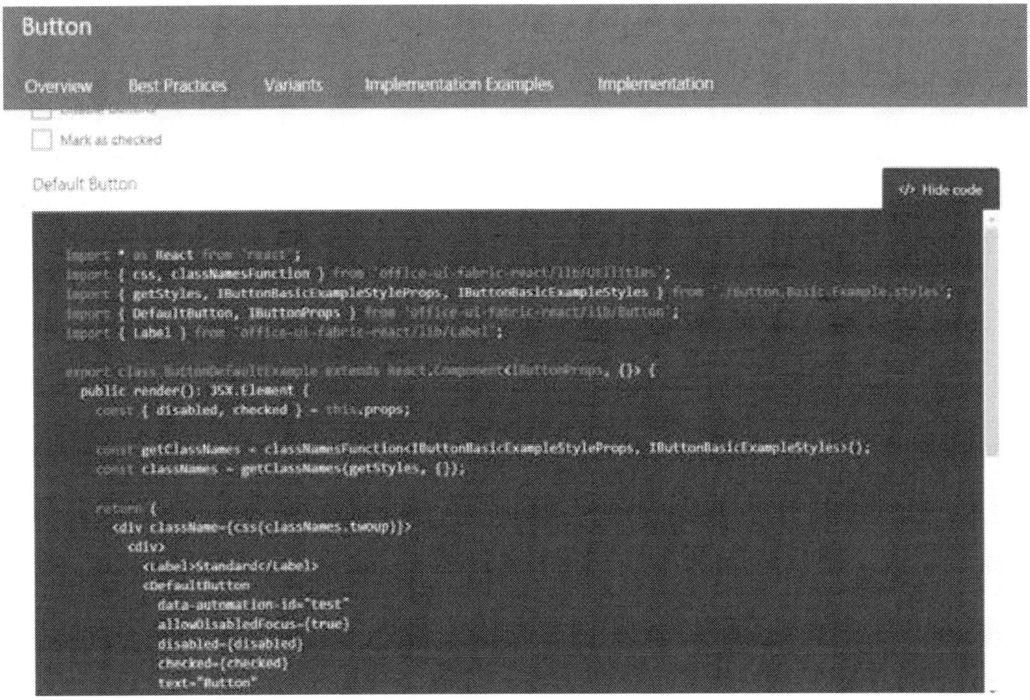

Figure 23.4: Office 365 UI Fabric component code

8. Copy the entire code or part of it to use in your SPFx solution.

Implement the Greet Message WebPart using Office UI Fabric

Using the Office UI Fabric components, we will implement a simple webpart having the following components:

- **Textbox:** This accepts the user name.
- **Button:** This button is with the text as **Greet** when clicked will show an alert greeting the text typed in the textbox.

Follow the given steps to add Office UI Fabric controls to the SPFx solution:

1. In the solution, add the `IComponentState.ts` file, which will represent the state of the entered user name:

    TypeScript
    ```
    exportinterface IComponentState {
        userName: string;
    }
    ```

2. Open OfficeUiFabricExamples.tsx under the "\src\webparts\ officeUiFabricExamples\components\" folder.
3. Import the Textfield and Button components:

   TypeScript

   ```
   // Import Textfield component
   import { TextField } from'office-ui-fabric-react/lib/TextField';

   // Import Button component
   import { IButtonProps, DefaultButton } from'office-ui-fabric-react/lib/Button';
   ```

4. Add components to the Render method:

   TypeScript

   ```
   Exportdefaultclass OfficeUiFabricExamples extends React.Component<IOfficeUiFabricExamplesProps, IComponentState> {
   constructor(props: IOfficeUiFabricExamplesProps, state: IComponentState) {
   super(props);
   this.state = ({userName: ''});
   this._greetClicked = this._greetClicked.bind(this);
     }

   public render(): React.ReactElement<IOfficeUiFabricExamplesProps> {
   return (
   <divclassName={ styles.officeUiFabricExamples }>
   <divclassName={ styles.container }>
   <divclassName={ styles.row }>
   <divclassName={ styles.column }>
   <divclassName="docs-TextFieldExample">
   <TextFieldrequired={true}name="txtUserName"
   placeholder="Your name please!"value={this.state.userName}
   onChanged={e =>this.setState({ userName: e })}
   />
   ```

```
<DefaultButton
data-automation-id="greet"target="_blank"
title="Greet the user!"onClick={this._greetClicked}
>
                Greet
</DefaultButton>
<p>{this.state.userName}</p>
</div>
</div>
</div>
</div>
</div>
    );
  }

private _greetClicked(): void {
    alert('Hello ' + this.state.userName);
    }
}
```

Test the WebPart

Follow below steps to test the web part on the SharePoint local workbench:
1. At the command prompt, type `gulp serve`.
2. The SharePoint local workbench will open.
3. Add the webpart to the page.

4. Enter the text in TextBox component, and then click on the **Greet** button. An alert message will appear greeting the value entered in a textbox:

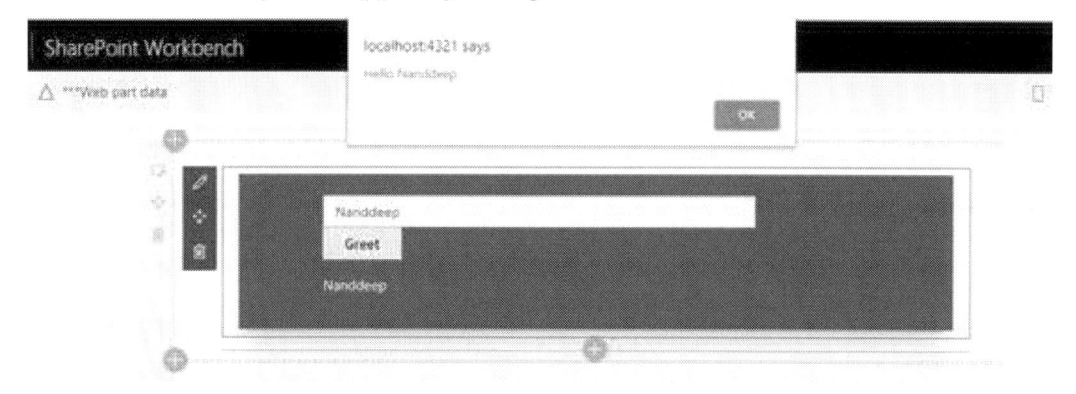

Figure 23.5: Test Office 365 UI Fabric components in the SPFx web part

Conclusion

In this chapter, we learned about the Office UI Fabric Components and used them in the SPFx web part for a reliable look and feel. The Office UI Fabric React components help to develop a robust and consistent design across SharePoint modern experiences. Office UI Fabric is available out of the box for developers in the SharePoint Framework.

CHAPTER 24
Provision SharePoint Assets in SPFx Solutions

SharePoint components like web parts ordinarily associate with the SharePoint artifacts like lists, libraries, content types, and so on. In the full trust solutions, we deploy these SharePoint assets alongside web parts in a deployable package (.wsp).

Similarly, the **SharePoint Framework (SPFx)** client-side web parts are associated with the underlying lists and libraries in SharePoint site. These SharePoint assets should be provisioned alongside the client side solution package. The SharePoint framework toolchain permits to package and deploy SharePoint assets with a client-side solution package.

Structure

- SharePoint Assets
- Add SharePoint Assets to the SPFx Solution
- Package Assets as part of the SPFx Solution

Objectives

- Add SharePoint assets to the SPFx solution
- Package the SharePoint assets needed for SPFx web parts

SharePoint Assets

A SharePoint asset is a non-exclusive term alluded to essential building blocks of SharePoint that comprises fields, content types, and list instances.

Fields (Site Columns):

A field is a metadata that portrays the property or attribute of the object we want to represent. For instance, an Employee can be represented with its ID, Name, Department, etc. Each field has a specific type such as text, number, Boolean, etc.

The following is an example of a field representing a number:

XML

```xml
<Field ID="{060E50AC-E9C1-4D3C-B1F9-DE0BCAC300F6}"
Name="SPFxAmount"
DisplayName="Amount"
Type="Currency"
Decimals="2"
Min="0"
Required="FALSE"
Group="SPFx Columns" />
```

Content types

A content type is a reusable collection of site columns. The following is an example of a content type that uses a site column:

XML

```xml
<ContentType ID="0x010042D0C1C200A14B6887742B6344675C8B"
Name="Cost Center"
Group="SPFx Content Types"
Description="Content types from SPFx">
<FieldRefs>
<FieldRef ID="{060E50AC-E9C1-4D3C-B1F9-DE0BCAC300F6}" />
</FieldRefs>
</ContentType>
```

List instance:

List instance is pre-defined SharePoint list with a well-known identifier. We can add, update, and delete items from the list:

XML

```xml
<ListInstance
FeatureId="00bfea71-de22-43b2-a848-c05709900100"
Title="SPFx List"
Description="SPFx List"
TemplateType="100"
Url="Lists/SPFxList">
</ListInstance>
```

List instance with custom schema:

We can create our own schema to define fields, content types, and views for the list instance. Use the Custom Schema attribute in the `ListInstance` element to reference custom schema:

XML

```xml
<ListInstance
CustomSchema="schema.xml"
FeatureId="00bfea71-de22-43b2-a848-c05709900100"
Title="SPFx List"
Description="SPFx List"
TemplateType="100"
Url="Lists/SPFxList">
</ListInstance>
```

Create the SPFx Solution

Open the command prompt. Follow the given steps to create the SPFx solution:

1. Create a directory for the SPFx solution:
   ```
   md spfx-provisionspassets
   ```
2. Navigate to the above-created directory:
   ```
   cd spfx-provisionspassets
   ```

3. Run the Yeoman SharePoint Generator to create the SPFx solution:

   ```
   yo @microsoft/sharepoint
   ```

4. The Yeoman generator will display the wizard by asking questions about the solution to be generated:

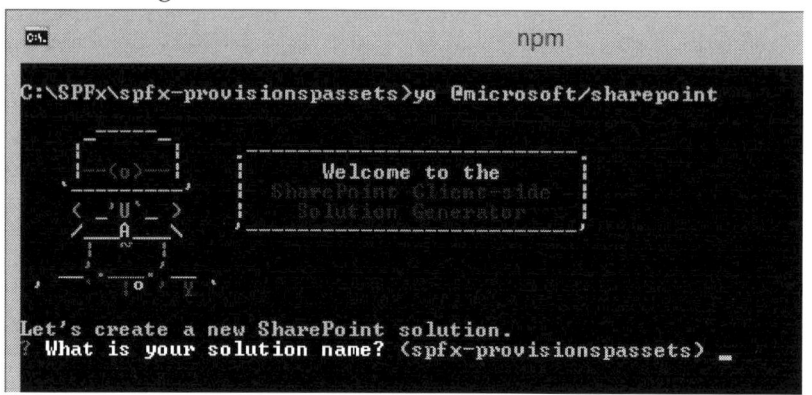

Figure 24.1: SPFx Yeoman generator

The SPFx Yeoman generator will display the following wizard of questions:

- **Solution Name:** Specify the name of the SPFx solution. Hit the *Enter* key to go ahead with the default name (`spfx-provisionspassets` in this case) or type in any other name for your solution.
    - **Selected choice:** Hit *Enter*
- **The target for the component:** Specify the target environment to develop and deploy the SPFx solution. Select SharePoint Online or SharePoint On-Premises environment.
    - **Selected choice:** SharePoint Online only (latest)
- **Place of files:** Choose the folder location for the SPFx project (either the same folder or a subfolder).
    - **Selected choice:** Same folder
- **Deployment option:** Specify Y to allow the deployment of the app instantly to all the sites, N otherwise.
    - **Selected choice:** N (install on each site explicitly)
- **Permissions to access web APIs:** Decide whether the components in the solution require permissions to access web APIs that are unique and not shared with other components in the tenant.
    - **Selected choice:** N (solution contains unique permissions)
- **Type of client-side component to create:** Choose to create a client-side web part or an extension.

            o   **Selected choice:** WebPart
   - **Web part name:** Specify the name of the web part. Hit the *Enter* key to go ahead with the default name or type in any other name.
            o   **Selected choice:** `ProvisionSPAssets`
   - **Web part description:** Specify the description of the web part. Hit the *Enter* key to go ahead with the default description or type in any other value.
            o   **Selected choice:** Provision SharePoint Assets with SPFx
   - **A framework to use:** Select any JavaScript framework to develop the component. The available choices are No JavaScript Framework, React, and Knockout.
      - **Selected choice:** No JavaScript Framework
5. The Yeoman generator will perform the scaffolding process to generate the solution. The scaffolding process will take a significant amount of time.
6. Once the scaffolding process is complete, lock down the version of project dependencies by running the following command:

   ```
   npm shrinkwrap
   ```

7. At the command prompt, type the following command to open the solution in the code editor of your choice:

   ```
   code .
   ```

Add SharePoint Assets to the SPFxSolution

Follow below steps to add SharePoint Assets to the SPFx Solution:

1. Create a folder structure as `'sharepoint\assets'`:

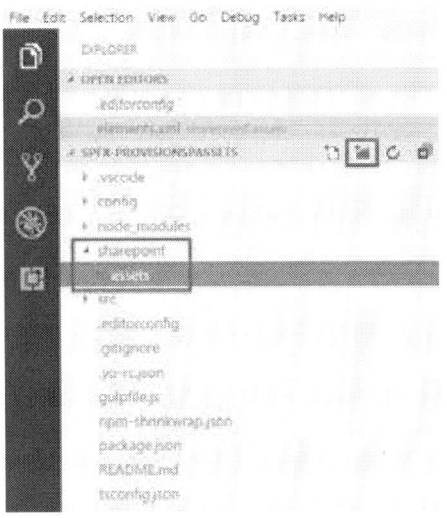

Figure 24.2: Add assets folder to SPFx solution

2. Add `theelements.xml` file under the 'sharepoint\assets' folder:

XML
```xml
<?xml version="1.0" encoding="utf-8"?>
<Elementsxmlns="http://schemas.microsoft.com/sharepoint/">

<FieldID="{060E50AC-E9C1-4D3C-B1F9-DE0BCAC300F6}"
Name="SPFxAmount"
DisplayName="Amount"
Type="Currency"
Decimals="2"
Min="0"
Required="FALSE"
Group="SPFx Columns"/>

<FieldID="{943E7530-5E2B-4C02-8259-CCD93A9ECB18}"
Name="SPFxCostCenter"
DisplayName="Cost Center"
Type="Choice"
Required="FALSE"
Group="SPFx Columns">
<CHOICES>
<CHOICE>Administration</CHOICE>
<CHOICE>Information</CHOICE>
<CHOICE>Facilities</CHOICE>
<CHOICE>Operations</CHOICE>
<CHOICE>Sales</CHOICE>
<CHOICE>Marketing</CHOICE>
</CHOICES>
</Field>

<ContentTypeID="0x010042D0C1C200A14B6887742B6344675C8B"
```

```xml
            Name="Cost Center"
            Group="SPFx Content Types"
            Description="Sample content types from web part solution">
            <FieldRefs>
            <FieldRefID="{060E50AC-E9C1-4D3C-B1F9-DE0BCAC300F6}"/>
            <FieldRefID="{943E7530-5E2B-4C02-8259-CCD93A9ECB18}"/>
            </FieldRefs>
            </ContentType>

            <ListInstance
            CustomSchema="schema.xml"
            FeatureId="00bfea71-de22-43b2-a848-c05709900100"
            Title="SPFx List"
            Description="SPFx List"
            TemplateType="100"
            Url="Lists/SPFxList">
            </ListInstance>

            </Elements>
```

We are provisioning two fields: content type and list instance with a custom schema. `FeatureId` in the `ListInstance` represents the ID of the feature, which contains the list definition. The `FeatureId` mentioned in the XML represents the ID for the custom list definition.

Custom Schema

Add the `schema.xml` file as our custom schema under the 'sharepoint\assets' folder:

XML

```xml
<Listxmlns:ows="Microsoft SharePoint"Title="Basic List"EnableContentTypes="TRUE"FolderCreation="FALSE"Direction="$Resources:Direction;"Url="Lists/Basic List"BaseType="0"xmlns= "http://schemas.microsoft.com/sharepoint/">

<MetaData>
```

```xml
<ContentTypes>
<ContentTypeRefID="0x010042D0C1C200A14B6887742B6344675C8B"/>
</ContentTypes>
<Fields></Fields>        <Views>
<ViewBaseViewID="1"Type="HTML"WebPartZoneID="Main
"DisplayName="$Resources:core,objectiv_schema_mwsidcamlidC24;"
DefaultView="TRUE"MobileView="TRUE" MobileDefaultView="TRUE"
SetupPath="pages\viewpage.aspx"ImageUrl="/_layouts/images/generic.png
"Url="AllItems.aspx">
<XslLinkDefault="TRUE">main.xsl</XslLink>
<JSLink>clienttemplates.js</JSLink>
<RowLimitPaged="TRUE">30</RowLimit>
<ToolbarType="Standard"/>
<ViewFields>
<FieldRefName="LinkTitle"></FieldRef>
<FieldRefName="SPFxAmount"></FieldRef>
<FieldRefName="SPFxCostCenter"></FieldRef>
</ViewFields>
<Query>
<OrderBy>
<FieldRefName="ID"/>
</OrderBy>
</Query>
</View>
</Views>
<Forms>
<FormType="DisplayForm"Url="DispForm.aspx"SetupPath="pages\form.aspx"WebPartZoneID="Main"/>
<FormType="EditForm"Url="EditForm.aspx"SetupPath="pages\form.aspx"WebPartZoneID="Main"/>
<FormType="NewForm"Url="NewForm.aspx"SetupPath="pages\form.aspx"WebPartZoneID="Main"/>
```

```
</Forms>
</MetaData>
</List>
```

Package the assets as part of the SPFx Solution

We created the assets and custom schema. We need to package these files as part of the solution.

Follow below steps to package the assets as part of the SPFx Solution:
1. Open the `package-solution.js` on file in the config folder.
2. Include the feature framework definition for the solution package:

   JSON

   ```
   {
   "$schema":    "https://developer.microsoft.com/json-schemas/spfx-build/package-solution.schema.json",
   "solution": {
   "name": "spfx-provisionspassets-client-side-solution",
   "id": "ea551656-9f74-4107-b049-e296e475932d",
   "version": "1.0.0.0",
   "includeClientSideAssets": true,
   "features": [{
   "title": "asset-deployment-webpart-client-side-solution",
   "description": "asset-deployment-webpart-client-side-solution",
   "id": "523fe887-ced5-4036-b564-8dad5c6c6e24",//Specify unique GUID
   "version": "1.0.0.0",
   "assets": {
   "elementManifests": [
   "elements.xml"
         ],
   "elementFiles":[
   ```

```
                    "schema.xml"
                ]
            }
        }]
    },
    "paths": {
        "zippedPackage": "solution/spfx-provisionspassets.sppkg"
    }
}
```

Please specify the unique GUID for the feature ID.

Deploy and Test the SPFx Web Part

Follow below steps to deploy and test the SPFx web part:

1. Package your client-side solution by running the following command:

   ```
   gulp bundle
   ```

2. Create a solution package by running the following command:

   ```
   gulp package-solution
   ```

   This command will create the package (.sppkg) inside the `sharepoint/solution` folder.

3. Deploy the package to the app catalog:

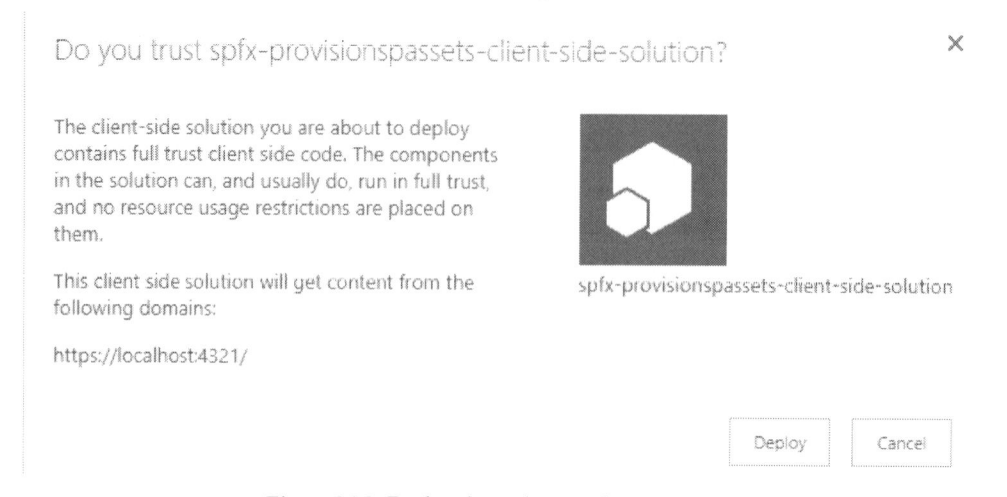

Figure 24.3: Deploy the package to the app catalog

4. Click on **Deploy**.
5. Open the SharePoint site. Click on **Add an app**.
6. Install the app.

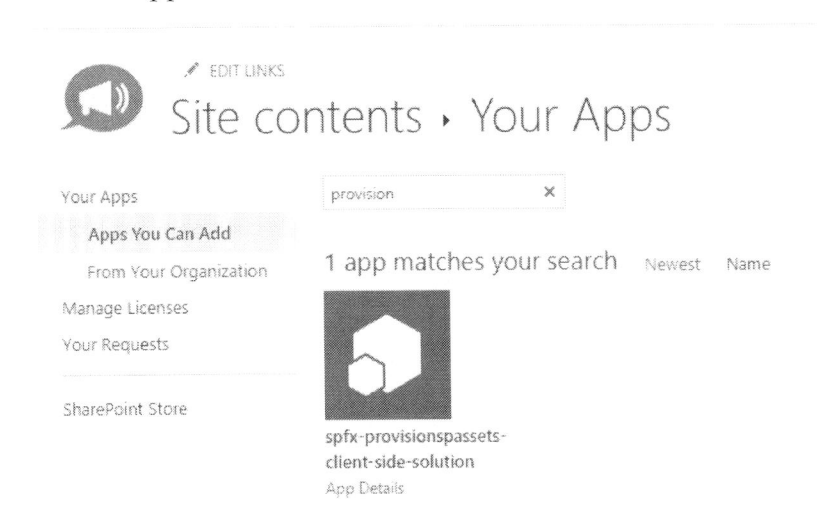

Figure 24.4: Add and install the app to the SharePoint site

7. When the installation finishes, refresh the page. The site should have **SPFx List** provisioned:

Figure 24.5: SharePoint asset provisioning

8. Open **SPFx List.** It should have our content type with the site columns inside it:

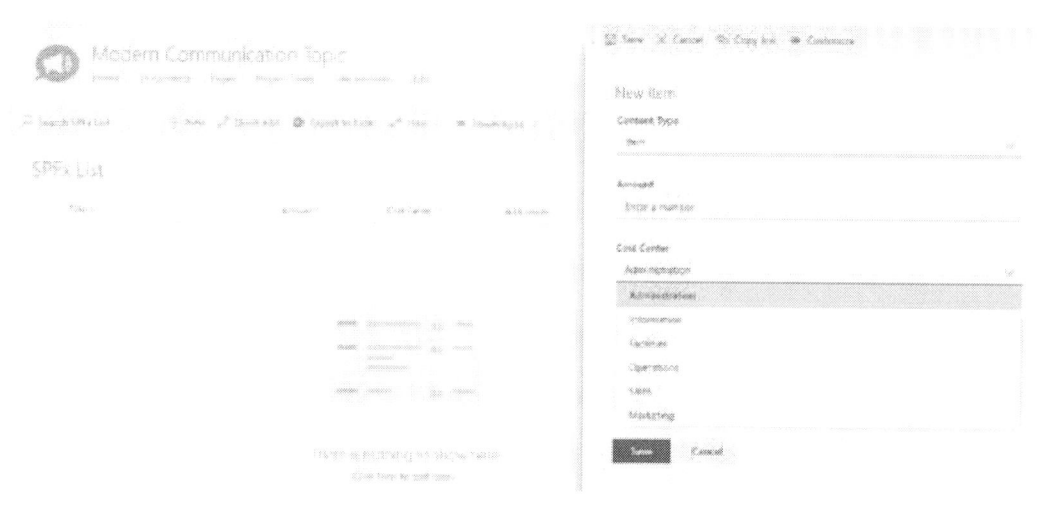

Figure 24.6: Verify the content type attached to the provisioned SharePoint list

Conclusion

In this chapter, we learned how SharePoint assets can be provisioned utilizing SPFx. We can define the required structure to provision on the SharePoint site, which can be used by SPFx web parts. The **SharePoint Framework (SPFx)** client-side web parts interact with the underlying lists and libraries in the SharePoint site. The SharePoint framework toolchain permits to package and deploy SharePoint assets with a client-side solution package.

CHAPTER 25
Connect to the MS Graph API with MSGraphClient

Microsoft Graph provides a unified set of REST APIs to access various content and services across Office 365. A common enterprise-level business scenario always includes connecting to MS Graph APIs from SPFx web parts and displays some meaningful information to the end users.

Structure
- Overview of Microsoft Graph
- Connect to the MS Graph API
- Consume User Details utilizing MS Graph
- API Management

Objectives
- Get Introduced to Microsoft Graph
- Consume the MS Graph in SPFx web parts

Brief information about Microsoft Graph

MS Graph is a unified set of REST APIs provided by Microsoft to access content and services over Office 365. For example, using Microsoft graph, we can access the mailbox, calendar and **one drive for business (OD4B)** of a user. Just like how we can access the Site collection, sites, and lists in SharePoint Online. Likewise, we can get access to Office 365 Groups and MS Teams utilizing MS Graph.

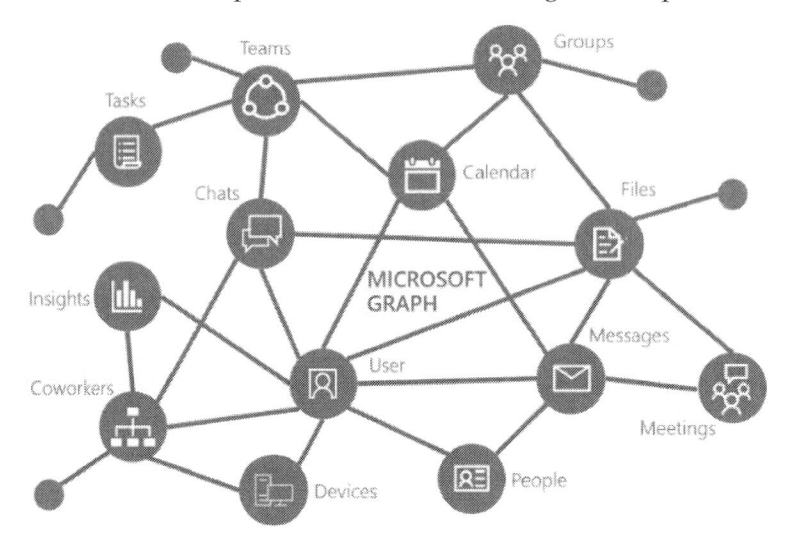

Figure 25.1: Microsoft Graph

Develop the SPFx Solution to consume the MS Graph API with MSGraphClient

Open the command prompt. Follow the given steps to make the SPFx solution:

1. Make a folder for the SPFx solution:

    ```
    md msgraph-using-msgraphclient
    ```

2. Change the path of the above folder:

    ```
    cd msgraph-using-msgraphclient
    ```

3. Execute the Yeoman Generator for SharePoint:

    ```
    yo @microsoft/sharepoint
    ```

4. The Yeoman generator will run through the wizard asking questions about the SPFx solution to be created:

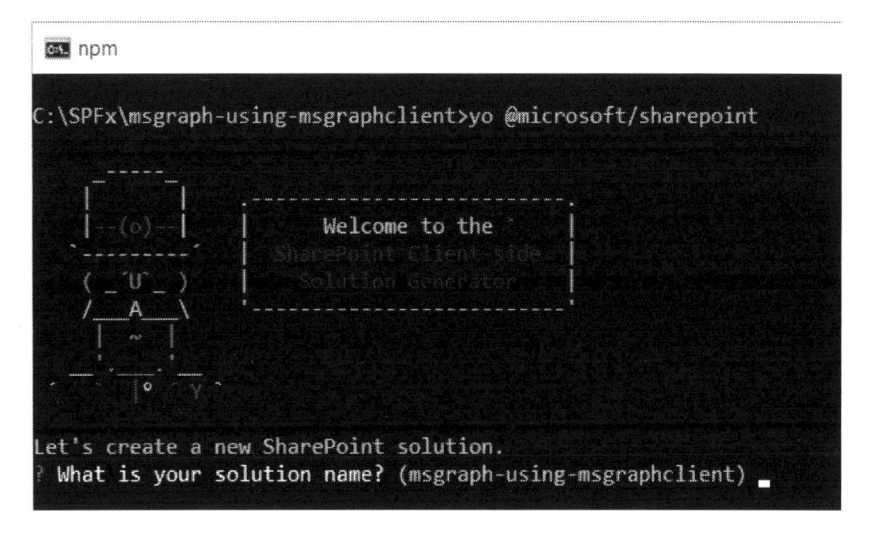

Figure 25.2: SPFx Yeoman generator

The SPFx Yeoman generator will display the following inquiries:

- **Solution Name:** Determine the SPFx solution name. Hit the *Enter* key to proceed with the default selection (msgraph-using-msgraphclient) or type another name.
    - o **Chosen decision:** Hit *Enter*
- **Target environment:** Specify the target environment to deploy the SPFx solution. Select any option from SharePoint Online or SharePoint On-Premises environment.
    - o **Chosen decision:** SharePoint Online only (latest)
- **Place of files:** Choose the folder location for the SPFx project (either the same folder or a subfolder).
    - o **Chosen decision:** Use the current folder
- **Deployment option:** Specify Y to deploy app instantly to all the sites, N otherwise.
    - o **Chosen decision:** N (install on each site explicitly)
- **Consents to access web APIs:** Decide whether the components in the solution need an explicit permission to access web APIs that are unique and not shared with other components in the tenant.
    - o **Chosen decision:** N (solution contains unique permissions)
- **Choice of client-side component:** Decide whether to develop a web part or an extension.
    - o **Chosen decision:** WebPart

- **Web part name:** Provide the web part name. Hit the *Enter* key to proceed with the default choice or type another name.
  - **Chosen decision:** `MSGraphWithMSGraphClient`
- **Web part description:** Provide the web part description. Hit the *Enter* key to proceed with the default choice or type another value.
  - **Chosen decision:** Consume MS Graph with **MSGraphClient**
- **Choice of framework:** Choose the JavaScript framework to develop the component from No JavaScript Framework, React, and Knockout.
  - **Chosen decision:** React

5. After the scaffolding is complete, lock down the version of project dependencies by executing the following command:

```
npm shrinkwrap
```

6. At the command prompt, execute the following command to open the SPFx solution in the preferred code editor:

```
code .
```

MSGraphClient to consume the Graph APIs

The native graph client (`MSGraphClient`) helps to consume MS Graph APIs. It is available to the SPFx projects built using v1.6.0 or later.

Include the following import statement in the "src\webparts\msGraphWithMsGraphClient\components\MsGraphWithMsGraphClient.tsx" file:

TypeScript

```
import { MSGraphClient } from '@microsoft/sp-http';
```

MS GraphTypings

At the command prompt, run the following command to include the typings for MS Graph:

```
npm install @microsoft/microsoft-graph-types --save-dev
```

Add the following import statement to the "\src\webparts\msGraphWithMSGraphClient\components\MSGraphWithMSGraphClient.tsx" file:

TypeScript

```
import * as MicrosoftGraph from '@microsoft/microsoft-graph-types';
```

Permission Scopes:

We explicitly need to mention the permission scopes inside the solution manifest available in the `config\package-solution.json` file to access a particular MS Graph API:

JSON

```
{
"$schema": "https://developer.microsoft.com/json-schemas/spfx-build/package-solution.schema.json",
"solution": {
"name": "msgraph-using-msgraphclient-client-side-solution",
"id": "7342a9b5-7513-427a-86a3-b65cab7e175e",
"version": "1.0.0.0",
"includeClientSideAssets": true,
"isDomainIsolated": false,
"webApiPermissionRequests": [
    {
"resource": "Microsoft Graph",
"scope": "User.ReadBasic.All"
    }
  ]
 },
"paths": {
"zippedPackage": "solution/msgraph-using-msgraphclient.sppkg"
  }
}
```

Each item in the `webApiPermissionRequests` array represents the following:
- **resource:** This is the resource name or the `ObjectId` in Azure AD. For example: Microsoft Graph.
- **scope:** This is the permission name or unique ID.

Define Props:

Under the "\src\webparts\msGraphWithMSGraphClient\components\" folder, define the context in IMSGraphWithMSGraphClientProps.ts file:

TypeScript

```typescript
import { WebPartContext } from '@microsoft/sp-webpart-base';

exportinterface IMSGraphWithMSGraphClientProps {
  description: string;
  context: WebPartContext;
}
```

Define State:

Under the "\src\webparts\msGraphWithMSGraphClient\components\" folder, add the IUser.ts interface to represent the user:

TypeScript

```typescript
exportinterface IUser{
    displayName: string;
email: string;
    userPrincipalName: string;
}
```

Under "\src\webparts\msGraphWithMSGraphClient\components\" folder, add the IMsGraphWithMsGraphClientState.ts file:

TypeScript

```typescript
import { IUser } from './IUser';

exportinterfaceIMsGraphWithMsGraphClientState {
    users: Array<IUser>;
}
```

Retrieve User Information using MS Graph

Implement the following method to get the user details from your tenant:

TypeScript

```
privateretrieveUserInfo(): void {
this.context.msGraphClientFactory
    .getClient()
    .then((client: MSGraphClient): void=> {
// get information about the current user from the Microsoft Graph client
        .api('users')
        .version("v1.0")
        .select("displayName,mail,userPrincipalName")
        .get((error, result: any, rawResponse?: any) => {
// handle the response
if (error) {
console.error(error);
return;
        }

// Prepare the output array
varusers: Array<IUser> = newArray<IUser>();

// Map the JSON response to the output array
result.value.map((item: any) => {
users.push({
displayName:item.displayName,
email:item.mail,
userPrincipalName:item.userPrincipalName,
          });
        });

// Update the component state accordingly to the result
```

```
this.setState(
            {
users:users,
            }
        );
    });
});
}
```

Once we have the user information set in the state, it can be bind to any control (e.g. `DetailsList`) to display the information on the web part.

Test the WebPart:

Follow below steps to test the web part on the SharePoint page:

1. At the command prompt, type "`gulp serve`".
2. Open the SharePoint site. Navigate to `/_layouts/15/workbench.aspx`.
3. Add the webpart to the page:

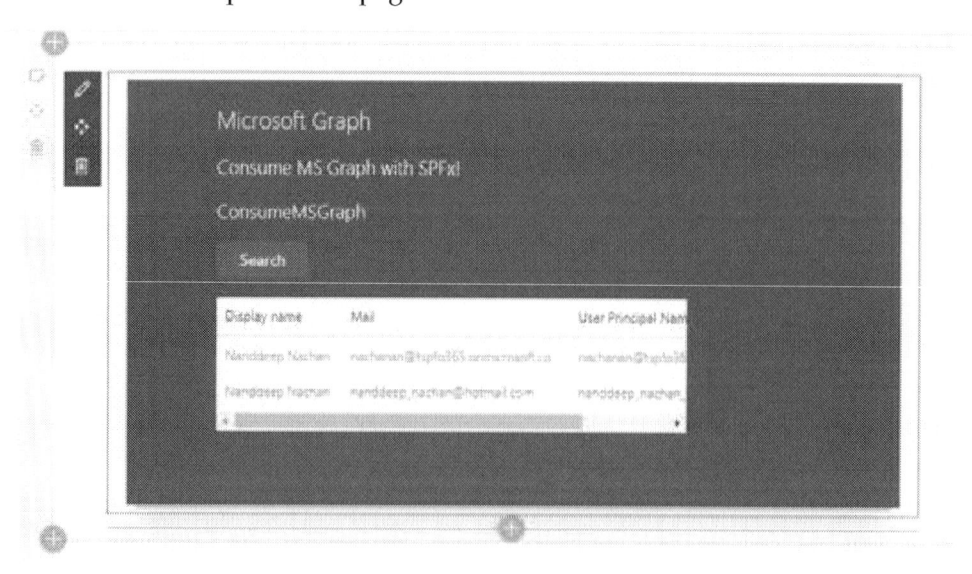

Figure 25.4: Verify the MS Graph API

API Management:

Post deploying the web part to the app catalog, follow the given steps to approve API requests:

1. Open SharePoint Admin Center (**https://[tenant]-admin.sharepoint.com**).
2. Click on **Try the preview** to open the modern SharePoint Admin center:

Figure 25.5: Try the preview of modern SharePoint Admin center

3. From the left navigation bar, click on **API Management**.
4. Approve pending requests, as shown in the following screenshot:

Figure 25.6: Approve pending requests

Conclusion

In this chapter, we discussed the essentials of MS Graph, how to use it in SPFx web parts to retrieve helpful data like user information, and so on. Microsoft Graph offers a wide scope of REST APIs to help access content and services given by Office 365.

CHAPTER 26
Connect to the MS Graph API with AadHttpClient

A typical business situation incorporates expending MS Graph APIs in SPFx web parts and shows some important data to the clients. `AadHttpClient` can be utilized to expend any REST API; though `MSGraphClient` can just devour MS Graph (native graph client).

Structure
- Access MS Graph using `AadHttpClient`
- Get User Details using MS Graph
- Enable Targeted Release on the Office 365 Tenant
- API Management

Objective
- Consume the MS Graph in SPFx web parts using `AadHttpClient`.

AadHttpClient vs MSGraphClient

`AadHttpClient` is utilized to get a client that is preconfigured with the '*Authorization*' request header with an OAuth access token acquired from Azure AD for the target endpoint with the allowed scopes in it. `AadHttpClient` is the same as `HttpClient`.

It simply has the extra auth mechanism in it. `HttpClient` is utilized to call any endpoint you need.

`MSGraphClient` utilizes a similar procedure that `AadHttpClient` uses to get an access token; however, in the case of the MS Graph, JS API from the MS Graph JS SDK are preconfigured/introduced with the access token.

To put it simply, you can utilize `AadHttpClient` to converse with the MS Graph and REST endpoint; though with the `MSGraphClient`, you get the MS Graph JS familiar API.

Create the SPFx Solution

Open the command prompt. Follow the given steps to create the SPFx solution:

1. Create a directory for the SPFx solution:

    ```
    md msgraph-using-aadhttpclient
    ```

2. Navigate to the above created directory:

    ```
    cd msgraph-using-aadhttpclient
    ```

3. Run the Yeoman SharePoint Generator to create the solution:

    ```
    yo @microsoft/sharepoint
    ```

4. The Yeoman generator will show you the wizard asking questions about the solution to be created:

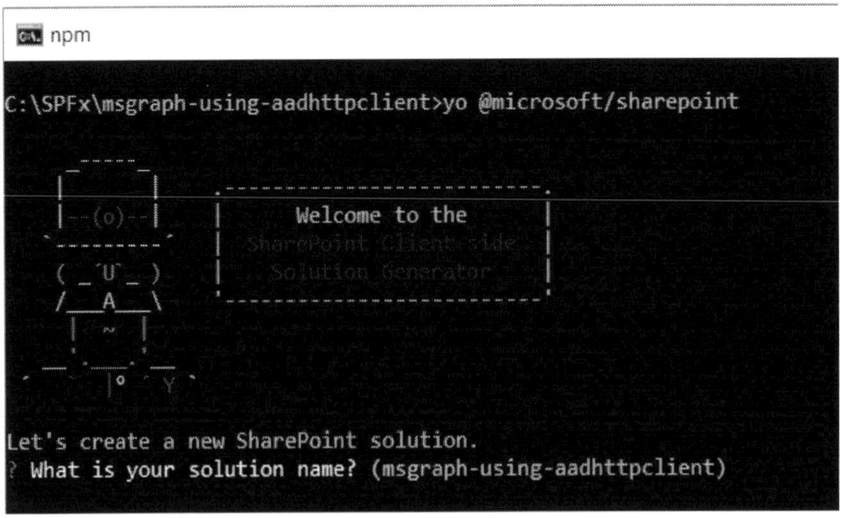

Figure 26.1: SPFx Yeoman generator

The SPFx Yeoman generator will display the following wizard of questions:

- **Solution Name:** Specify the name of the SPFx solution. Hit the *Enter* key to go ahead with the default name (`msgraph-using-aadhttpclient` in this case) or type in any other name for your solution.
    - o **Selected choice:** Hit *Enter*
- **The target for the component:** Select the target environment where we are planning to deploy the client web part, i.e. SharePoint Online or SharePoint On-Premises (SharePoint 2016 onwards).
    - o **Selected choice:** SharePoint Online only (latest)
- **Place of files:** Choose the folder location for the SPFx project (either the same folder or a subfolder).
    - o **Selected choice:** Same folder
- **Deployment option:** Selecting Y will allow the app to be deployed instantly to all sites and it will be accessible everywhere.
    - o **Selected choice:** N (install on each site explicitly)
- **Permissions to access web APIs:** Decide whether the components in the solution require permissions to access web APIs that are unique and not shared with other components in the tenant.
    - o **Selected choice:** N (solution contains unique permissions)
- **Type of client-side component to create:** Choose to create a client-side web part or an extension.
    - o **Selected choice:** WebPart
- **Web part name:** Specify the name of the web part. Hit the *Enter* key to go ahead with the default name or type in any other name.
    - o **Selected choice:** `MSGraphWithAADHttpClient`
- **Web part description:** Specify the description of the web part. Hit the *Enter* key to go ahead with the default description or type in any other value.
    - o **Selected choice:** `Connect MS Graph utilizingAADHttpClient`
- **A framework to use:** Select any JavaScript framework to develop the component. Available choices are No JavaScript Framework, React, and Knockout.
    - o **Selected choice:** React

5. After the scaffolding is complete, run the following command to lock down the version of project dependencies:

   ```
   npm shrinkwrap
   ```

6. At the command prompt, type the following command to open the solution in the code editor of your choice:

   ```
   code .
   ```

Access MS Graph using AadHttpClient

Microsoft Graph can be accessed by the low-level type used to access Azure AD secured REST API (`AadHttpClient`). The `AadHttpClient` client object can be utilized to devour any REST API, while the `MSGraphClient` client object can just consume Microsoft Graph.

Add the following import statement to the `MSGraphWithAADHttpClient.tsx` file in the "\src\webparts\msGraphWithAADHttpClient\components\" folder:

TypeScript

```
import { AadHttpClient } from '@microsoft/sp-http';
```

Permissions

To consume MS Graph, we should explicitly specify the permissions in the solution manifest. Under the config folder, in the `package-solution.json` file, set up the `webApiPermissionRequests` property to indicate the 'User.ReadBasic.All' consent:

JSON

```
{
"$schema": "https://developer.microsoft.com/json-schemas/spfx-build/package-solution.schema.json",
"solution": {
"name": "msgraph-using-aadhttpclient-client-side-solution",
"id": "f4123803-dc4b-42d9-b6c4-96e895ec02fe",
"version": "1.0.0.0",
"includeClientSideAssets": true,
"webApiPermissionRequests": [
      {
"resource": "Microsoft Graph",
"scope": "User.ReadBasic.All"
      }
    ]
  },
"paths": {
"zippedPackage": "solution/msgraph-using-aadhttpclient.sppkg"
  }
}
```

`webApiPermissionRequests` is an array of `webApiPermissionRequest`, where each item is characterized as follows:

- **resource:** This is the name or ObjectId (in Azure AD). For example, Microsoft Graph.
- **scope:** This is the name or unique ID of the authorization.

Configure Props:

Define the context property in IMSGraphWithAADHttpClientProps.ts under the "\src\webparts\MSGraphWithAADHttpClient\components\" folder:

TypeScript

```
import { WebPartContext } from '@microsoft/sp-webpart-base';

exportinterface IMSGraphWithAADHttpClientProps {
  description: string;
  context: WebPartContext;
}
```

Configure State:

Define the state for the React component by implementing an interface to represent the user. Under the '\src\webparts\ MSGraphWithAADHttpClient\components\' folder, add the IUserItem.ts file:

TypeScript

```
exportinterface IUserItem {
    displayName: string;
    mail: string;
    userPrincipalName: string;
}
```

Add the IMSGraphWithAADHttpClientState.ts file in the "\src\webparts\MSGraphWithAADHttpClient\components\" folder:

TypeScript

```
import { IUserItem } from './IUserItem';

exportinterface IMSGraphWithAADHttpClientState {
    users: Array<IUserItem>;
}
```

Get user details using MS Graph

Implement the following method to get the user details from your tenant:

TypeScript

```
private getUserDetails(): void {
const aadClient: AadHttpClient = new AadHttpClient(
this.props.context.serviceScope,
"https://graph.microsoft.com"
    );

// Get users with givenName, surname, or displayName
    aadClient
      .get(
`https://graph.microsoft.com/v1.0/users?$select=displayName,mail,userPrincipalName`,
        AadHttpClient.configurations.v1
      )
      .then(response => {
return response.json();
      })
      .then(json => {
// Prepare the output array
var users: Array<IUserItem> = new Array<IUserItem>();

// Map the JSON response to the output array
        json.value.map((item: any) => {
          users.push( {
            displayName: item.displayName,
            mail: item.mail,
            userPrincipalName: item.userPrincipalName,
          });
        });
```

```
// Update the component state accordingly to the result
this.setState(
      {
         users: users,
      }
    );
  })
  .catch(error => {
    console.error(error);
  });
}
```

Configure your Office 365 Tenant as the First Release Tenant

The MS Graph operation is part of an experimental or preview feature which is only available in the Targeted release (first release) tenants.

Follow below steps to configure the Office 365 tenant as the first release:

1. Open the Office 365 admin center.
2. Go to Settings > Organization profile.
3. Click on Edit against **"Release preferences"**
4. Select the preference:

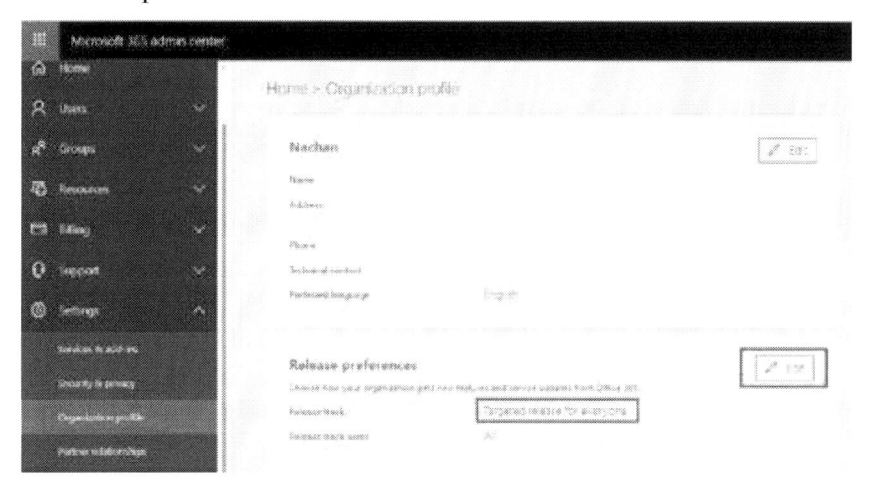

Figre 26.2: Enable Targeted Release on Office 365 Tenant

Test the WebPart

Follow below steps to test the web part on the SharePoint page:

1. At the command prompt, type **"gulp serve"**.
2. Open the SharePoint site. Navigate to /_layouts/15/workbench.aspx
3. Add the webpart to the page:

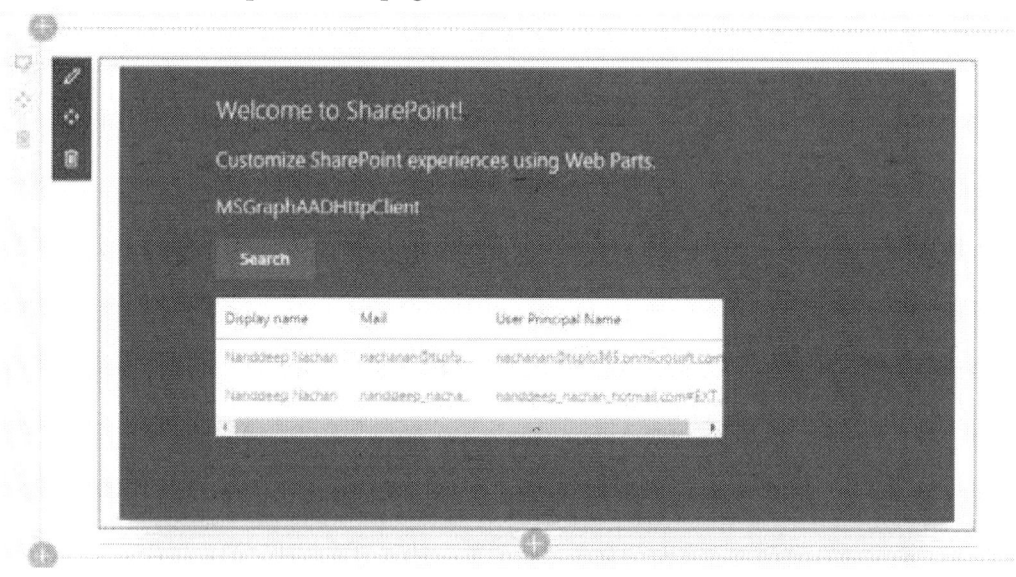

Figure 26.3: Verify the MS Graph API

API Management

In the Production environment, after deploying the web part, follow the given steps to approve API requests:

1. Open SharePoint Admin Center (**https://[tenant]-admin.sharepoint.com**).
2. Click on **Try the preview.**

Figure 26.4: Try the preview of the modern SharePoint Admin center

3. Click on **"API Management"** from the left navigation bar.

4. Approve the pending requests:

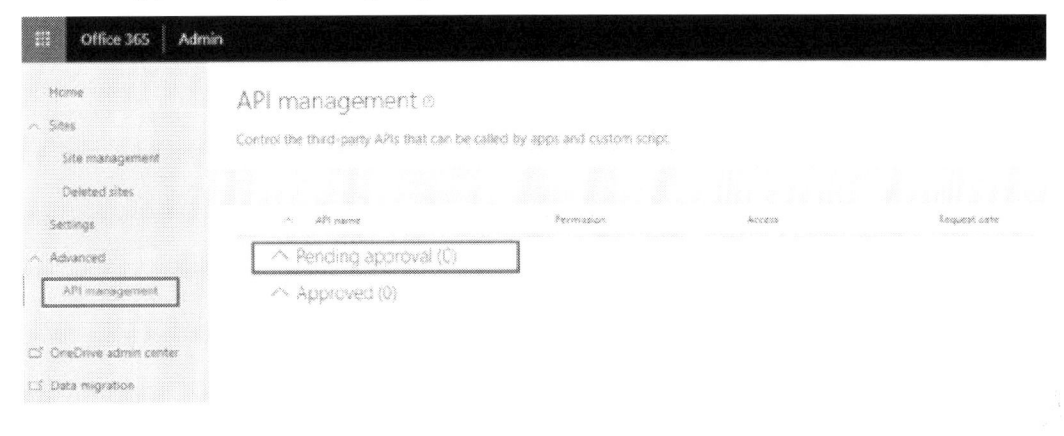

Figure 26.5: Approve pending requests

Conclusion

In this chapter, we explored how to utilize MS Graph in SPFx web parts to retrieve valuable information like user information, and so on. Microsoft Graph offers a wide scope of REST APIs to access appsand services providedby Office 365.

CHAPTER 27
SPFx Logging Mechanism

SharePoint web parts pursue their own lifecycle while executing user requests. Everything looks fine till the time all requests get executed with success and the web part serves the user interactions (with no error). The ungainly minute comes when any user requests come up short and the web part begins showing a blunder message.

SharePoint supports logging. The verbose logging is empowered. SharePoint tracks every action and it makes heaps of logs. In these circumstances, experiencing gigantic logs and finding related data about our mistakes is cumbersome. It is constantly prudent to have our very own logging mechanism executed.

The **SharePoint Framework (SPFx)** additionally has no exception to it and supports logging APIs which can be utilized during the lifecycle of the web part.

Structure
- Understand the Logging
- Overview of the Logging API

Objectives
- Understand logging
- Implementing the logging API in SPFx

Understand the Logging API

The logging levels are predefined:

Logging Level	Definition
Verbose	Denotes lengthy events. Logs nearly everything.
Information	No attention is needed. It gives significant information for monitoring the state of the solution.
Warning	Demonstrates a potential issue or issue that may require consideration. Whenever overlooked, cautioning may bring about an extreme blunder.
Error	Requires earnest consideration. All erroneous events need to be researched.
Critical	Demonstrates a genuine mistake that has caused significant failure in the solution.
None	No logging happens

Verbose is the least significant logging level pursued by information, warning, and error.

Develop the SPFx Solution for Implementing Logging

Open the command prompt. Follow the given steps to create the SPFx solution:

1. Create a directory for the SPFx solution:

    ```
    md logging-mechanism
    ```

2. Navigate to the above created directory:

    ```
    cd logging-mechanism
    ```

3. Run the Yeoman SharePoint Generator to create the SPFx solution:

    ```
    yo @microsoft/sharepoint
    ```

4. The Yeoman generator will display the wizard by asking questions about the solution to be generated:

```
C:\SPFx\logging-mechanism>yo @microsoft/sharepoint
```

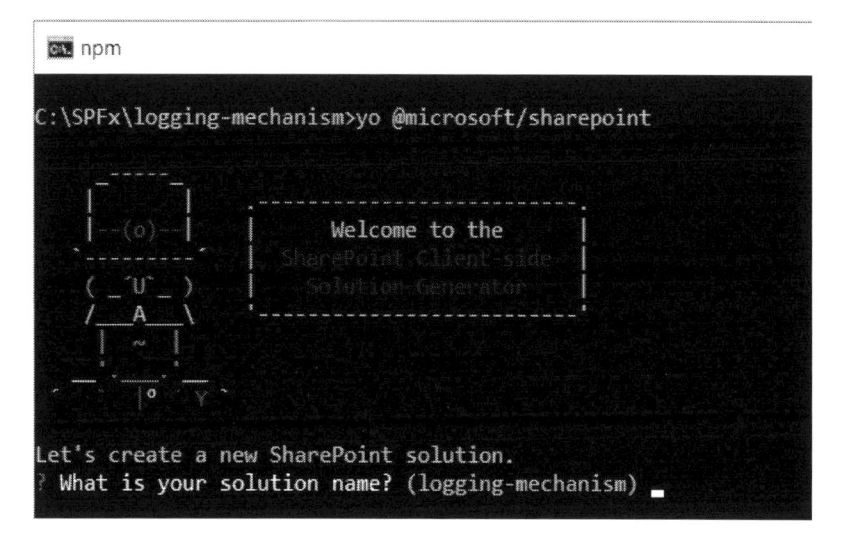

Figure27.1: SPFx Yeoman generator

The SPFx Yeoman generator will display the following wizard of questions:

- **Solution Name:** Specify the name of the SPFx solution. Hit the *Enter* key to go ahead with the default name (logging-mechanism in this case) or type in any other name for your solution.
    - o **Selected choice:** Hit *Enter*
- **The target for the component:** Select the target environment where we are planning to deploy the client web part, i.e. SharePoint Online or SharePoint On-Premises (SharePoint 2016 onwards).
    - o **Selected choice:** SharePoint Online only (latest)
- **Place of files:** Choose the folder location for the SPFx project (either the same folder or a subfolder).
    - o **Selected choice:** Same folder
- **Deployment option:** Selecting Y will allow the app to be deployed instantly to all sites and it will be accessible everywhere.
    - o **Selected choice:** N (install on each site explicitly)
- **Permissions to access web APIs:** Decide whether the components in the solution require permissions to access web APIs that are unique and not shared with other components in the tenant.
    - o **Selected choice:** N (solution contains unique permissions)
- **Type of client-side component to create:** Choose to create a client-side web part or an extension.
    - o **Selected choice:** WebPart

- **Web part name:** Specify the name of the web part. Hit the *Enter* key to go ahead with the default name or type in any other name.
    - **Selected choice:** `SPFxLogHelper`
- **Web part description:** Specify the description of the web part. Hit the *Enter* key to go ahead with the default description or type in any other value.
    - **Selected choice:** Logging with SPFx
- **A framework to use:** Select any JavaScript framework to develop the component. Available choices are No JavaScript Framework, React, and Knockout.
    - **Selected choice:** No JavaScript Framework

5. After the scaffolding is complete, run the following command to lock down the version of project dependencies:

    ```
    npm shrinkwrap
    ```

6. At the command prompt, type the following command to open the solution in the code editor of your choice:

    ```
    code .
    ```

Exploring the Logging API

Logging is supported out of the box in the SharePoint Framework solutions. To use logs in SPFx solution, add the following import statement:

TypeScript

```
import { Log } from'@microsoft/sp-core-library';
```

Define the log source to use as follows:

TypeScript

```
constSPFX_LOG_SOURCE: string = 'SPFxLogHelper';
```

Log the messages from the web part as follows:

TypeScript

```
@override
public onInit(): Promise<void> {
Log.info(SPFX_LOG_SOURCE, 'Hello from SPFx Log');
Log.info(SPFX_LOG_SOURCE, JSON.stringify(this.properties, undefined, 2));
Log.info(SPFX_LOG_SOURCE, `Access the strings as "${strings.BasicGroupName}"`);
```

```
return Promise.resolve<void>();
}
```

The Log class defines four strategies to log the data. Each one describes a comparing log level: verbose, information, warning, and error. The first parameter is the logging location. As a matter of fact, it is the name of the web part. In any case, it can be superseded. The following parameter is the message to be logged. Alternatively, we can determine the service scope.

The log message appears in the browser's console window during debugging:

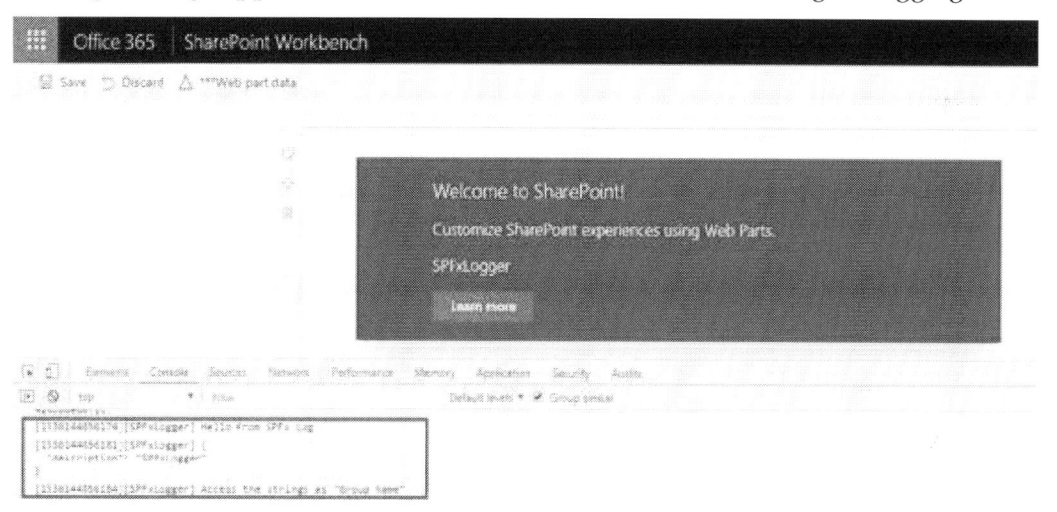

Figure 27.2: Logging in the browser console

Conclusion

In this chapter, we discussed about logging and the Logging API. We learned how to utilize the logs viably to get benefits out of it while investigating the cause of the error. We must try not to utilize the logging exorbitantly yet astutely to help get to the root cause effectively.

CHAPTER 28
Debug SPFx Solutions

In the developer's life, code working on one environment might not work on other environments. Every user and environment is unique, so this can be caused by anything. The best possible approach to tackle these issues is by debugging the situation and finding the root cause of the issue.

Structure

- Debugging with a Browser
- Debug While Developing
- Debug with Visual Studio Code
- Get the Debugger Extension
- Debugging on the Local Workbench
- Debugging on the Hosted Workbench

Objectives

- Debug the SPFx solutions with a browser
- Debug the solution while developing
- Debug the SPFx solutions with Visual Studio Code

Develop the SharePoint Framework Web Part

Open the command prompt. Follow the given steps to create the SPFx solution:

1. Create a directory for the SPFx solution:

   ```
   md debug-spfx-solution
   ```

2. Navigate to the above created directory:

   ```
   cd debug-spfx-solution
   ```

3. Run the Yeoman SharePoint Generator to create the SPFx solution:

   ```
   yo @microsoft/sharepoint
   ```

4. The Yeoman generator will run through the wizard by asking questions about the SPFx solution to be generated:

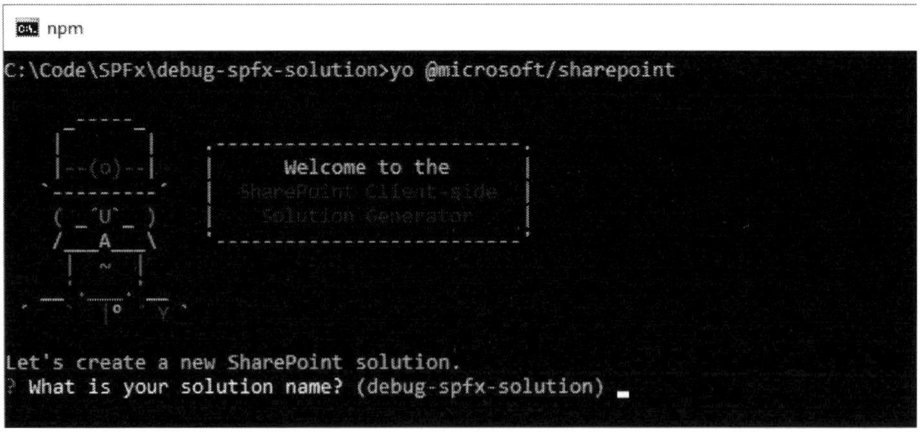

Figure 28.1: SPFx Yeoman generator

The SPFx Yeoman generator will display the following wizard of questions:

- **Solution Name:** Specify the name of the SPFx solution. Hit the *Enter* key to go ahead with the default name (`debug-spfx-solution` in this case) or type in any other name for your solution.
  - **Selected choice:** Hit *Enter*

- **The target for the component:** Specify the target environment to develop and deploy the SPFx solution. Choose from SharePoint Online or SharePoint On-Premises environment.
  - **Selected choice:** SharePoint Online only (latest)

- **Place of files:** Choose the folder location for the SPFx project (either the same folder or a subfolder).
    - **Selected choice:** Same folder
- **Deployment option:** Specify Y to allow the deployment of the app instantly to all the sites, N otherwise.
    - **Selected choice:** N (install on each site explicitly)
- **Permissions to access Web APIs:** Decide whether the components in the solution require permissions to access web APIs.
    - **Selected choice:** N (No explicit permissions are required)
- **Type of client-side component to create:** Choose to create a client-side web part or an extension.
    - **Selected choice:** WebPart
- **Web part name:** Specify the name of the web part. Hit the *Enter* key to go ahead with the default name or type in any other name.
    - **Selected choice:** DebugSPFx
- **Web part description:** Specify the description of the web part. Hit the *Enter* key to go ahead with the default description or type in any other value.
    - **Selected choice:** Debugging SPFx solutions
- **A framework to use:** Select any JavaScript framework to develop the component. The available choices are No JavaScript Framework, React, and Knockout.
    - **Selected choice:** React

5. After the scaffolding process is complete, run the following command to lock down the version of project dependencies:
```
npm shrinkwrap
```
6. At the command prompt, type the following command to open the solution in the code editor of your choice:
```
code .
```

Run the SPFx WebPart

Follow below steps to run the SPFx Web Part:
1. At the command prompt, type `'gulp serve'`.
2. Open the SharePoint site.
3. Navigate to `/_layouts/15/workbench.aspx`.

4. Add the webpart to the page:

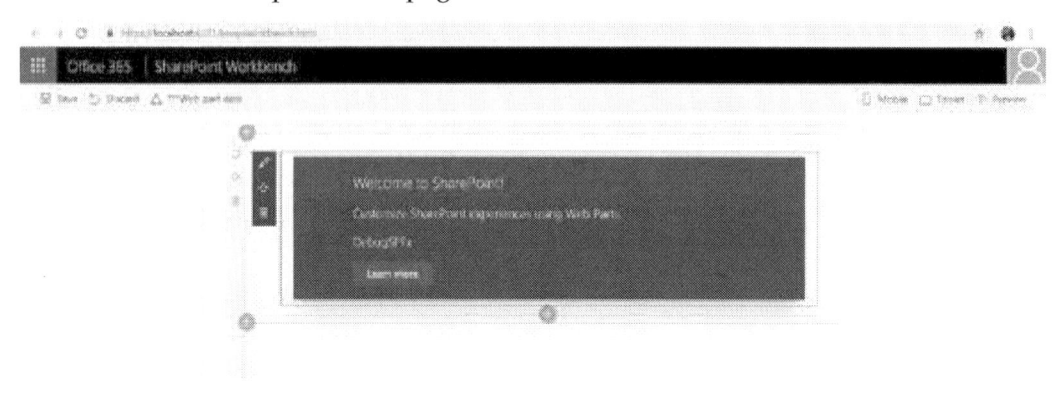

Figure 28.2: Add the SPFx web part to the SharePoint page

Debugging with a Browser

The SharePoint Framework is simply created using HTML and JavaScript code. The principal thought that rings a bell is open the developer tool of the browser and investigate the JavaScript code.

In the browser, hit *F12* to open the developer tool and observe the console:

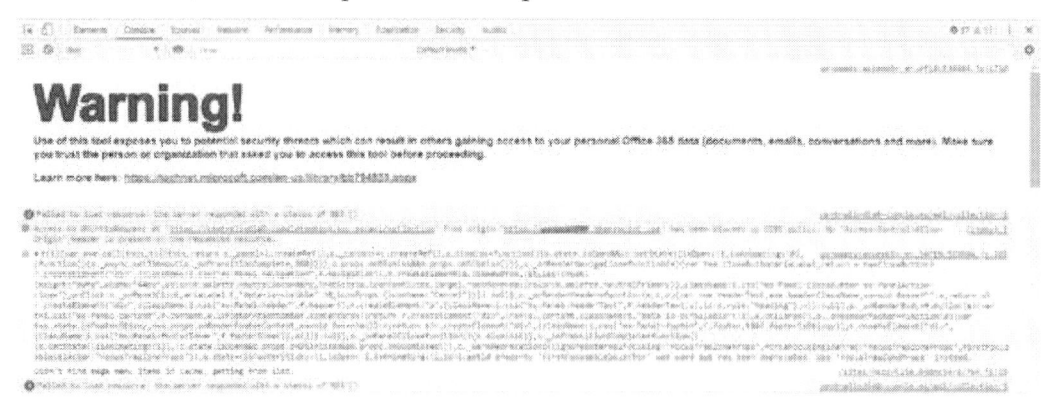

Figure 28.3: Debugging with browser

The console is loaded with a log. There are a few errors; however, these are not generated from our code, but they are generated from the workbench itself.

Additionally, note that the production bundles for SharePoint Framework solutions are minimized. Troubleshooting the minimized code is never simple to bring up the precise error. Google Chrome has the capacity to change this revolting code:

Figure 28.4: Pretty-print this minified file

Click on **Pretty-print this minified file?** and it will transform the minimized ugly code into pretty code.

Debug while developing

In usual cases, we need to debug our written code and not the minimized and bundled code.

1. At the command prompt, type '`gulp serve --nobrowser`'.
2. Append the following to the URL:

```
?loadSPFX=true&debugManifestsFile=https://localhost:4321/temp/manifests.js
```

3. Click on **Load debug scripts**:

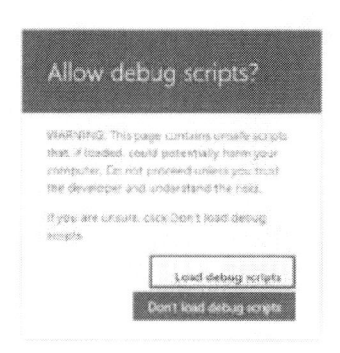

Figure 28.5: Debug in browser

4. From the **Sources** tab, open your code file and start debugging by setting up the debug points:

Figure 28.6: Debug in browser

In this way, we are loading the webpart to debug in our local instance of the browser. The enablement of debug points will not stop the work of any other developers as in the server-side object model days.

Debug with Visual Studio Code

SPFx solutions can be easily debugged in VS Code using debugger extensions. This gives the comfort of developing, testing and debugging the SPFx solution from the same IDE.

Get the Debugger Extension

Follow below steps to get the debugger extension:
1. In visual studio code, click on Extensions from the left-hand side menu.
2. Search for the debugger:

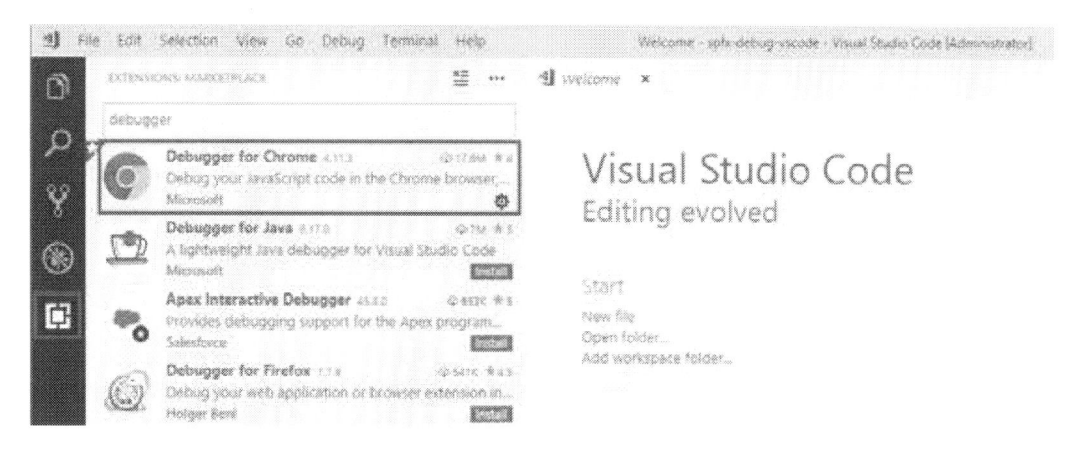

Figure 28.7: VS Code debugger extension

3. Select and install **Debugger for Chrome**, if not installed already.
4. Open launch.json from the .vscode folder. This file contains configurations for a local workbench and hosted workbench:

JSON

```
{
/**

    * Install Chrome Debugger Extension for Visual Studio Code to debug your components with the

    * Chrome browser: https://aka.ms/spfx-debugger-extensions

    */
"version": "0.2.0",

"configurations": [{

"name": "Local workbench",

"type": "chrome",

"request": "launch",

"url": "https://localhost:4321/temp/workbench.html",

"webRoot": "${workspaceRoot}",

"sourceMaps": true,

"sourceMapPathOverrides": {

"webpack:///../././src/*": "${webRoot}/src/*",

"webpack:///../../../src/*": "${webRoot}/src/*",
```

```
            "webpack:///../../../../../src/*": "${webRoot}/src/*",
            "webpack:///../../../../../../src/*": "${webRoot}/src/*"
                },
        "runtimeArgs": [
        "--remote-debugging-port=9222"
                ]
            },
            {
        "name": "Hosted workbench",
        "type": "chrome",
        "request": "launch",
        "url": "https://enter-your-SharePoint-site/_layouts/workbench.aspx",
        "webRoot": "${workspaceRoot}",
        "sourceMaps": true,
        "sourceMapPathOverrides": {
        "webpack:///../././src/*": "${webRoot}/src/*",
        "webpack:///../../../src/*": "${webRoot}/src/*",
        "webpack:///../../../../../src/*": "${webRoot}/src/*",
        "webpack:///../../../../../../src/*": "${webRoot}/src/*"
                },
        "runtimeArgs": [
        "--remote-debugging-port=9222",
        "-incognito"
                ]
            }
        ]
    }
```

Debugging on the Local Workbench

Follow below steps to start the debug process on the local workbench:

1. Open the main webpart file (src\webparts\spFxDebug\SpFxDebugWebPart.ts) and set the debug point to the render method.
2. Click on **View>Terminal** to open the terminal window:

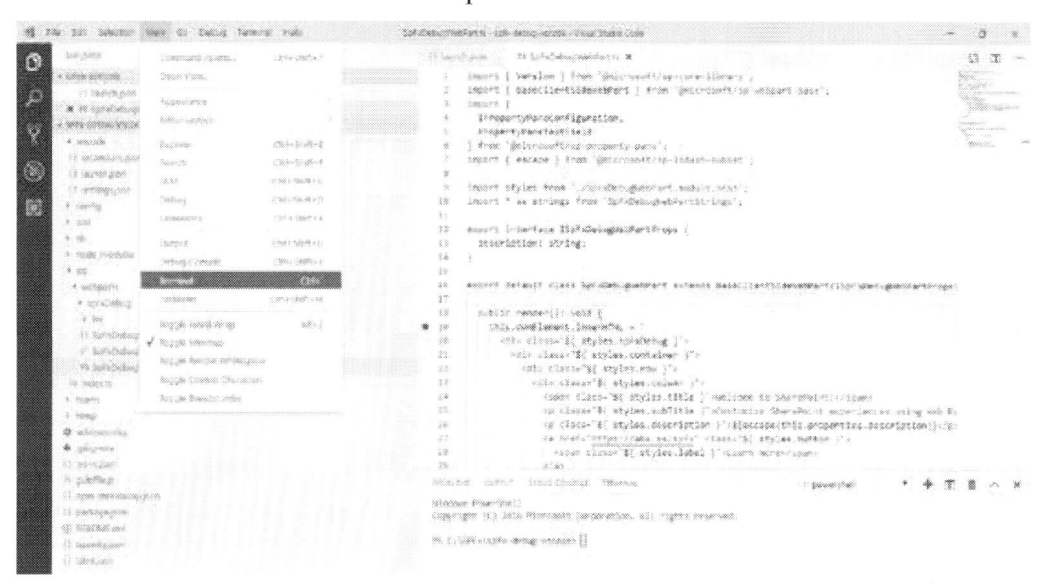

Figure 28.8: Debugging on Local Workbench

3. In the terminal window, type the following command:

```
gulp serve --nobrowser
```

Now that we are ready to debug our code in VS Code, use any of the following options to start debugging:

1. On the keyboard, press F5.
2. From the main menu, click on **Debug>Start Debugging**.

3. From the left-hand side menu, click on **Debug** and start debugging by clicking on the green arrow.

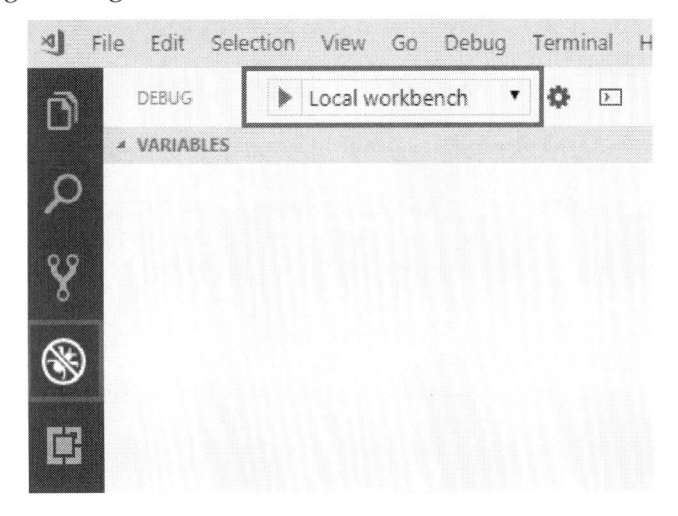

Figure 28.9: Start debugging on the Local Workbench

Debugging on the Hosted Workbench

Follow the given steps to debug on the real SharePoint site:

1. From VS Code, open `launch.js` on under the `.vscode` folder.
2. In the `Hosted workbench` configuration, type your SharePoint online site address for the URL property.
3. Optionally, remove `-incognito` from `runtimeArgs`:

```
{
  "name": "Hosted workbench",
  "type": "chrome",
  "request": "launch",
  "url": "https://contoso.sharepoint.com/_layouts/workbench.aspx",
  "webRoot": "${workspaceRoot}",
  "sourceMaps": true,
  "sourceMapPathOverrides": {
    "webpack:///../../src/*": "${webRoot}/src/*",
    "webpack:///../../../src/*": "${webRoot}/src/*",
    "webpack:///../../../../src/*": "${webRoot}/src/*",
    "webpack:///../../../../../src/*": "${webRoot}/src/*"
  },
  "runtimeArgs": [
    "--remote-debugging-port=9222",
    "-incognito"
  ]
}
```

Figure 28.10: Debugging on the Hosted Workbench

4. From the debug menu, select **Hosted workbench**:

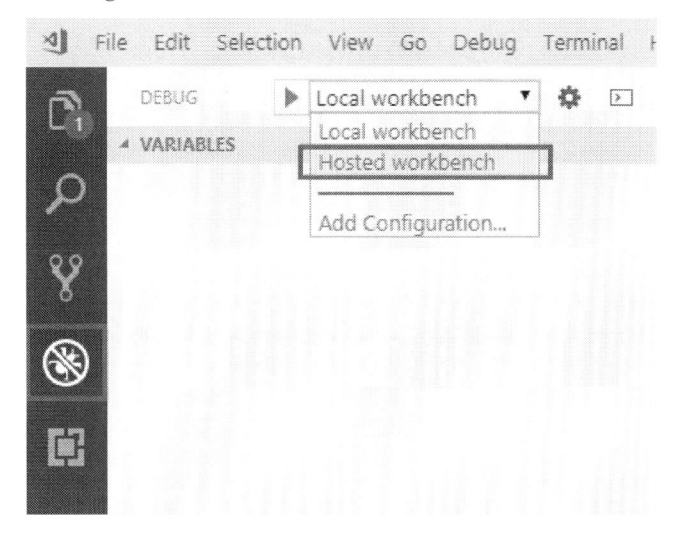

Figure 28.11: Debugging on the Hosted Workbench

Conclusion

In this chapter, we discussed the significance of troubleshooting/debugging. We learned how to debug the SPFx solutions with a browser, visual studio code debugger extension and troubleshooting the solution during development.

Troubleshooting is fundamental to identify and resolve the issues. As the SharePoint framework client-side web parts are created utilizing JavaScript, they can be effectively debugged in the browser. The `loadSPFx` and `debugManifestFile` query string parameters can be utilized to troubleshoot the code while implementation.

CHAPTER 29
Overview of SPFx Extensions

The **SharePoint Framework (SPFx)** was introduced in February 2017 that changed the perspectives of SharePoint developers. Developers by then started to build and deploy the modern client-side web parts utilizing SPFx solutions over their Office 365 tenants. In the classic SharePoint days, development scenarios were focused around Script Editor Web parts everywhere on SharePoint sites. Troubleshooting the issues to discover which script on the page gets executed in a sequence was questionable. The SharePoint Framework conveyed some governance to developers' lives to address these issues.

Structure
- Introduction to SPFx Extensions
- Develop SPFx Extensions Solutions

Objectives
- Overview of SPFx extensions
- Explore SPFx extension types

SharePoint Framework Extensions

SPFx Extensions help to expand the SharePoint modern UI, including support for site, list, command extensions, and the Graph HttpClient support. The SharePoint Framework consolidates the following extension types:

Application Customizers:
- Extends predefined HTML element placeholders with custom renderings
- Helps to embed JavaScript on the SharePoint site
- Can be added to any scope, including Site collection, site or list

Field Customizers:
- Allows us to modify the view for fields within a list
- Can be used to override the field presentation in the list
- Can be used with site columns or directly on the field in the list

Command Sets:
- Allows developers to extend command surfaces of SharePoint to add new actions, along with the client-side code that can be used to implement behaviors
- Can be used to provide action buttons to the list
- Supports the toolbar and context menu

Update the SPFxYeoman Generator

Microsoft releases frequent updates to the SharePoint Framework with new updates for web parts and extensions. Follow the given steps to check the available updates for SPFx:

1. Open the command prompt.
2. Type the following command:

```
yo
```

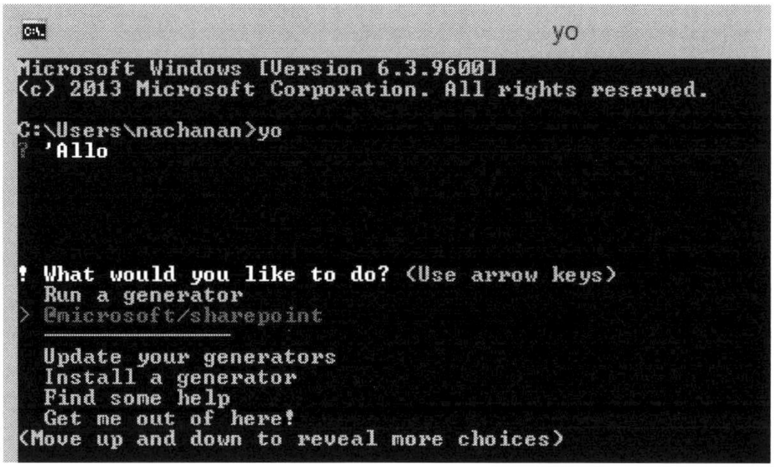

Figure 29.1: Check for updates

3. Select the '**Update your generators**' option.
4. Select @microsoft/generator-sharepoint.
5. Hit *Enter* to update the microsoft/generator-sharepoint.

Useful commands:

1. Update your SharePoint Framework Yeoman generator:

   ```
   npm update -g @microsoft/generator-sharepoint@latest
   ```

   If there are no updates available, the command will basically return.

2. Check the SharePoint Framework Yeoman Generator version:

   ```
   npm view @microsoft/generator-sharepoint version
   ```

3. Listthe specific npm package:

   ```
   npm list -g @microsoft/generator-sharepoint
   ```

This command displays information of the installed package on your workstation. Optionally, you may use the -g parameter to get information on the globally installed package.

Create the SharePoint Framework Extensions Project

Open the command prompt. Follow the given steps to create the SPFx solution:

1. Create a directory for the SPFx solution:

   ```
   md HelloWorldExtension
   ```

2. Navigate to the above created directory:

   ```
   cd HelloWorldExtension
   ```

3. Run the Yeoman SharePoint Generator to create the solution:

   ```
   yo @microsoft/sharepoint
   ```

4. The Yeoman generator will display the wizard by asking questions about the solution to be generated:

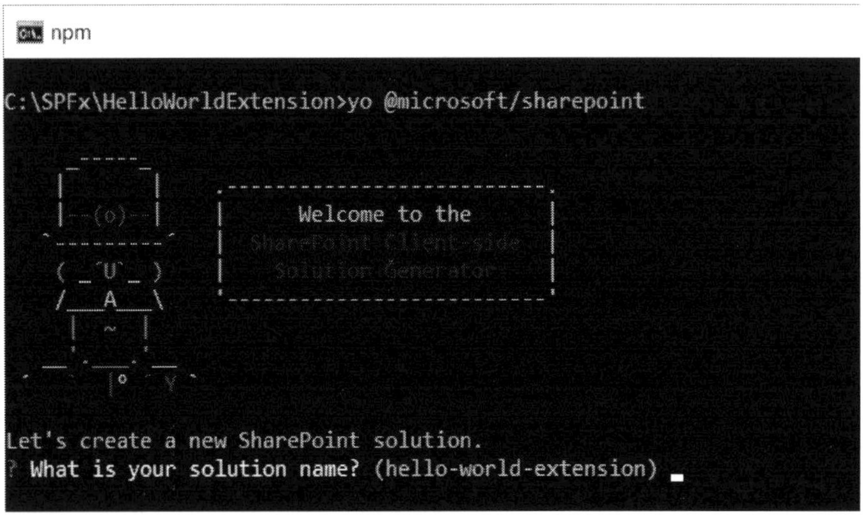

Figure 29.2: SPFx Yeoman generator

The SPFx Yeoman generator will display the following wizard of questions:
- **Solution Name:** Specify the name of the SPFx solution. Hit the *Enter* key to go ahead with the default name (`hello-world-extension` in this case) or type in any other name for your solution.
    - o **Selected choice:** Hit *Enter*
- **The target for the component:** Specify the target environment to develop and deploy the SPFx solution. Choose from SharePoint Online or SharePoint On-Premises environment.
    - o **Selected choice:** SharePoint Online only (latest)
- **Place of files:** Choose the folder location for the SPFx project (either the same folder or a subfolder).
    - o **Selected choice:** Same folder
- **Deployment option:** Specify Y to allow the deployment of the app instantly to all the sites, N otherwise.
    - o **Selected choice:** N (install on each site explicitly)

- **Permissions to access web APIs:** Decide whether the components in the solution require permissions to access web APIs that are unique and not shared with other components in the tenant.

    o **Selected choice:** N (solution contains unique permissions)

- **Type of client-side component to create:** Choose to create a client-side web part or an extension.

    o **Selected choice:** Extension

- **Type of client-side extension to create:** Choose to create the type of extension to create (Application customizer, Field customizer, or ListView Command Set).

    o **Selected choice:** Application customizer

- **Application customizer name:** Specify the name of the extension. Hit the *Enter* key to go ahead with the default name or type in any other name.

    o **Selected choice:** AppCustomizer

- **Application customizer description:** Specify the description of the extension. Hit the *Enter* key to go ahead with the default description or type in any other value.

    o **Selected choice:** SPFx Application Customier

5. After the scaffolding process is complete, run the following command to lock down the version of project dependencies:

    ```
    npm shrinkwrap
    ```

6. At the command prompt, type the following command to open the solution in the code editor of your choice:

    ```
    code .
    ```

Conclusion

In this chapter, we explored SPFx extensions and their types. SharePoint Framework extensions help to extend further the SharePoint modern UI. Application Customizers, Field Customizers, and Command Sets are the accessible extension types that help expand the SharePoint site.

In the subsequent chapters, we will explore each of the extension types in detail.

CHAPTER 30
SPFx Extensions- Application Customizer

SharePoint Framework (SPFx) Extensions permit expanding the SharePoint user experience. Utilizing SharePoint Framework Extensions, we can by and large modify the SharePoint user experience, including notification areas, list views, and toolbars. In this chapter, we will discuss the Application Customizer part of SharePoint extensions.

Structure
- Overview of an Application Customizer
- Develop an Application Customizer

Objectives
- Get introduced to an Application customizer
- Develop an Application customizer
- Explore extension types

Overview of an Application Customizer

The application customizer gives access to predefined areas on the SharePoint page and permits you to customize or extend them. In this chapter, we will include the header and footer section to the SharePoint site using the application customizer.

In the classic SharePoint, we used to broaden predefined HTML components or placeholders from the master page to show the custom substance. In the modern SharePoint, as JavaScript can't be utilized on the page as the application customizer executes these situations.

Page Placeholders:

The application customizer helps you to get access to the following zones on the Modern SharePoint page:
- **Top:** Header section of the page
- **Bottom:** Footer section of the page

Application Customizer the SPFx Solution

Open the command prompt. Follow the given steps to create the SPFx solution:

1. Create a directory for the SPFx solution:

    ```
    md spfx-extensions-applicationcustomizer
    ```

2. Navigate to the above created directory:

    ```
    cd spfx-extensions-applicationcustomizer
    ```

3. Run the Yeoman SharePoint Generator to create the solution:

    ```
    yo @microsoft/sharepoint
    ```

4. The Yeoman generator will display the wizard by asking questions about the solution to be generated:

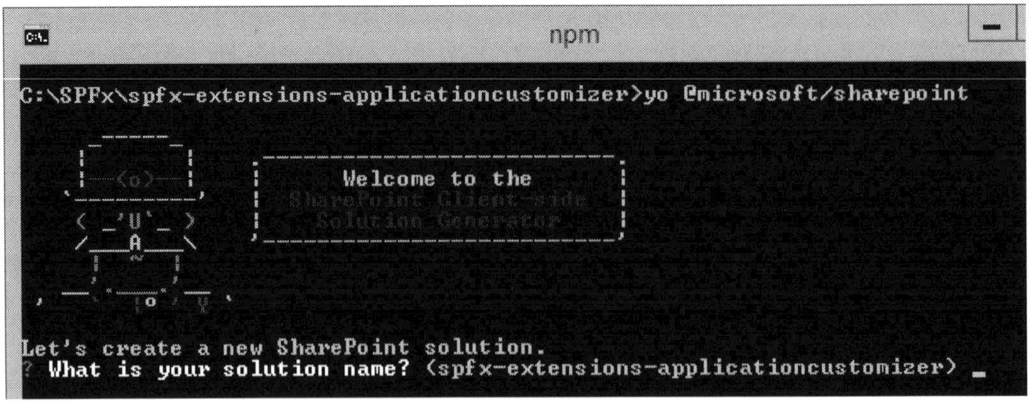

Figure 30.1: SPFx Yeoman generator

The SPFx Yeoman generator will display the following wizard of questions:

- **Solution Name:** Specify the name of the SPFx solution. Hit the *Enter* key to go ahead with the default name (`spfx-extensions-applicationcustomizer` in this case) or type in any other name for your solution.
    - **Selected choice:** Hit *Enter*
- **The target for the component:** Specify the target environment to develop and deploy the SPFx solution. Choose from any SharePoint Online or SharePoint On-Premises environment.
    - **Selected choice:** SharePoint Online only (latest)
- **Place of files:** Choose the folder location for the SPFx project (either the same folder or a subfolder).
    - **Selected choice:** Same folder
- **Deployment option:** Specify Y to allow the deployment of the app instantly to all the sites, N otherwise.
    - **Selected choice:** N (install on each site explicitly)
- **Permissions to access web APIs:** Decide whether the components in the solution require permissions to access web APIs that are unique and not shared with other components in the tenant.
    - **Selected choice:** N (solution contains unique permissions)
- **Type of client-side component to create:** Choose to create a client-side web part or an extension.
    - **Selected choice:** Extension
- **Type of client-side extension to create:** Choose to create the type of extension to be created (Application customizer, Field customizer, or ListView Command Set).
    - **Selected choice:** Application customizer
- **Application customizer name:** Specify the name of the extension. Hit the *Enter* key to go ahead with the default name or type in any other name.
    - **Selected choice:** `CustomHeaderFooter`
- **Application customizer description:** Specify the description of the extension. Hit the *Enter* key to go ahead with the default description or type in any other value.
    - **Selected choice:** Adds the custom header and footer to the SharePoint site

5. After the scaffolding process is complete, run the following command to lock down the version of project dependencies:

```
npm shrinkwrap
```

6. At the command prompt, type the following command to open the solution in the code editor of your choice:

```
code .
```

Solution Structure

The solution structure of an extension is similar to client-side web parts with comparative configuration options:

```
EXPLORER
▲ OPEN EDITORS
▲ SPFX-EXTENSIONS-APPLICATIONCUSTOMIZER
  ▷ .vscode
  ▷ config
  ▷ node_modules
  ▷ sharepoint
  ▲ src
    ▲ extensions
      ▲ customHeaderFooter
        ▲ loc
            en-us.js
            myStrings.d.ts
          CustomHeaderFooterApplicationCustomizer.manifest.json
          CustomHeaderFooterApplicationCustomizer.ts
      index.ts
  .editorconfig
  .gitignore
  .yo-rc.json
  gulpfile.js
  npm-shrinkwrap.json
  package.json
  README.md
  tsconfig.json
  tslint.json
```

Figure 30.2: Solution structure

The `CustomHeaderFooterApplicationCustomizer.manifest.json` file inside the '\src\extensions\customHeaderFooter\' folder defines the extension type and unique identifier for the solution. Please note down the id. We will need it later for debugging purpose:

JSON

```
{
"$schema": "https://developer.microsoft.com/json-schemas/spfx/
client-side-extension-manifest.schema.json",

"id": "f58a0902-c9d8-4cce-bd5e-4da887e21bed",

"alias": "CustomHeaderFooterApplicationCustomizer",

"componentType": "Extension",

"extensionType": "ApplicationCustomizer",


// The "*" signifies that the version should be taken from the
package.json
"version": "*",

"manifestVersion": 2,


// If true, the component can only be installed on sites where
Custom Script is allowed.

// Components that allow authors to embed arbitrary script code
should set this to true.

// https://support.office.com/en-us/article/Turn-scripting-
capabilities-on-or-off-1f2c515f-5d7e-448a-9fd7-835da935584f

"requiresCustomScript": false
}
```

Implement the Application Customizer

Open `CustomHeaderFooterApplicationCustomizer.ts` from the "\src\extensions\customHeaderFooter\" folder.

To get access to placeholders on the page, run the following imports:

TypeScript

```
import {
  BaseApplicationCustomizer,
  PlaceholderContent,
  PlaceholderName
} from '@microsoft/sp-application-base';
```

Update the `IAlertApplicationCustomizerProperties` interface to include the Top and Bottom properties:

TypeScript

```
exportinterface ICustomHeaderFooterApplicationCustomizerProperties {
  Top: string;
  Bottom: string;
}
```

Implement the `OnInit` method:

TypeScript

```
public onInit(): Promise<void> {
    Log.info(LOG_SOURCE, `Initialized ${strings.Title}`);

// Added to handle possible changes on the existence of placeholders.
this.context.placeholderProvider.changedEvent.add(this, this._renderPlaceHolders);

// Call render method for generating the HTML elements.
this._renderPlaceHolders();

return Promise.resolve();
  }
```

Implement the `_renderPlaceHolders` method to handle the top and bottom placeholders:

TypeScript

```
private _renderPlaceHolders(): void {
    console.log('HelloWorldApplicationCustomizer._renderPlaceHolders()');
      console.log('Available placeholders: ',
this.context.placeholderProvider.placeholderNames.map(name => PlaceholderName[name]).join(', '));

// Handling the top placeholder
if (!this._topPlaceholder) {
```

```
this._topPlaceholder =
this.context.placeholderProvider.tryCreateContent(
        PlaceholderName.Top,
        { onDispose: this._onDispose });

// The extension should not assume that the expected placeholder is available.
if (!this._topPlaceholder) {
        console.error('The expected placeholder (Top) was not found.');
return;
    }

if (this.properties) {
let topString: string = this.properties.Top;
if (!topString) {
        topString = '(Top property was not defined.)';
    }

if (this._topPlaceholder.domElement) {
this._topPlaceholder.domElement.innerHTML = `
<div class="${styles.app}">
<div class="ms-bgColor-themeDark ms-fontColor-white ${styles.top}">
<i class="ms-Icon ms-Icon--Info" aria-hidden="true"></i>${escape(topString)}
</div>
</div>`;
        }
      }
    }


// Handling the bottom placeholder
if (!this._bottomPlaceholder) {
```

```
this._bottomPlaceholder =
this.context.placeholderProvider.tryCreateContent(
        PlaceholderName.Bottom,
        { onDispose: this._onDispose });

// The extension should not assume that the expected placeholder is available.
if (!this._bottomPlaceholder) {
        console.error('The expected placeholder (Bottom) was not found.');
return;
    }

if (this.properties) {
let bottomString: string = this.properties.Bottom;
if (!bottomString) {
        bottomString = '(Bottom property was not defined.)';
    }

if (this._bottomPlaceholder.domElement) {
this._bottomPlaceholder.domElement.innerHTML = `
<div class="${styles.app}">
<div class="ms-bgColor-themeDark ms-fontColor-white ${styles.bottom}">
<i class="ms-Icon ms-Icon--Info" aria-hidden="true"></i>${escape(bottomString)}
</div>
</div>`;
        }
      }
    }
  }
```

Use `this.context.placeholderProvider.tryCreateContent` to get access to the placeholder, without assuming that the placeholder will exist.

Custom Styles:

Add the `CustomHeaderFooterApplicationCustomizer.module.scss` file under the "\src\extensions\customHeaderFooter\" folder:

scss

```scss
.app {
.top {
height:60px;
text-align:center;
line-height:2.5;
font-weight:bold;
display: flex;
align-items: center;
justify-content: center;
    }

.bottom {
height:40px;
text-align:center;
line-height:2.5;
font-weight:bold;
display: flex;
align-items: center;
justify-content: center;
    }
  }
```

Include the styles in the `CustomHeaderFooterApplicationCustomizer.ts` extension:

TypeScript

```typescript
import styles from './CustomHeaderFooterApplicationCustomizer.module.scss';
```

Test the extension

Follow below steps to test the extension on the SharePoint page:

1. Open serve.json under the config folder.
2. Update the properties section to include the Top and Bottom messages:

   JSON

   ```json
   {
   "$schema": "https://developer.microsoft.com/json-schemas/core-build/serve.schema.json",
   "port": 4321,
   "https": true,
   "serveConfigurations": {
   "default": {
   "pageUrl": "https://contoso.sharepoint.com/sites/mySite/SitePages/myPage.aspx",
   "customActions": {
   "f58a0902-c9d8-4cce-bd5e-4da887e21bed": {
   "location": "ClientSideExtension.ApplicationCustomizer",
   "properties": {
   "Top": "Header of the page",
   "Bottom": "Footer of the page"
   }
   }
   }
   }
   },
   "customHeaderFooter": {
   "pageUrl": "https://contoso.sharepoint.com/sites/mySite/SitePages/myPage.aspx",
   "customActions": {
   "f58a0902-c9d8-4cce-bd5e-4da887e21bed": {
   "location": "ClientSideExtension.ApplicationCustomizer",
   "properties": {
   ```

```
            "Top": "Header of the page",
            "Bottom": "Footer of the page"
                    }
                }
            }
        }
    }
}
```

3. At the command prompt, type the following command:

   ```
   gulp serve
   ```

4. The SharePoint site will open. Then, click on **"Load debug scripts"**.

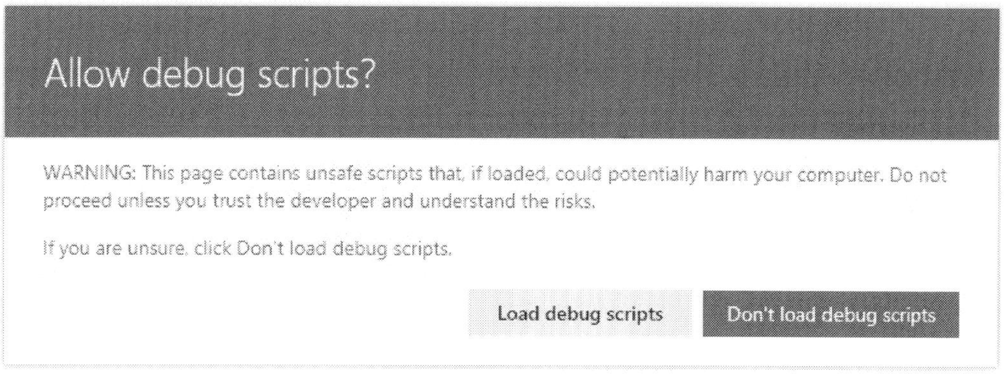

Figure 30.3: Load debug scripts

5. Take a look at the header and footer on the page:

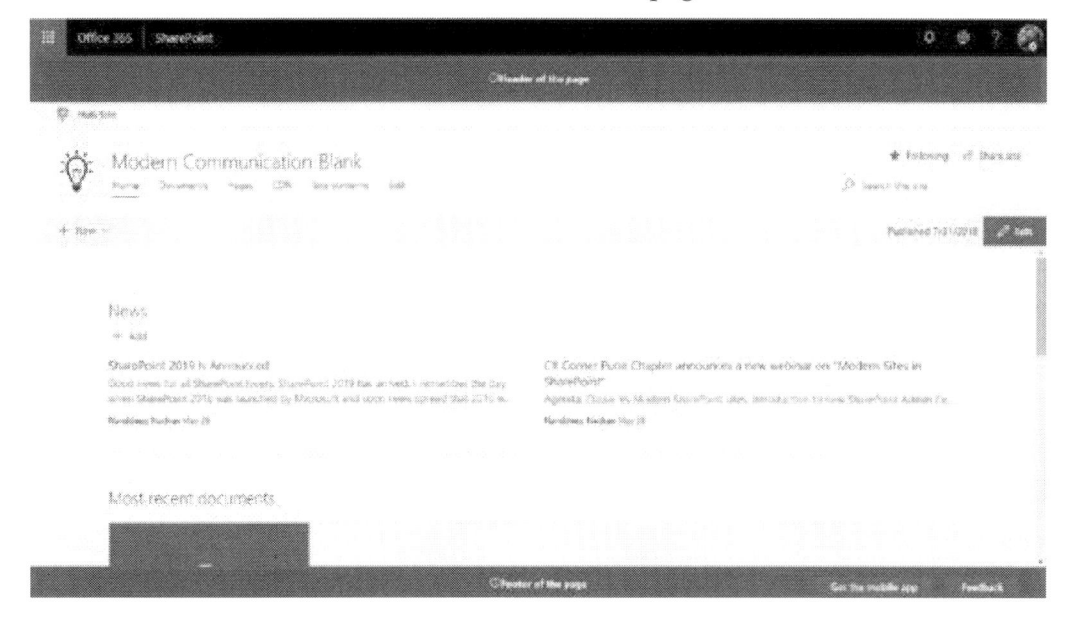

Figure 30.4: Header and footer implementation using the SPFx extension application customizer

Conclusion

In this chapter, we discussed the concept of the application customizer SPFx extension and introduced extension types. The application customizer SharePoint Framework extension broadens the predefined placeholders on the Modern SharePoint page. These extensions can be deployed tenant wide.

In the next chapter, we will go ahead, and use React parts in an application customizer.

CHAPTER 31
Extendan Application Customizer with React Components

SharePoint Framework Extensions broaden the SharePoint user experience by altering pre-defined placeholders of SharePoint portal. At the time of writing this book, we could only expand the top (header) and bottom (footer) placeholders to tweak the header and footer region. React components help to develop the functionality by keeping up the separation of concerns. React components can be utilized as components of an application customizer.

Structure

- Introduction to an Application Customizer
- Extend an Application Customizer with React Components

Objectives

- Application Customizer Implementation
- Utilize React components to extendan Application Customizer

Generate the SPFx Solution for an Application Customizer

Open a command prompt. Follow the given steps to make the SPFx solution:
1. Make a folder for the SPFx solution:

   ```
   md spfx-application-customizer-react
   ```
2. Change the path to the above folder:

   ```
   cd spfx-application-customizer-react
   ```
3. Execute the Yeoman Generator for SharePoint:

   ```
   yo @microsoft/sharepoint
   ```
4. The Yeoman generator will run through the wizard to ask questions about the SPFx solution to be created:

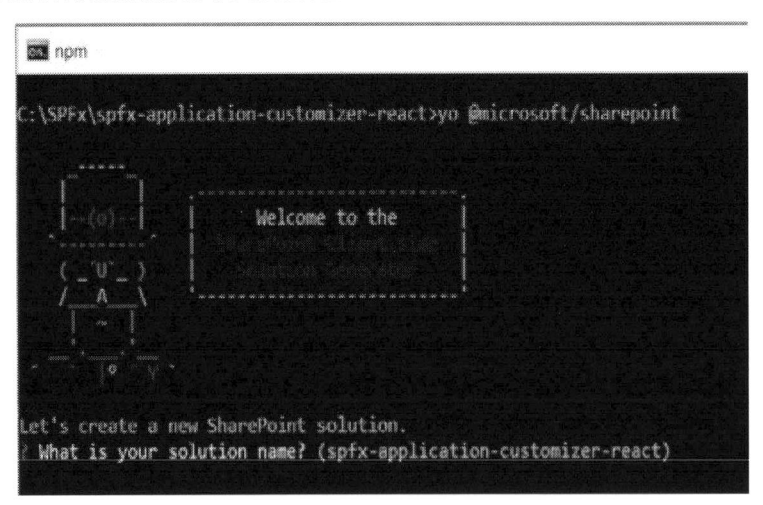

Figure 31.1: SPFx Yeoman generator

The SPFx Yeoman generator will display the following wizard of inquiries:
- **Solution Name:** Determine the SPFx solution name. Hit the *Enter* key to proceed with the default selection (`spfx-application-customizer-react`in this case) or type another name.
    - **Chosen decision:** Hit *Enter*
- **Target environment:** Specify the target environment to deploy the SPFx solution. Select any option from SharePoint Online or SharePoint On-Premises environment.
    - **Chosen decision:** SharePoint Online only (latest)

- **Folder location:** Choose the folder location for the SPFx project (either the same folder or a subfolder).
    - **Chosen decision:** Use the current folder
- **Deployment option:** Specify Y to deploy the app instantly to all the sites, N otherwise.
    - **Chosen decision:** Y
- **Consents to access web APIs:** Decide whether the components in the solution need explicit permission to access web APIs that are unique and not shared with other components in the tenant.
    - **Chosen decision:** N (solution contains unique permissions)
- **Choice of client-side component:** Choose to develop a web part or an extension.
    - **Chosen decision:** Extension
- **Choice of client-side extension:** Decide to develop a type of extension (Application customizer, Field customizer, or ListView Command Set).
    - **Chosen decision:** Application Customizer
- **Application customizer name:** Provide the extension name. Hit the *Enter* key to proceed with the default choice or type another name.
    - **Chosen decision:** `CustomHeaderFooterReact`
- **Application customizer description:** Provide the extension description. Hit the *Enter* key to proceed with the default choice or type another value.
    - **Chosen decision:** Adds the custom header and footer to the SharePoint site

5. After the scaffolding is complete, lock down the version of project dependencies by executing the following command:

    ```
    npm shrinkwrap
    ```

6. At the command prompt, execute the following command to open the solution in the code editor of your choice:

    ```
    code .
    ```

7. Install Office 365 UI Fabric controls with 5.x version:

    ```
    npm install office-ui-fabric-react@5.132.0 --save
    ```

Application Customizer Implementation

In the '\src\extensions\customHeaderFooterReact\' folder, open the CustomHeaderFooterReactApplicationCustomizer.ts file.

To access the placeholders on the SharePoint page, include the following imports:

TypeScript

```
import {
  BaseApplicationCustomizer,
  PlaceholderContent,
  PlaceholderName
} from'@microsoft/sp-application-base';
```

Include the Top and Bottom properties to the ICustomHeaderFooterReactApplicationCustomizerPropertiesinterface:

TypeScript

```
exportinterface ICustomHeaderFooterReactApplicationCustomizerProperties {
    Bottom: string;
}
```

The OnInit method is executed during the initiation of the web part and it is used here to bind the events to the placeholders. Implement the OnInit method:

TypeScript

```
private _footerPlaceholder: PlaceholderContent | undefined;

public onInit(): Promise<void> {
    Log.info(LOG_SOURCE, `Initialized ${strings.Title}`);

// Handle possible changes on the placeholders existence.
this.context.placeholderProvider.changedEvent.add(this, this._renderPlaceHolders);

// Generate HTML elements.
this._renderPlaceHolders();
return Promise.resolve();
    }
```

The _renderPlaceHolderscustom method finds the Bottom placeholder and renders its content. Implement the _renderPlaceHolders method:

TypeScript

```
private _renderPlaceHolders(): void {
    console.log('Accessible placeholders: ',
this.context.placeholderProvider.placeholderNames.map(name => PlaceholderName[name]).join(', '));

// Handle bottom (footer) placeholder
if (!this._footerPlaceholder) {
this._footerPlaceholder =
this.context.placeholderProvider.tryCreateContent(
        PlaceholderName.Bottom,
        { onDispose: this._onDispose });

// Do not assume existence of placeholder.
if (!this._footerPlaceholder) {
        console.error('The Bottom placeholder was not found.');
return;
    }
  }
}
```

Use this.context.placeholderProvider.tryCreateContent to access the placeholder on the SharePoint site. Do not assume the existence of the placeholder.

The _onDisposecustom method is called during the dispose of the custom placeholder. Implement the _onDispose method:

TypeScript

```
private _onDispose(): void {
  console.log('[CustomHeaderFooterReactApplicationCustomizer._onDispose] Disposed custom bottom placeholder.');
}
```

Implement the React Component as the Footer

Add a new file to the solution named `ReactFooter.tsx`:

TypeScript
```
import *as React from "react";
import { Link } from 'office-ui-fabric-react/lib/Link';
import { CommandBar } from 'office-ui-fabric-react/lib/CommandBar';

export interface IReactFooterProps {}

export default class ReactFooter extends React.Component<IReactFooterProps> {
constructor(props: IReactFooterProps) {
super(props);
  }

public render(): JSX.Element {
return (
<div className={"ms-bgColor-themeDark ms-fontColor-white"}>
<CommandBar
items={this.getItems()}
/>
</div>
    );
  }

// Data for CommandBar
private getItems = () => {
return [
    {
      key: 'microsoft',
      name: 'Microsoft',
      cacheKey: 'myCacheKey', // changing this key will invalidate this items cache
      iconProps: {
```

```
          iconName: 'AzureLogo'
        },
        href: 'https://www.Microsoft.com'
      },
      {
        key: 'officeUIFabric',
        name: 'Office UI Fabric',
        iconProps: {
          iconName: 'OneDrive'
        },
        href: 'https://dev.office.com/fabric',
        ['data-automation-id']: 'uploadButton'
      }
    ];
  }
}
```

Open the src\extensions\CustomHeaderFooterReact\CustomHeaderFooter ReactApplicationCustomizer.ts file.

Add the following imports:

TypeScript

```
import * as React from "react";

import * as ReactDOM from "react-dom";

import ReactFooter, { IReactFooterProps } from "./ReactFooter";
```

Update the _renderPlaceHolders method to include our React component:

TypeScript

```
private _renderPlaceHolders(): void {
    console.log('Accessible placeholders: ',
this.context.placeholderProvider.placeholderNames.map(name => PlaceholderName[name]).join(', '));

// Handling the bottom placeholder
```

```
if (!this._footerPlaceholder) {
this._footerPlaceholder =
this.context.placeholderProvider.tryCreateContent(
        PlaceholderName.Bottom,
        { onDispose: this._onDispose });

// The extension should not assume that the expected placeholder is available.
if (!this._footerPlaceholder) {
      console.error('The expected placeholder (Bottom) was not found.');
return;
      }

const elem: React.ReactElement<IReactFooterProps> = React.createElement(ReactFooter);
      ReactDOM.render(elem, this._footerPlaceholder.domElement);
   }
  }
```

Test the extension

Follow below steps to test the SPFx extension:

1. In the config folder, open serve.json.
2. Include the page URL to test under the properties section:

    JSON

    ```
    {
    "$schema": "https://developer.microsoft.com/json-schemas/core-build/serve.schema.json",
    "port": 4321,
    "https": true,
    "serveConfigurations": {
    "default": {
    "pageUrl": "https://contoso.sharepoint.com/sites/commsite/SitePages/Home.aspx",
    "customActions": {
    "c633afef-a94d-4970-89ca-30f403612550": {
    ```

```
            "location": "ClientSideExtension.ApplicationCustomizer",
            "properties": {
            "testMessage": "Test message"
                    }
                }
            }
        },
        "CustomHeaderFooterReact": {
        "pageUrl": "https://contoso.sharepoint.com/sites/commsite/SitePages/HomePage.aspx",
        "customActions": {
        "c633afef-a94d-4970-89ca-30f403612550": {
        "location": "ClientSideExtension.ApplicationCustomizer",
        "properties": {
        "testMessage": "Test message"
                }
                }
            }
        }
    }
}
```

3. At the command prompt, execute the following command:

    ```
    gulp serve
    ```

4. Click on **Load debug scripts**, when prompted:

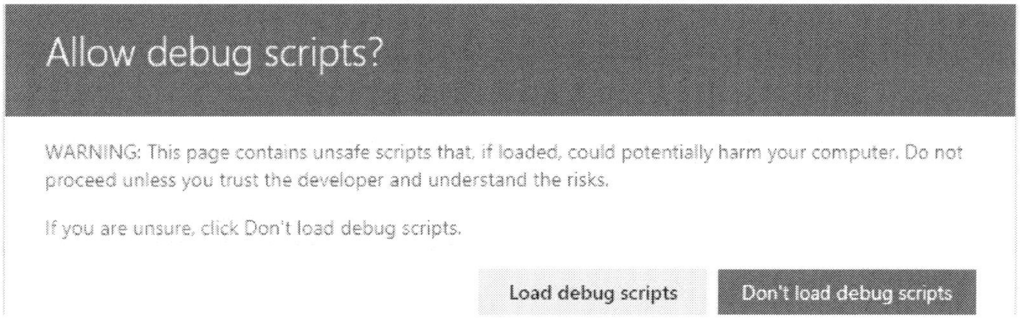

Allow debug scripts?

WARNING: This page contains unsafe scripts that, if loaded, could potentially harm your computer. Do not proceed unless you trust the developer and understand the risks.

If you are unsure, click Don't load debug scripts.

                                        Load debug scripts   Don't load debug scripts

Figure 31.2: Load debug scripts

5. The footer section is now customized:

Figure 31.3: Customized footer with React Components

Conclusion

In this chapter, we explored implementing an Application Customizer using the React component. The SPFx Application customizer extension broadens the predefined placeholders on the Modern SharePoint page. React components help to implement the separation of concerns.

CHAPTER 32
SPFx Extensions- Field Customizer

SharePoint Framework (SPFx) Extensions permit expanding the modern SharePoint experience. Using a field customizer, we can alter the behavior of the field or column inside the SharePoint list view. In this chapter, we will learn about the field customizer part of SharePoint extensions.

Structure
- Introduction to a Field Customizer
- Develop a Field Customizer

Objectives
- Get introduced to a Field customizer
- Develop a Field customizer
- Modify the look and feel of the field inside the SharePoint list view

Overview of a Field Customizer

A field customizer permits changing perspectives for the field inside the SharePoint list view. It may be utilized to abrogate the field representation in the list.

In the classic SharePoint, the representation of SharePoint list fields was customized utilizing JSLink. On the modern SharePoint portal, as JavaScript cannot be embedded, the field customizer is an alternative approach.

Column Formatting VS SPFx Field Customizer

Modern SharePoint supports multiple options to format the column in the SharePoint view. Column formatting is an out-of-the-box solution offered by modern SharePoint, whereas a field customizer requires custom coding efforts.

Column Formatting

Column formatting allows easy formatting of data displayed in the list columns of the SharePoint view. It does not need any extensive technical knowledge and coding skills other than JSON, HTML, and CSS. The user should have permissions to manage views in a list to use this feature.

The formatting option is available to most of the column types, but not for all (e.g. managed metadata, calculated fields, and filename, etc.). This feature is only available on the modern view of lists.

Field Customizer

A field customizer is more powerful than column formatting. It is implemented using custom code. It needs higher permissions to install and apply to the lists. The only disadvantage of this approach is that there might be a delay to display the information.

Develop the SPFx Solution for a Field Customizer

Open a command prompt. Follow the given guidelines to make the SPFx solution:

1. Make a folder for the SPFx solution:

    ```
    md spfx-extensions-fieldcustomizer
    ```

2. Change the path to the above folder:

    ```
    cd spfx-extensions-fieldcustomizer
    ```

3. Execute the Yeoman Generator for SharePoint:

    ```
    yo @microsoft/sharepoint
    ```

4. The Yeoman generator will run through the wizard to ask questions about the SPFx solution to be created:

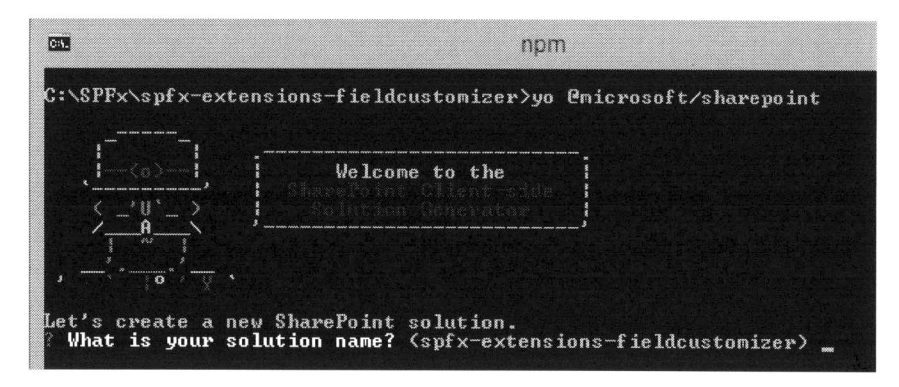

Figure 32.1: SPFx Yeoman generator

The SPFx Yeoman generator will display the following wizard of inquiries:
- **Solution Name:** Determine the SPFx solution name. Hit the *Enter* key to proceed with the default selection (spfx-extensions-fieldcustomizer in this case) or type another name.
    - o **Chosen decision:** Hit *Enter*
- **Target environment:** Specify the target environment to deploy the SPFx solution. Select any option from SharePoint Online or SharePoint On-Premises environment.
    - o **Chosen decision:** SharePoint Online only (latest)
- **Folder location:** Choose the folder location for the SPFx project (either the same folder or a subfolder).
    - o **Chosen decision:** Same folder
- **Deployment option:** Specify Y to deploy the app instantly to all the sites, N otherwise.
    - o **Chosen decision:** N (install on each site explicitly)
- **Consents to access web APIs:** Check whether the components in the solution need explicit permission to access web APIs that are unique and not shared with other components in the tenant.
    - o **Chosen decision:** N (solution contains unique permissions)
- **Choice of client-side component:** Choose to develop a web part or an extension.
    - o **Chosen decision:** Extension
- **Choice of client-side extension:** Decide to develop a type of extension (Application customizer, Field customizer, or ListView Command Set).

- o **Chosen decision:** Field customizer
- **Field customizer name:** Provide the extension name. Hit the *Enter* key to proceed with the default choice or type another name.
  - o **Chosen decision:** `NumberFieldCustomizer`
- **Field customizer description:** Provide the extension description. Hit the *Enter* key to proceed with the default choice or type another value.
  - o **Chosen decision:** Displays the field in percentage
- **A framework to use:** Select any JavaScript framework to develop the component. Available choices are No JavaScript Framework, and React.
  - o **Chosen decision:** No JavaScript Framework

5. After the scaffolding is complete, lock down the version of project dependencies by executing the following command:

```
npm shrinkwrap
```

6. At the command prompt, execute the following command to open the solution in the code editor of your choice:

```
code .
```

Solution Structure

The solution structure is like client-side web parts with similar configuration options.

Figure 32.2: Solution structure

The SPFx extension type and unique identifier of the solution is defined in the NumberFieldCustomizerFieldCustomizer.manifest.js on file inside the '\src\extensions\numberFieldCustomizer\' folder. Note down the id for future debugging purpose:

JSON

```json
{
"$schema": "https://developer.microsoft.com/json-schemas/spfx/client-side-extension-manifest.schema.json",

"id": "93defefb-1f32-4aa4-a402-0f93261c9d6b",

"alias": "NumberFieldCustomizerFieldCustomizer",

"componentType": "Extension",

"extensionType": "FieldCustomizer",

// The "*" signifies that the version should be taken from the package.json
"version": "*",

"manifestVersion": 2,

"requiresCustomScript": false
}
```

Implement the Field Customizer

In the '\src\extensions\numberFieldCustomizer\' folder, open NumberFieldCustomizerFieldCustomizer.ts. The class includes the following useful methods:

- The **onInit()** event occurs well before the page DOM is ready. It returns promise for asynchronous operations.
- The **onRenderCell()** event occurs when each cell is rendered. It gives event.domElement to customize the field representation. This event is invoked after the onInit() promise is resolved.
- The **onDisposeCell()** event avoids any resource leak by free up any utilized resources allocated during the rendering of the field.

Debug Field Customizer

To test the field customizer, we need a SharePoint site with needed list and fields, as it cannot be tested on the SharePoint local workbench.

Follow below steps to debug the field customizer:

1. Open the SharePoint site.

356 ■ Mastering SharePoint Framework

2. From site contents, create a new list named `Projects`:

Figure 32.3: Create a SharePoint list

3. To include a new number field, click on **Add column:**

Figure 32.4: Add a newcolumn to the SharePoint list

4. Name it as **Completion**:

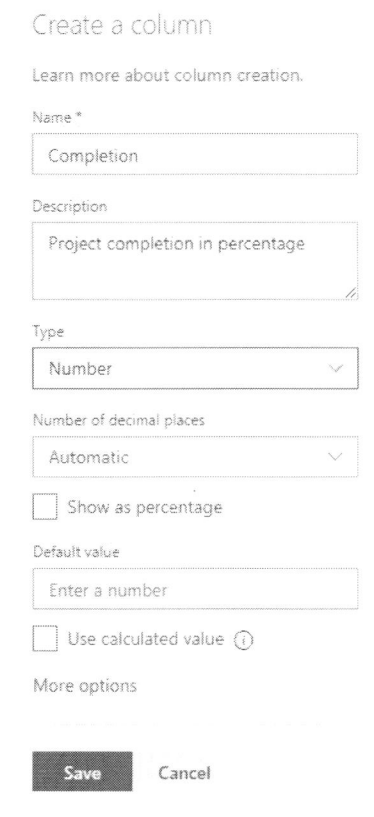

Figure 32.5: Create a column

5. Click on **Save**.
6. Add mock data to the list:

Projects

Title	Completion
Cold Fusion	20
Honeycomb	60
Liberation	75
Phoenix	45
Topaz	100
Whistler	56

Figure 32.6: Add test data to the SharePoint list

Update the Solution for Field changes

Follow below steps to update the InternalFieldName attribute with the name of our field:

1. In the config folder, open the `serve.json` file:

Figure 32.7: serve.json configuration

2. Update the `InternalFieldName` attribute with the name of our field, i.e. Completion:

   JSON

   {

   "$schema": "https://developer.microsoft.com/json-schemas/core-build/serve.schema.json",

   "port": 4321,

   "https": true,

   "serveConfigurations": {

   "default": {

   "pageUrl": "https://contoso.sharepoint.com/sites/mySite/SitePages/myPage.aspx",

   "fieldCustomizers": {

   "Completion": {

   "id": "93defefb-1f32-4aa4-a402-0f93261c9d6b",

   "properties": {

```
            "sampleText": "Value"
                    }
                }
            }
        },
    "NumberFieldCustomizer": {
    "pageUrl": "https://contoso.sharepoint.com/sites/mySite/SitePages/myPage.aspx",
    "fieldCustomizers": {
    "Completion": {
    "id": "93defefb-1f32-4aa4-a402-0f93261c9d6b",
    "properties": {
    "sampleText": "Value"
                }
            }
        }
    }
  }
}
```

3. At the command prompt, type the following command to execute the SPFx extension:

   ```
   gulp serve
   ```

4. Accept loading of debugging manifests by clicking on **Load debug scripts:**

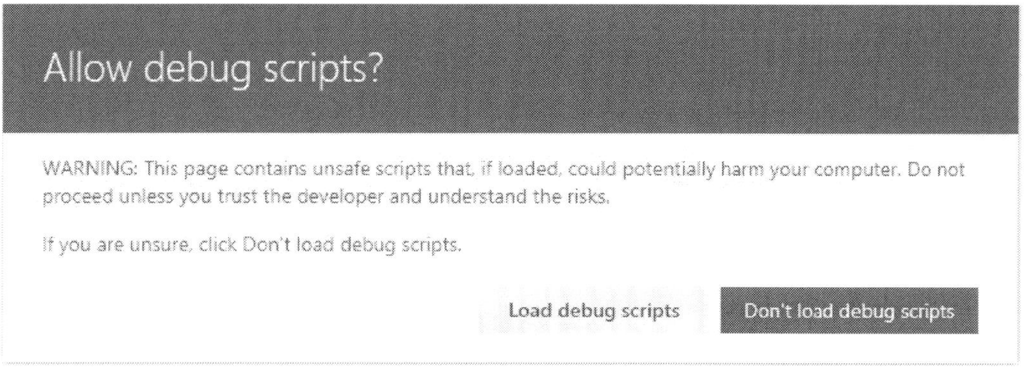

Allow debug scripts?

WARNING: This page contains unsafe scripts that, if loaded, could potentially harm your computer. Do not proceed unless you trust the developer and understand the risks.

If you are unsure, click Don't load debug scripts.

Load debug scripts   Don't load debug scripts

Figure 32.8: Load debug scripts

5. The formatted column (e.g. **Completion**) is rendered in the list view as shown in the following screenshot:

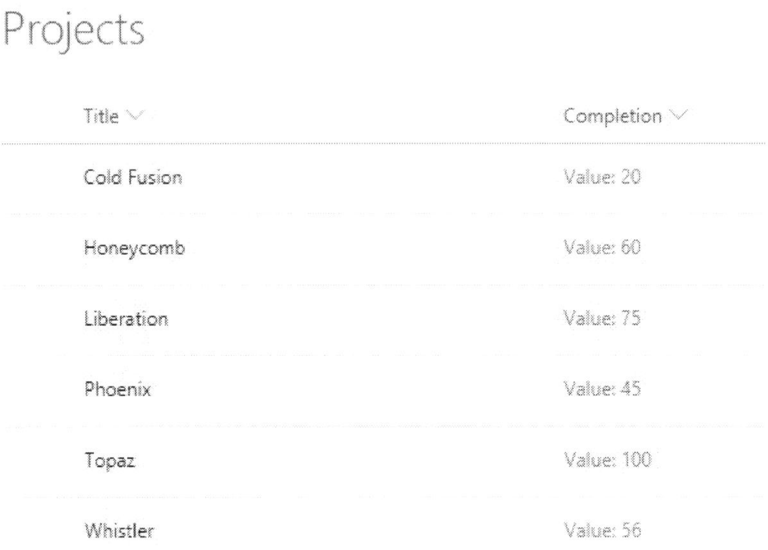

Projects

Title ∨	Completion ∨
Cold Fusion	Value: 20
Honeycomb	Value: 60
Liberation	Value: 75
Phoenix	Value: 45
Topaz	Value: 100
Whistler	Value: 56

Figure 32.9: List view with the formatted column

Apply Field Customization

Follow below steps to apply the customizations to the field:

1. Open the SPFx solution in the editor.
2. In the '\src\extensions\numberFieldCustomizer\' folder, open the `NumberFieldCustomizerFieldCustomizer.module.scss` file to update the CSS:

SCSS

```scss
.NumberFieldCustomizer {
.cell {
background-color: "[theme:themePrimary, default:#e5e5e5]";
display: 'inline-block';
  }
.full {
background-color: #e6e6e6;
width: 100px;
  }
}
```

3. Under the '\src\extensions\numberFieldCustomizer\' folder, open the NumberFieldCustomizerFieldCustomizer.ts file.
4. Update the onRenderCell method:

TypeScript

```typescript
public onRenderCell(event: IFieldCustomizerCellEventParameters): void {
// Use this method to perform your custom cell rendering.
    event.domElement.classList.add(styles.cell);
    event.domElement.innerHTML = `
<div class='${styles.NumberFieldCustomizer}'>
<div class='${styles.full}'>
<div style='width: ${event.fieldValue}px; background:#0094ff; color:#ffffff'>
  ${event.fieldValue}
</div>
</div>
</div>`;
}
```

5. Verify that the 'gulp serve' is running. Refresh the SharePoint list. The **Completion** field is rendered as progress completion:

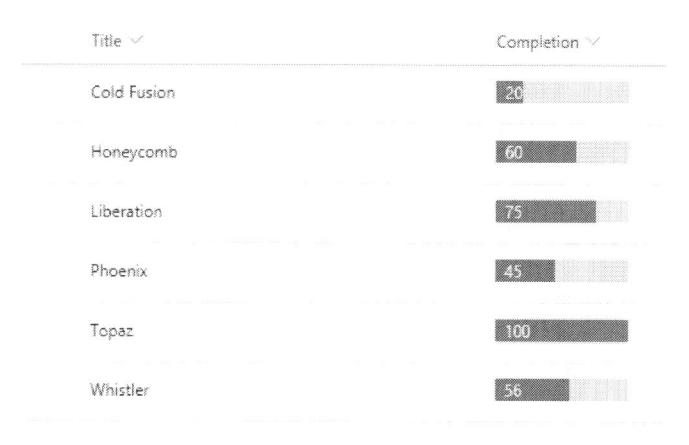

Figure 32.10: List view with the formatted column

Conclusion

In this chapter, we explored the field customizer and altered the rendering of the field in a list view. The SPFx field customizer extension helps to modify the representation of the field in the SharePoint list. This is an option in contrast to JS Link in the modern SharePoint sites.

CHAPTER 33
SPFx Extensions- ListView Command Set

SharePoint Framework Extensions permit expanding the SharePoint user experience. ListView Command Set permits adding newer actions to the command bar of a SharePoint list.

Structure
- Introduction to ListView Command Set
- Develop ListView Command Set

Objectives
- Get introduced to ListView Command Set
- Extend the command bar with new actions

Overview of ListView Command Set

ListView Command Set expands command surfaces of the SharePoint list by introducing new actions. It supports expanding the context menu and toolbar of the SharePoint list.

During classic SharePoint days, similar functionalities were implemented by developing the custom actions. The modern SharePoint offers ListView Command Set as an option to focus on these circumstances.

Develop the ListView Command Set SPFx Solution

Open a command prompt. Follow the given guidelines to make the SPFx solution:

1. Make a folder for the SPFx solution:

    ```
    md spfx-listview-commandset
    ```

2. Change the path to the above folder:

    ```
    cd spfx-listview-commandset
    ```

3. Execute the Yeoman Generator for SharePoint:

    ```
    yo @microsoft/sharepoint
    ```

4. The Yeoman generator will run through the wizard to ask questions about the SPFx solution to be created:

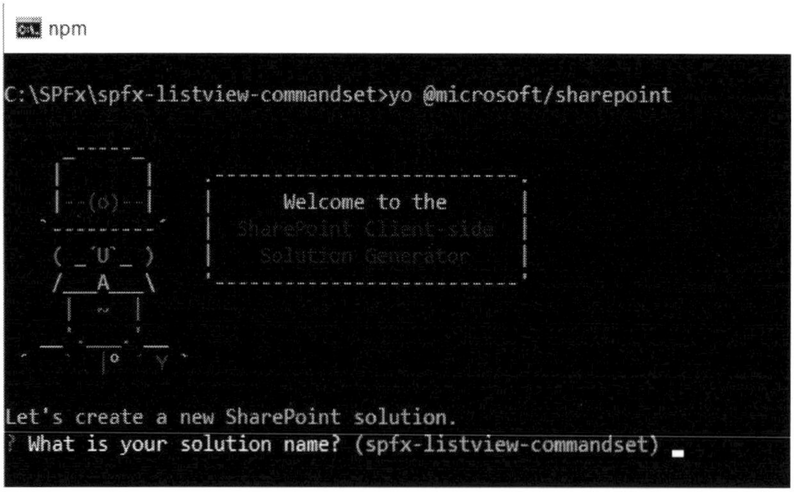

Figure 33.1: SPFx Yeoman generator

The SPFx Yeoman generator will display the following wizard of inquiries:

- **Solution Name:** Determine the SPFx solution name. Hit the *Enter* key to proceed with the default selection(`spfx-listview-commandset` in this case) or type another name.
    - **Chosen decision:** Hit *Enter*
- **Target environment:** Specify the target environment to deploy the SPFx solution. Select any option from SharePoint Online or SharePoint On-Premises environment.
    - **Chosen decision:** SharePoint Online only (latest)

- **Folder location:** Choose the folder location for the SPFx project (either the same folder or a subfolder).
  - **Chosen decision:** Same folder
- **Deployment option:** Specify Y to deploy the app instantly to all the sites, N otherwise.
  - **Chosen decision:** N (install on each site explicitly)
- **Consents to access web APIs:** Check whether the components in the solution need explicit permission to access web APIs that are unique and not shared with other components in the tenant.
  - **Chosen decision:** N (solution contains unique permissions)
- **Choice of client-side component:** Choose whether to develop a web part or an extension.
  - **Chosen decision:** Extension
- **Choice of client-side extension:** Decide to develop a type of extension (Application customizer, Field customizer, or ListView Command Set).
  - **Chosen decision:** ListView Command Set
- **Command Set name:** Provide the extension name. Hit the *Enter* key to proceed with the default choice or type another name.
  - **Chosen decision:** `CustomDialog`
- **Command Set description:** Provide the extension description. Hit the *Enter* key to proceed with the default choice or type another value.
  - **Chosen decision:** Modal dialog with a listview command set

5. After the scaffolding is complete, lock down the version of project dependencies by executing the following command:

   ```
   npm shrinkwrap
   ```

6. Execute the following command to open the solution in the code editor:

   ```
   code .
   ```

Solution Structure

The solution structure of an extension resembles client-side web parts with relative configuration choices:

Figure 33.2: SPFx Extension structure

The '\src\extensions\customDialog\CustomDialogCommandSet.manifest.json' file contains information about the SPFx extension type and unique identifier of the solution. Note down the id for future debugging purpose:

JSON

```json
{
"$schema": "https://developer.microsoft.com/json-schemas/spfx/command-set-extension-manifest.schema.json",

"id": "894b69eb-4edd-4f11-9dd9-9622f9ab2782",

"alias": "CustomDialogCommandSet",

"componentType": "Extension",

"extensionType": "ListViewCommandSet",
```

```
// The "*" signifies that the version should be taken from the
package.json
"version": "*",
"manifestVersion": 2,

// If true, the component can only be installed on sites where
Custom Script is allowed.
"requiresCustomScript": false,

"items": {
"FIRST_COMMAND": {
"title": { "default": "Command One" },
"iconImageUrl": "icons/request.png",
"type": "command"
},
"SECOND_COMMAND": {
"title": { "default": "Command Two" },
"iconImageUrl": "icons/cancel.png",
"type": "command"
    }
  }
}
```

Develop the ListViewCommand Set

In the "\src\extensions\customDialog\" folder, open the `CustomDialog CommandSet.ts` file. The class contains the following methods:

- The **onInit()** event occurs well before the page DOM is ready. It returns a promise for asynchronous operations.
- The **onListViewUpdated()** event occurs independently for every command. This event is invoked after the onInit() promise is resolved:

   TypeScript

   ```
   public onListViewUpdated(event:
   IListViewCommandSetListViewUpdatedParameters): void {
   const compareOneCommand: Command = this.tryGetCommand('FIRST_COMMAND');
   ```

```
if (compareOneCommand) {
```
// This command should be hidden unless exactly one row is selected.
```
    compareOneCommand.visible = event.selectedRows.length === 1;
  }
}
```
- **The onExecute()** method characterizes what happens when the command is excecuted:

TypeScript

```
public onExecute(event: IListViewCommandSetExecuteEventParameters): void {
switch (event.itemId) {
case 'FIRST_COMMAND':
    Dialog.alert(`${this.properties.sampleTextOne}`);
break;
case 'SECOND_COMMAND':
    Dialog.alert(`${this.properties.sampleTextTwo}`);
break;
default:
thrownew Error('Unknown command');
  }
}
```

Debuggingthe List View Command Set

List view command set customizer requires a SharePoint site with a needed list to test the functionality.

Follow below steps to debug the list view command set:

1. Open the SharePoint site.
2. Create a new list 'Projects':

Figure 33.3: New Projects list

3. Add a number column:

Figure 33.4: Adding a number column

4. Name the column as **Completion**:

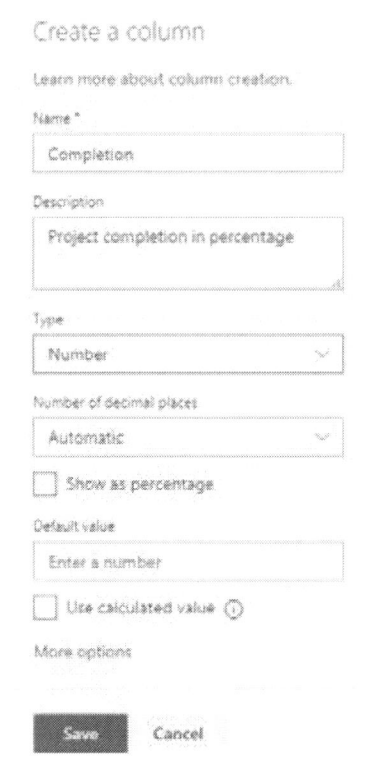

Figure 33.5: Column creation

5. Click on **Save**.
6. Add mock data to the list:

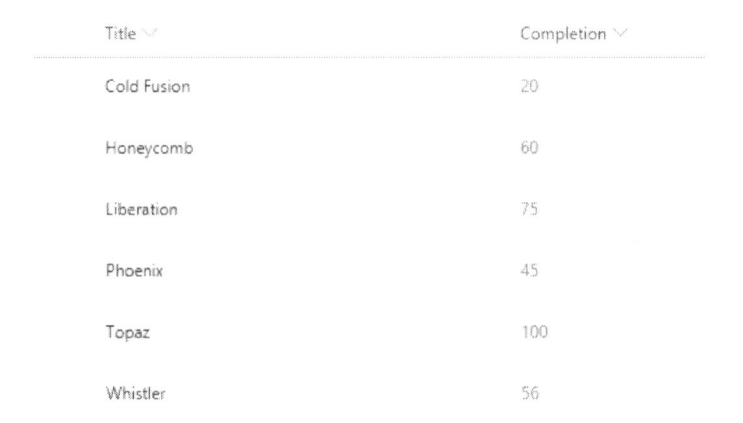

Title	Completion
Cold Fusion	20
Honeycomb	60
Liberation	75
Phoenix	45
Topaz	100
Whistler	56

Figure 33.6: Mock data

Define the ListView Command Sets

Follow below steps to define the list view command sets on SharePoint list:

1. Open the "config\serve.json" file. SetpageUrl to the Projects list URL:

   JSON

   ```
   {
   "$schema": "https://developer.microsoft.com/json-schemas/core-build/serve.schema.json",
   "port": 4321,
   "https": true,
   "serveConfigurations": {
   "default": {
   "pageUrl": "https://tenant.sharepoint.com/sites/ModernSite/Lists/Projects/AllItems.aspx",
   "customActions": {
   "9a068944-ea20-4e96-a102-a2525fed7e2e": {
   "location": "ClientSideExtension.ListViewCommandSet.CommandBar",
   "properties": {
   "sampleTextOne": "One item is selected in the list",
   "sampleTextTwo": "This command is always visible."
          }
         }
        }
       },
   "customDialog": {
   "pageUrl": "https://tenant.sharepoint.com/sites/ModernSite/Lists/Projects/AllItems.aspx",
   "customActions": {
   "9a068944-ea20-4e96-a102-a2525fed7e2e": {
   "location": "ClientSideExtension.ListViewCommandSet.CommandBar",
   "properties": {
   ```

```
            "sampleTextOne": "One item is selected in the list",
            "sampleTextTwo": "This command is always visible."
          }
        }
      }
    }
  }
}
```

2. Execute the SPFx extension:

   ```
   gulp serve
   ```

3. Click on the **Load debug scripts to load** debugging manifests:

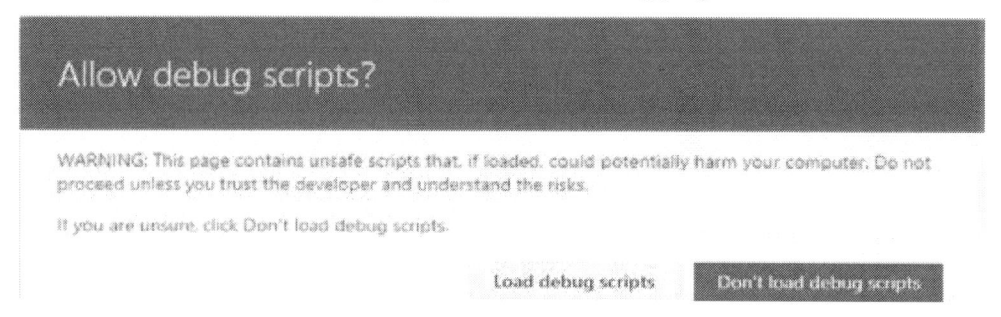

Figure 33.7: Load debugging manifests

4. The toolbar should display the **Command Two** button:

Figure 33.8: Toolbar with the custom button

5. **The Command One** button will be visible on selection of the item:

Figure 33.9: Display the button conditionally

6. An alert message will be displayed when you click on the **Command One** button:

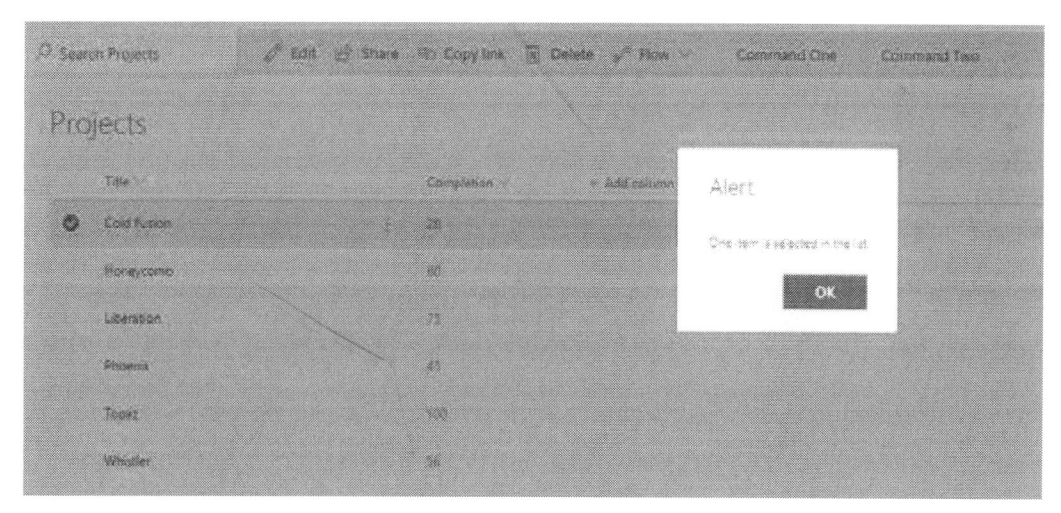

Figure 33.10: Alert on button click

Implement the ListView Command Set Customization

Follow below steps to implement and verify the ListView Command Set Customization:

1. Open the \src\extensions\customDialog\CustomDialogCommandSet.ts file.
2. Update the on Execute method:

   TypeScript

   ```typescript
   public onExecute(event: IListViewCommandSetExecuteEventParameters): void {

   switch (event.itemId) {

   case 'FIRST_COMMAND':

           Dialog.alert(`Clicked ${this.properties.sampleTextOne}`);

   break;

   case 'SECOND_COMMAND':

           Dialog.prompt(`Clicked ${strings.Command2}. Enter something to alert:`).then((value: string) => {

               Dialog.alert(value);

           });

   break;

   default:

   thrownew Error('Unknown command');
       }
     }
   ```

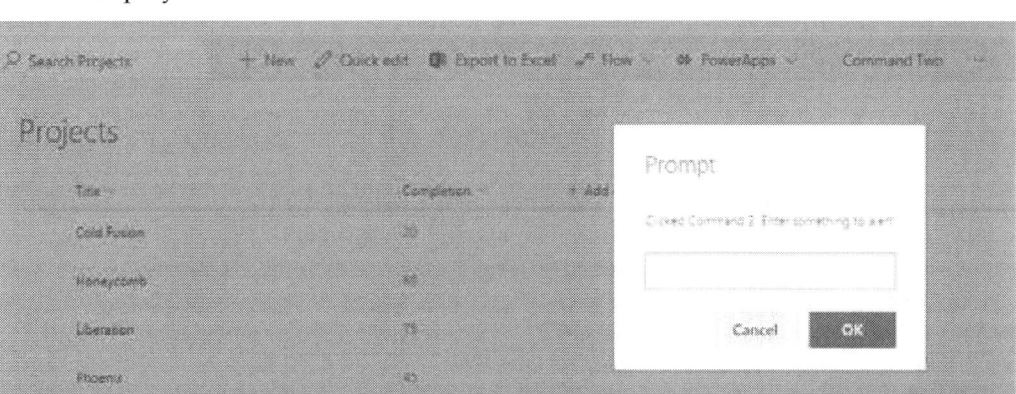

3. When you click on the **Command 2** button, the following prompt will be displayed:

Figure 33.11: Dialog Prompt

Conclusion

In this chapter, we learned abou tListView Command Set and the extended command bar to include new actions. The ListView Command Set SPFx extension expands the SharePoint list toolbar. This is an option in contrast to custom actions in the modern SharePoint sites.

CHAPTER 34
Anonymously Call MS Azure Functions

SharePoint Framework solutions help to create visual elements such as web partson classic and modern SharePoint portals. In certain situations, all the processing can't occur at the SharePoint end, and we need to play out certain handling outside of SharePoint. Azure Functions is one of the most comprehensively utilized alternatives in these situations.

Structure
- Introduction to Azure Functions
- Enabling CORS for Azure Functions
- Consume Azure Functions anonymously from the SPFx Web Part

Objectives
- Implementan Azure Function
- Consume it throughthe SPFx web part

Introduction to Azure Functions

Azure functions help to build the microservices architecture using serverless computing. It provides an event-driven and compute-on-demand experience.

Perform the following steps to create an Azure function app:

1. Login to the Azure Portal (**https://portal.azure.com**).
2. Click on **Create Resource**.
3. Under the **Compute** section, choose **Function App**:

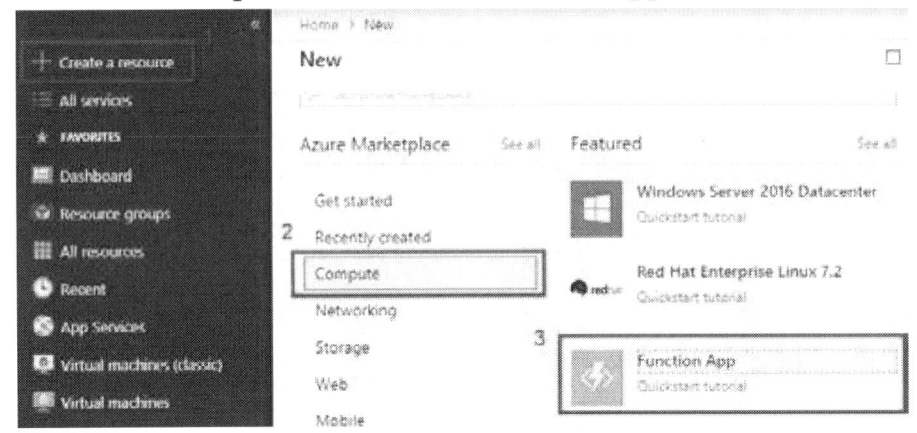

Figure 34.1: Azure Function app creation

4. Fill the form for the Function App creation:

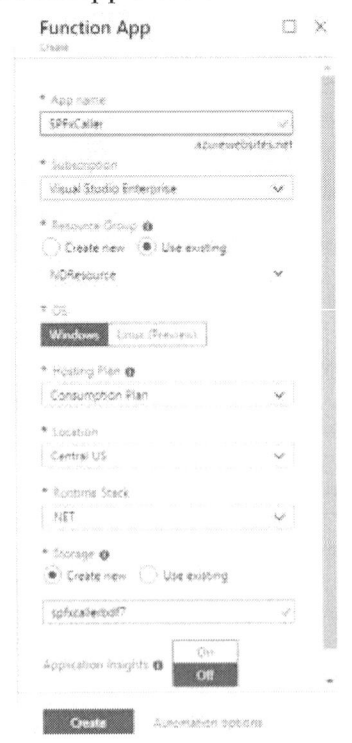

Figure 34.2: Function App creation form

5. Click on **Create**.
6. Post the Azure function creation, go to **Functions>New function**:

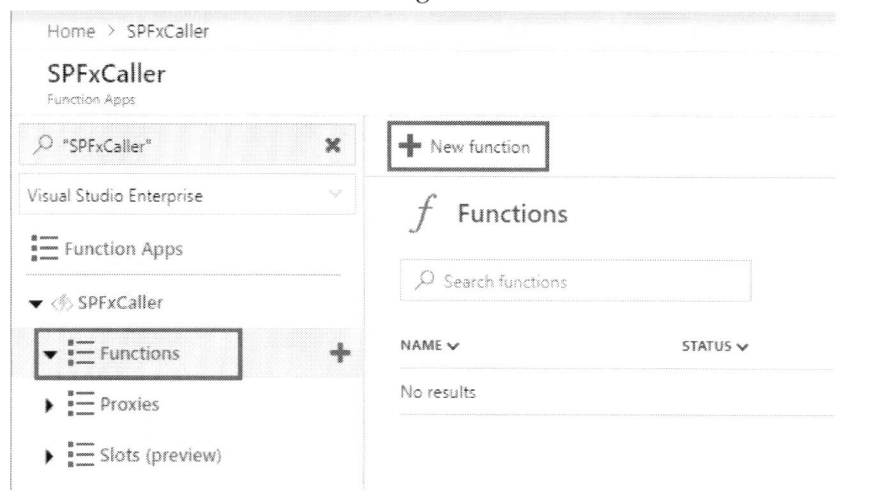

Figure 34.3: Create New Function

7. Select the template as **HTTP trigger**:

Figure 34.4: HTTP Trigger template

8. Provide the function name, and then select **Authorization level**.
9. Click on **Create**.

10. Click on **Run** to execute and test the Azure function:

Figure 34.5: Verify Azure Function

11. Confirm that the Azure function returns the expected output for a given set of input along with the status code as `200 OK`.
12. Select **Get function URL**.

Figure 34.6: Get function URL

13. Note down the function URL for anyfuture reference.

Empower CORS for the Azure Function

The Azure functions being hosted on MS Azure run in a different domain (e.g. azurewebsites.net) than the SharePoint site (e.g. sharepoint.com) hosting SPFx solutions. Naturally, cross-domain calls are not entertainedby SharePoint. To conquer this, we should empower **CrossOrigin Resource Sharing (CORS)** for the Azure function.

Enable CORS on the Azure function by following the given instructions:

1. Select **Platform features.**
2. Under the **API** section, click on **CORS:**

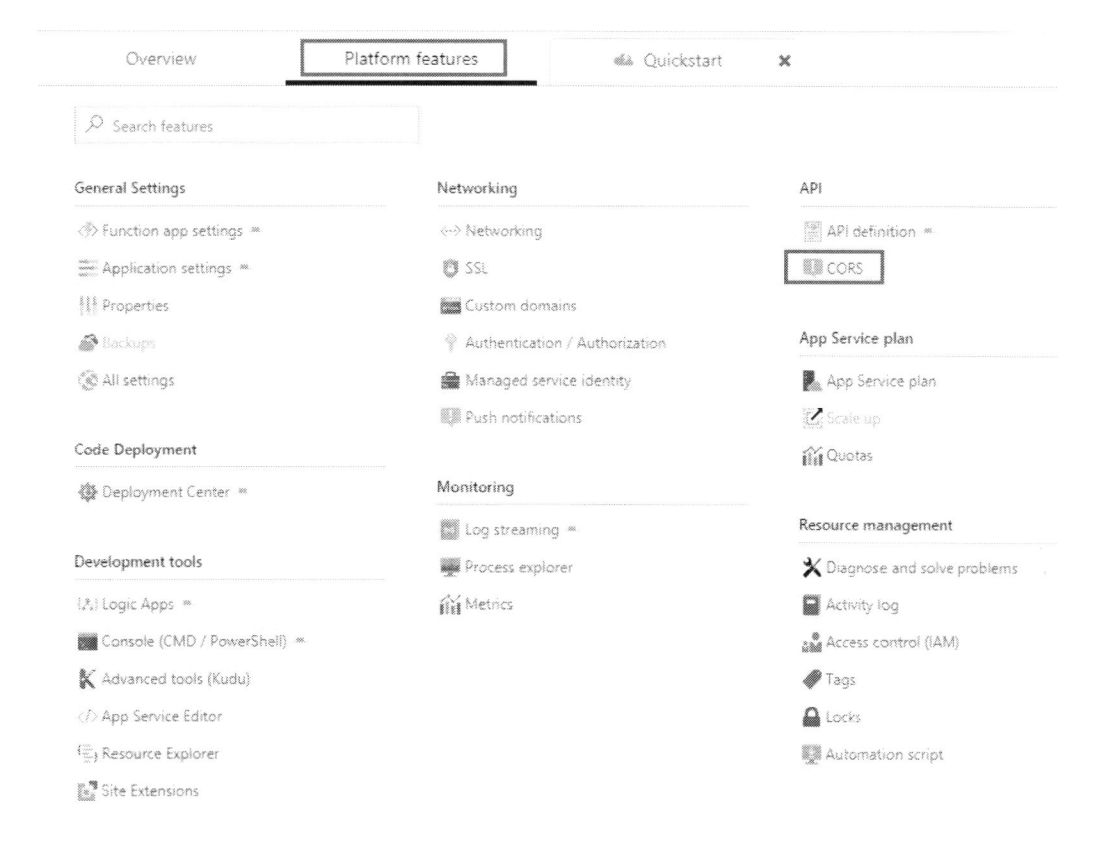

Figure 34.7: Enable CORS

3. Specify the URL of the SharePoint local workbench and Office 365 tenant domain:

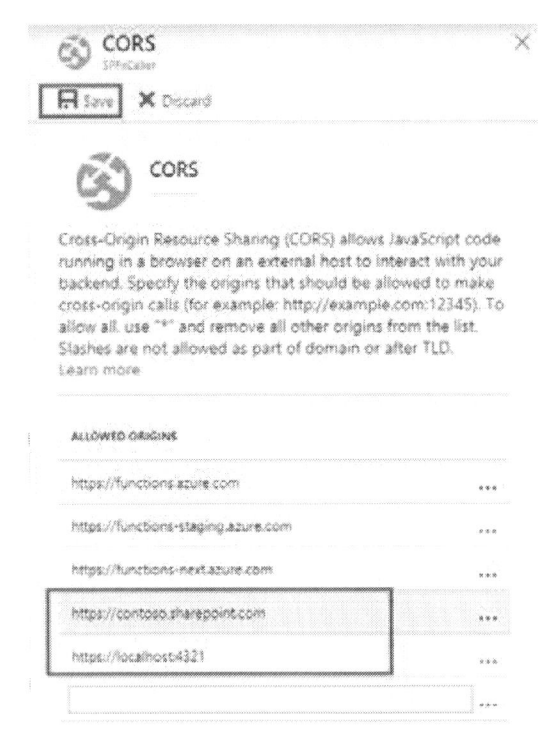

Figure 34.8: Specify allowed origins

4. Click on **Save**.

Call the Azure function from the SPFx Web Part

Open a command prompt. Follow the given guidelines to make the SPFx solution:

1. Make a folder for the SPFx solution:

   ```
   md call-anonymous-azurefunction
   ```

2. Change the path to the above folder:

   ```
   cd call-anonymous-azurefunction
   ```

3. Execute the Yeoman Generator for SharePoint:

   ```
   yo @microsoft/sharepoint
   ```

4. The Yeoman generator will run through the wizard to ask questions about the SPFx solution to be created:

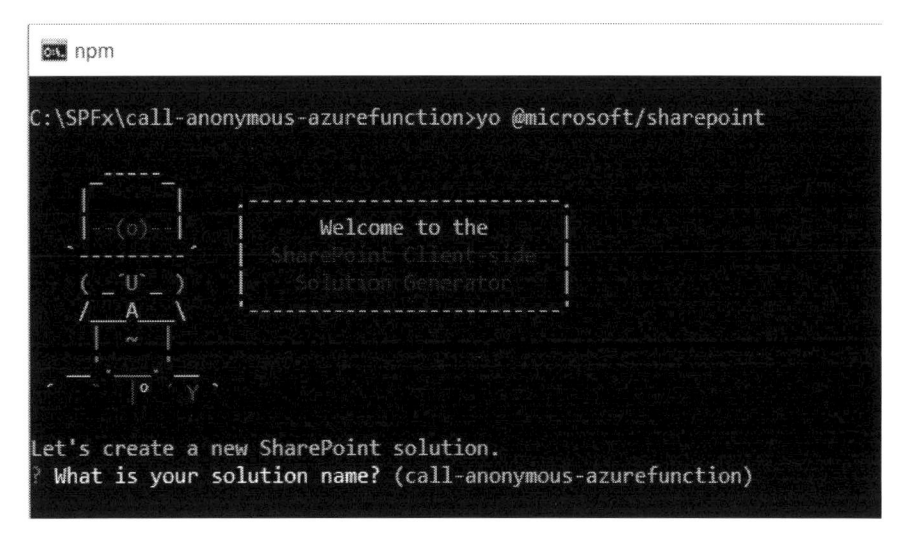

Figure 34.9: SPFx Yeoman generator

The SPFx Yeoman generator will display the following wizard of inquiries:

- **Solution Name:** Determine the SPFx solution name. Hit the *Enter* key to proceed with the default selection (`call-anonymous-azurefunction` in this case) or type another name.
    - **Chosen decision:** Hit *Enter*
- **Target environment:** Specify the target environment to deploy the SPFx solution. Select any option from SharePoint Online or SharePoint On-Premises environment.
    - **Chosen decision:** SharePoint Online only (latest)
- **Folder location:** Choose the folder location for the SPFx project (either the same folder or a subfolder).
    - **Chosen decision:** Same folder
- **Deployment option:** Specify Y to deploy the app instantly to all the sites, N otherwise.
    - **Chosen decision:** N (install on each site explicitly)
- **Consents to access web APIs:** Check whether the components in the solution need explicit permission to access web APIs that are unique and not shared with other components in the tenant.
    - **Chosen decision:** N (solution contains unique permissions)

- **Choice of client-side component:** Choose to develop a web part or an extension.
    - **Chosen decision:** WebPart
- **Web part name:** Provide the web part name. Hit the *Enter* key to proceed with the default choice or type another name.
    - **Chosen decision:** AnonymousAzureFunctionCaller
- **Web part description:** Provide the web part description. Hit the *Enter* key to proceed with the default choice or type another value.
    - **Chosen decision:** Call Azure Function from SPFx
- **Choice of the framework:** Choose a JavaScript framework to develop the component from No JavaScript Framework, React, and Knockout.
    - **Chosen decision:** No JavaScript Framework

5. After the scaffolding is complete, lock down the version of project dependencies by executing the following command:

```
npm shrinkwrap
```

6. At the command prompt, execute the following command to open the solution in the code editor of your choice:

```
code .
```

Call Anonymous Azure Function from the Web Part

Follow below steps to call an anonymous Azure function from the SPFx web part:

1. In the '\src\webparts\anonymousAzureFunctionCaller\AnonymousAzureFunctionCallerWebPart.ts' file, include the following imports:

    TypeScript
    ```
    import { HttpClient, SPHttpClient, HttpClientConfiguration, HttpClientResponse, ODataVersion, IHttpClientConfiguration, IHttpClientOptions, ISPHttpClientOptions } from '@microsoft/sp-http';
    ```

2. Implement the helper method as follows:

    TypeScript
    ```
    protectedinvokeAzureFunction(): void {

    const requestHeaders: Headers = new Headers();

        requestHeaders.append("Content-type", "application/json");
    ```

```
        requestHeaders.append("Cache-Control", "no-cache");

var siteUrl: string = this.context.pageContext.web.absoluteUrl;

var userName: string = (<HTMLInputElement>document.
getElementById("txtUserName")).value;

    console.log(`SiteUrl: '${siteUrl}', UserName: '${userName}'`);

const postOptions: IHttpClientOptions = {
        headers: requestHeaders,
        body: `{ name: '${userName}' }`
    };

let responseText: string = "";

letmsgResult: HTMLElement = document.
getElementById("responseContainer");

this.context.httpClient.post(this.functionUrl, HttpClient.
configurations.v1, postOptions).then((response:
HttpClientResponse) => {
        response.json().then((responseJSON: JSON) => {
            responseText = JSON.stringify(responseJSON);
if (response.ok) {
msgResult.style.color = "green";
            } else {
msgResult.style.color = "red";
            }
msgResult.innerText = responseText;
        })
        .catch ((response: any) => {
let errMsg: string = `WARNING - error calling URL ${this.
functionUrl}. Error = ${response.message}`;
msgResult.style.color = "red";
            console.log(errMsg);
```

```
    msgResult.innerText = errMsg;
        });
    });
}
```

3. Update the `render()` method to call the Azure function:

   TypeScript

   ```
   public render(): void {
   this.domElement.innerHTML = `
   <div class="${ styles.anonymousAzureFunctionCaller}">
   <div class="${ styles.container }">
   <div class="${ styles.row }">
   <div class="${ styles.column }">
   <span class="${ styles.title }">Call Azure Function</span>
   <p class="${ styles.subTitle }">Customize SharePoint experiences using Web Parts.</p>

   <div class="${styles.row}">
   <span class="ms-font-l  ms-fontColor-white  ${styles.label}">User name:</span>
   <input type="text" id="txtUserName"></input>
   </div>

   <button id="btnInvokeAzureFunction" class="${styles.button}">Say Hello!</button>
   <div id="responseContainer" class="${styles.label}"></div>

   </div>
   </div>
   </div>
   </div>`;
           document.getElementById("btnInvokeAzureFunction").onclick =
   ```

```
this.invokeAzureFunction.bind(this);
}
```

Test the WebPart

Follow the given steps to test the web part on the SharePoint page:

1. With 'gulp serve' running, open the SharePoint site.
2. Navigate to `/_layouts/15/workbench.aspx`.
3. Include the webpart in thepage:

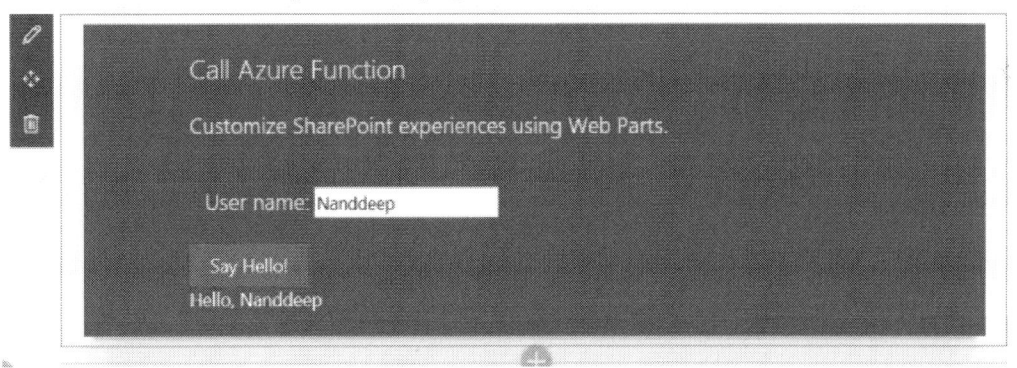

Figure 34.10: SPFx web part calling the Azure function

Conclusion

In this chapter, we actualized a straight forward Azure function and used it in the SPFx web part. Perplexing or long-running processing can be executed from Azure functions (outside SharePoint) and later they can be adequately used in the SharePoint Framework client web parts.

CHAPTER 35
Securing Azure Functions with Azure Active Directory

Azure function capacities are generally utilized to perform operations outside the context of SharePoint by connecting remotely. In the previous chapter, we executed an Azure function with anonymous access. However, in reality, we should not expose Azure functions with anonymous access but protect them with Azure Active Directory.

Structure
- Introductionto Azure Functions
- CORS enablement on Azure Functions

Objectives
- Understand your Azure Active Directory App Registration
- Securing Azure functions with Azure Active Directory

Azure Active Directory App Registration

Follow the given steps to create an Azure AD application registration:

1. From the MS Azure portal, create an application registration:

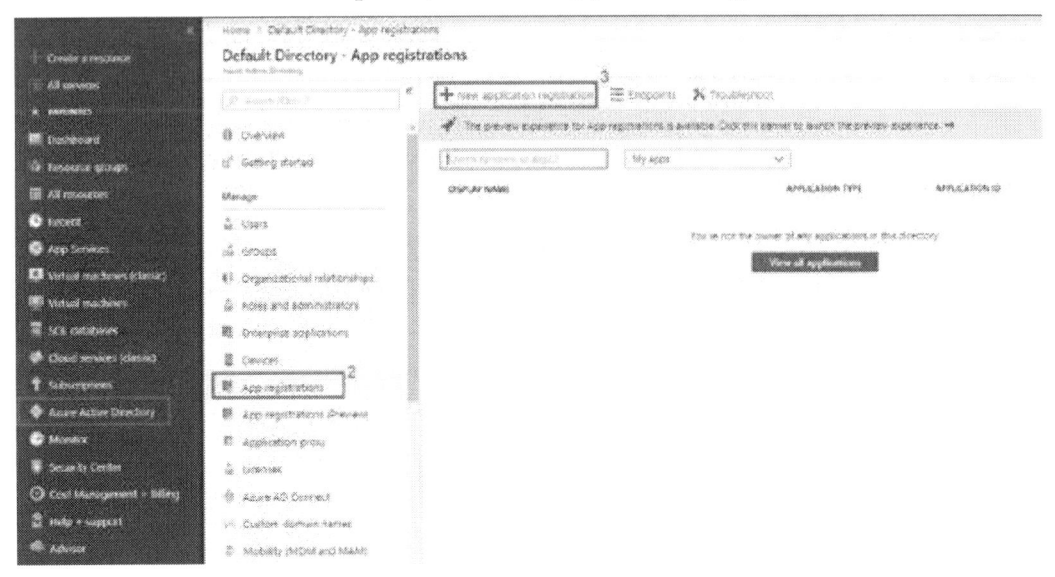

Figure 35.1: App registration

2. Provide the app registration name.
3. Choose **Application type** as **Web app / API**.
4. Provide the Azure function URL as **Sign-on URL**:

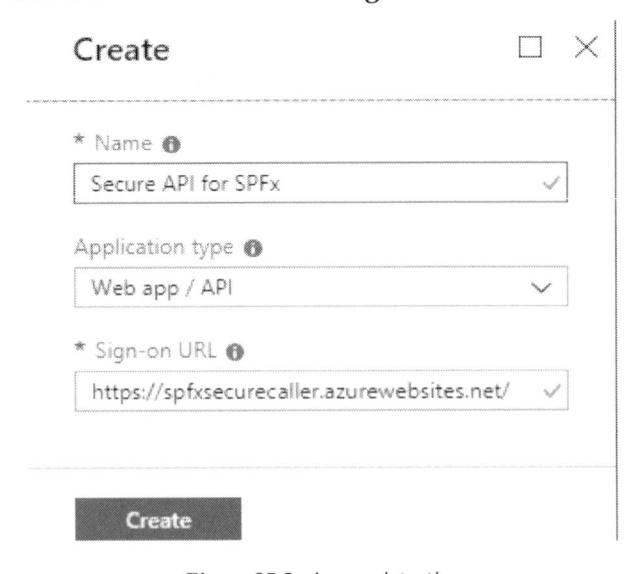

Figure 35.2: App registration

5. Select **Create**.

Get the App ID URI

Follow below steps to get the App ID URI:

1. Go to **Settings>Properties.**
2. Copy **App ID URI** to use it later:

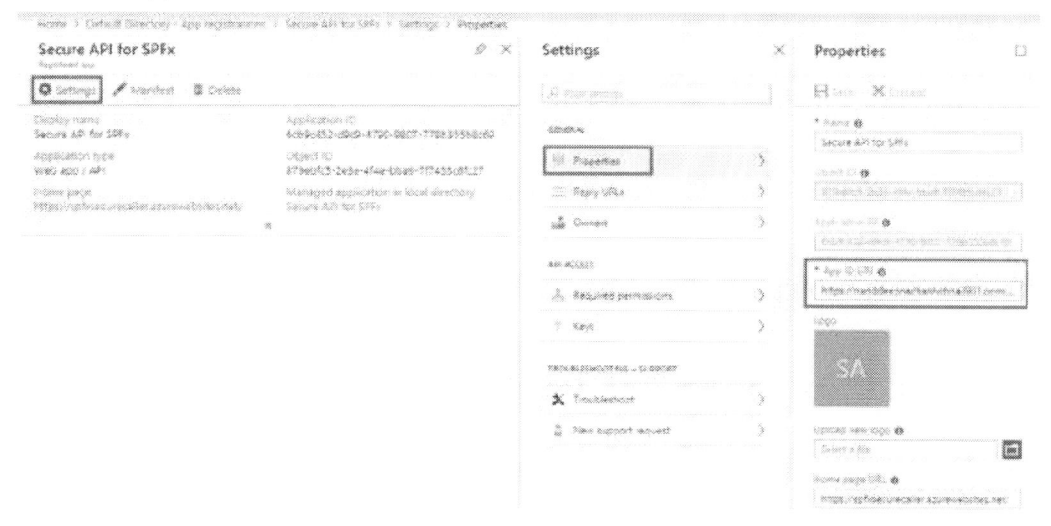

Figure 35.3: App ID URI

Set up the required permissions for App registration

The default permission assigned to app registration is **Sign in and read user profile**. Follow the given instructions to set new permissions:

1. Select Settings.
2. Under **API ACCESS**, select **Required permissions**.
3. Select **Add**.

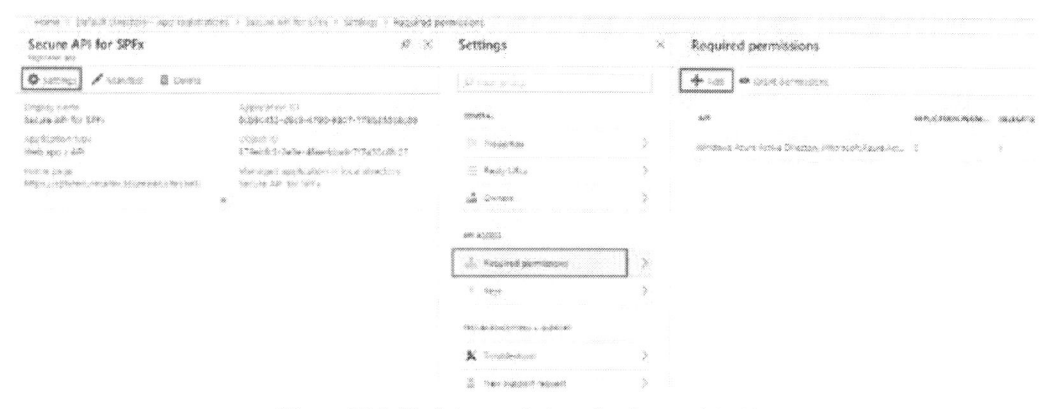

Figure 35.4: Update permissions for App registration

4. As required, add or update the permissions.

Assign consents for the App registration

Follow the given instructions to grant permissions with the administrator role to the App registration for each of the users:

1. Select Settings.
2. Under **API ACCESS**, select **Required permissions**.
3. Click on **Grant permissions**. Then, click on **Yes:**

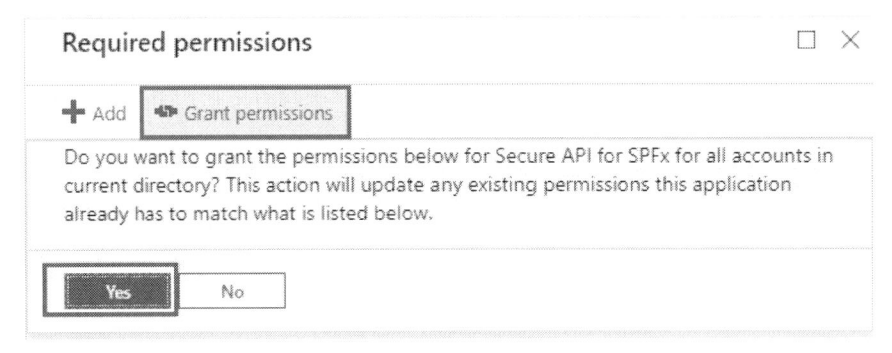

Figure 35.5: Required permissions

Implement the MS Azure Function

Azure functions help to build the microservices architecture using serverless computing.

Follow the given instructions to implement the Azure function:

1. From the Azure portal, Select **Create Resource**.

2. Under the **Compute** section, click on **Function App**:

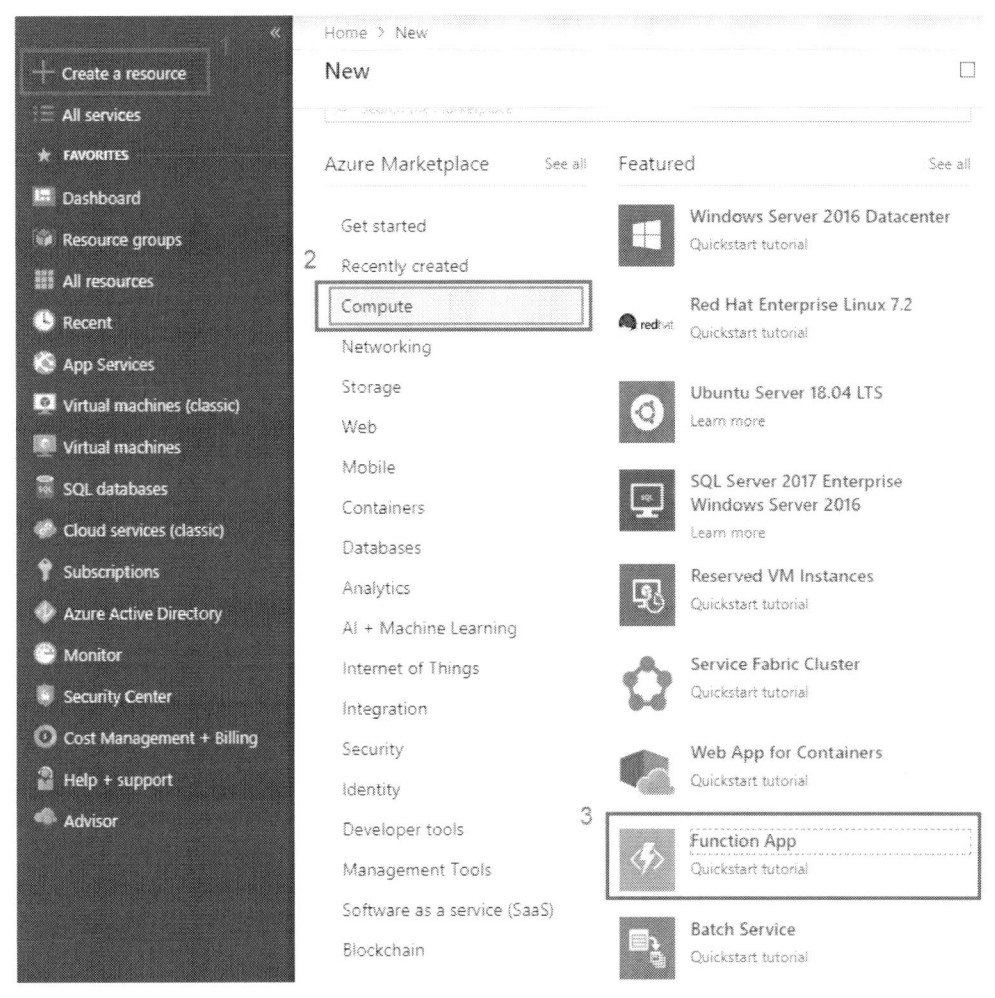

Figure 35.6: Function App

3. Fill in the details for **Function App**:

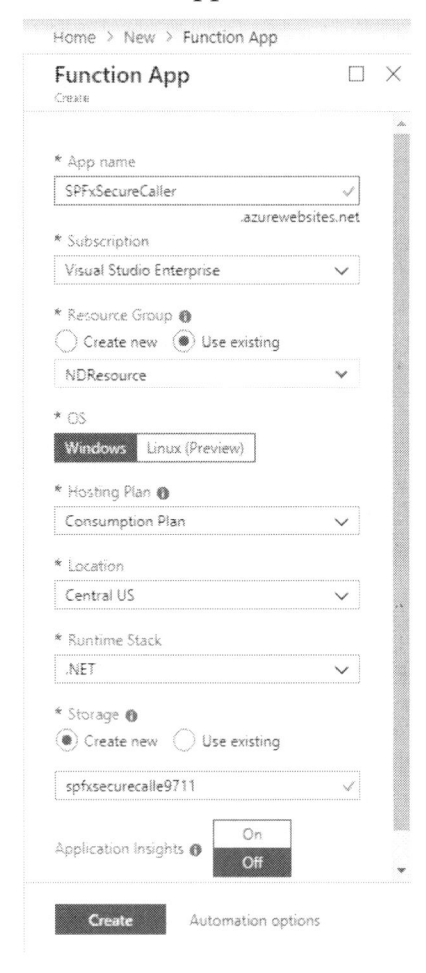

Figure 35.7: Function App

4. Click on **Create**.
5. Select the '**Platform features**' tab.

6. Under **Networking**, click on **Authentication / Authorization**.

Figure 35.8: Platform features

7. Set **App Service Authentication** to **ON**.

8. For **Action to take when a request is not authenticated**, select **Log in with Azure Active Directory**.

9. For **Authentication Providers**, choose **Azure Active Directory**:

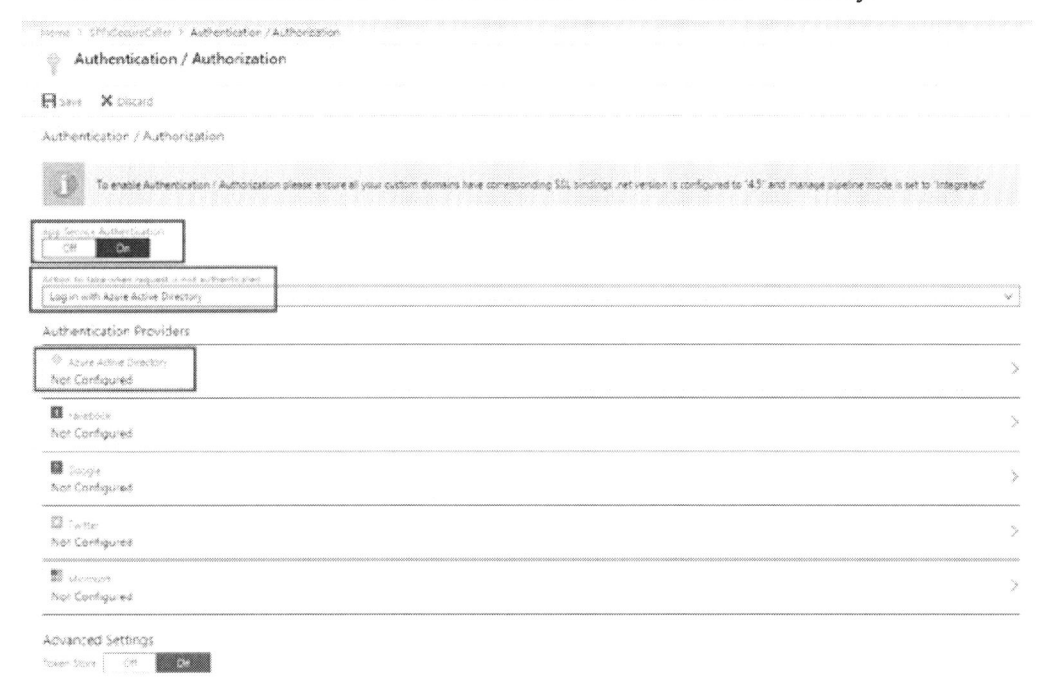

Figure 35.9: Authentication and Authorization

10. Set **Management mode** to **Advanced**.
11. Set **Client ID** as the Application ID created in the previous step.
12. Set **Allowed Token Audiences** to App ID URI created in the previous step:

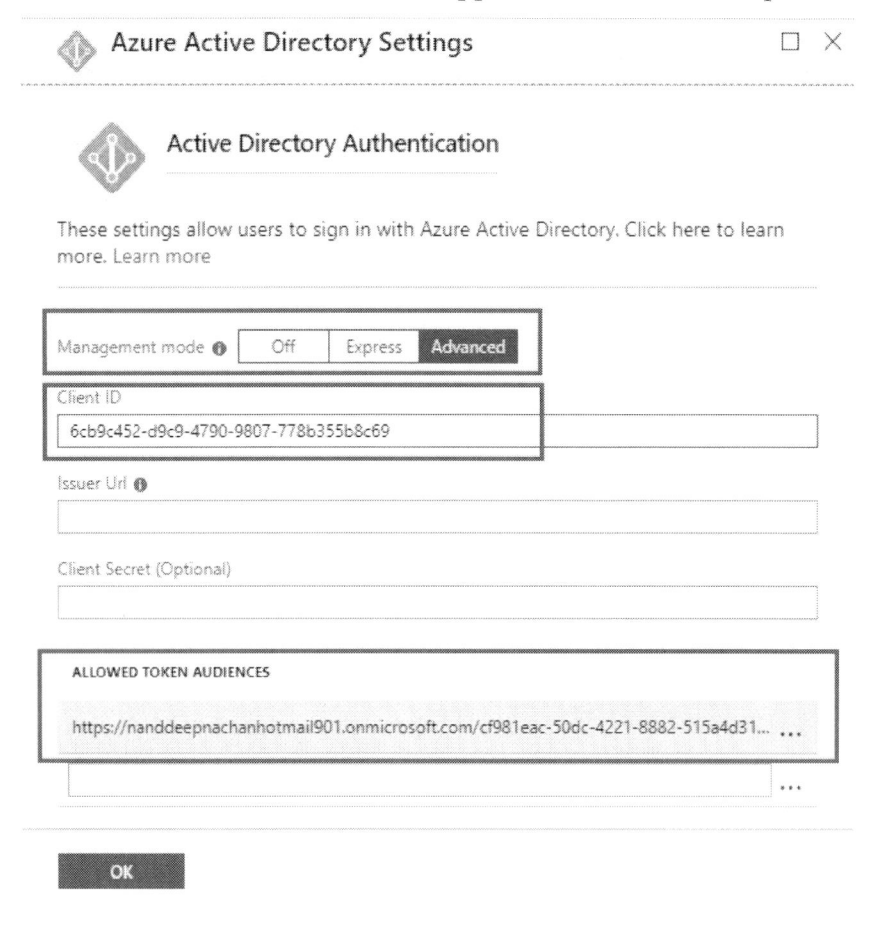

Figure 35.10: Azureactive directory settings

13. Then, click on **OK**.

CORS Enablement for Azure Function

As a matter of fact, cross-domain calls are not permitted from SharePoint. To conquer this, we should empower **Cross-Origin Resource Sharing (CORS)** in the Azure function.

Perform the following instructions to enable CORS to the Azure function:
1. Select **Platform features**.
2. Under **API**, select **CORS**:

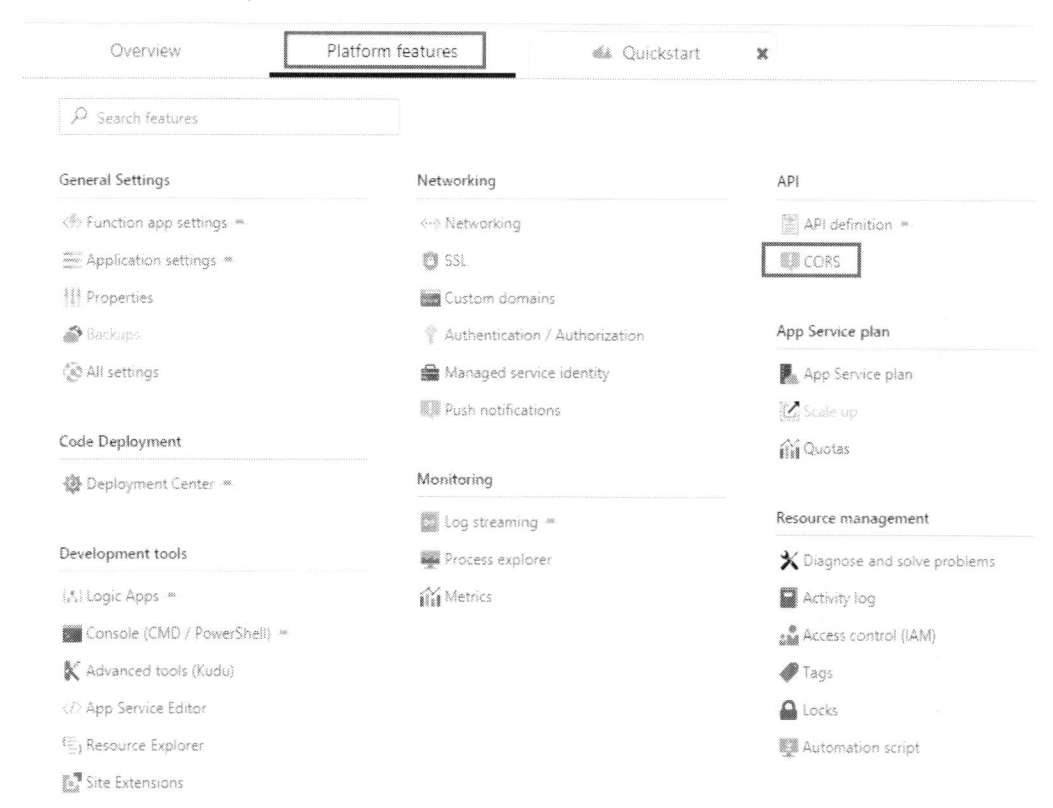

Figure 35.11: Platform features.

3. In the allowed origins, specify the URL of the SharePoint local workbench and Office 365 tenant.

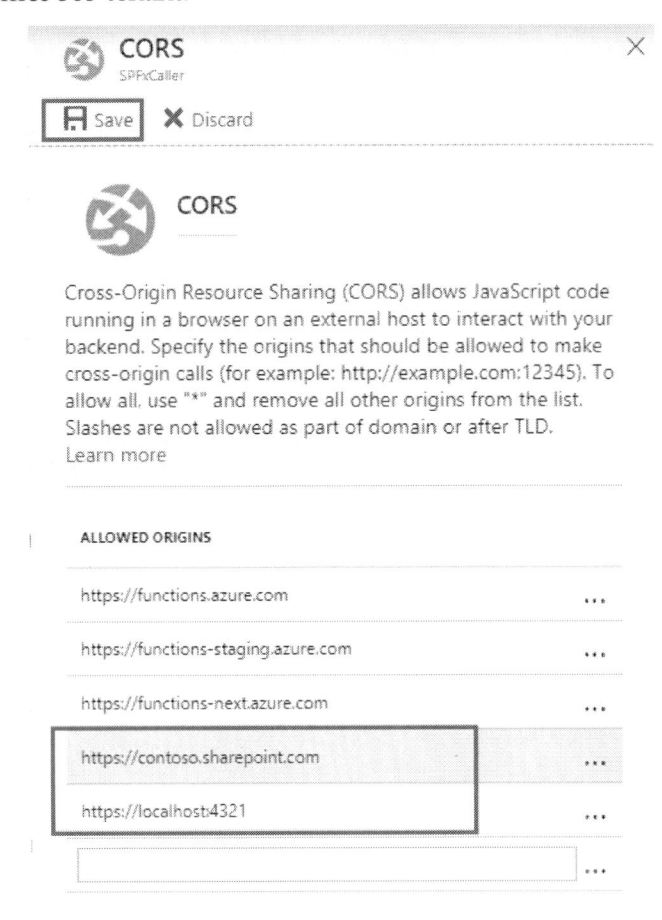

Figure 35.12: CORS allowed origins

4. Click on **Save**.

Develop the Azure Function with Visual Studio

Follow the given instructions to develop the MS Azure function using Visual Studio:

1. Create a new project in Visual Studio.
2. Under **Visual C#**, choose **Cloud>Azure Functions**.

Securing Azure Functions with Azure Active Directory

3. Specify the project name:

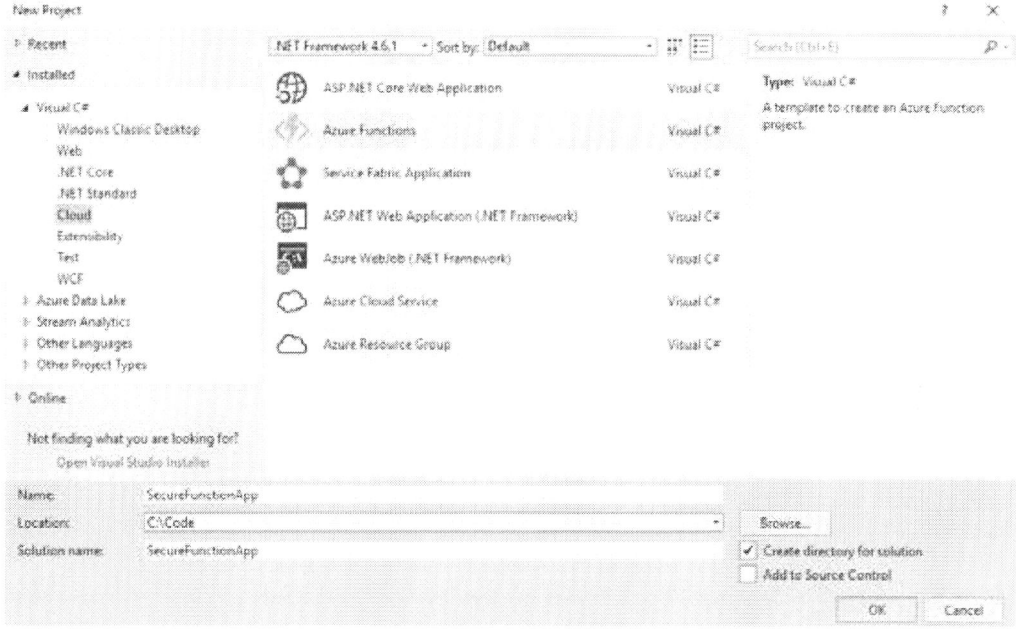

Figure 35.13: Develop Azure function with Visual Studio

4. Click on **OK**.
5. Add the Azure function by right-clicking on the project:

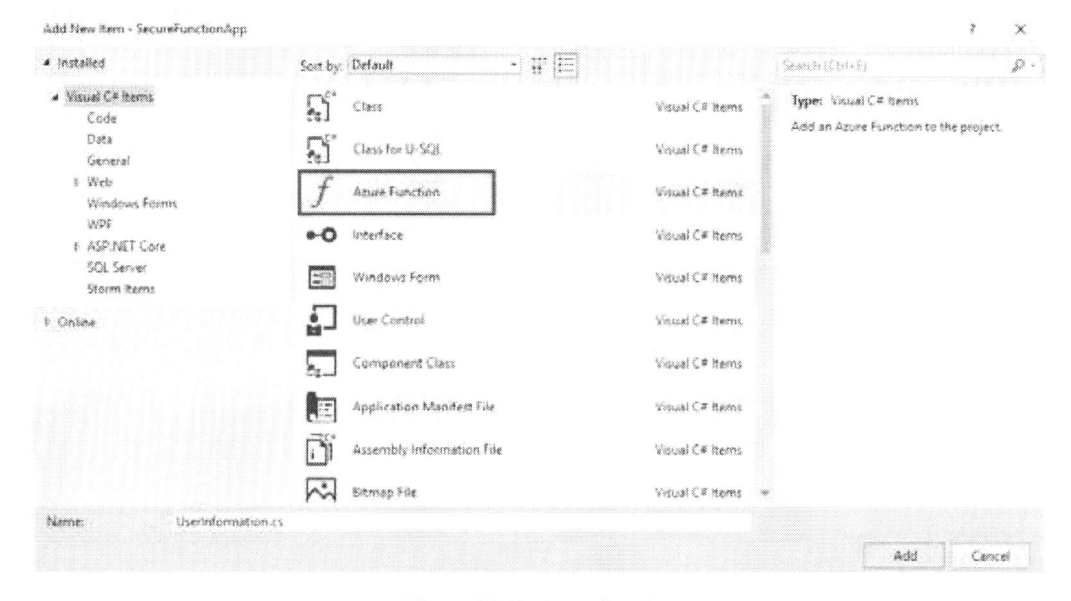

Figure 35.14: Azure function

6. Select the **Http trigger**.
7. Under **Access rights**, choose **Anonymous** as the function will be secured with Azure AD:

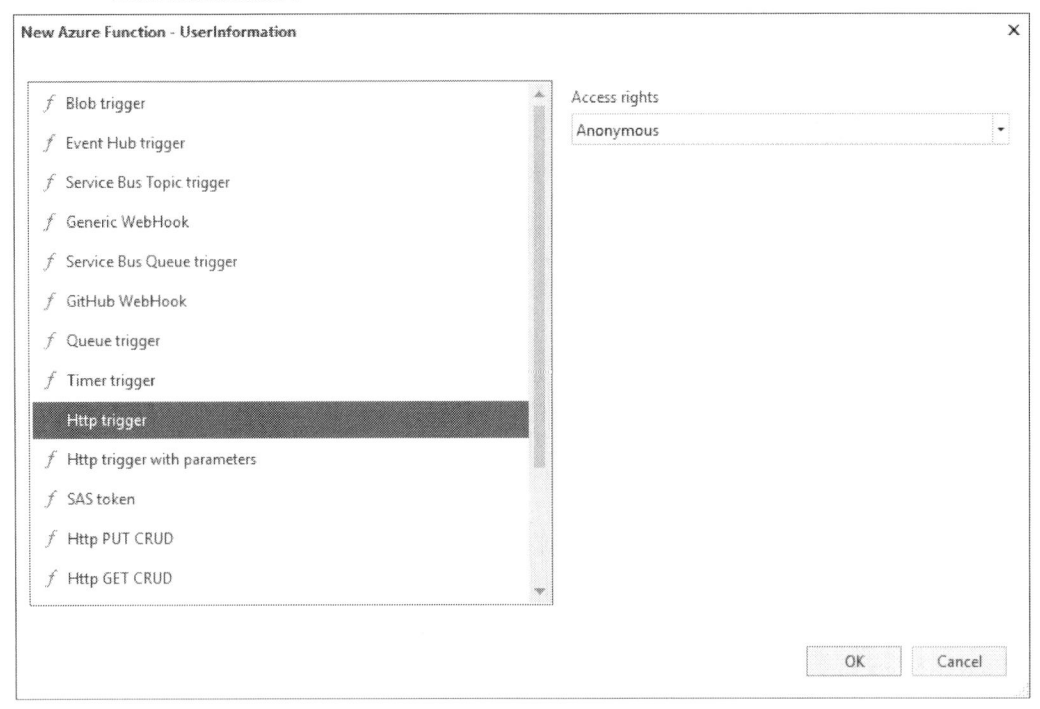

Figure 35.15: Http trigger

8. Implement the Function app as follows:

    C#

    ```
    using Microsoft.Azure.WebJobs;
    using Microsoft.Azure.WebJobs.Extensions.Http;
    using Microsoft.Azure.WebJobs.Host;
    using System.Collections.Generic;
    using System.Net;
    using System.Net.Http;
    using System.Net.Http.Formatting;
    using System.Security.Claims;
    using System.Threading.Tasks;

    namespace SecureFunctionApp
    ```

```csharp
{
publicstaticclassUserInfo
    {
        [FunctionName("UserInfo")]
publicstaticasyncTask<HttpResponseMessage>
Run([HttpTrigger(AuthorizationLevel.Anonymous, "get", "post",
Route = null)]HttpRequestMessage req, TraceWriter log)
        {
         log.Info("C# HTTP trigger function processed a request.");
var result = newDictionary<string, string>();
// Get current user claims
foreach (Claim claim inClaimsPrincipal.Current.Claims)
            {
                result.Add(claim.Type, claim.Value);
            }
return req.CreateResponse(HttpStatusCode.OK, result,
JsonMediaTypeFormatter.DefaultMediaType);
        }
    }
}
```

9. Publish by right-clicking on the project name.
10. Choose **Select existing**:

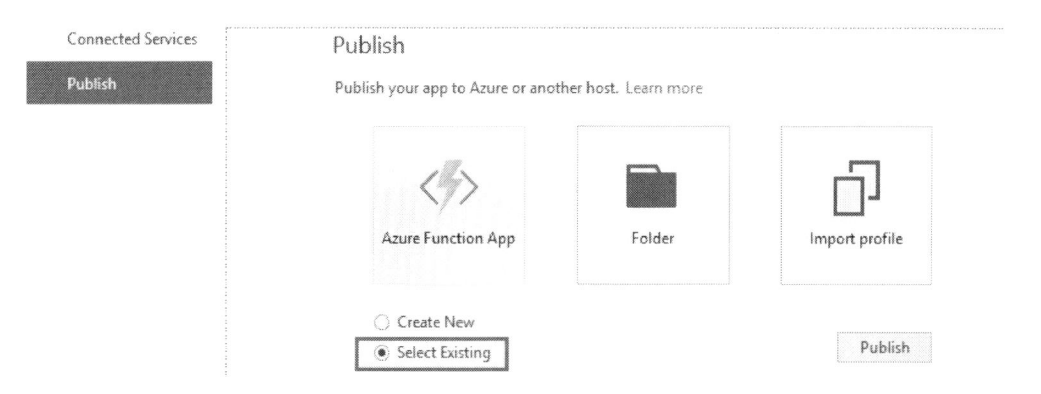

Figure 35.16: Publish the Azure function

11. Click on **Publish**.
12. Select the Function app implemented previously:

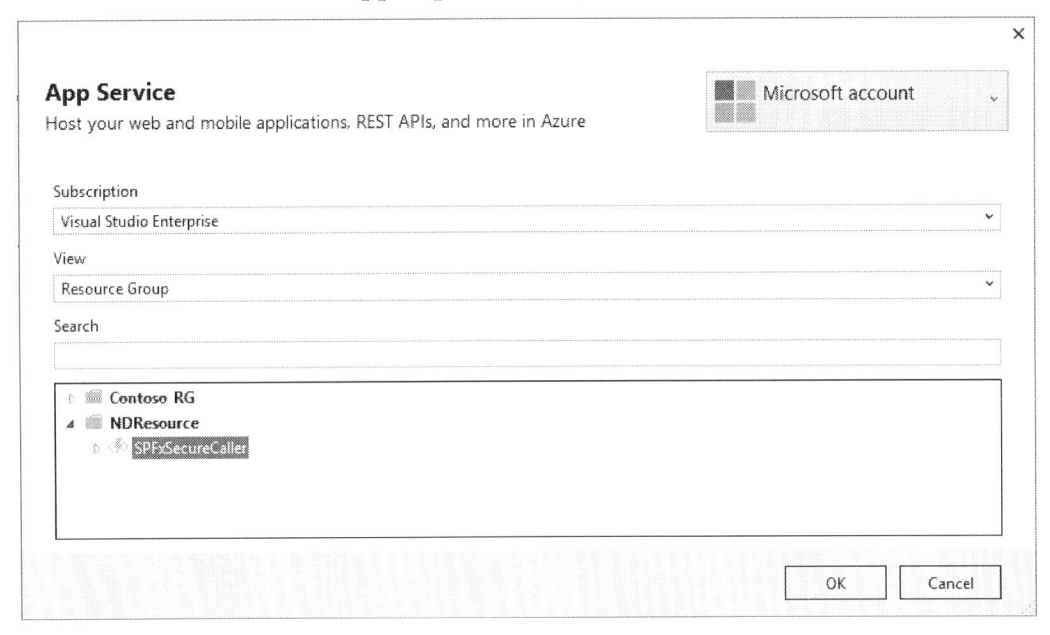

Figure 35.17: Publish Azure function

13. Click on **OK** to publish the Azure function app.

Conclusion

In this chapter, we learned about protecting the Azure Function with Azure Active Directory. The Azure functions deployed in a production environment should be secured. Azure AD is one of the most effective ways to achieve this.

CHAPTER 36
Consume Azure AD Secured Function with SPFx

Azure functions help to build the microservices architecture using serverless computing. They are commonly used to perform operations outside the context of SharePoint by connecting remotely. In the previous chapter, we secured an Azure function with Azure AD. Now, we will consume it in the SPFx web part.

Structure
- Consume Azure AD secured functions
- PowerShell to handle application permissions

Objectives
- Configure permissions on the SPFx web part
- Access resources with Azure functions

Consume the Azure function with the SPFx web part

Open a command prompt. Follow the given steps to make the SPFx solution:
1. Make a folder for the SPFx solution:

```
md consume-azuread-secured-function
```

2. Change path to the above folder:

   ```
   cd consume-azuread-secured-function
   ```

3. Execute the Yeoman Generator for SharePoint:

   ```
   yo @microsoft/sharepoint
   ```

4. The Yeoman generator will run through the wizard to ask questions about the SPFx solution to be created:

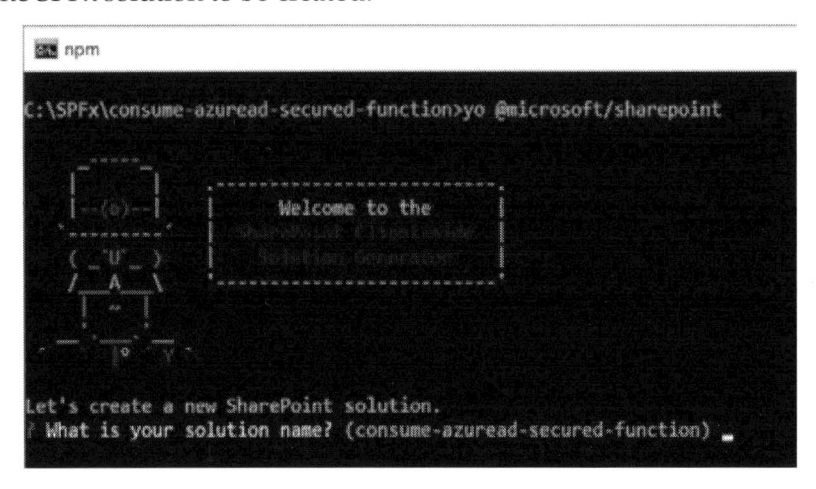

Figure 36.1: SPFx Yeoman generator

The SPFx Yeoman generator will display the following wizard of inquiries:

- **Solution Name:** Determine the SPFx solution name. Hit the *Enter* key to proceed with the default selection (`consume-azuread-secured-function` in this case) or type another name.
    - **Chosen decision:** Hit *Enter*

- **Target environment:** Specify the target environment to deploy the SPFx solution. Select any option from SharePoint Online or SharePoint On-Premises environment.
    - **Chosen decision:** SharePoint Online only (latest)

- **Place of files:** Choose the folder location for the SPFx project (either the same folder or a subfolder).
    - **Chosen decision:** Same folder

- **Deployment option:** Specify Y to deploy the app instantly to all the sites, N otherwise.
    - **Chosen decision:** N (install on each site explicitly)

- **Consents to access web APIs:** Check whether the components in the solution need an explicit permission to access web APIs that are unique and not shared with other components in the tenant.
    - **Chosen decision:** N (solution contains unique permissions)
- **Choice of client-side component:** Choose to develop a web part or an extension.
    - **Chosen decision:** WebPart
- **Web part name:** Provide the web part name. Hit the *Enter* key to proceed with the default choice or type another name.
    - **Chosen decision:** `ConsumeAzureADSecuredFunction`
- **Web part description:** Provide the web part description. Hit the *Enter* key to proceed with the default choice or type another value.
    - **Chosen decision:** Call Secure Azure Function from SPFx
- **Choice of framework:** Choose the JavaScript framework to develop the component from No JavaScript Framework, React, and Knockout.
    - **Chosen decision:** No JavaScript Framework

5. After the scaffolding is complete, run the following command to lock down the version of project dependencies:

```
npm shrinkwrap
```

6. At the command prompt, type the following command to open the solution in the code editor of your choice:

```
code .
```

Set permissions to the SPFx webpart

To set permissions for the web part to the resources utilizing Azure function, set the `webApiPermissionRequests` property to `config\package-solution.js` on file:

JSON

```
{

"$schema":"https://developer.microsoft.com/json-schemas/spfx-build/package-solution.schema.json",

"solution": {

"name": "consume-azuread-secured-function-client-side-solution",

"id": "91b58b57-7f80-432d-9ac7-f8f5cef0eed8",

"version": "1.0.0.0",
```

```
            "includeClientSideAssets": true,
            "isDomainIsolated": false,
            "webApiPermissionRequests": [
                {
"resource": "SPFx Secure API for SPFx",
"scope": "user_impersonation"
                },
                {
"resource": "Windows Azure Active Directory",
"scope": "User.Read"
                }
            ]
        },
        "paths": {
"zippedPackage": "solution/consume-azuread-secured-function.sppkg"
        }
    }
```

In the preceding config file:
- Provide resource as the Azure AD App registration.
- Set scopetouser_impersonationas the call will happen on behalf of the current user.

Code the webpart

Follow the given steps to consume the Azure AD secured function in the SPFx web part:

1. Open ConsumeAzureADSecuredFunctionWebPart.tsIn the \src\webparts\consumeAzureADSecuredFunction\ folder.
2. Add the following imports:

   TypeScript
   ```
   import { AadHttpClient, HttpClientResponse } from'@microsoft/sp-http';
   ```

3. Update the render() method as follows:

TypeScript

```
public render(): void {
this.domElement.innerHTML = `
<div class="${ styles.consumeAzureADSecuredFunction}">
<div class="${ styles.container }">
<div class="${ styles.row }">
<div class="${ styles.column }">
<span class="${ styles.title }">Welcome to SharePoint!</span>
<p class="${ styles.subTitle }">Current user claims from Azure function</p>
</div>
</div>
</div>
</div>
<div class="${styles.tableContainer}">
<table class='claimsTable'>
</table>
</div>
        `;

this.context.aadHttpClientFactory
      .getClient('https://tenant.onmicrosoft.com/cf981eac-50dc-4221-8882-515a4d31328d')
      .then((client: AadHttpClient): void => {
        client
            .get('https://spfxsecurecall.azurewebsites.net/api/UserInformation', AadHttpClient.configurations.v1)
.then((response: HttpClientResponse): Promise<JSON>=> {
return response.json();
      })
```

```
            .then((responseJSON: JSON): void => {
// Render JSON in table
var             claimsTable          =         this.domElement.
getElementsByClassName("claimsTable")[0];


for (var key in responseJSON) {
var trElement = document.createElement("tr");
    trElement.innerHTML = `<td class="${styles.tableCell}">${key}</
td><td class="${styles.tableCell}">${responseJSON[key]}</td>`;
             claimsTable.appendChild(trElement);
        }
     });
   });
}
```

Package the SPFx solution

Follow the given steps to build and package the solution:
1. Build the solution:

    ```
    gulp build
    ```

2. Minify the required assets:

    ```
    gulp bundle
    ```

3. Create the solution package (.sppkg) in the sharepoint\solution folder:

    ```
    gulp package-solution
    ```

4. Start local debugging:

    ```
    gulp serve --nobrowser
    ```

5. Upload the .sppkg file from the sharepoint/solution folder to the App Catalog.

Grant permissionsto test the webpart

Follow the given steps to grant permissions to the web part:
1. Open the SharePoint Admin Center (**https://[tenant]-admin.sharepoint.com**).

2. In classic experience only, click on Try it now:

Figure 36.2: SharePoint admin center

3. Select **API Management**:

Figure 36.3: API Management

4. Click on **Approve** for pending approval.

Handle permission requests using Power Shell

In the SharePoint Online Management Shell, execute the following set of commands to manage permission requests:

1. Connect to SharePoint Online:

   ```
   Connect-SPOService -Url "https://[tenant]-admin.sharepoint.com"
   ```

2. View the pending permission requests:

   ```
   Get-SPOTenantServicePrincipalPermissionRequests
   ```

3. Approve an individual permission request:

```
Approve-SPOTenantServicePrincipalPermissionRequest -RequestId
<Guid>
```

Conclusion

In this chapter, we learned how to connect to Azure active directory secured functions from SPFx solutions. `AadHttpClient` helps to connect securely to APIs without any OAuth implementation. We can specify the Azure AD applications and permissions the SPFx solution requires and the Office 365 tenant administrator can grant the permissions.

CHAPTER 37
Implementing Separation of Concerns (SoC)

SharePoint Framework solutions are created utilizing TypeScript and supporting JavaScript frameworks (for example, React, Angular, KnockOut, and so on.). The SPFx solution gives a fundamental structure to begin creating. We can take one stride further to execute best practices.

Structure
- Introduction to **Separation of Concerns (SoC)**
- Develop Mock Service
- Develop an SoC Example

Objectives
- Understand the concept of SoC
- Develop SoC in SPFx

Separation of Concerns (SoC)

Separation of Concerns is a structured guideline or design principle for isolating our program (or solution) into a distinct segment, where every segment tends to a separate concern. Code is split into segments with every segment in charge of its own usefulness as shown in the following image:

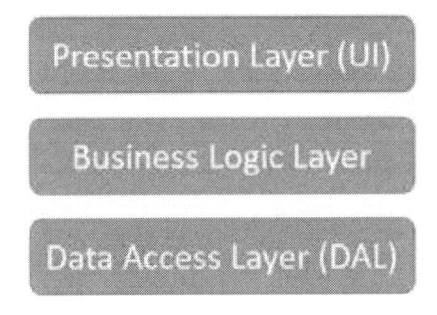

Figure 37.1: Separation of Concerns

Each section is independent with no knowledge about the internal implementation of the other section. They only need to realize how to speak with one another by passing certain data and get the ideal outcome.

Advantages of SoC:

With the implementation of SoC, each section:

- Is simpler to keep up
- Can be easily unit tested
- Can be revamped if necessary, without influencing other sections

In the SPFx solution, we can allude to each section as a Service.

Developan SoC scenario

In this chapter, we will change an existing SPFx solution (React-based Organogram) implemented later in this book to begin developing SoC.

The React component `OrganogramViewer.tsx` at `\src\webparts\Organogram Viewer\components\` has data access, business and presentation logic at one commonplace. To separate it, we will develop a service as an independent section.

Open the solution in the editor of your choice (for e.g. Visual Studio Code).

An Organogram Service class

Follow the given steps to implement the service:

1. Under src, make a new `services` folder.
2. Add the new `OrganogramService.ts` file:

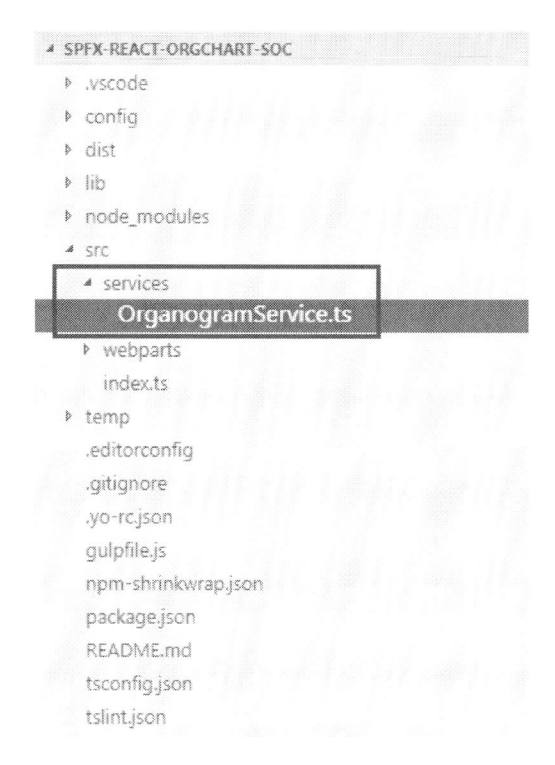

Figure 37.2: Implement service

3. The `OrganogramService` skeleton looks like the following screenshot:

```
import { ServiceScope, ServiceKey } from "@microsoft/sp-core-library";
import { IOrganogramItem, ChartItem } from './IOrganogramItem';
import { IDataService } from './IDataService';
import { SPHttpClient, SPHttpClientResponse } from '@microsoft/sp-http';
import { PageContext } from '@microsoft/sp-page-context';

export class OrganogramService implements IDataService {
    public static readonly serviceKey: ServiceKey<IDataService> = ServiceKey.create<IDataService>('Organogram:data-service', OrganogramService);
    private _spHttpClient: SPHttpClient;
    private _pageContext: PageContext;
    private _currentWebUrl: string;

    constructor(serviceScope: ServiceScope) {
        serviceScope.whenFinished(() => {
            // Configure the required dependencies
            this._spHttpClient = serviceScope.consume(SPHttpClient.serviceKey);
            this._pageContext = serviceScope.consume(PageContext.serviceKey);
            this._currentWebUrl = this._pageContext.web.absoluteUrl;
        });
    }
}
```

Figure 37.3: OrganogramService skeleton

4. Move all methods responsible for data retrieval from the React component to the above service:

```typescript
export class OrganogramService implements IDataService {

    public getOrganogramInfo(listName?: string): Promise<IOrganogramItem[]> {
        return new Promise<IOrganogramItem[]>((resolve: (itemId: IOrganogramItem[]) => void, reject: (error: any) => void): void => {
            this.readOrganogramItems(listName)
                .then((OrganogramItems: IOrganogramItem[]): void => {
                    resolve(this.processOrganogramItems(OrganogramItems));
                });
        });
    }

    private readOrganogramItems(listName: string): Promise<IOrganogramItem[]> {
        return new Promise<IOrganogramItem[]>((resolve: (itemId: IOrganogramItem[]) => void, reject: (error: any) => void): void => {
            this._spHttpClient.get(`${this._currentWebUrl}/_api/web/lists/getbytitle('${listName}')
                                    /items?$select=Title,Id,URL,Parent/Id,Parent/Title&$expand=Parent/Id&$orderby=Parent/Id asc`,
                SPHttpClient.configurations.v1,
                {
                    headers: {
                        'Accept': 'application/json;odata=nometadata',
                        'odata-version': ''
                    }
                })
                .then((response: SPHttpClientResponse): Promise<{ value: IOrganogramItem[] }> => {
                    return response.json();
                })
                .then((response: { value: IOrganogramItem[] }): void => {
                    resolve(response.value);
                }, (error: any): void => {
                    reject(error);
                });
        });
    }

    private processOrganogramItems(OrganogramItems: IOrganogramItem[]): any {
        let OrganogramNodes: Array<ChartItem> = [];

        var count: number;
        for (count = 0; count < OrganogramItems.length; count++) {
            OrganogramNodes.push(new ChartItem(OrganogramItems[count].Id
                , OrganogramItems[count].Title
                , OrganogramItems[count].Url
                , OrganogramItems[count].Parent ? OrganogramItems[count].Parent.Id : undefined));
        }

        var arrayToTree: any = require('array-to-tree');
        var OrganogramHierarchyNodes: any = arrayToTree(OrganogramNodes);
        var output: any = JSON.stringify(OrganogramHierarchyNodes[0]);

        return JSON.parse(output);
    }
}
```

Figure 37.4: Methods moved inside the React component

ServiceKey and ServiceScope:

These classes permit executing dependency injection. Rather than passing a reference to a single dependency, we can pass scope as an argument to the section and the section calls the `consume()` method to call the required service.

The following code declares the service key:

TypeScript

```
publicstaticreadonly serviceKey: ServiceKey<IOrganogramItem> =
ServiceKey.create<IOrganogramItem>('organogram:soc-dataservice',
OrganogramService);
```

The key will distinguish service inside a scope. To guarantee whether the default implementation consistently exists, call `expend()` inside a callback from `serviceScope.whenFinished()`.

Mock data service implementation

The mock data service feeds the dummy data to the web part, while it is running inside the local SharePoint workbench.

Under the `\src\services` folder, include the `MockDataService.ts` file.

```
import { ServiceScope, ServiceKey } from "@microsoft/sp-core-library";
import { IDataService } from "./IDataService";

export class MockDataService implements IDataService {
    public static readonly serviceKey: ServiceKey<IDataService> = ServiceKey.create<IDataService>('orgChart:mock-service', MockDataService);

    constructor(serviceScope: ServiceScope) {
    }

    public getOrgChartInfo(): Promise<any> {
        const initechOrg: any =
        {
            id: 1,
            title: "ROOT",
            url: {Description: "Microsoft", Url: "http://www.microsoft.com"},
            children:[
                {
                    id: 2,
                    title: "Parent 1",
                    url: null,
                    parent_id: 1,
                    children:[
                        { id: 3, title: "Child 11", parent_id: 2, url: null },
                        { id: 5, title: "Child 12", parent_id: 2, url: null },
                        { id: 6, title: "Child 13", parent_id: 2, url: null }
                    ]
                },
                {
                    id: 7,
                    title: "Parent 2",
                    url: null,
                    parent_id: 1,
                    children:[
                        { id: 8, title: "Child 21", parent_id: 7, url: null },
                        { id: 9, title: "Child 22", parent_id: 7, url: null }
                    ]
                },
                {
                    id: 10,
                    title: "Parent 3",
                    url: null,
                    parent_id: 1,
                    children:[
                        { id: 11, title: "Child 31", parent_id: 10, url: null },
                        { id: 12, title: "Child 32", parent_id: 10, url: null }
                    ]
                }
            ]
        };

        return new Promise<any>((resolve, reject) => {
            resolve(JSON.parse(JSON.stringify(initechOrg)));
        });
    }
}
```

Figure 37.5: Mock Data Service

Consume service inside the SPFxwebpart

Follow the given steps to consume the service from the SPFx web part:

1. Open the web part class `OrganogramViewer.tsx` under '\src\webparts\organogramViewer\components\' folder.
2. Consume the service from the web part class:

```
export default class OrganogramViewer extends React.Component<IOrganogramViewerProps, IOrganogramViewerState> {
  private dataCenterServiceInstance: IDataService;

  constructor(props: IOrganogramViewerProps, state: IOrganogramViewerState) {
    super(props);

    this.state = {
      OrganogramItems: []
    };

    let serviceScope: ServiceScope = this.props.serviceScope;

    switch (Environment.type) {
      case EnvironmentType.SharePoint:
      case EnvironmentType.ClassicSharePoint:
        // Based on the type of environment, return the correct instance of the IDataCenterService interface
        // Mapping to be used when webpart runs in SharePoint.
        this.dataCenterServiceInstance = serviceScope.consume(OrganogramService.serviceKey);

        this.dataCenterServiceInstance.getOrganogramInfo(this.props.listName).then((OrganogramItems: any) => {
          this.setState({
            OrganogramItems: OrganogramItems
          });
        });

        break;
      // case EnvironmentType.Local:
      // case EnvironmentType.Test:
      default:
        // Webpart is running in the local workbench or from a unit test.
        this.dataCenterServiceInstance = serviceScope.consume(MockDataService.serviceKey);

        this.dataCenterServiceInstance.getOrganogramInfo().then((OrganogramItems: any) => {
          this.setState({
            OrganogramItems: OrganogramItems
          });
        });
    }
  }

  public render(): React.ReactElement<IOrganogramViewerProps> {
    return (
      <div className={ styles.OrganogramViewer }>
        <div className={ styles.container }>
          <div className={ styles.row }>
            <div className={ styles.column }>

              <Organogram tree={this.state.OrganogramItems} NodeComponent={this.MyNodeComponent} />

            </div>
          </div>
        </div>
      </div>
    );
  }

  private MyNodeComponent = ({ node }) => {
    if (node.url) {
      return (
        <div className="initechNode">
          <a href={ node.url.Url } className={styles.link} >{ node.title }</a>
        </div>
      );
    }
    else {
      return (
        <div className="initechNode">{ node.title }</div>
      );
    }
  }
}
```

Figure 37.6: Consume service in the web part

Test the web part

Follow the given steps to test the web part:

SharePoint workbench

1. At the command window, execute gulp serve.
2. On the SharePoint site, browse to /_layouts/15/workbench.aspx.
3. Add the webpart to the page.
4. Configure the webpart property for the list name:

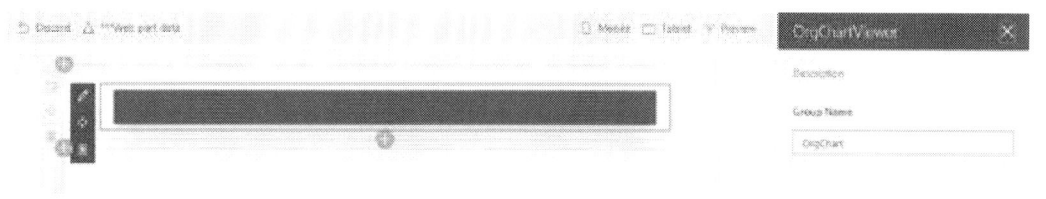

Figure 37.7: Web part added to the SharePoint page

5. The web part should show the information from the SharePoint list in an org chart:

Figure 37.8: SPFx web part showing the org chart

6. Click on the nodes with URL to navigate to the specified link.

Local workbench

1. Open the Local SharePoint workbench (**https://localhost:4321/temp/workbench.html**).

2. Add the webpart to the page:

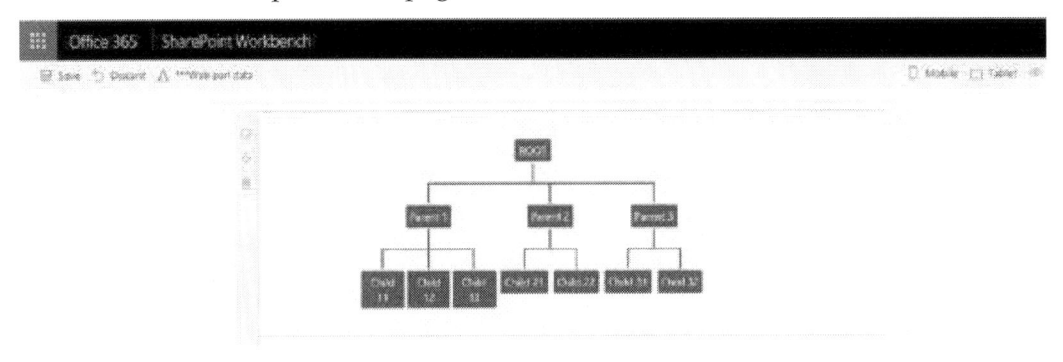

Figure 37.9: SPFx org chart on the local workbench

Conclusion

In this chapter, we discussed the ideology of **Separation of Concerns (SoC)** and actualized it in an existing SPFx solution. Implementing **Separation of concerns (SoC)** helps to isolate each section. Code is less difficult to keep and update without touching different segments. ServiceScope manufactures SoC in SharePoint Framework solutions.

CHAPTER 38
Localization Support for SPFx

SharePoint has supported localization in each of its version to help fabricate better content for clients around the world. The SharePoint Framework is not a special case to it. SPFx offers multilingual help with the assistance of localized resource files as a piece of a SPFx solution.

Structure
- Support for Localization
- Localize the contents

Objectives
- Multilingual support in SPFx
- Localization choices in SPFx

Develop localization solutions for SPFx

Open a command prompt. Follow the given steps to make the SPFx solution:
1. Make a folder for the SPFx solution:

```
md localization-support
```

2. Change the path to the above folder:

```
cd localization-support
```

3. Execute the Yeoman Generator for SharePoint:

```
yo @microsoft/sharepoint
```

4. The Yeoman generator will run through the wizard to ask questions about the SPFx solution to be created:

Figure 38.1: SPFx Yeoman generator

The SPFx Yeoman generator will display the following wizard of inquiries:

- **Solution Name:** Determine the SPFx solution name. Hit the *Enter* key to proceed with the default selection (`localization-support` in this case) or type another name.
    - **Chosen decision:** Hit *Enter*
- **Target environment:** Specify the target environment to deploy the SPFx solution. Select any option from SharePoint Online or SharePoint On-Premises environment.
    - **Chosen decision:** SharePoint Online only (latest)
- **Place of files:** Choose the folder location for the SPFx project (either the same folder or a subfolder).
    - **Chosen decision:** Same folder
- **Deployment option:** Specify Y to deploy the app instantly to all the sites, N otherwise.
    - **Chosen decision:** N (install on each site explicitly)

- **Consents to access web APIs:** Check whether the components in the solution need an explicit permission to access web APIs that are unique and not shared with other components in the tenant.
    - **Chosen decision:** N (solution contains unique permissions)
- **Choice of client-side component:** Choose to develop a web part or an extension.
    - **Chosen decision:** WebPart
- **Web part name:** Provide the web part name. Hit the *Enter* key to proceed with the default choice or type another name.
    - **Chosen decision:** SPFxLocalization
- **Web part description:** Provide the web part description. Hit the *Enter* key to proceed with the default choice or type another value.
    - **Chosen decision:** Localize SPFx web part
- **Choice of framework:** Choose the JavaScript framework to develop the component from No JavaScript Framework, React, and Knockout.
    - **Chosen decision:** React

5. After the scaffolding is complete, run the following command to lock down the version of project dependencies:

```
npm shrinkwrap
```

6. At the command prompt, type the following command to open the solution in the code editor of your choice:

```
code .
```

Support for localization

The localized texts are stored in the loc folder inside the `mystrings.d.ts` file:

TypeScript

```
declare interface ISPFxLocalizationWebPartStrings {
  PropertyPaneDescription: string;
  BasicGroupName: string;
  DescriptionFieldLabel: string;
}

declare module 'SPFxLocalizationWebPartStrings' {
```

```
const strings: ISPFxLocalizationWebPartStrings;
export = strings;
}
```

The default locale supported by the SharePoint Framework is English (en-US) and it is defined inside the en-us file. In order to include support for any other language, add the .js file per language.

Localize the web part property pane

Add the fi-fi.js under '\src\webparts\SPFxLocalization\loc\' file supporting the Finnish language:

TypeScript

```
define([], function() {
return {
"PropertyPaneDescription": "Kuvaus",
"BasicGroupName": "Ryhmän nimi",
"DescriptionFieldLabel": "Kuvauskenttä"
    }
  });
```

Localize the web part content

The web part content can be localized in a similar manner as that of the property pane. To localize every string, include the key inside the localization TypeScript definition file and localized values to locale .js files.

Follow the given steps to localize the web part content:

1. **Step 1: Add the localization key to the TypeScript definition file**

    Follow below steps to add the localization key to the TypeScript definition file:
    - Open mystrings.d.ts under '\src\webparts\spfxLocalization\loc\' folder.
    - Include the key representing the button text:

    TypeScript

    ```
    declareinterface ISPFxLocalizationWebPartStrings {
      PropertyPaneDescription: string;
    ```

```
  BasicGroupName: string;
  DescriptionFieldLabel: string;
  LearnMoreButtonLabel: string;
}

declare module 'SPFxLocalizationWebPartStrings' {
  const strings: ISPFxLocalizationWebPartStrings;
  export = strings;
}
```

2. **Step 2: Add the localized values to locale JS files**

   Follow below steps to add the localized values to locale JS files:
   - Include the file with English text at \src\webparts\ SPFxLocalization\loc\en-us.js:

   TypeScript

   ```
   define([], function() {
   return {
   "PropertyPaneDescription": "Description",
   "BasicGroupName": "Group Name",
   "DescriptionFieldLabel": "Description Field",
   "LearnMoreButtonLabel": "Learn more"
     }
   });
   ```
   - Include the file with language support at \src\webparts\SPFx Localization\loc\fi-fi.js:

   TypeScript

   ```
   define([], function() {
   return {
   "PropertyPaneDescription": "Kuvaus",
   "BasicGroupName": "Ryhmän nimi",
   "DescriptionFieldLabel": "Kuvauskenttä",
   "LearnMoreButtonLabel": "Lisätietoja"
   ```

3. **Step 3: Web part globalization**

   Follow below steps for web part globalization:
   - Open the file `SPFxLocalization.tsx` under `'\src\webparts\SPFxLocalization\components\'` folder.
   - Add reference to localized strings:

   TypeScript

   ```
   import*as strings from'SPFxLocalizationWebPartStrings';
   ```

   - Reference the localized strings:

   TypeScript

   ```
   exportdefaultclassSPFxLocalizationextends React.Component<ISPFxLocalizationProps, {}> {
   public render(): React.ReactElement<ISPFxLocalizationProps> {
   return (
   <divclassName={ styles.SPFxLocalization}>
   <divclassName={ styles.container }>
   <divclassName={ styles.row }>
   <divclassName={ styles.column }>
   <spanclassName={ styles.title }>Welcome to SharePoint!</span>
   <pclassName={ styles.subTitle }>Customize SharePoint experiences using Web Parts.</p>
   <pclassName={ styles.description }>{escape(this.props.description)}</p>
   <ahref="https://aka.ms/spfx"className={ styles.button }>
   <spanclassName={ styles.label }>{strings.LearnMoreButtonLabel}</span>
   </a>
   </div>
   </div>
   </div>
   ```

```
        </div>
    );
      }
}
```

Test the web part property pane

The default locale value is the value of `spPageContextInfo.currentUICulture Name`. The default locale supported by the SharePoint local workbench is en-US.

Run gulp serve with the locale parameter:

```
gulp serve --locale=fi-fi
```

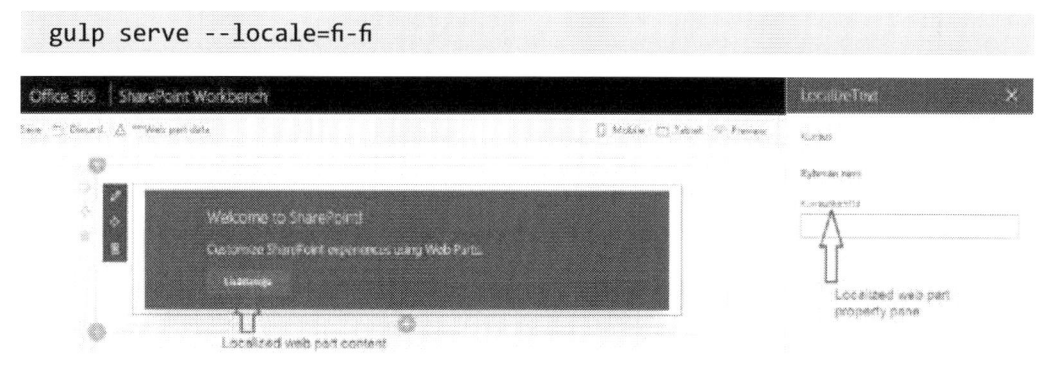

Figure 38.2: Localized the SPFx web part

Conclusion

In this part, we discussed the localization support for SPFx and localization alternatives with SPFx. Localization fabricates better substance for users around the world. The SharePoint Framework underpins localization by keeping localized values in discrete JavaScriptfiles per language.

CHAPTER 39
Office 365 CLI

The Microsoft innovation stack is widely known to be supported on Windows operating systems. PowerShell has been administrators and developers' closest companion in Office 365 to execute powerful commands and computerize the procedure. PowerShell is just bolstered on Windows platform.

The Office 365 CLI deals with the Office 365 and **SharePoint Framework (SPFx)** solutions platform independently. It can function admirably on Windows, Linux, or macOS. The Office 365 CLI is bolstered on PowerShell, Cmder, and Bash. The Office 365 CLI likewise supports to fabricate automation scripts.

Structure

- Introduction to the Office 365 CLI
- Installation and usage
- Managing the Office 365 Tenant
- Introduction to Cmdlets
- Upgrade the Office 365 CLI

Objectives

- Installation of the Office 365 CLI

- Explore Office 365 CLI Cmdlets
- Utilize the Office 365 CLI to manage Office 365 and SPFx solutions

Installation of the Office 365 CLI

The Office 365 CLI is accessible as the NPM bundle.

Execute the following command to install the Office 365 CLI globally:

```
npmi -g @pnp/office365-cli
```

Optionally, execute the following command to install the Office 365 CLI beta version. The beta version includes upcoming and experimental features:

```
npmi -g @pnp/office365-cli@next
```

Usage of the Office 365 CLI

To begin utilizing the Office 365 CLI, execute the following command:

```
office365
```

The Office 365 CLI will start its very own command prompt:

Figure 39.1: Office 365 CLI

Office 365 Tenant Management

Follow the given steps to set up the Office 365 tenant for using the Office 365 CLI:

1. Execute the following command to login to the Office 365 tenant:

   ```
   o365$ spo login https://[tenant]-admin.sharepoint.com
   ```

   In the preceding command, replace the token [tenant] with your Office 365 tenant name.

   Based on the site you want to manage, either provide the SharePoint admin site or normal SharePoint site.

2. Execution of the command will generate a unique code to authenticate against Office 365. Note down the code to be used later:

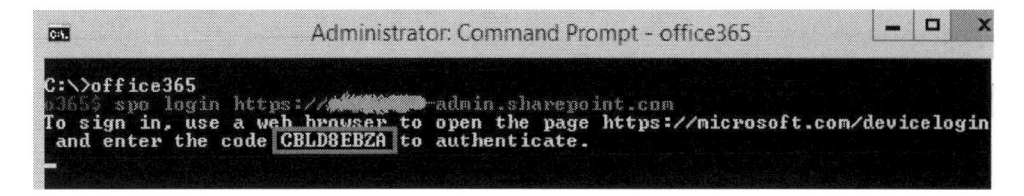

Figure 39.2: Unique generated code for authentication

3. In the browser, open URL (**https://microsoft.com/devicelogin**):

Figure 39.3: Login to O365

4. Provide the unique generated code:

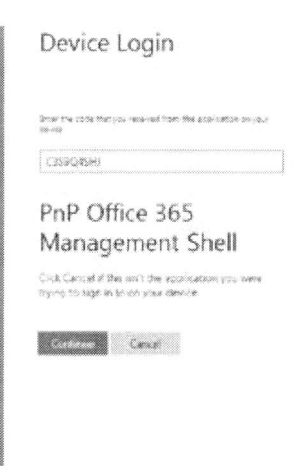

Figure 39.4: Enter the unique generated code

5. Select **Continue**.
6. Provide the Office 365 credentials:

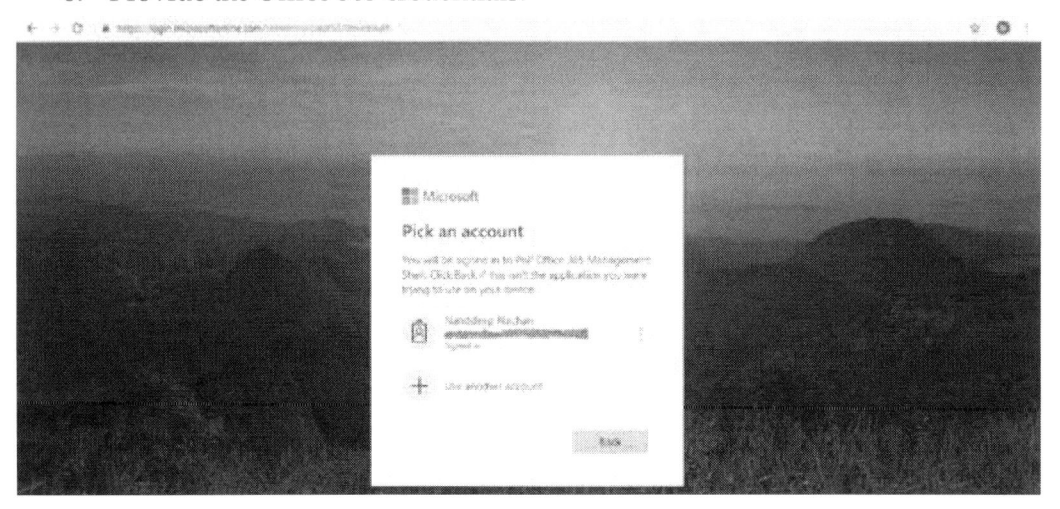

Figure 39.5: Authenticate to Office 365

7. Provide the consent for the app to access the data:

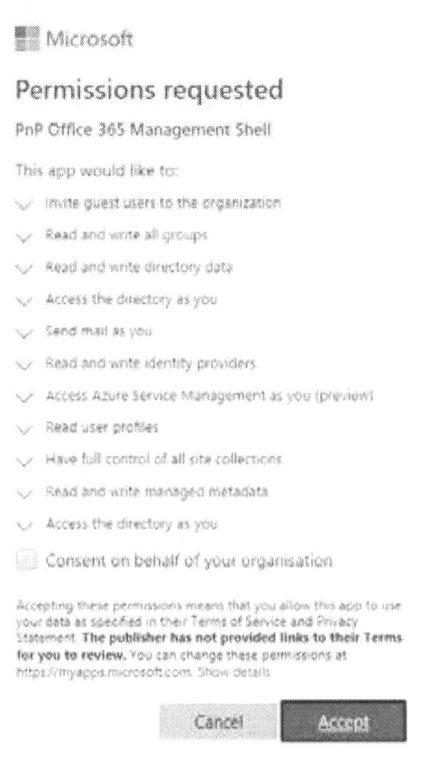

Figure 39.6: Consent for app

8. Select **Accept**.
9. You will be signed in to the PnP Office 365 management shell application:

Figure 39.7: Sign in to PnP Office 365 Management Shell

10. Optionally, close the browser and return to the command prompt.

Office 365 CLI Cmdlets

Get the list of available cmdlets:

```
o365$ help
```

Figure 39.8: Office 365 CLI Cmdlets

Azure Active Directory Management cmdlets:

The aad*cmdletsease to manage Azure AD:

Figure 39.9: AAD management cmdlets

Azure Management cmdlets:

The azmgmt*cmdlets ease to manageAzure Management Service:

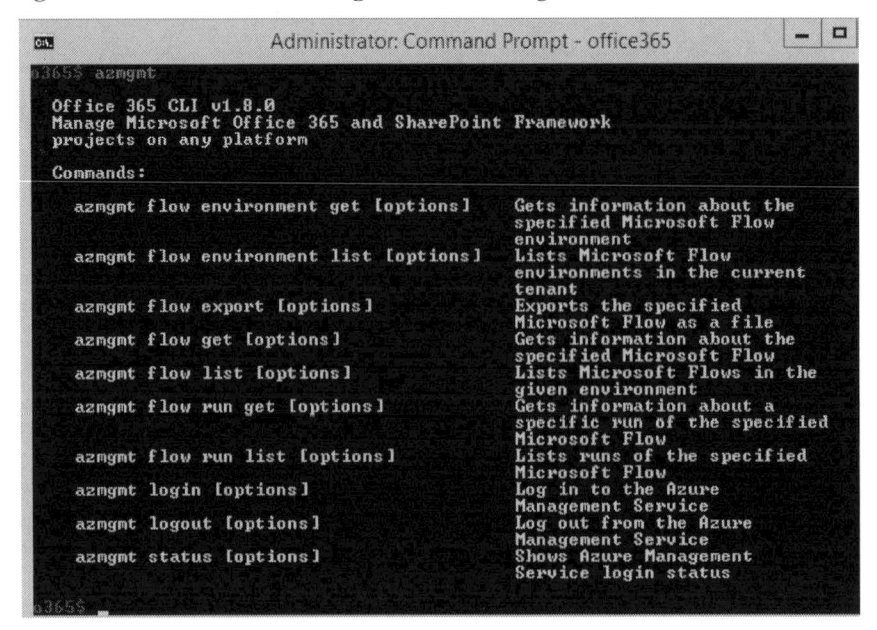

Figure 39.10: Azure Management cmdlets

MS Graph Management cmdlets:

The graph*cmdlets ease to manage Microsoft graph:

```
o365$ graph
Office 365 CLI v1.8.0
Manage Microsoft Office 365 and SharePoint Framework
projects on any platform

Commands:
  graph groupsetting add [options]            Creates a group setting
  graph groupsetting get [options]            Gets information about
                                              the particular group
                                              setting
  graph groupsetting list [options]           Lists Azure AD group
                                              settings
  graph groupsetting remove [options]         Removes the particular
                                              group setting
  graph groupsetting set [options]            Updates the particular
                                              group setting
  graph groupsettingtemplate get [options]    Gets information about
                                              the specified Azure AD
                                              group settings template
  graph groupsettingtemplate list [options]   Lists Azure AD group
                                              settings templates
  graph login [options]                       Log in to the Microsoft
                                              Graph
  graph logout [options]                      Log out from the
                                              Microsoft Graph
  graph o365group add [options]               Creates Office 365 Group
  graph o365group get [options]               Gets information about
                                              the specified Office 365
                                              Group
  graph o365group list [options]              Lists Office 365 Groups
                                              in the current tenant
  graph o365group remove [options]            Removes an Office 365
                                              Group
  graph o365group restore [options]           Restores a deleted Office
                                              365 Group
  graph o365group set [options]               Updates Office 365 Group
                                              properties
  graph siteclassification disable [options]  Disables site
                                              classification
  graph siteclassification enable [options]   Enables site
                                              classification
                                              configuration
  graph siteclassification get [options]      Gets site classification
                                              configuration
  graph status [options]                      Shows Microsoft Graph
                                              login status
  graph teams channel add [options]           Adds a channel to the
                                              specified Microsoft Teams
                                              team
  graph teams list [options]                  Lists Microsoft Teams in
                                              the current tenant
  graph user get [options]                    Gets information about
                                              the specified user
  graph user list [options]                   Lists users matching
                                              specified criteria
  graph user sendmail [options]               Sends e-mail on behalf of
                                              the current user
o365$
```

Figure 39.11: MS Graph cmdlets

SPFx Management cmdlets:

SPFx cmdlets ease to manage SharePoint Framework solutions. The only supported command as of today is to upgrade the SPFx solutions to the latest versions:

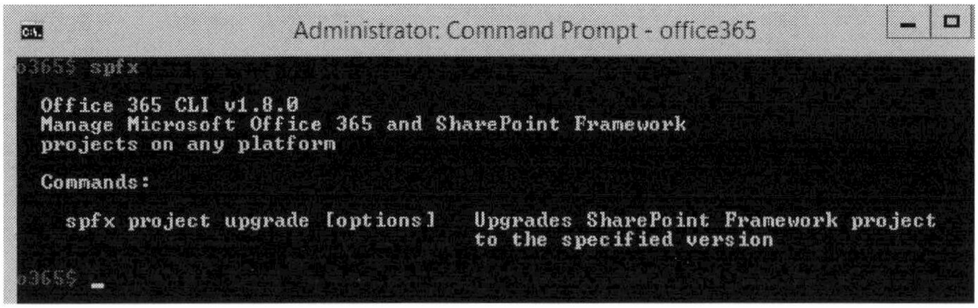

Figure 39.12: SPFx management cmdlets

SharePoint Online management cmdlets:

SharePoint Online (SPO) commands help to manage the SharePoint Online site:

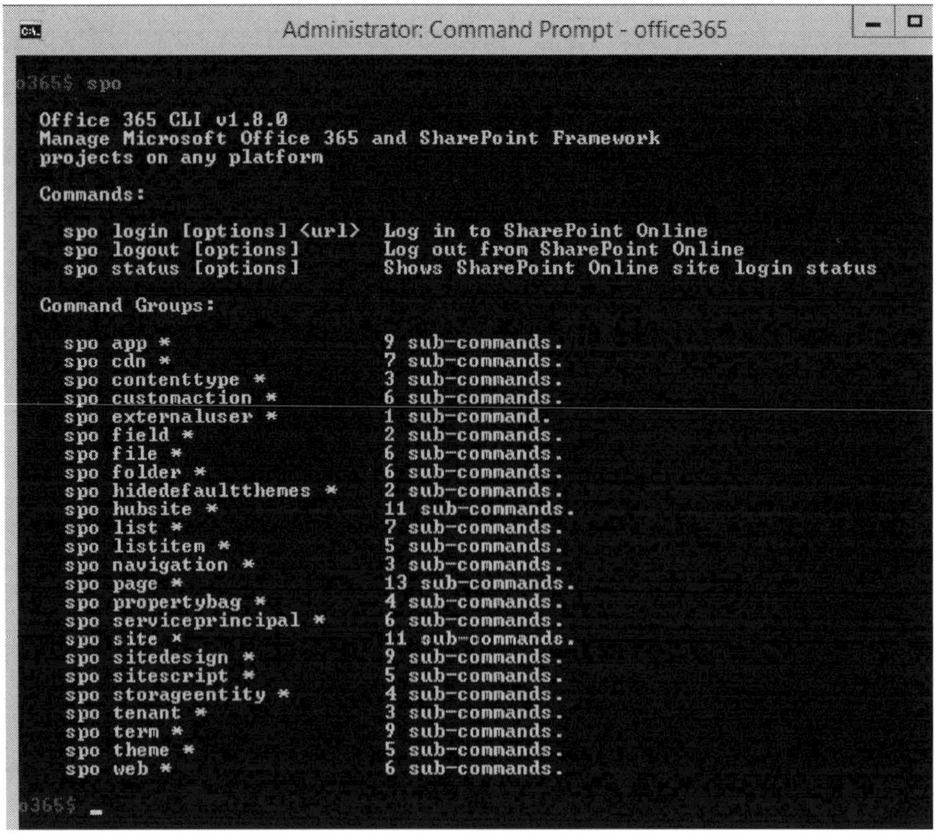

Figure 39.13: SPO management cmdlets

Execute the following command to exit the CLI:

```
o365$ exit
```

Office 365 CLI Upgrade

As the Office 365 CLI is accessible as the NPM bundle, the bug fixes and more current functionalities are discharged as another variant of the NPM bundle.

Execute the following command to check upgrades for the Office 365 CLI:

```
npm outdated --global
```

Update the Office 365 CLI:

```
npm update -g @pnp/office365-cli
```

Conclusion

In this chapter, we discussed the Office 365 CLI, different cmdlets accessible with it, and its utilization to manage Office 365 and SharePoint Framework solutions. The Office 365 CLI deals with the Office 365 and **SharePoint structure (SPFx)** solution platform independently. It can be utilized viably to upgrade SPFx solutions and manufacture automation scripts.

CHAPTER 40
SPFx Solutions Upgrade

The upgrade is an inevitable part of every product and the SharePoint Framework has no exemptions to it. SPFx gets refreshed on a regular basis. Each time with new updates, it offers better functionalities and bug fixes. SPFx web parts and extensions are created utilizing JavaScript packages from various vendors or publishers. The bundles are accessible At the npm repository (**https://www.npmjs.com/**). These bundles likewise receive successive updates. To utilize the most recent contributions, the need emerges to overhaul our current SPFx answers for the more up-to-date forms.

Structure
- The Upgrade Puzzle
- The Upgrade Plan

Objectives
- Analyze upgrade situations
- Upgrade to more up-to-date forms of JavaScript bundles

The upgrade puzzle
The primary question emerges to mind is that is there a genuine need for overhauling

a current solution which is tried and working fine for some time? The doubt is that you need to exploit the best in the class of the SharePoint Framework at that point when the update is fundamental.

It is an individual decision or a group choice to settle on the redesign. In any case, to be in a state of harmony with the SPFx happenings, it is smarter to redesign.

Is the upgrade process simple?

The appropriate response isn't generally. Upgrading the SPFx solution isn't simple consistently. You may frequently keep running into build errors.

The basic strides to upgrade

Take a case of any SPFx solution created with a prior adaptation of SPFx. Let us take the SPFx solution made with v1.5.1 and update it to v1.6.0 (the most recently available as an example).

Follow below steps to check the version of the SPFx solution:

1. At the command prompt, navigate to the SPFx solution folder location.
2. Open the solution in the code editor by executing the following command:

    code .

3. Open the package.json file:

Figure 40.1: package.json contents

4. SPFx packages can be recognized with the `@microsoft/sp-` prefix.
5. The above SPFx solution has v1.5.1.

The upgrade plan

The upgrade procedure will assist us with upgrading our solution for the most recent SPFx version (think about v1.6.0 as the most recent one for this upgrade situation).

Follow below steps to find out the outdated npm packages:

1. At the command prompt, navigate to the SPFx solution folder location.
2. To list the outdated packages, execute the following command:

```
npm outdated
```

Figure 40.2: Outdated npm packages

The output represents:
- **Current:** Present version of the bundle utilized.
- **Wanted:** Version required by the solution (referenced in package.json).
- **Latest:** The recent accessible version of the bundle.

Upgrading NPM packages:

Execute the following set of commands to upgrade each of the outdated packages.

Upgrade an individual package to a specific version:

```
npm install [package]@[version] --save
```

Upgrade the package to the latest version:

```
npm install [package]@latest --save
```

Example:

```
npm install @types/chai@latest --save
```

Or use another variant:

```
npm install [package] --save
```

Example:

```
npm install @microsoft/sp-core-library --save
```

Package updates verification:

Follow below steps to verify that the npm packages are updated:

1. At the command prompt, execute the following command to open the SPFx solution in the code editor:

   ```
   code .
   ```

2. Open package.json.
3. Check whether the package versions are updated:

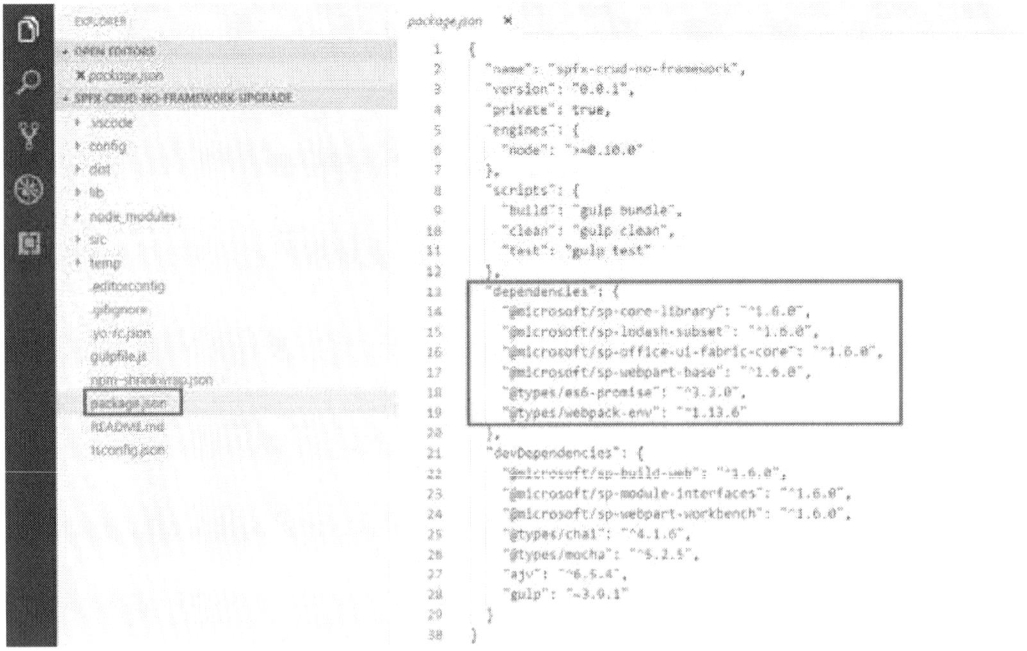

Figure 40.3: Package dependencies in package.json

4. Update config.json to the latest version:

   ```
   gulp --update
   ```

5. Clean the previous packages:

   ```
   gulp clean
   ```

6. Build the solution:

   ```
   gulp build
   ```

7. Run the project:

   ```
   gulp serve
   ```

In the event that this goes well, you have your SPFx solution updated to the new version. In the event that, for reasons unknown, the overhaul does not go well, follow the given steps:

1. Install or update to the most recent version of the Yeoman generator for SPFx:

   ```
   npm update -g @microsoft/generator-sharepoint@latest
   ```

2. Generate another SPFx solution.
3. The new solution references the most recent packages.
4. Compare and merge the `package.json` contents. (May be using something like the **Code Compare** tool from Devart):

Figure 40.4: Code compare

5. Compare and merge the contents of the `tsconfig.json` file.
6. Remove `package-lock.json` or `npm-shrinkwrap.json` from the SPFx solution.
7. Delete the `node_modules` folder.

8. Download the updated npm packages:

    ```
    npm install
    ```

9. Clean the output from the previous builds:

    ```
    gulp clean
    ```

10. Lock down the package versions:

    ```
    npm shrinkwrap
    ```

Conclusion

In this chapter, we learned about the upgrade procedure to a fresher adaptation of SPFx. It isn't required but it is wise to upgrade SPFx solutions to get advantages of more current functionalities from the most recent versions. The overhaul procedure probably won't be simple yet it can be carefully defined and executed.

CHAPTER 41
SPFx Solution Upgrade with the Office 365 CLI

The SharePoint Framework is regularly developing. With each one of its variants, it discharges more up-to-date usefulness and functionalities. Overhauling the SPFx solutions with every release is cumbersome. The manual endeavors to overhaul could conceivably work. Sometimes, we may need to rework the code in a more up-to-date form. The Office 365 CLI handles this situation smoothly and gives an adaptable alternative to developers to move up to any new versions of SPFx.

Structure
- Introduction to the Office 365 CLI
- Upgrading SPFx Solutions to the Latest Version
- Upgrading SPFx Solutions to a Specific Version

Objective
- Upgrading SPFx solutions utilizing the Office 365 CLI

Introduction to the Office 365 CLI

It is an open source venture from **Pattern and Practices (PnP)**. It helps to organize the Office 365 tenant and SPFx solutions platform independently (Windows, Linux, macOS, and so on). The Office 365 CLI is accessible as a distributable NPM bundle. Run the following command to globally install the Office 365 CLI:

```
npm i -g @pnp/office365-cli
```

SPFx Solution Upgrade to the Latest Version

We will take a case of the SPFx solution created with SPFx drop v1.7.1. In this chapter, we will overhaul this solution for the most recent SPFx v1.9.1 (most recent accessible at the time of writing this book).

Perform the following steps to update the SPFx solution to the most recent version:

1. At the command prompt, execute the following command:

   ```
   npm install -g @pnp/office365-cli@latest
   ```

2. At the command prompt, open the folder location of the SPFx solution and run the following command:

   ```
   o365 spfx project upgrade --output md > report.md
   ```

This will create a markdown document with the actions to be performed on the SPFx solution in order to overhaul it to the most recent version. The Office 365 CLI does not apply any changes to the SPFx solution. The progressions should be carried out physically.

3. Execute the given command to open the SPFx solution in the preferred code editor:

   ```
   code .
   ```

4. In the code editor, open the `report.md` file.

5. Select **Open Preview to the Side** (shortcut *Ctrl + K V*) to preview the markdown file:

Figure 41.1: Preview markdown file

6. The mark down file provides the simple steps to follow directions to upgrade the solution:

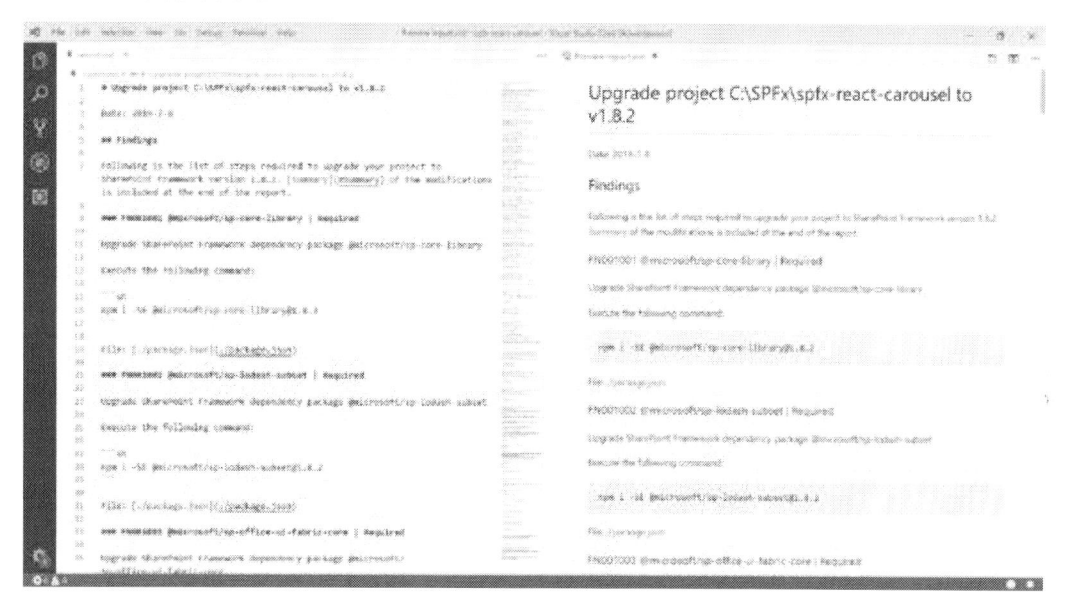

Figure 41.2: Upgrade directions

7. Carry out the guidelines as perthe markdown file instructions:

The guidelines contain a set of npm commands to be executed in order and the importance of the individual npm package for an upgrade. Follow the **Summary** section towards the end of the file to know the set of npm commands to be executed, as well as manual changes to be carried out:

Figure 41.3: Upgrade summary

SPFx Solution Upgrade to a Specific Version

In certain situations, we might not have any desire to move up to the most recent SPFx version but perhaps to some intermediate version adaptation. The Office 365 CLI under pins this situation. Use the following command to move up to a particular variant (for example v1.9.1 for this situation):

```
o365 spfx project upgrade --toVersion 1.9.1 --output md > report.md
```

SPFx Solution Downgrade?

No, the Office 365 CLI does not permit downgrading the SPFx solution. For instance, your SPFx solution is made utilizing adaptation v1.7.1, so running the following command won't downgrade the SPFx solution to v1.5.0.

```
o365 spfx project upgrade --toVersion 1.5.0 --output md > report.md
```

The upgrade report will show the message **Error: You cannot downgrade a project:**

Figure 41.4: SPFx solution downgrade scenario

Conclusion

The Office 365 CLI is an open-source venture from **Pattern and Practices (PnP)** which oversees the Office 365 tenant and SPFx solutions platform independently. The Office 365 CLI does not make any changes to SPFx solution, but gives the direction to the progressions to be carried out physically so as to upgrade the solution. Downgrading the SPFx solution is not supported.

CHAPTER 42
Common Issues and Resolutions with Upgrading npm Packages

The **SharePoint Framework (SPFx)** underpins modern tool chain, which utilizes different npm bundles. Upgrading the npm bundles to the most recent version is critical to get advantages of the best highlights offered by that npm bundle. This chapter isn't just explicit to the npm bundle upgrade with the SharePoint Framework. It tends to be utilized conventionally.

Structure

- Upgrade situations for npm packages
- Challenges and resolutions with npm upgrade

Objectives

- Understand benefits of upgrading npm packages
- Common issues and resolutions with upgrade

Why to upgrade npm packages?

The npm bundles get refreshed by the vendor dependent on the feedback received and issues raised now and again. Likewise, to begin utilizing more up-to-date capacities and functionalities offered by npm bundles, it is critical to refresh ourselves to the more up-to-date npm bundles.

One normal situation for the npm bundle update is the updates to the SharePoint Framework variant. Microsoft releases newer version of the SharePoint Framework with new capacities, bug fixes, and so on. The updates are not too frequent; however, they get discharged at ordinary interims, which is something worth being thankful for. In the long run, we need to move towards utilizing the new SharePoint Framework version.

By nature, not all npm package versions are compatible with one another. Subsequently, it is critical to comprehend the npm bundle dependencies and after that, plan the upgrade appropriately.

Upgrading npm packages

To discover the obsolete npm bundles at the global level, execute the following command:

```
npm outdated --global
```

The preceding command will list out the outdated packages. To upgrade each package, execute the given command:

```
npm update -g <package-name>
```

This is a perfect situation. In a genuine case, we may face difficulties getting the obsolete npm bundles.

Common Issues and Resolutions for npm Upgrade

There have been certain issues with npm to discover the obsolete bundles. The '`npm outdated`' command neglects to report the obsolete bundles. The error reported is: **Cannot read property 'length' of undefined:**

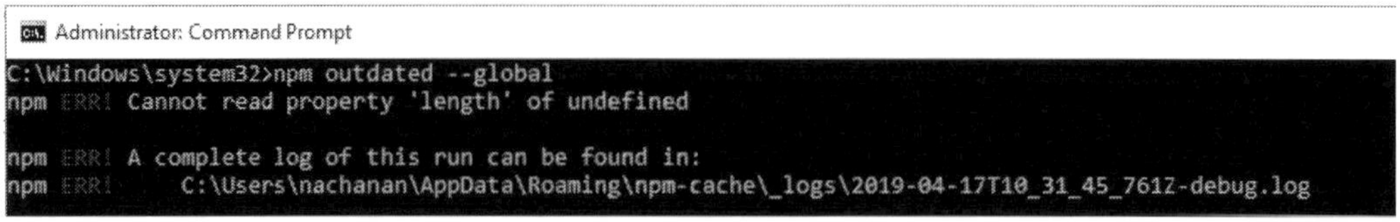

Figure 42.1: Issues with npm outdated

The error log is accessible at the referenced area under '`AppData\Roaming\npm-cache\_logs`'. It doesn't help to plainly comprehend the definite reason for the issue and its resolution:

Figure 42.2: npm upgradeerror log

In spite of the fact that npm fails to report the obsolete bundles, if you know the name of the npm bundle to upgrade, you can in any case use the 'npm update' command to upgrade that particular npm bundle.

Alternative 1: Upgrade npm

The simple and first choice is to upgrade the npm itself. Execute the following command to upgrade npm:

```
npm i -g npm
```

Alternative 2: Reinstall Node.js

In the event that upgrading the npm does not work, the subsequent choice is to uninstall and reinstall Node.js. Install the LTS version of Node.js 8.x or 10.x as supported by SPFx.

Alternative 3: Alter npm configuration

The globally installed npm bundles are accessible at 'C:\Users\<user-name>\ AppData\Roaming\npm\node_modules\'.

Physically alter the 'lib\outdated.js' record situated at 'npm\node_modules\ npm' location. (For example C:\Users\nanddeep\AppData\Roaming\npm\node_ modules\npm\lib\outdated.js)

Update the `makePretty` function as follows:

Figure 42.3: npm configuration

Execute the 'npm outdated' command again to view the outdated packages:

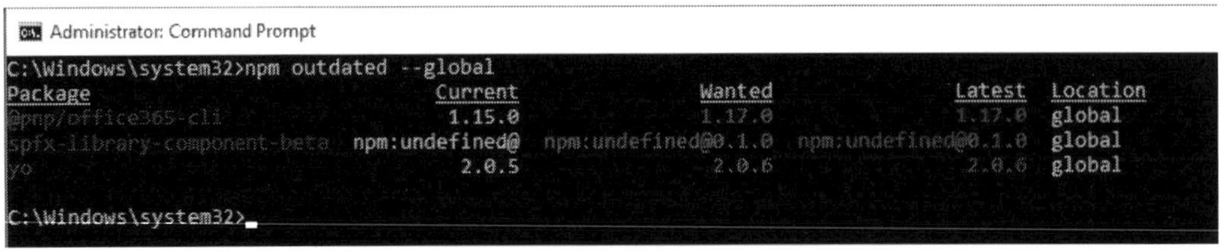

Figure 42.4: npm updated packages

Conclusion

In this chapter, we discussed the necessity for the npm bundle upgrade, how to upgrade the npm bundles, and basic issues and resolutions while refreshing to the most recent npm bundles.

It is imperative to upgrade SPFx solutions for more recent npm bundle adaptation to get the advantages of new improvements and bug fixes accessible as components of fresher bundles. Reporting the obsolete npm bundles command probably won't work sometimes. This can be settled by following any one of the choices referenced in this chapter.

CHAPTER 43
Extend MS Teams with SPFx

The SharePoint Framework v1.8.0 onwards facilitates the development of Microsoft Teams tabs. This gives the likelihood to different situations in creating Microsoft Teams tabs utilizing the SharePoint Framework.

Structure
- Extend MS Teams utilizing SPFx
- Make the SPFx web part accessiblein MS Teams

Objectives
- Implement the MS Teams tab utilizing SPFx
- Build and deploy common solutions to SharePoint and MS Teams utilizing SPFx

Develop the MS Teams Tab SPFx Solution

Open a command prompt. Follow the given guidelines to make the SPFx solution:
1. Make a folder for the SPFx solution:

```
md spfx-extend-msteams
```

2. Change the path to the above folder:

   ```
   cd spfx-extend-msteams
   ```

3. Execute the Yeoman Generator for SharePoint:

   ```
   yo @microsoft/sharepoint
   ```

4. The Yeoman generator will run through the wizard to ask questions about the SPFx solution to be created:

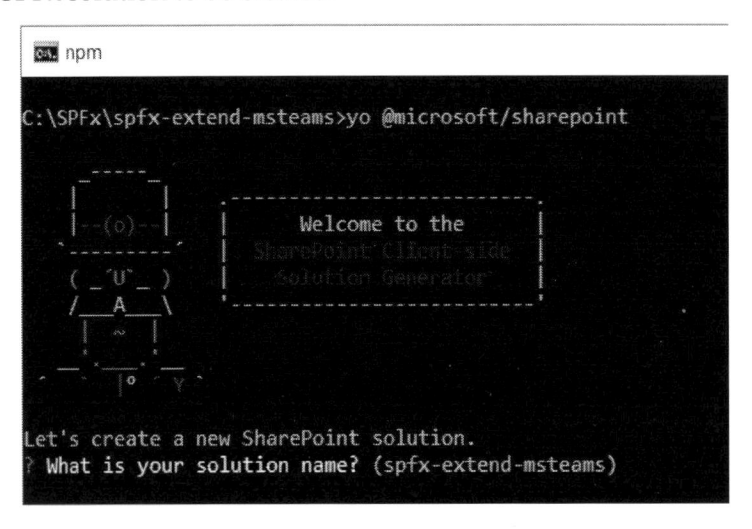

Figure 43.1: SPFx Yeoman generator

The SPFx Yeoman generator will display the following wizard of inquiries:

- **Solution Name:** Determine the SPFx solution name. Hit the *Enter* key to proceed with the default selection (`spfx-extend-msteams` in this case) or type another name.
  - **Chosen decision:** Hit *Enter*
- **Target environment:** Specify the target environment to deploy the SPFx solution. Select any option from SharePoint Online or SharePoint On-Premises environment.
  - **Chosen decision:** SharePoint Online only (latest)
- **Folder location:** Choose the folder location for the SPFx project (either the same folder or a subfolder).
  - **Chosen decision:** Use the current folder
- **Deployment option:** Specify Y to deploy the app instantly to all the sites, N otherwise.
  - **Chosen decision:** Y

- **Consents to access web APIs:** Check whether the components in the solution need explicit permission to access web APIs that are unique and not shared with other components in the tenant.
    - **Chosen decision:** N (solution contains unique permissions)
- **Choice of client-side component:** Choose to develop a web part or an extension.
    - **Chosen decision:** WebPart
- **Web Part Name:** Specify the name of the web part. Hit the *Enter* key to go ahead with the default name or type in any other name.
    - **Chosen decision:** `MSTeamsTab`
- **Web part description:** Specify the description of the web part. Hit the *Enter* key to go ahead with the default description or type in any other value.
    - **Chosen decision:** First Teams Tab
- **A framework to use:** Select any JavaScript framework to develop the component. Available choices are (No JavaScript Framework, React, and Knockout)
    - **Chosen decision:** No JavaScript Framework

5. After the scaffolding is complete, execute the following command to lock down the version of project dependencies:

```
npm shrinkwrap
```

6. At the command prompt, execute the following command to open the solution in the code editor:

```
code .
```

Support for MS Teams in SPFx

The SPFx solution structure supports the folder named teams containing default configurations to start developing against MS Teams:

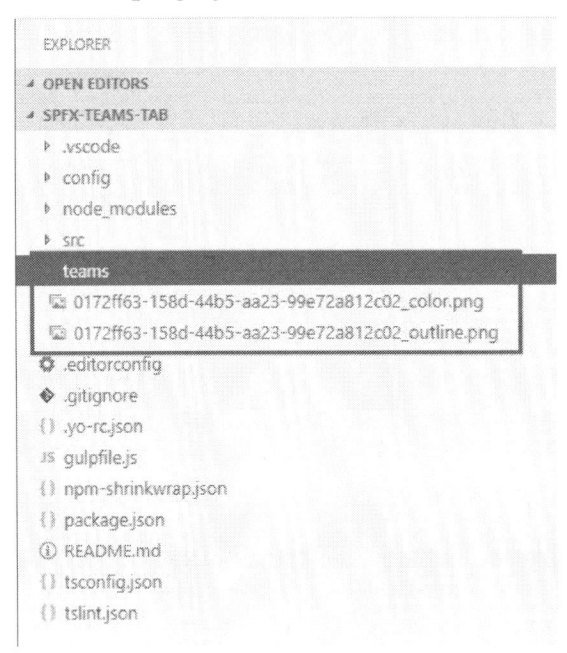

Figure 43.2: teams folder for MS Teams support

The teams folder contains two images representing default pictures for the MS Teams tab. The one ending with `_color.png` represents the small picture and the one ending with `_outline.png` represents the large picture. The prefix guid represents the web part `id`.

Enable MS Teams Support:

Follow below steps to enable the MS Teams support for SPFx solution:

1. Open the web part `manifest.json` file.
2. To the `supportedHosts` property, add the TeamsTab:

    JSON

    ```
    {
    "$schema":"https://developer.microsoft.com/json-schemas/spfx/client-side-web-part-manifest.schema.json",
    "id": "0172ff63-158d-44b5-aa23-99e72a812c02",
    "alias": "MSTeamsWebPart",
    ```

```
    "componentType": "WebPart",

    // The "*" signifies that the version should be taken from the
    package.json
    "version": "*",
    "manifestVersion": 2,

    // If true, the component can only be installed on sites where
    Custom Script is allowed.
    // Components that allow authors to embed arbitrary script code
    should set this to true.
    "requiresCustomScript": false,
    "supportedHosts": ["SharePointWebPart", "TeamsTab"],

    "preconfiguredEntries": [{
    "groupId": "5c03119e-3074-46fd-976b-c60198311f70", // Other
    "group": { "default": "Other" },
    "title": { "default": "MSTeamsTab" },
    "description": { "default": "MSTeams tab" },
    "officeFabricIconFontName": "Page",
    "properties": {
    "description": "Tab for MS Teams"
        }
      }]
    }
```

Handle MS Teams Context in the Web Part

Follow below steps to handle the MS Teams context in the SPFx web part:
1. To the web part file (src\webparts\spfx-extend-msteams\MSTeamsTabWebPart.ts), include the following import:

   TypeScript

   ```
   import*as microsoftTeams from'@microsoft/teams-js';
   ```

2. Define a variable to represent the MS Teams context:

   TypeScript

   ```typescript
   private _msTeamsContext: microsoftTeams.Context;
   ```

3. Set the MS Teams context inside the Init() method:

   TypeScript

   ```typescript
   protected onInit(): Promise<any> {
   letreturnValue: Promise<any> = Promise.resolve();
   if (this.context.microsoftTeams) {
   returnValue = new Promise((resolve, reject) => {
   this.context.microsoftTeams.getContext(context => {
   this._msTeamsContext = context;
        resolve();
      });
     });
   }
   returnreturnValue;
   }
   ```

4. Update the render() method:

   TypeScript

   ```typescript
   public render(): void {
   letwpTitle: string = '';
   letsubTitle: string = '';

   if (this._msTeamsContext) {
   // MSTeams context
   wpTitle = "Welcome to Teams!";
   subTitle = "Team: " + this._msTeamsContext.teamName;
     }
   else {
   ```

```
// SharePoint context
wpTitle = "Welcome to SharePoint!";
subTitle = "SharePoint site: " + this.context.pageContext.web.title;
    }
this.domElement.innerHTML = `
<div class="${ styles.teamsTab }">
<div class="${ styles.container }">
<div class="${ styles.row }">
<div class="${ styles.column }">
<span class="${ styles.title }">${wpTitle}</span>
<p class="${ styles.description }">${subTitle}</p>
<p class="${ styles.description }">Description property value - ${escape(this.properties.description)}</p>
<a href="https://aka.ms/spfx" class="${ styles.button }">
<span class="${ styles.label }">Learn more</span>
</a>
</div>
</div>
</div>
</div>`;
}
```

Package and Deploy the web part to SharePoint

Follow below steps to package and deploy the SPFx web part to the SharePoint:

1. At the command prompt, execute the following command to bundle the solution:

    ```
    gulp bundle --ship
    ```

2. Execute the following command to package the solution:

    ```
    gulp package-solution --ship
    ```

The `spfx-extend-msteams.sppkg` package will be generated At the 'sharepoint\solution' folder.

3. Navigate to the SharePoint App catalog site.
4. Upload the `spfx-extend-msteams.sppkg` to app catalog.
5. Select the `Make this solution available to all sites in the organization` option:

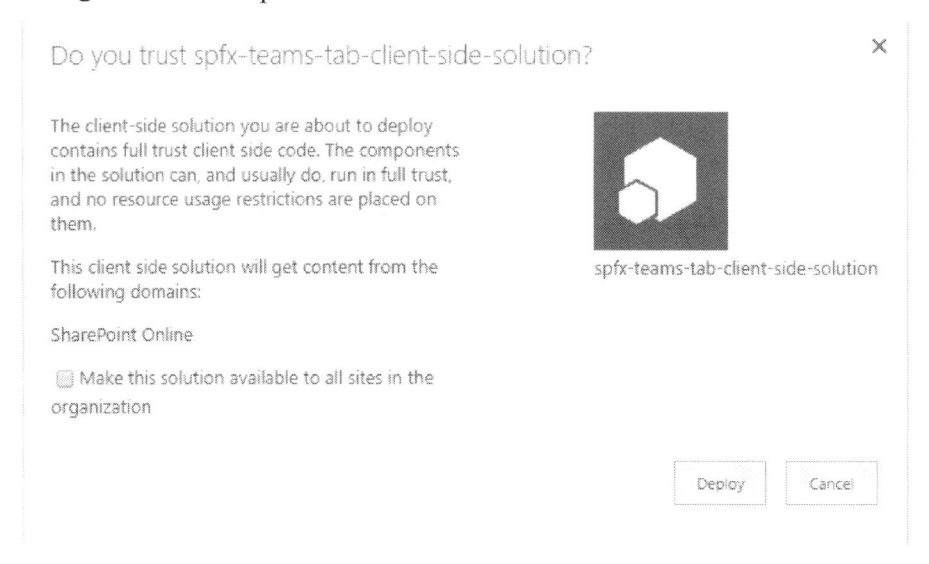

Figure 43.3: Add solution to app catalog

6. Select Deploy.

Validate the web part in SharePoint

Follow below steps to validate the SPFx web part on the SharePoint site:

1. On the SharePoint site, include our web part.
2. The web part should display the information with the SharePoint site context:

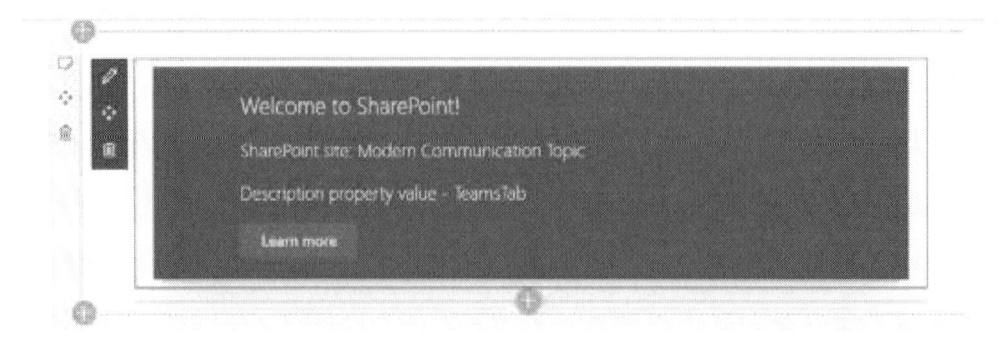

Figure 43.4: SharePoint context information in web part

Make the web part accessible in MS Teams

Follow below steps to synchronize the solution with MS Teams to make it accessible:

1. In the app catalog, choose the deployed solution.
2. With the **Files** option selected in the ribbon, select **Sync to Teams**:

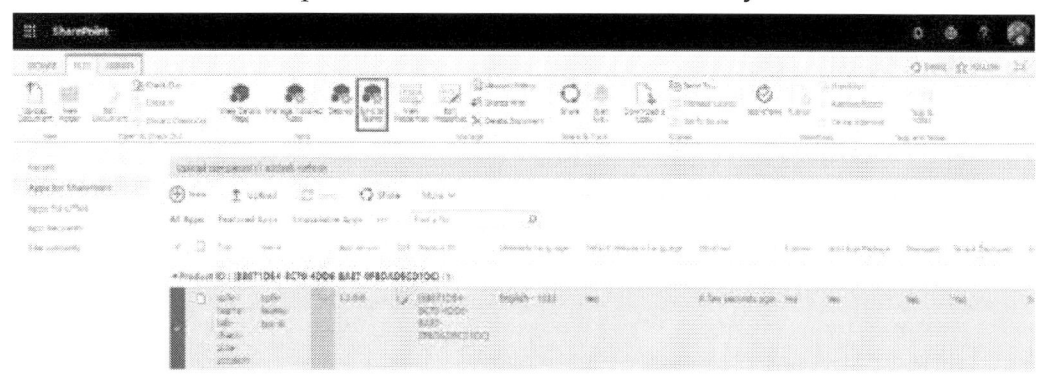

Figure 43.5: Make solution accessible in MS Teams

Validate the web part in Microsoft Teams

Follow below steps to validate the SPFx web part in MS Teams:

1. Open MS Teams.
2. Under any of the existing team, select a channel.
3. Add a new tab by clicking "+":

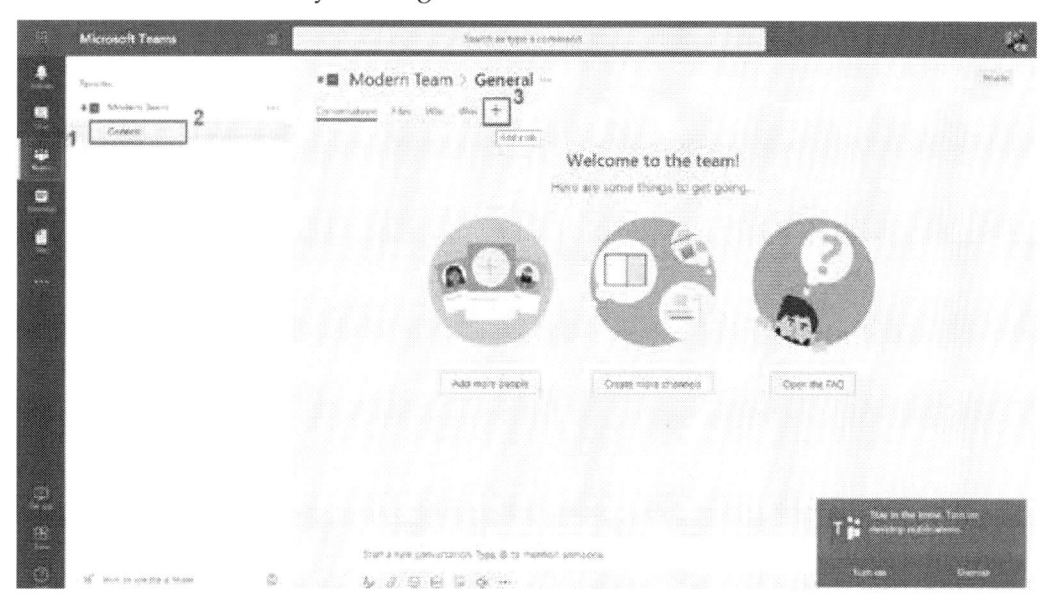

Figure 43.6: Include Teams tab

462 ■ *Mastering SharePoint Framework*

4. Choose the SPFx web part from the available apps:

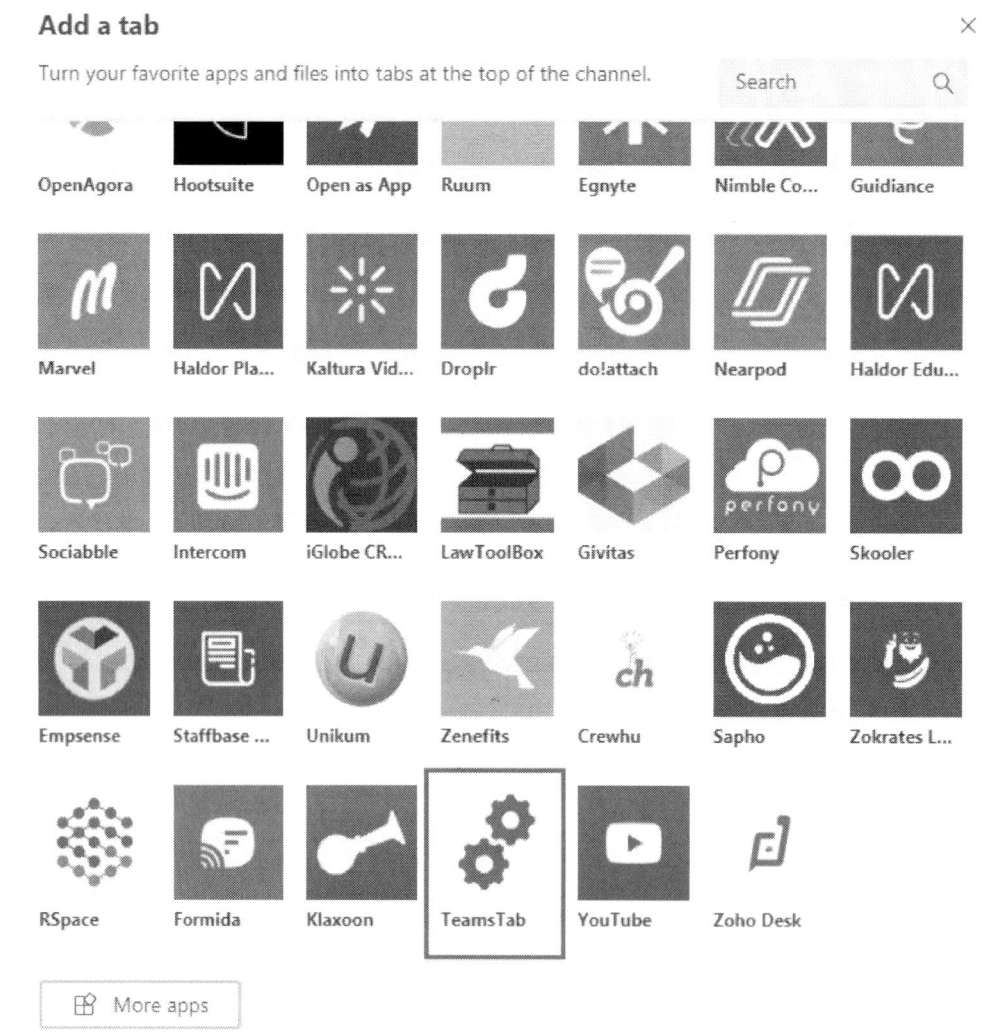

Figure 43.7: Choose SPFx web part

5. Click on **Install**:

Figure 43.8: Install the solution

6. Then, click on **Save**.

Figure 43.9: Add solution to tab

7. The SPFx web part shouldbe visible as a custom MS Teams tab showing the information from the MS Teams context:

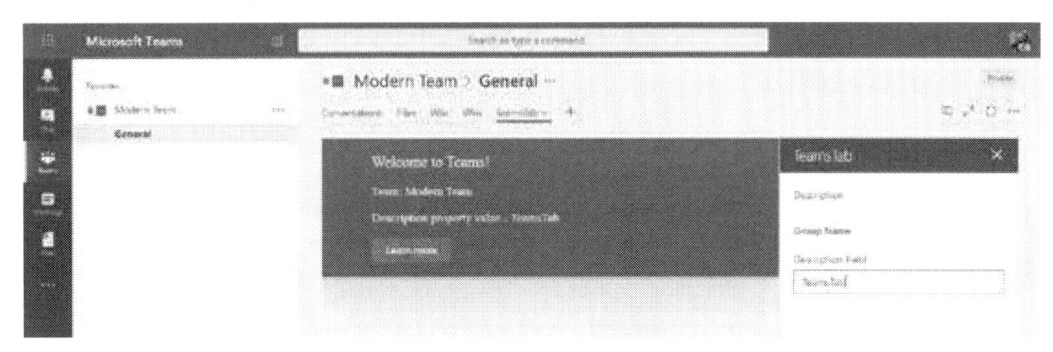

Figure 43.10: MS Teams context information in the web part

Conclusion

In this chapter, we learned about the MS Teams tab advancement with SPFx. SPFx v1.8.0 onwards facilitates the advancement of Microsoft Teams tabs. A similar web part arrangement can work at both SharePoint and Microsoft Teams dependently under which it is running.

CHAPTER 44
Library Component Types

The SharePoint Framework offers more up-to-date abilities with each new release. The SPFx release v1.8.0 has presented a library component type which exhibits a pleas ant choice to builda shared code. The library component is generally available with SPFx v1.9.1.

Structure
- Introduction to a Library Component
- Develop a Library Component
- Utilize Library in the SPFx web part

Objectives
- Overview of a library component
- Build a library component
- Utilize a library component

Introduction to a Library Component

Building a common code that can be shared by different components is advisable. A library component type offers an alternative to make shared code, which can be freely formed and conveyed. The excellence of the library component is that it may very well be referenced over all components in the tenant.

- A single version of a library component can be facilitated in a tenant at any given moment.
- A solution can contain only a single library component in it.
- To bundle library component dependent solutions, reference them from the package manager while development or use 'npmlink'.

Create the Library Component

At the command prompt, follow the given instructions:

1. Make a folder for the SPFx solution:

    ```
    md LibraryComponent\spfx-library
    ```

2. Change the path to the above folder:

    ```
    cd LibraryComponent\spfx-library
    ```

3. Run the Yeoman SharePoint generator to create the SPFx solution:

    ```
    yo @microsoft/sharepoint
    ```

    If you are using the SPFx version less than 1.9.0, execute the Yeoman Generator for SharePoint with the `--plusbeta` option to utilize the preview/beta features:

    ```
    yo @microsoft/sharepoint --plusbeta
    ```

4. The Yeoman generator will run through a wizard to ask questions about the SPFx solution to be created:

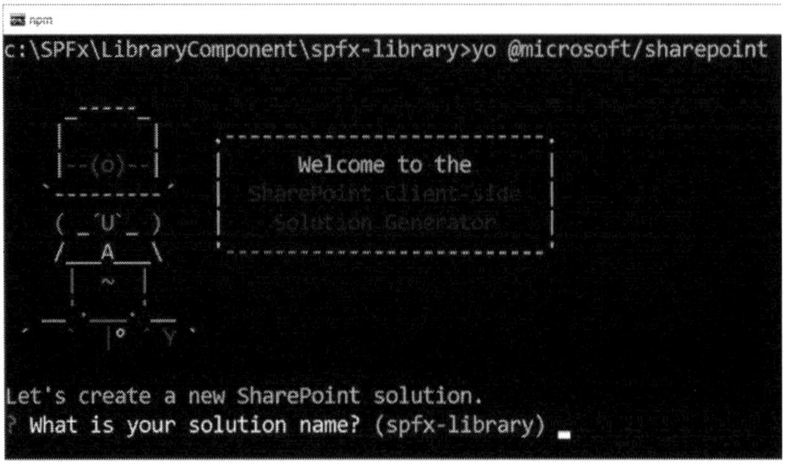

Figure 44.1: SPFx Yeoman generator

The SPFx Yeoman generator will give the following wizard of inquiries:

- **Solution Name:** Determine the SPFx solution name. Hit the *Enter* key to proceed with the default selection (`spfx-library` in this case) or type another name.
    - o **Chosen decision:** Hit *Enter*
- **Target environment:** Specify the target environment to deploy the SPFx solution. Select any option from SharePoint Online or SharePoint On-Premises environment.
    - o **Chosen decision:** SharePoint Online only (latest)
- **Folder location:** Choose the folder location for the SPFx project (either the same folder or a subfolder).
    - o **Chosen decision:** Use the current folder
- **Deployment option:** Specify Y to deploy the app instantly to all the sites, N otherwise.
    - o **Chosen decision:** Y
- **Permissions to access web APIs:** Check whether the components in the solution require permissions to access web APIs.
    - o **Chosen decision:** N (solution contains unique permissions)
- **Choice of client-side component:** Choose to develop a web part or an extension or Library.
    - o **Chosen decision:** `Library`

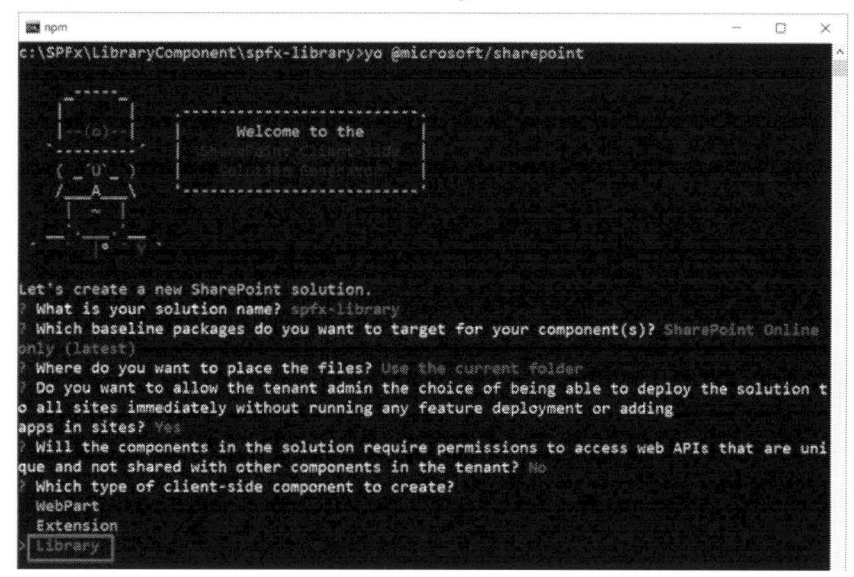

Figure 44.2: Library Component Type

- **Library Name:** Provide the library name.
    - **Chosen decision:** CommonLibrary
- **Library Description:** Provide the library description.
    - **Chosen decision:** Specify the library description

Develop the Library Component

Follow the given steps to develop the library component:

1. At the command prompt, execute the following command to open the solution in the code editor:

    ```
    code .
    ```

2. The src\CommonLibraryLibrary.manifest.json file records the component type as library:

JSON

```
{
"id": "e02dc42c-b48a-481b-be18-cc9908cc4a88",
"alias": "CommonLibraryLibrary",
"componentType": "Library",

// The "*" signifies that the version should be taken from the package.json
"version": "*",
"manifestVersion": 2
}
```

3. The `index.ts` file points to the responsible library class implementation:

Figure 44.3: index.ts file

4. Open `src\libraries\commonLibrary\CommonLibraryLibrary.ts`.
5. The library component contains the default method name, which returns the name of the library component. We will start by adding more methods:

TypeScript

exportdefaultclassCommonLibraryLibrary {

public name(): string {

return'CommonLibraryLibrary';

}

publicgetRandomNumber(): string {

// Generate and return random number between 1 to 100

    letrandomNumber = Math.floor(Math.random() * 100) + 1;

return'Random number returned from the common library is ' + randomNumber;

}

}

6. At the command prompt, compile the library component by executing the 'gulp' command.

Utilizethe library component in the SPFx-webpart

Follow the given steps to utilize the library component in the SPFxweb part:

1. At the command prompt, point to the library solution root folder. Execute the following command:

   ```
   npm link
   ```

   Figure 44.4: npm link

   This will create a local npm link to the library as highlighted in the preceding screenshot.

2. Create the web part project ina separate SPFx solution(not inside the library folder hierarchy):

   ```
   md LibraryComponent\spfx-library-consumer && cd LibraryComponent\spfx-library-consumer
   ```

3. At the command prompt, execute the following command:

   ```
   yo @microsoft/sharepoint
   ```

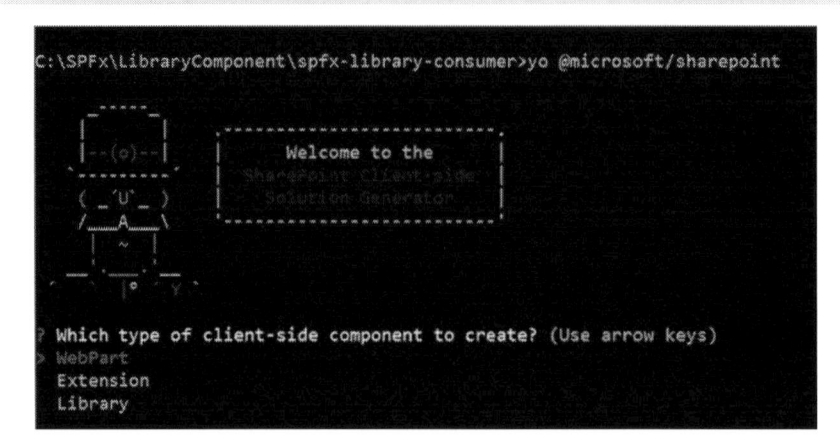

   Figure 44.5: Implement the SPFx web part

- **Choice of client-side component:** WebPart
- **Web part name:** LibraryConsumerWebPart
- **Web part description:** Consume common library
- **Choice of framework:** React

4. At the command prompt, pointto the web part solution root folder (i.e. src\webparts\libraryConsumer) and execute the following command:

    ```
    npm link spfx-library
    ```

Figure 44.6: npm link

5. At the command prompt, execute the following command to open the solution in the code editor:

    ```
    code .
    ```

6. Open the web part file src\webparts\libraryConsumer\components\LibraryConsumer.tsx.

7. Import the library:

    TypeScript

    ```
    import * as myLibrary from 'spfx-library';
    ```

8. Implement the render() method:

    TypeScript

    ```
    public render(): React.ReactElement<ILibraryConsumerProps> {
      const myInstance = new myLibrary.CommonLibraryLibrary();

      return (
        <div className={styles.libraryConsumer}>
          <div className={styles.container}>
            <div className={styles.row}>
              <div className={styles.column}>
    ```

```
                <span className={styles.title}>Welcome to SharePoint!</span>
                <p className={styles.subTitle}>Customize SharePoint experiences using Web Parts.</p>
                <p>${myInstance.getRandomNumber()}</p>
              </div>
            </div>
          </div>
        </div>
    );
}
```

Verify the webpart

Follow below steps to test the web part on the SharePoint page:
1. At the command, execute 'gulp serve'.
2. On the SharePoint site, browse to /_layouts/15/workbench.aspx.
3. Add the webpart to the page:

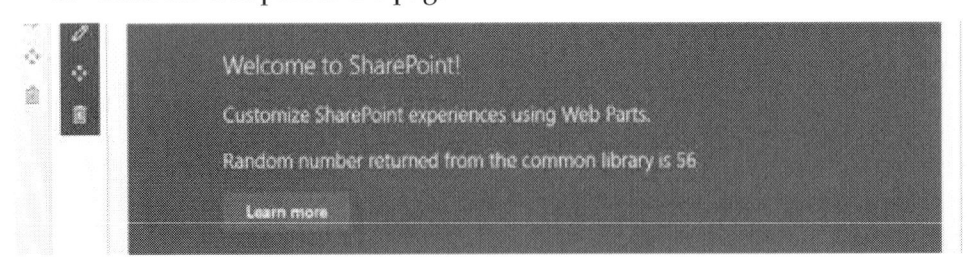

Figure 44.8: SPFx web part utilizing the library component

Deploy a library to the tenant app catalog

Follow the given steps to deploy the library to the tenant app catalog:
1. At the command prompt, navigate to the root folder of the library component.
2. Execute the following commands to bundle and package the library component:

   gulp bundle --ship

   gulp package-solution --ship

3. Deploy the package to the tenant app catalog as tenant wide.

Consume the Library from the Tenant App Catalog

Follow the given steps to consume the library inside the SPFx web part from the tenant app catalog:

1. Open the package.json file from the SPFx web part.
2. Add the following entry under the dependencies section to reflect the library and it's version:

JSON

```json
"dependencies": {
  "spfx-library": "0.0.1", // Reference to the library
  "react": "16.8.5",
  "react-dom": "16.8.5",
  "@types/react": "16.8.8",
  "@types/react-dom": "16.8.3",
  "office-ui-fabric-react": "6.189.2",
  "@microsoft/sp-core-library": "1.9.1",
  "@microsoft/sp-webpart-base": "1.9.1",
  "@microsoft/sp-lodash-subset": "1.9.1",
  "@microsoft/sp-office-ui-fabric-core": "1.9.1",
  "@types/webpack-env": "1.13.1",
  "@types/es6-promise": "0.0.33"
}
```

Conclusion

In this chapter, we discussed the ideology of a library component. We built our very own library component for code sharing and expended it in the SPFx web part.

SharePoint Framework v1.8.0 has introduced the library component as one of the useful features. It is generally available with SPFx v1.9.x. It is an elective choice to make shared code.

CHAPTER 45
Develop Custom App Pages with SPFx

Single part application pages are as of now lately available in Modern SharePoint. Default page templates can be extended to have own custom templates. In any case, they are constrained to just that particular site. To utilize the page layouts all over the tenant, we should make custom application pages utilizing the SharePoint framework. We can uncover application pages by utilizing the new page layout choice with the SPFx web part on it.

Structure
- Develop custom app pages with SPFx
- Configure the Web Part for a Single Part Page
- Custom App Page Creation

Objective
- Develop and deploy SPFx built custom app pages

Develop custom app pages with SPFx

Open a command prompt. Follow the given guidelines to make the SPFx solution:

1. Make a folder for the SPFx solution:

```
md custom-apppage
```

2. Change the path to the above folder:

    ```
    cd custom-apppage
    ```

3. Execute the Yeoman Generator for SharePoint:

    ```
    yo @microsoft/sharepoint
    ```

4. The Yeoman generator will run through the wizard to ask questions about the SPFx solution to be created:

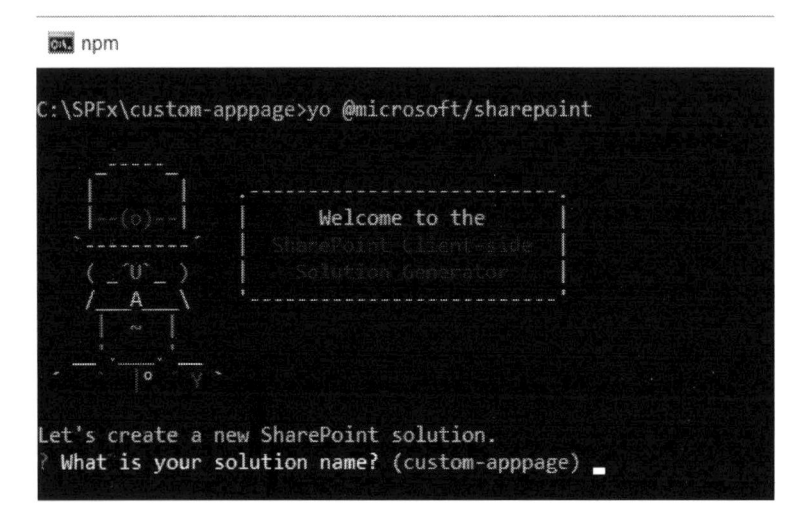

Figure 45.1: SPFx Yeoman generator

The SPFx Yeoman generator will give the following wizard of inquiries:

- **Solution Name:** Determine the SPFx solution name. Hit the *Enter* key to proceed with the default selection (`custom-apppage` in this case) or type another name.
    - o **Chosen decision:** Hit *Enter*
- **Target environment:** Specify the target environment to deploy the SPFx solution. Select any option from SharePoint Online or SharePoint On-Premises environment.
    - o **Chosen decision:** SharePoint Online only (latest)
- **Folder location:** Choose the folder location for the SPFx project (either the same folder or a subfolder).
    - o **Chosen decision:** Use the current folder
- **Deployment option:** Specify Y to deploy the app instantly to all the sites, N otherwise.
    - o **Chosen decision:** Y

- **Consents to access web APIs:** Check whether the components in the solution need explicit consent to access web APIs that are unique.
    - **Chosen decision:** N (solution contains unique permissions)
- **Choice of client-side component:** Choose to develop a web part or an extension.
    - **Chosen decision:** WebPart, since single part app pages are web parts
- **Web part name:** Provide the web part name. Hit the *Enter* key to proceed with the default choice or type another name.
    - **Chosen decision:** SinglePartPage
- Web part description: Provide the web part description. Hit the *Enter* key to proceed with the default choice or type another value.
    - **Chosen decision:** Hit *Enter*
- **Choice of the framework:** Choose a JavaScript framework to develop the component from No JavaScript Framework, React, and Knockout.
    - **Chosen decision:** No JavaScript Framework

5. After the scaffolding is complete, lock down the version of project dependencies by executing the following command:

```
npmshrinkwrap
```

6. At the command prompt, execute the following command to open the solution in the code editor of your choice:

```
code .
```

Configure the web part for a single part page

Follow the given instructions to configure the web part as a single part page:

1. In \src\webparts\singlePartPage folder, open the SinglePartPageWebPart.manifest.json file.

2. To the `supportedHosts`, `includeSharePointFullPage`:

Figure 45.2: supported Hosts choice

We will proceed with the default usage of the custom application page with no customization to perceive what it looks like by default.

Deploy the Package

Bundle the solution:

At the command prompt, execute the following command:

```
gulp bundle --ship
```

Package the solution:

At the command prompt, execute the following command:

```
gulp package-solution --ship
```

The `custom-apppage.sppkg` package will be available at `\custom-apppage\sharepoint\solution`.

Deploy the package to the app catalog

Follow below steps to deploy the package to the SharePoint app catalog:

1. Browse to the SharePoint Online App Catalog site.
2. Add custom-apppage.sppkg to the app catalog.

3. Select **Make this solution available to all sites in the organization** to make the solution available to tenant-wide.
4. Select **Deploy:**

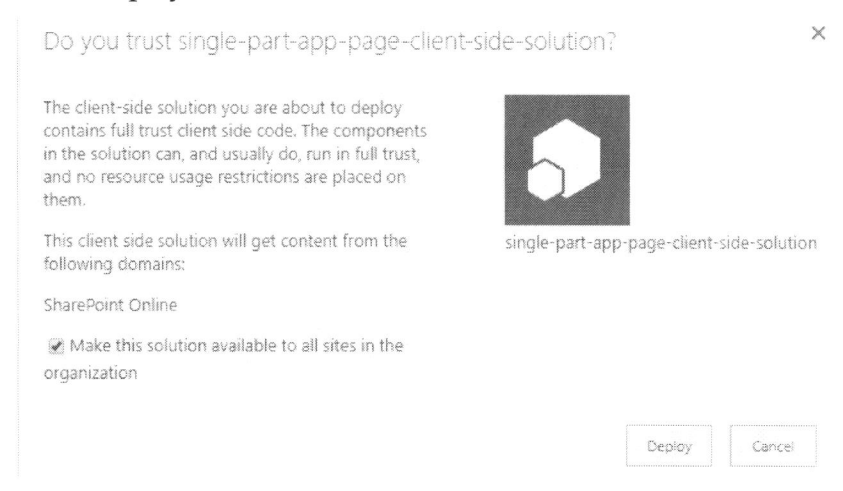

Figure 45.3: Deploy the package

Verify the Custom App Page Creation

Follow the given steps to verify the custom app page creation:

1. Open the Modern SharePoint site.
2. Go to **New>Page**:

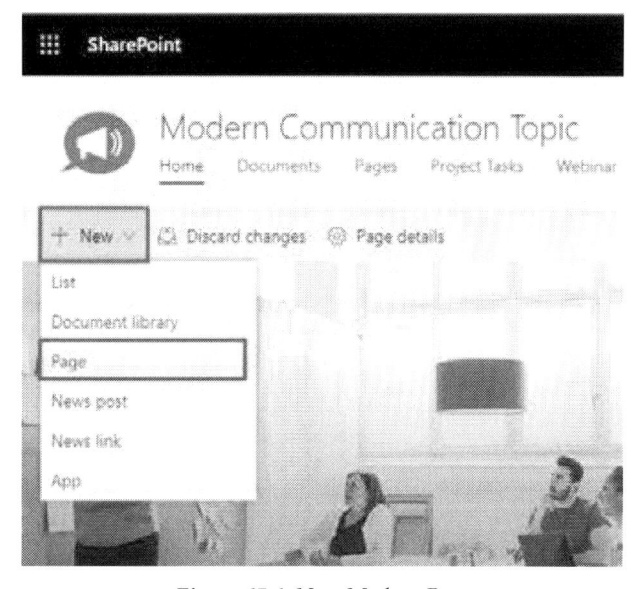

Figure 45.4: New Modern Page

480 ■ *Mastering SharePoint Framework*

3. Default templates are visible, as shown in the following screenshot:

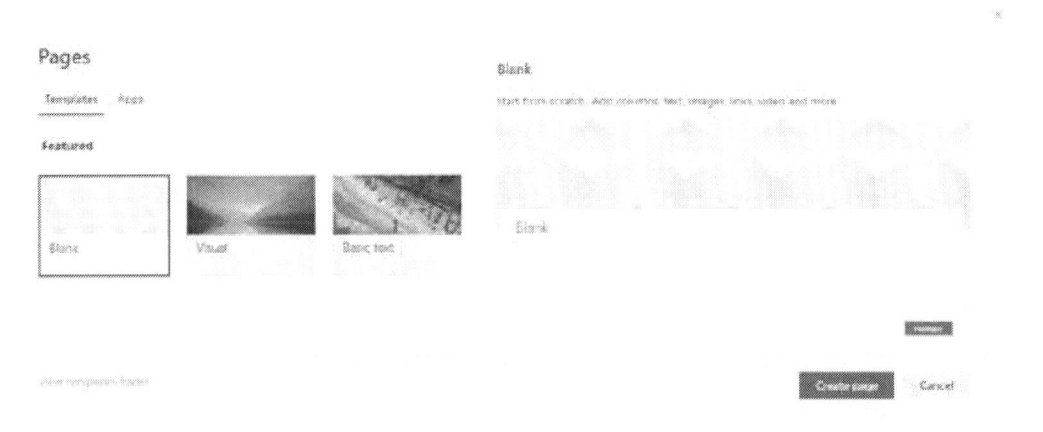

Figure 45.5: Default templates

4. Click on the **Apps** tab. It is available subject to custom app pages deployment to the tenant.
5. Click on custom app to see the preview:

Figure 45.6: Custom app page preview

6. Select **Create page**:
7. Provide the **Title**:

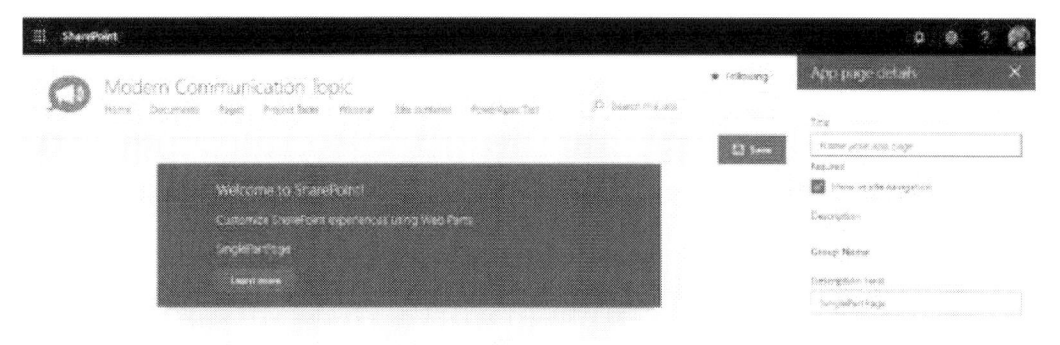

Figure 45.7: Custom app page creation

The custom app page is available with the SPFx web part on it.

Conclusion

In this chapter, we learned how to develop, deploy, and utilize custom application pages assembled utilizing SPFx. We can extend default page templates by creating our own. In any case, they are restricted to just that site. To utilize the page formats all over the tenant, we should make custom application pages utilizing the SharePoint Framework.

CHAPTER 46
Optimizing SPFx Solutions

The SharePoint Framework has turned out to be prevalent in a limited ability to focus on time and it has been broadly embraced. SPFx is being created utilizing modern toolchain and client-side technologies and conveys the functionality quickly. When we are usinga number of web parts on a website, we generally need to think of the overall performance and optimization strategies.

Structure
- Common concerns with the SPFx solution implementation
- Optimizing SPFx solutions

Objective
- Explore methods to optimize SPFx solutions

SPFx implementation common issues

There can be numerous reasons behind poorly developed SPFx solutions:
- Poor structure or design
- Less contemplating about the impact on the tenant
- Heavy bundles packaging all assets together

- Third-party libraries reference
- Developer interest

Because of at least one of the reasons mentioned above, the SPFx solution optimization prioritizes lower. Here are a few common perceptions and proposals to enhance SPFx solutions.

Tip# 1: Splitting web parts to load individually

A single SPFx solution many contain several web parts and extensions. These are regularly referenced in the config\config.json document as follows:

```
{
    "$schema": "https://developer.microsoft.com/json-schemas/spfx-build/config.2.0.schema.json",
    "version": "2.0",
    "bundles": {
        "spfx-webparts": {
            "components": [
                {
                    "entrypoint": "./lib/webparts/webpartOne/webpartOne.js",
                    "manifest": "./src/webparts/webpartOne/webpartOne.manifest.json"
                },
                {
                    "entrypoint": "./lib/webparts/webpartTwo/webpartTwo.js",
                    "manifest": "./src/webparts/webpartTwo/webpartTwo.manifest.json"
                }
            ]
        }
    },
    "externals": {},
    "localizedResources": {}
}
```

Figure 46.1: Multiple web parts in a single SPFx solution

Both the web parts get packaged as one single JavaScript file. This circumstance has the following points to consider:
- Both the web parts are loaded on the page although only single one is added.
- The load time will be reduced if both the web parts are added to the page.

It is smarter to split both the web parts in independent files to lessen what is loaded on the page:

```
{
    "$schema": "https://developer.microsoft.com/json-schemas/spfx-build/config.2.0.schema.json",
    "version": "2.0",
    "bundles": {
        "spfx-webparts-one": {
            "components": [
                {
                    "entrypoint": "./lib/webparts/webpartOne/webpartOne.js",
                    "manifest": "./src/webparts/webpartOne/webpartOne.manifest.json"
                }
            ]
        },
        "spfx-webparts-two": {
            "components": [
                {
                    "entrypoint": "./lib/webparts/webpartTwo/webpartTwo.js",
                    "manifest": "./src/webparts/webpartTwo/webpartTwo.manifest.json"
                }
            ]
        }
    },
    "externals": {},
    "localizedResources": {}
}
```

Figure 46.2: Bundle web parts independently

Tip# 2: Dynamic loading of third-party libraries

The SharePoint Framework utilizes a webpack to package the solution. Webpack permits the dynamic import of part of an application. Consider a case of the Moment library utilized in our SPFx web part to carry out date activities.

Ordinary import:

In the following example, the Moment library will be incorporated into the final bundle, regardless of whether `GetTimeInLongFormat` is called or not:

TypeScript

```
import * as moment from moment;
.
.
export default class DateTimeConverter {
    public GetTimeInLongFormat(dateTimeValue: string){
        return moment(dateTimeValue).format("LLLL");
    }
}
```

Dynamic import:

In the following example, the Moment library is loaded asynchronously just when the `GetTimeInLongFormat`function is invoked:

TypeScript

```
exportdefaultclassDateTimeConverter{
publicasyncGetTimeInLongFormat(dateTimeValue:string){
constmoment = awaitimport(
/* webpackChunkName: 'my-moment' */
'moment'
        );
returnmoment(dateTimeValue).format("LLLL");
  }
}
```

Tip# 3: Externally Reference External Libraries

We regularly utilize outside libraries (for example jQuery) in our SPFx solution. Including these external libraries as npm bundles and including them inside the final bundle makes it massive. Refer to the libraries externally as follows:

1. Open the `config\config.json` file.
2. Load the jQuery via CDN location by making an entry to the externals section:

```
{
  "entries": [
    {
      "entry": "./lib/webparts/externalReference/ExternalReferenceWebPart.js",
      "manifest": "./src/webparts/externalReference/ExternalReferenceWebPart.manifest.json",
      "outputPath": "./dist/externalReference.bundle.js"
    }
  ],
  "externals": {
    "@microsoft/sp-client-base": "node_modules/@microsoft/sp-client-base/dist/sp-client-base.js",
    "@microsoft/sp-client-preview": "node_modules/@microsoft/sp-client-preview/dist/sp-client-preview.js",
    "@microsoft/sp-lodash-subset": "node_modules/@microsoft/sp-lodash-subset/dist/sp-lodash-subset.js",
    "jquery": "https://code.jquery.com/jquery-3.1.0.min.js"
  },
  "localizedResources": {
    "externalReferenceStrings": "webparts/externalReference/loc/{locale}.js"
  }
}
```

Figure 46.3: Externally reference jQuery

Import jQuery in the SPFx web part as follows:

TypeScript

`import * as $ from 'jquery';`

Tip# 4: Dissecting the SPFx Bundle

Expand the Webpack configuration in your SPFx solution to comprehend the bundle.

Run the following command to install the `webpack-bundle-analyzer` bundle to the SPFx solution:

```
npm install webpack-bundle-analyzer --save-dev
```

Modify the `gulp file.js` contents as follows:

```
'use strict';

const gulp = require('gulp');
const path = require('path');
const build = require('@microsoft/sp-build-web');
const bundleAnalyzer = require('webpack-bundle-analyzer');

build.configureWebpack.mergeConfig({
  additionalConfiguration: (generatedConfiguration) => {
    const lastDirName = path.basename(__dirname);
    const dropPath = path.join(__dirname, 'temp', 'stats');
    generatedConfiguration.plugins.push(new bundleAnalyzer.BundleAnalyzerPlugin({
      openAnalyzer: false,
      analyzerMode: 'static',
      reportFilename: path.join(dropPath, `${lastDirName}.stats.html`),
      generateStatsFile: true,
      statsFilename: path.join(dropPath, `${lastDirName}.stats.json`),
      logLevel: 'error'
    }));

    return generatedConfiguration;
  }
});

build.initialize(gulp);
```

Figure 46.4: Webpack configuration

The gulp bundle command will create a perception file at '.\temp\stats\[spfx-solution].stats.html'.

Conclusion

In this chapter, we discussed the regularly observed practices and enhancement techniques to construct better SPFx solutions. The performance of the SPFx solution can be improved by following basic strategies. This will keep the bundle size inside points of confinement and improve the general execution.

CHAPTER 47
Unit Test with Jest and Enzyme

There is an unsaid theory that irrespective of how effectively you as a single developer or a team of experts write a code using available industry best practices and design patterns, a time will come when your code will become unmanageable, difficult to follow and test (independently or as a whole). Having significant supporting test cases for your code will always help you to unit test your code and build it further.

Testing is an important part of programming life cycle. It is a piece of persistent advancement and arrangement to accomplish better outcomes. A SPFx solution is no exemption to this. As a piece of the SPFx solution advancement, we need to have supporting experiments to test the usefulness freely or as relapse testing. Having noteworthy experiments help to grow new functionalities by guaranteeing the trustworthiness of the current usefulness.

Structure
- Role of Unit Testing
- Implement Unit Tests

Objectives
- Implement unit tests utilizing Enzyme and Jest
- Execute Tests against SPFx solutions

Need of unit tests

The following are important reasons to have unit tests:
- It helps to make code extensible and flexible to change.
- Helps to test solutions for the regression.
- Reduces bugs while changing the existing functionality.
- Early bug identification.
- Better code quality.
- Facilitates, changes, and simplifies integration.
- Provides documentation of the system.
- Simplifies debugging.

Writing test cases involves initial effort. But once they are in place, they pay off in time.

SPFx is JavaScript-based and it does not provide any testing framework by default. In a way, it is good because we can take liberty of using any JavaScript-based testing framework (e.g. Jest, Chai).

Implement Unit Tests

Open a command prompt. Follow the given guidelines to make the SPFx solution:

1. Make a folder for the SPFx solution:

   ```
   md test-with-jest-enzyme
   ```

2. Change the path to the above folder:

   ```
   cd test-with-jest-enzyme
   ```

3. Execute the Yeoman Generator for SharePoint.

   ```
   yo @microsoft/sharepoint
   ```

4. The Yeoman generator will run through the wizard to ask questions about the SPFx solution to be created:

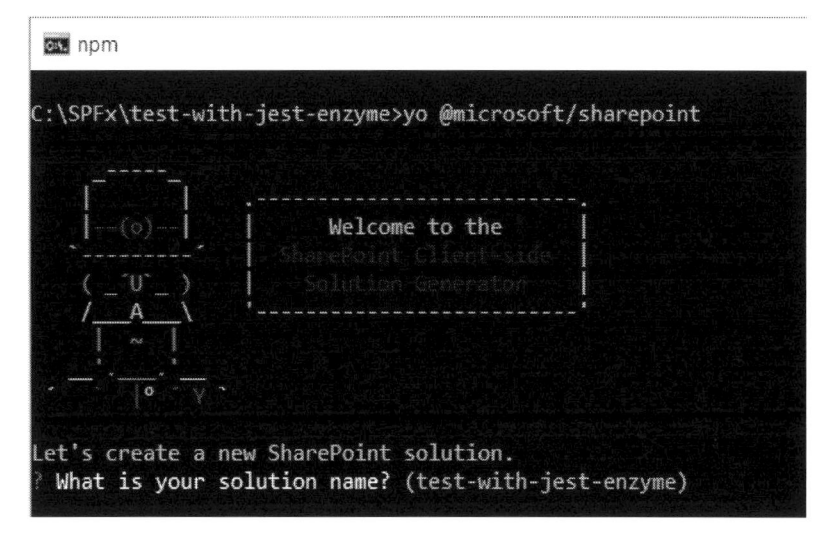

Figure 47.1: SPFx Yeoman generator

The SPFx Yeoman generator will give the following wizard of inquiries:

- **Solution Name:** Determine the SPFx solution name. Hit the *Enter* key to proceed with the default selection(test-with-jest-enzyme in this case) or type another name.
    - o **Chosen decision:** Hit *Enter*
- **Target environment:** Specify the target environment to deploy the SPFx solution. Select any option from SharePoint Online or SharePoint On-Premises environment.
    - o **Chosen decision:** SharePoint Online only (latest)
- **Folder location:** Choose the folder location for the SPFx project (either the same folder or a subfolder).
    - o **Chosen decision:** Same folder
- **Deployment option:** Specify Y to deploy the app instantly to all the sites, N otherwise.
    - o **Chosen decision:** N (install on each site explicitly)
- **Consents to access web APIs:** Check whether the components in the solution need explicit consent to access web APIs that are unique.
    - o **Chosen decision:** N (solution contains unique permissions)
- **Choice of client-side component:** Choose to develop a web part or an extension.
    - o **Chosen decision:** WebPart

- **Web part name:** Provide the web part name. Hit the *Enter* key to proceed with the default choice or type another name.
    - **Chosen decision:** UnitTestSPFx
- **Web part description:** Provide the web part description. Hit the *Enter* key to proceed with the default choice or type another value.
    - **Chosen decision:** Test with Jest and Enzyme
- **Choice of the framework:** Choose a JavaScript framework to develop the component from No JavaScript Framework, React, and Knockout.
    - **Chosen decision:** React

5. After the scaffolding is complete, lock down the version of project dependencies by executing the following command:

```
npmshrinkwrap
```

6. At the command prompt, execute the following command to open the solution in the code editor of your choice:

```
code .
```

7. Update the render() method inside the React component 'src\webparts\unitTestSPFx\components\UnitTestSPFx.tsx' to setup the test scenarios (e.g. added id 'UnitTestSPFx' to parent div and set web part title as '**SPFx Unit Test**'):

```
public render(): React.ReactElement<IUnitTestSPFxProps> {
  return (
    <div className={ styles.unitTestSPFx } id="UnitTestSPFx">
      <div className={ styles.container }>
        <div className={ styles.row }>
          <div className={ styles.column }>
            <span className={ styles.title }>Welcome to SharePoint!</span>
            <p className={ styles.subTitle }>Unit Test SPFx Solutions</p>
            <h1 className={styles.title}>SPFx Unit Test</h1>
            <p className={ styles.description }>{escape(this.props.description)}</p>
            <a href="https://aka.ms/spfx" className={ styles.button }>
              <span className={ styles.label }>Learn more</span>
            </a>
          </div>
        </div>
      </div>
    </div>
  );
}
```

Fig 47.2: Set up test scenarios

NPM Dependencies

Enzyme:

We need to install additional developer dependencies for Enzyme. Enzyme is designed by Air bnb which provides test utilities for React.

At the command prompt, execute the following command:

```
npm install enzyme enzyme-adapter-react-16 react-test-renderer @types/enzyme --save-dev --save-exact
```

Jest:

Jest is one of the good choices as it supports asserts, mocking, code coverage, coverage threshold for continuous deployment, and summary report:

```
npm install jest jest-junitts-jest @types/jest --save-dev --save-exact
```

identity-obj-proxy:

Allows to test SASS / LESS / CSS imports:

```
npm install identity-obj-proxy --save-dev --save-exact
```

Setup Jest for SPFx:

Follow below steps to set up the Jest for SPFx:

1. Open the `package.json` file.
2. Under the '`scripts`' section, for the 'test' configuration, replace '`gulp test`' with '`jest`':

Figure 47.3: package.json test configuration

3. Add the '`jest`' configuration after '`devDependencies`':

```json
"jest": {
  "moduleFileExtensions": [
    "ts",
    "tsx",
    "js"
  ],
  "transform": {
    "^.+\\.(ts|tsx)$": "ts-jest"
  },
  "testMatch": [
    "**/src/**/*.test.+(ts|tsx|js)"
  ],
  "collectCoverage": true,
  "coverageReporters": [
    "json",
    "lcov",
    "text",
    "cobertura"
  ],
  "coverageDirectory": "<rootDir>/jest",
  "moduleNameMapper": {
    "\\.(css|less|scss|sass)$": "identity-obj-proxy"
  },
  "reporters": [
    "default",
    "jest-junit"
  ],
  "coverageThreshold": {
    "global": {
      "branches": 100,
      "functions": 100,
      "lines": 100,
      "statements": 100
    }
  }
},
"jest-junit": {
  "output": "./jest/summary-jest-junit.xml"
}
```

Figure 47.4: *jest configuration*

Include tests in the SPFx webpart

In Visual Studio Code, perform the instructions to add a few tests to our SPFx solution:

1. In the '`src\webparts\UnitTestSPFx\`' path, include the '`test`' folder.

2. Inside the 'test' folder, add the 'essential.test.ts' file:

```ts
/// <reference types="jest" />

import * as React from 'react';
import { configure, mount, ReactWrapper } from 'enzyme';
import * as Adapter from 'enzyme-adapter-react-16';

configure({ adapter: new Adapter() });

import UnitTestSPFx from '../components/UnitTestSPFx';
import { IUnitTestSPFxProps } from '../components/IUnitTestSPFxProps';

describe('Enzyme essentials', () => {

  let reactComponent: ReactWrapper<IUnitTestSPFxProps, {}>;

  beforeEach(() => {

    reactComponent = mount(React.createElement(
      UnitTestSPFx,
      {
        description: "SPFx Test"
      }
    ));
  });

  afterEach(() => {
    reactComponent.unmount();
  });

  it('should root web part element exists', () => {

    // define the css selector
    let cssSelector: string = '#UnitTestSPFx';

    // find the element using css selector
    const element = reactComponent.find(cssSelector);
    expect(element.length).toBeGreaterThan(0);
  });

  it('should has the correct title', () => {
    // Arrange
    // define contains/like css selector
    let cssSelector: string = 'h1';

    // Act
    // find the element using css selector
    const text = reactComponent.find(cssSelector).text();

    // Assert
    expect(text).toBe("SPFx Unit Test");
  });
});
```

Test case# 1 — Setup

Test case# 2

Figure 47.5: Test cases

Execute Test Cases

At the command prompt, execute the following command to run the test cases:

```
npm test
```

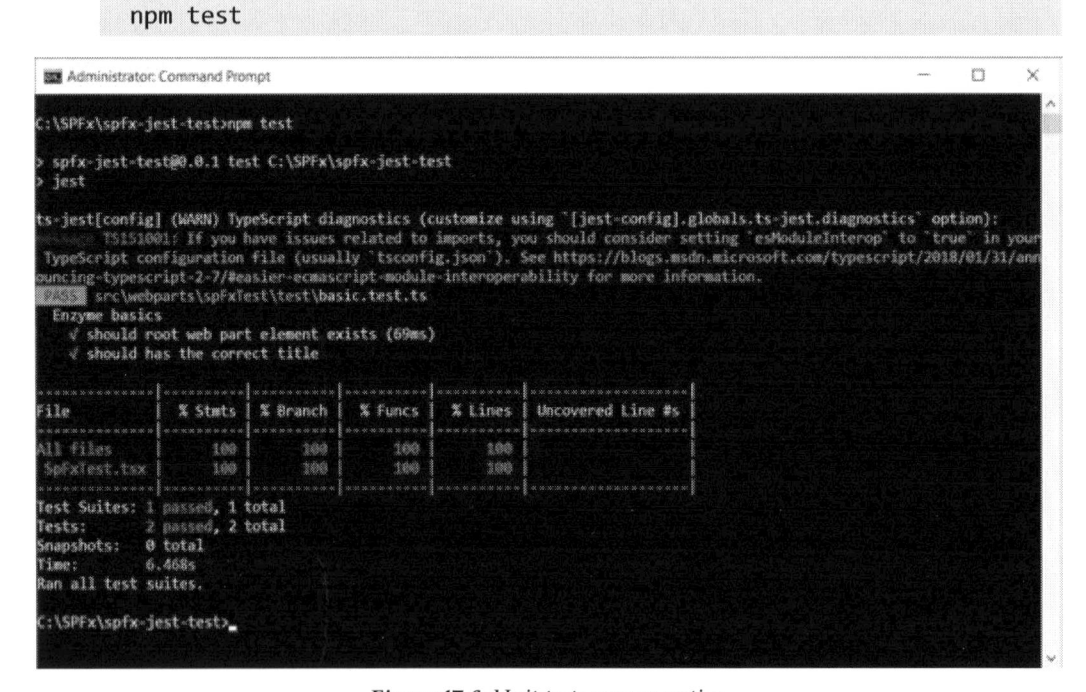

Figure 47.6: Unit test cases execution

Automate Unit Testing with Azure DevOps

We will cover the Azure DevOps with SharePoint in depth in thenext chapter. However, we will touch base on automating unit testing with Azure DevOps in continuation with the topic of discussion of this chapter.

Changes to the SPFx solution for automated testing using Azure DevOps

Follow the given steps to make changes to the SPFx solution:

1. At the command prompt, execute the following command to open the SPFx solution in the code editor:

    ```
    code .
    ```

2. Execute the following command to install the `jest-junit` dependency to get test reports which Azure DevOps can process:

    ```
    npmi jest-junit --save-dev --save-exact
    ```

3. Inside the `package.json` file, add the following jest configuration after the `devDependencies` section:

   ```
   "jest": {
   "reporters": [
       [
   "jest-junit", {
   "suiteName": "SPFx Unit Testing",
   "outputDirectory": "./reports/",
   "outputName": "./junit.xml"
       }
      ]
     ]
   }
   ```

4. At the command prompt, execute the following command to locally verify the configuration:

   ```
   npm test
   ```

5. It will create a new folder named 'reports' and the `junit.xml` file.

Azure DevOps Build Pipeline Configuration

Create a repository in Azure DevOps projects and add the code. Once the repository is created, create a new build pipeline by adding the following tasks:

Install Node JS:

Follow below steps to install Node JS:
- On the default agent, click on the + sign.
- Search for '**Node**'.
- Add **Node.js tool installer**.

- Specify the version as `8.x` or `10.x`:

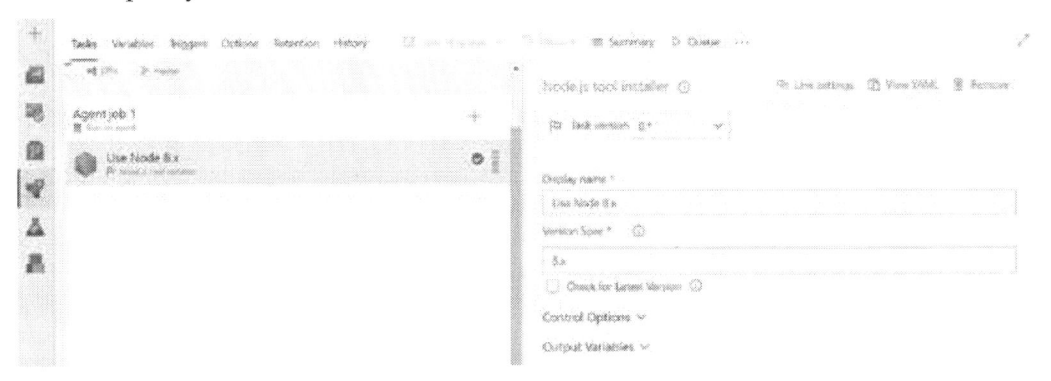

Figure 47.7: Install Node.js

Install npm packages:

Restore the required npm packages before starting the build process:
- Add the **npm** task.
- Check whether the **Command** is set to **install**:

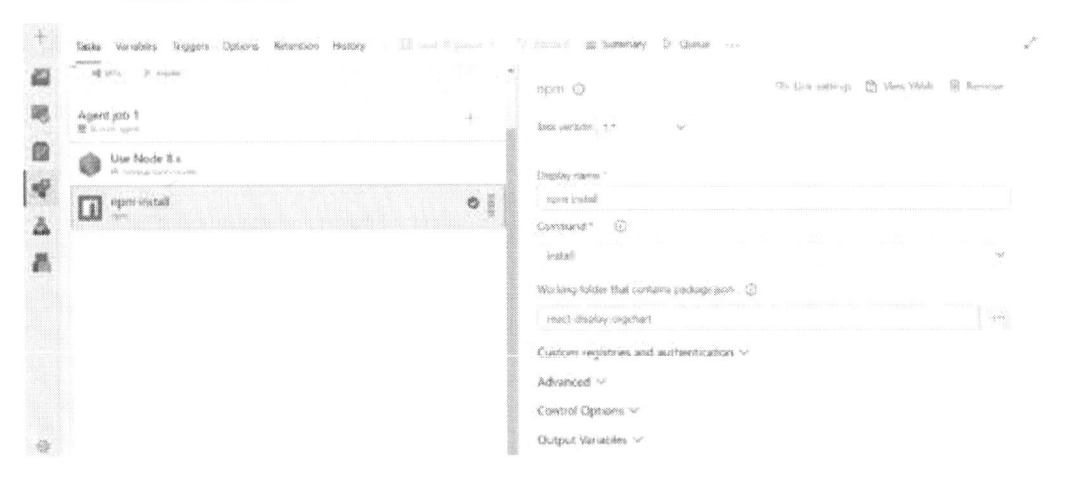

Figure 47.8: Restore npm Packages

Execute Test Cases:

Follow below steps to execute the test cases:
- Add the **npm** task.
- Set **Command** to **custom**.
- In the '**Command and arguments**', type '**test**':

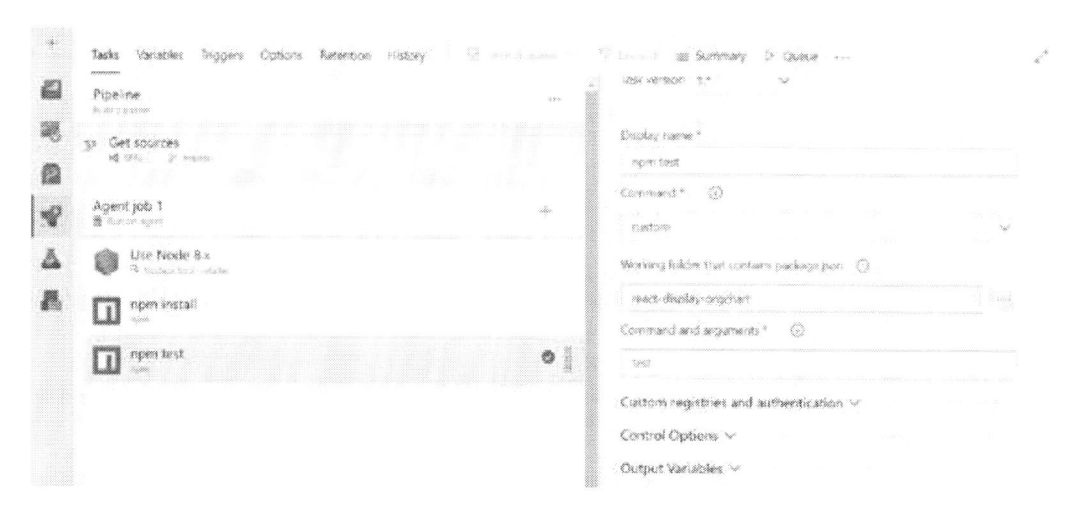

Figure 47.9: Execute Test Cases

Publish Test Results:

Follow below steps to publish the test results:
- Add the **'Publish Test Results'** task.
- Select **'Test result format'** as JUnit.
- In the **'Test results files'**, specify '`**/junit.xml`':

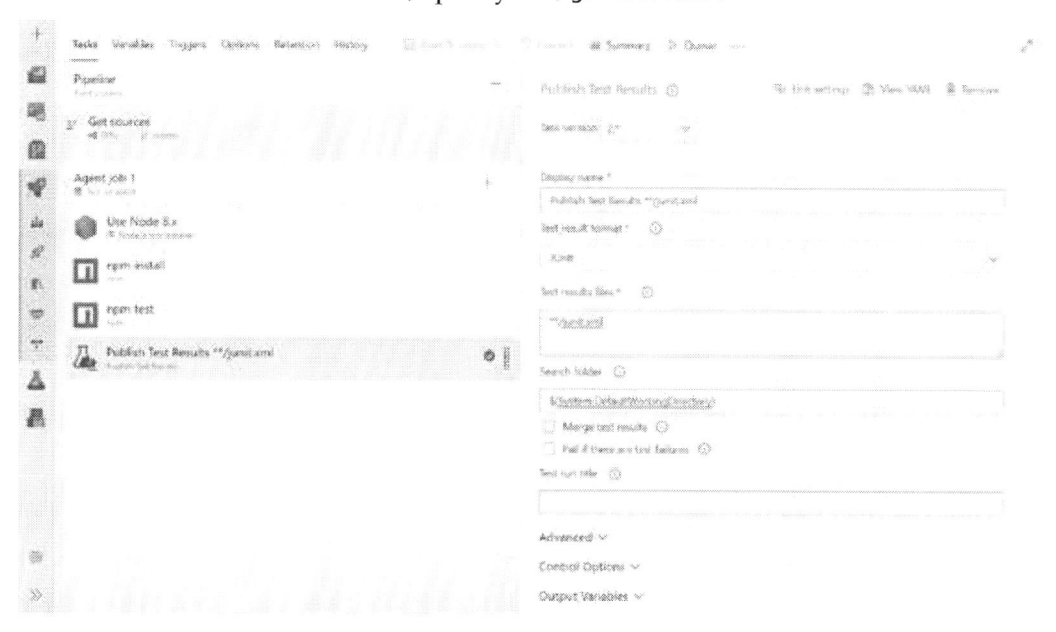

Fig 47.10: Publish Test Results

Execute Test Cases with Azure DevOps:

Queue a new build and wait for the output:

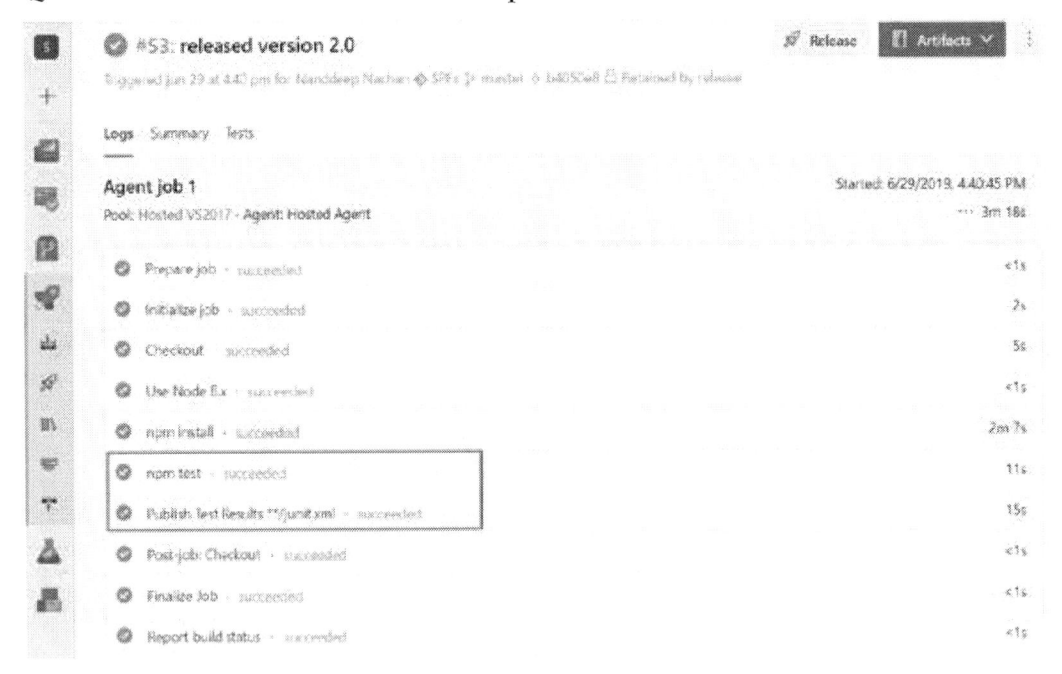

Figure 47.11: Azure Build Output

Click on the '**Tests**' tab to view the test outcome:

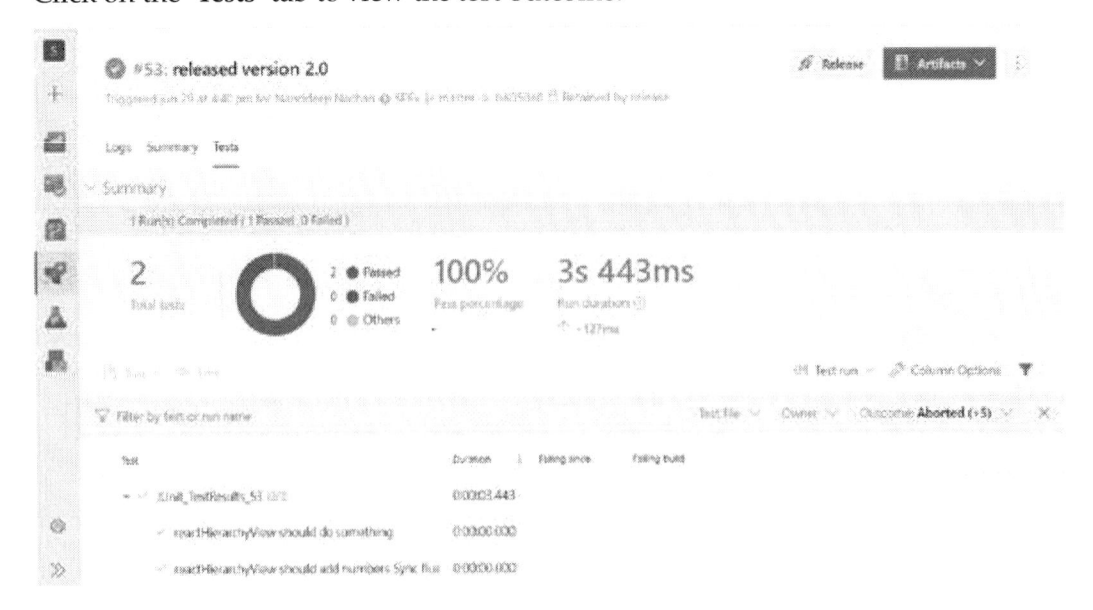

Figure 47.12: Test Outcome

The test outcome will display the number of passed and failed tests along with the run duration and pass percentage. Click on each of the test case to view the details of each test case run.

Conclusion

Unit tests help to implement new functionalities by guaranteeing the integrity of the existing functionalities. It can be created utilizing the Jest JavaScript Testing Framework. We can automate the execution of the test cases using Azure DevOps. The test outcome from Azure DevOps summarizes the number of passed and failed test cases.

CHAPTER 48
DevOps for SPFx

Developing SharePoint Framework solutions is simple. Maintaining the SPFx solutions for their coherence as they develop are continually demanding. At the point when the SPFx solution is worked upon by a group of impressive size and it experiences constant advancement endeavors, testing, and deployment of the most recent released bundle is a gigantic undertaking. Setting up **Continuous Integration (CI)** and **Continuous Deployment (CD)** automates the process and takes away the burden of manual efforts.

Structure

- Introduction to CI/CD
- Design a Build Definition
- Design a Release Definition
- Setup a Trigger for Deployment

Objectives

- Understand the importance of CI/CD
- Implement CI/CDutilizing Azure DevOpsforSPFx

Continuous Integration (CI)

It is the way toward automating the build process and code testing when an engineer commits changes to source control. Every submission to source control invokes a mechanized build which snatches the most recent code from the version control, builds it, and runs tests against it (whenever arranged). The following are advantages of actualizing CI:

- Improved developer efficiency
- Reduction in bugs count
- Early detection of bugs
- Early to market release

Build pipeline

Build pipeline incorporates the following major steps:

1. Constructa build definition
2. Install Node JS
3. Restore npm packages
4. Build the solution
5. Package the solution
6. Prepare the Artifacts
7. Publish the Artifacts

Create a Build Definition

Build definition representsa build configuration. Follow the given steps to make a new build definition:

1. Login to Azure DevOps (**https://visualstudio.microsoft.com/vso/**)
2. Choose a project to createa build definition.
3. From the left menu, select **Pipelines>Builds**.

4. Select **New pipeline**:

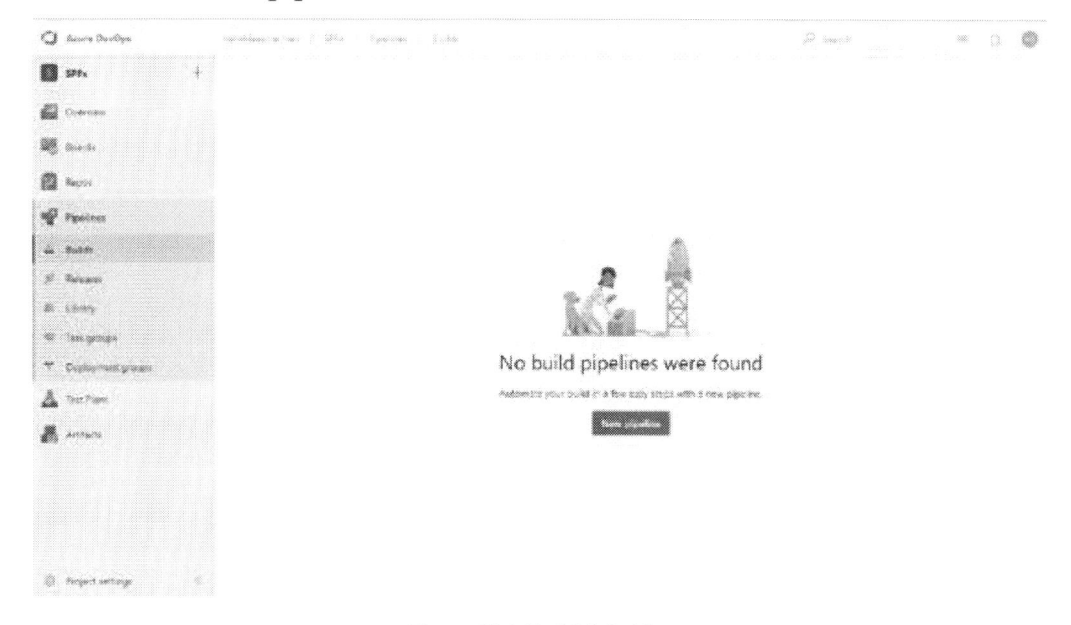

Figure 48.1: Build definition

5. Connect to the source repository. Click on **continue**:

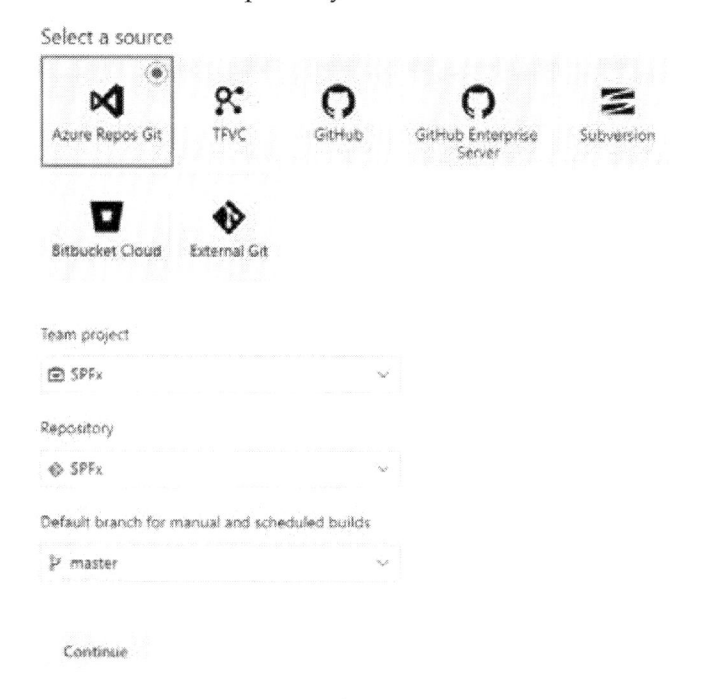

Figure 48.2: Select source repository

6. Select **Empty Pipeline** as the template to begin with:

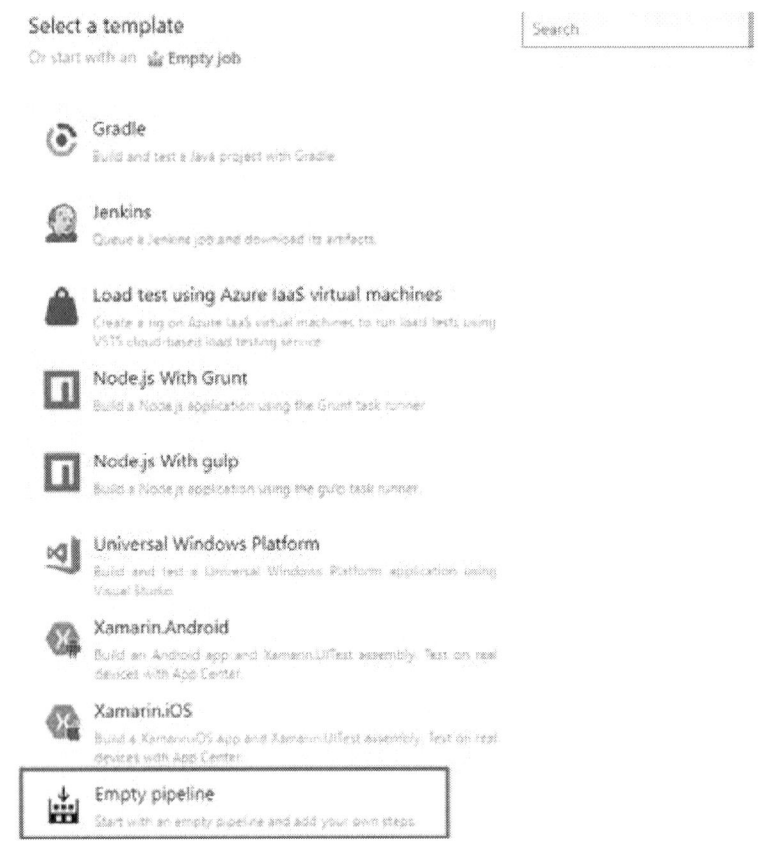

Figure 48.3: Select a template

7. Each build definition offers a default agent. Multiple tasks can be added to an agent to compose build:

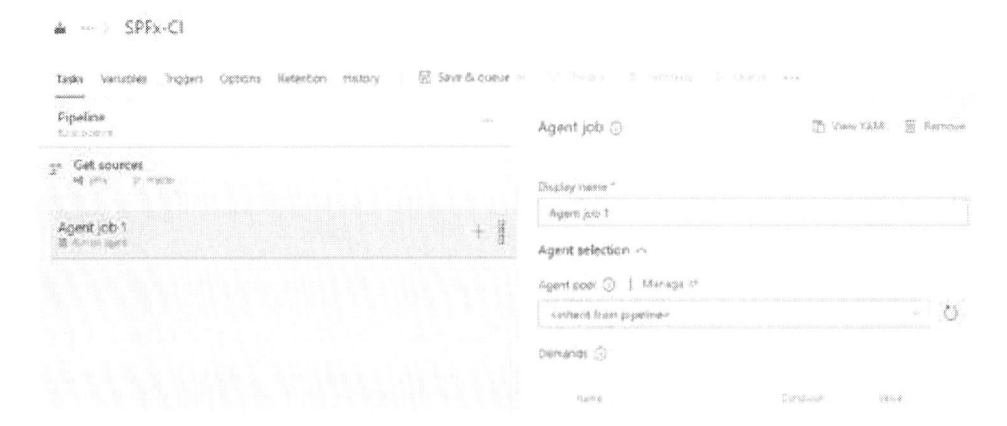

Figure 48.4: Default agent for the build definition

Install Node JS

Follow the below steps to install the Node JS:
1. On the default agent, choose+ sign.
2. Search and include **Node.js Tool Installer**:

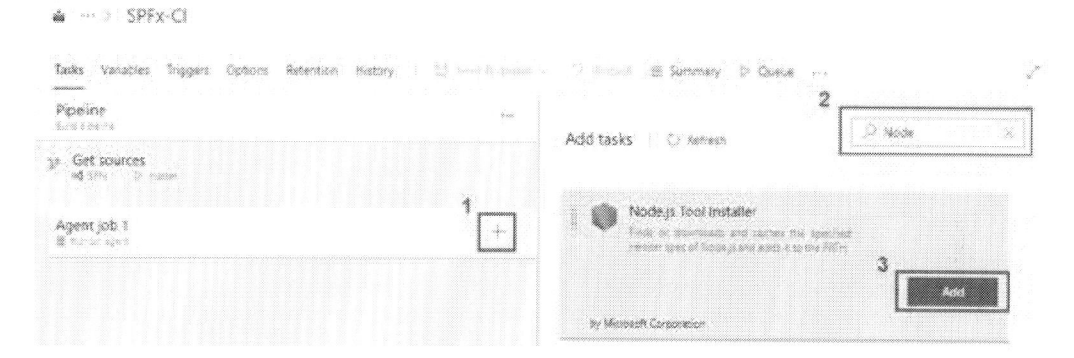

Figure 48.5: Install Node.js

3. Set the Node version as 8.x or 10.x, which is supported by SPFx:

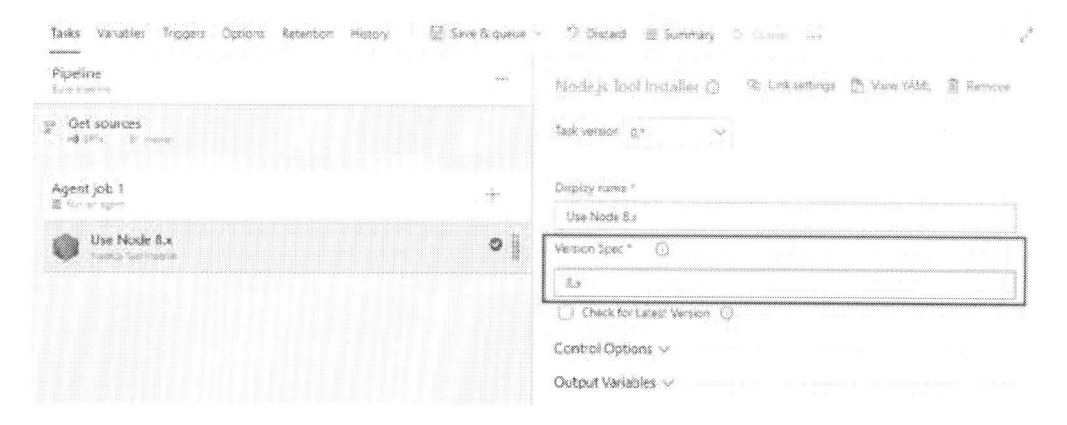

Figure 48.6: Specify Node.js version as 8.x

Restore npm Packages

SPFx solutions may utilize third-party npm bundles. Those should be restored before the actual build process kicks in:
1. Include the **'npm'** task.

2. Set the command to '**install**':

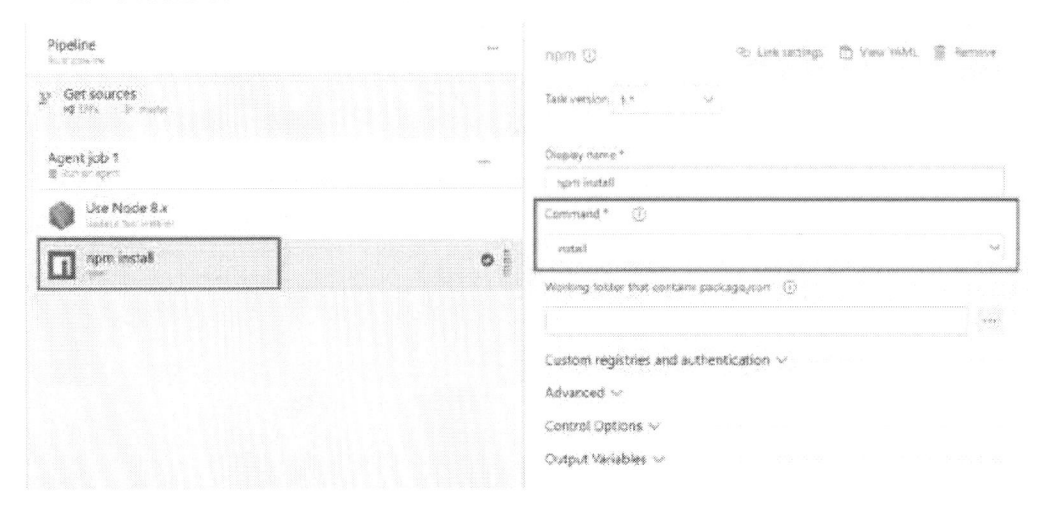

Figure 48.7: Restore npm Packages

Build the Solution

The build process minifies the assets to be uploaded to CDN. Follow the below steps to build the solution:

1. Add the '**gulp**' task.
2. Specify '**Gulp File Path**' as gulp file.js in our solution.
3. Specify '**Gulp task**' as 'bundle'.
4. Specify '**Arguments**' as '--ship':

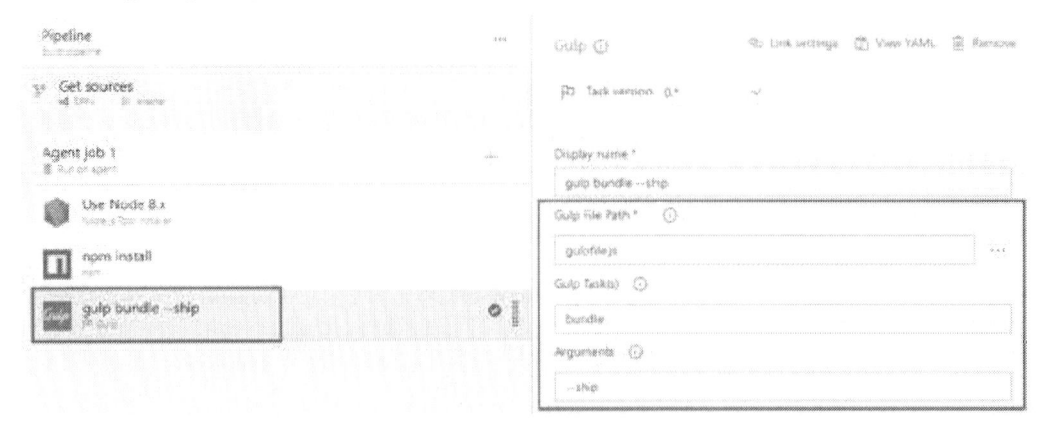

Figure 48.8: Build the solution

Package the Solution

Combine the assets into a package. Follow the below steps to package the solution:

1. Add the '**gulp**' task.
2. Specify '**Gulp File Path**' as gulpfile.js in our solution.
3. Specify '**Gulp Task(s)**' as 'package-solution'.
4. Specify '**Arguments**' as '--ship':

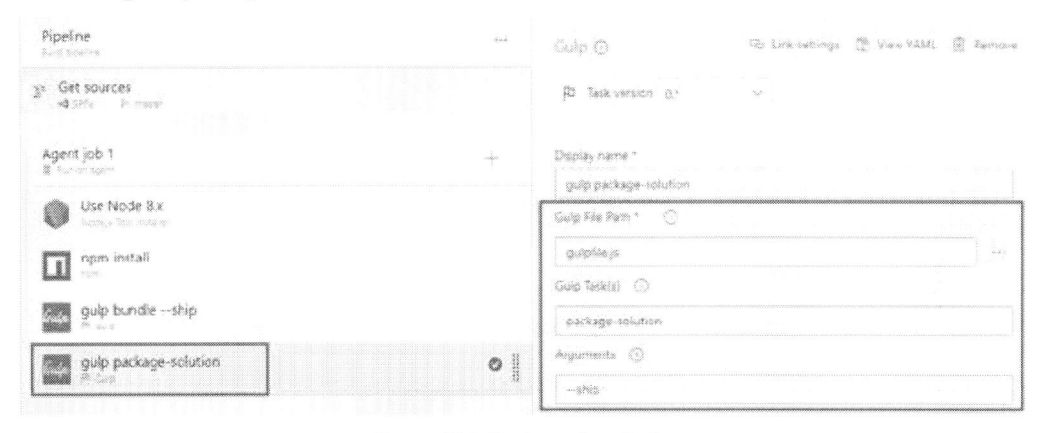

Figure 48.9: Package the solution

Prepare the Artifacts

The Azure DevOps build does not hold back any files. The .sppkg file generated needs to be copied to the staging directory to make it available to release the pipeline. Follow the below steps to prepare the artifacts:

1. Add the '**Copy Files**' task.
2. Specify '**Source Folder**' as $(Build.Repository.LocalPath)/sharepoint/solution.
3. Specify **Contents** as *.sppkg.
4. Specify target folder as $(Build.ArtifactStagingDirectory)/drop:

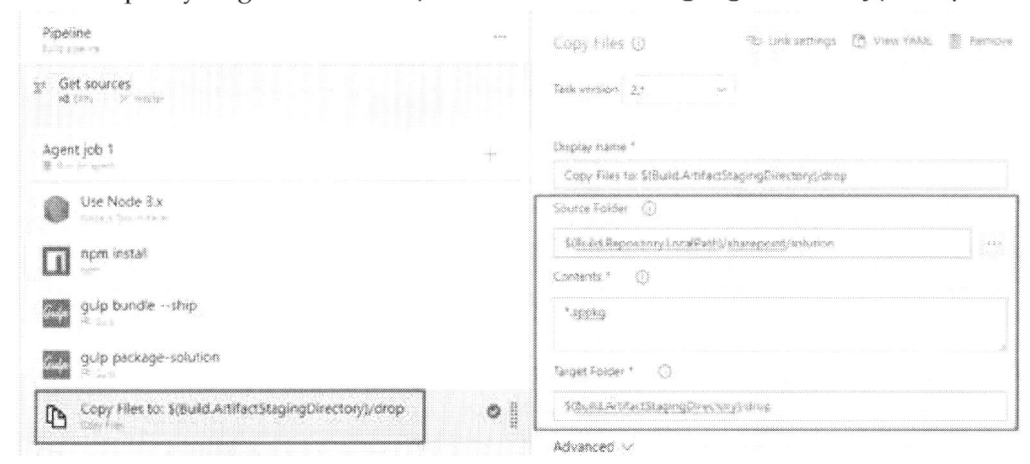

Figure 48.10: Prepare the Artifacts

Publish the Artifacts

Instruct Azure DevOps to keep the files after build execution. Follow the below steps to publish the artifacts:

1. Add task '**Publish Build Artifacts**'.
2. Specify '**Path to publish**' as $(Build.ArtifactStagingDirectory)/drop.
3. Specify '**Artifact name**' as drop:

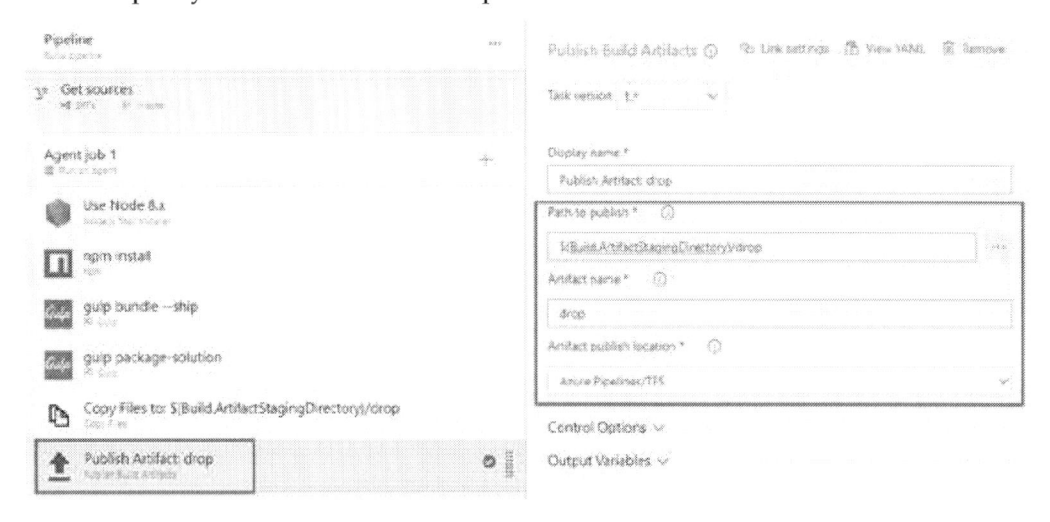

Figure 48.11: Publish the Artifacts

Continuous Deployment

Continuous Deployment (CD) gets the solution package from a build and deploys it to the specified environment. The deployment status can be tracked.

Continuous Deployment with SPFx includes the following steps:

1. Create the release definition
2. Link the build artifact
3. Create the environment
4. Install NodeJS
5. Install the Office 365 CLI
6. Connect to the App Catalog
7. Add solution package to the app catalog
8. Deploy the app
9. Set environment variables

Create the Release Definition

Follow the below steps to create the release definition:

1. From the left navigation, choose **Pipelines>Releases**.
2. Choose **New pipeline**:

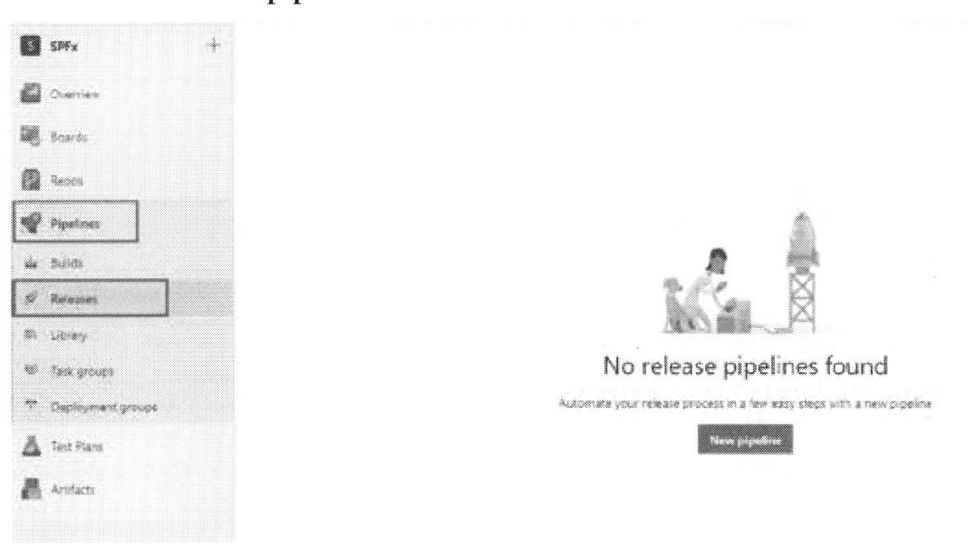

Figure 48.12: Create Release definition

3. Start by creating a new release definition as an empty template:

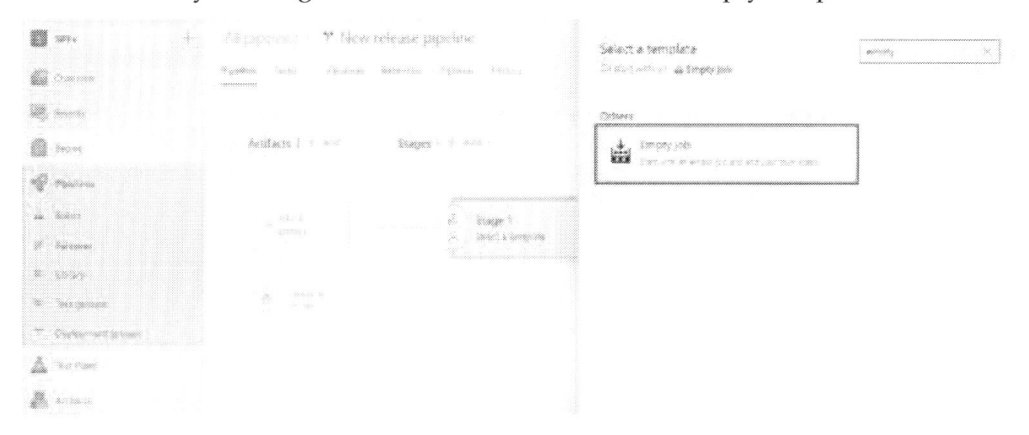

Figure 48.13: Empty template

Link the Build Artifact

Follow the below steps to link the build artifact:

1. Choose '**Add an artifact**'.
2. Under '**Source (build pipeline)**', choose the build definition created in the earlier step.
3. Make a note of '**Source alias**' to use later.
4. Choose '**Add**':

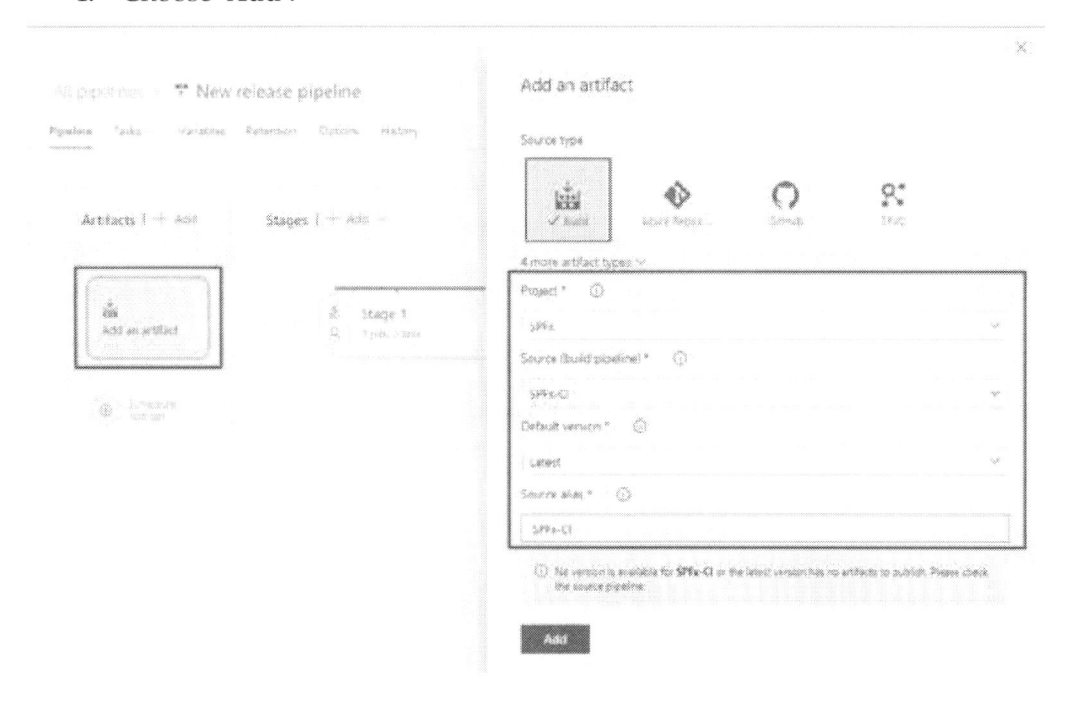

Figure 48.14: Link the Build Artifact

Create the Environment

Define an environment to deploy the build artifacts. Follow below create an environment:

1. Under **Stages**, choose '**Stage 1**'.

2. Specify the environment name:

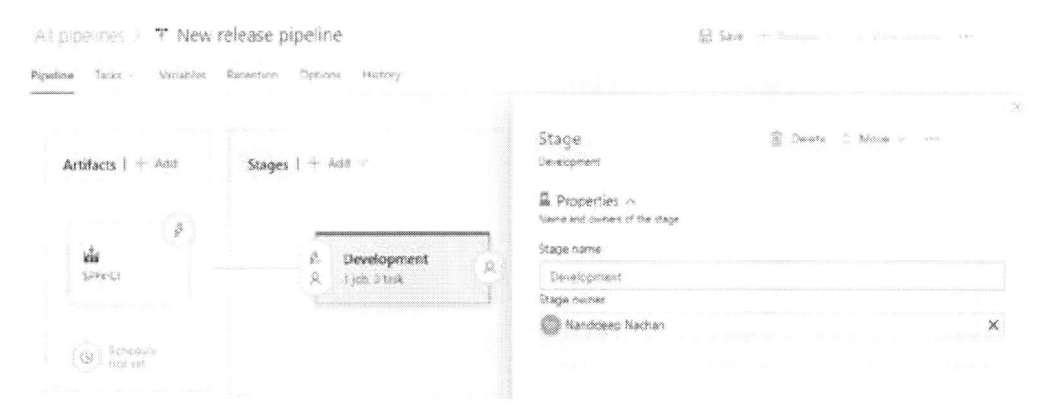

Figure 48.15: Create the environment

Install Node JS

Follow the below steps to install the Node JS:
1. Under the environment, choose '**1 job, 0 task**'.
2. Under the default agent, choose the '+' sign.
3. Search for task '**Node**'.
4. Add **Node.js Tool Installer**.
5. Set the Node version as `8.x` or `10.x`, which is supported by SPFx:

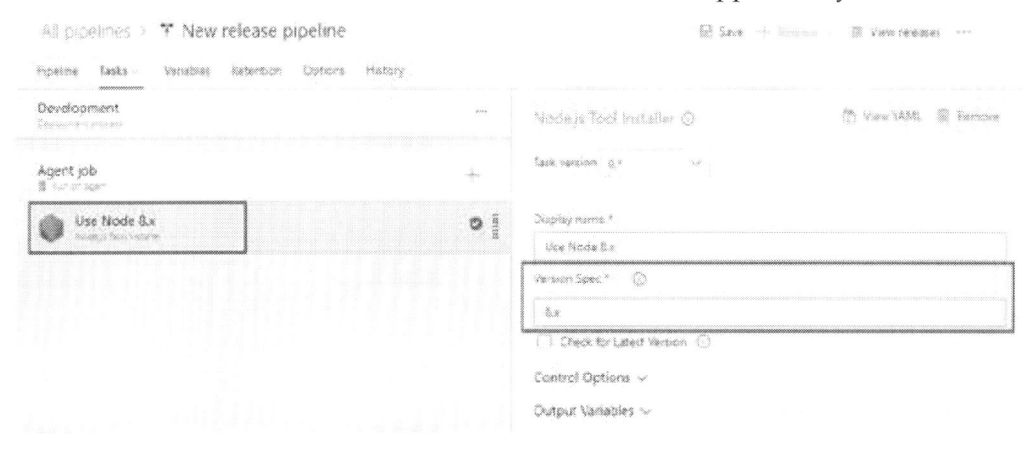

Figure 48.16: Install Node.js

Install the Office 365 CLI

The Office 365 CLI is an open source project from the OfficeDev PnP Community which helps to manage Office 365 and the SharePoint framework solutions platform independently. Follow the below steps to install the Office 365 CLI:

1. Add the '**npm**' task.
2. Under '**Command**', select custom.
3. In the '**Command and Arguments**', type `install -g @pnp/office365-cli`:

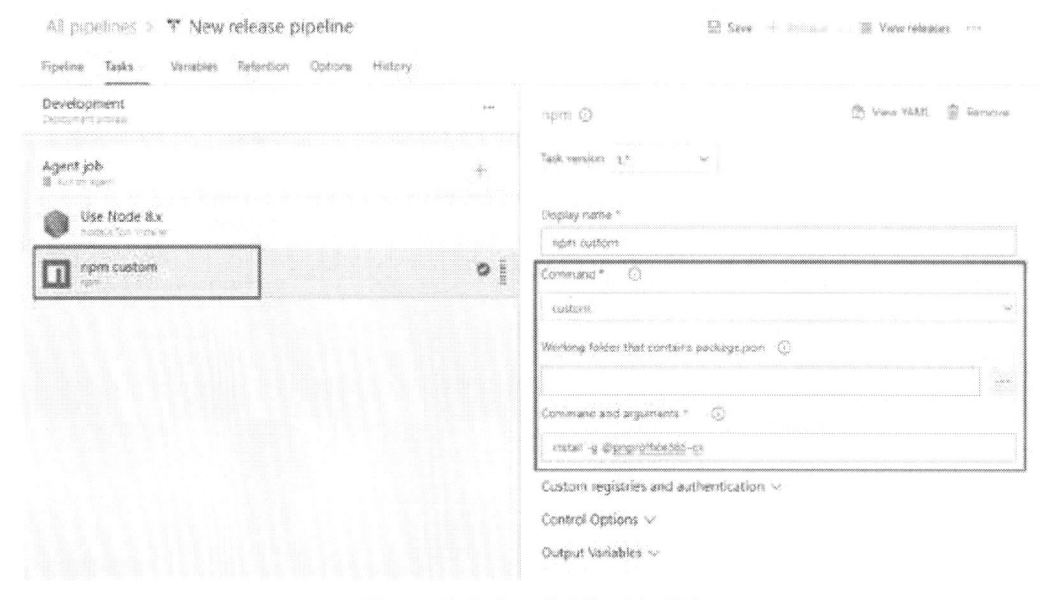

Figure 48.17: Install Office 365 CLI

Connect to the SharePoint App Catalog

Authenticate against the SharePoint App Catalog. Follow the below steps to connect to the SharePoint app catalog:

1. Add the '**Command Line**' task.
2. Specify the following command as the '**Script**' parameter:

```
o365 login https://$(tenant).sharepoint.com/$(catalogsite) --authType password --userName $(username) --password $(password)
```

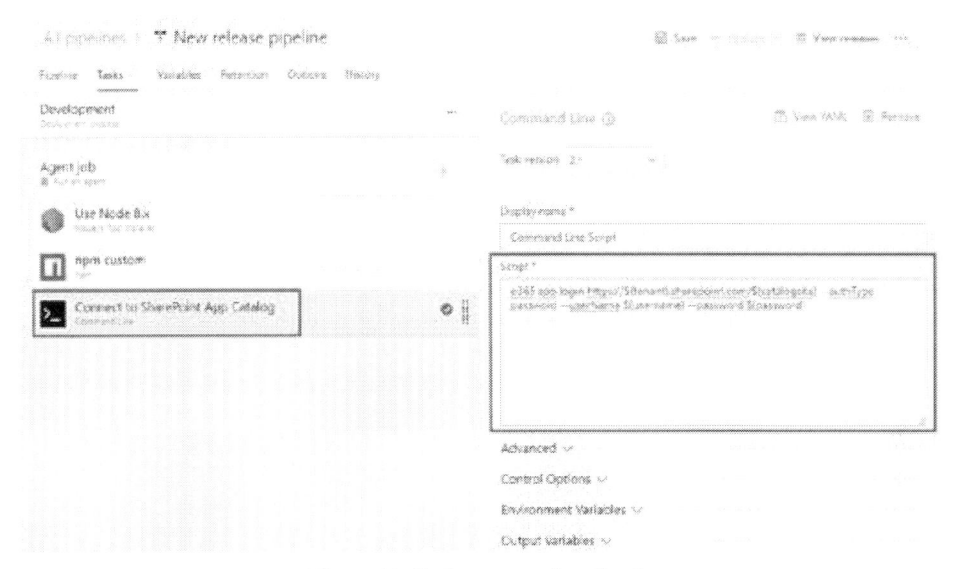

Figure 48.18: Connect to App Catalog

Deploy Solution Package to the App Catalog

Follow the below steps to upload the solution package to the SharePoint app catalog.

1. Add the '**Command Line**' task.
2. Specify the following command as the '**Script**' parameter:

```
o365 spo app add -p $(System.DefaultWorkingDirectory)/SPFx-CI/drop/SharePoint/solution/spfx-ci.sppkg --overwrite
```

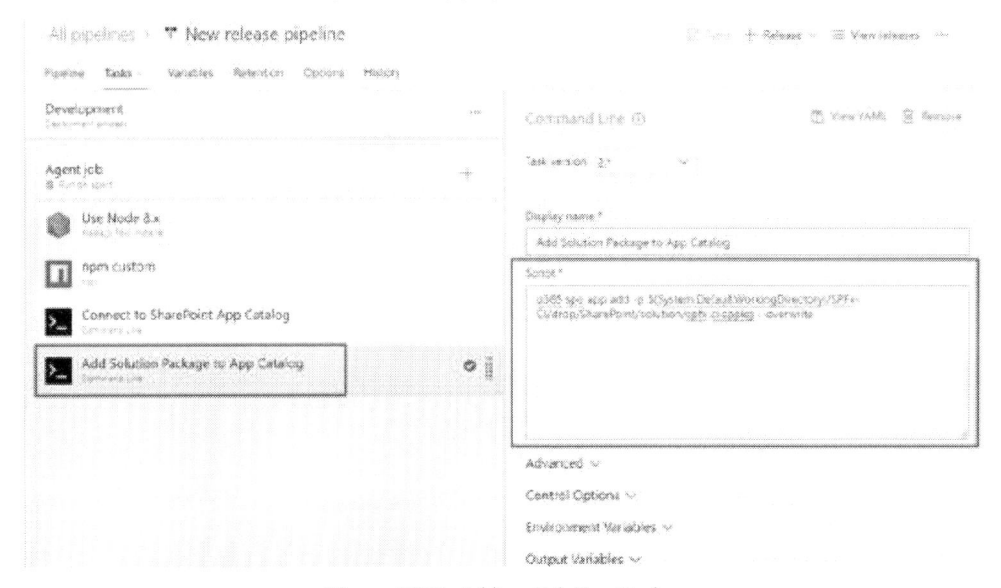

Figure 48.19: Adding Solution Package

Deploy the App:

Follow below steps to deploy the app to the SharePoint app catalog to be accessible for all site collections across the tenant:

1. Include the '**Command Line**' task.
2. In the '**Script**' field, specify the following command:

    ```
    o365 spo app deploy --name spfx-ci.sppkg --appCatalogUrl
    https://$(tenant).sharepoint.com/$(catalogsite)
    ```

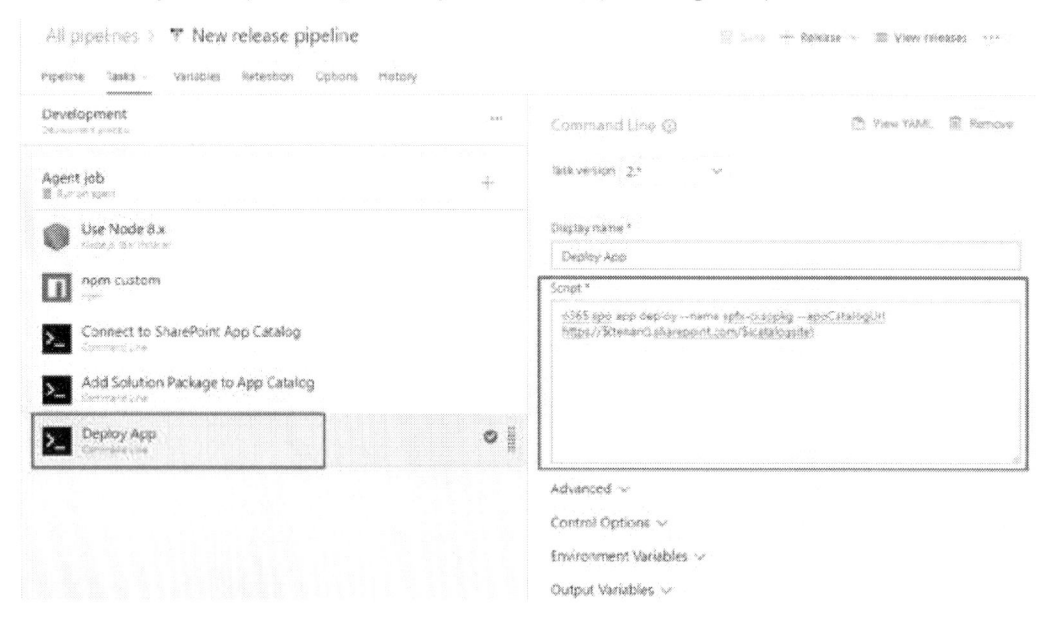

Figure 48.20: App Deploy

Set Environment Variables:

Follow the below steps to define the process variables used in the previous steps:

1. Choose the **Variables** tab.
2. Under '**Pipeline variables**', include the following variables:

Figure 48.21: Environment variables

Verify Continuous Deployment:

Follow the given steps to test the continuous deployment:
1. Under '**Pipelines**', choose '**Builds**'.
2. Choose '**Queue**':

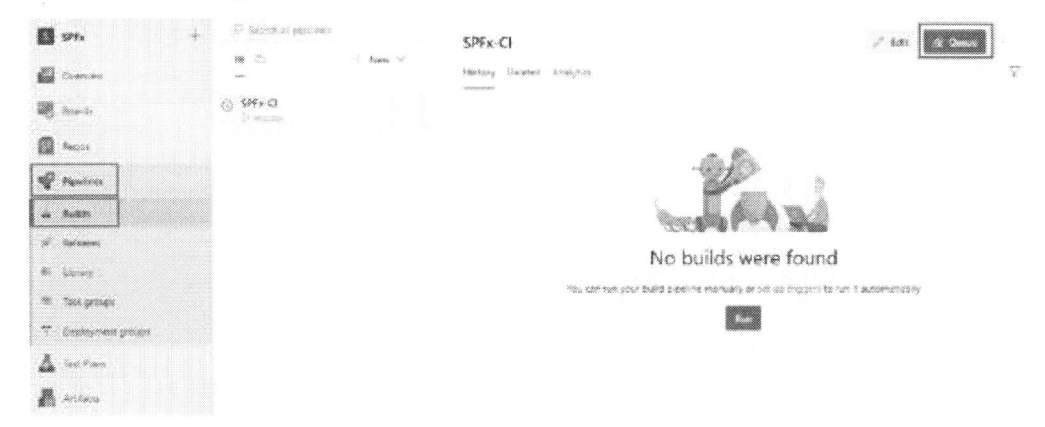

Figure 48.22: Queue new build

3. Select the branch. Then, click on **Queue**:

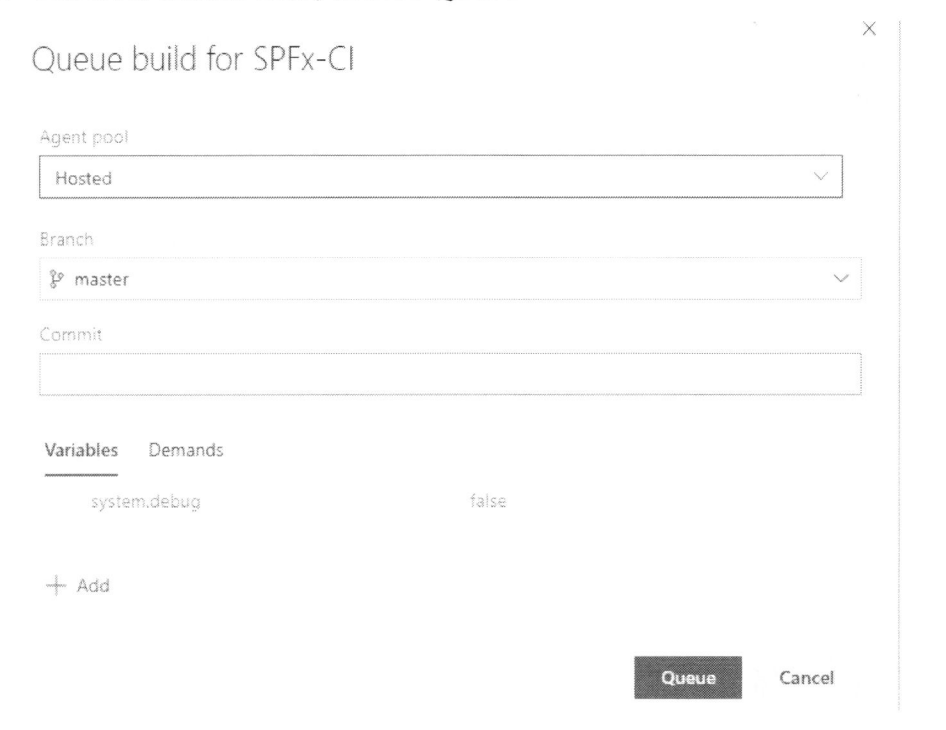

Figure 48.23: Select branch for queue

4. When the build executes, observe the logs and fix the issues, if any.
5. After a successful build, the auto-deployment will trigger:

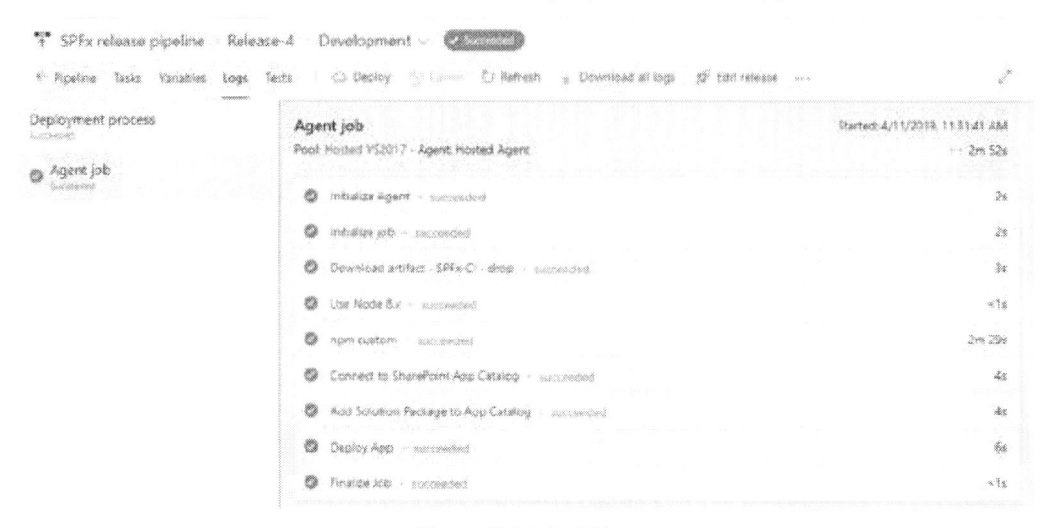

Figure 48.24: Build logs

6. Verify the app (.sppkg) is deployment to the SharePoint app catalog.

Setup Deployment Trigger

We can physically trigger the deployment. In any case, the perfect situation is to trigger the deployment on successful build completion. Follow the given steps to setup a trigger:

1. Choose **Pipelines>Releases**.
2. Edit the earlier created **Release** pipeline:

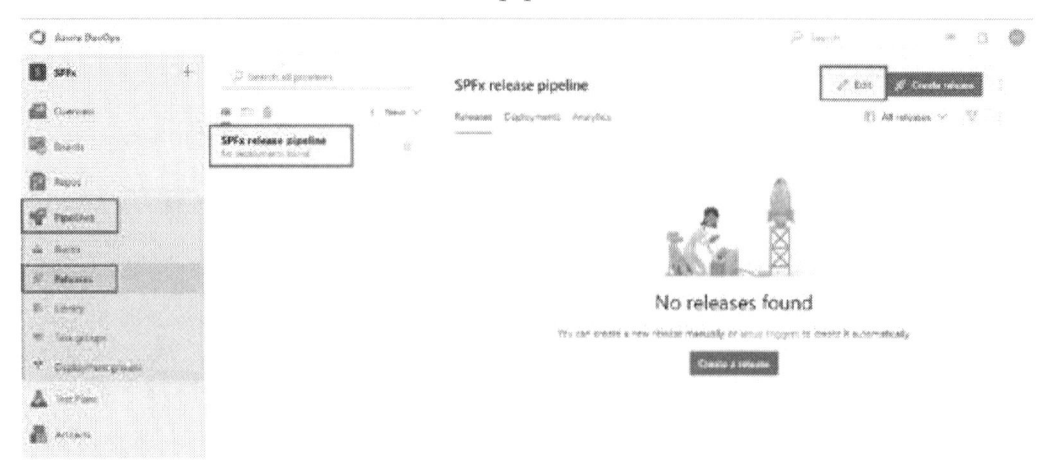

Figure 48.25: Setup Deployment Trigger

3. Under '**Artifacts**', choose '**Continuous deployment trigger**'.
4. Enable continuous deployment:

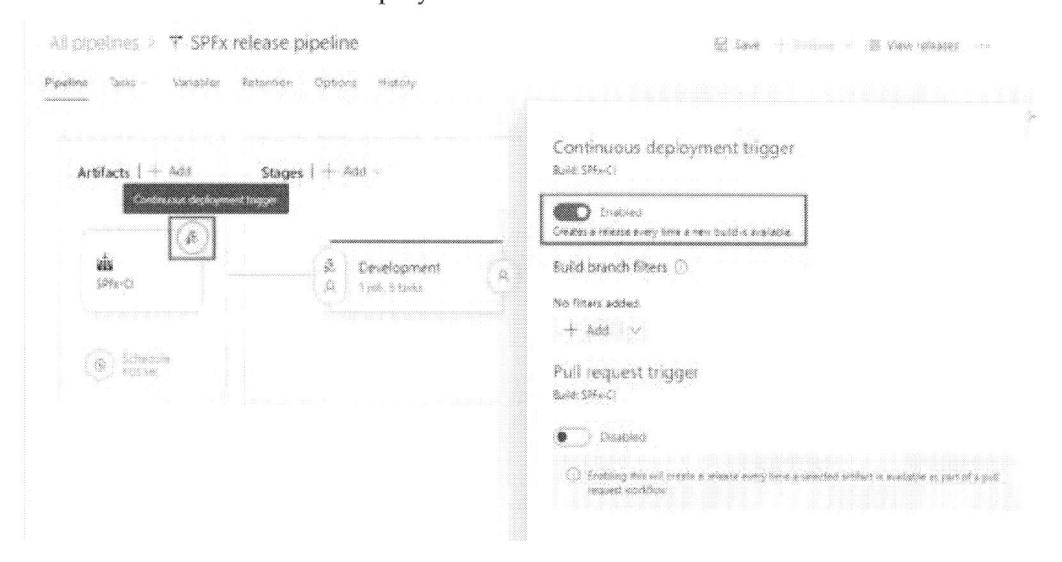

Figure 48.26: Enable continuous deployment

5. Choose '**Save**'.

Conclusion

In this chapter, we discussed the significance of CI/CD and how to execute **Continuous Integration (CI)** and **Continuous Deployment (CD)** utilizing Azure DevOps to automate the SPFx build and deployment.

CI/CD computerizes the build and deployment process when a solution is being taken a shot at by the team and is experiencing constant changes.

CHAPTER 49

Query User Profile Details

User Profile service in SharePoint is helpful to keep user-specific information. SharePoint by default gives different user profile properties as attributes (for example Id, First Name, Last Name, Manager, and so on.). We can likewise make our very own custom user profile properties.

Structure

- Outline of User Profile Service
- Query User Profile Details from SPFx

Objectives

- Query user profile details
- Implement a practical scenario utilizing ReactJS

User Profile Service Outline

Follow the given steps to explore the user profile service:

1. Browse the SharePoint Online Admin Center (**https://<tenant>-admin.sharepoint.com**).

2. Choose **'user profiles'** available on the left menu:

Figure 49.1: User profiles

Query User Profile Details from SPFx

Open a command prompt. Follow the given guidelines to make the SPFx solution:

1. Make a folder for the SPFx solution:

   ```
   md query-user-profile
   ```

2. Change the path to the above folder:

   ```
   cd query-user-profile
   ```

3. Execute the Yeoman Generator for SharePoint:

   ```
   yo @microsoft/sharepoint
   ```

4. The Yeoman generator will run through the wizard to ask questions about the SPFx solution to be created:

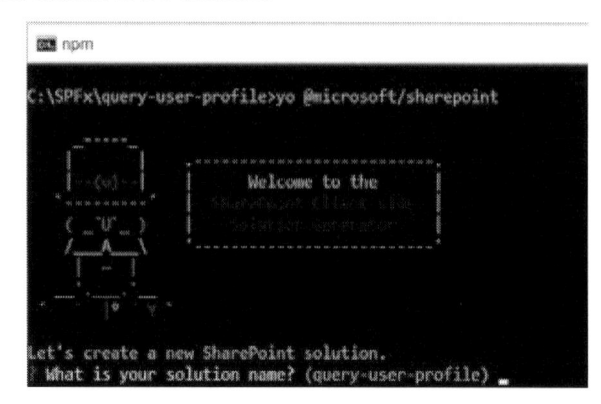

Figure 49.2: SPFx Yeoman generator

The SPFx Yeoman generator will display the following wizard of inquiries:

- **Solution Name:** Determine the SPFx solution name. Press the *Enter* key to proceed with the default selection (`query-user-profile` in this case) or type another name.
    - **Chosen decision:** Type *Enter*
- **Target environment:** Specify the target environment to deploy the SPFx solution. Select any option from SharePoint Online or SharePoint On-Premises environment.
    - **Chosen decision:** SharePoint Online only (latest)
- **Folder location:** Choose the folder location for the SPFx project (either the same folder or a subfolder).
    - **Chosen decision:** Same folder
- **Deployment option:** Specify Y to deploy the app instantly to all the sites, N otherwise.
    - **Chosen decision:** N (install on each site explicitly)
- **Consents to access web APIs:** Check whether the components in the solution need explicit permission to access web APIs that are unique.
    - **Chosen decision:** N (solution contains unique permissions)
- **Choice of client-side component:** Choose to develop a web part or an extension.
    - **Chosen decision:** WebPart
- **Web part name:** Provide the web part name. Press the *Enter* key to proceed with the default choice or type another name.
    - **Chosen decision:** `DisplayUserProfileInfo`
- **Web part description:** Provide the web part description. Press the *Enter* key to proceed with the default choice or type another value.
    - **Chosen decision:** Fetch user profile values with SPFx
- **Choice of the framework:** Choose a JavaScript framework to develop the component from No JavaScript Framework, React, and Knockout.
    - **Chosen decision:** React

5. After the scaffolding is complete, lock down the version of project dependencies by executing the following command:

```
npm shrinkwrap
```

6. At the command prompt, execute the following command to open the solution in the code editor:

```
code .
```

Define Model representing User Profile Information

To define a model representing the user profile properties, include the IUserInfo.ts file under the 'src\webparts\displayUserProfileInfo\components\' folder:

TypeScript

```
exportinterfaceIUserInfo {
    FirstName: string;
LastName: string;
    Email: string;
    Title: string;
WorkPhone: string;
    DisplayName: string;
    Department: string;
PictureURL: string;
UserProfileProperties: Array<any>;
}
```

Update IDisplayUserProfileInfoProps.ts under the 'src\webparts\displayUserProfileInfo\components\' folder to include the following properties:

TypeScript

```
import { ServiceScope } from '@microsoft/sp-core-library';

exportinterfaceIDisplayUserProfileInfoProps {
  description: string;
userName: string;
serviceScope: ServiceScope;
}
```

Define State

Add the IDisplayUserProfileInfoState.ts file under the 'src\webparts\displayUserProfileInfo\components\' folder:

TypeScript

```
import{IUserInfo } from'../components/IUserInfo';

exportinterfaceIDisplayUserProfileInfoState {
userProfileItems: IUserInfo;
}
```

Define Service

Follow below steps to define a service to fetch user profile values:

1. In the solution, create a new folder 'services' at the level of the 'components' folder.
2. Add a new file 'UserInformationService.ts' below it:

Figure 49.3: Service implementation

Code the WebPart

Open `DisplayUserProfileInfo.tsx` under the `'src\webparts\displayUserProfileInfo\components\'` folder.

Implement the `componentWillMount` method:

```
public componentWillMount(): void {
  let serviceScope: ServiceScope = this.props.serviceScope;
  this.dataCenterServiceInstance = serviceScope.consume(UserProfileService.serviceKey);

  this.dataCenterServiceInstance.getUserProfileProperties().then((userProfileItems: IUserProfile) => {
    for (let i: number = 0; i < userProfileItems.UserProfileProperties.length; i++) {
      if (userProfileItems.UserProfileProperties[i].Key == "FirstName") {
        userProfileItems.FirstName = userProfileItems.UserProfileProperties[i].Value;
      }

      if (userProfileItems.UserProfileProperties[i].Key == "LastName") {
        userProfileItems.LastName = userProfileItems.UserProfileProperties[i].Value;
      }

      if (userProfileItems.UserProfileProperties[i].Key == "WorkPhone") {
        userProfileItems.WorkPhone = userProfileItems.UserProfileProperties[i].Value;
      }

      if (userProfileItems.UserProfileProperties[i].Key == "Department") {
        userProfileItems.Department = userProfileItems.UserProfileProperties[i].Value;
      }

      if (userProfileItems.UserProfileProperties[i].Key == "PictureURL") {
        userProfileItems.PictureURL = userProfileItems.UserProfileProperties[i].Value;
      }
    }

    this.setState({ userProfileItems: userProfileItems });
  });
}
```

Figure 49.4: componentWillMount method

Implement the `render()` method to display user profile values:

```
public render(): React.ReactElement<IUserProfileViewerProps> {
  return (
    <div className={ styles.userProfileViewer }>
      <div className={ styles.container }>
        <div className={ styles.row }>
          <div className={ styles.column }>
            <span className={ styles.title }>Welcome to SharePoint!</span>
            <p className={ styles.subTitle }>Fetch User Profile Properties</p>

            <img src={this.state.userProfileItems.PictureURL}></img>

            <p>
              Name: {this.state.userProfileItems.LastName}, {this.state.userProfileItems.FirstName}
            </p>

            <p>
              WorkPhone: {this.state.userProfileItems.WorkPhone}
            </p>

            <p>
              Department: {this.state.userProfileItems.Department}
            </p>
          </div>
        </div>
      </div>
    </div>
  );
}
```

Figure 49.5: render method

Verify the WebPart:

Follow below steps to test the web part on the SharePoint page:

1. At the command prompt, execute 'gulp serve'.
2. On the SharePoint site, browse '/_layouts/15/workbench.aspx'
3. Add the webpart to the page.
4. The web part shows the currently logged-in user details:

Figure 49.6: User profile details

Conclusion

In this chapter, we analyzed the practical scenario of retrieving the user profile details using React. Showing user profile detailsis a common practice in SharePoint and it can be implemented in the SPFx web partutilizing the out-of-the-box accessible REST APIs.

Chapter 50
Querying SP Search Results

Search is a fundamental piece of SharePoint throughout the years. Search encourages getting the security trimmed outcomes across SharePoint sites. Modern SharePoint does not support any Search based web part. This chapter will help you to create your own Search based SPFx solution.

Structure

- QueryingSP Search Results from SPFx
- Develop Service to Query Search Results

Objectives

- Query the Search REST API
- Implement a practical scenario utilizing ReactJS

SPFx Web Part to Query Search Results

Open a command prompt. Follow the given guidelines to make the SPFx solution:
1. Make a folder for the SPFx solution:

```
md retrieve-spsearchresults
```

2. Change the path to the above folder:

    ```
    cd retrieve-spsearchresults
    ```

3. Execute the Yeoman Generator for SharePoint:

    ```
    yo @microsoft/sharepoint
    ```

4. The Yeoman generator will run through the wizard to ask questions about the SPFx solution to be created:

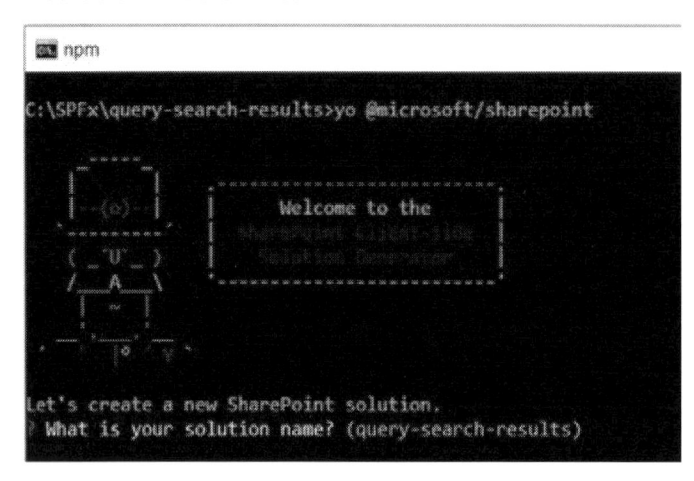

Figure 50.1: SPFx Yeoman generator

The SPFx Yeoman generator will display the following wizard of inquiries:

- **Solution Name:** Determine the SPFx solution name. Hit the *Enter* key to proceed with the default selection(`retrieve-spsearch results` in this case) or type another name.
    - **Chosen decision:** Hit *Enter*
- **Target environment:** Specify the target environment to deploy the SPFx solution. Select any option from SharePoint Online or SharePoint On-Premises environment.
    - **Chosen decision:** SharePoint Online only (latest)
- **Folder location:** Choose the folder location for the SPFx project (either the same folder or a subfolder).
    - **Chosen decision:** Same folder
- **Deployment option:** Specify Y to deploy the app instantly to all the sites, N otherwise.
    - **Chosen decision:** N (install on each site explicitly)

- **Consents to access web APIs:** Check whether the components in the solution need explicit permission to access web APIs that are unique.
    - **Chosen decision:** N (solution contains unique permissions)
- **Choice of client-side component:** Choose to develop a web part or an extension.
    - **Chosen decision:** WebPart
- **Web part name:** Provide the web part name. Hit the *Enter* key to proceed with the default choice or type another name.
    - **Chosen decision:** `DisplaySearchResults`
- **Web part description:** Provide the web part description. Hit the *Enter* key to proceed with the default choice or type another value.
    - **Chosen decision:** Retrieve search results using REST API
- **Choice of the framework:** Choose a JavaScript framework to develop the component from No JavaScript Framework, React, and Knockout.
    - **Chosen decision:** React

5. After the scaffolding is complete, lock down the version of project dependencies by executing the following command:

```
npmshrinkwrap
```

6. At the command prompt, execute the following command to open the solution in the code editor:

```
code .
```

Define a Model for Search Result

Follow below steps to characterize an interface foran SP search result item:

1. Include an interface (`ISearchItem.ts`):

   TypeScript

   ```
   exportinterfaceISearchItem
   {
       Title: string;
       Description: string;
       Url: string
   }
   ```

2. Include the state to our solution (IDisplaySearchResultsState.ts):

   TypeScript

   import {ISearchItem} from'./ISearchItem';

   exportinterfaceIDisplaySearchResultsState {
       status: string;
   searchText: string;
       items: ISearchItem[];
   }

3. Configure `DisplaySearchResults.tsx` to use the state:

```
SearchResultsViewer.tsx
 1   import * as React from 'react';
 2   import styles from './SearchResultsViewer.module.scss';
 3   import { ISearchResultsViewerProps } from '../ISearchResultsViewerProps';
 4   import { ISearchResultsViewerState } from '../ISearchResultsViewerState';
 5   import { escape } from '@microsoft/sp-lodash-subset';
 6
 7   export default class SearchResultsViewer extends React.Component<ISearchResultsViewerProps, ISearchResultsViewerState> {
 8
 9     constructor(props: ISearchResultsViewerProps, state: ISearchResultsViewerState) {
10       super(props);
11
12       this.state = {
13         status: "Ready", searchText: "",
14         items: []
15       }
16     }
17
18     public render(): React.ReactElement<ISearchResultsViewerProps> {
19       return (
20         <div className={ styles.searchResultsViewer }>
21           <div className={ styles.container }>
22             <div className={ styles.row }>
23               <div className={ styles.column }>
24                 <span className={ styles.title }>Welcome to SharePoint!</span>
25                 <p className={ styles.subTitle }>Customize SharePoint experiences using Web Parts.</p>
26                 <p className={ styles.description }>{escape(this.props.description)}</p>
27                 <a href="https://aka.ms/spfx" className={ styles.button }>
28                   <span className={ styles.label }>Learn more</span>
29                 </a>
30               </div>
31             </div>
32           </div>
33         </div>
34       );
35     }
36   }
```

Figure 50.2: Configure Display Search Results.tsx for state

Add Controls to WebPart

Follow below steps to add controls to the web part:

1. Open DisplaySearchResults.tsx under the '\src\webparts\display SearchResults\components\' folder.
2. Update the Render method to include the needed controls:

   Text field:

   TypeScript

   import { TextField } from'office-ui-fabric-react/lib/TextField';

   import'./TextField.Examples.scss';

   <TextField
       required={true}
       name="txtSearchText"
       placeholder="Search..."
       value={this.state.searchText}
   onChanged={e =>this.setState({ searchText: e })}
   />

   Button:

   TypeScript

   import { IButtonProps, DefaultButton } from'office-ui-fabric-react/lib/Button';

   <DefaultButton
   data-automation-id="search"
   target="_blank"
   title="Search"
   onClick={this._searchClicked}
   >
       Search
   </DefaultButton>

   private _searchClicked(): void {
   }

List:

TypeScript

import { FocusZone, FocusZoneDirection } from'office-ui-fabric-react/lib/FocusZone';

import { List } from'office-ui-fabric-react/lib/List';

import { Link } from'office-ui-fabric-react/lib/Link';

<FocusZonedirection={FocusZoneDirection.vertical}>

<divclassName="ms-ListGhostingExample-container"data-is-scrollable={true}>

<Listitems={this.state.items}onRenderCell={this._onRenderCell}/>

</div>

</FocusZone>

private _onRenderCell(item: ISearchItem, index: number, doesScroll: boolean): JSX.Element {

return (

<divclassName="ms-ListGhostingExample-itemCell"data-is-focusable={true}>

<divclassName="ms-ListGhostingExample-itemContent">

<divclassName="ms-ListGhostingExample-itemName">

<Linkhref={item.Url}>{item.Title}</Link>

</div>

<divclassName="ms-ListGhostingExample-itemName">{item.Description}</div>

<p></p>

</div>

</div>

);

}

3. At the command prompt, type '`gulp serve`' to see the controls on the webpart:

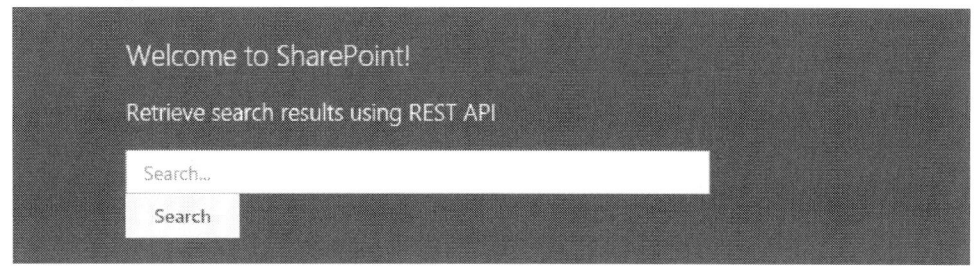

Figure 50.3: SPFx web parts with controls placed on it

Implement Service to Query Search Results

Follow the below steps to implement the service to query the search results:

1. In the solution, include a folder '`services`'.
2. Include a file `SearchService.ts` under it.
3. Utilize the REST API to query the search results:

```
import { SPHttpClient, SPHttpClientResponse } from '@microsoft/sp-http';
import { IWebPartContext } from '@microsoft/sp-webpart-base';
import { ISPSearchResult } from '../components/ISPSearchResult';
import { ISearchResults, ICells, ICellValue, ISearchResponse } from './ISearchService';

export default class SearchService {
    constructor(private _context: IWebPartContext) {
    }

    public getSearchResults(query: string): Promise<ISPSearchResult[]> {
        let url: string = this._context.pageContext.web.absoluteUrl + "/_api/search/query?querytext='" + query + "'";

        return new Promise<ISPSearchResult[]>((resolve, reject) => {
            // Do an Ajax call to receive the search results
            this._getSearchData(url).then((res: ISearchResults) => {
                let searchResp: ISPSearchResult[] = [];

                // Check if there was an error
                if (typeof res["odata.error"] !== "undefined") {
                    if (typeof res["odata.error"]["message"] !== "undefined") {
                        Promise.reject(res["odata.error"]["message"].value);
                        return;
                    }
                }

                if (!this._isNull(res)) {
                    const fields: string = "Title,Path,Description";

                    // Retrieve all the table rows
                    if (typeof res.PrimaryQueryResult.RelevantResults.Table !== 'undefined') {
                        if (typeof res.PrimaryQueryResult.RelevantResults.Table.Rows !== 'undefined') {
                            searchResp = this._setSearchResults(res.PrimaryQueryResult.RelevantResults.Table.Rows, fields);
                        }
                    }
                }

                // Return the retrieved result set
                resolve(searchResp);
            });
        });
    }
}
```

Figure 50.4: Search service

4. Implement the supporting methods:

```ts
/**
 * Retrieve the results from the search API
 *
 * @param url
 */
private _getSearchData(url: string): Promise<ISearchResults> {
    return this._context.spHttpClient.get(url, SPHttpClient.configurations.v1, {
        headers: {
            'odata-version': '3.0'
        }
    }).then((res: SPHttpClientResponse) => {
        return res.json();
    }).catch(error => {
        return Promise.reject(JSON.stringify(error));
    });
}

/**
 * Set the current set of search results
 *
 * @param crntResults
 * @param fields
 */
private _setSearchResults(crntResults: ICells[], fields: string): any[] {
    const temp: any[] = [];

    if (crntResults.length > 0) {
        const flds: string[] = fields.toLowerCase().split(',');

        crntResults.forEach((result) => {
            // Create a temp value
            var val: Object = {}
            result.Cells.forEach((cell: ICellValue) => {
                if (flds.indexOf(cell.Key.toLowerCase()) !== -1) {
                    // Add key and value to temp value
                    val[cell.Key] = cell.Value;
                }
            });

            // Push this to the temp array
            temp.push(val);
        });
    }

    return temp;
}

/**
 * Check if the value is null or undefined
 *
 * @param value
 */
private _isNull(value: any): boolean {
    return value === null || typeof value === "undefined";
}
```

Figure 50.5: Supporting methods

Verify the WebPart:

Follow below steps to test the web part on the SharePoint page:
1. At the command prompt, execute 'gulp serve'.
2. On the SharePoint site, browse '/_layouts/15/workbench.aspx'
3. Include the webpart on the page.
4. Verify the search results against search texts:

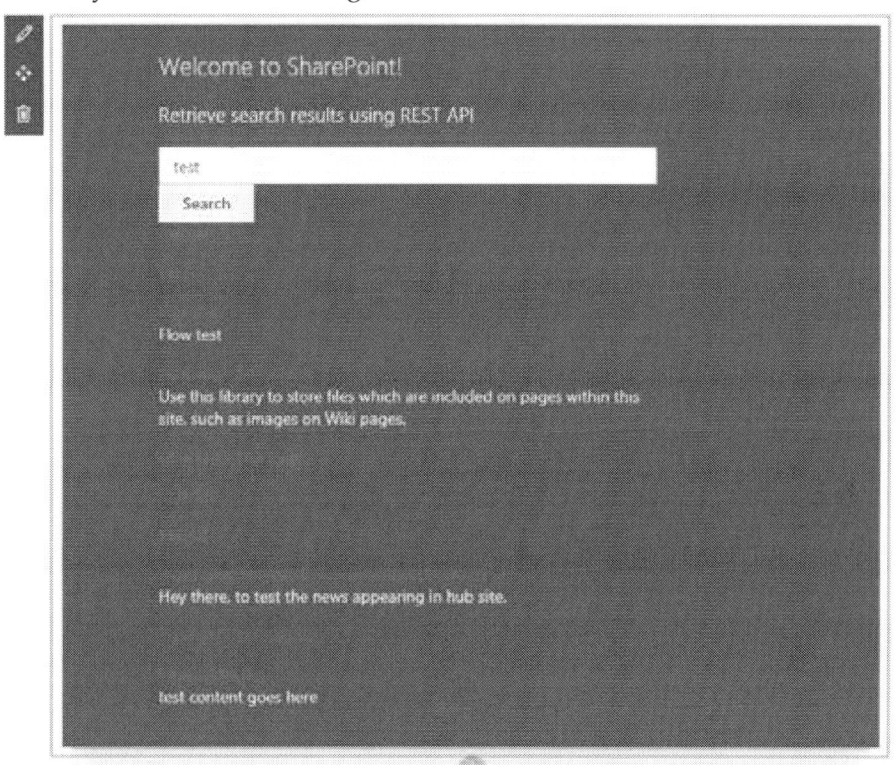

Fig 50.6: Search results in the SPFx web part

Conclusion

In this chapter, we discussed the pragmatic situation of querying the list items utilizing React. Search results can be displayed by utilizing SharePoint REST APIs. Modern SharePoint does not offer any web part for search. By utilizing the Search REST API, the outcomes can be accomplished effectively.

CHAPTER 51
React-based Tree View

Web parts created in SharePoint utilizes different controls to portray the functionality on the UI. The Office 365 UI Fabric provides most of the UI controls that can be utilized with SharePoint Framework web parts. However, there are certain UI controls which are not available to use out of the box. The tree view is one such example of a UI control.

Structure

- Develop a SPFx Solution for a React-based Tree View
- Tree View Control - npm package

Objectives

- Build a tree view control
- Use ReactJS to implement the practical scenario

Develop a SPFx Solution for a React-based Tree View

Open a command prompt. Follow the given guidelines to make the SPFx solution:

1. Make a folder for the SPFx solution:

   ```
   md tree-view-control
   ```

2. Change the path to the above folder:

   ```
   cd tree-view-control
   ```

3. Execute the Yeoman Generator for SharePoint:

   ```
   yo @microsoft/sharepoint
   ```

4. The Yeoman generator will run through the wizard to ask questions about the SPFx solution to be created:

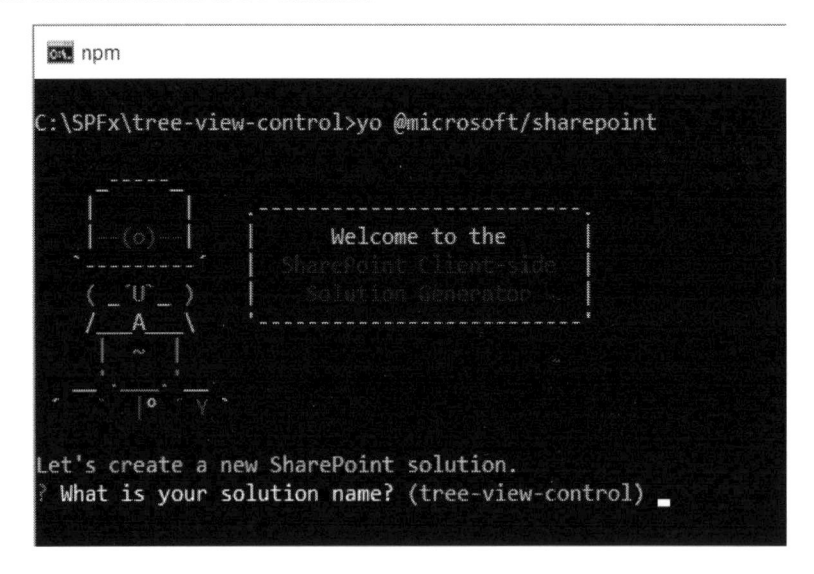

Figure 51.1: SPFx Yeoman generator

The SPFx Yeoman generator will display the following wizard of inquiries:

- **Solution Name:** Determine the SPFx solution name. Hit the *Enter* key to proceed with the default selection (`tree-view-control` in this case) or type another name.
    - **Chosen decision:** Hit *Enter*
- **Target environment:** Specify the target environment to deploy the SPFx solution.
    - **Chosen decision:** SharePoint Online only (latest)
- **Folder location:** Choose the folder location for the SPFx project (either the same folder or a subfolder).
    - **Chosen decision:** Same folder

- **Deployment option:** Specify Y to deploy the app instantly to all the sites, N otherwise.
    - **Chosen decision:** N (install on each site explicitly)
- **Consents to access web APIs:** Check whether the components in the solution need explicit permission to access web APIs that are unique.
    - **Chosen decision:** N (solution contains unique permissions)
- **Choice of client-side component:** Choose to develop a web part or an extension.
    - **Chosen decision:** WebPart
- **Web part name:** Provide the web part name. Hit the *Enter* key to proceed with the default choice or type another name.
    - **Chosen decision:** TreeViewControl
- **Web part description:** Provide the web part description. Hit the *Enter* key to proceed with the default choice or type another value.
    - **Chosen decision:** Tree view control with React
- **Choice of the framework:** Choose a JavaScript framework to develop the solution.
    - **Chosen decision:** React

Tree View Control

While writing this book, the tree view control wasn't available in Office 365 UI Fabric controls. We will utilize the npm package 'react-super-treeview'.

Install the tree view control by executing the following command:

```
npm install react-super-treeview --save
```

Code the webpart

Follow the below steps to develop the tree view control:

1. Open the TreeViewControl.tsx file under the '\src\webparts\treeViewControl\components\' folder.
2. Import the tree view control:

    TypeScript

    ```
    importSuperTreeviewfrom'react-super-treeview';
    ```

3. Define a tree structure in a state:

TypeScript

```
this.state = {
  data: [
    {
        id: 1,
        name: 'Parent A'
    },
    {
        id: 2,
        name: 'Parent B',
        isExpanded: true,
        isChecked: true,
        children: [
            {
                id: 21,
                name: 'Child 1',
                isExpanded: true,
                children: [
                    {
                        id: 5,
                        name: "Grand Child",
                        isExpanded: true
                    }
                ]
            },
            {
                id: 22,
                name: 'Child 2'
            },
            {
                id: 23,
                name: 'Child 3'
            },
            {
                id: 24,
                name: 'Child 4'
            }
        ]
    }
  ]
};
```

Figure 51.2: State representing the tree structure

4. Render the tree structure:

   TypeScript

```
public render(): React.ReactElement<ITreeViewControlProps> {
  return (
    // RENDER THE COMPONENT
    <div className={ styles.treeViewControl }>
      <div className={ styles.container }>
        <div className={ styles.row }>
          <div className={ styles.column }>

            <SuperTreeview
              data={ this.state.data }
              noChildrenAvailableMessage=''
              isDeletable= {(node, depth) => {
                return false;
              }}
              onUpdateCb={(updatedData) => {
                this.setState({data: updatedData});
                let selectedNodeName: string = sessionStorage.getItem(sessionStorageSelectedNodeKey);

                resetNodes(updatedData);

                function resetNodes(nodes){
                    nodes.forEach((node)=>{
                        if (node.name !== selectedNodeName) {
                          node.isChecked = false;
                        }

                        if(node.children){
                          resetNodes(node.children);
                        }
                    });
                }
                sessionStorage.removeItem(sessionStorageSelectedNodeKey);
              }}
              onCheckToggleCb={(nodes, depth)=>{
                  sessionStorage.setItem(sessionStorageSelectedNodeKey, nodes[0].name);
              }}
            />
          </div>
        </div>
      </div>
    </div>
  );
}
```

Figure 51.3: render method implementation

Verify the web part

Follow the given steps to test the web part on the SharePoint page:
1. At the command prompt, type 'gulp serve'.
2. On the SharePoint site, browse '/_layouts/15/workbench.aspx'.

3. Include and verify the webpart on the page:

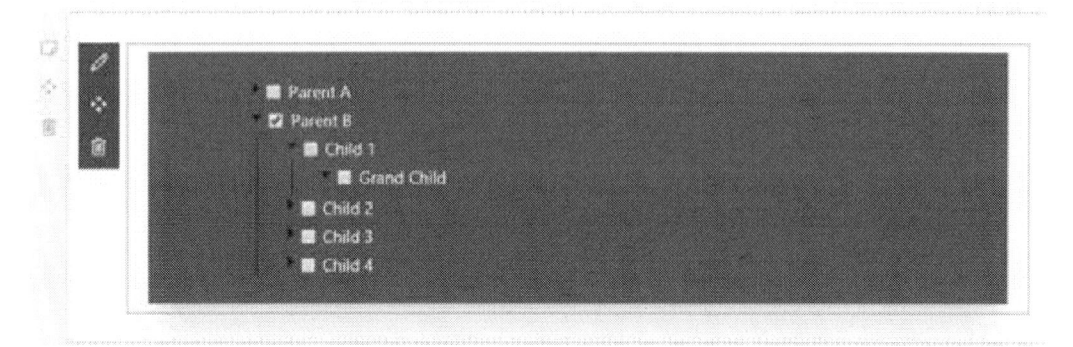

Figure 51.4: Tree view representation in the SPFx web part

Conclusion

In this chapter, we explored the practical scenario of displaying the hierarchical information in a tree view structure using React. The Office 365 UI fabric provides most of the controls. However, we can utilize third-party controls to address customer business requirements.

CHAPTER 52
React-based Carousel

SharePoint offers numerous web parts showing content to the users. They are either out-of-the-box web parts arranged to demonstrate the substance or specially created web parts. Carousel is one such ordinarily utilized web part. The Carousel web part regularly looks over the pictures in an endless circle and enables clients to look through. Carousels are utilized to turn the news or declarations on a landing page of the SharePoint site. We can utilize npm packages to implement the custom Carousel web part.

Structure
- Develop SPFx Solutions for a React-based Carousel
- NPM Carousel Package

Objectives
- Build a Carousel in SPFx
- Use ReactJS to implement the practical scenario

Develop the SPFx Solution for Carousel

At the command prompt, follow the given guidelines to make the SPFx solution:

1. Make a folder for the SPFx solution:

   ```
   md carousel-control
   ```

2. Change the path to the above folder:

   ```
   cd carousel-control
   ```

3. Execute the Yeoman Generator for SharePoint:

   ```
   yo @microsoft/sharepoint
   ```

4. The Yeoman generator will run through the wizard to ask questions about the SPFx solution to be created:

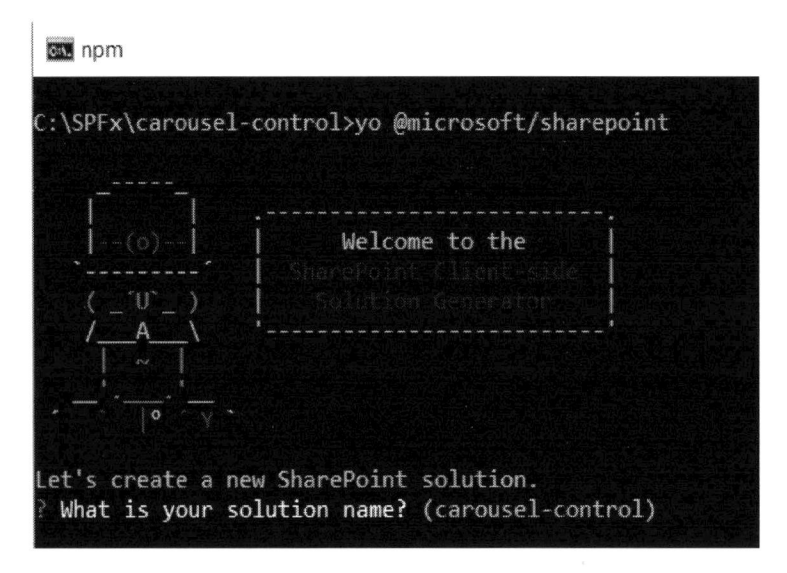

Figure 52.1: SPFx Yeoman generator

The SPFx Yeoman generator will display the following wizard of inquiries:

- **Solution Name:** Determine the SPFx solution name. Hit the *Enter* key to proceed with the default selection (carousel-control in this case) or type another name.
    - **Chosen decision:** Hit *Enter*
- **Target environment:** Specify the target environment to deploy the SPFx solution.
    - **Chosen decision:** SharePoint Online only (latest)
- **Folder location:** Choose the folder location for the SPFx project (either the same folder or a subfolder).
    - **Chosen decision:** Use the current folder

- **Deployment option:** Specify Y to deploy the app instantly to all the sites, N otherwise.
    - o **Chosen decision:** N (install on each site explicitly)
- **Consents to access web APIs:** Check whether the components in the solution need explicit permission to access web APIs that are unique.
    - o **Chosen decision:** N (solution contains unique permissions)
- **Choice of client-side component:** Choose to develop a web part or an extension.
    - o **Chosen decision:** WebPart
- **Web part name:** Provide the web part name. Hit the *Enter* key to proceed with the default choice or type another name.
    - o **Chosen decision:** Carousel Control
- **Web part description:** Provide the web part description. Hit the *Enter* key to proceed with the default choice or type another value.
    - o **Chosen decision:** React-based Carousel
- **Choice of the framework:** Choose a JavaScript framework to develop the solution.
    - o **Chosen decision:** React

NPM Carousel Package

We will utilize the npm package 'react-responsive-carousel'. Install the npm package by executing the following command:

```
npm install react-responsive-carousel --save
```

Code the webpart

Follow the below steps to develop the carousel:

1. Open `CarouselControl.tsx` file under the '\src\webparts\carousel Control\components\' folder.
2. Import the `Carousel` control:

    TypeScript
    ```
    import{ Carousel } from'react-responsive-carousel';
    ```

3. Import Carousel styles:

    TypeScript
    ```
    import"react-responsive-carousel/lib/styles/carousel.min.css";
    ```

Define State

Follow the below steps to define the React state:

1. Create a new file ICarouselControlState.ts under the '\src\webparts\carouselControl\components\' folder:

    TypeScript

    ```
    exportinterfaceICarouselControlState {
    imageURLs: string[];
    }
    ```

2. Update our '\src\webparts\carouselControl\components\CarouselControl.tsx' component to use the state:

    TypeScript

    ```
    exportdefaultclassCarouselControlextendsReact.Component<ICarouselControlProps, ICarouselControlState> {
    publicconstructor(props: ICarouselControlProps, state: ICarouselControlState) {
    super(props);

    this.state = {
    imageURLs: []
        };
      }
    }
    ```

Implement Service to fetch Image information:

Let us implement the service to fetch the image URLs to display in the carousel:

1. Create the 'services' folder under the 'src' folder.
2. Add the IDataService.ts file under the 'services' folder:

    TypeScript

    ```
    exportinterfaceIDataService {
    getImages: (listName?: string) =>Promise<any>;
    }
    ```

3. Under the 'services' folder, implement the ImageService.ts service:

TypeScript

```
import { ServiceScope, ServiceKey } from "@microsoft/sp-core-library";
import { IDataService } from "./IDataService";
import { SPHttpClient, SPHttpClientResponse } from "@microsoft/sp-http";
import { PageContext } from "@microsoft/sp-page-context";
import { ICarouselImage } from "./ICarouselImage";

export class ImageService implements IDataService {

    public static readonly serviceKey: ServiceKey<IDataService> = ServiceKey.create<IDataService>('carousel-data-service', ImageService);

    private _spHttpClient: SPHttpClient;
    private _pageContext: PageContext;
    private _currentWebUrl: string;

    constructor(serviceScope: ServiceScope) {
        serviceScope.whenFinished(() => {
            // Configure the required dependencies
            this._spHttpClient = serviceScope.consume(SPHttpClient.serviceKey);
            this._pageContext = serviceScope.consume(PageContext.serviceKey);
            this._currentWebUrl = this._pageContext.web.absoluteUrl;
        });
    }

    public getImages(listName: string): Promise<string[]> {
        var images: string[] = [];
        return new Promise<string[]>((resolve: (items: string[]) => void, reject: (error: any) => void): void => {
            this.readImages(listName)
                .then((carouselItems: ICarouselImage[]): void => {
                    var i: number = 0;
                    for (i = 0; i < carouselItems.length; i++) {
                        images.push(this._currentWebUrl + carouselItems[i].FileRef);
                    }
                    resolve(images);
                });
        });
    }

    private readImages(listName: string): Promise<ICarouselImage[]> {
        return new Promise<ICarouselImage[]>((resolve: (items: ICarouselImage[]) => void, reject: (error: any) => void): void => {
            this._spHttpClient.get(`${this._currentWebUrl}/_api/web/lists/getbytitle('${listName}')/items?$select=FileRef/FileRef&$filter=FSObjType eq 0`,
                SPHttpClient.configurations.v1,
                {
                    headers: {
                        'Accept': 'application/json;odata=nometadata',
                        'odata-version': ''
                    }
                })
                .then((response: SPHttpClientResponse): Promise<{ value: ICarouselImage[] }> => {
                    return response.json();
                })
                .then((response: { value: ICarouselImage[] }): void => {
                    resolve(response.value);
                }, (error: any): void => {
                    reject(error);
                });
        });
    }
}
```

Figure 52.2: Service implementation

Update the web part class to consume the service

Follow the below steps to consume the service from the web part:

1. Open the CarouselControl.tsx file under the '\src\webparts\carouselControl\components\' folder.
2. Consume the above service:

TypeScript

```typescript
import * as React from 'react';
import styles from './CarouselControl.module.scss';
import { ICarouselControlProps } from './ICarouselControlProps';
import { escape } from '@microsoft/sp-lodash-subset';
import { Carousel } from 'react-responsive-carousel';
import "react-responsive-carousel/lib/styles/carousel.min.css";
import { ICarouselControlState } from './ICarouselControlState';

import { ServiceScope } from '@microsoft/sp-core-library';
import { ImageService } from '../../../services/ImageService';
import { IDataService } from '../../../services/IDataService';

export default class CarouselControl extends React.Component<ICarouselControlProps, ICarouselControlState> {
  private dataCenterServiceInstance: IDataService;

  public constructor(props: ICarouselControlProps, state: ICarouselControlState) {
    super(props);

    this.state = {
      imageURLs: []
    };

    let serviceScope: ServiceScope = this.props.serviceScope;
    this.dataCenterServiceInstance = serviceScope.consume(ImageService.serviceKey);

    this.dataCenterServiceInstance.getImages('Site Collection Images').then((carouselItems: any) => {
      this.setState({
        imageURLs: carouselItems
      });
    });
  }

  public render(): React.ReactElement<ICarouselControlProps> {
    return (
      <div className={styles.CarouselControl}>
        <div className={styles.container}>
          <div className={styles.row}>
            <div className={styles.column}>
              <span className={styles.title}>Welcome to SharePoint!</span>
              <p className={styles.subTitle}>React based Carousel</p>
              <p className={styles.description}>{escape(this.props.description)}</p>

              <Carousel showThumbs={false} >
                {this.state.imageURLs.map((imageList) => {
                  return (<div>
                    <img src={imageList} />
                  </div>)
                })}
              </Carousel>
            </div>
          </div>
        </div>
      </div>
    );
  }
}
```

Figure 52.3: Consume service

Verify the web part

Follow the given steps to test the web part on the SharePoint page:
1. At the command prompt, type '`gulp serve`'.
2. On the SharePoint site, browse '`/_layouts/15/workbench.aspx`'.
3. Include the web part in the page:

Figure 52.4: Add the SPFx web part to the SharePoint page

4. Check whether the **Carousel** is rotating the pictures:

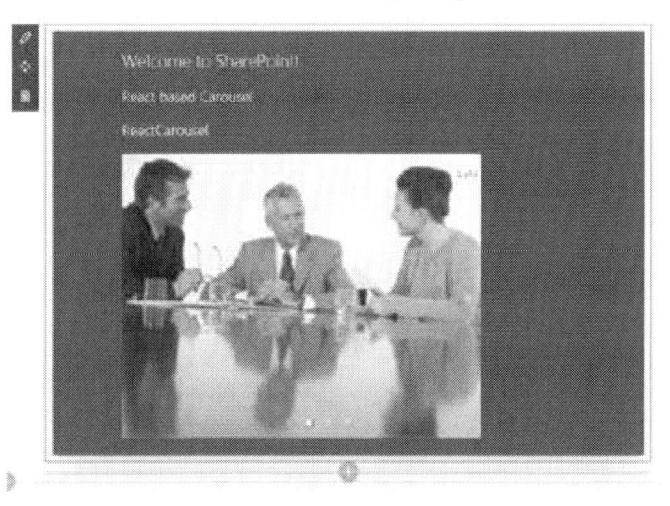

Figure 52.5: SPFx Carousel web part

Conclusion

In this chapter, we explored the practical scenario of displaying images in Carousel using React. Showing scrolling pictures is a typical situation in SharePoint and it can be actualized in the SharePoint Framework web part utilizing third-party npm packages.

CHAPTER 53
Implement a React-based Organogram

SharePoint Framework web parts are focused to handle business situations. The Office 365 UI fabric component offers consistent coordination with Office 365 and offers a wide scope of UI segments. In any case, it doesn't offer an organogram sort of controls yet. In these situations, we can utilize open source npm bundles offerings.

Structure
- Develop a React-based Organogram
- NPM Packages - Organization Chart Control and Array to Tree

Objectives
- Build an organization chart
- Use ReactJS to implement the practical scenario

Develop the SPFx Solution for an Organogram

At the command prompt, follow the given guidelines to make the SPFx solution:

1. Make a folder for the SPFx solution:
   ```
   md spfx-react-orgchart
   ```

2. Change the path to the above folder:

   ```
   cd spfx-react-orgchart
   ```

3. Execute the Yeoman Generator for SharePoint:

   ```
   yo @microsoft/sharepoint
   ```

4. The Yeoman generator will run through the wizard to ask questions about the SPFx solution to be created:

Figure 53.1: SPFx Yeoman generator

The SPFx Yeoman generator will display the following wizard of inquiries:

- **Solution Name:** Determine the SPFx solution name. Hit the *Enter* key to proceed with the default selection (`spfx-react-orgchart` in this case) or type another name.
  - o **Chosen decision:** Hit *Enter*
- **Target environment:** Specify the target environment to deploy the SPFx solution.
  - o **Chosen decision:** SharePoint Online only (latest)
- **Folder location:** Choose the folder location for the SPFx project (either the same folder or a subfolder).
  - o **Chosen decision:** Same folder
- **Deployment option:** Specify Y to deploy the app instantly to all the sites, N otherwise.
  - o **Chosen decision:** N (install on each site explicitly)

- **Consents to access web APIs:** Check whether the components in the solution need explicit permission to access web APIs that are unique.
    - **Chosen decision:** N (solution contains unique permissions)
- **Choice of client-side component:** Chooseto develop a web part or an extension.
    - **Chosen decision:** WebPart
- **Web part name:** Provide the web part name. Hit the *Enter* key to proceed with the default choice or type another name.
    - **Chosen decision:** `OrganogramViewer`
- **Web part description:** Provide the web part description. Hit the *Enter* key to proceed with the default choice or type another value.
    - **Chosen decision:** Organization chart with React
- **Choice of the framework:** Choose a JavaScript framework to develop the solution.
    - **Chosen decision:** React

Development Scenario

We will utilize SharePoint to store the various leveled (hierarchy) data for the chart and render it on the SPFx web part.

A SharePoint list (**OrgChart**) is utilized to store the various leveled information. The list schema is as follows:

Columns

A column stores information about each item in the list. The following columns are currently available in this list:

Column (click to edit)	Type	Required
Title	Single line of text	✓
Parent	Lookup	
Url	Hyperlink or Picture	
Modified	Date and Time	
Created	Date and Time	
Created By	Person or Group	
Modified By	Person or Group	

Figure 53.2: SharePoint list structure

The **Parent** column is a lookup on the **Title** column. Include the test data in the list:

Figure 53.3: Test data

NPM Packages

Organization Chart Control:

We will utilize the npm package 'react-orgchart'. Install the npm package by executing the following command:

```
npm install react-orgchart --save
```

Array to Tree:

The npm package 'array-to-tree' helps to convert a plain array of nodes to a nested data structure. Install the npm package by executing the following command:

```
npm install array-to-tree --save
```

Code the webpart

Follow the below steps to develop the organogram:

1. Import the org chart control and CSS to '\src\webparts\organogram Viewer\components\OrganogramViewer.tsx':

   TypeScript

   ```
   importOrgChartfrom'react-orgchart';
   ```

2. Render the tree control:

   TypeScript

```
public render(): React.ReactElement<IOrganogramViewerProps> {
  return (
    <div className={ styles.organogramViewer }>
      <div className={ styles.container }>
        <div className={ styles.row }>
          <div className={ styles.column }>

            <OrgChart tree={this.state.orgChartItems} NodeComponent={this.MyNodeComponent} />

          </div>
        </div>
      </div>
    </div>
  );
}

private MyNodeComponent = ({ node }) => {
  if (node.url) {
    return (
      <div className="initechNode">
        <a href={ node.url.Url } className={styles.link} >{ node.title }</a>
      </div>
    );
  }
  else {
    return (
      <div className="initechNode">{ node.title }</div>
    );
  }
}
```

Figure 53.4: render method

3. Implement a method to read items from the SharePoint list:

   TypeScript

```typescript
private readOrgChartItems(): Promise<IOrgChartItem[]> {
    return new Promise<IOrgChartItem[]>((resolve: (itemId: IOrgChartItem[]) => void, reject: (error: any) => void): void => {
        this.props.spHttpClient.get(`${this.props.siteUrl}/_api/web/lists/getbytitle('${this.props.listName}')/items?$select=Title,Id,Url,Parent/Id,Parent/Title&$expand=Parent/Id&$orderby=Parent/Id asc`,
            SPHttpClient.configurations.v1,
            {
                headers: {
                    'Accept': 'application/json;odata=nometadata',
                    'odata-version': ''
                }
            })
            .then((response: SPHttpClientResponse): Promise<{ value: IOrgChartItem[] }> => {
                return response.json();
            })
            .then((response: { value: IOrgChartItem[] }): void => {
                resolve(response.value);
            }, (error: any): void => {
                reject(error);
            });
    });
}
```

Figure 53.5: Read SharePoint items

4. Implement a method to process the items and convert it to the org chart:

   TypeScript

```typescript
private processOrgChartItems(): void {
    this.readOrgChartItems()
        .then((orgChartItems: IOrgChartItem[]): void => {

            let orgChartNodes: Array<ChartItem> = [];
            var count: number;
            for (count = 0; count < orgChartItems.length; count++) {
                orgChartNodes.push(new ChartItem(orgChartItems[count].Id
                    , orgChartItems[count].Title, orgChartItems[count].Url
                    , orgChartItems[count].Parent ? orgChartItems[count].Parent.Id : undefined));
            }

            var arrayToTree: any = require('array-to-tree');
            var orgChartHierarchyNodes: any = arrayToTree(orgChartNodes);
            var output: any = JSON.stringify(orgChartHierarchyNodes[0]);

            this.setState({
                orgChartItems: JSON.parse(output)
            });
        });
}
```

Figure 53.6: Process SharePoint items

Verify the webpart

Follow the given steps to test the web part on the SharePoint page:

1. At the command prompt, type '`gulp serve`'.
2. On the SharePoint site, browse '`/_layouts/15/workbench.aspx`'.
3. Include the web part in the page.
4. Edit the webpart and update the web part property with the list name (i.e. **OrgChart**):

Figure 53.7: Configure the list name property

5. The web part will render the organization chart from the list:

Figure 53.8: Org chart information in SPFx web part

6. Click the nodes with the URL for navigation.

Conclusion

In this chapter, we explored the practical scenario of displaying the hierarchical information in an OrgChart format using React. Displaying the hierarchical information is a common scenario in SharePoint and it can be implemented in the SharePoint Framework webpart using third-party npm packages.

CHAPTER 54
Integrating Adaptive Cards with SPFx

The **SharePoint Framework (SPFx)** based web parts under pins a combination with different JavaScript frameworks and libraries. We can incorporate the npm bundle in our solution for utilizing the different functionalities offered by that npm bundle. The browser-based Adaptive cards define newer dimensions to SPFx.

Structure
- Introduction to Adaptive Cards
- Integrate Adaptive Cards with SPFx

Objectives
- Integration of Adaptive Cards with SPFx
- Use ReactJS to implement the practical scenario

Introduction to Adaptive Cards

Adaptive Cards are a new way for the developers to exchange card content in a common and consistent way. Adaptive cards are an extra ordinary fit for Bot. Notwithstanding; they can be viably utilized with SPFx to render the content. You can read more about Adaptive Cards at **https://adaptivecards.io/**.

Develop the SPFx web part for Adaptive Cards integration

At the command prompt, follow the given guidelines to make the SPFx solution:

1. Make a folder for the SPFx solution:

    ```
    md adaptive-cards-integration
    ```

2. Change the path to the above folder:

    ```
    cd adaptive-cards-integration
    ```

3. Execute the Yeoman Generator for SharePoint:

    ```
    yo @microsoft/sharepoint
    ```

4. The Yeoman generator will run through the wizard to ask questions about the SPFx solution to be created:

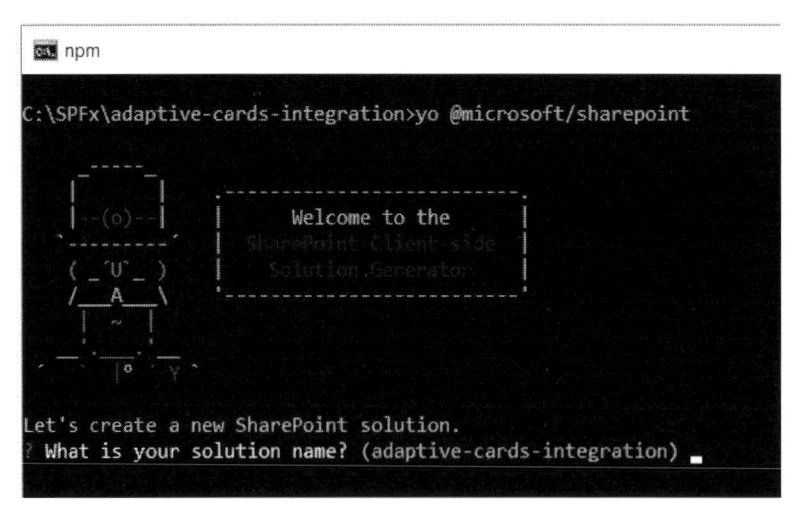

Figure 54.1: SPFx Yeoman generator

The SPFx Yeoman generator will display the following wizard of inquiries:

- **Solution Name:** Determine the SPFx solution name. Hit the *Enter* key to proceed with the default selection (`adaptive-cards-integration` in this case) or type another name.
    - o **Chosen decision:** Hit *Enter*
- **Target environment:** Specify the target environment to deploy the SPFx solution.
    - o **Chosen decision:** SharePoint Online only (latest)

- **Folder location:** Choose the folder location for the SPFx project (either the same folder or a subfolder).
  - o **Chosen decision:** Same folder
- **Deployment option:** Specify Y to deploy the app instantly to all the sites, N otherwise.
  - o **Chosen decision:** N (install on each site explicitly)
- **Consents to access web APIs:** Check whether the components in the solution need explicit permission to access web APIs that are unique.
  - o **Chosen decision:** N (solution contains unique permissions)
- **Choice of client-side component:** Choose to develop a web part or an extension.
  - o **Chosen decision:** WebPart
- **Web part name:** Provide the web part name. Hit the *Enter* key to proceed with the default choice or type another name.
  - o **Chosen decision:** `ImageGalleryAdaptiveCards`
- **Web part description:** Provide the web part description. Hit the *Enter* key to proceed with the default choice or type another value.
  - o **Chosen decision:** Adaptive Cards based Image Gallery
- **Choice of the framework:** Choose a JavaScript framework to develop the solution.
  - o **Chosen decision:** React

NPM Packages

Adaptive cards:

Install the npm package by executing the following command:

```
npm install adaptivecards --save
```

@pnp/sp:

Install the npm package by executing the following command:

```
npm install @pnp/logging @pnp/common @pnp/odata @pnp/sp --save
```

SharePoint Information Architecture

Create a SharePoint list (named '**Adaptive Card Images**') to store the image data. The list schema is as follows:

Columns

A column stores information about each item in the list. The following columns are currently available in this list:

Column (click to edit)	Type	Required
Title	Single line of text	✓
Modified	Date and Time	
Created	Date and Time	
Image Link	Hyperlink or Picture	✓
Navigation URL	Hyperlink or Picture	✓
Sort Order	Number	✓
Created By	Person or Group	
Modified By	Person or Group	

Figure 54.2: List Schema

- The '**Image Link**' column stores the URL of a picture to be shown in an adaptive card.
- The '**Navigation URL**' column speaks to the URL to explore by tapping on the picture in the adaptive card.
- The '**Sort Order**' column speaks to the request where pictures can be shown in an adaptive card.

Define State:

Under the '\src\webparts\imageGalleryAdaptiveCards\components\' folder, add the IImageGalleryAdaptiveCardsState.ts file:

TypeScript

exportinterfaceIImageGalleryAdaptiveCardsState {

galleryItems: any[];

isLoading: boolean;

showErrorMessage: boolean;

}

Define Properties:

Update IImageGalleryAdaptiveCardsProps.ts under the '\src\webparts\imageGalleryAdaptiveCards\components\' folder as follows:

TypeScript

import { ServiceScope } from'@microsoft/sp-core-library';

```
exportinterfaceIImageGalleryAdaptiveCardsProps {

serviceScope: ServiceScope;

imageGalleryName: string;

imagesToDisplay: number;

}
```

Define Service:

Implement a service to the querySharePoint list:

TypeScript

Figure 54.3: Implement service

Code the web part:

Follow below steps to develop the Adaptive cards based image gallery:

1. Open the main webpartImageGalleryAdaptiveCards.tsx under '\src\webparts\imageGalleryAdaptiveCards\components\'.

2. Add the needed imports:

    TypeScript

```typescript
import * as React from 'react';
import styles from './ImageGalleryAdaptiveCards.module.scss';
import { IImageGalleryAdaptiveCardsProps } from './IImageGalleryAdaptiveCardsProps';
import { IImageGalleryAdaptiveCardsState } from './IImageGalleryAdaptiveCardsState';
import { escape } from '@microsoft/sp-lodash-subset';

import * as AdaptiveCards from "adaptivecards";
import { ImageGalleryService, IImageGalleryService } from '../services/ImageGalleryService';
import { ServiceScope, Environment, EnvironmentType } from '@microsoft/sp-core-library';
import { Spinner, SpinnerSize } from 'office-ui-fabric-react/lib/Spinner';
```

Figure 54.4: Imports

3. Implement the render() method:

    TypeScript

```typescript
public render(): React.ReactElement<IImageGalleryAdaptiveCardsProps> {
  return (
    <div className={styles.adaptiveCardsImageGallery}>
      <div className={styles.container}>
        {this.state.isLoading && <Spinner className={styles.spinner} size={SpinnerSize.large} />}
        {!this.state.isLoading && <div ref={(n) => { n && n.appendChild(this.renderedCard) }} />}
      </div>
    </div>
  );
}
```

Figure 54.5: Render method

4. In the constructor, create an AdaptiveCard instance as follows:

    TypeScript

```typescript
// Create an AdaptiveCard instance
var adaptiveCard = new AdaptiveCards.AdaptiveCard();

// Set its hostConfig property unless you want to use the default Host Config
// Host Config defines the style and behavior of a card
adaptiveCard.hostConfig = new AdaptiveCards.HostConfig({
  fontFamily: "Segoe UI, Helvetica Neue, sans-serif"
});

// Set the adaptive card's event handlers. onExecuteAction is invoked
// whenever an action is clicked in the card
adaptiveCard.onExecuteAction = function(action) {
  window.location.href = action.iconUrl;
};

// Parse the card
adaptiveCard.parse(this.card);

// Render the card to an HTML element
this.renderedCard = adaptiveCard.render();
```

Figure 54.6: Adaptive Card instance

5. Define the card as follows:

   TypeScript

```typescript
this.card = {
  "$schema": "http://adaptivecards.io/schemas/adaptive-card.json",
  "type": "AdaptiveCard",
  "version": "1.0",
  "body": [
    {
      "type": "TextBlock",
      "text": "Adaptive Image Gallery",
      "size": "medium"
    },
    {
      "type": "ImageSet",
      "imageSize": "medium",
      "images": this.imagesJSON
    }
  ]
};
```

Figure 54.7: Adaptive card definition

6. Consume the service as follows:

TypeScript

```
let serviceScope: ServiceScope;
serviceScope = this.props.serviceScope;

this._galleryListName = this.props.imageGalleryName;
this._noOfItems = this.props.imagesToDisplay;

// Based on the type of environment, return the correct instance of the ImageGalleryServiceInstance interface
if (Environment.type == EnvironmentType.SharePoint || Environment.type == EnvironmentType.ClassicSharePoint) {
    // Mapping to be used when webpart runs in SharePoint.
    this.ImageGalleryServiceInstance = serviceScope.consume(ImageGalleryService.serviceKey);
}

this.ImageGalleryServiceInstance.getGalleryImages(this._galleryListName, this._noOfItems).then((galleryImages: any[]) => {
    galleryImages.forEach(adaptiveImage => {
        let image = {};
        image["type"] = "Image";
        image["url"] = adaptiveImage.ImageLink.Url;

        // Compose image action
        let imageAction = {};
        imageAction["title"] = adaptiveImage.NavigationURL.Description;
        imageAction["type"] = "Action.OpenUrl";
        imageAction["url"] = adaptiveImage.NavigationURL.Url;
        imageAction["iconUrl"] = adaptiveImage.NavigationURL.Url;

        image["selectAction"] = imageAction;
        this.imagesJSON.push(image);
    });
});
```

Figure 54.8: Consume the service

Verify the SPFx web part

Follow the given steps to test the web part on the SharePoint page:

1. At the command prompt, type '`gulp serve`'.
2. On the SharePoint site, browse '`/_layouts/15/workbench.aspx`'.
3. Include the web part in the page:

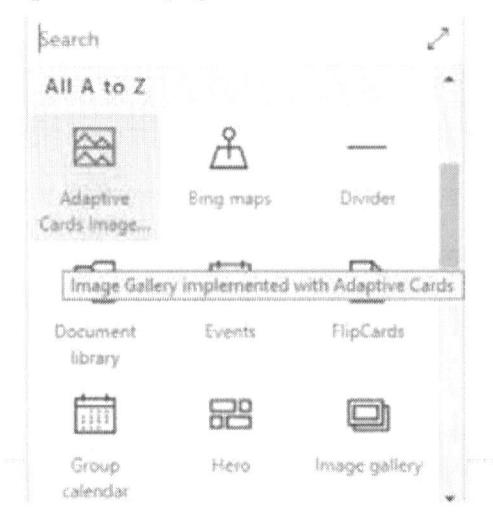

Figure 54.9: Add the SPFx web part to the SharePoint page

4. Edit the web part and update **Image Gallery** and **Number of images to display** properties:

Figure 54.10: SPFx web part with Adaptive cards – image gallery

Conclusion

In this chapter, we discussed the implementation of Adaptive cards in the SPFx web part. Adaptive Cards are another way for the engineers to trade the card content in a typical and reliable manner. This model exhibits the capacity of utilizing Adaptive Cards (**https://adaptivecards.io/**) with the SharePoint Framework.

CHAPTER 55
Integrating the Google API with SPFx

Google and Microsoft are two different platforms. Google exposes various services and APIs to access those programmatically. These Google APIs can be consumed inside SPFx solutions. Google has vast services to offer. However, in this chapter, we will concentrate on one of the services – **Google Fit.**

Structure

- Introduction to Google REST API
- Google Developer Playground
- SPFx Web Part to query Google REST API

Objectives

- Explorethe Google Fit REST API
- Develop the SPFxweb part to display Google Fit information

Google Fit REST API

In this quick paced world and feverish life plan, wellness is ofutmost significance. With innovation propels, we can follow our wellness exercises. There arevarious wellness bands and applications accessible in the market and application stores.

We can follow all our everyday activities by utilizing these wellness bands or applications. As a developer, we need to feel free to begin programming with our wellness information so we can utilize it in any applications and shape it further.

Overview of the Google Fit REST API

The Google Fit REST API empowers to store and access user data from the fitness store. Here are a few related important keywords:

- **Data Source:** This denotes an interesting well spring of sensor information. Data sources uncover crude information produced from equipment sensors. It can likewise uncover determined information by changing or consolidating different data sources.
- **Dataset:** This denotes a set of points from a specific data source. It represents data at fixed boundaries.
- **Data Point:** This denotes tests from specific data sources. Data Point holds an incentive for each field per timestamp.
- **Session:** This denotes the time interim. It permits questioning the information. The start time and end time for sessions is constrained by applications and is utilized to represent user-friendly information like walking, running, bicycling, and so forth.
- **Data Type:** This denotes the mapping for the information being recorded. It just characterizes the portrayal and arrangement of information. For instance, com.google.step_count.delta information type represents the step count as delta between the start and end time, whereascom.google.step_count.cumulative as the total number of steps between the start and end time.

Beginning with Google Fitness REST APIs

Google Fit will assist you in tracking your wellness information. The Google Fitness REST APIs enable engineers to broaden it further and make claim dashboards. Google Fitness REST APIs are valuable on the off chance that you have a wellness application and you need to coordinate your information with Google Fit or on the off chance that you simply need to gather Fitness information and show some data to the clients.

We will explore Google Fitness REST APIs and the Google developer playground.

Get Started with REST API

Google Account:

The most importantis that you need to have a Google account.

Generate OAuth 2.0 client ID:

Follow the below steps to generate OAuth 2.0 client ID:

1. Browse Google API Console (**https://console.developers.google.com/flows/enableapi?apiid=fitness**).
2. Choose an existing project or create a new one.
3. Choose **Continue**:

Figure 55.1: OAuth 2.0 client ID generation

4. After the project is created, select '**Go to credentials**':

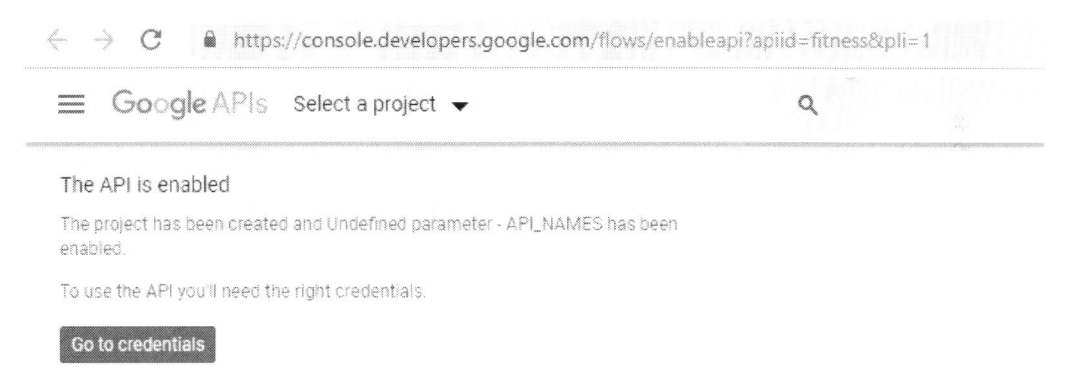

Figure 55.2: Go to credentials

5. Choose the following options:

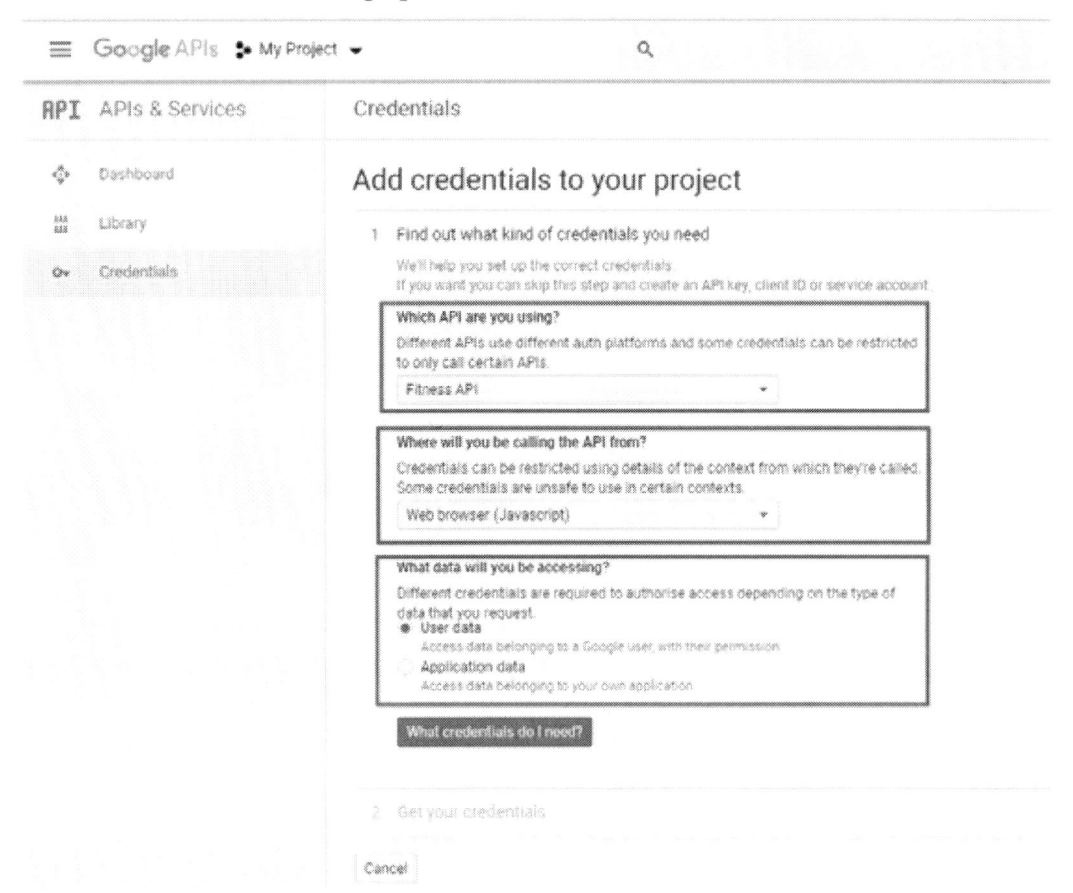

Figure 55.3: Add credentials to project

6. Select '**What credentials do I need?**'
7. Under Authorized JavaScript origins, add **https://developers.google.com**.

8. Under the Authorized redirect URI, add **https://developers.google.com/oauthplayground**:

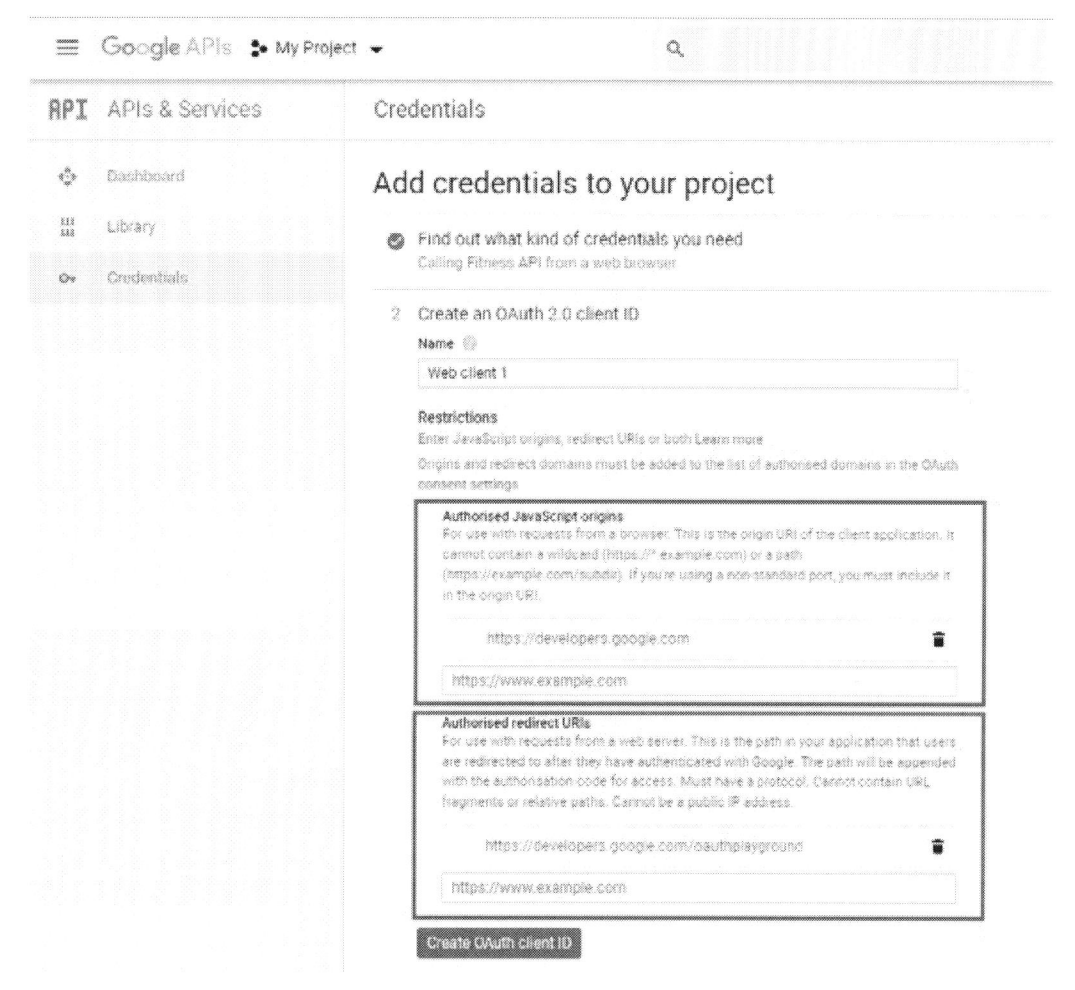

Figure 55.4: Add Authorized JavaScript origins and redirect URIs

9. Select '**Create an OAuth client ID**'.

10. Set up the OAuth 2.0 consent screen:

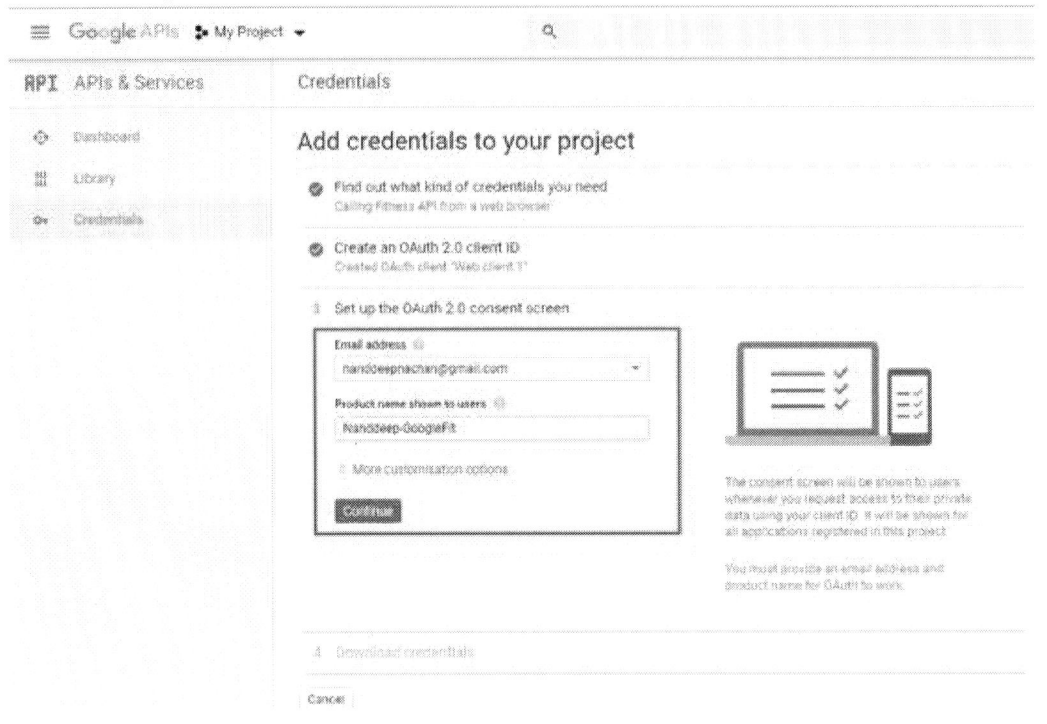

Figure 55.5: Set up OAuth 2.0 consent screen

11. Select **Continue**.
12. The **Client id** will be generated. Note it down for future use:

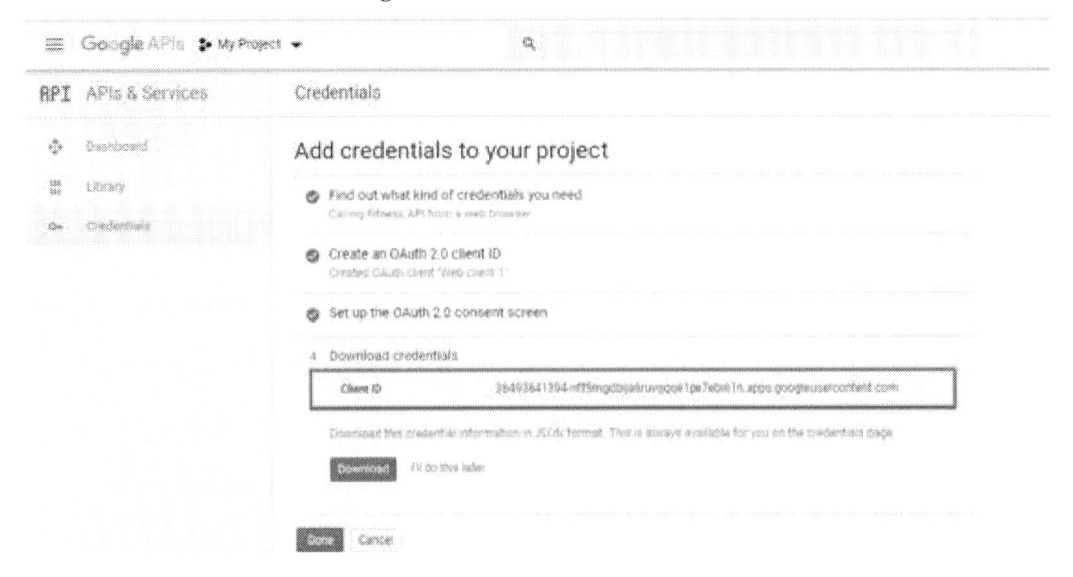

Figure 55.6: Generate client id

13. Select **Done**.

Google Developer Playground

The OAuth 2.0 Playground for Google developers is available at (**https://developers.google.com/oauthplayground/**). This play area will assist engineers in exploring different Google APIs, comprehend their request, response, and query the APIs to bring the information.

Follow below steps toexplorethe various Fitness APIs:

1. Open OAuth 2.0 Playground.
2. Locate the '**Fitness V1**' API.
3. Select the scopes you want to query to:

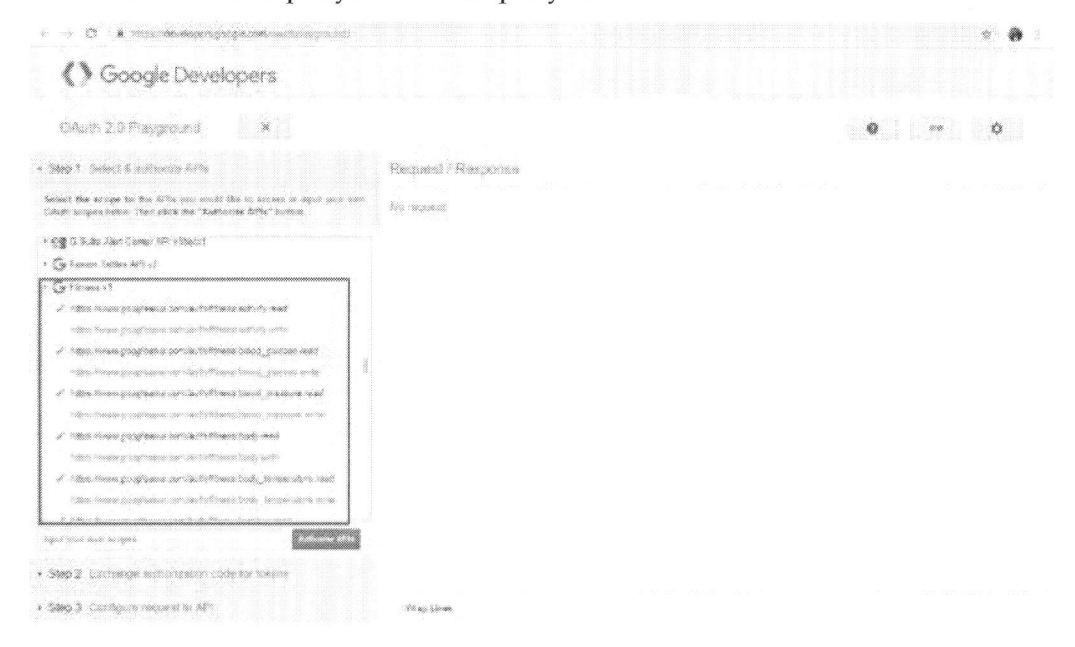

Fig 55.7: Google Developer Playground

4. Select **Authorize APIs**.
5. On the next screen, choose the Google account to be used:

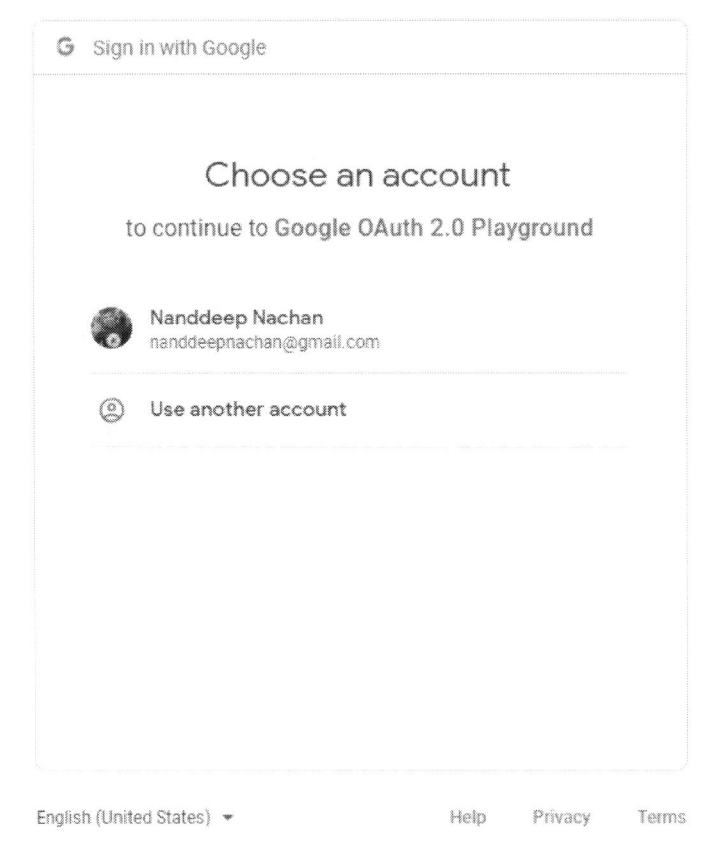

Figure 55.8: Login to Google

6. On the confirmation screen, verify the selected scopes:

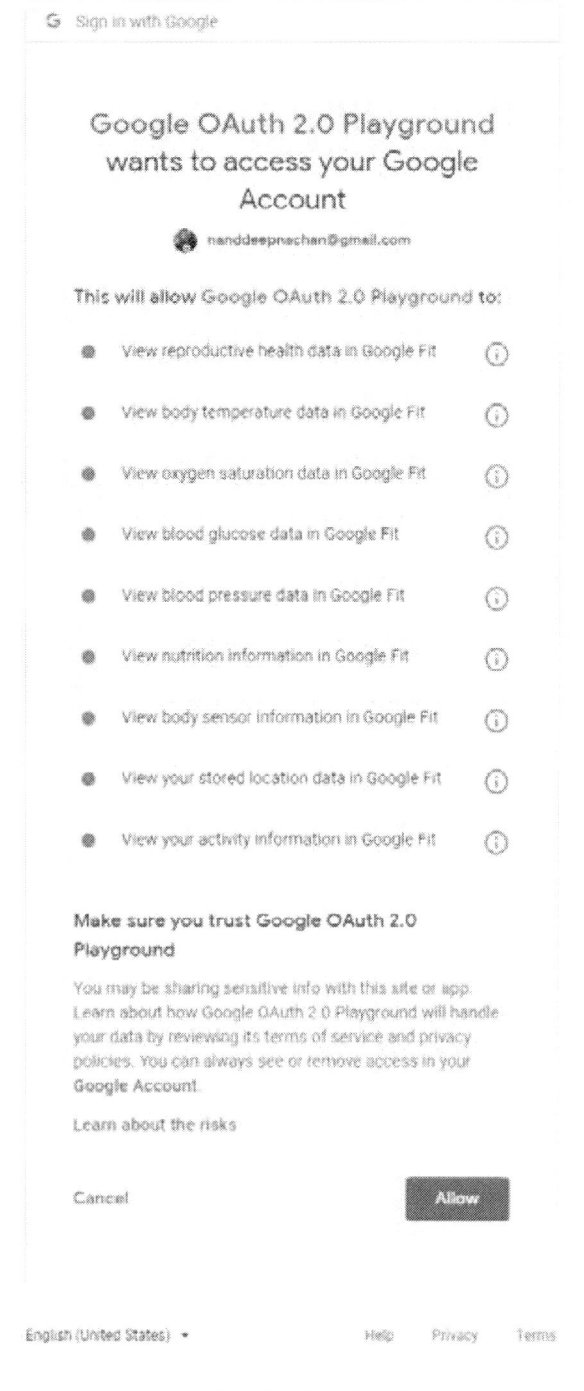

Figure 55.9: verify the selected scopes

7. Select **Allow**.
8. On the next screen, select '**Exchange authorization code for tokens**':

Figure 55.10: Exchange authorization code for tokens

List all data sources

Google over sees information through data sources. You can view the data sources using the following URI:

```
https://www.googleapis.com/fitness/v1/users/me/dataSources
```

Figure 55.11: List all data sources

Get the Number of Steps

We will use the available data source derived:com.google.step_count.delta:com.google.android.gms:estimated_steps to get the steps.

Follow the below steps to get the number of steps from data source:
1. Change the HTTP method to POST.
2. In the Request URI, type **https://www.googleapis.com/fitness/v1/users/me/dataset:aggregate.**
3. Select '**Enter request body**'. Enter the following request body:

Figure 55.12: Get the Number of Steps

4. Select **Close**.
5. Select **Send the request**.

6. The response will appear on the right-hand side of the page:

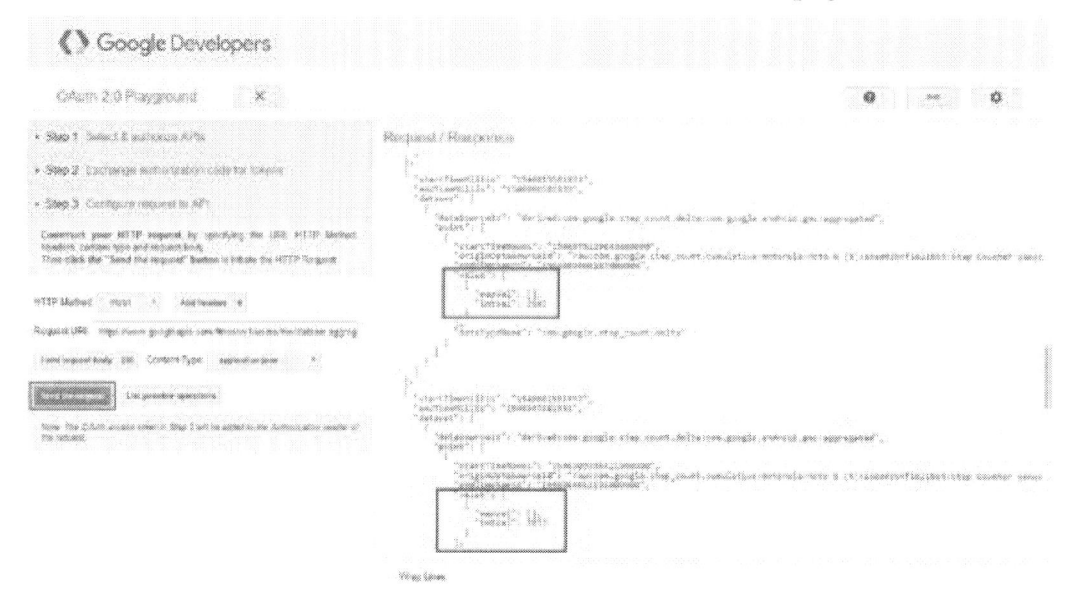

Figure 55.13: Send the request

7. Total up all the `intVal` (featured above) to get the steps count. Each `intVal` demonstrates the step activity at an alternate time inside a predefined time range.

Get the start date and end date

We can use the plan JavaScript to get the start date:

```
new Date().getTime()
```

The end date can be `1000000000` less than the start date (which is approx. one day).

Develop the SPFx web part to display Google Fit information

Open a command prompt. Follow the given guidelines to make the SPFx solution:

1. Make a folder for the SPFx solution:

    ```
    md spfx-consume-googleapi
    ```

2. Change the path to the above folder:

    ```
    cd spfx-consume-googleapi
    ```

3. Execute the Yeoman Generator for SharePoint.

    ```
    yo @microsoft/sharepoint
    ```

4. The Yeoman generator will run through the wizard to ask questions about the SPFx solution to be created:

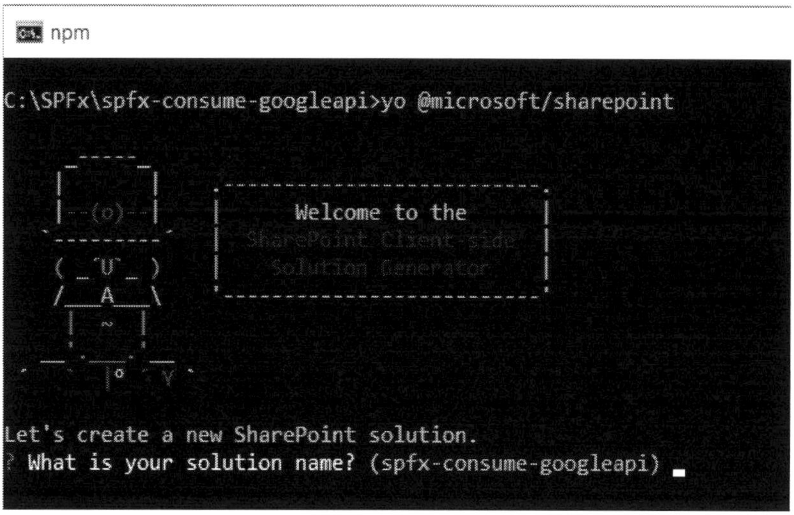

Figure 55.14: SPFx Yeoman generator

The SPFx Yeoman generator will display the following wizard of inquiries:
- **Solution Name:** spfx-consume-googleapi
- **Target environment:** SharePoint Online only (latest)
- **Folder location:** Use the current folder
- **Deployment option:** N (install on each site explicitly)
- **Consents to access web APIs:** N (solution contains unique permissions)
- **Choice of client-side component:** WebPart
- **Web part name:** GoogleFitActivityViewer
- **Web part description:** Display Google Fit Activities
- **Choice of the framework:** React

NPM Packages Used

react-google-authorize (**https://www.npmjs.com/package/react-google-authorize**) can be used to authenticate and authorize against Google:

1. Include the to '\src\webparts\googleFitActivityViewer\components\ GoogleFitActivityViewer.tsx' package:

TypeScript

```
import { GoogleAuthorize } from 'react-google-authorize';
```

2. Use the GoogleAuthorize component in the render method:

TypeScript

```
public render(): React.ReactElement<IGoogleFitActivityViewerProps> {
  const responseGoogle = (response) => {
  };

  return (
    <div className={styles.googleFitActivityViewer}>
      <div className={styles.container}>
        {
          !this.state.isGoogleAuthenticated && this.state.accessToken == "" &&
          <GoogleAuthorize
            scope={'https://www.googleapis.com/auth/fitness.activity.read https://www.googleapis.com/auth/fitness.location.read'}
            clientId={this.props.clientId}
            onSuccess={responseGoogle}
            onFailure={responseGoogle}
          >
            <span>Login with Google</span>
          </GoogleAuthorize>
        }
      </div>
    </div>
  );
}
```

Figure 55.15: GoogleAuthorize component

Let us include the following scopes:

- **https://www.googleapis.com/auth/fitness.activity.read:** To read the fitness activities (calories burned, step count).
- **https://www.googleapis.com/auth/fitness.location.read:** To read the activity time spent and distance traveled.

Define State

Follow the below steps to define the state:

1. Under '\src\webparts\googleFitActivityViewer\components\', add the IGoogleFitActivityViewerState.ts file:

   TypeScript

   ```
   export interface IGoogleFitActivityViewerState {
       isGoogleAuthenticated: boolean;
       accessToken: string;
       stepCount: number;
       calories: number;
       distance: number;
       activityTime: number;
   }
   ```

   Figure 55.16: Google Fit State

2. Update our component '\src\webparts\googleFitActivityViewer\
   components\ GoogleFitActivityViewer.tsx' to use the state:

   TypeScript

   ```
   import { IGoogleFitActivityViewerState } from './IGoogleFitActivityViewerState';

   export default class GoogleFitActivityViewer extends React.Component<IGoogleFitActivityViewerProps, IGoogleFitActivityViewerState> {
       constructor(props) {
           super(props);
           this.state = {
               isGoogleAuthenticated: false,
               accessToken: "",
               stepCount: 0,
               calories: 0,
               distance: 0,
               activityTime: 0
           };
       }
   }
   ```

   Figure 55.17: Utilize the State in the React Component

Implement the Service

Under 'src\services', define service (`IFitnessActivity.ts`) to query Google REST APIs:

TypeScript

```
export interface IFitnessActivity {
    dataSourceId: string;
    maxEndTimeNs: string;
    minStartTimeNs: string;
    point: IFitnessPoint[];
}

export interface IFitnessPoint {
    dataTypeName: string;
    endTimeNanos: string;
    modifiedTimeMillis: string;
    value: IFitnessPointValue[];
}

export interface IFitnessPointValue {
    intVal: number;
    fpVal: number;
}
```

Figure 55.18: Fitness Activity Model

Implement Generic Interface:

Follow the below steps to implement the generic interface to represent the methods for Google Fit:

1. Add the `IDataService.ts` file under the '\src\services' folder:

   TypeScript

   ```typescript
   export interface IDataService {
       getStepCount: (accessToken: string) => Promise<any>;
       getCalories: (accessToken: string) => Promise<any>;
       getDistance: (accessToken: string) => Promise<any>;
       getActivityTime: (accessToken: string) => Promise<any>;
   }
   ```

Figure 55.19: DataService interface

Implement Google Fit Interface:

Follow the below steps to implement the above defined interface:

1. Under '\src\services', include the `GoogleFitService.ts` file:

   TypeScript

   ```typescript
   import { ServiceScope, ServiceKey } from "@microsoft/sp-core-library";
   import { IDataService } from "./IDataService";
   import { HttpClient, HttpClientResponse, IHttpClientOptions } from "@microsoft/sp-http";
   import { PageContext } from "@microsoft/sp-page-context";
   import { IFitnessActivity, IFitnessPoint, IFitnessPointValue } from "../IFitnessActivity";

   export class GoogleFitService implements IDataService {
       public static readonly serviceKey: ServiceKey<IDataService> = ServiceKey.create<IDataService>('googlefit:data-service', GoogleFitService);
       private _httpClient: HttpClient;
       private _pageContext: PageContext;

       constructor(serviceScope: ServiceScope) {
           serviceScope.whenFinished(() => {
               // Configure the required dependencies
               this._httpClient = serviceScope.consume(HttpClient.serviceKey);
               this._pageContext = serviceScope.consume(PageContext.serviceKey);
           });
       }
   }
   ```

Figure 55.20: Google Fit Service

2. Implement the `IDataService` interface:
   TypeScript

   Figure 55.21: IDataService interface implementation

Code the web part

Follow the below steps to develop the SPFx web part to show Google Fit information:
1. Open the webpart `GoogleFitActivityViewer.tsx` under the '\src\webparts\googleFitActivityViewer\components\' folder.
2. Implement the `render()` method:

TypeScript

Figure 55.22: render method implementation

3. Implement the helper methods and set the states from it:
   TypeScript

```
private readStepCount(accessToken: string): void {
  let serviceScope: ServiceScope = this.props.serviceScope;
  this.dataCenterServiceInstance = serviceScope.consume(GoogleFitService.serviceKey);

  this.dataCenterServiceInstance.getStepCount(accessToken).then((stepCount: number) => {
    this.setState(() => {
      return {
        ...this.state,
        stepCount: stepCount
      };
    });
  });
}

private readCalories(accessToken: string): void {
  let serviceScope: ServiceScope = this.props.serviceScope;
  this.dataCenterServiceInstance = serviceScope.consume(GoogleFitService.serviceKey);

  this.dataCenterServiceInstance.getCalories(accessToken).then((calories: number) => {
    this.setState(() => {
      return {
        ...this.state,
        calories: calories
      };
    });
  });
}

private readDistance(accessToken: string): void {
  let serviceScope: ServiceScope = this.props.serviceScope;
  this.dataCenterServiceInstance = serviceScope.consume(GoogleFitService.serviceKey);

  this.dataCenterServiceInstance.getDistance(accessToken).then((distance: number) => {
    this.setState(() => {
      return {
        ...this.state,
        distance: distance
      };
    });
  });
}

private readActivityTime(accessToken: string): void {
  let serviceScope: ServiceScope = this.props.serviceScope;
  this.dataCenterServiceInstance = serviceScope.consume(GoogleFitService.serviceKey);

  this.dataCenterServiceInstance.getActivityTime(accessToken).then((activityTime: number) => {
    this.setState(() => {
      return {
        ...this.state,
        activityTime: activityTime
      };
    });
  });
}
```

Figure 55.23: Helper method implementation

Include Authorized JavaScript Origins

Follow the below steps to include the authorized javascript origins:

1. Browse Google Developer Dashboard (**https://console.developers.google.com/apis/dashboard**).
2. Choose a previously created project.
3. Select **Credentials**:

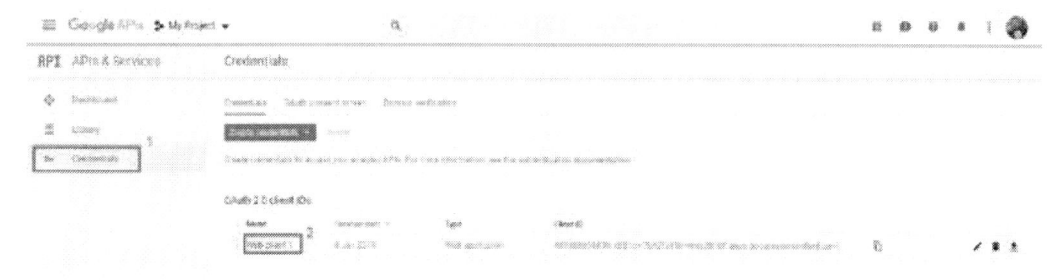

Figure 55.24: Web client

4. Under **Authorized JavaScript origins**, include the SharePoint Online site URL (e.g. https://<tenant>.sharepoint.com) or **https://localhost:4321** In the SharePoint local workbench.
5. Under **Authorized redirect URI**, include **https://localhost:4321/auth/google/callback** in the SharePoint local workbench:

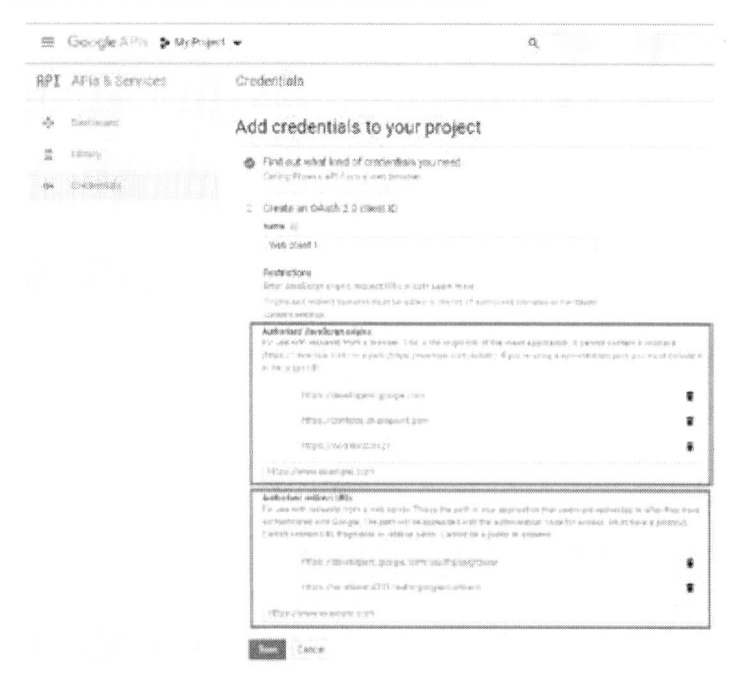

Figure 55.25: Include Authorized JavaScript Origins

6. Select **Save**.

Verify the web part

Follow below steps to test the web part on the SharePoint page:
1. Add the **'Google Fit Activity Viewer'** web part on the SharePoint page.
2. Specify OAuth 2.0 client ID to the **'ClientId Field'** web part property:

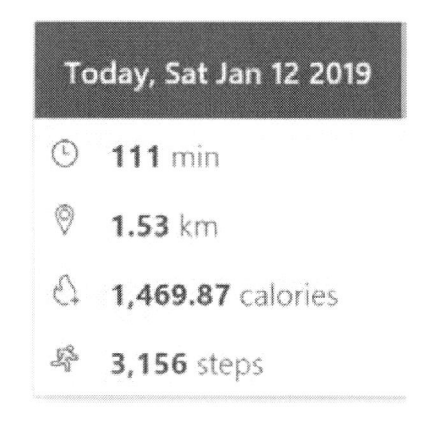

Figure 55.26: Google fit information inside the web part

Conclusion

In this chapter, we explored Google API coordination with SPFx. Google Fit gives the REST APIs to store and access client information in a wellness store. Google Fit has predefined information types to speak to the wellness information. Google Fitness REST APIs permits performing tasks on different accessible data sources. The Google engineer play area begins programming with REST APIs to get the real information. Google Fit REST APIs can be expended in the SPFx web part to show the key wellness data (activity time spent, distance traveled, calories burned, step count) from the Google fit data source.

CHAPTER 56
SPFx Development with SharePoint On-Premises

The **SharePoint Framework (SPFx)** is prevalent for building solutions for modern sites in SharePoint Online. However, it isn't just constrained to the cloud infrastructure. The SharePoint Framework development is additionally upheld on the SharePoint On-Premises environment (SharePoint 2016 onwards).

Structure

- SharePoint On-Premises Readiness for SPFx
- SPFx Solutions for SharePoint On-Premises
- Common Issues and Resolutions

Objectives

- Prepare the SharePoint On-Premises environment for SPFxdevelopment
- Start developing SPFx solutions against SharePoint On-Premises

Decide the SPFx Version

SharePoint Online follows regular release cycles in contrast with SharePoint On-Premises. SharePoint online consistently utilizes the most recent version of the SharePoint Framework. On the other hand, SharePoint On-Premises supports the version with matching server-side dependencies. Because of this reason, the SharePoint on-premises SPFx version might not catch up with the latest SPFx version.

Prepare SharePoint On-Premises for SPFx

SharePoint 2016:

'**SharePoint 2016 Feature Pack 2**' is a pre-requisite to get started with the development on the SharePoint 2016 on-premises version. This should get installed as a part of Windows update.

SharePoint 2019:

SharePoint Server 2019 out of the box supports the SPFx development, with no extra feature pack installation.

Follow the given instructions to install the needed software and tools.

Install NodeJS:
- Install version 8.x or 10.x from **https://nodejs.org**.
- Verify the installed version by executing the following command:

```
node -v
```

Install Code Editor

Install any of the following code editor:
- Visual Studio Code (**https://code/visualstudio.com**)
- Atom (**https://atom.io**)
- Webstorm (**https://www.jetbrains.com/webstorm**)

Install Yeoman and gulp

Execute the following command:

```
npm install -g yo gulp
```

Install the Yeoman Generator for SharePoint

Execute the following command:

```
npm install -g @microsoft/generator-sharepoint
```

Develop the SPFx Web Part

At the command prompt, follow the given guidelines to make the SPFx solution:
1. Make a folder for the SPFx solution:

SPFx Development with SharePoint On-Premises

```
md spfx-onprem
```

2. Change the path to the above folder:

```
cd spfx-onprem
```

3. Execute the Yeoman Generator for SharePoint:

```
yo @microsoft/sharepoint
```

4. The Yeoman generator will run through the wizard to ask questions about the SPFx solution to be created:

Figure 56.1: SPFx Yeoman generator

The SPFx Yeoman generator will display the following wizard of inquiries:

- **Solution Name:** Determine the SPFx solution name. Hit the *Enter* key to proceed with the default selection (`spfx-onprem` in this case) or type another name.
    - o **Chosen decision:** Hit *Enter*
- **Target environment:** Specify the target environment to deploy the SPFx solution.
    - o **Chosen decision:** SharePoint 2016 onwards, including 2019 and SharePoint Online
- **Folder location:** Choose the folder location for the SPFx project (either the same folder or a subfolder).
    - o **Chosen decision:** Same folder

- **Deployment option:** Specify Y to deploy the app instantly to all the sites, N otherwise.
  - **Chosen decision:** N (install on each site explicitly)
- **Choice of client-side component:** Choose to develop a web part or an extension.
  - **Chosen decision:** WebPart

  Please note that SharePoint 2016 does not support creating an extension. However, SharePoint 2019 supports both web parts and extensions.
- **Web part name:** Provide the web part name. Hit the *Enter* key to proceed with the default choice or type another name.
  - **Chosen decision:** `HelloWorldOnPrem`
- **Web part description:** Provide the web part description. Hit the *Enter* key to proceed with the default choice or type another value.
  - **Chosen decision:** SPFx on SharePoint on-premises
- **Choice of the framework:** Choose a JavaScript framework to develop the solution.
  - **Chosen decision:** React

5. After the scaffolding is complete, lock down the version of project dependencies by executing the following command:

```
npmshrinkwrap
```

6. At the command prompt, execute the following command to open the solution in the code editor:

```
code .
```

SPFx Support for SharePoint 2019

If you utilize the SharePoint Framework v1.7, you can target the scaffolded solution to SharePoint 2019, which will make sure that packages are correct for your target environment.

Open `package.json` file and observe the SPFx version being used (~1.4.0).

```json
{
  "name": "spfx-sp-2019-onprem",
  "version": "0.0.1",
  "private": true,
  "engines": {
    "node": ">=0.10.0"
  },
  "scripts": {
    "build": "gulp bundle",
    "clean": "gulp clean",
    "test": "gulp test"
  },
  "dependencies": {
    "react": "15.6.2",
    "react-dom": "15.6.2",
    "@types/react": "15.6.6",
    "@types/react-dom": "15.5.6",
    "@microsoft/sp-core-library": "~1.4.0",
    "@microsoft/sp-webpart-base": "~1.4.0",
    "@microsoft/sp-lodash-subset": "~1.4.0",
    "@microsoft/sp-office-ui-fabric-core": "~1.4.0",
    "@types/webpack-env": "1.13.1",
    "@types/es6-promise": "0.0.33"
  },
  "resolutions": {
    "@types/react": "15.6.6"
  },
  "devDependencies": {
    "@microsoft/sp-build-web": "~1.4.1",
    "@microsoft/sp-module-interfaces": "~1.4.1",
    "@microsoft/sp-webpart-workbench": "~1.4.1",
    "gulp": "~3.9.1",
    "@types/chai": "3.4.34",
    "@types/mocha": "2.2.38",
    "ajv": "~5.2.2"
  }
}
```

Figure 56.2: Package.json

Verify the SPFx webpart on the local SharePoint workbench

Follow below steps to test the web part on the local SharePoint workbench:

1. At the command prompt, execute '`gulp serve`'.
2. On the SharePoint site, browse '`/_layouts/15/workbench.aspx`'.

3. Add the webpart to the page:

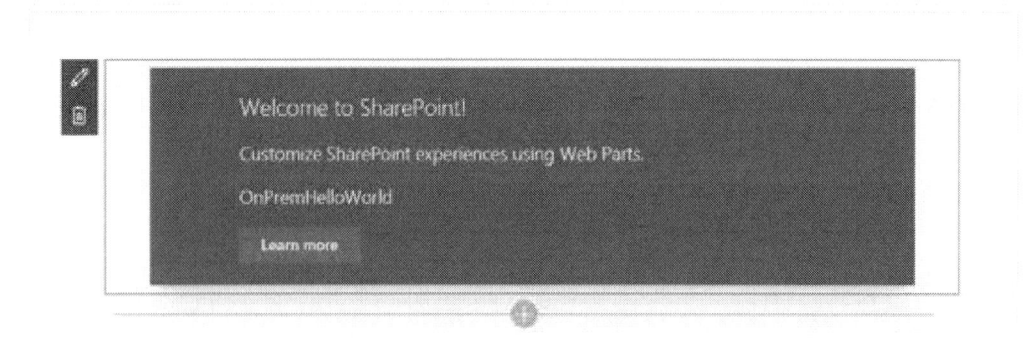

Figure 56.3: SPFx web part on SharePoint local workbench

Set up App Catalog

Follow the given instructions as the SharePoint farm administrator to set up an App catalog to add the SPFx solution:

1. Open the SharePoint Central Administration site.
2. Under the left navigation, select '**Apps**'.
3. Under '**App Management**', select '**Manage App Catalog**':

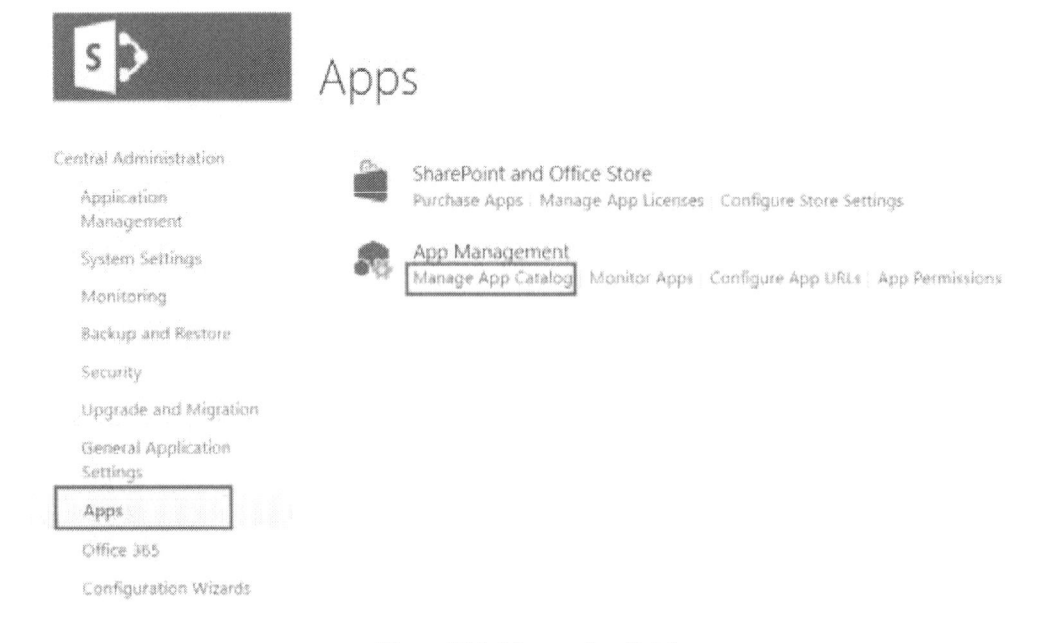

Figure 56.4: Manage App Catalog

4. Choose web application.
5. Choose '**Create a new app catalog site**':

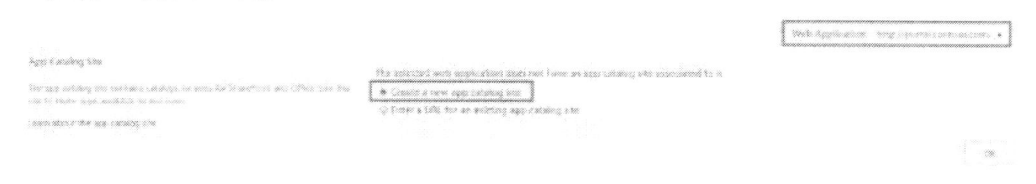

Figure 56.5: Manage App Catalog

6. Select **OK**.
7. Provide the details to set up an App catalog:

Figure 56.6: App catalog details

8. Select **OK**.

Enable Scripting Capabilities (SharePoint 2019 only)

Optionally, if you are targeting SPFx solutions on classic SharePoint sites, then follow the given instructions. Skip this step if you are planning deployment on modern SharePoint.

1. Open SharePoint 2019 Management Shell as an administrator.
2. Run the following command:

   ```
   (Get-SPSite -Identity "http://portal.contoso.com/sites/
   ModernSite").DenyPermissionsMask = [Microsoft.SharePoint.
   SPBasePermissions]::EmptyMask
   ```

Prepare the Package

Follow the given instructions to prepare a package (.sppkg) to be deployed to the SharePoint app catalog:

Bundle the solution

At the command prompt, execute the following command:

```
gulp bundle --ship
```

This will minify the needed assets in the 'temp\deploy' folder.

Package the solution:

At the command prompt, execute the following command:

```
gulp package-solution --ship
```

This will create the solution package (.sppkg) in the 'sharepoint\solution' folder.

Upload the Package to the App Catalog

Follow the given instructions to upload the SPFx package to the app catalog in order to make it accessible on all sites:

1. Browse the **SharePoint App Catalog** site.
2. From the left menu, select '**Apps for SharePoint**'.

3. Upload the SPFx package from '\sharepoint\solution':

Figure 56.7: Upload the SPFx package to the app catalog

4. Select **OK**:

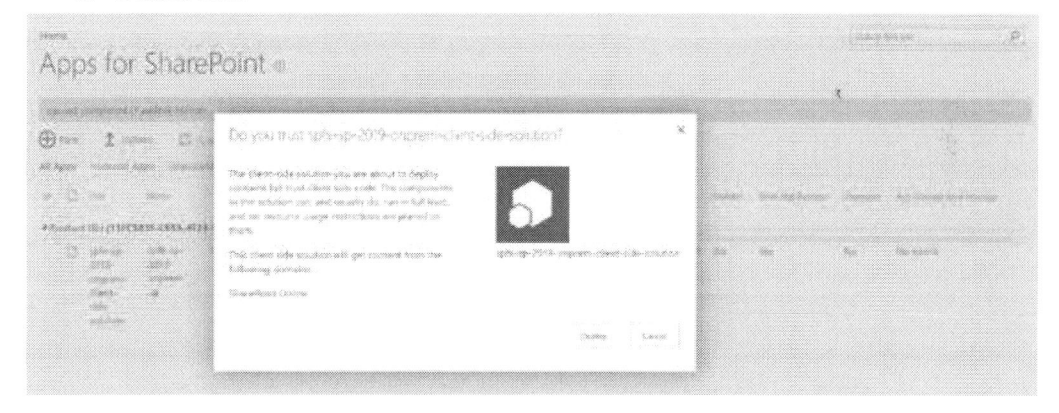

Figure 56.8: Deploy the package

5. Select **Deploy**:

Add the SPFx Solution to the SharePoint Site

Follow the given instructions to add the SPFx solution to the Modern SharePoint site in SP2019. The instructions more or less remain the same on classic SharePoint sites in SP2016 and SP2019:

1. On the SharePoint site, browse '**Site contents**':

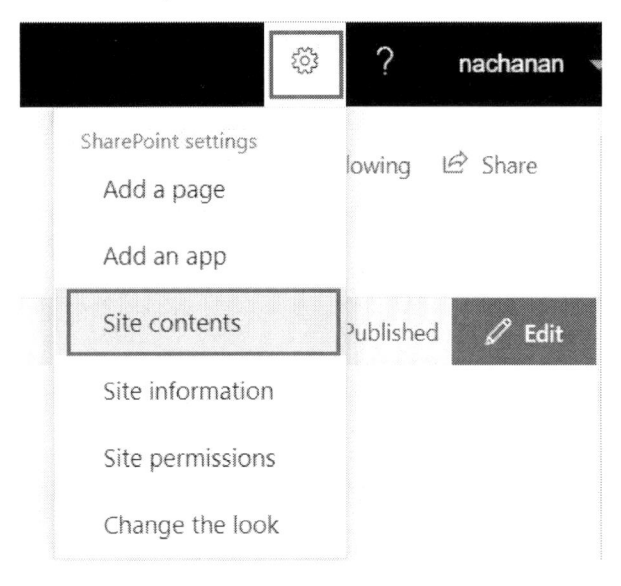

Figure 56.9: Browse to Site contents

2. Go to **New>App**:

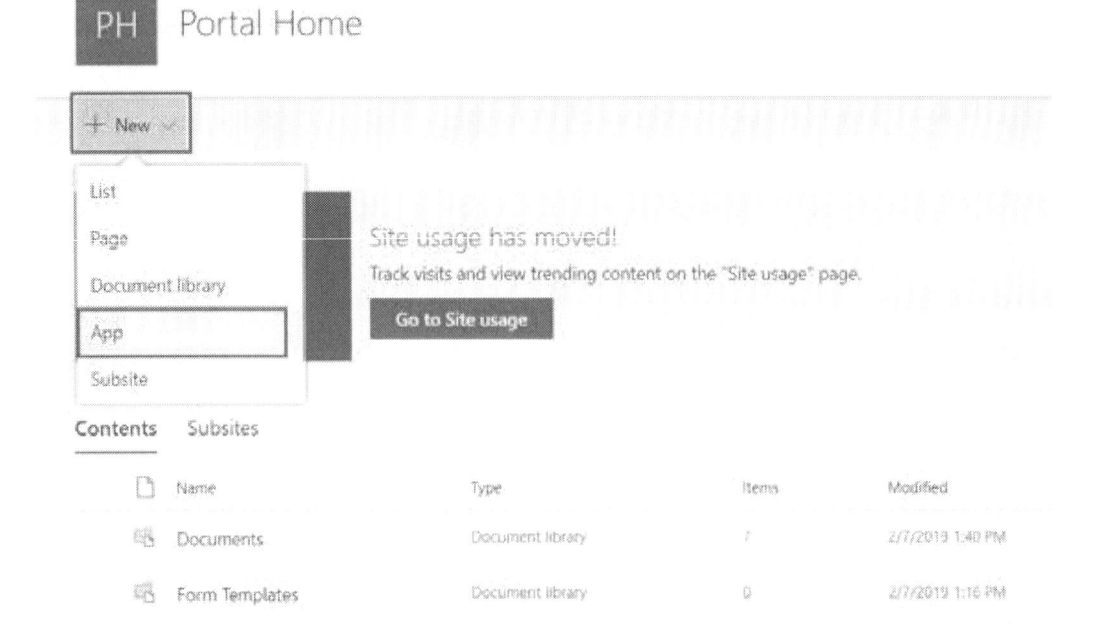

Figure 56.10: Add a new app

3. Select the SPFxapp to add to the site.

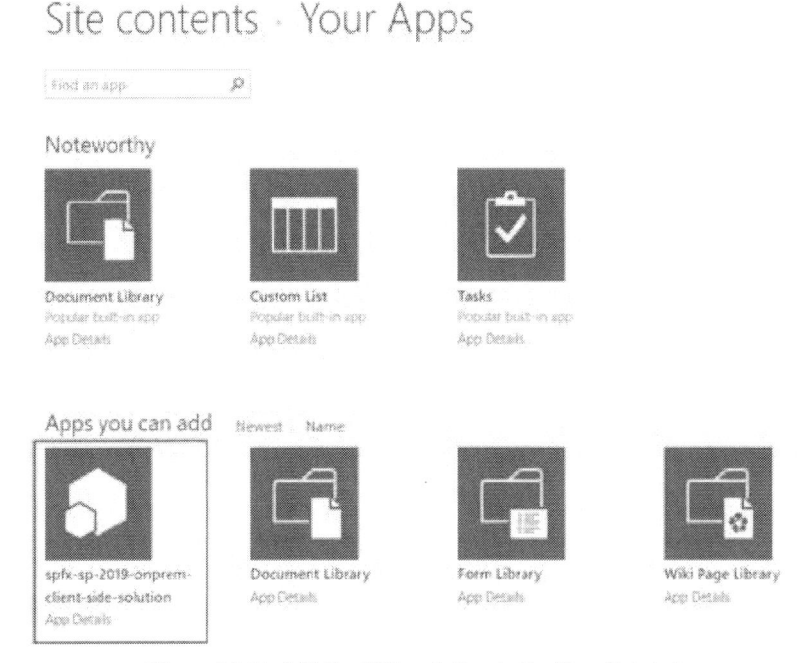

Figure 56.11: Add the SPFx solution to the SharePoint site

Place SPFx web part on the modern page

After the SPFx solution is deployed to the SharePoint site, let us add the web part to the SharePoint page:

1. Open an existing page or create a new page:

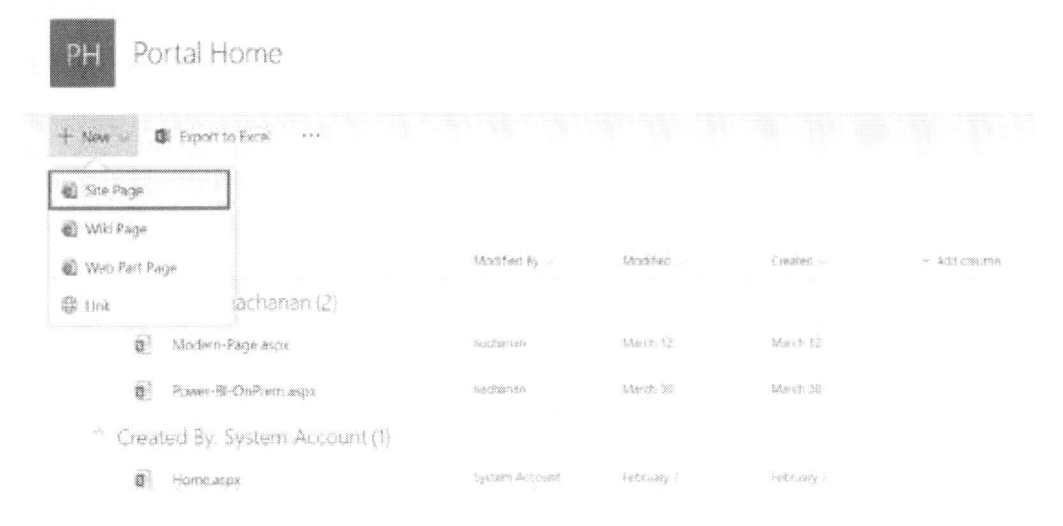

Figure 56.12: Create a new modern page

604 ■ *Mastering SharePoint Framework*

2. Select the + sign to include a web part to the page:

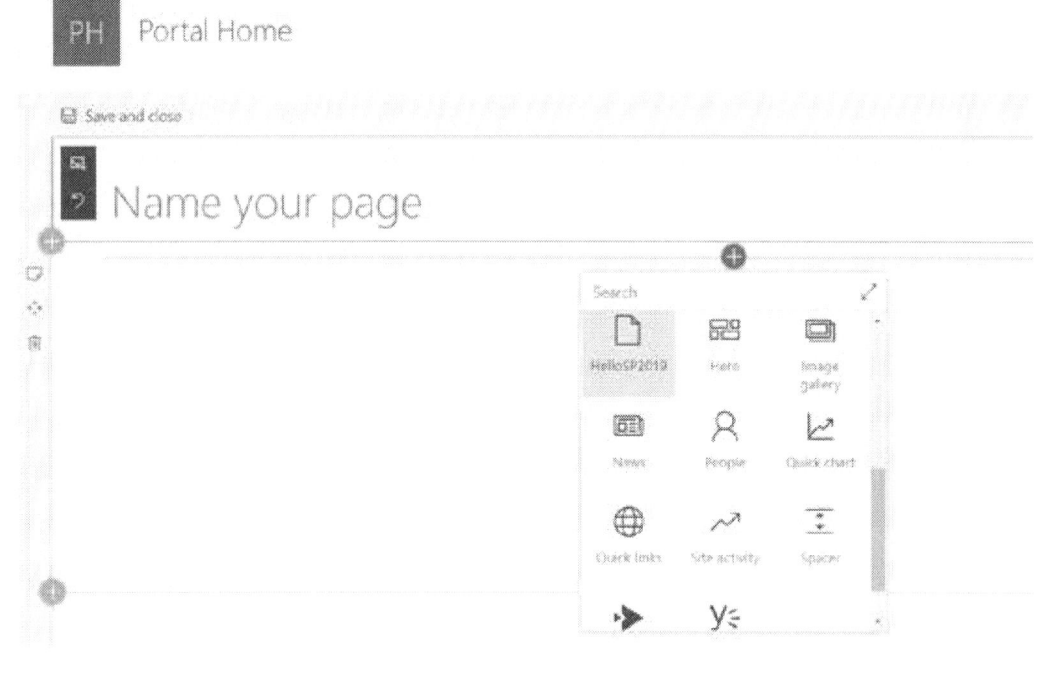

Figure 56.13: Include SPFx web part on the page

3. The web part renders the default content:

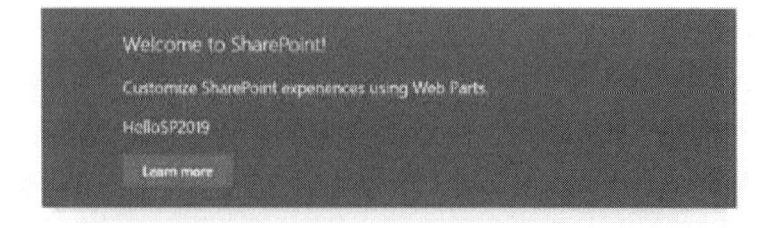

Figure 56.14: SPFx web part in the action

4. Open the developer dashboard (F12) and observe the assets CDN location:

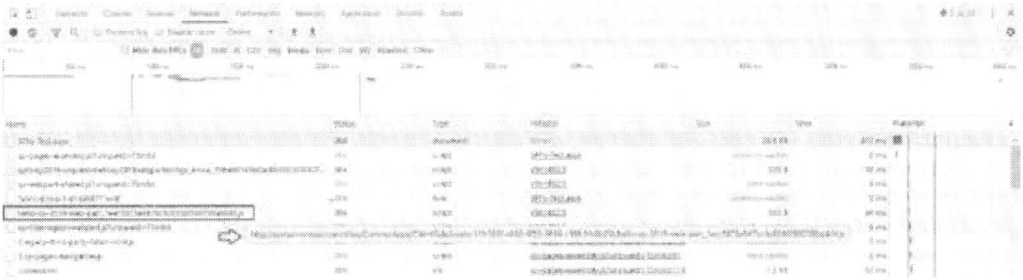

Fig 56.15: Developer dashboard

Conclusion

In this chapter, we explored SPFx readiness with SharePoint on-premises (SharePoint 2019 and 2016). For future compatibility, it is prescribed to begin utilizing the SharePoint Framework based development on SharePoint On-Premises. Likewise, one thing to take note isthat SPFxsolution developed for SharePoint Online probably won't work for SharePoint On-Premises.

Appendix

SPFx Commands Cheat Sheet

Let us revise all the useful commands for SharePoint Framework.

Node.js Commands

Node.js is an open source JavaScript runtime, used to build and run the applications.

Command	Description	Example
-v, --version	Display node's version.	node -v
-h, --help	Display node command line options	node -h

NPM Commands

Node Package Manager installs modules and its dependencies.

NPM Install

Install a package.

Outline

```
npm install (with no args, in package directory)

npm install [<@scope>/]<package-name>
```

aliases: npmi, npm add

Command	Description	Example
npmi -g <package-name>	Install a package globally	npmi -g @microsoft/ generator-sharepoint
npm install --global <package-name>		
npmi -g <package-name1><package-name2>	Install multiple packages at once	npmi -g yo gulp
npm install --global <package-name1><package-name2>		
npm install (with no args, in package directory)	Install all modules listed as dependencies in package.json	npmi
npmi -g npm	Update npm itself	npmi -g npm
npmi<package-name>--save	Enable NPM to include the packages to dependencies section of the package.json file	npmijquery--save
npmi<package-name>--save-exact **npmi<package-name>-E**	Avoid caret or tilde dependencies only at first level	
npmi<package-name>--save-dev **npmi<package-name> -D**	Package will appear in your devDependencies	
npmi<package-name>--save-optional **npmi<package-name> -O**	Package will appear in your optional Dependencies	
npmitsd -g	TSD is a package manager to search and install TypeScript definition files	

NPM Update

Update a package.

Outline

```
npm update [-g] [<package-name>...]
```
aliases: up, upgrade

Description	Command	Example
Report globally outdated packages	npm outdated --global	
Report locally outdated packages	npm outdated	
Update the package globally	npm update -g <package-name>	npmupdate -g @microsoft/generator-sharepoint
Update the package globally	npm update<package-name>	npm update jquery
Update all dependencies to the minimum required version	npm update --save	

Other NPM commands

Command	Description
npm ls <package-name> -g --depth=0	Check the version of installed package
npmshrinkwrap	Lockdown the package dependencies
npm link	symlink a package folder (library component)
npm ls -g <library-name>	Check the folder location of SPFx library
npm unlink<library-name>	Unlink anSPFx library that was symlinked during development in your SPFx project, navigate to SPFx project root folder and run the command.
npm unlink	Remove local npm link to the library, navigate to the SPFx library root folder and run the command

Gulp

Automates SPFx development and deployment tasks.

gulp <command> [optional pararms]

Command	Description
gulp bundle	Creates a new build and writes manifest to the temp folder. This will minify the required assets to upload to CDN. The minified assets are located at "temp\deploy" folder.
gulp bundle --ship	The ship switch denotes distribution.
gulp package	Create the packages inside ./dist folder
gulp package-solution	Create the solution package (sppkg) in sharepoint\solution folder
gulp package-solution --ship	The ship switch denotes distribution.
gulp deploy-azure-storage	Deploy the assets (JavaScript, CSS files) to Azure CDN
gulp --update	Update config.json to the latest version
gulp clean	Removes all files from previous builds
gulp clean-build	Clean the build folder.
gulp serve	Serve code for testing in the browser
gulp serve --nobrowser	Will not automatically launch the SharePoint Workbench
gulp build	Build all of the packages
gulp test	Runs the tests specified in each package's tests folder

Yeoman SharePoint Generator

Scaffolding tool for Modern web apps. Used as SPFx solution generator and builds the required project structure.

yo @microsoft/sharepoint[optional pararms]

Optional Parameter	Description
--help	See the list of command-line options available for the SharePoint generator.
--skip-cache	Do not remember prompt answers.
--skip-install	Do not automatically install dependencies.
--component-type	The type of component ("webpart", "extension", or "library")
--component-name	Name of the component. (Web part name)

--component-description	Description of the component. (Web part description)
--framework	Framework to use for the solution. ("none", "react", or "knockout")
--plusbeta	Use the beta packages
--extension-type	The type of extension (ApplicationCustomizer, FieldCustomizer, ListViewCommandSet)
--solution-name	SPFx solution name
--environment	Target environment for SPFx solution ("onprem", "onprem19" or "spo")
--package-manager	The package manager for the solution ("npm", "pnpm", or "yarn")
--skip-feature-deployment	Allow the tenant admin the choice of being able to deploy the components to all sites immediately without running any feature deployment or adding apps in sites.
--is-domain-isolated	The web part will be rendered in isolated domain using IFrame.

Other Useful Commands

Command	Description	Example
tsd install <package-name> --save	TSD is a package manager to search and install TypeScript definition files. Typings will help for auto complete while writing the code in the code editor.	tsd install jquery --save
code .	Open the solution in the code editor of your choice.	

Glossary

A

AAD	Azure Active Directory
AadHttpClient	Used to perform REST calls against an Azure AD Application.
Adaptive Cards	A new way for the developers to exchange card content in a common and consistent way.
ALM	Application lifecycle management is the product lifecycle management (governance, development, and maintenance) of computer programs.
Angular JS	A JavaScript framework which extends HTML with new attributes.
App catalog	A SharePoint document library that administrators can use to distribute apps for Office and SharePoint to their end users.
Application Customizer	Provides access to predefined locations on the SharePoint page and allows to customize them.
Atom	A free and open-source text and source code editor.
Authentication	The process of recognizing a user's identity.
Authorization	The process of specifying access rights/privileges to resources.

Azmgmt	Azure Management Service
Azure Active Directory	Microsoft's cloud-based identity and access management service.
Azure Function	An event-driven, compute on demand experience.

B

BLOB	Binary Large Object, a collection of binary data stored as a single entity in a database management system.

C

CDN	Content Delivery Network refers to a geographically distributed group of servers that work together to provide fast delivery of Internet content.
Classic SharePoint	Classic SharePoint is developed on the ASP .Net platform with the request, response model.
CLI	A command-line interface for interacting with a computer program.
Cmdlets	A lightweight command used in the Windows PowerShell environment.
config	Configuration files.
Continuous Deployment (CD)	Takes a package from the build and deploys it to a designated environment.
Continuous Integration (CI)	The process of automating the build and testing of code when a developer commits changes to source control.
CORS	Cross-Origin Resource Sharing is a specification that enables truly open access across domain-boundaries.
CRUD	Create, Read, Update, and Delete operations.
CSOM	Client Side Object Model to build client applications and remotely connect to SharePoint.
CSS	Cascading Style Sheets is a language that describes the style of an HTML document.
Custom action	Defines an extension to the user interface, such as a button on a toolbar or a link on a site settings page.

D

dist Distributable files (e.g. TypeScript files compiled into bundled JavaScript files).

DOM The Document Object Model (DOM) is the data representation of the objects that comprise the structure and content of a document on the web.

E

Encoding The process of converting data from one form to another.

F

Field Customizer Used to override the field representation in the list.

G

Gulp Automates development and deployment tasks.

I

IDE An integrated development environment (IDE) is a software application that provides comprehensive facilities to computer programmers for software development.

iframe An HTML element that creates an inline frame, which embeds an independent HTML document into the current document.

J

JavaScript injection A process by which we can insert and use our own JavaScript code in a page.

JSOM SharePoint JavaScript Object Model to communicate with SharePoint.

K

Knockout JS A standalone JavaScript implementation of the Model-View-ViewModel pattern with templates.

L

lib Intermediate files that are being used by SharePoint in the project build process.

Lightweight Developed using JavaScript libraries and HTML.

ListView Command Set	Allows extending command surfaces of SharePoint to add new actions.
Localization	Refers to the adaptation of an application to meet the language, cultural requirements of a specific locale.
LTS	Long-term support is a product lifecycle management policy in which a stable release of computer software is maintained for a longer period of time than the standard edition.

M

Microsoft Azure	An open, flexible, enterprise-grade cloud computing platform.
Minify	Compress CSS and JS files to make it load faster.
Modern SharePoint	A whole new user experience offered by SharePoint.
MS Graph	A rich and fast-growing set of REST APIs provided by Microsoft to access content and services provided by Office 365.
MS Teams	The hub for team collaboration in Office 365.
MSGraphClient	Used to perform REST calls against Microsoft Graph.

N

Node.js	Open source JavaScript runtime to build and run the applications.
node_modules	NPM installs packages for the project locally into the node_modules folder.
node_modules	Contains npm package dependencies in a complex hierarchy of files and folders.
NPM	Node Package Manager is a package manager for the JavaScript programming language.
npmshrinkwrap	Freezes the entire tree of dependencies.
NuGet	The package manager for .NET

O

Office 365	A line of subscription services offered by Microsoft.
Office 365 CLI	Helps to manage the Office 365 tenant and SharePoint framework (SPFx) projects on any platform.

Office UI Fabric	An official front-end framework for building experiences that fit seamlessly into Office and Office 365.

P

PnP	SharePoint Patterns and Practices Developer Community.
PowerShell	A task-based command-line shell and scripting language built on .NET.
Property Pane	Allows defining custom properties for SPFx web part.

R

React	a JavaScript library for building user interfaces, maintained by Facebook.
Responsive	Responsive Web Design is about using HTML and CSS to automatically resize a website, to make it look good on all devices.
REST API	Representational State Transfer is a software architectural style that defines a set of constraints to be used for creating Web services.

S

Sass	Syntactically Awesome Style Sheets, CSS extension language.
Scaffolding	A process of generating initial project files and folders structure.
SharePoint Assets	A generic term referred to basic building blocks of SharePoint that constitute fields, content types, list instances.
SharePoint Workbench	The HTML page is served from a local filesystem by Node.js
SoC	Separation of Concerns is a design principle for separating our program (or solution) into a distinct section.
Solution Package	A SharePoint solution is deployed to a SharePoint server by using a solution package (.wsp) file.
SPFx	The SharePoint Framework (SPFx) is a page and web part model that provides full support for client-side SharePoint development, easy integration with SharePoint data, and support for open source tooling.
SPFx Extensions	Used to customize more facets of the SharePoint experience, including notification areas, toolbars, and list data views.

SPFx Toolchain	Set of build tools, framework packages, and other items that manages the building and deploying client-side projects.
SPO	SharePoint Online
sp-pnp-js	A JavaScript library for SharePoint development (Deprecated).
src	Contains source files.

T

temp	Contains temporary files.
Theme	Defines the overall look and feel of the SharePoint site.
TSD	A tool to acquire and manage type definitions.
TypeScript	A strict syntactical superset of JavaScript.
typings	TypeScript typing information.
Typings	Help for auto complete while writing the code in the code editor.

U

User Profile Application	The service in SharePoint to store information related to users.

V

Virtual DOM	An abstraction of the true DOM.
Visual Studio Code	A code editor redefined and optimized for building and debugging modern web and cloud applications.

W

Webstorm	A lightweight and intelligent IDE for front-end development and server-side JavaScript.

Y

Yeoman	Scaffolding tool for Modern web apps.

Index

A

AadHttpClient 261-268

Adaptive Cards 489

ALM 18

Angular JS 163-182

App / Add-ins Model 12, 13

Application Customizer 295-304, 305-312

Atom 14, 19

AutoBind 231-236

C

Call MS Azure Function 337-346, 347-368

Carousel 471

CDN 97

Classic SharePoint 14

Continuous Deployment (CD) 18, 436

Continuous Integration (CI) 18, 429

CRUD Operations 127-142, 143-162, 163-182, 183-200, 201-214

CSS 73-76

Custom App Pages 423

D

Debugging 281-290

Deployment 97-106, 107-112, 113-118

DOM 14, 15

F

Field Customizer 313-324

Full Trust Farm Solutions 12

G

Google API 499

Gulp 17, 19

I

IDE 14, 19

iframe 14, 15

J

JavaScript injection 14

JavaScript XML (.jsx)   226

Jquery 119

K

Knockout JS 183-200

L

Library component 415

ListView Command Set 325-336

Localization 378

Logging 277-280

LTS 16

M

Modern SharePoint 11

MS Graph 261-268, 269-276

MS Teams 405

MSGraphClient 269-276

N

No Framework 127-142

Node.js 16, 19

node_modules 16

NPM 16, 19, 35-38

npmshrinkwrap 35-38

NuGet 16

O

Office 365 CLI 384

Office UI Fabric 73, 82, 243-

OrgChart 481

P

Project Upgrade 395, 401

Property Pane 39-49, 50-62, 63-68, 69-72

R

React 21

React Component 225

React Element 224

React JS 143-162, 221-226, 227-230, 231-236, 237-242, 305-312, 447, 455, 465, 471, 481, 489

React Props 224

React State 225, 237-242

Responsive 14, 21

REST API 13

S

Sandbox Solutions 12

Sass 74

Scaffolding 23, 24

Index   621

Search Results   455

Separation of concerns 369

SharePoint Workbench 17

Solution Package 12

SPFx 13, 14, 21

SPFx Extensions   291-294, 295-304, 305-312, 313-324, 325-336

SPFx Toolchain 13, 15, 16

sp-pnp-js 201-214

Spread operator 242

T

Tree view 465

TypeScript 17

Typings 120

User Profile 447

Visual Studio Code 14, 19

Webstorm 14, 19

Yeoman 17, 19

Recommendations
- Learn TypeScript!
- Use SPHttpClient to connect to SharePoint
- HttpClient for other API's
- Use frameworks and libraries that already have typings
- Office UI Fabric available for consistent styling

Resources
- SPFx Articles by Author

  https://www.c-sharpcorner.com/members/nanddeep-nachan/articles
- SPFx Overview

  https://dev.office.com/sharepoint/docs/sharepoint-framework-overview
- SPFx Tutorials

  http://aka.ms/spfx-tutorials
- Build your first webpart

  https://dev.office.com/sharepoint/docs/spfx/web-parts/get-started/build-a-hello-world-web-part
- SharePoint Framework API

  https://dev.office.com/sharepoint/reference/spfx/sharepoint-framework-reference-overview
- Get an introduction to the SharePoint Framework

  https://channel9.msdn.com/Events/Ignite/2016/BRK2114-TS
- SharePoint PnP Community

  http://aka.ms/sppnp-community

  http://aka.ms/spdev-docs

The Final Words

SharePoint Framework is the future of SharePoint. The directions from Microsoft is to use the SPFx.I hope this book has helped you to get started your journey with SPFx. Thanks for sticking with me on this journey, and hopefully we'll cross paths again in the future.

Printed in Great Britain
by Amazon